ETHICS IN PSYCHOLOGY

ETHICS IN PSYCHOLOGY

Professional Standards and Cases

Patricia Keith-Spiegel

Ball State University, Muncie, IN

Gerald P. Koocher

Children's Hospital Medical Center, Boston, MA

Distributed exclusively by
Lawrence Erlbaum Associates, Inc., Publishers
Hillsdale, New Jersey, and London

McGraw-Hill, Inc.
New York St. Louis San Francisco Auckland Bogotá
Caracas Lisbon London Madrid Mexico City Milan
Montreal New Delhi San Juan Singapore
Sydney Tokyo Toronto

We owe gratitude to our colleagues and mentors who have inspired, encouraged, and guided us throughout the years. With much affection and appreciation, we dedicate this book to Brenda Allen, Stuart Cook, Fred McKinney, Freda Rebelsky, and M. Brewster Smith.

ETHICS IN PSYCHOLOGY

First Edition

0 AGM AGM 9987654

Design/Production: *The Cambridge Studio*

Library of Congress Cataloging-in-Publication Data

Keith-Spiegel, Patricia.
  Ethics in psychology.

  Includes index.
    1. Psychology — Practice — Moral and ethical aspects.
  2. Psychology — Research — Moral and ethical aspects.
  3. Psychology — Study and teaching — Moral and ethical
  aspects. 4. Psychology — Standards. I. Koocher,
  Gerald P. II. Title. [DNLM; 1. Ethics, Medical.
  2. Psychology — standards. BJ 45 K28e]
  BF76.4.K46 1985   174'.915   84 – 27542
  ISBN 0-07-554879-8

Contents

CHAPTER 9

Knowing Thyself: Competence and Weakness   223

CHAPTER 10

Dual-Role Relationships and Conflicts of Interest   251

CHAPTER 11

Relationships with Colleagues, Cohorts, and Collaborators   291

CHAPTER 12

Ethical Dilemmas in Special Work Settings   319

CHAPTER 13

Scholarly Publishing and Teaching   351

CHAPTER 14

Research Issues   383

Foreword

Psychologists are increasing in number and in the variety of roles and functions that they fill in our society. Almost 60,000 members now belong to the American Psychological Association—a doubling in the last 14 years.

The scope of psychology is expanding at what sometimes seems to be an exponential fashion. Psychologists continue to fill their rather traditional roles as teachers, researchers, diagnosticians, therapists, measurement experts, curriculum designers, and so forth. The number of psychologists in these traditional roles is increasing. In addition, new and more uncharted roles for psychologists also exist in health maintenance organizations (HMOs), in changing health-related behaviors in general medical settings, in mental health prevention and consultation, as expert witnesses in the courtroom, as consultants to management, and so on. The sheer size of the psychological enterprise has thrust many psychologists into management roles where they experience new and different pressures and expectations. Perhaps the most extraordinary growth has been in the independent practice of psychology on both a full- and part-time basis.

Notwithstanding the changes in their field in both size and scope, psychologists have insisted on maintaining and enforcing a code of ethics for all psychologists, especially those psychologists who are either members of the American Psychological Association or who are licensed by a state or provincial licensing board that insists that its licensees adhere to such a code. Although this code, officially adopted by the American Psychological Association, is brief and easy to read, its application in specific situations is often difficult; thus many of the implicit and necessary ethical dilemmas are left for the individual psychologist to resolve. Until the publication of this volume, no comprehensive guide to the understanding and application of the code existed, either for teaching purposes or for use by the individual psychologist in particular situations. Consequently, the need that this book serves is a large and important one. There could be no more appropriate people to write such a volume than Patricia Keith-Speigel and Gerald Koocher. Both of them are distinguished psychologists with substantial academic and writing credentials; both are former members of the American Psychological Association's Ethics Committee; and both have a commitment and depth of understanding in this area that has made this book the contribution to the field that it is.

Leonard D. Goodstein

Preface

To be good is noble, but to teach others to be good is nobler—and less trouble.

Mark Twain

WHY ETHICS NOW?

The general use definition of ethics refers to a set of guidelines that provide directions for conduct. Students and professionals alike may react to this topic with groans and yawns since heated diatribes or prissy, rigid moralizing are often associated with the term "ethics."

Ethics study, however, has burgeoned in recent years, perhaps reflecting the complexities of today's world. As a pluralistic and mobile "nation of strangers," the availability of trusted advisors has diminished. It is increasingly difficult to find guideposts in a fast-changing world, yet moral guidance seems to be needed most during confusing times. We may react by turning inward and searching for inner fulfillment or self-pleasure, but we may also remain unaware that others may be harmed by a personal philosophy of "do whatever feels good or right." Cultural relativism occasionally results in unstable or feeble ethical values, which are no more comforting than absolutist doctrines that may be anachronistic or inappropriate in a particular situation.

Despite today's uncertainties, ethical guidelines are essential to maintaining the integrity and cohesiveness of a profession. The growing distrust of professionals and their potential misuse of power by the general public has also forced a more careful self-examination of our conduct. Students and professionals alike are increasingly eager for the clear signposts that indicate appropriate and inappropriate conduct under various conditions.

PURPOSE AND GOALS OF THE BOOK

Our primary purpose is to present the full range of contemporary ethical issues in psychology as not only relevant and intriguing, but also as integral and unavoidable aspects of the professional role of a psychologist. Regardless of one's training specialty or the work setting, ethical dilemmas will arise—probably with some regularity—and action decisions must be made. By providing an awareness of the ethical standards of the profession, and by revealing how they apply to specific situations, we hope to achieve a useful and practical guide.

After serving for many years on ethics committees, we began to realize that many people who are already functioning as fully trained psychologists are not as well attuned to the expectations for ethical conduct and how the profession monitors itself as they could be. We also observed that inquiries to ethics committees or calls for consultation on ethical matters often arrive after-the-fact and that the resolution primarily involves reactive or remedial, rather than preventative, steps. Consequently, this book sensitizes readers to the monitoring and redress mechanisms available when ethical violations occur, and it also provides information and decision-making strategies that will assist in avoiding or preventing ethical misconduct.

Nonetheless, we cannot provide solutions to every conceivable ethical problem that might arise in psychology practice, research, or teaching. Many specific situations are, in fact, so complicated that no ethics code, policy guideline, or law can deftly point the way to a satisfactory and "correct" resolution. In some situations, for example, one ethical principle may seem to be pitted *against* another, or upholding an ethical principle may be at variance with a legal requirement, leaving the psychologist dangling somewhere in the middle. Moreover, the discipline of psychology in particular, as well as our society in general, is constantly emerging and changing, which causes profound ethical dilemmas that neither the ethics code nor the profession is fully equipped to handle. Rapid computerization, new and untested therapeutic techniques, changing consent procedures, and the increasing involvement of psychology with the mass media are only a few of the phenomena that have yet to be fully explored in terms of ethical implications. We do assume, however, that the more information and sensitization to issues made available to psychologists or psychologists in training, the better they will be able to sort out even the most complex ethical problems and make the best possible professional judgment.

AN EXPLANATION OF SOME SPECIFIC FEATURES OF THIS BOOK

This book is developed around the most recent version of the ethics code of the American Psychological Association, *Ethical Principles of Psychologists* (1981). This code is cited extensively throughout the text and is reproduced, in its entirety, as Appendix A.* We refer to it simply as the *Ethical Principles* in the text. Or, when we wish to refer parenthetically to a *specific* principle or

---

*The Ethical Principles, copyright © 1981 by the American Psychological Association, are reprinted in Appendix A by permission of APA.

subprinciple, we designate that as *EP* followed by the corresponding number and letter of the principle and subprinciple: for example, *EP*: 6a refers to Principle 6 (Client Welfare) of the ethics code and subsection *a* of that principle dealing with dual-role relationships and exploitation. This notation makes it easy for the reader to look up the exact wording of the code relevant to the text discussion.

Because ethical problems often overlap or cluster around several principles, it is difficult to create neat piles of material from which to develop discrete chapters. Whereas each chapter has a specific focus, some cross-referencing was necessary to inform readers whether additional information about a particular topic could be found in another chapter. Furthermore, it was not possible to cover every conceivable ethical situation that psychologists might face in a single volume. The omission of specific topics, however, does not mean they are unimportant, and the neglect of some forms of conduct does not mean that such behaviors are implicitly condoned.

We use case vignettes as a way to illustrate violations of APA's *Ethical Principles* and other ethical dilemmas. Our case examples are adapted either from ethics committees' case files or from actual incidents known to us. We have disguised the material in a variety of ways, such as through combining the features of one case with another, switching the sex of one or more principals, or altering contexts in which the activity occurred. It should also be noted that we often "trimmed" cases by focusing on only one aspect of the charge or violation. In fact, most cases brought to the attention of ethics committees involve charges of violating two or more *Ethical Principles*. A single incident of misconduct that violates five or six principles and subprinciples of the *Ethical Principles* is not an uncommon occurrence.

We decided to avoid routine methods of designating the principal characters in our case material (e.g., "Dr. A." or "the client"), but we also wanted to reduce the risk of using bogus names that might correspond to those of real people. Hence, most of our pseudonyms are highly contrived. Nevertheless, it was *not* our intent to trivialize the seriousness of the matters under discussion, but rather to enhance interest and recall of specific cases. Any resulting resemblance between the names of our characters and those of actual people is purely coincidental. The names used in particular cases, however, do *not* even remotely resemble the names of the actual principals.

In a few instances, we have cited cases that are in the public domain because of associated litigation. These cases use the real names of the principals and are accompanied in the text by citation of the relevant law or public source.

ACKNOWLEDGMENTS

A book aspiring to provide appropriate decisions and actions when ethical dilemmas arise in professional activity carries a heavy responsibility. We felt obligated to submit our chapters to extensive external review by experts in specific topic areas. We are deeply indebted to our reviewers for their invaluable assistance in ensuring the accuracy and integrity of our book. Our appreciation is extended to the following people:

Brenda Allen, Ph.D.

Kenneth M. Austin, Ph.D.

Bruce E. Bennett, Ph.D.

Frank H. Boring, Ph.D.

Jacqueline C. Bouhoutsos, Ph.D.

Douglas W. Bray, Ph.D.

William L. Claiborn, Ph.D.

David L. Cole, Ph.D.

Louis Everstine, Ph.D.

Ellen C. Fitzgerald, M.S., R.R.A.

Leonard D. Goodstein, Ph.D.

Rachel T. Hare-Mustin, Ph.D.

Eric Harris, J.D., Ed.D.

Jean C. Holroyd, Ph.D.

Hannah Lerman, Ph.D.

Hanna Levenson, Ph.D.

Wilbert J. McKeachie, Ph.D.

Gary B. Melton, Ph.D.

Ruth Ochroch, Ph.D.

Richard H. O'Connell, Ph.D.

Barbara M. Pedulla, Ph.D.

Philip S. Pierce, Ph.D.

Kenneth S. Pope, Ph.D.

Gerald M. Rosen, Ph.D.

Bruce Dennis Sales, J. D., Ph.D.

Joseph R. Sanders, Ph.D.

Kenneth Shapiro, Ph.D.

Joan E. Sieber, Ph.D.

Max Siegel, Ph.D.

David W. Simmonds, Ph.D.

Suzanne B. Sobel, Ph.D.

Norman D. Sundberg, Ph.D.

Ryan D. Tweney, Ph.D.

Alexander Tymchuk, Ph.D.

Louis A. Weithorn, Ph.D.

We also wish to extend appreciation to the American Psychological Association's Ethics Officer, David H. Mills, Ph.D., and to the two APA Ethics Committee Chairs, Judy E. Hall, Ph.D., and Wilsie B. Webb, Ph.D., who served during our writing period. They evaluated the case file material and made many useful suggestions for every chapter.

We must note that reviewers may not necessarily endorse the entire content of the book or even the particular chapter reviewed. Our colleagues did not always agree with us or among themselves, leaving the authors with the final content decisions for which we assume full responsibility.

We also wish to acknowledge Ann Kilbride, M.A., who supervised the editorial-production and design of the text. In addition, we wish to thank Mary Falcon, acquisitions editor, and Mary Shuford, project editor, from McGraw-Hill, Inc., for their support in ensuring prompt publication of this book.

Finally, we wish to thank Carla Millhauser for the major responsibility she accepted for manuscript preparation and the students in Dr. Keith-Spiegel's ethics classes for volunteering to read and comment on early drafts of the manuscript.

Northridge, CA   **P.K.S.**
December 1984   **G.P.K.**

About The Authors

PATRICIA KEITH-SPIEGEL is a Professor of Psychology at California State University, Northridge. She received her Ph.D. degree from Claremont Graduate School. She has served three terms as Chair of the Ethics Committee of the American Psychological Association and was a participating author of the 1977 *Ethical Principles for Psychologists* and its 1981 revision. She has served as President of the Western Psychological Association. Other professional interests include the effects of early experience and teaching skills.

GERALD P. KOOCHER is Associate Professor of Psychology at Harvard Medical School and Director of Training in Psychology at Boston's Children's Hospital and Judge Baker Guidance Center. A native of Cambridge, Massachusetts, he completed undergraduate work at Boston University and his Ph.D. in clinical psychology at the University of Missouri, Columbia. He is editor of the *Journal of Pediatric Psychology*, and formerly served on the Ethics Committee of the American Psychological Association. His areas of professional interest also include children's adaptation to chronic illness, forensic psychology, and ethical problems regarding consent and substituted judgment.

Current Status of APA Ethics Code [February, 1991]

This book is based on the 1981 version of the *Ethical Principles for Psychologists*, the ethics code of the American Psychological Association. In response to pressure from the Federal Trade Commission, the Board of Directors of the American Psychological Association declared an emergency on June 2, 1989 and acted in place of the Council of Representatives to rescind several provisions of the code. A copy of the amended *Ethical Principles* was published in the August, 1989 issue of the *American Psychologist*, 45, 557-563. Unfortunately, no commentary or explanation for the changes accompanied the publication leaving some readers confused about exactly what had been changed and why.

The changes involve no added text, but rather *deletions* from Principles 4, 6, and 7. The following items from Principle 4 have been rescinded: 4. b. v; 4 b vi; 4 b vii; 4. b. viii. The phrase, "they neither give nor receive any remuneration for referring clients from professional services" has been rescinded from Principle 7. b. and the phrase "If a person is receiving similar services from another professional, psychologists do not offer their own services directly to such a person." Although the deliberations were complicated, the primary reasoning behind rescinding these portions of the code was not because the points have no ethical relevance, but rather because they may constitute restraint of trade. Keith-Spiegel and Koocher, however, continue to stand behind their analysis of the ethical dilemmas related to the rescinded sections and phrases.

The rest of the code currently in force is the same as the version used in this textbook. Whereas, the American Psychological Assocation is in the process of substantially revising its ethics code, the 1989 version does not constitute that major revision. Hence, the analyses and references to the APA code in this book are valid until the major revision is completed and approved by the APA Council of Representatives. This is not likely to occur before mid-1992 at the earliest.

Codes, Controls, and Ethical Decision Making

1

*Always do right; this will gratify
some people and astonish the rest.*

Mark Twain

We begin with an overview of ethical principles developed to guide the professional conduct of psychologists, a consideration of conditions that create ethical dilemmas, and an overview of the available monitoring mechanisms. Ethical codes and monitoring mechanisms alone, however, cannot ensure the maintenance of the integrity of the profession. Informal peer monitoring is a responsibility incurred by all psychologists. We will present the alternative courses of action and the dilemmas faced by those who witness or learn of ethical misconduct committed by colleagues. Finally, we will examine how one's own awareness of ethical issues and the process of decision making when ethical dilemmas arise constitute the essential ingredients of "self-monitoring."

ETHICS CODES

A profession has been described as a unique body of theory or knowledge with its members possessing specific skills or techniques based on this knowledge. Ethics code development is considered an essential step in professionalization of an occupation (Wilensky, 1964). A profession such as psychology requires an ethics code because society sustains a different relationship with professions than with a commercial enterprise or ventures. The public may hold a *caveat emptor* ("Let the buyer beware!") attitude when either purchasing a washing machine or engaging the services of a TV

1

repair shop. As professions developed, however, people began to expect professionals to be trustworthy and competent and to cause no harm. Professions must then instigate mechanisms that balance their self-interests against the interests of the people with whom they work.

Ethics codes, which have been described as moral guides to self-regulation, attempt to ensure the appropriate use of skills and techniques. Codes have also been defined as principles specifying the rights and responsibilities of professionals in their relationships with each other and with the people they serve, as well as stating prescriptive, normative values reflecting the consensus of the profession. Charles Levy, for example, proposed an especially frank description of the nature and function of ethics codes:

> Codes of ethics are once the highest and lowest standards of practice expected of the practitioner, the awesome statement of rigid requirements, and the promotional materials issued primarily for public relations purposes. They embody the gradually evolved essence of moral expectations, as well as the arbitrarily prepared shortcut to professional prestige and status. At the same time, they are handy guides to the legal enforcement of ethical conduct and to punishment of unethical conduct. They are also the unrealistic, unimpressive, and widely unknown or ignored guides to wishful thinking. The motivation to create a code of ethics may be a zeal for respectability. However, occupational groups are most often moved by a genuine need for guides to action in situations of agonizing conflict and by sincere aspirations to deal justly with clients, colleagues, and society. (Levy, 1974, p. 207)

Indeed, ethics codes are fairly blunt instruments and may create conceptual confusion in their attempt to be all things to all people (Clouser, 1975). We do expect a great deal from our ethics code—perhaps too much. The code of the American Psychological Association, entitled *The Ethical Principles of Psychologists* (see Appendix A), has the same major goal as those of other professions; namely, sensitization to an ethical way of professional life and the provision of a structural guide and alerting mechanism to ethical issues and dilemmas (Moore, 1978). In addition, it is the document of reference for the identification of unethical acts brought to the attention of ethics committees. It also attempts to describe the ethical conduct of psychologists with different training backgrounds (e.g., clinical service providers and researchers) functioning in various work settings in the public and private sectors. It further attempts to prescribe how to protect the welfare of a variety of publics including psychotherapy clients, students, supervisors and employees, employers and employing agencies, human and animal research participants, and society in general, as well as protecting psychologists from each other.

It is easy to find fault with a code that attempts to do so much. Critics have noted that it contains internal inconsistencies that could lead to potential conflict when one attempts to apply the code to certain situations.

Principles are worded abstractly leading to different interpretations or insufficient specificity for application to actual problems. The code mixes the highest moral values with matters that could be described as "professional etiquette." Sometimes, the code is vague and requires individual professional judgment, while other times it is rigid and detailed. Despite the criticisms, however, the American Psychological Association's code has been praised by other professional societies, which have often included its basic premises in their own ethics codes.

Ethics codes among professional societies range in length from ten sentences describing the seven *Principles of Medical Ethics* (1980) of the American Medical Association, to the forty-eight pages of tiny print, issued by the American Bar Association (1980). (The American Psychiatric Association has adopted the seven principles of the AMA code, but each code has been heavily annotated for application to psychiatry, resulting in a six-page document.) Most codes contain about one full page of text, although the six-page code of the American Psychological Association is one of the longer and more detailed codes. Despite the variations in length and specificity, most professional ethics codes echo similar themes: to promote the welfare of consumers served, to maintain competence, to protect confidentiality and/or privacy, to act responsibly, to avoid exploitation, and to uphold the integrity of the profession through exemplary conduct.

Although the American Psychological Association (APA) established an ethics committee in 1938, it did not adopt a formal ethics code until 1953. The first code was developed in a unique, quasi-empirical manner. APA solicited input from the membership and forged the first code using the more than one thousand cases received as a data base. The code has since undergone a number of minor, as well as several major, revisions with the latest version issued in 1981. (See Golann, 1969, 1970, and Holtzman, 1979 for more details on the history of the APA ethics codes.) The current *Ethical Principles of Psychologists* (1981) consists of a preamble and ten annotated principles under the following headings: *Responsibility; Competence; Moral and Legal Standards; Public Statements; Confidentiality; Welfare of the Consumer; Professional Relationships; Assessment Techniques; Research with Human Participants;* and *Care and Use of Animals.*

The APA code is a "living document" reflecting in each revision some newly emerged issues within the profession or society. Examples of such contemporary features in the more recent APA code revisions include a new principle devoted exclusively to the use of nonhuman participants in research, specific prohibitions against sexual intimacies with clients and sexual harassment, and relaxed provisions related to the previously more stringent controls on advertising services and advice-giving via media channels.

The APA ethics code and its ethics committee are not, of course, the sole publication and group concerned with ethical matters within the organization. Other APA guidelines dealing, at least in part, with ethical matters include the *Standards for Providers of Professional Services* (1977), *Ethical Principles in the Conduct of Research with Human Participants* (1982), and *Standards for Educational and Psychological Tests* (1984). In addition, other major APA boards, committees, and task forces have been active in dealing with the ethical matters relevant to their mandates, often in cooperation with the ethics committee.

HOW DO ETHICAL DILEMMAS ARISE?

Sometimes psychologists willfully, even maliciously, engage in acts they know to be in violation of the ethical standards of the profession. Avarice, expediency, and other self-serving motives that blur judgments and boundaries are common among those guilty of ethical violations. Nevertheless, well-meaning psychologists are also vulnerable to ethical dilemmas. Sieber (1982) outlined six common conditions that result in ethical problems, which we have adapted and expand on in the following list:

1. An ethical problem may simply be unforeseen. Inexperience and ignorance of specific ethical principles can be the cause. But, at other times, an ethical issue was simply not predictable: for example, when a psychologist's published research findings are applied inappropriately by another party.

2. An ethical problem may be inadequately anticipated. The psychologist may have underestimated the magnitude of the problem and/or decided that safeguards were unnecessary or too costly. For example, a psychologist consulting an individual, occasionally with the spouse, through a divorce with the potential for a child custody dispute must be alert to the possible confidentiality dilemmas that could develop if one parent later subpoenas the psychologist for testimony in his or her behalf. Or a psychologist may decide to save time by not removing identities from research questionnaires. Ethical problems may never materialize, but, if they do, the psychologist may be faulted for not clarifying information with affected parties or for not taking reasonable precautions.

3. An ethical problem may be foreseen, but there may be no apparent way to avoid it. A psychologist may see no alternatives to the use of deception in a research design. Or a clinical psychologist may recognize the potential for no other course of action except to share information obtained in confidence to protect the welfare of a client.

4. In a variation of the anticipated ethical problem, what to do may be unclear because of ambiguities of the consequences of available alternatives. The use of innovative or controversial techniques, for example, often causes this dilemma because the risks, if any, are simply unknown or unpredictable.

5. An ethical problem may arise whenever available guidelines and/or laws are inadequate or nonexistent relative to the situation. The generality

or nonspecificity of ethics codes and other regulations may cause confusion in a particular instance. For example, the ethics code for psychologists permits them to give advice to individuals through mass media channels, as long as they do not provide diagnoses or psychotherapy in the process. Nonetheless, the distinction between "advice" and "therapy" is not easy to discern.

6. An ethical problem may arise whenever one responds to the demands of a law, governmental policy, or even an ethical principle that simultaneously jeopardizes the welfare of people with whom one works. This thorny ethical dilemma typically causes considerable distress because the psychologist must choose between legitimate loyalties.

ENFORCEMENT OF ETHICAL CONDUCT IN PSYCHOLOGY

Various mechanisms have been established by law and within the profession itself to protect the public from unlawful, incompetent, and unethical actions perpetrated by psychologists. Hess (1980) has outlined five sources of control:

1. Control through *general criminal and civil law* that is applicable to all citizens including, of course, psychologists.
2. Control exerted on psychologists by their *peers*, with ethics committees emerging as the most relevant peer control mechanism.
3. Profession-specific *legal controls* emerging from *state licensing boards* and the accompanying establishment of entry standards, definitions of practice, delineation of offenses and sanctions, and means of enforcement under criminal law.
4. Additional control through *civil litigation of malpractice complaints* resulting from both the definition of practice that accomplished the evolvement of licensure and the higher visibility of the profession of psychology.
5. Controls imposed by or derived from *federal laws and regulations,* such as the policies issued on the protection of human participants in social and behavioral science research and the mandated establishment of peer standards review committees.

(These five sources of control will be discussed in detail in the following sections.)

The existence of several levels of control and protection reveals that the issue has both pros and cons. The primary asset is that each level has its own focus, which ideally allows each incident or issue to have a most appropriate focus for a hearing and resolution. For example, if a psychologist extorts money from a client, adjudication by criminal law would probably result in the most appropriate sanction. If an insurance company questions treatment applicability or claims, peer standard review committees are particularly well-suited forums for evaluation. Nevertheless, it is not difficult to generate a list of reprehensible, highly objectionable, and blatantly unethical acts that are neither illegal nor in violation of any policy *except* the ethics code. In such cases, ethics committees are the sole source of redress.

This is not to say that only one level of control is applicable to any single incident. Indeed, an ethics committee of a professional association would probably investigate complaints of extortion against a member. In fact, it is theoretically possible for a single case to be investigated at all five levels (including levels within levels if, for example, the psychologist involved is a member of several professional associations, each of which has an ethics of professional standards committee). Herein lies a primary liability associated with the existence of so many avenues of control. Efforts may be duplicated resulting in unnecessary expense and confusion. Moreover, investigators at each level may expect that another level involved is in control of the matter, resulting in diffusion of responsibility and inadequate investigations by all concerned. Or one level of investigation may interfere with another, leading to impediments and/or procedural errors that could later release an offender on technical or procedural violations.

Territoriality, the need for confidentiality, and poor communication channels among levels of control can cause additional obfuscation and confusion. The public may well be perplexed by the array of monitoring levels. In addition, psychologists and complainants involved in multiple-level actions may be appropriate in cases involving serious violations with potential for public harm, experiences of undue harassment, and "overkill"; of course, multiple-jeopardy may also result. The many hazards for client–plaintiffs and psychotherapist–defendants in the network of professional, administrative, and legal procedures have been illustrated by Sinnett and Linford (1982b). Recommendations for improving intercontrol level communication and cooperation have been proposed (e.g., Hess, 1980; Wellner and Albidin, 1981), but implementation follows slowly and unevenly.

Law versus Ethical Standards

General criminal and civil law do not adequately protect consumers from unethical conduct by psychologists. As Clouser (1973) noted, morality is external to law despite an apparent overlap. The illusory similarity is caused by morals and laws that have almost the same purpose—namely, to outline rules of conduct that assist in harmonious living and the facilitation of achievement of individual aims and desires in a socially acceptable manner. But, as Clouser observes, laws have been criticized and even overturned because they were immoral and unjust, and frequently laws deal with matters that are not moral concerns at all. In addition, many matters of morality and ethics cannot be sanctioned by law because of inconvenience or the impossibility of enforcement.

Thus the correspondence between "legal-ethical" and "illegal-unethical" is frequently incongruent. Of course, ethical professional conduct often involves perfectly legal and even exemplary "good citizen" actions. In addition, unethical professional conduct is also often illegal. A psychologist who is found guilty of a felony can be both delicensed and expelled from state and national psychological associations for that reason alone. However, conviction on a misdemeanor will usually not be handled in the same manner, unless the offense also involved the violation of an ethical principle as well (Hare-Mustin and Hall, 1981). Differences among state legal statutes allow for discrepancies in these cases. For example, engaging in sexual intimacies with psychotherapy clients is a criminal offense in some jurisdictions but not in others.

The situation is further complicated when one begins to note the many instances of fully legal conduct (or, perhaps more correctly, conduct not in violation of any criminal or civil law) that would be defined as unethical according to the profession's code. Lecturing from outdated notes, advertising services in gawdy or outlandish ways, administering psychological assessment techniques without adequate training, failing to give adequate or timely feedback to supervisees, or diagnosing people who call into a radio talk show are only a few of the hundreds of possible examples illustrating acts that are not illegal, but which the profession of psychology considers unethical.

Finally, some instances exist that may place psychologists in a most unfortunate dilemma. These situations involve those relatively rare occasions when upholding the spirit of the ethics code might also be in violation of the law. For example, refusing to report information shared in confidence as mandated by law may be judged by a psychologist to be in the best interests of a client as well as that client's family and society. A more frequent occurrence involves a variation of the theme in which psychologists face a conflict between what they believe to be their professional ethical obligations and the policies of their employers. Upholding the ethical standards may carry unpleasant sanctions, such as the loss of a job or position. But condoning the unethical practices of an employer could result in negative consequences, such as facing an ethics inquiry by one's peers or difficulty facing oneself in the mirror. (See Chapters 12 and 15 for descriptions, obligations, and examples of exposing unethical practices and "whistle-blowers.")

Ideally, ethical behavior prescribed by a group within the context of a larger society should conform to the law and not defy it. Yet ethical professional standards also expect behavior that is more correct or more stringent than is required by law. In this respect, ethical standards are higher than the law (Ballantine, 1979).

Licensing Boards versus Ethics

State licensing boards establish and monitor the entry-level qualifications required to offer services to the public for a fee under the protected title of "psychologist." The relevance of this function to ethical principles of the profession is that licensing boards may help ensure competence, although critics such as Gross (1979) and Koocher (1979) disagree with that assertion. State licensing boards also monitor the conduct of psychologists whom they have already licensed. In general, state boards promulgate the APA ethics code; thus the same misconduct may qualify for sanctioning at both levels. But, as Wellner and Albidin (1981) have documented in a survey of the 50 state regulations, reasons specified for denial, revocation, or suspension of licensure vary significantly. Furthermore, the distinctions between ethical or professional conduct violations and legal violations are not always sharp. Table 1–1 illustrates conduct that would clearly violate the *Ethical Principles*. None of these violations, however, is sanctioned by every state, and many are sanctioned by only a few.

TABLE 1–1
Conduct Violating Ethical Principles

Reasons for Denial, Revocation, or Suspension of Licensure as Specified in Laws	Number of States
Fraud or deception in applying for license or passing exam.	45
Use of alcoholic beverage or any drug to the extent that it impairs ability to perform professional duties.	44
Conviction of a felony.	41
Conviction of a crime involving moral turpitude.	24
Impersonation of another person holding a license or allowing another person to use license.	23
Legally adjudged to be mentally ill or incompetent.	17
The aiding or abetting of any person to engage in the unlawful practice of psychology.	15
Gross negligence in professional practice.	14
Fraud or deception in rendering services or obtaining fees.	13
Practicing under a false or assumed name.	11
Practicing in an area inappropriate to license.	11
Acceptance of rebates for referral to other professional persons.	9
Willful, unauthorized communication of information received in professional confidence.	6
Professional connection with anyone acting contrary to state law concerning professional practice.	4
Violation of the Medical Practices Act.	3
Advertising in a way that deceives or is harmful to the public.	3
Conviction of a crime related to the practice of psychology.	2

(Wellner and Albidin, 1981)

State regulatory boards governing the practice of psychology rarely have access to the resources and/or the inclination to deal with more minor violations of the ethics code or violations that may be offensive to the profession but not necessarily harmful to the public. Furthermore, many psychologists are not required to be licensed, such as psychology professors or research psychologists. Thus ethics committees can fill the monitoring gap for psychologists who are not required to be licensed but who are members of a psychological association with a peer monitoring system. Nonmember, nonlicensed psychologists fall through the cracks and are subject only to criminal or civil law or, if not self-employed, to the quality-control mechanisms at their place of employment. (For more information on licensing and malpractice, see Chapter 9.)

Peer Monitoring: Ethics Committees

The APA established an ethics committee in the late 1930s, although an ethics code was not formalized until much later. Today, APA is the only professional organization spending more than $100,000 per year on matters relating to ethics, including monitoring and complaint processing (Chalk, Frankel, and Chafer, 1980), although this is still less than one percent of the association's annual budget.

Ethics committees consist of psychologists (typically experienced, senior people well regarded for their sensitivity to ethical matters and sense of fairness) who are elected or appointed by the governing body of the professional association. Committee members serve without pay and, at the state and local levels, often without reimbursement for expenses incurred. The task of serving on an ethics committee is not, of course, an easy one. The dilemmas committee members face are often extremely difficult, both in terms of the issues and in dealing with the parties involved who are often distressed or vulnerable.

All state psychological associations, as well as a few of the larger city or county associations, have ethics committees. These organizations are loosely affiliated with APA and have generally adopted its ethics code. But rules and procedures used vary widely and, according to a 1981 survey by APA, 17 of the 40 states responding noted no formal rules and procedures at all. Nevertheless, state and local associations may have several advantages over the national association when it comes to handling complaints. These smaller groups can meet frequently and more easily arrange for face-to-face interviews with complainants and/or the psychologists against whom a complaint was lodged ("respondents") due to closer geographical proximity. The APA committee meets only in Washington, D.C., and it operates almost exclusively on the basis of written documents. (See Appendix B for the complete rules and procedures of the APA Ethics Committee.)

State and local associations may be the preferred level of processing when peer pressure or monitoring is likely to be most effective. Unfortunately, as also revealed by the APA survey, many state committees are afflicted with chronic procedural and financial problems resulting in a marginal level of functioning. The APA has far more resources, including a full-time psychologist serving as the Administrative Officer for Ethics who has access to expert legal counsel. Local, state, and national level committees can cooperate with each other by transmitting cases to a more appropriate group. For example, when a complaint is received by an association to which the respondent does not belong, it can be given to an association in which the respondent does hold membership. When a conflict-of-interest exists within the group receiving the complaint (a situation most likely to arise in a state or local association when close personal ties may exist between the committee members and the respondent), a case may be given to a more objective committee, if the respondent is also a member. Currently, efforts are underway to streamline the communication and cooperation among local, state, and the national committees to increase efficiency and avoid unnecessary duplication of efforts.

Although ethics committees are uniquely able to pick up some of the slack that other levels of control may be unwilling or unable to handle, whether professional association ethics committees are effective and efficient means of peer control and public protection is a debatable question. Specific criticisms include the assessment of "token penalties" that have no genuine impact; conflict-of-interest or bias among committee members; the lack of training and experience of most psychologists to function adequately in a quasi-judicial capacity; allegations of precedence of protective guild interests and due process rights of respondents over the welfare of the complainants; extended time frame for adjudicating cases that may result in harm to the public in the interim; insufficient investigatory and other resources to do the job properly; timid procedures as a result of fears of lawsuits; and reactive rather than proactive procedures. (For more detailed criticisms of self-regulation in general and/or ethics committees in particular, see Taylor and Torrey, 1972; Derbyshire, 1974; Clouser, 1975; Zitrin and Klein, 1976; Moore, 1978; Hogan, 1979; Chalk, Frankel, and Chafer, 1980; Hess, 1980; Zemlick, 1980; Sinnett and Linford, 1982a).

Without denying that some of the criticisms are valid in some situations, we sustain a more positive view of the effectiveness of peer monitoring. Indeed, we strongly suspect that some critics have never served on an ethics committee. We also assert that some critics are unduly harsh and others single out ethics committees for shortcomings that exist, unfortunately, at any level of monitoring.

The "token penalties" criticism, for example, requires a closer examination. A letter of reprimand may not *seem* like much to someone who has never received one, but any negative sanction can have considerable impact as revealed in correspondence from numerous respondents. Both malpractice insurance renewal forms and license renewal forms clearly ask whether any ethics charges have been sustained against the practitioner in the intervening period. Thus even a reprimand would have to be reported and explained with some attendant risk of nonrenewal and embarrassment.

In his admittedly disdainful account, Rosenthal (1976) describes his reaction to being questioned by the APA ethics committee despite the fact that no charges were ultimately pressed against him:

> The experience has created an indelible mark on me. To one degree or another, I carry that ethics committee with me as a Tribunal perpetually in session. . . . My judges accost me most often during the psychotherapy hour whenever they sense I am near or about to trespass the boundaries of propriety or common practice. . . . Terror comes when I realize I am on my own and that what I am doing may not stand up in court. (pp. 3–4)

This description is no doubt an overstatement. However, vows of no recurrences and of having learned a lesson are common reactions among respondents who have been sanctioned by ethics committees.

We also disagree with the criticism that ethics committees hide and protect psychologists, while appearing to be dealing forcefully with the issue at hand. Whereas it is unfortunately true that ethics committees may not be able to determine all of the facts, our insider perspective reveals that this is not due to failure to explore every avenue available to them.

Ethics committees are, in fact, often more advantageous than other monitoring methods for several reasons. They are composed of psychologists with different training and backgrounds who assist in ensuring that the full range of concerns brought before the committees is properly represented. They also have access to other consultative resources within the association. The flexibility of ethics committee proceedings, compared with legal and administrative procedures, permits a wider range of data-gathering methods, without forcing one to use stringent evidence and examination requirements. Ethics committees stay in business from year to year, without a concern that legislators or other nonpsychologists will eliminate their budgets. Ethics committees can remain proconsumer without being antipsychology. An investment in protecting the profession does not eliminate a concern for the welfare of consumers and society, because the reputation of a profession is based primarily on the public's image of it. Thus it is in the profession's best interests to maintain high standards and to police itself effectively. (We shall return to a description of the internal workings of ethics committees in Chapter 2.)

INFORMAL PEER MONITORING

The Ethical Principles (EP: 7g) actively deputize psychologists to monitor peer conduct, although in a somewhat cautious and protective manner. Previous versions of the ethics code mandated that psychologists attempt to deal with ethics violations committed by colleagues on their own as the first line of action. Only if an informal attempt proved unsuccessful should an ethics committee be contacted. It was not an uncommon occurrence for complaints pressed by APA members to be either returned to the complainant or tabled by the ethics committee until after the complaining psychologist had attempted to resolve the matter independently.

The 1981 version of the *Ethical Principles,* however, issued a more guarded obligation, noting that individual psychologists acting on no real authority may not always be the most appropriate remediation agents. Currently, the psychologist is given the option of deciding whether he or she is the appropriate party to deal with the matter directly. The code recommends that misconduct either of a minor nature or due to lack of sensitivity, knowledge, or experience is probably amenable to informal resolution. If an informal solution seems unlikely (for reasons left unspecified in the code), or if the violation is of a more serious nature, then the psychologist should contact a local, state, or national ethics committee.

Although no data base exists, it is likely that the earlier versions of the ethics code stifled the entire process of informal peer monitoring. Psychologists observing or suspecting ethical misconduct by peers were on their own in waters that may have felt dangerous and cold, especially if the suspected violator was litigious or antisocial. We do know of several instances of threatened legal action for harassment and slander against psychologists who attempted to report ethical misconduct of colleagues, and these incidents were instrumental in the more recent decision to alter the obligations of psychologists.

Biases and Risks

Whenever one observes or learns of a colleague's unethical behavior, a decision to intervene is unlikely to be made dispassionately. Several factors, in addition to the alleged misconduct itself, often intrude and thus may alter the course of action substantially (Keith-Spiegel, Note 1). The following two vignettes, for example, reveal the role of the nature of the relationship between the psychologist who suspects that an ethical misconduct has occurred and the alleged violator.

Vignette A

Your colleague, Professor X, is a person you have never liked or respected. He is arrogant and absorbed with his own self-promotion. He contributes virtually nothing to the department or its spirit. In social situations he usually either ignores you or, if he does acknowledge your existence, makes statements such as "Did you ever manage to finish that little study you were trying to run last year?"

His student assistant has recently approached you with a problem. He has noticed that the data Dr. X supposedly analyzed are not the same data he collected. Furthermore, Dr. X is reporting twice the number of subjects actually used in the procedure. He has the evidence in hand. Dr. X has submitted a manuscript based on the apparently fraudulent data to a journal for publication. How would you advise the student, and what action would you consider?

Vignette B

Your colleague, Dr. Y, is a good friend. He is a gentle man who prefers teaching to research, but is facing pressure to do research since his tenure evaluation is coming up next year. You and Dr. Y see each other socially about twice a month. You share an interest in football and chat about it constantly during the season.

His student assistant has recently approached you with a problem. He has noted that the data Dr. Y supposedly analyzed are not the same data he collected. Furthermore, Dr. Y is reporting twice the number of subjects actually used in the procedure. He has the evidence in hand. Dr. Y has submitted a manuscript based on the apparently fraudulent data to a journal for publication. How would you advise the student, and what action would you consider?

When colleagues were asked to respond only to the Professor X vignette, their perceptions of the incident were harsh, and their intended responses were formal and direct. Most stated that they would form an alliance with the student assistant and together they would plot a course of action that would lead to the full exposure of the transgression and the transgressor. Another group of colleagues responded only to the Professor Y vignette, and the responses were *markedly* different. One person became so distressed at the thought of facing such a prospect that he said he could not deal with it at all. The others responded with a general theme that involved two basic actions. First, the student assistant would be disengaged entirely from the matter by convincing the student that it would be "dealt with appropriately." Next, Professor Y would be approached and asked to withdraw his manuscript from consideration and the matter would be considered closed. Several people, however, proposed assisting Professor Y either in developing new studies or in working on the data legitimately collected so that something could be completed in time for Professor Y's tenure evaluation.

In addition to "like" and "dislike" dimensions, other relationships could alter the action a psychologist may take toward a suspected violator of ethical standards. For example, the offending psychologist could be a family member, a competitor for a promotion slot, or someone who holds a position of power or authority over the concerned psychologist. Each situation may evoke a different set of reactions that may, in turn, affect the attributes assigned to the suspected violator.

The personal biases, attitudes, beliefs, and personality traits of the psychologist witnessing or learning of an ethics violation committed by a colleague are also powerful determinants of what action (if any) might be taken. Because psychologists differ in their definitions of and commitments to professional obligations and responsibilities, they may have different reactions to either direct experiences or reports of ethical misconduct of peers. Psychologists also probably vary on assessments of seriousness, including the potential for harm, of violations of the various ethical principles promulgated by the profession. Decisions to take action may reflect differences in beliefs about the reprehensibility of a particular act. Indeed, we have observed such discrepancies during actual ethics committee deliberations!

The ethical ideologies held by an individual may be a major determinant in a psychologist's decision to become involved with informal peer monitoring. A useful scheme created by Forsyth (1980) can be used to illustrate how one's degree of idealism and relativistic views may influence how one perceives a particular act and what type of decision or action may follow. (See Table 1-2.) For example, the "exceptionalist" would probably respect the *Ethical Principles* but make allowances for a particular set of circumstances, whereas the "absolutist" would not be so swayed by mitigating circumstances. The "situationist" may or may not advocate the *Ethical Principles* depending on his or her analysis of a particular situation, whereas the "subjectivist" may never have even read the *Ethical Principles*.

Standards people employ when making moral judgments have also been related to basic differences in personality structure (Hogan, 1970). Other traits, such as assertiveness, anxiety level, tolerance, and courage, are

TABLE 1-2
Taxonomy of Ethical Ideologies

Idealism	High	Relativism Low
High	**Situationists** Rejects moral values; advocates individualistic analysis of each act in each situation; relativistic.	**Absolutists** Assumes that the best possible outcome can always be achieved by following universal moral rules.
Low	**Subjectivists** Appraisals based on personal values and perspective, rather than on universal moral principles; relativistic.	**Exceptionists** Moral absolutes guide judgments, but pragmatically open to exceptions to these standards; utilitarian.

(Forsyth, 1980. Reprinted with permission of the author and the American Psychological Association.)

also determinants of what action a psychologist will or will not take toward a colleague.

Whether a psychologist was directly victimized by the conduct of a colleague is probably another major determinant of what action will be contemplated. As discussed in detail in Chapter 2, those who are angered by a psychologist's conduct appear to compromise the vast majority of complainants. When psychologists complain against colleagues to ethics committees, more often than not they are personally affected in some way by the alleged unethical conduct. This reporting pattern may be partially due to the more salient evidence available when the violation was experienced directly as opposed to hearing about a violation secondhand. Although no data are available regarding the frequency of informal intervention by psychologists *not* personally involved in or affected directly by the ethical misconduct of another psychologist, it is possible that variations of the "bystander apathy" phenomenon described by social psychologists may operate: in essence, psychologists may diffuse responsibility if they see themselves as only one of a large pool of psychologists who know of the possible ethical misconduct of a colleague. Rusch's (1981) survey reveals that the majority of the psychologists sampled indicate that action would be taken after witnessing a *serious* ethical violation and that direct contact with the violator was the most preferred option. However, for less serious violations, any action at all was unlikely.

Several other factors might contribute to a reluctance to become involved in informal peer monitoring. These factors include fear of retribution or other personal consequences, in addition to conflicts concerning the duty to report or intervene versus maintaining a loyal and protective stance toward one's colleagues (Bok, 1978).

Another set of problematic factors involves the assessment of the misconduct itself. Ethical infractions, particularly the most serious ones, are seldom committed openly before a host of witnesses. With few exceptions, such as plagiarism or inappropriate advertisement of services offered, no tangible exhibits corroborate that an unethical event ever occurred. If the evidence is unverifiable or ambiguous, a psychologist may feel uneasy about becoming involved with informal peer monitoring. Another related problem that sometimes occurs is difficulty in determining whether a given act constitutes an ethics violation. The distinction between the merely unorthodox or poor professional etiquette and unethical behavior is not always easy to discern.

Hints for Engaging in Informal Peer Monitoring

Despite the biases and risks that may operate when informal peer monitoring is contemplated, we encourage active involvement in this professional responsibility. (See Chapter 11 for case examples involving informal peer monitoring.) Although it is not possible for us to make the task of confronting colleagues about their unethical conduct easy, we offer the following suggestions that may facilitate a successful outcome:

1. Locate the relevant section of the *Ethical Principles* that applies to the suspected violation. Use this at the onset as the framework for evaluating the situation.

2. Assess the strength of the evidence that a violation has been committed. Is it mostly hearsay? How credible is the source of information? Are there any substantial, verifiable facts? This process is important because it assists in formulating the appropriate approach to the offender. Weak or hearsay evidence would dictate a mild introduction to the topic, whereas overwhelming, credible evidence would necessitate setting a more formal initial tone.

3. Be in touch with your own motivations to engage in (or to avoid) a confrontation. In addition to any fears, anger, or other emotional reaction, do you perceive that the conduct, either as it stands or if it continues, will potentially undermine the integrity of the profession and/or harm one or more of the people served by the psychologist? If the answer to this question is affirmative, then *some* action is mandated.

4. Consultation with a trusted and experienced colleague who has demonstrated a sensitivity to ethical issues is recommended. If you personally do not know such a person, state psychological associations or the APA may be able to provide names of individuals available to help psychologists with ethics-related problem solving. Do homework if necessary. This book and other writings may help to clarify the nature of the violation and may assist in educating the offender.

5. Schedule the confrontation in advance, although not in a menacing manner. (For example, do *not* say: "Something has come to my attention about you that causes me grave concern. What are you doing a week from next Thursday?") Simply indicate to the offender that you would like to speak with her or him privately and schedule a face-to-face meeting. A business setting would normally be more appropriate than a home or restaurant. (Handling such matters on the phone is not recommended, unless geographical barriers preclude a direct meeting.)

6. When entering into the confrontation phase, remain calm and self-confident. The offender-psychologist may display considerable emotion. Expect that, but do not become involved in it. Be as nonthreatening as possible. Avoid a rigidly moralistic, higher-than-thou demeanor, since most people find this approach obnoxious.

7. Set the tone for a constructive and educative session. Your role is *not* that of accuser, judge, jury, or penance-dispenser; instead, perceive your role as one of informing and educating and as a teammate in problem solving. The session will probably develop better if you see yourself as having an alliance with the offender—not in the usual sense of consensus and loyalty, but as

facing a problem together. The demeanor resulting from this role perception will assist in facilitating a favorable outcome.

8. Describe your ethical obligations, noting the relevant section of the *Ethical Principles* that encourages your intervention. Rather than equivocating or beating around the bush, state your concerns directly and present the evidence on which they are based. If confidences require protection (e.g., another person agreed to allow you to confront the psychologist, but insisted that his or her identity be protected), explain this and expect an uncomfortable reaction since no one relishes an unseen and unknown accuser. Do not attempt to play detective by trying to trap your colleague through asking leading questions or by withholding relevant information. Such tactics will lead only to defensiveness and resentment and diminish the possibility of a favorable outcome.

9. Allow the offender time to explain and defend in as much detail as required. The colleague may be flustered and repetitive. Be patient with this response.

10. If the offender is abusive or theatening, attempt to lead her or him to a more constructive state. Although some people need a chance to vent feelings, they often settle down if the confronting person remains steady and refrains from becoming abusive and threatening in return. If the negative reaction continues, it may be appropriate to say something calming, such as: "I see you are very upset right now and I regret that we cannot explore this matter together in a way that would be satisfactory to both of us. I would like you to think about what I have presented and if you would reconsider talking more about it, please contact me within a week." If a return call is not forthcoming, then other forms of action must be taken. Action might involve another appropriate person, or it might include pressing formal charges to some duly constituted monitoring body and informing the offender of your next step.

11. If the offender is a friend or acquaintance with whom there has been no previous problematic interactions, the "teammate role" described above is easier to effect. You can express how you wanted to be the one to deal with the matter because you care about the person and her or his professional standing. The danger, of course, is that you may feel that you are risking an established, positive relationship. If your friend can be handled effectively by you, however, you have done a colleague a favor by protecting him or her from embarrassment or from more public forms of censure. Moreover, if you have lost respect for your friend after learning of possible ethical misconduct, the relationship has been altered anyway. Discomfort, to the extent that it ensues, will probably be temporary. If the confrontation was successful, and clarifications and remediations were explored, however, the relationship would remain intact.

12. If the offender is someone you do not know personally, the confrontation will be, by definition, more formal. But expressing a motivation of concern and a willingness to work through the problem together may still be quite effective.

13. If the offender is someone you do know but dislike, your dilemma is more difficult. If the information is known to others or can be appropriately

shared with others, you might consider approaching someone who has a better relationship with this person to intercede. If that is not feasible, and a careful assessment of your own motivations reveals a conclusion that the misconduct requires intervention on its own merits, then you must take some form of action. It may still be possible to approach this individual yourself and, if you maintain a professional attitude, it may work out. We know of one psychologist who approached his longstanding nemesis with concern about her ethical conduct, and the two eventually became friends as a result of working through the matter together!

While facing a dilemma whether to confront a colleague, one might be *tempted* to engage in one of two covert activities. The first temptation is to gossip about the suspected or known ethical violation to others. This behavior may *feel* as though action has been taken because other people have been informed or warned. Although gossip may provide a sense that duty has been fulfilled, it is more likely that responsibility has only been diffused, and gossip certainly cannot guarantee that the offender has been affected in any constructive way. Moreover, to the extent that the conduct was misjudged, it may cause a colleague unfair harm. The second temptation is to engage in more direct but anonymous action. This action may include sending an unsigned note or delivering a relevant document (e.g., a copy of the *Ethical Principles* with one or more sections circled in red). Constructive results, however, are not guaranteed, and the recipient may not even receive a clear message. Even if the information was absorbed, the reaction to an anonymous charge may be counterproductive. In fact, it may only assist the offender in perfecting the art of nondetection, and/or it may instill a certain amount of paranoia that could result in additional negative consequences (such as adding suspiciousness to the individual's character). Thus, although both of these covert actions feel safe and proactive, we recommend neither.

SELF-MONITORING AND ETHICAL DECISION MAKING

A complete familiarity with and commitment to upholding the *Ethical Principles* are by themselves major hedges against engaging in ethical misconduct. One must know and be prepared to obey the rules of professional and ethical expectations before one can uphold the principles. Many violators of the *Ethical Principles* have attempted to defend their acts by arguing that they were unaware of the provisions of the ethics code. Similar to legal liability, however, ignorance is no excuse. Yet the fact remains that knowledge of the code, as well as a sincere motivation to follow it, will not fully insulate psychologists from questionable conduct.

As described earlier, ethics codes are general, prescriptive guides and may not always provide answers to ethical conflicts arising in specific circumstances. Indeed, they were never intended to cover every conceivable eventuality, and it is unlikely that such a comprehensive guideline could ever be created. In addition, ethics codes often do not deal adequately with many contradictions that can arise. For example, although the code stresses consumer welfare, it is not unusual for a circumstance to arise wherein protecting a consumer may simultaneously place another person, group, or even the public-at-large at risk. Psychologists incur ethical responsibilities to their clients (including students, supervisees, and research participants), their employers, the law, and society in general, as well as to their profession and their colleagues. It is often difficult, if not impossible, to protect the rights and fulfill the legitimate needs of all sectors simultaneously (Roston, 1975; Freedman, 1978).

A careful reading of the *Ethical Principles* reveals a recurring explicit or implicit requirement to use one's professional judgment in the course of upholding the mandates of the code. Thus psychologists must develop some decision-making strategies to assist in coping with each ethical matter when it arises. We expect that such a process will maximize the chances to effect an ethical outcome, but we are also quick to note that this may not necessarily be the case. Some outcomes remain problematical no matter how much effort was expended in resolving the conflict. Ethical decision-making strategies do not actually *make* the decision, but they permit a systematic examination of the situation and the factors that may influence the final decision (Tymchuk, 1981). At the *very least*, engaging in an ethical decision-making procedure provides protection for psychologists themselves, because it can be used later to explain what factors were taken into consideration prior to reaching a decision and taking action (Tymchuk et al., 1982).

A Suggested Ethical Decision-Making Process

Ethical dilemmas faced by social and behavioral science researchers are usually quite different on the surface from those faced by psychotherapists whose dilemmas, in turn, appear unlike those of teaching psychologists, and so forth. The underlying issues, however, are often similar, thereby allowing us to adapt from a basic procedural guideline developed by Alexander Tymchuk (1981; and Note 2).

1. *Describe the parameters of the situation.* Initially one should obtain information from the parties involved and/or from sources relevant to the matter, such as literature papers or collegial consultation.

2. *Define the potential issues involved.* From the information assembled from the first phase, the resulting critical issues should be described.

3. *Consult the guidelines, if any, already available that might apply to the resolution of each issue.* These guidelines may include the *Ethical Principles* or other codes or policy statements issued by APA or related professional organizations; federal law or policy, such as the Department of Health and Human Services

regulations regarding research procedures with human or animal participants; local and state laws, including those related to the regulation of the
profession; research evidence, including clinical case studies that may apply
to the particular situation; and value systems, including religious, political,
philosophical, and economic orientations. The "right answer" might not, of
course, necessarily emerge at this point. One may discover contradictions or
may find no relevant application from any source and may become even more
confused than before this process was started! Nevertheless, this is a critical
step to take conscientiously since a disregard for extant policy may well have
future consequences.

4. *Evaluate the rights, responsibilities, and welfare of all affected parties* (including
   institutions and the general public). It is not unusual to discover that a flawed
   decision resulted from the lack of awareness of a party's right to confidentiality,
   informed consent, or evaluative feedback.

5. *Generate the alternative decisions possible for each issue.* This phase should be
   conducted *without* a focus on whether each option is ethical or feasible, but
   may include alternatives that the psychologist would consider useless, too
   risky, or inappropriate. The decision *not* to make a decision or to do nothing
   should also be included. Establishing an array of options allows for the
   occasional finding that a decision initially considered unacceptable may later
   be the best one after all.

6. *Enumerate the consequences of making each decision.* Whenever relevant, these
   consequences should include economic, psychological, and social costs; short-
   term, ongoing, and long-term effects; the time and effort necessary to effect
   each decision, including any resource limitations; any other risks, including
   the violation of individual rights; and any benefits.

7. *Present any evidence that the various consequences or benefits resulting from each
   decision will actually occur.* To the extent possible, estimate the probability of
   such occurrences. Often no evidence exists, because the rapidly changing
   discipline is characterized by the frequent emergence of new and not-fully-
   tested innovative techniques. Lack of evidence must be considered in and of
   itself a risk, since the decision outcome is not predictable.

8. *Make the decision.* If the above phases have been completed conscientiously, a
   full informational display should now be available. Ideally, one should share
   this information with all people affected by the decision, or at least some
   subset of representatives if a larger population is involved. Their input
   should be solicited and considered. If affected parties cannot be contacted or
   cannot participate or cannot give consent due either to age or to physical,
   mental, or other limitations (e.g., small children, prisoners, or developmentally disabled people), the psychologist incurs responsibilities to ensure
   that their welfare is protected. Special advocates or other safeguards may be
   required. In some cases, the psychologist's role may be limited to the information presentation, since those affected have the right to make the final
   decision themselves.

Some decision options can be quickly dismissed because they involve
flagrant violations of someone's rights or other respectable governing poli-

cies, or because the risks far outweigh the possible benefits. Sometimes, however, several decisions appear to be equally feasible or correct; in these cases, collegial consultation may again prove useful. Or, at other times, the best decision is not feasible due to various factors, such as resource limitations; in these instances, another, less preferable decision would have to be considered.

Whenever the final decision requires implementation during a period of time, the plan must be carefully developed and communicated to all affected parties. The plan should be monitored through its completion and, in some cases, follow-up may also be desirable.

Sources of Variability in Ethical Decision Making

No matter how objectively and carefully psychologists may attempt to follow an ethical decision-making process, such as the one we have just described, many factors will influence it. Except in those instances in which the issues are clear-cut, salient, and definitively defined by established guidelines, psychologists will probably differ among themselves regarding the decision. In a survey requiring respondents to make ethical decisions on various treatment issues, Tymchuk et al. (1982) found that the inconsistencies among psychologists were greatest when the treatments described were novel or when no guidelines existed.

Some variability will probably be due to the amount of professional experience a psychologist has accumulated. Morrison, Layton, and Newman (Note 3) found that more experienced psychologists reported fewer ethical conflicts arising in their work than did newcomers to the profession. Perhaps the experienced group was more self-confident and competent, but this is not the only explanation possible. It is also possible that newcomers have received more training in ethical matters, since formal ethics training is a rather recent phenomenon within the profession, and they may be more sensitized to the issues. Newcomers may also be somewhat more idealistic.

The criteria used to make the final decision can also vary, leading to different outcomes. Some people may focus on the *Ethical Principles*, while others focus on the individual client, the welfare of society, loyalty to ones' employer, scientific rigor, and so forth. The psychologist's orientation within the discipline may be a major determinant of principal criteria revealing differences among those with, for example, humanistic, behavioral, and psychoanalytic leanings.

As indicated in the preceding section on informal peer monitoring, personality and values will significantly influence one's own ethical decision-making process. These personal characteristics might include criteria used to assign innocence, blame, and responsibility; personal needs and goals, including emotional involvement; a need to avoid censure; and the level of risk one is willing to take. Intertwined in most sources of variability in ethical decision making are differences in value systems among psychologists. Although this book does not approach ethical principles from the perspective of moral philosophies and their relative merits, limitations, and uses, we will make frequent references to the potential for power abuse and coercion whenever psychologists exercise their personal value systems in ways that bias them against the welfare of individuals or groups with whom they work.

Ethical Decision Making under Crisis Conditions

When ethical conflicts arise, the most appropriate resolution is far more likely to be satisfying if several other conditions simultaneously pertain. These conditions include the following: (1) sufficient time available to collect systematically all pertinent information, to consider strategies or plan for change, and to intervene and follow-up; (2) the involvement of all relevant parties; (3) the proper identification of the "client" to whom primary allegiance is owed; (4) freedom from stress and the possibility of keeping sufficient distance to maximize objectivity; and (5) maintenance of an ongoing evaluation, which allows for midcourse corrections or other changes to resolve satisfactorily the dilemma (adapted from Babad and Salomon, 1978). In most instances involving ethical dilemmas, decisions do not have to be rushed into before the above conditions can be met. But sometimes a situation will arise, usually for psychologists who provide clinical services, that requires immediate determinations and action in the absence of sufficient time to consult, consider all alternatives, and plan appropriate strategies. Ethical issues imbedded in the following case examples include confidentiality, client welfare, invasion of privacy, and protection of either identifiable others or the public in general.

> **Case 1−1:** A psychotherapy client who had expressed considerable suicidal ideation and who had made numerous suicidal gestures appeared uncommonly "flat" and resigned during a session. The psychologist was aware that the stressors in her life were exceptionally intense at this point and was concerned that the client's apathy and apparent calm could indicate a commitment to suicide rather than be a sign of improvement. The psychologist questioned the woman about her plans, but her answers were vague, and any intent to do herself harm was denied.

> **Case 1−2:** A female client burst into tears during the initial therapy session and insisted that if she returned to her home, her abusive and alcoholic husband would kill her.

> **Case 1−3:** A 10-year-old female client, brought in by the mother because the child was behaving "in an uncommonly reserved and withdrawn manner and could offer

no explanation for this abrupt change in personality," told the therapist that for the past three months her stepfather had been entering her room every night after everyone else was asleep, touching her body, and requesting that she fondle his genitals. The stepfather had warned the girl not to tell the mother or her brothers because if she did she would be responsible for breaking up the family.

Case 1–4: One student threatened to do harm to another student and to the professor during an intense outburst in a geography classroom. Another geography professor called the dean who, in turn, called a clinical psychologist in the psychology department requesting that the psychologist determine the appropriate course of action immediately since he was "an expert when it comes to dealing with crazy kids."

Case 1–5: A psychotherapy client expressed considerable anger toward an ex-boss who had recently fired him. During a late evening session, the client announced that the ex-boss was an exploiter of the working classes and deserved "to be exterminated." The client then detailed a plan to perform the execution himself as soon as the therapy session was over. The psychologist was unable to convince him otherwise and, while in the process of trying, the client abruptly bolted from the room and disappeared down the hall.

As each of the above cases illustrates, crises with some ethical implications occur most often when an element of immediate danger is present. Although it has been debated whether mental health professionals can ever hope to predict "dangerousness" accurately (Daley, 1975; Peszke, 1975; Shah, 1978), a professional judgment regarding whether the danger is "clear and present" must be made. If the determination is affirmative, the psychologist is released from the obligation to maintain confidentiality and may involve "appropriate others" in whatever actions are deemed necessary to protect the individual or others or society. In addition, the psychologist may be required by law to reveal information shared in confidence under certain circumstances. Unfortunately, the *Ethical Principles* offer minimal assistance in formulating appropriate actions beyond relieving the psychologist from the confidentiality mandated in the usual circumstances that involve no danger. Moreover, other sources of assistance, even if one has the time to consult them, do not provide an unequivocal course of action either. Legal case precedents involving people threatening harm to others with whom a psychologist has a professional relationship, such as *Tarasoff* (see Chapter 3), are muddled regarding outcome and relevance to similar situations with slight variations; thus, as Winslade (in press) concludes:

> The profession [psychotherapists] would do well to maintain a skeptical attitude about any theoretical framework purporting to solve complex, unique, and atomistically irreducible episodes that call for sensitive, thoughtful, and responsible clinical judgments. . . . The complexity of factual situations, the inevitable uncertainties of human conduct, the difficulties in orchestrating patients, potential victims, families, police, and mental health institutions, are

likely to defy any neat categorization or fixed plan of action. . . . Therapists would be wise to make decisions about each such case on an individual basis rather than trying to find a formula to apply in every instance.

Patient suicides, involving later legal actions by the patients' families, reveal sufficiently unclear determinations of appropriate professional and ethical decision making, thereby leading to a similar conclusion that no *set* course of action has been agreed on for people threatening harm to themselves (Slawson, Flinn, and Schwartz, 1974; Berman and Cohen-Sandler, 1983).

Psychologists are among the few professionals who are especially vulnerable to requirements to perform and to make decisions with ethical ramifications under crisis conditions. This problem can occur even if the psychologist is not directly involved in the emergency situation itself. Rubin (1975) vividly describes an instance (from which *Case 1–4* cited previously was adapted) in which he was called in by the administrators of his employment institution to manage a threatening and armed student. Time was of the essence. Even the determination of "client" could not be carefully considered. Was the client the violent student, the people he was menacing, the university, or society in general? The psychologist could hardly maintain "professional distance," since his own life was in danger. Although this is an extreme case, most psychologists will face, at least once in their professional careers, situations requiring ethical decision making under less-than-optimal conditions.

Although we cannot describe crisis techniques in detail, we would like to propose the following suggestions for *preventative* action that may be useful for making decisions under conditions of time restraint, crisis, or emergency:

1. Know the emergency resources available in your community. Keep the names, numbers, and descriptions of services offered in an easy-to-access location. The prudent psychologist will also check the *quality* of the resources as well. Sometimes promotional materials promise more than they actually deliver. Some resources are known to be slow or disorganized, ineffective, or even inhumane in actual crisis situations. This list should be updated at least once a year, since some of the well-meaning and enthusiastic community support services are short-lived, and others lose their funding and disband. If such resources are used during a crisis, follow-up on their services and monitor the client carefully.

2. Form an alliance of colleagues, each of whom agrees to be available for consultation when emergencies arise. Ideally, a mental health professional who has experience in working with people in crisis should be included. Keep these names and numbers in the emergency resource file.

3. Know the laws and policies in your state or locale relating to matters that are likely to concern emergency conditions (such as the state evidence code

mandating the conditions under which information obtained in confidence must be reported and commitment procedures). Frantic searches through one's files or phone calls to colleagues or lawyers are no substitute for preexisting knowledge. Any sections of the law of policies that are unclear should be clarified *before* it is necessary to understand them.

4. Locate an attorney in your community who is knowledgeable about matters that may have legal implications relevant to the practice of psychology.

5. Actively seek out learning experiences that will sharpen knowledge about the kinds of crises that may arise in professional practice. Case histories, strategies, and descriptions of clinical skills required under such conditions may not be totally relevant to a specific situation one might actually face, but they may expand the repertoire of alternatives and provide a better understanding of the dynamics of such situations.

6. Pay special attention to defining your own areas of competence, then practice within the confines of these areas. Although this is, of course, an ethical requirement in and of itself (see Chapter 9), it may also provide an additional advantage because crises, as well as the psychologist's ability to function properly during them, may often be related to the psychologist's level of expertise and experience with a particular clientele population or diagnostic group. "Competency containment" is not, of course, a surefire safeguard against crises arising, but it does reduce the probabilities of facing a crisis that one is unable to manage.

7. Carefully monitor the relationship between yourself and those with whom a close and trusting alliance has been built. Therapists mishandling transferences or techniques have been traced to the *cause* of crises, including completed suicides (Skodol, Kass, and Charles, 1979; Stone, 1971).

To the extent possible, given the time and other restraints operating in crises, use an ethical decision-making model. We also suggest that each instance be carefully documented, including decisions made and their rationale, for the psychologist's protection, as well as for possible future use during similar episodes, and/or for helping other professionals cope with such matters.

NOTES

1. Keith-Spiegel, P. *Moral conundrums, shibboleths, and Gordian knots: Current issues in ethical standards for psychologists*. Presidential address presented at the Western Psychological Association, Sacramento, California, 1982.

2. Tymchuk, A. J. *Ethical decision making and primary prevention*. Paper presented at the NIMH Conference on Ethics and Primary Prevention, Los Angeles, California, 1983.

3. Morrison, J. K.; Layton, D. B; and Newman, J. *Reported ethical conflict among mental health professionals in the community*. Paper presented at the American Psychological Association meeting, Toronto, 1978.

REFERENCES

American Bar Association. *Model Code of Professional Responsibility and Code of Judicial Conduct*. Washington, DC: ABA, 1980.

American Medical Association. *Principles of Medical Ethics*. Chicago: AMA, 1980.

American Psychiatric Association. *The Principles of Medical Ethics with Annotations Especially Applicable to Psychiatry*. Washington, DC: APA, 1981.

American Psychological Association. *Standards for Providers of Psychological Services*. Washington, DC: APA, 1977.

———. *Ethical Principles of Psychologists*. Washington, DC: APA, 1981. (See also *American Psychologist*, 1981, *36*, 633–638).

———. *Ethical Principles in the Conduct of Research with Human Participants*. Washington, DC: APA, 1982.

———. *Standards for Education and Psychological Tests*. Washington, DC: APA, 1984.

Babad, E. Y., and Salomon, G. Professional dilemmas of the psychologist in an organizational emergency. *American Psychologist*, 1978, *33*, 840–846.

Ballantine, H. T. Annual discourse—The crisis in ethics, Anno Domini 1979. *The New England Journal of Medicine*, 1979, *301*, 634–638.

Berman, A. L., and Cohen-Sandler, R. Suicide and malpractice: Expert testimony and the standard of care. *Professional Psychology*, 1983, *14*, 6–19.

Bok, S. *Lying: Moral Choice in Public and Private Life*. New York: Vintage, 1978.

Chalk, R.; Frankel, M. S.; and Chafer, S. B. *AAAS Professional Ethics Project*. Washington, D.C.: American Association for the Advancement of Science, 1980.

Clouser, K. D. Some things medical ethics is not. *Journal of the American Medical Association*, 1973, *223*, 787–789.

———. Medical ethics: Some uses, abuses, and limitations. *The New England Journal of Medicine*, 1975, *297*, 384–387.

Daley, D. W. Tarasoff and the psychotherapist's duty to warn. *San Diego Law Review*, 1975, *12*, 932–951.

Derbyshire, R. C. Medical ethics and discipline. *Journal of the American Medical Association*, 1974, *228*, 59–62.

Forsyth, D. R. A taxonomy of ethical ideologies. *Journal of Personality and Social Psychology*, 1980, *39*, 175–184.

Freedman, A. M. Ethics in psychiatry: A question of allegiance. *Psychiatric Annals*, 1978, *8*, 48–57.

Golann, S. E. Emerging areas of ethical concern. *American Psychologist*, 1969, *24*, 454–459.

———. Ethical standards for psychology: Development and revision, 1938–1968. *Annals of the New York Academy of Sciences*, 1970, *169*, 398–405.

Gross, S. The myth of professional licensing. *American Psychologist*, 1979, *33*, 1009–1016.

Hare-Mustin, R. T., and Hall, J. E. Procedures for responding to ethics complaints against psychologists. *American Psychologist*, 1981, *36*, 1494–1505.

Hess, H. F. Enforcement: Procedures, problems and prospects. *Professional Practice of Psychology*, 1980, *1*, 1–10.

Hogan, D. *Regulation of Psychotherapists*. Cambridge, MA: Ballinger, 1979.

Hogan, R. A dimension of moral judgment. *Journal of Consulting and Clinical Psychology*, 1970, *35*, 205–212.

Holtzman, W. H. The IUPS project on professional ethics and conduct. *International Journal of Psychology*, 1979, *14*, 107–109.

Koocher, G. P. Credentialing in psychology: Close encounters with competence? *American Psychologist*, 1979, *34*, 696–702.

Levy, C. S. On the development of a code of ethics. *Social Work*, 1974, *19*, 207–216.

Moore, R. A. Ethics in the practice of psychiatry: Origins, functions, models, and enforcement. *American Journal of Psychiatry*, 1978, *135*, 157–163.

Peszke, M. A. Is dangerousness an issue for physicians in emergency commitment? *American Journal of Psychiatry*, 1975, *132*, 825–828.

Rosenthal, V. A bare branch with buds. *Voices*, Spring, 1976, 2–10.

Roston, R. A. Ethical uncertainties and "technical" validities. *Professional Psychology*, 1975, *6*, 50–54.

Rubin, J. A psychologists dilemma: A real case of danger. *Professional Psychology*, 1975, *6*, 363–366.

Rusch, P. C. *An empirical study of the willingness of psychologists to report ethical violations*. Unpublished doctoral dissertation, University of Southern California, 1981.

Shah, S. A. Dangerousness: A paradigm for exploring some issues in law and psychology. *American Psychologist*, 1978, *33*, 224–238.

Sieber, J. E. Ethical dilemmas in social research. In J. E. Sieber (Ed.) *The Ethics of Social Research: Surveys and Experiments*. New York: Springer-Verlag, 1982.

Sinnett, E. R., and Linford, O. Is there a crisis in professional self-regulation of the practice of psychology? *Professional Psychology*, 1982a, *13*, 332–333.

———. Processing of formal complaints against psychologists. *Psychological Reports*, 1982b, *50*, 535–544.

Skodol, A. F., Kass, F., and Charles, E. S. Crisis in psychotherapy: Principles of emergency consultation and intervention. *American Journal of Orthopsychiatry*, 1979, *49*, 585–597.

Slawson, P. F.; Flinn, D. E.; and Schwartz, D. A. Legal responsibility for suicide. *Psychiatric Quarterly*, 1974, *48*, 50–64.

Stone, A. Suicide precipitated by psychotherapy: A clinical contribution. *American Journal of Psychotherapy*, 1971, *25*, 18–26.

Taylor, R. L., and Torrey, E. F. The pseudo-regulation of American psychiatry. *American Journal of Psychiatry*, 1972, *129*, 658–663.

Tymchuk, A. J. Ethical decision making and psychological treatment. *Journal of Psychiatric Treatment and Evaluation*, 1981, *3*, 507–513.

———. Strategies for resolving value dilemmas. *American Behavioral Science*, 1982, *26*, 159–175.

————; Draphkin, R.; Major-Kinglery, S.; Ackerman, A. B.; Coffman, E. W., and Baum, M. S. Ethical decision making and psychologist's attitudes toward training in ethics. *Professional Psychology*, 1982, *13*, 412–421.

Wellner, A. M., and Albidin, R. R. Regulation/enforcement/discipline of professional practice in psychology: Issues and strategies. *Professional Practice of Psychology*, 1981, *2*, 1–16.

Wilensky, H. L. The professionalization of everyone? *American Journal of Sociology*, 1964, *70*, 137–158.

Winslade, W. J. After Tarasoff: Legal directions and psycho-therapeutic reactions. In L. Everstine and D. S. Everstine (Eds.), *Psychotherapy and the Law*. New York: Grune and Stratton (in press).

Zemlick, M. J. Ethical standards: Cosmetics for the face of the profession of psychology. *Psychotherapy, Theory, Research and Practice*, 1980, *17*, 448–453.

Zitrin, A., and Klein, H. Can psychiatry police itself effectively? The experience of one district branch. *American Journal of Psychiatry*, 1976, *133*, 653–656.

Inside Ethics Committees 2

*One cool judgment is worth
a thousand hasty councils.*

Thomas Woodrow Wilson

In this chapter, we will reveal what occurs behind the closed doors of
ethics committee meetings. Many psychologists, including some of those
who write articles about ethics committees, are unclear or in error about
procedures, sanctions, and decision-making strategies. Most of the cases
presented throughout the book were taken from ethics committee files.
Consequently, information about the internal workings of ethics committees will also assist in understanding and evaluating the illustrative case
examples.

MAJOR UNDERLYING THEMES OF COMPLAINTS AGAINST PSYCHOLOGISTS

In our experience, the basic thematic patterns that characterize the nature of
alleged misconduct fall into five major categories: i.e., *exploitation, insensitivity, incompetence, irresponsibility*, and *abandonment*. Often these themes are
not mutually exclusive. A psychologist, for example, may be insensitive to a
client's needs because he or she is not competent to provide the services
offered. Or perhaps the psychologist's irresponsible character may lead to
abandonment of the client.

Exploitation occurs whenever psychologists take advantage of consumers by abusing a position of trust, expertise, or authority. Specific examples
include sexual exploitation of clients, charging excessive fees, deceiving

research participants in a manner that may cause them harm, or failing to credit coworkers for their contributions.

Insensitivity involves harm caused by a lack of regard or concern for the needs, feelings, rights, or welfare of others. Specific examples include rude or abusive behavior directed inappropriately toward clients or students or coworkers, biased attitudes toward minority groups that adversely affect the quality of treatment rendered, or such excessive concentration on one's own needs that adequate consideration of the needs of others with whom one works is impeded.

Incompetence occurs when psychologists are not fully capable of providing the services being rendered for reasons ranging from inadequate training or inexperience to personal unfitness, such as a character defect or an emotional disturbance. Specific examples include delivering psychotherapy services without adequate background or training in the modality used, teaching courses in areas about which one has little knowledge, or continuing to provide services while under considerable stress resulting in poor professional judgment.

Irresponsibility arises in several forms, including lack of reliable or dependable execution of professional duties, attempts to blame others for one's mistakes, shoddy or superficial professional work, or excessive delays in delivering necessary feedback, assessments, reports, or services.

Abandonment occurs when psychologists fail to follow through with their duties or responsibilities, thereby causing consumers to become vulnerable or to feel discarded or rejected. Consumers often charge that such abdication of duties either left them resourceless or caused them considerable harm. Specific examples include premature termination of psychotherapy services, refusal to fulfill commitments, deserting a position in which dependencies had been formed without adequate preparation or time to locate a replacement, or leaving a position with the tasks involved in disarray.

WHO COMPLAINS TO ETHICS COMMITTEES?

The number of complaints brought before ethics committees has been escalating in recent years. This phenomenon may be partially due to the increase in the number of psychologists and partially due to a public that may be becoming more informed about and aware of ethical issues and the rights of consumers of services.

Based on our experience with serving on ethics committees, we have arrived at several solid impressions about the characteristics of people who press ethics complaints against psychologists, (i.e., "complainants"). The majority of complaints, at least 60%, are from people who are (or were) psychotherapy clients (or family members of psychotherapy clients) and who were dissatisfied with the conduct, technique, competence, or payment policies of the psychotherapist. A substantial minority of complainants, perhaps 25%, are other psychologists or closely allied professionals who are concerned about the conduct of colleagues. The remainder are divided almost equally among students or supervisees and private citizens who were dissatisfied with their professional relationship with the psychologists delivering nonclinical services. These complaints include concerns about teaching methods, quality of business consultations, or upsetting research procedures.

Almost all complaints are instigated by individuals (sometimes banded into small, informal groups) rather than by formal organizations. The vast majority of complainants have had direct, personal interactions with the psychologists against whom they are charging ethical misconduct. However, a minority of the cases (perhaps 15%) involve complaints against psychologists by people the respondent has never met. In such instances, the complainants are usually other psychologists or allied professionals. For example, psychologists may send in advertisements they notice in newspapers or telephone directories, because they question the propriety of the content. Psychologists may mail in newspaper accounts of misconduct or lawbreaking by other psychologists, and they may suggest that the ethics committee undertake an investigation if they have not already done so. Most cases of plagiarism are discovered by psychologists or psychology students in the course of their own literature searches. Sometimes psychologists will assist a client in pressing charges against the client's previous therapist, teacher, or employer.

People who complain to ethics committees usually share several common characteristics. They tend to be knowledgeable about redress procedures, are quite capable of clearly describing the situation as they see it, and are sufficiently motivated to sustain themselves throughout the various stages of the formal ethics inquiry process. A striking similarity among complainants who were personally involved with the accused psychologists is *anger*. Often such feelings are explicitly described (e.g., "I have never felt such intense rage before in my life"), while at other times they are easily inferred (e.g., "Dr. Porky is a destructive, slovenly, moronic asshole").

It appears that angry feelings may be the primary fuel that triggers taking of formal action against a psychologist and provides the energy that sustains complainants through what is often, for them, an arduous process. Leveling a complaint with an ethics committee, however, is not an easy weapon for perturbed consumers or disgruntled colleagues to wield capriciously against psychologists. Only the truly committed will stick with the process.

Thus ethics committees tend to hear from complainants who are resourceful, articulate, rankled, and persevering. They may well comprise a highly selective group. Consumers who may have legitimate grievances of an ethical nature against psychologists, but who are hurt, frightened, unassertive, unresourceful, or inarticulate may never report them to the ethics committees or to any other redress mechanism.

Many psychologists, as well as other people, often believe that the number of extremely disturbed or delusional complainants is quite high. In fact, however, few people who complain to ethics committees could be characterized, solely on the basis of their correspondence, as seriously impaired. When committees receive complaints, such as the ones illustrated in the following examples, the most common recourses are either to ask the person for more specific details or evidence or to contact the psychologist for an impression of what has occurred.

Case 2–1: A woman complained that her psychologist had claimed the souls of her cat, two dogs, and the canary.

Case 2–2: A retired military officer charged two VA psychologists with attempting to brainwash him to "kill small boys, homosex, overthrow the British Empire, and bomb Los Angeles."

Case 2–3: A secretary wrote a long and rambling letter charging her psychologist ex-employer with following her everywhere she went, tapping her home telephone, stealing small items from her apartment, and hiring someone to drive by her place at all hours of the day and night on a motorcycle.

These are clearly unfortunate situations. But ethics committees do not simply dismiss complaints without trying to ascertain additional details about the situation and to ensure that the psychologist had attempted to protect the individual's welfare.

Occasionally ethics committees press charges *sua sponte*; that is, on the basis of information in the public domain (e.g., newspaper articles, advertisements, or courts records), the committee initiates the investigation itself. The following two cases illustrate cases handled *sua sponte*.

Case 2–4: A large envelope was sent to an ethics office with no identifying information about the sender. The contents consisted of a 1969 journal article describing the results of a survey on teenage runaways and a microfilm copy of a 1975 psychology doctoral dissertation, authored by someone else, which contained the same data and most of the text duplicated exactly as it appeared in the earlier journal article.

Although ethics committees do not normally pursue anonymous complaints, this was an exception since it did not matter who provided the evidence. The committee has received sufficient information to investigate a possible plagiarism violation.

Case 2–5: Several psychologists and students sent an ethics committee a local newspaper article containing a quote from a psychology professor who admitted to having frequent sexual relationships with undergraduate students in his classes.

In this instance, the committee again decided to investigate the matter independently, since the people who brought it to the committee's attention were not involved in the alleged improprieties but were merely supplying the committee with information from the public domain.

THE PERILS OF BEING A COMPLAINANT

The full cooperation of complainants, whether they are consumers or professional colleagues, is absolutely necessary if ethics committees are to function properly. Consequently, complainants must accept the committee's rules and procedures for processing the complaint. Because the committee's procedures are designed to protect the due process rights of the respondent, as well as the rights of the complainant, they contain several policies that may cause complainants some discomfort (see Appendix B).

Complainants must be willing to allow their identities and the nature of their complaint to be shared with the accused party. They must also sign a waiver allowing the respondent to share information relevant to the case, often involving material originally shared in confidence (i.e., therapy notes or diagnoses or psychological assessment records) with the committee. This procedure may feel especially uncomfortable to the complainant since such information will be shared as a defense against the charge rather than as a substantiation of it. Sometimes the respondent does not offer a defense and agrees that the ethical violation did occur precisely as the complainant described it. Occasionally, in an attempt to create a defense, the respondent will unwittingly offer additional incriminating data. However, predictions about a respondent's reaction cannot be made in advance of obtaining the waivers of confidentiality from the complainant.

Although the waiver requirement was not designed to discourage pursuit of ethics charges, some complainants drop their charges when asked to sign and return waivers. Some complainants never return the forms, while others write the committee indicating that they have decided not to pursue the case. In one instance, a potential complainant wrote that she would be afraid for her life if the psychologist knew that she had written to an ethics committee. Another person wrote that she could not bear the thought of the psychologist discussing her personal turmoils with "a bunch of strangers" (i.e., ethics committee members). Another person dropped a complaint when he was told that the psychologist's correspondence to the committee could not be shared directly with him.

It is possible that some frivolous or contrived complaints may be reconsidered when complainants realize that pursuing an ethics charge is a serious and complicated business. Occasionally, however, the reasons for not pursuing a complaint never become known and cause feelings of frustration and powerlessness in committee members. Those complainants who persist, as most do, agree to have their identities known to the respondent; in addition, they also agree to have their identities shared with the respondent and to allow the respondent to share relevant material about them with the committee.

Then the complainants must *wait*. Cases may take three months to several years to adjudicate, with the average case lasting six to eight months. This delay may be distressing to the complainant (and the respondent as well), because the act of pressing a charge (as well as having one pressed) establishes an uncomfortable anticipation while waiting for a resolution. When the investigation is complete and the decision has been reached, the complainant will be informed, but feedback about the details may be more scanty than the person expects.

Occasionally complainants have expressed dissatisfaction after learning that ethics committees cannot award financial damages, terminate employment, or revoke licenses. Although the rules and procedures made available to all complainants at the onset of the process state the types of sanctions available to impose on guilty respondents, some complainants apparently do not fully understand or accept these limitations.

Sometimes the accused psychologists heap additional difficulties on complainants after the investigation is initiated. On rare occasion, threats ranging from verbal abuse to law suits have been reported by complainants, after the ethics committee had contacted the respondent. When the complainant is in an ongoing relationship with the respondent and occupies the less powerful position, such as in the case of an employee or student, fears of adverse evaluations or other retaliation are commonly expressed. Consequently, these complainants often wait until after the relationship has been terminated before pressing charges.

When the complainant is also a psychologist, the respondent sometimes files a countercharge against the complaining psychologist, often appearing to be "harassment." A recent change in the APA procedures, however, does not allow for adjudicating any countercharges until the original complaint is resolved. Sometimes, as described more fully in Chapter 11, instigating an ethics charge is a way to wage an interpersonal battle between psychologists. Committees are uncomfortable when the role of "weapon" is thrust upon them, and they attempt to minimize opportunities for being used in this manner.

By candidly sharing these perils of complaining to an ethics committee, we do not wish to discourage people from pressing complaints against psychologists who have violated the ethical principles. Rather, we urge consideration of Moore's (1978) concept regarding the function of complainants. Moore contends that complainants have only one function; namely, to notify a profession that something may be awry with one of its members. Notification should lead to remedial action that will help ensure the integrity and standards of the profession and, in turn, benefit society. The complainant may obtain few benefits, but should receive altruistic satisfaction from helping the profession to improve itself.

COMPLAINTS ETHICS COMMITTEES DO NOT PURSUE

In general, ethics committees do not pursue complaints included in any of the following seven categories: (1) when the nature of the complaint has no relevant or corresponding provision in the *Ethical Principles*; (2) when the person's alleged infraction was *not* committed while he or she was functioning in the role of a psychologist; (3) when the committee members agree that a professional association to which the complaint was directed is not an appropriate mediator; (4) when complaints are filed against nonmembers of the professional association; (5) when complaints are made against groups, agencies, corporations, or institutions rather than against identifiable individuals; (6) when the complaints are anonymous (but not in the public domain, as previously noted); and (7) when the statutes of limitations have passed.

No Relevant Provision in the Ethics Code

Despite the intentionally broad concepts found in the *Ethical Principles*, an occasional complaint does not fit into the code.

> **Case 2–6:** Tim Nopenny, a graduate student, complained that Don Staunch, Ph.D., director of a clinical internship program, discriminated against him and any other applicant with limited financial resources living a considerable distance from the facility. The program required applicants to appear for a personal interview. Tim claimed that he did not have enough money to make the trip and requested the facility to pay for his travel expenses, or for the staff director to come to him, or that the interview be conducted over the phone. Dr. Staunch rejected these alternatives on the grounds that the budget was insufficient to pay for the applicants' travel expenses, the entire staff was involved with the evaluation process, and that on-site applicant visits were critical to the determination of suitability for training.

Although an ethics committee sympathized with Tim Nopenny's predicament, nothing in the ethics code prohibits a psychologist, acting in this case as an agent for an internship program, from administering selection policies that can be reasonably justified.

> **Case 2–7:** Kitty Friend complained to an ethics committee about a psychologist she read about in the newspaper who was doing research on evoked potentials in cat brains. She asserted that the use of domesticated cats in research was unethical, inhumane, and immoral.

The ethics committee would have pursued such a complaint if evidence indicated that the animals had been subjected to unjustified discomfort, were poorly cared for, or endured surgical procedures without appropriate anesthesia—all actions explicitly proscribed by the ethics code (*EP*: 10). It is not unethical *per se*, however, to do research on cats or on any other infrahuman species.

Conduct Outside the Professional Role

Usually, with some types of exceptions noted later, an ethics committee will not consider complaints involving psychologists who were functioning outside a professional role when the alleged infraction occurred.

> **Case 2–8:** A recently divorced woman, who worked in the same office building with Ted Jilt, Psy. D., complained to an ethics committee that the psychologist had exploited her and was responsible for her current anxiety state. The two had started dating and spent the night together on several occasions. Then, she claimed, Dr. Jilt called less frequently and finally stopped making contact altogether.

After clarifying with the complainant that she was not and never had been a client or supervisee of the psychologist, the ethics committee informed her that it would not intervene in relationship problems between consenting adults functioning in their roles as private citizens.

The professional/private role situation is not always clear-cut. Individuals who serve on ethics committees do not always agree that cases should be rejected when psychologists are acting as private citizens or in some other nonpsychologist role, especially if the misconduct was of an especially grave nature. One argument contends that, whenever a person who happens to be a psychologist engages in an act that has serious consequences, the person's competence and fitness to be a psychologist can also be questioned. A second argument maintains that if the person's conduct is of an extremely menacing nature or becomes highly publicized, and reference to the person's identity as a psychologist is highlighted, then the public trust in psychology and psychologists may be reduced (see Chapter 15). To refrain from any action under these circumstances might reflect poorly on our profession. Consequently, the committee's procedures permit expulsion of a member who has committed a felony, regardless of the relevance of the crime to that person's professional identity.

> **Case 2–9:** Andrew Bumpoff, Ph.D., was convicted of the attempted murder of his wife, after a young man who was hired to do the killing confessed during questioning by the police. The man claimed that Dr. Bumpoff had bought a large insurance policy on his wife's life and promised the man one-quarter of the payoff if he would break into the house on a particular evening when Dr. Bumpoff was seeing clients,

shoot his wife, and take a few expensive items to make it appear to be a robbery. The trial was widely publicized, and Dr. Bumpoff's profession was prominently woven into every story.

In this case, the ethics committee acted *sua sponte* (initiating the case itself) since after verifying the media information, it judged that such a person was not fit to function as a psychotherapist. Thus, in actual practice, psychologists' private lives remain unscrutinized by ethics committees *except* in instances where their behavior "may compromise the fulfillment of their professional responsibilities or reduce the public trust in psychology or psychologists" (*EP:* 3 preamble).

Ethics Committees as Inappropriate Mediators

Sometimes an ethics committee refuses to process complaints when it becomes clear that the committee will be unable to make any reasonable contribution to the solution of the problem. This problem occurs most often under the following circumstances: (1) when two or more psychologists are involved in an intense interpersonal conflict that affects their professional relationship with each other; (2) when the infraction involves acts that might conceivably be unethical, but which are virtually impossible for ethics committees to evaluate or investigate; (3) when the issues are related to non-ethical aspects of standards of practice or interprofessional political disputes; or (4) when other sources of redress are clearly more appropriate.

Case 2–10: Edgar Potshot, Ed.E., who had a longstanding and intense dislike for a colleague, complained that the colleague engaged in unprofessional conduct when he had told a department secretary that the complainant had "shit for brains." When the committee asked the colleague about the incident, he countercharged that Dr. Potshot had been making horrendous remarks about him to others for years and produced corroborative witnesses.

The committee realized that it could not resolve the ethical issues or the intense and ingrained interpersonal difficulties between the two men, given the limitations of its scope and function. A duplicate letter was sent to both psychologists indicating that it was withdrawing from the case and noting that this was a no-win situation for all concerned. The letter stressed the professional responsibilities of both parties and urged them to embark on some course of action that would lead to a neutralization of the destructive nature of their relationship.

Case 2–11: A student complained that a psychology professor gave her a B in a course when she thought she had deserved an A.

Some complaints, including most involving grading disputes, are virtually impossible for ethics committees to assess adequately (see Chapter 13). The appropriateness of ethics committees' intervention in some cases that might be better handled closer to the source through established channels can also be raised. The student in the above case was encouraged to speak with the professor about the matter and, if she was not satisfied, to seek appropriate redress within the university.

Other complaints reaching ethics committees involve disputes regarding acceptable standards of practice or intraprofessional disagreements. Unless incompetence or malicious intent are clearly involved, committees typically send the parties back to their respective arenas to resolve the issues among themselves.

Case 2–12: A Ph.D. psychologist complained that another psychologist hired a M.A. level person as an agency counselor. The Ph.D. level psychologist had applied for the job and felt that he should have received it because of his higher degree.

Case 2–13: A psychologist complained that other members of the board of directors of a local professional association criticized him for the quality of the performance of his assigned tasks during an executive session.

Degree status *per se* cannot be conclusively designated as *the* marker of competency or fitness for a particular job. Unless a prospective employee can demonstrate that he or she was the victim of discriminatory hiring practices, an ethics committee has no place in personnel decision making. The ethics code does not also automatically protect psychologists from negative evaluation by peers, unless such evaluations were unfairly biased or delivered in an inappropriate context.

Ethics committees may also inform complainants that other sources of redress are more appropriate and suggest that these be pursued. In such instances, the committee assumes the role of facilitator by serving as a resource and/or referral agent. For example, in cases where legal action against a respondent seems clearly indicated, the committee may encourage the complainant to pursue the matter in the courts or state licensing boards, since the sanctions available to these alternatives are more fitting than those available to ethics committees.

Case 2–14: An ethics committee received a charge against the complainant's psychologist-cousin alleging that Rob Filch, Ph.D., had bilked the complainant's mentally incompetent daughter out of a large inheritance. Dr. Filch responded that the money was a gift from the complainant's daughter. The complainant provided documentation indicating that her daughter was seriously impaired and had been institutionalized on a number of occasions to bolster her argument that the young woman possessed neither the capacity to give such a gift in a fully voluntary and informed manner nor the capacity to pursue a complaint independently.

An ethics committee does not have the resources necessary to explore fully or to resolve such a complaint, nor does it have the authority to make appropriate restitution if it is warranted. The complainant was encouraged to seek legal counsel.

Complaints Filed against Nonmembers

Professional psychological associations are *voluntary* membership organizations, and the jurisdiction of their ethics committees extends only to current members. It is not an uncommon occurrence for complaints to be filed against psychologists who are not members of the association to which the complaint is sent. Such complaints cannot be processed, although information can be offered to the complainant about alternative sources of redress possessing jurisdiction. On some occasions, the complainant believes the offender to be a psychologist when he or she is, in fact, a psychiatrist, social worker, or other allied professional. In these instances, the complainant is usually provided the name and address of the appropriate organization representing the discipline.

Complaints against licensed psychologists can also be referred to state boards when the psychologist does not hold a membership in any professional organization with an ethics complaint mechanism. However, as we have noted earlier, in these instances the complaint may lie dormant indefinitely unless the alleged infraction is extremely serious. Unfortunately, some of the most serious or bizarre complaints have been leveled against psychologists (or untrained persons representing themselves to the public as "psychologists" or as "psychotherapists" or "counselors") who are not members of any professional association, hold no license or certification, and who are self-employed.

Case 2−15:   A group of students complained that Sam Scam, Psy.D., who owned a consulting firm, was supplying letters of reference for students he had never even met in support of their applications to graduate school for a one-hundred-dollar fee.

Case 2−16:   A client and her attorney gathered considerable evidence to substantiate that Ransom Fleece, "Ph.D.," (later identified as unlicensed and holding a "doctorate" supplied by a diploma mill) was extorting large sums of money to buy her silence. "Dr." Fleece told the woman that he would inform her influential and wealthy husband of her many affairs and follies as revealed to him during the course of "psychotherapy," unless she complied with his demands for payment.

The second case involved obviously illegal behavior and could be pursued in a court of law if the client so desired. The first case, however, is more difficult to resolve because, despite the impropriety of the service being performed, its illegality is not clear-cut.

Professional association membership does not guarantee competence or ethical behavior, nor does nonmembership in professional organizations indicate incompetence or unethical behavior. Nevertheless, consumers do have additional protection and redress channels when the psychologists providing services for them voluntarily agree to ethical scrutiny by virtue of their membership in organizations with peer-control mechanisms.

Complaints Against Groups, Agencies, Corporations, or Institutions

Whereas a complainant may name more than one person in a single complaint, each respondent must be known to the committee by name, and the specific involvement of each person in the dispute must be provided. The ethics committee mechanisms are not equipped to deal with a group or corporation, unlike legal procedures used in court. Even a cursory reading of the *Ethical Principles* reveals that the focus is on the *individual's* ethical responsibility. Consequently, when complaints are received against the United States Army, a state psychology examining committee, an entire psychology department, or a mental health clinic, the material is returned to the complainant requesting that the particular psychologists be identified by name and that the conduct of each be described. Unless the specific behavior of such individuals can be linked to ethical violations, the case cannot be processed by an ethics committee.

Anonymous Complaints

Occasionally an ethics committee receives an unsigned complaint against a psychologist. Usually the reason for anonymity (typically a fear of retribution) is noted. Ethics committees are often concerned, especially when a letter is well documented and the alleged infraction is serious. But the rules and procedures of ethics committees permit the respondent the right to know one's accuser. Thus, unless the complaint contains information that can be substantiated via another route, the committee cannot pursue the case.

Related to the anonymous complainant is the person who does reveal his or her identity, but insists that the committeee not inform the respondent. In this instance, the committee explains the procedure (including the safeguards the committee can extend) and defends the requirement for making identities known to respondents. Some complainants then agree to pursue the case according to the necessary procedures, while others withdraw their complaints. Only in extremely unusual circumstances may the committee, at its discretion, pursue a case without identifying the complainant.

Beyond the Statute of Limitations

Ethics committees expect that complaints should be filed within a reasonable time frame after the alleged violation either occurred or came to the complainant's attention. The APA rules and procedures permit an elapsed time of one year when the complaint is issued by an APA member. For nonmember complainants, the time frame is extended to five years. The discrepancy favoring the nonmember reveals that members are expected to be more aware of the ethics code and redress procedures and to act promptly. Nonmembers, on the other hand, usually do not possess equivalent knowledge, and it may not become available to them for a considerable period of time. In addition, other factors could interfere with punctual reporting. In some cases, the nonmember suffered emotionally in ways that were immobilizing for an extended time period; thus the person was incapable of pursuing a complaint until the trauma either had been worked through or had dissipated.

WHO VIOLATES ETHICAL STANDARDS OF THE PROFESSION?

The stereotype of the "unethical psychologist" is quite unsavory. Informal polling of some colleagues revealed that the most often checked adjectives describing *A Violator of the Ethical Standards of Our Profession* were "greedy," "stupid," "psychopathic," "devious," and "immoral." In our experience, the prevailing portrait is far more muted and variable, even including people of decency, intelligence, and fitness. Based on our experience in serving on ethics committees, we present our impressions of the major categories of psychologists who become ethics violators.

The Uninformed/Unaware Psychologist

A substantial number of violators appear to be naive or out-of-touch with their professional identity. Offenses can be quite minor attesting more to the psychologist's lack of understanding or knowledge of one or more of the provisions of the ethics code (Keith-Spiegel, 1977). Some of the most serious infractions are also committed by psychologists in this group, however. For example, one psychologist who routinely administered a controlled drug to his clients was puzzled when he discovered that his action was not only unethical but illegal.

For the minor violators in this category, educative procedures are sufficient to ensure that the behavior will not recur. But for those who have lost touch with their professional identity, remediation is more difficult.

The Troubled Psychologist

Psychologists who are suffering from their own emotional difficulties or from situational stressors in their private lives also account for a substantial number of violators. Their problems may lead to incompetent performance of their professional duties and/or poor judgment. Although this is an unfortunate group, considerable harm can be done by them to vulnerable consumers. The matter is further complicated by the fact that ethics committees are not the appropriate mechanism for rehabilitation of troubled psychologists. A sanction may include the suggestion of seeking psychotherapy as one means of remediation, but more appropriate mechanisms must be established to assist the psychologists whose own turmoil has resulted in unethical conduct. (See Chapters 9 and 10 for more detailed discussions of the troubled psychologist.)

The Overzealous and/or Avaricious Psychologist

Psychologists who become overzealous or who put the lure of financial gain above the welfare of consumers best fit the stereotype of "the unethical psychologist." The percentage of violators falling into this category, however, is actually relatively low. Even among those who fit the stereotype, many of the violators are what we term "Green Menaces," inexperienced psychologists too anxious to "make a splash." Fortunately, most of these new entrants into the field are amenable to constructive, educational approaches, and their misconduct is usually not serious, such as flashy or tasteless advertising of services.

The veteran psychologists in this category are usually recalcitrant and difficult to educate. Their infractions are typically more serious, such as defrauding insurance companies, accepting kickbacks, using bait-and-switch techniques, or making unsubstantiated claims about their effectiveness.

The Vengeful Psychologist

Violators in this category, which also occurs relatively infrequently, are psychologists who become outraged and allow their emotions to supersede their judgment. Usually their infraction was an impulsive act, rather than a premeditated plot to retaliate against their antagonist. The acts often have an immature quality to them, such as when a psychologist could not control his temper after being criticized by a client and retorted with a barrage of colorful pejoratives. Often such psychologists feel foolish later and frequently apologize for their loss of control. Unfortunately, damage may already have been done since outbursts cannot always be easily rectified.

The Insufficiently Trained/Inexperienced Psychologist

This group of violators accounts for a significant number of complaints. Their misconduct arises from their incompetence to perform the services being rendered. Competence is not easy for psychologists to assess in themselves (see Chapter 9). Many violators reported to ethics committees have vastly miscalculated the level of their skills either in general or in the application of specific techniques.

The Psychologist Who "Slips"

The last category, comprising a fairly substantial percentage of ethics violators, is composed of psychologists whose *usual* conduct is ethical and competent. All psychologists are vulnerable to membership in this category, and it is the most difficult type to predict or prevent. For some reason, often based on immediate situational demands, they committed an act that has serious, but almost always unintended, consequences. For example, a psychologist may unwittingly have provided sufficient data during a case discussion to permit a positive identification that could, in turn, harm the client if this information were distributed.

DISPOSITIONS AND LEVELS OF SANCTIONS AVAILABLE TO ETHICS COMMITTEES

If a case is accepted for investigation by an ethics committee, three dispositions are ultimately available: (1) The respondent may be judged innocent of any ethical misconduct; (2) Insufficient evidence may preclude a finding of guilt or innocence; and (3) The respondent may be judged guilty of ethical misconduct and, although committees strive to be educative rather than punitive, one or more sanctions may be imposed. (See Appendix B for the APA ethics committee rules and procedures, and Appendix C for the APA Bylaws describing the ethics committee scope and function. These documents, as well as the ethics code itself, undergo minor revisions continuously and major revisions periodically.)

Regardless of the truth or falseness of the charge, psychologists must promptly and completely reply to an ethics committee inquiry. Failure to do so can itself result in an ethics violation (*EP:* Preamble).

Finding of Innocence

If an investigation reveals no evidence of wrongdoing, the psychologist and complainant are so informed and the case is closed. In cases where the psychologist is found innocent, the complainant typically misunderstood the psychologist's conduct or did not understand the psychologist's responsibilities in certain difficult situations. At other times, the psychologist's conduct (and often that of the complainant as well) could hardly be characterized as exemplary, but was judged not to be outside the realm of tolerable expression of human emotion or behavior given the context of the situation. Three cases illustrate the typical conditions in which the decision of innocence is appropriate.

Case 2–17: Mazy Pickle complained that she was tricked into committing herself to expensive psychotherapy through a "bait-and-switch" technique. She said she was seeing a therapist at no charge because her company agreed to pay for it. But during the tenth session the psychologist announced that the fee would now be $30 per hour. Mazy suspected that he was collecting from both the company and from her. The psychologist explained, and the company's personnel director corroborated, that he was part of a referral network for the company that agreed to pay for the first ten sessions for their employees. Then the psychologist agreed to continue to see clients, if appropriate, at a reasonable fee based on the employee's ability to pay. This arrangement was described in the company's benefits brochure and, according to the psychologist, discussed briefly during the initial session. Inquiry revealed that the client remained confused, but did remember "something about ten sessions but then didn't think any more about it."

Case 2–18: Jen Frantic complained that her psychologist, Leslie Concerned, Ph.D., called the paramedics and police and told them she was suicidal when she claimed she was in fact only a "little agitated" and only wanted to "get the psychologist's attention." Ms. Frantic claimed she suffered extreme embarrassment and her landlord asked that she move elsewhere because of the commotion caused by the incident. She also complained that the psychologist violated his duty to keep information shared between them confidential. Dr. Concerned responded that the client called him at 3:00 A.M., claiming that she took "lots of pills" and that he should come right over. But because he feared for her safety and could not get her to tell him what kind of pills or how many were ingested, he decided that other forms of assistance should be marshaled as well. When he arrived, the police (called by the paramedics) were there, and the client was throwing things at the men and screaming that they should leave her alone. A hospital report indicated that the woman had not taken any pills. The psychologist's careful account of the evening and some of the other dynamics between the two people persuaded the committee that he had exercised acceptable professional judgment, given the apparent emergency circumstances.

Case 2–19: Billy Blunt, an employee at a state mental facility, complained that a staff psychologist had called him an "incompetent boob" in front of patients and other staff. The psychologist admitted that she was extremely angry at the employee, but that his behavior deserved that outburst. She was able to document that Mr. Blunt had just struck a severely regressed schizophrenic in the face, because the man had ignored his orders to follow him into the day room.

Insufficient Evidence

Despite their most vigorous investigatory efforts, ethics committees may not be able to obtain sufficient evidence to render a verdict one way or the other. By definition, the respondent has denied the charges. Thus, unless any credible witnesses or supporting documents can be produced, it boils down to one person's word against another's. Both the complainant and respondent are informed that definitive evidence is lacking and that any additional evidence either person may possess should be shared with the committee. But, too often, the alleged infraction occurred in private and no evidence beyond hearsay or opinion is available to either party or to the committee.

These cases are closed without a finding. The respondent and complainant are so informed. Both people are also reminded that an ethics committee, unlike a court of law, may reopen a case if evidence that would substantiate the veracity of the complaint (or its groundlessness) becomes available in the future.

This disposition is frustrating both to the individual who made a valid complaint and to an innocent psychologist respondent. In the first instance, the complainant who was indeed abused by the respondent no doubt experiences further stress when an ethics committee is unable to substantiate the charge. In these unfortunate cases, the consumer suffers an additional insult when the profession apparently takes the psychologist-offender off the hook. This perception on the part of the consumer is understandable, though not entirely accurate. The records in such cases are not destroyed for an extended period of time and, if similar complaints arise against that same psychologist in the future, the initial complaint is revived and reviewed. In addition, ethics committee members are hopeful that, in such instances, the investigatory process had a salutary effect on the psychologist. Even though denial may have allowed escape *this* time, sufficient sensitization to the issues and the noxious experience of undergoing an ethics inquiry by one's peers may preclude a recurrence of such infractions.

Regarding the unjustly accused psychologist who could not substantiate his or her innocence, a lingering feeling of unrest may persist, even though no finding was made and, hence, no sanction was imposed. It is unfortunate that a psychologist who committed no infraction has to undergo an inquiry by peers who close the case in doubt. Perhaps these psychologists learn something about consumers who, because of misunderstanding or malice, press spurious charges, and they may be more able to avoid such situations in the future.

Of course, ethics committee members are disappointed when cases are closed on grounds of insufficient evidence. The committee members are aware that someone was not served well—the dilemma is that they could not determine who that someone was.

Sustained Charges

When an ethics committee determines that a psychologist has violated the ethical standards of the profession, a number of sanctions are available to the committee. In general, considering the degree of seriousness as a criterion for determination of sanctions is useful, although, as we shall illustrate, numerous other factors may mitigate the type of penalty that is ultimately imposed.

An American Psychological Association's *Task Force on Ethics System Procedures* (Koocher et al., 1981) developed guidelines to conceptualize levels of seriousness of infractions, appropriateness of sanctions, and mediating factors to consider. As evident from even a cursory reading of the *Ethical Principles*, violation of some principles creates far more harm than does violation of others. Therefore we first examine the *levels* of seriousness, starting with the least problematical, as summarized in Table 2−1.

TABLE 2−1
Levels of Ethical Sanctions and Categories

Level	Sanction	Rationale/Mediating Factors
Level IA	Educative Advisory	Not clearly unethical, but in poor taste or insufficiently cautious, this offense might fall in "gray areas" or deal with newly emerging issues and problems.
Level IB	Educative Warning	A "cease and desist" notice from an ethics committee might accompany a finding that a mild or minor infraction had occurred.
Level IIA	Reprimand	A finding of clearly ethical misconduct, when the psychologist should have known better, although the consequence of the action or inaction may have been minor.
Level IIB	Censure	Deliberate or persistent behavior that could lead to substantial harm to the client or public, although little harm may actually have accrued.
Level IIIA	Stipulated Resignation or Permitted Resignation	Continuing or dramatic misconduct producing genuine hazard to clients, the public, and the profession; questionable motivation to change or demonstrate concern for the behavior in question. May include "no reapplication" stipulation.
Level IIIB	Expulsion (Voided Membership)	Individual clients or others with whom one worked are substantially injured with serious questions about the potential rehabilitation of the psychologist in question.

(Adapted from Koocher, Keith-Spiegel, and Klebanoff, 1981)

Level I deals essentially with *malum prohibitum* offenses: namely, behavior that is wrong because it is proscribed in the code of ethics, rather than behavior that is either inherently evil (*mala in se*) or involves moral turpitude. *Category IA* involves behavior that might be in poor taste, involve an arguable point, or simply be stupid, compared to prevailing standards. No malicious intent can be ascribed to the psychologist in question, and an ethics committee may respond by educating the individual or by suggesting better ways to handle such matters in the future.

Category IB, which carries *IA* a step further, addresses behavior that is unquestionably inappropriate and somewhat offensive. Nevertheless, the committee may still believe that the offense is relatively minor, that the individual in question may not have fully realized the nature of the problem, and that an educative stance, rather than a punitive one, is still warranted. Such cases might include advertising infractions, inappropriate public statements, or mild uncollegiality. A "cease and desist" notice may be issued, clearly noting that a more serious finding could result if the practices continue.

Level II (as well as *Level III*) involves *malum in se* offenses; namely, behavior that is unethical in itself in the view of the professional/scientific community. This category is applied whenever an ethics committee finds that a substantive violation did indeed occur. In *Level II* offenses the psychologist clearly should have "known better," although the action or inaction did not result in substantial harm beyond remedy. "Reprimand" is the more mild sanction issued when apparently no harm or damage resulted from the unethical act. "Censure" is the more severe sanction issued when some harm or damage accrued as a result of the unethical act. Each sanction should be applied with an appropriate educational or remedial action when indicated.

Remedial steps assigned by an ethics committee might include mandated supervision, probation, referral for psychotherapy, mandated apology, or even homework or assignments to specific continuing education courses.

Level III is applied whenever substantial harm accrues to others as a result of the respondent's unethical behavior and the respondent seems less prone to rehabilitation. In some cases, it might be appropriate to permit resignation with stipulations, while in other cases explusion from the organization may be involved as the ultimate sanction. These sanctions may be used educatively when appropriate by the use of the "stayed" or "suspended" sanction, especially when remediative steps are possible. For example, an individual might be told that her "expulsion" may be recommended, but that this will be delayed for a period of time while she demonstrates her sincere good faith in remediating the situation.

The system we have described above provides a helpful framework to assist in curbing either capricious punishment or excessive leniency relative to the specific violation. Nonetheless, violations that appear identical may be decided differently for various reasons. Common mitigating factors that might lead to different sanctions for similar violations include the following: the motivation or intent of the respondent; actual or potential harm caused as a result of the infraction; number of prior complaints against the respondent; degree of experience in the field; and the respondent's self-initiated attempts at remediation. Ethics committees may be lenient (e.g., apply an educative approach) on a first offender who is not malevolent but who committed a relatively minor offense due to inexperience. If the same offenses were committed by a recalcitrant, experienced psychologist, more severe sanctions might be considered appropriate.

Furthermore, most ethical principles can be violated in degrees ranging from minor to extremely serious. Thus different sanctions may be imposed for violations of the same specific principle by different individuals. We shall illustrate this phenomenon with two cases involving sections of the ethics code admonishing psychologists to refrain from issuing advertising that appeals to consumer's fears and anxieties, creates expectations of favorable results, and implies unique or one-of-a-kind abilities (*EP*: 4b).

> **Case 2–20:**   A psychologist ran an ad in the local paper that read as follows: "Do you have trouble getting out from being down in the dumps? If so, short-term psychotherapy using a special technique I have developed will help you control bouts with mild depression."

> **Case 2–21:**   A psychologist issued a flyer distributed to homes in his city that read as follows: "Stress is the number one killer in the country today and everyone, adult and child, is functioning under some form of stress. My unique program of stress management is not available anywhere else and is guaranteed to alleviate *all* forms of stress for good. Can *you* afford *not* to inquire further?"

Both advertisements are a violation of the *Ethical Principles*. The last case presented, however, is the more flagrant of the two, and the sanctions issued would probably reflect the difference.

Most of the sanctions imposed are made known only to the respondent and, usually, to the complainant. Sanctions have impact only if the respondents have been educated, sensitized, embarrassed, or shamed into ameliorating their behavior. Expulsion, the most severe sanction, does involve the dissemination of the violator's identity to others. Expulsion is professional banishment, historically regarded as the most powerful form of ostracism any group of people or a society can issue.

When a member is expelled or dropped from the American Psychological Association, the entire membership is informed, by mail, of the person's identity and the general nature of the offense. In addition, *all* state licensing and certification boards are informed. At its discretion, APA may also inform other parties if it is determined that additional sharing of information would be in the best interests of the public or of the profession. Ethics committees cannot expel a member directly, although they can independently issue all of the lesser sanctions. Committees characteristically recommend expulsion to the association's board of directors. At that point, respondents are given an opportunity for another defense hearing before the board, and the ethics committee assumes the role of the prosecutor.

Although expulsion involves termination of the individual's status as a member, another term, *membership voided*, is occasionally used. This term applies to instances in which the individual is not even qualified to be a member of the association. Sometimes the basis may possibly have been an inadvertent mistake by the applicant. More often, the individual willfully and fraudulently obtained entry into the profession and the association through misrepresentation, such as claiming credentials that were later discovered to be fabricated. In one case, a "psychologist," who also gained entry into APA, was found to have had minimal formal education or training, although he had claimed an impressive background. He had also functioned as a physician, astronomer, history professor, and in several other professional roles. In such instances, the cumbersome expulsion procedure machinery did not have to be activated. The individual is simply dropped from the membership roster.

Critics of ethics committees' effectiveness with serious violators have argued that even the most severe sanction of expulsion has minimal meaningful impact on the respondent. Membership in voluntary professional organizations is not, in fact, a prerequisite for professional practice or employment. When thousands of one's colleagues are informed, however, some impact on professional status accrues. Referrals may quickly stop in the respondent's locale, and casual observation reveals that professionals gossip about the individual for years. When state licensing boards take action based on the expulsion, financial loss may also result since the psychologist may be barred from practicing. Expulsion often leads to additional inquiries or hearings. Most expelled psychologists are either forced out of psychology because of the loss of licensure and reputation, or they leave the profession voluntarily, or they remain in the discipline while maintaining a low profile.

Expulsion is recommended if the offender is considered to be beyond remediation and is posing a potential threat to the public, as illustrated in the following three cases.

Case 2–22: Benny Dope, Ph.D., was charged with routinely administering drugs to clients for purposes of "enhancing" the dynamics of group encounters. One client had almost died from an overdose of a muscle relaxant. During the ethics hearing, he appeared to be unaware of the fact that psychologists are not allowed to administer prescription or illegal drugs. Dr. Dope also revealed that he had severed all interpersonal ties with colleagues because they did not seem to understand or approve of his techniques. When asked if he would be willing to be supervised by a local psycho-therapist for a period of time, he said that would be fine as long as the committee could locate someone who would agree with his ideas. When asked how he would conduct himself in the future, Dr. Dope said that he would not alter his methods, but would "be more careful."

Case 2—23:   Seymour Fraud, Ph.D., who was found guilty of defrauding Medicare out of thousands of dollars, was simultaneously investigated by the state regulatory agency and an ethics committee. During the period when both investigations were actively open, other charges were incontrovertibly documented by a major insurance company that Dr. Fraud had billed for more than 50 client sessions that had never transpired.

Case 2—24:   Harlan Stud, Ph.D., was charged by several women with sexual exploitation. Dr. Stud admitted engaging in sexual relations with these women, but denied that he was exploitative. He claimed that they all needed sexual activity to function effectively, and he then attempted to elucidate some vague theoretical justification regarding why *he* was the appropriate person to provide these "services." Despite the claims by the clients that he forced his sexual attentions on them and that the experiences were traumatic, Dr. Stud continued to deny wrongdoing or poor professional judgment. The only issue on which he would agree was that his form of therapy "did not work on these four women, but," he added, "it has worked beautifully on scores of others."

Critics have noted that, because so few expulsions occur each year at both national and state levels, the truly morally defective and/or incompetent among us are left untouched. Nonetheless, critics rarely discuss one important factor that may account for why many psychologists who commit serious offenses are not ejected from the professional association. Ethics committees often determine that, despite the seriousness of the offense, evidence suggests that the respondent may be amenable to rehabilitation. In these instances, it would be a *disservice* to the public, and perhaps even an irresponsible act, to expel the member. Once a member is dropped, the association can no longer monitor that individual's behavior. Unless another regulatory body intervenes (and this intervention cannot be guaranteed), the violator may continue to function as a psychologist. As we noted previously, for unlicensed persons, the number of bodies that have any jurisdiction over the violator is diminished or nonexistent except for certain legal channels.

By keeping a respondent with rehabilitation potential in the ranks, the association can issue the kinds of sanctions (e.g., careful supervision for an extended time, with periodic supervisor feedback to the committee) that help to ensure that the member regains fitness to be an effective, competent, and ethical psychologist. For those offenders who express a willingness to undergo the remediation recommended by an ethics committee, a lesser sanction than expulsion may be in everyone's best interests.

The following two cases illustrate and explain the decision to retain serious violators in the ranks.

Case 2−25: Rocky Slip, Psy.D., was charged with sexual intimacies with a client. The psychologist upheld the veracity of the complaint and expressed considerable guilt about it. He noted that he became swept away with the affectionate nature of the client and, due to personal turmoil in his marriage, allowed sexual intimacies to transpire on a single occasion. Realizing what he had done, he terminated the client and made several referrals available to her. He discussed with her the unethicality of his act and informed her that he was no longer the appropriate person to help her. Before the complaint was issued, Dr. Slip had entered psychotherapy on his own initiative to deal with what had transpired. His therapist confirmed this fact and expressed that the psychologist was highly motivated to ensure that this conduct would never surface again, and he was making good progress in therapy in general.

In this instance, the case was tabled for one year, while Dr. Slip continued in treatment, and his therapist provided quarterly reports to the committee. At the end of the year, the therapist's report was favorable, and Dr. Slip appeared to have considerable insight into his problems. A strong letter of censure was entered into the psychologist's file, rather than invoking the more usual penalties of a forced resignation or expulsion recommendation.

Case 2−26: Alan Jumbled, Ph.D., was discovered by an insurance company to have overbilled clients. Dr. Jumbled admitted the wrongdoing, but also provided documentary evidence that he had underbilled many other clients. He explained that he had been extremely agitated about personal matters that revealed itself in several ways, including erroneous record-keeping. He had reimbursed the insurance company for the $1,000 in overcharges. His pastor and many other community members sent letters attesting to how highly he was regarded in the community and documented his record of free community service.

Whereas insurance fraud is a serious offense, the ethics committee carefully considered the other factors. The portrait of an individual trying to make "fast money" by fraudulent means simply did not emerge. The committee requested that Dr. Jumbled begin treatment to work out his personal problems and mandated supervision of his work (including billing records and procedures) for one year. At the end of this period, considerable progress had been made in psychotherapy, and the supervisor attested to his high level of skills and moral character. In the meantime, he had joined and was functioning effectively in a group practice and was able to relinquish the billing procedures to a bookkeeper/receptionist hired by the group. The ethics committee entered a reprimand letter into his files.

A variation on this less-than-expulsion theme for serious violators who the committee believes *may* have some potential for remediation, but remains more dubious or concerned, is the imposition of *stipulated resignations*.

In these cases, the violator is asked to resign from the association for a specific period of time (usually three to five years). At the end of this period, the committee reexamines the case to see if the psychologists can demonstrate that major steps were taken on their own initiative to ensure that the nature of their difficulties have been worked through and are unlikely to resurface. At its option, the committee can act to restore the psychologist to membership in good standing.

How Publicly Should Violators of Ethical Principles Be Exposed?

The question of how much, if any, information about any sustained violation (not only those leading to expulsion or membership drops) should be shared and with whom is currently being debated. In the past, complainants were informed that the case had been investigated, decided, and closed. Rarely was more information made known to the complainants. Many individuals, however, contend that complainants have the right to know the outcome of the inquiry. One concern associated with revealing findings to complainants is that the letter, sent in confidence, may be displayed to others by the complainant in ways the ethics committee never intended, since the recipient cannot be ordered to treat the information confidentially. Revealing this information would be especially disconcerting if the committee believed that its own actions were sufficient to remediate the situation and to protect the public. Nevertheless, committees are increasingly sharing more details with complainants in the belief that the complainants' right to know supersedes any potential misuse of the information.

Should the public in general have access to the identity of individuals who have committed serious offenses and thereby be forewarned if the psychologist is still practicing? Legal and medical associations issue such information in professional publications that are available to the public. Professional psychology associations and those of many other related disciplines have not yet followed suit. Some believe that the profession does protect the public from truly incompetent people through the various mechanisms already available. Others have argued that more direct dissemination of information to the public is needed.

In bizarre or newsworthy cases, the media may obtain details either through complainant contact or through ongoing legal proceedings. In these instances, the psychologist (who may or may not have been fully adjudicated) is instantaneously notorious. Most people would agree, however, that the commercial media is neither the most reliable nor the most appropriate forum for protecting the public.

ADVISORY AND EDUCATIONAL FUNCTIONS OF ETHICS COMMITTEES

Although ethics committees spend most of their time functioning as a "complaint department," many members of professional associations (and probably most consumers) appear unaware that ethics committees also serve in an advisory role. We recommend that psychologists use this resource when they feel the need for assistance with ethical decision making, although sometimes feedback is delayed when the issue is not of an emergency nature or is extremely complicated. If a full committee opinion is sought, inquirers must wait for the item to appear on the agenda, which could mean a delay of several months. When immediate assistance is desired, a phone call to the office of the local, state, or national professional organization is advisable. Associations usually keep rosters of ethics committee members who can speak in an informal capacity about ethical dilemmas or noncommittee experts who specialize in a particular ethics-related area. We are aware of numerous incidents in which contact and advice received during the ethical decision-making process assisted psychologists in clarifying their responsibilities or in avoiding conduct that might have been ethically or legally questionable. Nonetheless, individual ethics committee members consulted for informal advice *cannot* speak for the ethics committee itself. Sometimes confusion has resulted from misunderstanding the critical distinction between the advice given by a knowledgeable individual who also happens to be serving on an ethics committee and the committee's opinion, which can be formulated only by a majority vote. It is not appropriate, however, to contact ethics committee members individually for advice or comment if one is already a complainant or respondent in a pending action with the committee. Once a case is opened, it is the province of the committee-as-a-whole, and members cannot act on their own unless specifically mandated to do so.

Ethics committees are also in a unique position to provide educational materials to psychologists. Recent publications, for example, include material published by Sanders (1979), Sanders and Keith-Spiegel (1980), and Hare-Mustin and Hall (1981).

REFERENCES

Hare-Mustin, R. T., and Hall, J. E. Procedures for responding to ethics complaints against psychologists. *American Psychologist*, 1981, 36, 1494–1505.

Keith-Spiegel, P. Violation of ethical principles due to ignorance or poor professional judgment versus willful disregard. *Professional Psychology*, 1977, 8, 288–296.

Koocher, G. P.; Keith-Spiegel, P.; and Klebanoff, L. *Levels and Sanctions*. Unpublished report of the APA Task Force on Ethics System Procedures, 1981.

Moore, R. A. Ethics in the practice of psychiatry: Origins, functions, models, and enforcement. *American Journal of Psychiatry*, 1978, *135*, 157–163.

Sanders, J. R. Complaints against psychologists adjudicated informally by APA's Committee on Scientific and Professional Ethics and Conduct. *American Psychologist*, 1979, *34*, 1139–1144.

———, and Keith-Spiegel, P. Formal and informal adjudication of ethics complaints against psychologists. *American Psychologist*, 1980, *35*, 1096–1105.

Privacy, Confidentiality, and Record-Keeping 3

Three may keep a secret, if two of them are dead.

Benjamin Franklin

The confidential relationship between psychologist and client has long been regarded as a cornerstone in the helping relationship (*EP*: 5). The trust conveyed through assurance of confidentiality is so critical, according to some theorists, that psychotherapy may be worthless without it (Epstein et al., 1977). Without assurance of confidentiality, many potential clients might not seek psychological services. Once services are sought, the lack of confidentiality might lead to concealment of information resulting in potentially ineffectual treatment or compromised consultative opinions (Woods and McNamara, 1980; DeKraai and Sales, 1981). The changing nature of societal values has evoked numerous concerns about the traditional meaning of confidentiality in psychological practice, which, in turn, raises many questions regarding the nature and degree of confidentiality obligations across a variety of situations.

One need not look far back in American history for important public examples of how breaches in the confidentiality of mental health records have had major implications for both the clients and the society. Thomas Eagleton, a United States Senator from Missouri, was dropped as George McGovern's vice-presidential runningmate in 1968, when it was disclosed that he had previously been hospitalized for the treatment of depression. Dr. Lewis J. Fielding, perhaps better known as "Daniel Ellsberg's psychiatrist," certainly did not suspect that the break-in at his office on September 3, 1971, might ultimately lead to the conviction of several high officials in the Nixon White House and contribute to the only resignation of an American

President (Morganthau et al., 1982). The special sensitivity of information gleaned by psychologists in the routine performance of their work, whether it be assessment, psychotherapy, consultation, research, or teaching cannot be ignored. Unfortunately, the complexity of the issues that are related to the general theme of confidentiality often appears to defy facile analysis.

The era of the computer, which has created the potential to cross-tabulate a vast amount of data, poses new threats to individual privacy and confidentiality on numerous issues (Parker, 1976; Sawyer and Schechter, 1968). As psychologists begin to computerize their records, test scores, research data, and patients' accounts, new potential risks arise. The existence of vast data banks and the consumer movement in America have certainly contributed to increasing requests for all types of information on people, including requests for information by individuals on themselves. This phenomenon leads to a whole new subset of problems regarding actual records. Who should keep them? For how long? Who has access? What is in them? What are the legal implications? How do record-keeping practices affect the ethical principle of confidentiality? What are the rights of the psychologists' students and research participants? These are a few of the problems addressed in this chapter.

THE PROBLEM OF DEFINITIONS

The entire area of confidentiality-related ethical problems is complicated by several misunderstandings about commonly used terms; such as confidentiality, privacy, and privilege. At least part of the confusion arises because some of these terms have legal meanings that are quite distinct from meanings attached by psychologists or other mental health practitioners. Many difficulties are related to a failure on the part of the psychologist to discriminate among the different terms and meanings. Other difficulties develop because, as discussed in Chapter 1, one's legal obligations are not always fully congruent with one's ethical responsibilities.

Privacy

The concept of privacy is often considered a basic right granted by the Fourth Amendment and other sections of the United States Constitution. It is basically the right of an individual to make the decision about how much of his or her thoughts, feelings, or personal data should be shared with others. Privacy has often been considered essential to ensure human dignity and freedom of self-determination. Considerable attention has been devoted to the topic of privacy, including a special issue of the *American*

Psychologist (May 1967, Volume 22, Number 5) and a special number of the *Journal of Social Issues* (1977, Volume 33, Number 3).

The concepts of both confidentiality and privilege develop from the concept of an individual's right to privacy, although privacy is obviously a broader topic. Concerns regarding wiretapping, electronic surveillance, the use of lie detectors, and various other observational or data-gathering activities influence privacy issues. The issues involved in public policy decisions regarding the violation of privacy rights parallel concern expressed by psychologists regarding confidentiality violations. In general, one's privacy rights may be subject to violation when one's behavior seriously violates the norms of society or somehow endangers others. An example would be the issuance of a search warrant based on "probable cause" that a crime has been or is about to be committed. This problem will be discussed in greater detail from the psychological perspective in the following pages; however, psychologists must also consider the concept of privacy as a basic human right due to all people and not simply limited to their clients.

Confidentiality

Confidentiality refers to a general standard of professional conduct that obliges a professional not to discuss information about a client with anyone. Confidentiality may also be based in statute or case law (Swoboda et al., 1978), but if cited as an ethical principle it implies an explicit contract or promise not to reveal anything about a client, except under certain circumstances agreed to by both source and subject. Although the roots of the concept are in professional ethics rather than in law, the nature of the psychologist/client relationship does have legal recognition (DeKraai and Sales, 1982). It is conceivable, for example, that a client whose confidence was violated could sue a psychologist in a civil action for breach of confidence or other action and seek specific criminal penalties mandated under state law. A New York appeals court ruled that a patient may bring a tort action against a psychiatrist who allegedly disclosed confidential information to the patient's spouse. If successful, the patient would be allowed to recover damages for mental distress, loss of employment, and the deterioration of his marriage (*MacDonald v. Clinger*, 1982; *Mental Disability Law Reporter*, 1982).

The degree to which one should, if ever, violate a client's confidentiality is a matter of some controversy (Siegel, 1979), although there is uniform agreement on one point: i.e., the client's right to know the parameters of the relationship. We believe that the initial interview with any client (individual or organizational) should include a direct and candid discussion of limits that may exist with respect to any confidences communicated in the relationship. Interviews with our colleagues and other anecdotal reports indicate that few practitioners actually define limits this early in a professional relationship. Although this is not unethical in itself, failure to provide such information in the beginning may lead to problems later on. The information may be given orally or as "new client information" in a pamphlet or written statement. Each psychologist should give sufficient thought to this matter before formulating a policy for his or her practice. This policy should be derived on the basis of applicable law, ethical standards, and personal conviction integrated in as meaningful a way as possible, considering the legal precedents and case examples discussed in the following pages.

Privilege

Distinguishing between privilege and confidentiality—two frequently confused concepts—is critical to understanding a variety of ethical problems. Privilege (or privileged communication) is a legal term that describes the quality of certain specific types of relationships that prevent information, acquired in such relationships, from being disclosed in court or other legal proceedings. Privilege is granted by law and belongs to the client in the relationship. Normal court rules provide that anything relative and material to the immediate issue can and should be admitted as evidence. Where privilege exists, however, the client is protected from having the communications covered by it revealed without explicit permission. If the client waives this privilege, the psychologist may be compelled to testify on the nature and specifics of the material discussed. The client is not permitted to waive privilege in part. In most courts, once a waiver is given it includes all of the relevant privileged material.

Traditionally, such privilege has been extended to attorney-client, husband-wife, physician-patient, and priest-penitent relationships. Some jurisdictions now extend privilege to psychologist-client or psychotherapist-client relationships, but the actual laws vary widely, and it is incumbent on each psychologist to know the statutes in force for her or his practice. In a survey of legislation and key case law affecting the primary mental health professions (i.e., psychologists, psychiatrists, social workers, and psychiatric nurses) in all fifty states, DeKraai and Sales (1982) noted that nurses were hardly ever mentioned, though physicians in general were frequently mentioned, with respect to privileged communication. The same authors also note that there are no federally created privileges for any mental health profession; the federal courts in general look to applicable state laws.

Almost all of the statutes providing privileges expressly require licensing, certification, or registration of psychologists under state law, although California, Hawaii, Nevada, and Texas provide for the application of privilege when the client reasonably believes the alleged psychologist to be licensed (DeKraai and Sales, 1982). Massachusetts, on the other hand, specifies that privilege does not apply unless the psychologist is both licensed and holds a doctorate, thus excluding masters-level psychologists licensed under that state's "grandparenting" period. In general, students, including psychology interns, trainees, or supervisees, are not specifically covered by statute.

Some jurisidictions (e.g., New Hampshire, New York, and Virginia) permit the judge discretion to overrule privilege between psychologist and client after determining that the interests of justice outweigh the interests of confidentiality. Some jurisidictions limit privilege exclusively to civil actions, while others may include criminal proceedings, except when homicide is involved. Just as some physicians are compelled under state law to report gunshot wounds or certain communicable diseases, psychologists may be obligated to report certain cases, such as those involving child abuse, to state authorities. These restrictions could certainly affect a therapeutic relationship adversely, but the client has a right to know of any limitations in advance, and the psychologist has the responsibility both to know the relevant facts and to inform the client as indicated.

EXCEPTIONS

As noted above, certain laws may mandate violations of client privilege and confidentiality in specific ways. Other circumstances, such as a suit alleging malpractice, may constitute a waiver of privilege and confidentiality. In some circumstances, a client may waive some confidentiality or privilege rights without fully realizing the extent of potential risk. In some dramatic circumstances, a psychologist may also face the dilemma of violating a confidence to prevent some imminent harm or danger from occurring. These matters are not without controversy, but it is important for the psychologist to be aware of the issues and to think prospectively about how to handle such problems.

When law and ethical standards diverge (e.g., when a confidential communication is not privileged in the eyes of the law), the situation becomes extremely complex, but it would be difficult to fault a psychologist ethically for divulging confidential material if ordered to do so by a court of competent authority. On the other hand, one might ask whether it is appropriate to violate the law if one believes that it is necessary in order to behave ethically. Consider, for example, the psychologist who is required by state law or court order to disclose some information learned about a client during the course of a professional relationship. If the psychologist claims that the law and ethical principles are in conflict, then by definition the ethical principles in question are illegal. The psychologist may choose civil disobedience as one course of action, but does so at his or her own peril in terms of the legal consequences.

Students of ethical philosophy will immediately recognize a modern psychological version in the controversy developed in the writings of Immanuel Kant and John Stuart Mill. Is it the *intention* of the actor that should be the basis for judgment, or solely the final *outcome* of the behavior that matters? Each situation is different, of course, but the most appropriate approach to evaluating a case would be to consider the potential impact of each alternative course of action and choose in terms of what outcomes might reasonably be expected.

Perhaps the best guidepost that can be offered is a type of balancing test in which the psychologist attempts to weigh the relative risks and vulnerabilities of the parties involved. (*Cases 3−7* and *3−12*, for example, especially highlight these difficult decisions.)

Statutory Obligations

As noted above, in some circumstances the law specifically dictates a duty to notify certain public authorities of information that might be acquired in the context of a psychologist-client relationship. The general rationale on which such laws are predicated maintains that certain individual rights must give way to the greater good of society or to the rights of a more vulnerable individual (e.g., in child abuse or child custody cases). Statutes in some states address the waiver of privilege relative to clients exposed to criminal activity—whether they are the perpetrator, victim, or third party. One might presume that violation of a confidence by obeying one's legal duty to report such matters (in the states where such a duty exists) could certainly hinder the psychologist-client relationship, yet the data on this point are limited (Woods and McNamara, 1980; DeKraai and Sales, 1982).

Psychologists have also been concerned about the potential obligation to disclose "future crime"—the client's stated intent to commit some crime sometime in the future. Shah (1969) has argued that in most cases this type of behavior is essentially help-seeking, rather than an actual intent to commit a crime. Siegel (1979) has also argued that interventions short of violating a confidence are invariably possible and more desirable, although he acknowledges that one must obey any applicable laws. No jurisidictions currently mandate that psychologists must disclose such information (DeKraai and Sales, 1982). The case in which a particular client may pose a danger to self or others creates a special circumstance, which is discussed below as the "duty to warn."

Malpractice and Waivers

Although only a few states have technically enacted malpractice actions as an exception to privilege, it is unreasonable not to allow psychologists to defend themselves by revealing communications of clients during their sessions. Likewise, no ethics committee could investigate a claim against a psychologist unless the complainant were willing to waive any duty of confidentiality that the psychologist might owe to him or her. In such instances, the waiver by the client of the psychologist's duty of confidentiality or legal privilege is a prerequisite for full discussion of the case. Although some people might fear that the threat to reveal an embarrassing confidence would deter clients from reporting or seeking redress from offender-psychologists, this problem can easily be handled procedurally. Ethics committees, for example, generally conduct all proceedings in confidence and may offer assurances to the client who wishes to complain about a psychologist. Sensitive testimony in a malpractice case could be held *in camera* (i.e., a proceeding where all spectators are excluded from court and records are sealed from the public).

In other circumstances, when a client is willing to waive his or her privilege or confidentiality, the psychologist may wish to advise against it or warn the client of potential problems.

Case 3–1: Barbara Bash, age 23, suffered a concussion in an automobile accident, experiencing a memory loss, and various neurological problems. Her condition improved gradually, although she developed symptoms of depression and anxiety, because she worried about whether she would fully recover. She had an initial consultation with Martha Muzzle, Ph.D., to assess her cognitive and emotional state, and she subsequently entered psychotherapy with Dr. Muzzle to deal with her anxiety and depression. Ms. Bash informed Dr. Muzzle that she had previously sought psychotherapy at age 18–20 to assist her in overcoming anxiety and depression linked to various family problems. Approximately ten months after the accident, Bash is still being treated by Muzzle and has made considerable progress. A lawsuit is pending against the other driver in the accident, and Bash's attorney wonders whether to call Dr. Muzzle as an expert witness at the trial to document the emotional pain Ms. Bash suffered and thereby secure a better financial settlement.

If consulted, the psychologist should remind Ms. Bash's attorney and inform her that, if called to testify on Ms. Bash's behalf, she would have to waive her privilege rights. Under cross-examination, the psychologist might then be asked about preexisting emotional problems, prior treatment, and various other personal matters that Ms. Bash might prefer not to have discussed in court. The potential danger is that such testimony might damage the client's credibility. In such situations, it is more likely that the case would be settled out of court, but the client should know the risks of disclosure.

Various types of pressures often exist that may be applied by employers, schools, clinics, or other agencies for clients to sign waivers of privilege or confidentiality. Moreover, the client may not want to sign the form, but may simply be complying with the requests of an authority figure or be afraid that requested help would otherwise be turned down (Rosen, 1977). If a psychologist has doubts about the wisdom or validity of a client's waiver in such circumstances, the best course of action would be to consult with the client about the reservations prior to supplying the requested information.

The Duty to Warn

No discussion of confidentiality in the mental health arena can be complete without reference to the Tarasoff case (i.e., *Tarasoff* v. *Regents of the University of California*, 1976) and several other, subsequent cases (*Mental Disability Law Reporter*, 1980). Detailed analyses of the legal case are provided by Stone (1976) and Leonard (1977), but the facts of the Tarasoff case are as follows:

> **Case 3-2:** In the fall of 1969, Prosenjit Poddar, a citizen of India and a naval architecture student at the University of California's Berkeley campus, shot and stabbed to death Tatiana Tarasoff, a young woman who had spurned his affections. Poddar had been in psychotherapy with a psychologist at the university's student health facility, and the psychologist had concluded that Poddar was quite dangerous. This conclusion stemmed from an assessment of Poddar's pathological attachment to Tarasoff and evidence that he intended to purchase a gun. After consultation with appropriate colleagues at the student health facility, the psychologist in question notified police both orally and in writing that Poddar was dangerous. He requested that Poddar be taken to a facility to be evaluated for civil commitment under California civil commitment statutes. The police allegedly interrogated Poddar and found him to be rational. They concluded that he was not really dangerous and secured a promise that he would stay away from Ms. Tarasoff. After his release by the police, Poddar never returned for further psychotherapy and two months later he killed Ms. Tarasoff. (Stone, 1976)

Subsequently, Ms. Tarasoff's parents attempted to sue the Regents of the University of California, the student health center staff members involved, and the police. Both trial and appeals courts dismissed the complaint, holding that despite the tragedy there was no legal basis in California law for the claim. The Tarasoff family appealed to the Supreme Court of California, asserting that the defendants had a duty to warn Ms. Tarasoff or her family of the danger and that they should have persisted to ensure his confinement. In a 1974 ruling, the court held that the therapists indeed did have a duty to warn Ms. Tarasoff. When the defendants and several *amici curiae* petitioned for a rehearing, the court took the unusual step of granting one. In their second ruling (*Tarasoff*, 1976), the court released the police from liability without explanation and more broadly formulated the duty of therapists, imposing a duty to use reasonable care to protect third parties against dangers posed by patients.

Although the impact of this decision outside California was not immediately apparent, the issue of whether psychologists must be police, protectors, or otherwise have a "duty to protect" rapidly became a national concern (Bersoff, 1976; Paul, 1977; Leonard, 1977). Siegel (1979) contends that, if Poddar's psychologist had accepted the absolute and inviolate confidentiality position, Poddar could have been kept in psychotherapy and the life of Tatiana Tarasoff might have been saved. Siegel believes the therapist "betrayed" his client and observes that if the psychologist had not considered Poddar "dangerous," he could not have been held liable for "failure to warn." This may be a valid position; however, many psychologists would argue the need to protect the public welfare with direct action. The key test of responsibility is whether the psychologist knew or should have known (in a professional capacity) of the client's dangerousness. No single, ethically correct answer may exist in such cases, but the psychologist must also consider his or her potential obligations.

Perhaps the ultimate irony of the Tarasoff case in terms of outcome is what happened to Poddar. His original conviction for second-degree murder was reversed because the judge had failed to give adequate instructions to the jury concerning the defense of "diminished capacity" (*People* v. *Poddar*, 1974). He was convicted of voluntary manslaughter and confined to the Vacaville Medical facility in California. He has since been released from confinement and "has returned to India, and by his own account is now happily married" (Stone, 1976, p. 358).

Various other decisions since the Tarasoff case have explored the duty of psychotherapists to warn potential victims of violence at the hands of their patients (Knapp and Vandecreek, 1982; *Mental Disability Law Reporter*, 1980). The cases are both fascinating and troubling from an ethical standpoint.

Cases 3-2, 3-3, 3-4, and 3-5 are not disguised or synthesized examples; instead, they are drawn from legal records, and they form a portion of the expanding case law on the duty to warn. The cases themselves do not necessarily reveal ethical misconduct. Rather, they are cited to reveal the legal cases that interface with the general principle of confidentiality.

> **Case 3-3:**   Dr. Shaw, a dentist, was in group therapy with Mr. and Mrs. Billian. Shaw became romantically involved with Mrs. Billian, only to be discovered at 2:00 A.M. one morning in bed with her by Mr. Billian, who had broken into Shaw's apartment. After finding his wife in bed nude with Dr. Shaw, Mr. Billian shot Shaw five times, but did not kill him.

Dr. Shaw sued the psychiatric team in charge of the group therapy program because of the team's alleged negligence in not warning him that Mr. Billian's "unstable and violent condition" presented a "foreseeable and immediate danger" to him (*Shaw* v. *Glickman*, 1980). In this case, the Maryland courts held that, although the therapists knew Mr. Billian carried a handgun, they could not necessarily have inferred that Billian might have had a propensity to invoke the "old Solon law" (i.e., a law stating that shooting the wife's lover could be considered justifiable homicide) and may not even have known that Billian harbored any animosity toward Dr. Shaw. The court also noted, however, that even if the team had received this information, they would have violated Maryland law if they had disclosed it.

> **Case 3—4:**   Lee Morgenstein, age 15, was in psychotherapy with a New Jersey psychiatrist, Dr. Milano, for two years. Morgenstein was involved with drugs and related fantasies of using a knife to threaten people. He also told Dr. Milano of sexual experiences and emotional involvement with Kimberly McIntosch, a neighbor five years his senior. Morgenstein frequently expressed anxiety and jealousy when Ms. McIntosch dated other men, and he reported to Dr. Milano that he once fired a BB gun at a car in which she was riding. One day Morgenstein stole a prescription blank from Dr. Milano and attempted to purchase 30 Seconal tablets with it. The pharmacist became suspicious and called Dr. Milano, who advised the pharmacist to send the boy home. Morgenstein obtained a gun after leaving the pharmacy and later that day shot and killed Kimberly McIntosch. (*Mental Disability Law Reporter*, 1979)

Dr. Milano had reportedly tried to reach his client by phone to talk about the stolen prescription blank, but it was too late to prevent the shooting. Ms. McIntosch's father, a physician who was familiar with the Tarasoff decision, and his wife ultimately filed a civil damage suit against Dr. Milano for the wrongful death of their daughter, asserting that Milano should have warned Kimberly or taken reasonable steps to protect her.

Dr. Milano attempted to dismiss the suit, claiming that the Tarasoff principle should not be applied in New Jersey for four reasons. First, to do so would impose an unworkable duty, since the prediction of dangerousness is unreliable. Second, violating the client's confidentiality would have interfered with effective treatment. Third, assertion of the Tarasoff principle could deter therapists from treating potentially violent patients. Finally, Milano claimed that the number of commitments to institutions might increase unnecessarily. The court rejected each of these arguments and denied the motion to dismiss the case (*McIntosch* v. *Milano*, 1979). The court noted that the duty to warn was a valid concept; in addition, although therapists cannot be 100 percent accurate in making predictions, they should be able to weigh the relationships of the parties. An analogy was drawn comparing the situation with warning communities and individuals about carriers of a contagious disease, and the court stated that confidentiality is not absolute and must yield to the greater welfare of the community, especially in the case of an imminent danger.

> **Case 3—5:**   James, a juvenile, was incarcerated for 18 months at a county facility. During the course of his confinement, James threatened to murder a child in the neighborhood if released, although no particular individual was mentioned. James was paroled and did indeed kill a child shortly thereafter.

In the litigation that resulted from this case (*Thompson* v. *County of Alameda*, 1980), the primary concern was whether the county had a duty to warn the local police, neighborhood parents, or James's mother of his threat. While recognizing the duty of the county to protect its citizens, the California Supreme Court declined to extend the Tarasoff doctrine to this case, noting that it would be impractical and negate rehabilitative efforts to provide general public warnings of nonspecific threats for each person paroled. Warning the custodial parent was also deemed futile since one would not expect her to provide constant supervision (*Mental Disability Law Reporter*, 1980).

Imminent Danger and Confidentiality

The current *Ethical Principles* authorize the disclosure of confidential material without the client's consent only "in those unusual circumstances in which not to do so would result in clear danger to the person or others" (*EP*: 5, preamble). Even then, one should only disclose information to the extent necessary to remove the danger. Consider the following case examples:

> **Case 3–6:** Bernard Bizzie, Ed.D., was about to leave for the weekend when he received an emergency call from a client who claimed to have taken a number of pills in an attempt to kill herself. Bizzie told her to telephone her physician and come in to see him at 9:00 A.M. on Monday morning. He made no other attempt to intervene. The client died later that evening, without making any other calls for assistance.

> **Case 3–7:** Mitchell Morose, age 21, was being treated by Ned Novice, a psychology intern at a university counseling center. Morose had been increasingly depressed and anxious about academic failure and dependency issues regarding his family. During one session, Morose told Novice that he was contemplating suicide, had formulated a plan to carry it out, and was working on a note that he would leave in order "to teach my parents a lesson." Novice attempted to convince Morose to enter a psychiatric hospital for treatment in view of these feelings, but Morose accused Novice of "acting like my parents," and left the office. Novice immediately called George Graybeard, Psy.D., his supervisor, for advice. Graybeard agreed with Novice about the risk of suicide; thus, acting under a provision of their state's commitment law, they contacted Morose's parents who could legally seek an emergency, involuntary hospitalization as his next-of-kin. The parents were told only that their son was in treatment, that he was having suicidal ideation, and that he was refusing care. They then assisted in having Morose committed for treatment. After discharge, Morose filed an ethical complaint against Novice and Graybeard for violating his confidentiality, especially by communicating with his parents.

Dr. Bizzie was clearly unethical in his negligence by not attending more directly to his client's needs. Even those psychologists who assert that one should *never* disclose confidential information without the informed consent of the client would not counsel inaction in the face of such a risk (Dubey, 1974; Siegel, 1979). There are many other actions Bizzie could have implemented, without violating the client's confidentiality. He should have at least attempted to learn the patient's location and ensure himself that help would reach her if he were unable to do so. While there are times when suicidal threats or gestures are "manipulative" and do not represent a genuine risk, it is a foolish and insensitive psychologist who ignores the threats or glibly attempts to send the patient to another colleague.

Mr. Morose represents a variation on the same theme. Novice certainly had reason to be concerned and to discuss the matter with his supervisor. (Moreover, we must assume that, early in their work together, Novice had explained his "intern" status to Morose, including the fact that the case would be discussed routinely with his supervisor.) Novice had attempted to ensure the safety of his client through voluntary hospitalization, but the client declined. Since the state laws, well known to Dr. Graybeard, provided a mechanism that permitted the involvement of next-of-kin, the decision to contact the parents was not inappropriate, despite the client's wishes. Morose had provided ample reason to consider him at risk, and the responsible parties disclosed only those matters that were deemed absolutely necessary to ensure his safety (i.e., that their son was at risk for suicide and refusing treatment). The parents were not given details or other confidential material. Morose's confidence was, of course, violated, and he was angry. Under the circumstances, however, Novice and Graybeard had behaved in an ethically appropriate fashion.

If there is a way to anticipate and avoid such dilemmas in one's practice, three separate issues are probably involved. First, each psychologist must review the circumstances under which she or he will breach confidentiality or privilege. Consultation with an attorney about the law in the jurisdiction where the psychologist practices, for example, would be helpful. Second, the psychologist should make these conditions or limitations clear to potential clients at the beginning of any professional relationship, either orally or in written form (Hare-Mustin et al., 1979; Everstine et al., 1980). Finally, if an actual circumstance arises that affects these issues, consultation with colleagues to determine alternatives that may not have appeared initially is appropriate. These steps will not solve all problems, but they can help reduce their likelihood.

ACCESS TO RECORDS

Psychologists maintain records on their work and clients for various reasons, such as legal obligation, reluctance to rely on memory, communication to other professionals, availability of important data, and documentation of services provided. By definition, such records will often contain confidential material, and, as long as they exist, someone other than the psychologist who collected the material may seek access to them. How should such access be provided to the client, members of the client's family, the courts, or other agencies? In addressing this issue we must first consider the process of securing a client's informed consent for the release of information (*EP*: 5c). We must then consider the claims and circumstances under which various parties might seek access, as well as the nature of the information being sought. Finally, we shall consider the use of client records for teaching or research purposes, including the use of tape recordings and photographic materials.

Informed Consent for the Release of Records

The existence of transferable records can be of considerable assistance or substantial detriment to clients, depending on what is contained in them and how they are used. Often the process of obtaining consent is so hurried or perfunctory that clients may not fully understand what they are authorizing or why. Some people may even sign release-of-information forms against their wishes, because of various subtle and obvious pressures or because no alternatives were offered (Rosen, 1977). The psychologist has an important role in educating and helping to safeguard the client's interests in such cases.

A consent or release-of-information form should contain several key elements, including the following: the name of the person to whom the records are to be released; which records are to be sent; the purpose or intended use; the date the form was signed; an expiration date; any limitations on the data to be provided; the name and signature of the person authorizing the releases, as well as that person's relationship to the client (if not the client him/herself); and the signature of a witness. If a psychologist receives a release or request for information that does not seem valid or might present some hazard to the client, it would be appropriate to contact the client directly prior to releasing any material.

Some psychologists have advocated the use of contracting for services with clients (Hare-Mustin et al., 1979; Everstine et al., 1980). These "contracts" may be either oral or written, but they should discuss important aspects and mutual expectations of the relationship. Although these issues are discussed in additional detail in Chapter 5, such contracts should include clear mention of confidentiality and any potential exceptions. Because of such cases as *Tarasoff* (1976) and *McIntosch* v. *Milano* (1979), some psychologists are providing clients with specific statements about potential violations of confidence and asking clients to sign an authorization for the disclosure of information necessary to prevent them from harming themselves or others.

These open-ended consent forms are probably not particularly useful for most clients who will rarely be dangerous, but they do serve to communicate any limitations placed on the relationship.

Whenever a consent form is signed, the client should be given a copy, and the psychologist should make the original part of that client's files. The psychologist should also keep a record of which materials were sent, to whom, and when. The materials should be appropriately marked as confidential, and the recipient should be aware of their confidentiality. One should also exercise caution to see that only material appropriate to the need is sent. Consider the following case:

> **Case 3–8:** Kurt Files, Psy.D., had evaluated eight-year-old Sheldon Sputter at his family's request because of school problems. The evaluation included taking a developmental and family history, meeting with both parents, reviewing school progress reports, and the administration of cognitive and personality tests. Dr. Files discovered that Sheldon has a mild perceptual learning disability and that he was also reacting to various family stresses, including his mother's reaction to paternal infidelity, the father's recent discovery that Sheldon was not his child, and numerous other family secrets that had recently been exposed. Dr. Files recommended appropriate psychotherapeutic intervention, and the family followed through with his recommendations. Several weeks later, Dr. Files received a signed release form from the school Sheldon attended, asking for "any" information he had on Sheldon's problem. Dr. Files responded with a letter describing the cognitive test results and referring in general terms to "emotional stresses in the family that are being attended to."

In this situation, the psychologist recognized the school's valid need to know information that could help serve Sheldon better. At the same time, Dr. Files recognized that some of the material was not relevant to the school's role, and he made the appropriate discrimination, despite the vague and broad request for "any" information.

Client Access to Records

Clients' access to their own mental health records remains a matter of some controversy, although the issues vary somewhat as a function of the precise type of records involved. The three general types of records are as follows: institutional (e.g., hospital, clinic, school, government agency), private practitioners' office records, and working notes. Access to institutional records is often governed by institutional policy and statute. The federal freedom-of-information act and state patients' rights laws often specify a right of access to institutional, agency, or medical records. Although medical and mental health records were exempted in the past, this trend has been reversing (Roth et al., 1980). The records retained by private practitioners in their offices are usually not covered by specific legislation, although patients certainly can be expected to ask occasionally for information from them (e.g., copies of formal reports). Some portions of psychologists' office records might include material that should be safeguarded from disclosure to nonprofessionals (e.g., copies of scored intelligence tests or other, similar materials that could compromise test security if released). In general, however, it is the category of records we have termed "working notes" that causes the most concern.

By working notes, we refer to those impressions, hypotheses, and half-formed ideas that a psychologist jots down to assist in formulating more comprehensive reports or later recommendations. Often these notes are reworked into a report, used for discussion with a supervisor, or simply discarded as new data are considered. Because of the speculative and impressionistic nature of such working notes, they would not be meaningful or useful to anyone except the person who made them. Such notes are definitely not the type of material that should be released to anyone. They should be temporary documents, which are occasionally reworked into more formal office or institutional records. The original notes are then destroyed. Psychologists should be aware that at least some risk always exists and that any written materials might some day be disclosed in public through a court proceeding. A regular pattern of reviewing and consolidating detailed working notes into less sensitive summaries should be the rule for all cases. This procedure avoids the danger of an accusation that a case file has been selectively edited simply because court action was pending. (The reasons for this suggestion will become clearer in the following pages.)

Most important, the records do not belong to the client, but rather are the property of the institution or private practitioner who has kept them, depending on the setting involved. Although clients may have a right to copies of, or access to, their records, the records do not belong to the client unless expressly transferred to the client for a particular reason. Clients may occasionally assert the claim to a record, because the person "paid for that report" or "those services." In fact, the client paid for services rendered and perhaps received a copy of a report, but does not receive the actual, original records unless that was a specific part of the agreement.

Opponents of free client access to records make two general types of claims. First, they assert that, to be creative, one must be free to speculate and jot down any thought or comments. Some of these impressions will invariably be erroneous or misleading if taken out of context. Second, opponents of open access might claim that harm may be done by sharing technical psychological information with clients who are not equipped to understand or to handle the information (Strassburger, 1975). Consider, for example, the following case from *Gotkin* v. *Miller* (1975):

Case 3−9:   On several occasions between 1962 and 1970, Janet Gotkin had been a voluntary mental patient at three different New York hospitals. After she and her husband decided to write a book about her experiences, they sought access to her records to verify some of the material. The requests were refused and led to a lawsuit against the New York State Commissioner of Mental Hygiene and the directors of the hospitals involved (*Medical World News*, 1975).

The judge in the case agreed with the refusal to provide the records when the hospitals expressed a preference for releasing the records to another professional, rather than to the client herself, for the following reasons: the records would be unintelligible to the layperson; some of the information might prove detrimental to the individual's current well-being; and the records could contain reference to other individuals who might be harmed by disclosure (Roth et al., 1980). The judge also noted that records are the property of the practitioner or the hospital and that a client consults the practitioner for services, not for records (*Medical World News*, 1975).

Those advocating more open access to records cite the legitimate interest of the client in obtaining information, and they regard such access as a way to help clients and to improve their consumer behavior (Roth et al., 1980). Other arguments in favor of this position include the point that providing such records to clients can improve the efficiency of delivering service by avoiding delays when the client is able to share the records directly with other practitioners. Studies performed at the University of Vermont and Pittsburgh's Western Psychiatric Institute suggest that a more open access policy may yield clients who are more cooperative, less anxious, and generally relieved. No adverse effects were documented (Roth et al., 1980). Other psychologists have argued against the assumptions that "professionals know best" or "clients are fragile" (Brodsky, 1972) or that secrecy might actually help the client in some way (Fisher, 1972).

The point is often made that some clients may obtain records with or without the psychologist's full cooperation: thus the records should be kept and written with this possibility in mind, and the psychologist should be willing to share the contents, along with an explanation of terms, and so forth. In a study conducted on an inpatient psychiatric unit, the effects of client access to records were definitely positive. The clients reported feeling better informed and more involved in their treatment, while the staff became more thoughtful about their notes in the charts (Stein et al., 1979).

There may exist circumstances, such as notes on group therapy sessions or records collected on behalf of a corporate client regarding many individuals, when full access to records could violate the privacy and confidentiality of another party. There may also exist a few rare instances when access to some recorded data might cause substantial and concrete detriment to an individual client.

Case 3–10: During an acute psychotic episode, Tyrone Propper penned a series of bizarre, sexually explicit notes to his psychotherapist. Since the notes seemed clinically relevant at the time, they were kept in the therapist's private case files. Mr. Propper later recovered fully and returned to his job as a bank officer. He visited the therapist for a follow-up session and asked to review the case file to help gain perspective on what had happened to him. Propper had few memories from the psychotic period.

Case 3–11: Barry Icarus had been raised by his aunt and uncle since his parents died when he was a year old. He had suffered a reactive depression since his uncle's death from a heart attack on his 16th birthday. Six months of psychotherapy had helped him to deal with the loss successfully and to enter college away from home. A few years later, Barry's aunt died, and he returned to have a few additional sessions with the same psychologist who had helped him earlier. Barry expressed some interest in reviewing his records with respect to his prior treatment. In the psychologist's file was a developmental history given by the aunt and uncle when Barry was 16. This file included the fact, still unknown to Barry, that his mother had been shot to death by his father who later committed suicide.

In these cases, it would be appropriate for the practitioners in question to delete material (e.g., the sexually explicit notes and the circumstances of the parents' deaths) from the files prior to reviewing them with the clients. The notes could prove embarrassing to the recovered client, and revealing them would serve no useful purpose while possibly creating emotional stress for him. The information on Barry's parents is irrelevant to his reason for seeking treatment now, but at age sixteen, it was part of a thorough developmental history required at the time. Providing him with this material now would add stress, without any immediately constructive purpose. He can always choose to research his family background, if he wishes, but to provide the data now would merely add stressful material tangential to his reason for seeking treatment.

When this type of situation occurs, it should be possible to supply the client with the information being sought, while deleting those sections that might violate the rights of others. In the case of the detrimental material, the residual content could be shared directly with the client. A decision about the actual degree of detriment, however, should first be made by a professional in a position to offer an unbiased consultation on the matter. If records are appropriately kept in a factual manner, with a minimum of speculation, written in clear language, and well documented, there should be minimal need to fear client access.

Psychologists who choose to make records available to clients should give serious consideration to the manner in which this disclosure will be done. Do you insist on being present? Do you charge for your time, or is it considered part of your service? Do you make your policy on such matters clear to clients before therapy (or other service delivery) starts? We believe that it is desirable to explain policies to clients early in the course of the professional relationship. We also believe that it is desirable for the psychologist to be present during the record review in order to offer elaboration, to explain technical terms, or to deal with the client's feelings related to the material. If a significant amount of time is involved, it is appropriate to charge for this service; however, this should be tempered with an understanding of the client's financial situation, balanced with his or her needs and rights of access in a particular situation. The client who has terminated treatment due to lack of funds, for example, should not be barred from a file review for inability to pay.

Access by Family Members

Occasionally, a concerned family member will seek access to a client's records. When the client is a child or has been deemed legally incompetent, parents or guardians may actually be entitled to legal access. Psychologists should recognize the unique problems that arise when working with minors or families, and they should be sensitive to each individual's right to privacy and confidentiality in such circumstances (EP: 5d). From the beginning of any such relationship, all parties should be informed about the specific nature of the confidential relationship. A discussion about what types of information might be shared and with whom should be raised early. This is not a difficult or burdensome process when dealt with as a routine practice (Koocher, 1976).

> **Case 3–12:** Cynthia Childs, Psy.D., has been treating seven-year-old Max Bashem for about a month. Max was referred for treatment because of secondary enuresis and acting-out behaviors that are of recent onset. The birth of a new sibling in the Bashem family several weeks ago seems to have been a precipitating factor. Near the end of the fifth therapy session, Max expresses some anger about his new sib and tells Dr. Childs: "Tonight after my parents go to bed, I'm gonna kill that little weasel!"

> **Case 3–13:** Donna Rhea, age 15, was also in psychotherapy with Dr. Childs. Donna feels alienated from her parents and is sexually active. Her parents discover that she has contracted a venereal disease and in a moment of emotional distress she accuses them of not being as "understanding as Dr. Childs." The parents are furious that the psychologist knew their daughter was sexually active and did not tell them. They claim that, unless they receive a full briefing from Dr. Childs, they will remove their daughter from treatment. They also threaten to file an ethics complaint.

These two cases illustrate several difficult, though not insolvable, problems. In the case of Max, Dr. Childs must consider several factors, not the least of which is the seriousness of Max's threat. Does Max have a history of violence toward others? Is he exaggerating his anger in the context of therapy for emphasis? Although Dr. Childs will certainly want to explore this issue with Max before ending the session, suppose she feels that there is some risk to the sibling? Suppose Max cannot commit himself not to do anything in the week intervening between sessions? Childs could express her concern and discuss with Max the need to do something to help him from doing something he might later regret. She could talk about alternatives with him and explore a variety of them, such as scheduling a family conference where Max could be encouraged to share some of his angry feelings more directly. If all else fails and Childs believes that she cannot otherwise stop Max from hurting his sibling, she must discuss the matter with his parents as a "duty to warn" issue. Not to do so would constitute malpractice. Although such a circumstance would be rare indeed, Childs should at least discuss the matter with Max, including her need to violate the confidence for his ultimate benefit.

In the case of Donna, the problem is more complex. Dr. Childs almost certainly would have lost the trust of her client if she had chosen to violate Donna's confidence. The parents may well be jealous of the trust and respect their daughter seems to have in the psychologist, while being angry and disappointed at her sexual activity and infection. A conference would not be inappropriate, although it would probably be best conducted as a family meeting with Donna present. Dr. Childs could attempt to be supportive and therapeutic in such a session, without necessarily breaking a confidence. It is unclear what type of information the parents are seeking. A better alternative would have been a pretreatment family conference, including a discussion of the treatment relationship and any attendant limitations. An outright refusal to meet with the parents in this circumstance would not serve the interests of any of the parties. Many state laws do permit minors to obtain treatment for venereal disease or birth control information without parental consent and in confidence. Dr. Childs' behavior does not appear to have been unethical.

When access to records is sought by family members of an adult, it should usually be denied, unless there is some particular reason to consider the request. Special reasons might include the "imminent danger" test, as discussed previously, or the incapacity of the client. The surviving line of consent generally recognized by courts is as follows: first, the spouse (even if living apart from the client, as long as they are not divorced); second, the children of legal age, with each child having equal voice; third, parents or grandparents, followed by siblings, each having equal voice. If none of the above survive, courts will occasionally designate the next nearest relative or closest friend.

Case 3–14: Marla Noma was a cancer patient for many years and, during that period, she occasionally consulted Michael Tact, Ph.D., about her fears and concerns related to the illness. During a surgical procedure, Marla was left comatose and was being kept alive on life-support equipment, although there was little chance of any recovery. Members of her family plan to seek court authorization to discontinue mechanical life-support equipment, and they wonder whether any of Tact's records or conversations with Marla might provide some guidance to them and the court about her wishes.

In such a case, where the client cannot speak for herself, it would probably not be unethical for Dr. Tact to respond openly to a duly authorized request for information from a next-of-kin.

Court Access to Records

The concept of privileged communication discussed earlier in this chapter is, in fact, rather narrow regarding what material is protected from disclosure in court. Nevertheless, courts or litigants may seek privileged information or other confidential material. Although psychologists must certainly respect appropriate requests emanating from the courts, they must also reasonably safeguard material from inappropriate release. Personal working notes are usually not subject to disclosure in court, especially in civil cases. In criminal cases, however, it is not unusual for a *subpoena duces tecum* to be issued, demanding that the psychologist appear in court and bring "any and all files, documents, reports, papers, and notes" regarding the case in question.

The first thing that a psychologist should do when a subpoena is served is nothing: that is, nothing should be surrendered to the party serving the subpoena no matter how aggressive the request. The document should be accepted, and the psychologist should then consult legal counsel regarding applicable law and resulting obligations. If it is ultimately determined that the call for the records has been appropriately issued by a court of competent authority, a psychologist may be placed in an awkward position, especially if the client does not wish to have the material disclosed.

Case 3−15: Arnold and Anita Abuser were being treated in marital therapy by Samuel Silent, Ed.D., when their child died of apparently inflicted injuries. Dr. Silent was subpoenaed to appear before a Grand Jury investigating the child's death, and he was questioned about the content of his sessions with the Abusers by the district attorney who sought incriminating evidence about the couple. There was no privileged communication statute in Dr. Silent's state, and a judge ordered him to testify or be held in jail for contempt of court. The Abusers did not wish Dr. Silent to discuss in court any material from their sessions.

Case 3−16: John and Sandra Spleen filed for divorce under circumstances that were less than amicable. John is a psychologist, and Sandra believed that he was lying about his income in the process of reaching a negotiated financial statement. She sought a court order for her spouse to disclose the names, addresses, and billing records of his clients so that she and her attorney could check on the actual income from his practice.

Dr. Silent is in a particularly difficult situation. If he bows to the court order, he may be seen as violating his clients' confidentiality (ethical violation). If the Abusers are guilty, and the psychologist's silence precludes prosecution, he may be protecting his clients to the detriment of society as a whole. If he does not comply with a valid court order to testify, he can be fined or jailed for contempt and may be accused of breaking the law (also an ethical violation). This example illustrates how ethical behavior may be at variance with legal requirements. If Dr. Silent believes he should not testify, the best advice would be to resist disclosure of confidential material, using all legitimate legal avenues. When such avenues are exhausted, and if they fail, Dr. Silent would probably not be faulted for ultimately disclosing the material. On the other hand, if he chooses to go to jail on a matter of principle, rather than disclose the confidential material, it also seems unlikely that he would be found to have violated professional ethics solely because of a resulting contempt citation. If he chose to disclose details from the outset under a statutory authorization or obligation specific to child abuse, he would also not be considered unethical.

Dr. Spleen is also in a difficult position, even if he has nothing personal to hide. Disclosing the names and addresses of his clients could certainly prove embarrassing and stressful to the clients themselves. Perhaps there are ways for his records to be audited in confidence by a bonded professional, without the need to contact clients individually or to otherwise disclose their names. In any event, the Spleens' dispute is a civil matter, and courts are less likely to pursue disclosure than they would be in a criminal or malpractice case. In a similar case, a California appellate court protected the confidentiality of the psychologist's records from the spouse, noting that public disclosure of client status itself might prove harmful to a client.

These examples clearly illustrate the importance of the recommendation made earlier in this chapter that personal notes containing speculation, hypotheses, and other tentative jottings be purged or synthesized frequently into more permanent and factual records. The best defense against harm caused by informal-type notes is to limit their life span. Files should be routinely culled of obsolete material, especially of informal information.

Third-Party Access: Insurers and Peer Review

The role of so-called "third-parties" is reviewed in Chapter 6 from the financial perspective. Clients, however, may sometimes authorize the release of information to third parties without fully realizing the implications of their actions. When a client decides to submit a claim for mental health benefits to an insurance company, for example, he or she may not realize that this submission authorizes the provider of services to share certain information (e.g., diagnosis, type of service offered, dates services were rendered, duration of treatment, and so forth). In some circumstances, insurers and other so-called "peer review" groups may be authorized to seek detailed information from case files, including a client's current symptom status, details of a treatment plan, or other sensitive material. After information leaves a psychologist's office, it is beyond his or her control, and insurance companies may not exercise the same caution and responsibility as the individual practitioner. Some insurance companies, for example, participate in rating services or similar pools of data on individuals that may be made available to other companies at some future date (Grossman, 1971; Jagim et al., 1978).

It is not always clear to clients that they are authorizing such a release when they give an insurance policy number or sign a claim form, although a specific general release statement invariably exists, just as it does whenever an American applies for life insurance coverage. Psychologists often fail to fully comprehend the differences between privilege and confidentiality, as well as the implications of providing some detailed data to insurers (Jagim et al., 1978). This yields an interesting problem when psychologists attempt to inform clients about the implications of using insurance coverage to pay for psychological services.

Case 3–17:   Victor Vigilant, Ph.D., routinely informs his clients about the issue of disclosure to insurance companies in the following manner. He tells clients who have coverage: "If you choose to use your coverage, I shall have to file a form with the company telling them when our appointments were and what services I performed (i.e., psychotherapy, consultation, or evaluation). I will also have to formulate a diagnosis and advise the company of that. The company claims to keep this information confidential, although I have no control over the information once it leaves this office. If you have questions about this you may wish to check with the company providing the coverage. You may certainly choose to pay for my services out-of-pocket and avoid the use of insurance altogether, if you wish."

Some clients may be unconcerned about the issue. A parent whose child is being assessed for perceptually-based learning disabilities, for example, may be unconcerned. On the other hand, a client holding a sensitive public office might well wish to avoid informing any third party that a psychologist was being consulted. In some companies, further complications arise whenever claim forms must be processed through the employer. This procedure creates an additional risk because staff in the personnel office might have access to the information. This possibility may not constitute a significant threat, but, for certain clients and some diagnoses, it might be best to avoid any type of disclosure without first checking on the channels through which the information will flow.

Professional Standards Review Committees (PSRCs) and other peer-review groups, such as professional association ethics committees, constitute a different type of third party in which the matter of disclosing confidential material occasionally becomes an issue. Psychologists are obligated to respond to inquiries from such duly constituted bodies, although they are obligated to first observe the basic principle of confidentiality. When asked to respond by such a committee, the psychologist should first determine whether an appropriate waiver of confidentiality has been obtained. No ethics committee or PSRC can press an inquiry about a client, unless it first obtains a signed release from the client of the psychologist's obligation of confidentiality. The same procedure applies to complaints to licensing boards or other regulatory groups. The principle is identical to the one involved in malpractice litigation: i.e., the psychologist cannot defend his or her case, unless the freedom to discuss the content of the relationship in question is granted.

> **Case 3–18:**   Roger Control filed an ethics complaint against a psychologist who allegedly "made my problems worse instead of better." Mr. Control complained about one session in particular that "caused me strong mental anguish and insomnia for several weeks." Mr. Control asserted that the dozen prior sessions with the psychologist were irrelevant and would only agree to let the psychologist talk about the one traumatic session he had cited. The ethics committee, noting that this limitation would not permit a sufficient response to their inquiry by the psychologist, declined to investigate the case without a broader authorization.

CONFIDENTIAL MATERIAL IN CLASSROOM AND LABORATORY

Ethical issues related to the classroom and psychological research are addressed in Chapters 13 and 14; however, it is important to note at least a few special issues related to confidential material in such settings. The first point discussed involves confidential materials that are adapted for teaching purposes, and the second point focuses on confidentiality problems involving research data.

Classroom Materials

Ideally, any materials prepared for teaching that use sensitive or confidential material involve the full informed consent of the client. When video or audio tapes, detailed summaries of case material, or other accounts of psychological material not otherwise in the public domain are adapted, the client or client's guardian should have consented to the use of the material for teaching purposes. This procedure is especially important when the nature of the material (e.g., visual reproductions or recognizable facts) might make it possible to identify the client(s). Formal consent may not be necessary if the material is disguised sufficiently to make recognition of the client impossible. This volume presents an appropriate example. Some of the cases cited here involve actual legal decisions in the public domain and are cited as such, but others are disguised or synthesized versions of actual situations or case material. These cases are presented in a sufficiently general manner so that real people are not recognizable, except perhaps to themselves.

> **Case 3−19:** Emily Barrassed entered psychotherapy with Will U. Tell, Psy.D., and was seen several times per week for nearly two years. During the course of these sessions, Ms. Barrassed shared a number of intimate and sensitive fantasies and life events with Dr. Tell. At the end of their work together, both felt that impressive progress had been made. Dr. Tell asked if Ms. Barrassed might permit him to mention some details of their work together in a book he was writing, providing he disguised the material so that she could not be recognized. She agreed and signed a release form he had prepared. Several years later, Dr. Tell's book became a popular best seller, and Ms. Barrassed discovered to her shock that she was easily recognized in the book by people who knew her. Dr. Tell had changed some details, such as the name, city, and so forth, but described her family, upbringing, occupation, and one-eyed amputee spouse without disguise.

> **Case 3−20:** Irwin Klunk, Ph.D., shared the test data obtained in an evaluation of a disturbed child with his graduate psychology class. He passed around copies of drawings, test protocols, and interpretations. All of the sheets bore the child's full name and other identifying information. One of the students in the class was a friend of the boy's mother and told her. The mother filed an ethics complaint against the professor for violating her son's confidentiality. The professor responded that since the testee was a minor and since the students were at a graduate level, he had not believed it necessary to remove identifying data.

The chances of having a relative, friend, acquaintance, or colleague of a client in the audience is not as small as one might imagine, and the consequences of revealing a confidence or sharing intimate details of a client's personal life in a recognizable fashion may be devastating. There are times when this is unlikely, such as during a classroom discussion of a response to the Rorschach Inkblots in which the client is identified only by age and sex, or through the use of a case history that has been thoroughly blinded, and actual individual consent may not be needed for such material. When in doubt, however, the material should be reviewed with a colleague to be certain that identifying facts have not inadvertently been included. Furthermore, any superfluous facts that might help to identify the client, while not adding meaningful detail to the example, should be omitted.

Research Data

Perhaps the best example of the difficulties resulting with respect to confidential research data is the case of Samuel Popkin.

> **Case 3–21:**   On November 21, 1972, Samuel L. Popkin, an assistant professor of government at Harvard University, was imprisoned under a U.S. District Court order for refusing to answer several questions before a federal grand jury investigating the publication of the "Pentagon Papers." Popkin asserted a First Amendment right to refuse to provide the information collected as part of his scholarly research on Vietnam and U.S. involvement in that country. He was released from jail seven days later when the grand jury was discharged, and the U.S. Supreme Court later refused to review the order that led to his confinement (Carroll, 1973).

Popkin was a political scientist, but he might have been a psychologist conducting attitude research or interviews on the personality structure of "political radicals." Despite the fact that such research might not be able to take place without some pledge of confidentiality to respondents, "national security interests" led the courts to overrule any claim of privilege or assertion of confidentiality. Consider, for example, the case that follows:

> **Case 3–22:**   Seb Terfuge, Ph.D., was conducting a field study of homosexual encounters in a public men's lavatory. Using a set of unobtrusive timing devices and a periscopic videotape apparatus, Dr. Terfuge concealed himself in a toilet stall and recorded a variety of casual homosexual encounters throughout a period of several months. When he published an account of his findings in a professional journal, the local district attorney attempted to subpoena his videotapes in order to prosecute the people studied under an "unnatural acts" statute.

Dr. Terfuge should have anticipated such difficulties, considering the sensitive nature of the matters he was studying, and he should have attempted to determine whether it was possible to collect the data in any other fashion. Assuming that it was not possible to do so and assuming that the potential hazards to the people under study were not sufficient to warrant cancellation of the project, he should have taken steps to protect their anonymity. Dr. Terfuge was not simply conducting a field study, but was actually placing his intended subjects at some risk to themselves without their knowledge and consent. One could argue that a police officer might have made arrests, if one had been present, but Terfuge was not a police officer and is obligated to consider the welfare of those he studies in the course of his research.

Not all confidential data are so threatening, and, in fact, there are times when the revelation of sensitive or confidential research data can have significant social benefits (Gordis and Gold, 1980). Epidemiological research presents a good example. While the National Research Act (Public Law 93–348) and the Privacy Act of 1974 (Public Law 93–579) specify many complex protective mechanisms, various medical studies have illustrated the importance of being able to break the confidential code from time to time. The studies of diethylstilbestrol (DES) and its association to vaginal cancers one generation later, studies of occupational cancers with long-dormancy intervals, and studies of long-term use of contraceptive pills are only three examples. In each type of study cited, it would be necessary to locate and track an identifiable individual over time in order to establish data of meaningful, long-term risk to clients as individuals and to society as a whole (Gordis and Gold, 1980).

Safeguards are indeed needed, but one must be prepared to seek advice and consultation from institutional review boards (IRBs) or other appropriate bodies when conducting such studies. Knerr (1982) offers considerable information and advice on what to do if one's data are ever subpoenaed. An attorney should also be consulted regarding the impact of laws, such as the Freedom of Information Act. Above all, the rights of the individual participant in the research must be considered (see Chapter 14).

RECORD RETENTION AND DISPOSITION

Retention

How long should one retain records? This question is difficult to answer easily, because the number and type of records kept by psychologists, clinics, and other agencies vary widely in both content and purpose, as discussed earlier in this chapter. The answer to this question will vary as a function of the type of record, nature of the client's need for documentation of prior services, probability of need for future services, validity of the data in the records, and the applicable state or federal regulations. In any given legal jurisdiction, for example, the responsibilities on a professional might vary widely, depending on whether the records in question are considered business files, medical records, school records, or research data. The two key factors a psychologist should consider in making a decision about retention or disposition of records are applicable legal obligations and client welfare.

Legal obligations are best determined by consulting with an attorney familiar with the statutes that apply to one's practice. A review of state laws (Springer, 1971) suggests that dramatic differences exist from location to location. Considering only "hospital records," Springer notes that Massachusetts permits the destruction of records thirty years after the discharge or final treatment of the patient. California requires retention of such hospital records for seven years after discharge or until the patient reaches age 21, but never less than seven years. New York's statute is similar to the California requirement except that the time frame is six years. In Texas, the law specifies 10 years general retention, while Pennsylvania specifies keeping the record itself for 15 years and keeping a permanent case file on each patient. Some states, such as South Dakota, specify that hospital records be kept permanently.

Laws dealing with practitioners themselves usually are less specific and often require less prolonged retention of patient or client files. Many state laws do not specifically mention psychologists and their records by name. Massachusetts seems to be typical in its statute (Mass. G.L. Ch.111, Sec. 70), requiring that a physician must maintain a "medical record" for a minimum of at least three years from the date of last patient encounter, "in a manner which permits the former patient or a successor physician access to them."

The U.S. Internal Revenue Service imposes yet another type of obligation on virtually all professionals through its seven-year record-keeping requirement. Although these obligations refer to business and financial records, some ability to access client names and payments is necessary. A client being audited might have to seek confirmation of payments made to the psychologist, or the psychologist might have to document certain financial data regarding his or her practice to the I.R.S.

Client welfare concerns affect the matter of record retention in two ways. First, one must consider the client need and benefit to the client of such records. Second, one must consider the risks and hazards of such records to clients, especially when they contain obsolete or potentially harmful data and may pass beyond the originating psychologist's control.

Records benefit the client in various ways, including their potential to assist in the continuity of care across providers and over time. Even after a client has improved and left the psychologist's care, a need might arise to document the fact that there had been a period of treatment, disability, treatment costs, and so forth. Records do, after all, have the potential to recall events better than and to survive longer than the provider who prepared them.

Potential problems with records, aside from the access issues mentioned earlier in this chapter, often arise as the result of invalid or obsolete information. Determining what is "obsolete" can be a problem, however. One must resist the temptation, inherent in the psychologist's research training, to save any potentially analyzable data indefinitely.

Case 3–23: An agency serving children maintained its clinical files, including psychological test data, indefinitely. A request for information, validly executed, is received from a government agency requesting copies of reports on a now forty-year-old job applicant who was seen at the agency thirty years earlier. The question of whether IQ and other tests or psychological information should be released is raised.

In fact, the agency may be obligated to release the information under the circumstances cited above, because it exists and the authorization is valid. On the other hand, one should legitimately question whether full test data and detailed notes should be kept this long and thus be available for such requests. The IQ data obtained at age 10 will have no bearing on the person's current employability, and any treatment or personality test data will have questionable value in light of the intervening 30 years. If the records had been destroyed or purged of data no longer valuable to the agency, there would be minimal danger to the former client that such information could return from the past to be used against him or her. Likewise, facts of interest to treatment team members, while a client is being seen, may be mere gossip years later (e.g., "paternal aunt suffered from melancholia," "intense sibling rivalry is present," "parents have difficulty with sexual intimacy").

A survey by Noll and Hanlon (1976) demonstrated widespread disagreements and confusion among mental health center administrators on the matter of record retention, with usual responses ranging from "three years" to "permanent" retention. In general, the best recommendation we can offer is twofold. First, check your legal obligations based on state law with respect to any statute of limitations on business and medical records. Given I.R.S. rules, we suggest a minimum of seven years' retention, even if your state permits shorter periods. The retention clock should start ticking at the end of the final professional service to the client. Second, when the client is treated prior to the age of majority, the records should be kept at least a few years longer than the date when majority is attained, even if this exceeds the suggested seven-year guideline.

Disposition

When records or obsolete contents culled from records are to be disposed of, the deed must be done in a manner consistent with their confidential nature. Shredding, burning, recycling, or other destructive actions should be carried out or contracted for, although actual responsibility for the destruction should reside with the practitioner or agency head in charge of the material.

> **Case 3–24:** An agency planned to dispose of many clinical records that were several years old. The records were tied in plastic trash bags and inserted in an outdoor receptacle, intended for trash pick-up. Neighborhood dogs tore several bags open, and the wind blew out many reports and notes bearing client names and other identifying material. Many of the clients whose records were strewn about still resided in the same community.

In this case, it is evident that minimal care was taken to see that the sensitive material was disposed of properly. The material should have been stored securely until it could be picked up by a responsible disposal agent.

The death of a psychologist can also raise a complex set of problems with respect to individual client records. In some cases, records have simply been destroyed by a surviving spouse or executor. In other cases, the records have been kept, but no arrangements were made available for the orderly processing and screening of requests to access information from them. This is another reason why psychologists who have such files should specify disposition instructions in their wills. One alternative could be an arrangement with a professionally responsible colleague for the care and management of the records. Other alternatives would be to instruct one's spouse or executor, to seek advice from others on record management, or to ask a professional association to assist in managing the files for a period of time after the client's death.

SUMMARY GUIDELINES

1. It is especially important for a psychologist to understand the distinctions between confidentiality (an ethical principle) and privilege (a legal concept) as they apply in his or her own state.

2. Psychologists should be aware of any exceptions and limitations, such as the so-called "duty to warn," obligations to report child abuse, collection of bills, or other special conditions bearing on confidentiality, and they should share such limitations with clients as necessary.

3. Prior to releasing records, psychologists should secure written informed consent from the client, and they should attempt to alert the client regarding any potential hazards to the release.

4. Psychologists should recognize the different types of formal and informal records that exist, and they should attempt to ensure that the contents remain factual, appropriate, and current.

5. There is an increasing trend toward freer client access to records, a fact that should be remembered when reports are prepared and files are maintained.

6. When confidential material is properly released, the psychologist should carefully consider the need-to-know basis of the intended recipient and the manner in which the information will probably be used.

7. Special consideration must be given to the rights of minors and legally incompetent individuals in considering their requests for access to their personal psychological files.

8. A psychologist should become informed regarding the appropriate mode of response to requests for information from courts or other third parties.

9. When using case materials for teaching purposes, care must be taken to secure proper permission and to disguise material sufficiently to protect the client.

10. In the conduct of psychological research, the welfare of those under study must be given careful consideration with respect to confidentiality.

11. Psychologists must take proper steps to ensure that the retention and disposition of records occurs within the context of the clients' best interests.

REFERENCE NOTE

1. Parker, D. B. Proposal for Research on Computer Science and Technology Ethics Workshop. SRI No. ISU 76–54, dated February 27, 1976. Stanford Research Institute, Menlo Park, California.

REFERENCES

Bersoff, D. N. Therapists as protectors and policemen: New roles as a result of Tarasoff. *Professional Psychology*, 1976, 7, 267–273.

Brodsky, S. L. Shared results and open files with the client. *Professional Psychology*, 1972, 3, 362–364.

Carroll, J. D. Confidentiality of social science research sources and data: The Popkin Case. *Political Science*, 1973, VI.

DeKraai, M. B., and Sales, B. D. Privileged communications of psychologists. *Professional Psychology*, 1982, 13, 372–388.

Dubey, J. Confidentiality as a requirement of the therapist: Technical necessities for absolute privilege in psychotherapy. *American Journal of Psychiatry*, 1974, 131, 1093–1096.

Epstein, G. N.; Steingarten, J.; Weinstein, H. D.; and Nashel, H. M. Panel Report: Impact of law on the practice of psychotherapy. *Journal of Psychiatry and Law*, 1977, 5, 7–40.

Everstine, L.; Everstine, D. S.; Heymann, G. M.; True, R. H.; Frey, D. H.; Johnson, H. G.; and Seiden, R. H. Privacy and confidentiality in psychotherapy. *American Psychologist*, 1980, 35, 828–840.

Fisher, C. T. Paradigm changes which allow sharing of results. *Professional Psychology*, 1972, 3, 364–369.

Godkin v. *Miller*, 379 F Supp 859 (ED NY, 1974), affirmed 514 F 2d 123 (2d Cir, 1975).

Gordis, L., and Gold, E. Privacy, confidentiality, and the use of medical records in research. *Science*, January 11, 1980, 207, 153–156.

Grossman, M. Insurance reports as a threat to confidentiality. *American Journal of Psychiatry*, 1971, 128, 96–100.

Hare-Mustin, R. T.; Marecek, J.; Kaplan, A. G.; and Liss-Levinson, N. Rights of clients, responsibilities of therapists. *American Psychologist*, 1979, 34, 3–16.

Jagim, R. D., Wittman, W. D., and Noll, J. O. Mental health professionals' attitudes toward confidentiality, privilege, and third-party disclosure. *Professional Psychology*, 1978, 9, 458–466.

Knapp, S., and Vandecreek, L. Tarasoff: Five years later. *Professional Psychology*, 1982, 13, 511–516.

Knerr, C. R. What to do before and after a subpoena of data arrives. In J. E. Sieber (Ed.), *The Ethics of Social Research: Surveys and Experiments.* New York: Springer-Verlag, 1982.

Koocher, G. P. A bill of rights for children in psychotherapy. In G. P. Koocher (Ed.), *Children's Rights and the Mental Health Professions.* New York: Wiley, 1976.

Leonard, J. B. A therapist's duty to warn potential victims: A nonthreatening view of Tarasoff. *Law and Human Behavior,* 1977, *1,* 309—318.

MacDonald v. *Clinger,* No. 991/1981 (N.Y. App. Div. Jan. 22, 1982).

McIntosch v. *Milano,* 403 A. 2d 500 (N.J. Super. Ct. 1979).

Medical World News. Doctor and the law: On patient's right to read own medical records. February 10, 1975.

Mental Disability Law Reporter. Tarasoff duty to warn third parties applied to therapists in New Jersey. 1979, *3,* 313—314.

———. Tarasoff duty to warn discussed in three cases; no such duty found in Maryland. 1980, *4,* 313—315.

———. Disclosure of confidential information gives rise to tort action against psychiatrist. 1982, *6,* 79.

Morgenthau, T.; Lindsay, J. J; Michael, R.; and Givens, R. The unanswered questions. *Newsweek,* 1982, *99,* 40.

Noll, J. O., and Hanlon, M. J. Patient privacy and confidentiality at mental health centers. *American Journal of Psychiatry,* 1976, *133,* 1286—1289.

Paul, R. E. Tarasoff and the duty to warn: Toward a standard of conduct that balances the rights of clients against the rights of third parties. *Professional Psychology,* 1977, *8,* 125—128.

People v. *Poddar,* 10 Ca. 3d 750, 518, P.2d 342, 111 Cal. Rptr. 910 (1974).

Rosen, C. E. Why clients relinquish their rights to privacy under sign-away pressures. *Professional Psychology,* 1977, *8,* 17—24.

Roth, L. H.; Wolford, J.; and Meisel, A. Patient access to records: Tonic or toxin? *American Journal of Psychiatry,* 1980, *137,* 592—596.

Sawyer, J., and Schechter, H. Computers, privacy, and the national data center: The responsibility of social scientists. *American Psychologist,* 1968, *23,* 810—818.

Shah, S. Privileged communications, confidentiality, and privacy: Privileged communications. *Professional Psychology,* 1969, *1,* 56—59.

Shaw v. *Glickman,* 415A. 2d 625 (Md. Ct. Spec. App. 1980).

Siegel, M. Privacy, ethics, and confidentiality. *Professional Psychology,* 1979, *10,* 249—258.

Springer, E. W. *Automated Medical Records and the Law.* Germantown, MD.: Aspen Systems Corp., 1971.

Stein, E. J.; Furedy, R. L.; Simonton, M. J.; and Neuffer, C. H. Patient access to medical records on a psychiatric inpatient unit. *American Journal of Psychiatry,* 1979, *136,* 327—329.

Stone, A. A. The Tarasoff decisions: Suing psychotherapists to safeguard society. *Harvard Law Review,* 1976, *90,* 358—378.

Strassburger, F. Problems surrounding "informed voluntary consent" and patient access to records. *Psychiatric Opinion*, 1975, *12*, 30–34.

Swoboda, J. S.; Elwork, A.; Sales, B. D; and Levine, D. Knowledge and compliance with privileged communication and child abuse reporting laws. *Professional Psychology*, 1978, *9*, 448–457.

Tarasoff v. *Board of Regents of the University of California*, 551 P. 2d 334 (Cal. Sup. Ct. 1976).

Thompson v. *County of Alameda*, 614 P. 2d 728 (Cal. Sup. Ct. 1980).

Waters, K. A., and Murphy, G. F. *Medical Records in Health Information*. Germantown, MD.: Aspen Systems Corp., 1979.

Woods, K. M., and McNamara, J. R. Confidentiality: Its effect on interviewee behavior. *Professional Psychology*, 1980, *11*, 714–721.

Psychological Assessment: Testing Tribulations 4

Nothing is so good as it seems beforehand.

George Eliot

Many professions have studied human behavior and capabilities, but in the realm of psychological assessment or testing the contributions of psychology have been unique. The use of small samples of human behavior, collected in standardized fashion, then scientifically evaluated to categorize, diagnose, evaluate, or predict future behavior, is certainly one of the most noteworthy accomplishments by behavioral scientists in this century. At times, such tests have seemed to be powerful tools for advancing human welfare, but occasionally great concern about the real, imagined, or potential abuses of tests has become a public policy issue. One of the earliest and most striking series of comments came from a 24-year-old writer, named Walter Lippmann, in a series of six articles on "The Mental Age of Americans" and "Mr. Binet's Test," which were published between October 25 and November 19, 1922 in *The New Republic*. Lippmann stressed the potential misunderstanding and "great mischief" that might follow if parents and school authorities became confused about the nature and validity of the assessment techniques devised either by Binet, or by Terman:

> If, for example, the impression takes root that these tests really measure intelligence, that they constitute a sort of last judgment on the child's capacity, that they reveal "scientifically" his predestined ability, then it would be a thousand times better if all the intelligence testers and all their questionnaires were sunk without warning in the Sargasso Sea. (Lippmann, 1922, p. 297)

87

The ethical problems that develop from the use and potential abuse of psychological tests and assessment techniques are as varied as the many different types of instruments, users of them, uses to which they are put, and consequences to those on whom they are used (*EP:* 8). As a general definition, we shall consider a *psychological test* to be any questionnaire, examination, or similar sample of behavior collected in a prescribed or standardized fashion for the purposes of describing, classifying, diagnosing, evaluating, or predicting behavior. We are referring, however, only to those techniques devised and routinely employed by psychologists in the course of their professional work. This definition excludes, for example, scientific anthropological or sociological survey and measurement techniques, as well as astral charts, tea-leaf readings, biorhythms, or fondling the viscera of certain animals as a means to predict future events.

TYPES OF TESTS

Test instruments can be classified across a number of dimensions, including the purpose for which they are designed, the population for which they are standardized, the nature of their administration, mode of interpretation, and psychometric properties. Types of tests (listed according to intended use) include the following: personnel selection, promotion, or classification; professional licensure or certification; educational admission and placement; certification testing in elementary and secondary schools; ability and achievement testing in schools; special education testing (including instruments designed for use with the blind, hearing-impaired, and other handicapped people); clinical assessment (including cognitive, neuropsychological, and personality testing); counseling and guidance (including vocational interest inventories); and specialized instruments designed for program evaluation and programmatic decision making. Within each of these general categories, still more specific types of tests could be identified by intended use.

Regarding standardization samples, some tests are designed for use only by literate, English-speaking adults. Other tests are intended for children under age seven or for individuals with advanced typing skills. Without specific knowledge of the population for whom the test is intended and on whom the norms are based, test scores may be meaningless. This presumes, of course, both that the test does have norms available and that it is properly validated.

Tests may be administered either in large groups or individually, with one examiner and one client. They may be timed or untimed, paper-and-pencil or oral, required forced-choice or open-ended responses. Some tests require a skilled administrator, while others may be self-administered or monitored by a person without psychological training. Some tests are administered completely by direct client interaction with a computer.

Similarly, test interpretation or data use may also vary widely. Some tests may be administered, scored, and interpreted quite simply by a person with little or no formal psychological training (e.g., tests of typing speed and accuracy). Other tests may not require skilled administrators, but demand sophisticated clinical training for proper interpretation (e.g., paper-and-pencil personality inventories). Still other tests may require high levels of psychological skill for their administration and interpretation (e.g., projective personality assessment techniques, such as the Rorschach Inkblots).

Key Concepts in Tests and Measurements

Many important technical concepts are necessary to understand the proper use of psychological tests (*EP*: 8c). Although this chapter is not intended as a substitute for formal coursework in test construction and measurement statistics, we will summarize those key terms that are important to understand in test use. Portions of this chapter may seem rather basic to some psychologists, especially to those who are thoroughly familiar with concepts related to tests and measurements. Unfortunately, however, it is just such basics that are too often at the heart of ethical complaints related to testing or assessment. These problems include the concepts of reliability, validity, sources of error, and standard error of measurement.

Reliability is the property of repeatable results. In essence, will the test dependably measure whatever it measures throughout time and across populations? Tests of relatively stable phenomena, for example, should have high test–retest reliability. If a person earns a certain score on a mathematics achievement test on Monday, that same student should earn a similar score on re-administration of the same test several days later (assuming no special studying or presentation of additional material occurred during the interval). Likewise, the test should yield similar scores for people of relatively equal ability when tested under similar conditions, whether or not they differ on the basis of other extraneous characteristics (e.g., age, sex, race, etc.). If the test does not measure something reliably, it is useless, since we would never know whether differences in score were related to the skill or trait being measured or to the unreliable instrument.

Validity refers to the concept of whether a reliable test does, in fact, measure what it is supposed to measure. A test cannot possibly be a valid measure of anything, unless it is reliable. At the same time, a test may yield reliable scores, yet not be a valid indicator of what it purports to measure. Test developers, therefore, are responsible for demonstrating that a particular test is appropriately valid for the uses recommended for it.

Content and *construct validity* refer to the issue of whether the test samples behavior representative of the skill, trait, or other characteristic to be measured. Content validity means the degree to which the items in the test are drawn from the domain of behavior that is of interest. This issue addresses the following question: Are the test tasks related to the performance ability we wish to gauge? The degree to which test scores may be used to infer how well any given construct describes individual differences is the key factor in construct validity (Guion, 1974; Green, 1981). The existence of many hypothetical constructs (e.g., ego-strength, trait-anxiety, or even intelligence) is controversial, with the result that tests predicated on these constructs are subject to question. For example, a test predicated on psychoanalytic concepts (e.g., The Blacky Test in which a dog named Blacky is depicted acting-out various Freudian concepts, such as oral gratification, anal rage, or castration anxiety) would be laughingly discounted by a behaviorally inclined clinican who is unwilling to consider constructs that are not directly observable in behavior. The responsibility for establishing whether the test measures the construct or reflects the content of interest is the burden of the developers and publishers.

Criterion-related validity concerns whether a particular test's outcome is related to other criteria in predictive or concurrent fashion. Adequate demonstration of this type of relationship is also the responsibility of the test developers and publishers. For example, graduate departments of psychology have long been interested in what aspects of data will best predict success in graduate school. They collect test scores, undergraduate grades, references, and other data in order to predict (and thereby select) those applicants who have the best likelihood to do well in, and successfully complete, the program. Individual test users also have a responsibility to use test data in ways that reflect well-established predictive or criterion-related relationships.

There are many *sources of error* to which test scores are subject. One person may be more motivated to try on one particular occasion. Another person may be a good guesser. Still another might be feeling ill, hungry, anxious, or have greater familiarity with specific test items on one form of an instrument. The importance of any particular source of error depends on the specific use of the test in the context of the specific individual who took it. The goal of studies of reliability is to estimate the magnitude of the errors of measurement from assorted sources. Any particular test has many *standard errors*, and the user is responsible for being familiar with these and considering the appropriate one(s) for consideration depending on the comparisons to be made. A standard error of measurement is a score interval that, given certain assumptions, has a certain probability of including any individual's true score. Consider, for example, the following cases related to these concepts as ethical issues.

Case 4-1: Norma Skew, Ph.D., develops a detailed interview schedule that is scorable in objective fashion, yielding a set of numbers that she describes as a "leadership quotient," a "motivation index," and a "likelihood of success rating." The items were selected from a variety of existing personality assessment tools and questionnaires. Dr. Skew proceeds to advertise this instrument for use in "selecting executive talent," although as yet she has collected no validity data and simply presumes reliability, "because the items are all based on questions asked in other reliable instruments."

Case 4-2: Amos Quark, Psy.D., retested a child who had been given the Wechsler Intelligence Scale for Children–Revised by another examiner a few months earlier. The youngster, who was mildly mentally retarded, earned IQ scores 3 to 5 points higher when Quark tested him, and Quark told the child's parents that this was "a sign that he could be making some real intellectual progress."

Case 4-3: Tanya Shallow, Ed.D., is a school psychologist charged with selecting a few dozen intellectually talented youngsters from the Plainville Regional School District to be offered access to a special summer enrichment program. She decides that the simplest way to select candidates is to group-administer a standardized paper-and-pencil IQ test and select students from among the high scorers.

Psychologists trained to use tests or who are familiar with assessment and measurement theory will no doubt wince at the prospect that any practitioner could behave as doctors Skew, Quark, and Shallow have, but these types of problems occur all too frequently.

Dr. Skew may be "creative" and "innovative" in designing her assessment plan, but she has not bothered to validate it. The fact that she has used items of known validity for something on other instruments does not mean that these items are valid for the uses in her context. We shall give her the benefit of the doubt and assume that she has secured permission to use any copyrighted material. On the other hand, unless she has specifically valid data to show that her items measure the constructs of "leadership, motivation, and likelihood of success," and that the scores her instruments yield are related to some meaningful criterion of success in selecting talented executives, she is abusing the use of psychological tests.

Dr. Quark is one of the most frightening kinds of practitioners, since he is offering illusory gains of hope to the family of a handicapped child, perhaps with the result of promoting unfortunate expectations. The "new scores" are within the standard error of the differences for each as described in detail in the WISC-R test manual. In essence, the upward shift is most probably related to some chance variable or other trivial factor, rather than a sign of intellectual gain. Quark's naivete about mental retardation and the proper use of the test manual data hints strongly at incompetence.

Dr. Shallow's choice of a group-administered paper-and-pencil measure of intelligence as the sole criterion in selection is an error. To begin with, many intellectually talented youngsters may not score well on such tests. One youngster, for example, may have been distracted by spitballs from a classmate, another might be preoccupied by family stresses, and still another might have an insufficient grasp of written English to do well on the test. Instead of using multiple criteria suited to the nature of the program and the type of students sought, Dr. Shallow appears to have sought the easiest solution. She is using an instrument that was designed primarily for another purpose, and she is ignoring potential drawbacks to the instrument as a valid indicator of the one variable she is actually measuring (i.e., the ability to do well on a group-administered paper-and-pencil task). At the least, she should not rely on a single data source.

Primary Reference Sources

Three major reference works exist that are important sources of information for anyone with a substantial interest in the proper use of psychological tests. The first two sources are the *Mental Measurement Yearbook* (Buros, 1978) and *Tests in Print*. Both have been routinely updated under the editorship of Oscar K. Buros and are published by the University of Nebraska Press. *Tests in Print* provides a rapid way to locate test publishers and to identify different types of tests, but the *Mental Measurement Yearbook* is the definitive source. The most recent (i.e., eighth edition), published in two volumes in 1978, contains information on 1,184 tests, with reviews of tests and books on testing, as well as 17,481 references on the construction, use, and validity of specific tests.

The third major reference work is the *1984 Joint Technical Standards for Educational and Psychological Testing*. This document is the joint product of a committee representing the American Psychological Association, the American Educational Research Association, and the National Council on Measurement in Education. This document contains a comprehensive set of standards addressing test development, text use, and special issues related to linguistic/cultural differences, testing the handicapped, testing the aged, and computerized adaptive testing. In addition, a special issue of the *American Psychologist*, devoted to "Testing: Concepts, Policy, Practice, and Research" (October, 1981), contains twenty invited articles including overviews and discussion of current controversies, and it contains the most recent collection of opinions from psychologists with expertise in assessment.

TEST ADEQUACY

The question of whether any given psychological assessment instrument is a "good test" or a "bad test" is quite complex. A test, which is reliable, valid, and quite useful for one purpose, may be useless or inappropriate for another purpose. An instrument that is quite adequate for its intended use in the hands of a trained examiner could be subject to substantial abuse in the hands of less well-trained users. This section will focus solely on the adequacy of particular instruments themselves and the factors that contribute to, or detract from, the appropriateness of the test (*EP:* 8b).

The Test Manual

Each psychological assessment instrument should have at least a test manual that contains detailed information for potential users, including the following: the development and purpose of the test; information on the standard administration and scoring conditions; data on the sample used to standardize the test; information on its reliability and measurement error; documentation of its validation; and any other information needed to enable a qualified user or reviewer to evaluate its appropriateness and adequacy for its intended use. The manual may have supplemental sections addressing particular issues or audiences (e.g., a technical measurement section or a section written in lay terms to help test-takers understand the meaning of their scores). It should also include references for all relevant published research on the instrument to which the test user may wish to refer. Publication or distribution of a test without the availability of such documentation is unethical.

Test manuals should also include data on potential biases, along with cautions to users regarding improper or unvalidated test applications. In advertising the test to professional or public audiences, the publisher must be careful to avoid any suggestion that the instrument can do more or has more uses than the existing research base warrants. Implying that any given test satisfies federal guidelines or requirements, for example, would not be appropriate, since even tests that have some type of official recognition or approval are limited to certain specific contexts (Bersoff, 1981; Novick, 1981).

Case 4–4: Guy Grand, Ed.D., developed a personnel selection instrument that proved to have some validity for selecting middle-level managers in a large consumer goods manufacturing company. In that context, the use of the test was later deemed appropriate by the Equal Employment Opportunity Commission and the U.S. Department of Labor. These rulings were touted in advertisements for the test sent to personnel officers of several other large corporations.

Case 4–5: The manual for the Omnibus Achievement Tests provides the numbers, grade levels, and ages of the school children on whom it was standardized. It fails to mention, however, ethnic/racial composition, geographic diversity, socioeconomic status, or similar demographic variables.

Case 4-6:   Joyce Nerd, Ph.D., is the primary author of the National Nonsequitur Personality Inventory, which has been widely used as a personality screening tool for many years. In revising the test manual, Dr. Nerd omits references to several articles published in peer-reviewed journals that are critical of the NNPI's stated uses and validity studies. She reasons that the "overwhelming body of data" documents the use of the test, while the "few polemic studies" critical of the test are not worthy of mention.

The point of all three cases cited above is that they involve tests that may be useful or valid, although all are presented or handled in an unethical fashion. Dr. Grand's advertising may lead to unwarranted generalizations regarding the governmental "approval" of his test. The recipients of his announcements most likely will be individuals who will not have sufficient knowledge of tests and measurements to conceptualize the issues needed to evaluate intelligently his claims or to discriminate between the "recognized" and potentially unrecognized uses of the test.

The Omnibus Achievement Tests severely handicap any potential user by omitting crucial demographic data on the basic population sampled. This omission effectively vitiates any potential application of the test, valid and reliable though it might be, because there is no basis for any user to conclude that the population to be tested resembles the population for which norms exist. By omitting such critical data from the manual, any user of this test would employ it at his or her own peril, since general conclusions cannot be drawn. Marketing such a test with an incomplete manual is an unethical act, since it might lead an unsophisticated potential user to think that it has some appropriate use.

Dr. Nerd may be letting her personal bias and investment in her own work to cloud her competence. She should not intentionally delete questions about the instrument raised in scholarly publications. These questions should be cited so that the informed test user may make an independent decision. It is not inappropriate for Nerd to rebut such citations in her manual, but the conscious omission of this information represents an act of deception and misrepresentation, regardless of Nerd's rationalization.

Test Administration

One important scientific value of a psychological assessment technique develops because it provides a means for assessing a standard sample of behavior. This standardization implies a specific test ecology, adherence to administration rules, and specific scoring criteria. Consider the following examples of variations in the administration of certain tests:

Case 4-7:   Erika, age six, is having trouble academically in grade one. Her parents call Mr. Blitz, the school principal, to request a conference regarding their daughter's progress. In a hurry to obtain some data before the conference with the parents, Mr. Blitz has Erika sent to a third-grade classroom one morning without prior notice to take paper-and-pencil IQ and achievement tests being administered to the third graders. When her scores are compared to first-grade norms, they are low, and Blitz concludes that her abilities are inherently poor.

Case 4−8: Sidney Mute is a deaf, nonverbal adult who is arrested as a suspect in a crime. There is some question concerning whether he is mentally retarded or psychotic, and psychological testing is sought. Alice Stanine, Ph.D., is asked to do a psychological assessment, and she discovers that Mr. Mute can read and write at an elementary school level. She administers a test battery using IQ and personality tests intended for hearing/speaking clients by providing Mr. Mute with specially prepared cards on which the test questions or instructions have been written. Her behavioral observations note that "Mr. Mute engaged in considerable hand-waving and finger-twitching, tic-like behaviors suggestive of psychosis."

Case 4−9: A state psychology board scheduled a nationally administered, multiple-choice, licensing examination. Candidates were told to arrive promptly at 8:00 A.M.; however, disorganized operations at the testing site resulted in delays of 2-½ hours to 3 hours before people were seated for the test. The test was scheduled for a roped-off section of the corridor in the lobby of a large state office building. During the course of the examination period, there was considerable pedestrian traffic through the lobby and corridor, people waited for elevators to arrive with bells ringing when the doors opened, and food aromas permeated the air during most of the test session from a cafeteria 100 feet away from the roped-off area. When complaints were filed against the psychologist-members of the state licensing board, they replied that the testing area was assigned by a different branch of state government, over which they had no control.

When Mr. Blitz removed Erika without warning from her first-grade class and placed her with a strange group of children to take a test that was not explained to her, he placed her at a substantial emotional disadvantage. Even if we assume that the test used is valid for the intended purpose, it would be inappropriate to base a conclusion about the child's ability solely on a paper-and-pencil test, without also considering such other factors as teacher reports, individual stresses on the child, and so on. The primary error in this case, however, was the altering of the child's ecology during the sampling of her behavior, while not making any effort to assist her adjustment. More appropriate actions would have been to provide the child with an explanation and to schedule testing with a group of peers or with an individual examiner who could establish rapport with Erika and make individual observations of her work during the test itself.

Dr. Stanine certainly attempted a creative approach to evaluating Mr. Mute. She is deviating from the test administration condition prescribed in the manual, and she must note that deviation in any report of results. More important, she is using a test on an individual for whom it has not been validated. Some of the data she collects may be useful, although clearly not in the same fashion as when the client is able to hear and speak. More troubling, however, is the fact that Dr. Stanine did not attempt to use one or more of the specific tests designed for use with the hearing impaired (e.g., the *Hiskey-Nebraska Test of Learning Aptitude*). She apparently did not consult anyone knowledgeable about assessing deaf clients, and she seems to have overlooked attempts by Mr. Mute to use sign language, misinterpreting these signals as suggesting psychopathology. Although this case has major implications regarding Dr. Stanine's competence, it also illustrates the problem of applying a standardized test instrument in a nonstandard fashion.

The state licensing board is also ignoring important aspects of test ecology. The examination was clearly administered in a setting and under conditions that could be expected to hinder concentration and potentiate the stress on the candidates taking it. Since the board is legally responsible for the licensing process, members cannot absolve themselves of responsibility for unsatisfactory testing conditions by deferring responsibility. If the board cannot ensure that the examination is given under the circumstances for which it was intended (e.g., a quiet, reasonably comfortable setting without extraneous distractions), they should postpone or defer testing until proper facilities are arranged. To do otherwise is a violation of proper test administration requirements.

Test Bias

The problem of test bias has received intense scientific and public scrutiny throughout the years, generating considerable scholarly and public debate. Even the definition of the term *test bias* has many disparate facets (Flaugher, 1978). Bias may manifest itself as a function of the skill or trait being tested, as a statistical phenomenon, as a selection model, as test-content problems, as an overinterpretation issue, as the use of wrong criteria, or even as test atmosphere or test ecology issues. When discussing ethical problems related to the matter of test bias, it will therefore be critical to consider what definition and which issues one is using.

Frederiksen (1984) notes increasing evidence that economical multiple-choice tests have driven other testing procedures out of school evaluation programs to the detriment of students. He argues that such testing in education has led to teacher and student behavioral changes less conducive to practice with feedback and the development of higher-level cognitive skills. He terms the adverse influence of testing on teaching and learning the ''real bias'' in psychological testing programs.

Cole (1981) presents an excellent overview of the scholarly research on test bias, including analyses of subtle differences in the content of test items to which individuals react differently. She argues that the basic issue in the matter of test bias is, in fact, one of validity. She makes a careful distinction between whether a test is valid for some use on the one hand, and whether it should be used (even if valid) on the other. Tests, of course, have often served as a kind of lightning rod or focal point of anger related to difficult social policy questions. Testing by itself will never provide answers to the broader social policy matters that must be resolved regardless of whether tests are used.

Cole (1981) cites several examples of recent social policy problems. In selecting for employment or promotion, what is the best way to meet current employer needs while compensating for past wrongs and current individual rights? What role should selective admissions play in higher education, and how should broad opportunities be provided? What form should education for handicapped children take? How should we deal with people for whom English is not a native language (Cole, 1981, p. 1074)? We agree with Cole's assertion that the bias issues are fundamentally questions of validity. The ethical problems are more clearly linked to the test developers and test users, who hold ultimate responsibility for remaining sensitive to the proper and improper use of the instruments they devise and use. Psychologists should certainly speak out on major public policy issues, both as individual citizens and as scientists who may have data to assist in resolving problems beneficially, but the solution to complex problems will rarely be found through a psychological test.

> **Case 4–10:**   Chi Minh was orphaned in Southeast Asia and relocated in the United States, where he was adopted by an American couple at age 16. Shortly after arriving in the U.S., he was referred for psychological evaluation and tested, using, among other instruments, the Wechsler Adult Intelligence Scale and the Rorschach Ink-blots. On the basis of IQ scores in the 60–70 range and unelaborated "explosion" or "fire" responses on the Rorschach, Chi was described by the psychologists who saw him as "most likely mildly retarded and prone to violent acting-out."

Once again, the issue is not clear-cut in terms of testing problems. One could argue, as in the case of Dr. Stanine (*Case 4–8*), that a question of user competence is involved. It is also evident that a test standardized and designed for adult, English-speaking Americans is not the instrument to use for ability testing with a recent immigrant whose contact with English was primarily in informal contacts with U.S. service people. In fact, Chi proved to be a very bright youngster whose receptive and expressive language skills were limited in English. Because he was socialized not to complain and to be compliant, he did not ask for clarification or protest his lack of understanding of instructions and test questions. Most of Chi's family had been killed during a rocket attack on their village, and he still suffered nightmares of that episode. In that context, his "explosion" responses to the Rorschach seem less subject to the usual interpretation. If the psychologist who saw Chi had given careful thought to these issues, or at least had included adequate cautionary statements in discussing the test data, the use of the tests might have been at least partially justified. In the context of Chi's situation, the evaluation and tests were certainly culturally and linguistically biased, and this was unethically ignored.

The revised *Joint Technical Standards for Educational and Psychological Testing* cites two cogent examples related to cultural and language differences that might result in test bias. The English word peach (i.e., a fruit) has two common translations in Spanish. *Durazno* is the word children from Mexico would use to name the fruit, while children from Puerto Rico would call it *melocoton*. In teaching reading comprehension, instructors of programs in the United States stress the concept of the *main idea*. Schools in Israel, on the other hand, stress the *moral lesson* of a given story. It is easy to see how tests keyed in one direction or the other could seriously underrate a person from a different cultural or linguistic background.

Key Litigation

Since major litigation has centered on the issue of test bias, we shall summarize two major cases in which issues of test bias were raised.

The first case is *Griggs* v. *Duke Power Company* (1971). This case was the first major challenge to employment tests (Bersoff, 1981) and developed from an objection to the legality of using general ability tests to hire and promote employees in a private company. Black employees cited the 1964 Civil Rights Act, claiming that the practice of test usage constituted a form of racial discrimination. Although the employer acknowledged that few blacks were employed or promoted and that the test may have had a prejudicial impact, the company claimed no intent to discriminate. A unanimous Supreme Court held that discriminatory practices were actionable regardless of whether the form is fair, as long as the result is discriminatory. When statistical data were produced showing the disproportionate impact on black workers, the court faulted the company for using broad and general testing devices (Bersoff, 1981). The court introduced the concept of "job-relatedness" as critical to the valid use of personnel testing. (An excellent summary of these issues may be found in Zedeck and Cascio, 1984.)

In another important case, known as *Larry P.* v. *Riles*, a federal court prohibited the use of standardized intelligence tests as a means for identifying EMR (i.e., Educable Mentally Retarded) black children or placement of such children in EMR classes (Bersoff, 1981; Lambert, 1981). This case evolved for two reasons: (1) because the primary basis for placement of children in California's EMR classes were these tests, and (2) because black children were heavily overrepresented in such classes. The plaintiffs argued that the test items were drawn from white, middle-class culture, that whites had better advantages and opportunities than blacks, that the language used by black children may not be the same as that on the test, that children's motivation may have been adversely influenced by the race of the examiners (mostly white), and that only token numbers of blacks were included in the most recent standardization samples. Lambert testified for the defense and published the gist of her arguments (1981), although the courts found for the defendants and against the test usage.

We would argue that these types of problems do ultimately represent validity issues. The test in both *Griggs* and *Larry P.* were being improperly used. In part, this impropriety developed because they were not well suited for the equitable differentiation that was needed: in part, it was because scores were being used inappropriately as paramount criteria in making complex decisions affecting the lives of people; and, in part, the problems occurred because psychologists were not sufficiently sensitive to the flaws in their instruments and the manner in which these flaws could adversely affect the lives of others. There was little recognition of the tests' contribution to broader repressive social policies. It is incumbent on the psychologist who uses such instruments to be sensitive to these issues and to take steps to ensure that his or her assessment work is not used to the detriment of the person tested.

USER COMPETENCE

Although we have thus far focused primarily on basic concepts in testing and issues in test adequacy, many of the examples we have cited raise issues of "user competency." It should also be evident that there is more involved in appropriate use of psychological tests than simply recording responses and adding up the score. The competence issues discussed in Chapter 9 are related in general to this point; however, testing also involves a special subset of competency problems. Many standardized psychological instruments are deceptively easy to administer and score, requiring little or no formal training. Nevertheless, the accurate interpretation and application of these instruments is another matter entirely. In addition to training issues, special problems, which are also related to diagnosis, test security, and sale of tests to unqualified users, raise ethical questions.

Training Issues

How much training and what types of training should be required of a person as a prerequisite to being designated as a "qualified" user of psychological tests? The answer is complicated and includes the type of test, the use to which it is subjected, and the setting in which it is applied. It is possible, for example, for a psychologist to graduate from an "APA-approved" doctoral program in clinical psychology without ever having administered a projective personality assessment technique (e.g., the Rorschach Inkblots or Thematic Apperception Test). Some theorists would argue that courses in statistics, individual differences, personality theory, abnormal psychology, and cognitive processes should be mandatory prior to undertaking comprehensive psychological assessments. If the evaluator intends to practice in organizational or industrial settings, coursework in organizational behavior, personnel law, and similar fields might be required. If a school setting is to be the primary workplace, a psychologist may require coursework in curriculum planning and educational theory prior to undertaking assessments. Few standards, however, specify the minimum competency needed to perform each assessment task adequately, and psychologists are usually expected to handle this matter on the basis of their own awareness of their own competencies and limitations. Sometimes this is an effective means of control, but at other times it is not.

> **Case 4–11:**   George Gargarmel, Psy.D., hired Mary Smurf to work in his private practice. Ms. Smurf had a B.A. degree in psychology, and Dr. Gargarmel gave her a few hours of training in the administration of the Wechsler tests, Thematic Apperception Test, and Rorschach Inkblots. Gargarmel would interview referred clients for about ten minutes and then send them to Ms. Smurf who would administer the tests he prescribed. Gargarmel would then prepare and sign evaluation reports based on the data Smurf collected.

> **Case 4–12:**   Sandra Toddler, Ph.D., had been trained in clinical child psychology, although her coursework and practice had always involved school-aged children and their families. When she began to receive referrals for assessment of developmentally delayed infants and children under age four, she ordered copies of several developmental instruments (e.g., Bayley Scales of Infant Development), read the manuals, and began using them in her practice.

> **Case 4–13:**   Norris Nemo, Ph.D., was trained in counseling psychology, and his doctoral program included supervised coursework in the use of IQ, personality, and vocational guidance assessment tools. He approached several large companies to offer "placement counseling" services to their personnel offices.

Each of the cases cited above demonstrates a lack of awareness of adequate or necessary training concerning a variety of assessment activities. Gargarmel has provided only minimal supervision and training to his relatively unqualified assistant (*EP:* 8f). He then bases his reports on a superficial interview and on data collected by a person who is not sufficiently trained to administer complex tests or to note the subtler aspects of meaningful variations in test behavior. The reactions of the client to certain test stimuli may go unrecorded, the nuance of a response that may tend to suggest one meaning or interpretation, rather than another, could be lost, and there seems to be no effort to ensure quality-control of the process. In some ways, Dr. Gargarmel is offering an impersonal service and giving the impression that he has conducted an evaluation, when he has, in fact, had only minimal direct contact with the client.

Dr. Toddler may be bright and sensitive enough to learn the administration of new instruments from their manuals rather quickly. Is she qualified, however, to assess the meaning of the data and to integrate it with other information to produce a valid and useful assessment? We cannot tell from the information provided. If Toddler were more attentive to her ethical responsibilities, she would have sought some consultation, supervision, and/or training from a colleague with expertise in infant assessment. Toddler could then, with a meaningful basis of comparison, be able to gauge the level of her own competency.

Dr. Nemo seems rather naive. We are not sure what he means by "placement counseling," and it is not clear that he has any background in personnel assessment or organizational consultation. He may not even recognize that he is offering to provide services beyond his qualifications. On the other hand, he may be competent to offer the services he proposes, but these might not be what the potential client-company needs. Perhaps Nemo mistakenly assumes that vocational preference and IQ are the most important factors in successful job functioning. All we know for certain is that Nemo seems to be reaching out to offer assessment in areas for which his training has not adequately prepared him.

Diagnosis

Assigning a diagnostic label to a client can have extremely serious consequences for him or her. This issue is alluded to in our discussion of confidentiality (Chapter 3), but the point is best illustrated in Hobbs's sourcebooks (1975) on issues in the classification of children. Szasz (1970) and Goffman (1961) highlight the problem of labeling mentally ill adults, while Mercer (1973) documents similar adverse consequences for those labeled mentally retarded. Anyone using psychological test data as the basis for applying diagnostic labels should be appropriately cautious and sensitive to potential alternatives.

Case 4–14: Kevin Bartley, age 15, was brought to a psychiatric facility by his mother who demanded that he be hospitalized. She was overwhelmed by her life situation, including a divorce in progress and other younger children at home. Kevin's truancy and problem behavior at home was too much for her to handle. Because Kevin was a minor, he was admitted to the hospital despite his objections and in the process assigned a psychiatric diagnosis. Several months later, the courts ordered Kevin's discharge. Sometime after his eighteenth birthday, Kevin was denied a municipal job because of his "history of psychiatric illness."

Case 4–15:   Carla Split sought the services of Jack Label, Ph.D., to assist her in coping more effectively with various emotional issues. Dr. Label asked her to complete some paper-and-pencil personality inventories and then offered her his diagnostic impression. Ms. Split was, according to Dr. Label, "a psychopath from the waist down and schizoid from the waist up." Ms. Split was extremely upset by these rather unusual diagnoses. She had never heard of them, could not find reference to them in books she consulted, and began to believe that she was particularly disturbed because of their serious sounding nature.

Case 4–16:   Ivan Meek, age 7, transferred to the Rocky Coast School when his family moved to town from another part of the country. Ivan was shy, socially withdrawn, and was not able to establish much rapport with Helen Brash, Ed.D., the school psychologist assigned to assist in placing him in the proper class. Dr. Brash was busy with the start of the new school year and recommended that Ivan be placed in a special education class on the basis of a fifteen-minute interview during which she administered some "screening tests." Ivan spent three years in classes with mildly to moderately retarded youngsters before he was fully evaluated and found to be of average intellectual ability. During the three years, no effort was made to assess his potential or to investigate the emotional issues that contributed to his shyness and withdrawal, since most of the personnel simply assumed he was retarded by virtue of the placement Dr. Brash had suggested.

The case of Kevin Bartley is important because his hospitalization was more a function of his family situation than it was of any psychopathology he may have had. He was "diagnosed" and that diagnosis had adverse consequences for him when he later sought employment, despite a court decision that suggested he should not have been hospitalized in the first place.

Dr. Label appears to be a proponent of the creative school of diagnostic psychopathology. It appears that he offered a rather rapid diagnosis of Ms. Split, but failed to explain it adequately. In addition, he used an idiosyncratic, jargon-laden term that was more frightening than helpful to his client. Even when a diagnosis is based on a legitimate classification system properly applied, the terms should not be glibly mentioned to clients. In Dr. Label's case, one wonders how much thought he gave to the actual assessment or to the creative terminology.

The situation in the case of Ivan Meek and Dr. Brash illustrated two major problems with labels and diagnoses. They can be applied easily or by inference, and they may remain for a long time, to the client's detriment. If we assume that Dr. Brash was overworked, we might excuse some initial haste and misjudgment. Apparently, however, she forgot about Ivan, failed to check with his prior school, did not order any follow-up evaluation, and did not apply any of a number of standardized assessment tools that might have proven to be more accurate than her quick judgment. Teachers and parents will often defer to professional judgment, and in Ivan's case a meaningful recognition of his needs did not occur for three years.

Cases 4–7, 4–8, and *4–10* can all be used as additional examples of the risks of misdiagnosis based on psychological test data. Discussion of actuarial prediction and automated test-scoring programs later in this chapter illustrate an extension of this hazard. Certainly any psychologist who intends to use psychological test instruments for psychodiagnostic purposes should have completed formal studies related to these issues.

Test Security

Psychological measures that are well drafted and carefully standardized require considerable developmental work and expense. Many such instruments could be compromised if their security were violated. Some tests also have substantial potential for abuse in the hands of untrained individuals and, therefore, should be made available only to individuals trained in their use and application. This security is not always easy to maintain, and any persistent person can obtain substantial "secure" test information by accessing journals or textbooks in major university libraries. There is ample documentation that a moderately clever nonprofessional can obtain copies of such test materials with ease (Oles and Davis, 1977). Recent so-called "Truth in Testing" statutes enacted in some states have mandated public access to certain types of group-administered educational placement, achievement, and admissions tests (e.g., Scholastic Aptitude Tests and Graduate Record Examinations), in addition to the correct answers. Consider the following cases in which the security of specialized clinical instruments was violated.

Case 4–17:   A reporter working on a story about IQ testing sought an interview with Harlan Simp, Ph.D. During the course of the interview, Dr. Simp showed the reporter a test manual and many items from the Wechsler Adult Intelligence Scale. Subsequently, the reporter wrote an article for a national magazine on "How to Score High on IQ Tests." In the article, the reporter revealed 70–80% of the verbal questions on the test, along with practice hints and other clues linked to the items he had seen.

Case 4–18:   A popular book about notorious criminals written for public consumption included reduced black and white reproductions of the Rorschach Inkblots, along with lists of common responses to the same stimuli.

Case 4–19:   An executive of a large corporation was one of a group of candidates for promotion to a major position in the organization. All candidates were required to take some psychological tests as part of the selection process. The executive consulted Seb Vert, Ph.D., a psychologist with training in personnel selection, to help him prepare for the tests. Dr. Vert discussed a number of the potential test instruments, suggesting response styles that might help the executive to seem most appealing in the final data.

Dr. Simp was outraged and embarrassed when he saw the reporter's article, but there was little he could do. In attempting to be "open and candid with a member of the press," he had inappropriately shared material that he should have treated as confidential. The impact of the article in terms of producing invalidly inflated scores is obviously unknown. (Chapter 8 contains related discussion and suggestions for psychologists who agree to interviews with the media.)

In the book on notorious criminals, the psychologist authors had sought and been given permission by the publisher to reprint copies of the Rorschach plates in achromatic reduced format. Many clinicians would assert that reprinting these plates, as well as listing common responses, represents a serious unethical act. Others would note that more detailed Rorschach textbooks are available in many public libraries, and they note that the impact of the book on potential test takers is questionable. While a psychologically well-adjusted individual of sophisticated ability might be able to fake a disturbed Rorschach protocol, it is unlikely that a troubled client could muster the psychological resources to simulate a psychologically sound protocol no matter what information had been available in the public domain. The impact of this disclosure remains unknown, of course, although the authors certainly used questionable professional judgment.

Dr. Vert regards himself as being helpful to *his client*, the executive. While consulting on the general matter of how to "look good" in a specific type of interview situation is not necessarily unethical, Dr. Vert could be considered unethical to the extent that he reveals confidential test items, obtained in his role as a psychologist, to the client. In essence, he is invalidating an instrument in secret with the intent of undermining the objective work of a colleague.

THE TESTING INDUSTRY

Psychological testing is big business. We are not referring to the many psychologists using testing in their practices who are paid for these services; instead, we mean the test publishers and companies offering automated scoring systems. Kohn (1975) notes that American school systems spend more than $24 million annually on testing secondary and elementary school children. While many publishers are secretive about income related directly to their testing services, Kohn uncovered some interesting figures: in 1974, for instance, Houghton Mifflin's measurement and guidance division had sales of more than $5.5 million; in the same year, related services sold by Harcourt Brace Jovanovich surpassed $20.8 million; the American College Testing Program netted nearly $11.3 million; and the Educational Testing Service reported its annual income as $53.9 million. Two other test publishers, McGraw-Hill and SRA (Science Research Associates), did not provide test-related revenue data for any recent year.

The spread of consumerism in America has seen increasing assaults on the testing industry (Kaplan, 1982) and well-intellectualized papers on test ethics from within the industry itself (Messick, 1980). Most of the ethical complaints leveled at the larger companies fall into the categories of marketing, sales to unauthorized users, and the problem of so-called *impersonal services*. Publishers claim that they make good-faith efforts to police sales so that only qualified users obtain tests. They note that they cannot control the behavior of individuals in institutions where tests are sent, and one could argue that documented episodes of improper sales (e.g., Oles and Davis, 1977) involved at least a modicum of deception. Since test publishers must advertise in the media provided by organized psychology in order to influence their prime market, most major firms are also especially responsive to letters of concern from psychologists and committees of APA. The use of automated testing services, however, raises a number of potential ethical issues that lead to frequent inquiries.

Automated Testing Services

The advent of the computer age made possible the bulk scoring and analysis of test data, creation of new profile systems, and even computer-generated reports from the electronic printer. As this period dawned, psychologists argued about the advantages of clinical versus actuarial prediction (Meehl, 1954; Holt, 1970). In essence, can a computer-generated, statistically driven, actuarial diagnosis or prediction be more accurate and useful than predictions of clinicians in practice? We shall not take sides in that debate, but simply note more recent developments.

Several large testing corporations (and even the subsidiary of a pharmaceutical company) now offer test scoring by mail. The user may ask for a "score report only" or for an "interpretive report." In the latter instance, the computer is programmed to score the test instrument and print out narrative paragraphs or simple statements describing the client diagnostically, in terms of personality traits, according to vocational interests, or in any of a number of other declarative or predictive ways. Several companies are willing to rent or sell terminals for the psychologist's office that may be used to administer the test themselves in automated fashion, with questions appearing on a screen and the client responding with a keyboard stroke.

Commenting on the ready availability of computerized personality assessment packages, Lanyon (1984) notes that the overwhelming problem is a lack of demonstrated validity for the printed interpretations they generate. His phone calls to several companies offering such services were "met with self-serving statements or papers that did not directly address validity" (p. 690). Lanyon suggests that perhaps it is time for federal regulation of the testing industry as a consumer protection measure.

There has been at least one complaint similar to the problem described in *Case 4—11*, with a slight variation. Instead of using an assistant to collect data, the psychologist used computer-generated reports and then plagiarized the computer's comments word-for-word in his own summary. A recent mailing brought us news of a new office system available to psychologists who wish to find "improved patient care, increased interaction time, and cost efficiency" by administering and interpreting twenty different scales, indexes, checklists, surveys, inventories, and schedules. Areas covered included intelligence, child development, personality, vocational preference, somatic problems, symptoms, and a measure of "depression and hopelessness." All of these instruments were intended for use by competent practitioners as *adjuncts* to firsthand clinical contact.

One obvious hazard is the lazy or incompetent practitioner who relies on artificial intelligence and programmers' skills. Other problems include the potential abuse by untrained individuals and the need to have a qualified professional evaluate the accuracy of such reports. Can a commercial enterprise ignore a marketplace expansion opportunity for the sake of ethics, even if it is unregulated by government? Consider, for example, the following cases.

> **Case 4—20:** A firm providing computer-generated, MMPI interpretive reports runs an advertisement in the *APA Monitor* offering a "sample kit" and everything one needs to use their service for a $5 trial offer. The coupon states that one must be a qualified user, but does not specify what that means, and seeks no evidence from responders. Subsequently, the same company solicits psychiatrists in a direct-mail invitation to use the service.

> **Case 4—21:** A licensed social worker makes use of computer-generated, vocational-guidance-interest blank reports to offer job counseling to her clients, as an added service.

Both of these cases illustrate the availability of the automated testing services to professionals outside psychology, as well as an emphasis on attracting new clients with little attention given to the nuance of qualifications. The companies would argue that this is a clinician-to-clinician service and that the practitioner is responsible for how the material is used. They would note that the reports are replete with cautions and warnings about the use of data. They might also argue that psychiatrists (or other physicians) and social workers, as independent professionals, have a right to such services. On the other hand, since so many psychologists are not fully trained to use complex psychometric tools, we must wonder how many nonpsychologist mental health service providers understand the complexities and proper use of these tools. Such sales represent a serious ethical problem (*EP*: 8e).

> **Case 4–22:**   An urban police department was planning a civil service examination for new recruits and was sensitive to the need for screening out psychologically troubled individuals. Since they could not provide indepth interviews for several hundred candidates, the department decided to use a computer-scored personality inventory as a sieve. Those candidates with deviant scores would be selected for personal screening interviews.

This case represents a fairly appropriate use of the instrument, but something interesting happened. A substantial portion of the applicants obtained "grossly deviant" scores. Apparently the 566 true–false items on the personality inventory were placed at the end of a day-long exam. Many of the candidates were exhausted and found the items "silly" or "stupid." The purpose of the test was not explained by the civil service clerks proctoring the examination, so many candidates left most of the items blank, responded randomly, or "checked off the weird answers to gross out" the administrators of the program.

USE OF TEST RESULTS

Problems of Consent

The issue of informed consent is raised several times in this book, and it is probably important in all decision-making behavior by clients of psychologists. Regarding assessment, clients have a right to know the purpose of the evaluation and the use that will be made of the results (*EP*: 8a). They are also entitled to know who is likely to have access to the information they are providing to the evaluator. Such use and consent problems often arise when the psychologist who conducts the assessment does so as an agent of an institution or organization.

Consent implies three separate aspects: knowledge, voluntariness, and capacity (Bersoff, 1983). In essence, the person seeking the consent must disclose sufficient information for the person granting consent to understand what is being asked. It is not necessary to disclose every potential aspects of the situation, but only those facts that a reasonable person might need to formulate a decision. Voluntariness refers to the absence of coercion, duress, misrepresentation, or undue inducement (Bersoff, 1983). Capacity refers to legal competence to give consent. Although all adults are deemed competent to grant consent, unless they are adjudged to be incompetent, children are not.

Chapter 12 will include detailed discussion of ethical dilemmas in special work settings, such as prisons, schools, and industry. Consent as an issue is also discussed in the chapters on confidentiality, psychotherapy, and research (Chapters 3, 5, and 14). The following cases, however, illustrate a few of the special consent problems associated with psychological testing.

Case 4–23:   Sean Battery, Ed.D., was hired to consult with the Central City Fire Department. He combined a series of tests, including the Minnesota Multiphasic Personality Inventory, Rorschach Inkblots, Thematic Apperception Test, Draw-a-Person, and a sentence completion series (i.e., all personality assessment tools) to be administered to potential fire-fighters, along with the civil service examination. Several of the fire-fighters protested that such tests would be an invasion of their privacy.

Case 4–24:   Patricia Popquiz, Psy.D., is a school psychologist for the Central City School Department. She scheduled and supervised the administration of standardized achievement testing and IQ testing for all students in grades 3, 5, 7, and 9, which has been done routinely throughout the years. She is shocked when several parents complain that their children have been tested without their consent, arguing, "But it was only routine testing!"

Case 4–25:   As part of an evaluation to determine whether he is competent to stand trial for murder, Roger Slugo agrees to cooperate in a psychological assessment by Arnold Transfer, Ph.D. Mr. Slugo is found fit to be tried and is convicted of murder. During the subsequent "penalty phase" of the trial, the prosecutor attempts to use portions of Dr. Transfer's assessment of Slugo as a basis for seeking imposition of the death penalty.

These situations all involve consent issues relating to assessment. In the case of the fire department applicants, the complaint is quite appropriate. It may be considered an invasion of privacy to ask an applicant to reveal personal information that is not clearly relevant to the job in question (London and Bray, 1980). When asked whether requiring potential employees to submit to a battery of tests (including personality tests) as a condition of employment-violated ethical standards (if such tests have not been demonstrated to be validated for the tasks involved in the position), the APA's ethics committee unanimously agreed that it did (Gurel, Note 1). Unless Dr. Battery has some basis for documenting the validity of the personality assessment techniques as fire-fighter selection tools, he is behaving unethically.

Dr. Popquiz sees no problem in continuing what has been the routine practice of the school system for many years. The fact that no one has complained previously does not immunize Popquiz from her responsibility to solicit appropriate consent and to remove from the routine testing program any child whose parents or guardians refuse to give consent (Bersoff, 1983; Pryzwansky and Bersoff, 1978). Even routine test data can have a lasting impact on a child's education and life (Hobbs, 1975). If parents do not know that their child has been tested, they might never know the scores existed. Inappropriate or erroneous data could not be challenged. While courts have ruled that the right of parents to veto testing is not absolute (Pryzwansky and Bersoff, 1978), not notifying them at all is unquestionably unethical and seeking cooperative consent is certainly good psychological practice, if inconvenient from time to time.

The case of Mr. Slugo seems to pose the rare situation where psychological test data can have life or death implications. Whatever the outcome, it is clear that Slugo was never informed that the test data might be used in this manner. He certainly might have declined to cooperate, if he had known of this risk. If Dr. Transfer routinely does evaluations of this sort, he should have been aware of the potential use of his report and so advised Slugo. If Dr. Transfer had not done such work before, he was practicing beyond his realm of competence by not first informing himself of the full implications of the report he had agreed to prepare.

Use of Test Results

Earlier in this chapter it became evident that a "good test" may be improperly used, either by inappropriate application or by misuses of the resulting scores. In this final section, we would like to raise special questions about access to test results and the potential use or misuse that can result. We shall also discuss the problem of obsolete or outdated test files.

> **Case 4–26:**   Helen Duration began working for General Tool and Power Company eight years ago. She had been given some paper-and-pencil general ability tests during the hiring period. She has recently applied for a higher-level opening within the company, but the personnel department is not seriously considering her because the test scores of eight years earlier are below those required for the new position.

> **Case 4–27:**   As part of a diagnostic evaluation, Dr. Ira Median administered intellectual and personality assessment tools to eight-year-old Victor Vector. Victor's parents were dissatisfied with Dr. Median's evaluation and recommended that Victor was in need of psychotherapy. They demanded a copy of all the tests and answers that Victor gave, along with a copy of Dr. Median's report, while they prepared to seek a second opinion.

> **Case 4–28:**   The Detroit Edison Company posted notice of six vacancies for the job classification of "Instrument Man B" at a new power plant. All ten employees who applied for the openings failed to achieve the acceptable cut-off score the Company had set on a battery of psychological aptitude tests, so the vacancies were filled by promoting employees with less seniority who had scored at or above the recommended cutoffs. A union grievance was filed and the union sought copies of the tests, employees' answer sheets, scores, and other related data, claiming that this information was essential for arbitration. (Eberlein, 1980).

Obsolete Scores

The case of Helen Duration (*Case 4–26*) illustrates the problem of obsolescence (*EP*: 8d). Test scores should be retained in a client's file only as long as they serve a valid and useful purpose, and they continue to reflect the status of that client (London and Bray, 1980). Occasionally some instruments do yield data that may be valid predictors eight or more years after they were collected (Bray et al., 1974), but that is a rare exception. The consulting psychologist who supervised the testing program at General Tool and Power Company should have cautioned the personnel department that Ms. Duration's scores should not be a basis for promotional decisions made years later. In fact, efforts should have been made to ensure removal of the obsolete test data from her file.

A recent survey of professional psychologists (Berndt, 1983) was a "good news—bad news story." The good news is that most of the psychologists surveyed seemed to manage their testing practices in keeping with established ethical principles. They also seemed willing to give appropriate feedback on test results to clients. The bad news was that few of those surveyed had attempted to handle the problem of obsolete data. The results also suggested that 76% expressed a willingness to release old test information to agencies with the consent of the client. This procedure implied minimal recognition that such old records might be inaccurate or harmful.

It is difficult to formulate firm rules regarding when a particular set of data is no longer useful; however, the 1984 version of the *Joint Technical Standards for Educational and Psychological Tests* provides several helpful examples. Broad test scores used for initial employment screening have minimal usefulness if more detailed evaluation follows, and they certainly have no value after a year or more of employment. Likewise, college placement test scores have minimal value after the college coursework is completed. Retention of such data (particularly low scores) could have a long-term stigmatizing effect. It is certainly possible to code data for use in long-term archival research, when indicated, while at the same time removing all trace of the same information from individual files.

Access to Test Data

Fairly uniform agreement among professionals maintains that clients have the right of access to information about themselves, and that parents have similar access to information about their minor children. The specific nature of the information has sometimes been raised as a question. Although this topic is addressed in Chapter 3, test data present some special difficulties since they seldom are interpreted alone. In essence, the test scores themselves may well be meaningless or misinterpreted by a layperson. One way of handling this problem is to frame reports in plain language, remembering that the reports will probably be read by the people about whom they are written. Likewise, psychologists who work with children must frame their reports with the parents' right of access in mind.

If Victor Vector's test protocols, for example, include themes of "murderous rage," "Oedipal anger," or similar psychodynamic concepts, one would hope that Dr. Median will deal with the meaning or basic issues, rather than saying something else, such as "Victor told stories in which a murderous boy kills evil father figures." Instead, Dr. Median might write: "Victor's test data suggest that he has difficulty dealing with angry feelings, especially in his relationship with his father." This type of writing can convey all appropriate meaning, while avoiding jargon that may be misunderstood by or upsetting to the client.

At the same time, however, Dr. Median would be correct in refusing to supply copies of the actual test material and protocols (i.e., raw data) to the parents, since they are not trained to use it. Dr. Median should be willing to discuss the results of the evaluation with the parents (or any adult client) and to prepare a report for them if that was part of the agreed-upon service. Nonetheless, he should refuse the raw data, while expressing a willingness to send it to another psychologist who is trained to use it, if they wish to obtain a second opinion.

The case involving Detroit Edison (4–28) went to the Supreme Court, with APA filing an *amicus* (i.e., "friend of the court") brief in support of withholding the requested information (*Detroit Edison Co.* v. *National Labor Relations Board*, 1979). The implications are discussed in detail elsewhere (Eberlein, 1980; London and Bray, 1980), but the Supreme Court rulings generally supported the Company. By a 5–4 vote the Court agreed that the "undisputed and important interests in test secrecy" did not justify asking that the test battery and answer sheets be given directly to the union. The court noted that retaining test security represented a greater benefit to the public than would open disclosure of the test contents. By a 6–3 vote, the Court also ruled that the union's need for information was not sufficient to require breach of the promise of confidentiality to the examinees or breach of the psychologists' code of ethics and resulting potential embarrassment to the examinees.

SUMMARY GUIDELINES

1. Although many different types of tests exist, each should adhere to the *Joint Technical Standards for Educational and Psychological Testing* insofar as they present facts through a user's manual. Psychologists should also adhere to these standards when using tests.

2. Different types of technical test data include reliability and validity findings. Any test user should be familiar with these data for any instrument used, and they should be aware of limitations on the appropriate use of the instrument.

3. Test users should exercise caution in the selection and interpretation of assessment techniques to ensure that each technique is valid for the intended purpose and specific situation in question.

4. Anyone developing new instruments has a scientific responsibility to ensure that potential users have the information necessary to use the test properly.

5. Those people administering psychological tests are responsible for ensuring that the tests are given and scored according to standardized instructions.

6. Test users should also be aware of potential test bias or client characteristics that might reduce the validity of the instrument for a client in that particular context. Specific cautions should be reported, along with test data in any situations, if bias or other problems with validity are suspected.

7. No psychologist is competent to use every standardized assessment tool. It is important to be self-critical and not attempt to use instruments without proper training. Nor should one employ assistants to administer tests, unless they are appropriately trained and supervised with those instruments.

8. The validity and confidence of test results often rely on the security of certain test information or items. This secure information should be protected carefully.

9. Automated testing services create a hazard to the extent that they may be misused by individuals who are not fully knowledgeable regarding the instruments in use. Psychologists operating or using such services should observe the same stringent safeguards required with manually administered testing.

10. Automated testing services are appropriate only as a professional-to-professional service, and they should never be offered directly to a client as an impersonal service.

11. A client who is to be tested should be informed of the purpose and intended use of the tests and test data in understandable terms.

12. A client has a right to know the results of an evaluation and the right to have test data kept confidential within the limits promised when consent is obtained.

REFERENCE NOTE

1. Gurel, B. D. Memorandum on telephone ballot of APA's Committee on Scientific and Professional Ethics and Conduct, dated June 29, 1977.

REFERENCES

American Psychological Association. *Standards for Educational and Psychological Tests.* Washington, D.C.: APA, 1974.

Berndt, D. J. Ethical and professional considerations in psychological assessment. *Professional Psychology: Research and Practice,* 1984, *14,* 580–587.

Bersoff, D. N. Testing and the law. *American Psychologist,* 1981, *36,* 1047–1056.

————. Children as participants in educational assessments. In Melton, G.B., Koocher, G. P., and Saks, M. (Eds.), *Children's Competence to Consent.* New York: Plenum, 1983.

Bray, D. W.; Campbell, R. J.; and Grant, D. L. *Formative Years in Business.* New York: Wiley, 1974.

Buros, O. K. (Ed.). *The Eighth Mental Measurement Yearbook.* Lincoln: University of Nebraska Press, 1978.

————. *Tests in Print.* Lincoln: University of Nebraska Press, 1974.

Cole, N. S. Bias in testing. *American Psychologist,* 1981, *36,* 1067–1077.

Detroit Edison Company v. *National Labor Relations Board,* 99 S. Ct. 1123, 1132 (1979).

Eberlein, L. Confidentiality of industrial psychology tests. *Professional Psychology,* 1980, *11,* 749–754.

Flaugher, R. L. The many definitions of test bias. *American Psychologist,* 1978, *33,* 671–679.

Frederiksen, N. The real test bias: Influences of testing on teaching and learning. *American Psychologist,* 1984, *39,* 193–202.

Goffman, E. *Asylums.* Garden City, New York: Anchor Books, 1961.

Green, B. F. A primer of testing. *American Psychologist,* 1981, *36,* 1001–1011.

Griggs v. *Duke Power Company,* 401 U.S. 424 (1971).

Guion, R. M. Open a new window: Validities and values in psychological measurement. *American Psychologist,* 1974, *28,* 287–296.

Hobbs, N. (Ed.). *Issues in the Classification of Children* (Vols. I & II). San Francisco: Jossey-Bass, 1975.

Holt, R. R. Yet another look at clinical and statistical prediction: Or, is clinical psychology worthwhile? *American Psychologist,* 1970, *25,* 337–349.

Kaplan, R. M. Nader's raid on the testing industry: Is it in the best interests of the consumers? *American Psychologist,* 1982, *37,* 15–23.

Kohn, S. D. The numbers game: How the testing industry operates. *National Elementary Principal,* 1975, July–August, pp. 11–23.

Lambert, N. M. Psychological evidence in *Larry P.* v. *Wilson Riles. American Psychologist,* 1981, *36,* 937–952.

Lanyon, R. I. Personality assessment. *Annual Review of Psychology,* 1984, *35,* 667–701.

Larry P. v. *Riles,* 343 F. Supp. 1306 N.D. Cal. 1972. (preliminary injunction), *affirmed,* 502 F. 2d 963 (9th Cir. 1974), opinion issued No. C-71-2270 RFP (N.D. Cal. October 16, 1979).

Lippmann, W. The abuse of tests. *The New Republic*, November 15, 1922, pp. 297–298.

London, M., and Bray, D. W. Ethical issues in testing and evaluation for personnel decisions. *American Psychologist*, 1980, *35*, 890–901.

Meehl, P. E. *Clinical versus Statistical Prediction*. Minneapolis: University of Minnesota Press, 1954.

Mercer, J. R. *Labeling the Mentally Retarded: Clinical and Social System Perspective on Mental Retardation*. Berkeley: University of California Press, 1973.

Messick, S. Test validity and the ethics of assessment. *American Psychologist*, 1980, *35*, 1012, 1027.

Novick, M. R. Federal guidelines and professional standards. *American Psychologist*, 1981, *36*, 1035–1046.

Oles, H. J., and Davis, G. D. Publishers violate APA standards on test distribution. *Psychological Reports*, 1977, *41*, 713–714.

Pryzwansky, W. B., and Bersoff, D. N. Parental consent for psychological evaluations: Legal, ethical, and practical consideration. *Journal of School Psychology*, 1978, *16*, 274–281.

Szasz, T. S. *The Manufacture of Madness*. New York: Harper & Row, 1970.

Zedeck, S., and Cascio, W. F. Psychological issues in personnel decisions. *Annual Review of Psychology*, 1984, *35*, 461–518.

Ethics in Psychotherapy 5

It is with disease of the mind, as with those of the body; we are half dead before we understand our disorder, and half cured when we do.

Charles Caleb Colton

Ask psychotherapists about the ethics of their work and they become philosophers. Writing on the ethics of their craft, psychotherapists have referred to the practice of therapy as a science (Karasu, 1980), an art (Hale, 1976), the purchase of friendship (Schofield, 1964), a means of social control (Hurvitz, 1973), a source of honest and nonjudgmental feedback (Kaschak, 1978), and even as a means of exploring one's "ultimate values" (Kanoti, 1971). Questions about the worth of psychotherapy or the need to use trained experts to provide it have spanned more than three decades of debate in the scientific literature (Eysenck, 1952; Marshall, 1980; Garfield, 1981). Garfield (1981) noted, after reviewing forty years of development, that the field has seen no significant breakthroughs, despite a large number of diverse therapies. Still, many clients seek and apparently benefit from psychotherapy, while many professionals also offer such services and train others to do so as well.

A placebo effect probably exists in psychotherapy; in fact, research studies indicate that seemingly inert "agents" or "treatments" may have psychotherapeutic effects (Piper and Wogan, 1970; Shapiro and Struening, 1973; O'Leary and Borkovec, 1978). From the client's viewpoint, it may matter little whether improvement results from newly acquired empathic insights or from a placebo effect. From the ethical standpoint, the central issue is client benefit. If the client improves as a result of the therapist's placebo value, so much the better. If, however, the client fails to improve, or if his or her condition becomes worse while under a psychologist's care, the therapist is ethically obliged to take corrective action. Moreover, if the client's condition seems to be worsening, consultation with more experienced colleagues in an effort to find alternative treatment approaches becomes an urgent necessity. If the client is merely not benefitting, however, the appropriate action involves terminating the relationship and offering to help the consumer locate alternate sources of assistance.

Recognizing a problem in the therapeutic relationship is not always easy, and it may be even more difficult to handle a sensitive problem after it is noticed. Recognizing, preventing, and remediating problems in the client-therapist relationship is the crux of ethical concern for client welfare in psychotherapy. We shall not attempt to answer basic questions about the nature of psychotherapy, such as the following: "What is it?" "Does it work?" "If so, how?" "Can it make you worse?" Although these are important issues, they are *not ethical* issues.

The *Ethical Principles* contain numerous specific references to psychologists as practitioners, including their social responsibilities and influence (*EP*: 1f), legal responsibilities (*EP*: 3d), public statements (*EP*: 4a, b, and k), responsibilities to clients (*EP*: 6), and cooperation with other professionals (*EP*: 7a and b).

We will discuss five substantive areas of ethical problems in psychotherapy: the nature of the treatment contract; the special obligations of the therapist; the special difficulties of multiple-client treatment (i.e., group, marital, and family therapy); technique-related ethical problems (e.g., sex therapy, hypnosis, behavioral approaches, etc.); and unproven or *fringe* therapies. (Sexual relationships with psychotherapy clients are discussed in Chapter 10.)

THE THERAPEUTIC CONTRACT

To develop a therapeutic alliance, a client and psychologist must share some basic goals and understandings about their work together. In warning psychotherapists about how not to fail their clients, Strupp (1975) notes three major functions of the psychologist. First is the *healing function* or the alleviation of emotional suffering through understanding, support, and reassurance. Second is an *educational function*, which includes promoting growth, insight, and maturation. Finally, there is a *technological function* whereby various techniques may be applied to change or modify behavior. As Strupp notes, "the client has a right to know what he [sic] is buying, and the therapist, like the manufacturer of a product or seller of a service, has a responsibility to be explicit on this subject" (p. 39).

The notion of a client-therapist contract is not new, although attempts to define the parameters of such contracts are relatively recent (Hale, 1976; Hare-Mustin et al., 1979; Everstine et al., 1980; Liss-Levinson et al., 1980).

Defining parameters, however, does not imply that therapists and clients should have formal or written documents outlining their relationship. Instead, it suggests that the therapist should be responsible for providing clients with the information they need to make decisions about therapy. The therapist should be willing to treat the client in a manner that any consumer of services has a right to expect (*EP*: 6 preamble). This response may include responding to clients' challenges about one's competence, attempting to resolve clients' complaints, and even using formal written contracts when indicated (Hare-Mustin et al., 1979).

The Client's Frame of Reference

Implicit in the contracting process is the assumption that the therapist will be able to understand the client's unique frame of reference and personal psychosocial ecology before deciding whether and how to treat a particular client. Therapists unfamiliar with the social, economic, and cultural pressures confronting women, minority group members, and the poor may well fail to recognize the impact of these stresses in creating psychological problems (Hare-Mustin et al., 1979; see also Chapter 3).

Conventional psychotherapy training often emphasizes the client's own contributions to his or her problems, while occasionally neglecting to consider the external forces that help to shape the client's behavior. Counseling clients of culturally diverse backgrounds by psychologists who are not trained to work with such groups has been cited as unethical behavior (Pedersen and Marsella, 1982). Many subgroups of society, including women (Brodsky and Hare-Mustin, 1980), children (Koocher, 1976; Glenn, 1980; and Melton, 1981), the elderly, gays (Davison, 1976; Meredith and Riester, 1980), and certain disadvantaged minorities (Jones and Seagull, 1977; Korchin, 1980), are socialized in a manner that may accustom them to having their individual rights to self-determination denied (Liss-Levinson et al., 1980). The therapist must be sensitive to these issues and the general reluctance that an emotionally troubled client may have in asking important questions or in discussing certain needs (*EP*: 1f). In such cases, the therapist must elicit basic information required to conclude a meaningful treatment contract.

Case 5-1:   Marsha Young, a recent law school graduate, had been hired by a prestigious law firm. She soon developed anxiety attacks and insomnia in the highly competitive office. At times, she felt as though she were the "token woman" in the organization, and she feared that her work was being scrutinized far more critically than that of recently hired male lawyers. She sought consultation with Jack Chauvan, Ph.D. Dr. Chauvan soon concluded that Ms. Young suffered from "penis envy" and was afraid of heterosexual intimacy. He advised her that it was critical for her to address these matters in therapy, if she ever hoped to be able to be married and bear a child, thus fulfilling herself as a woman.

Case 5−2:   Yochi Tanaka was the eldest son of a proud Japanese family, who was sent off to attend college in the United States at age 17. He had some difficulty adjusting at the large state university, and he failed midterm exams in three courses. Mr. Tanaka, who sought help at the college counseling center, was seen by Hasty Focus, M.A., a psychology intern. Mr. Focus was deceived by Tanaka's excellent command of English, western-style fashion consciousness, and a tendency to nod in seeming assent whenever Focus offered a suggestion or interpretation. Focus failed to recognize the subtle, but stressful, acculturation problem, or to detect the growing sense of depression and failure Tanaka was experiencing. Tanaka was apparently unwilling to assert his concerns regarding the interpretations of the ''expert.'' Five sessions and six weeks later, fearing failure on his final exams and disgrace in the eyes of his family, Tanaka committed suicide.

In both of these cases, the psychologists failed to sense and incorporate the client's psychosocial needs into the treatment plan. Dr. Chauvan seems to have ignored several real life stresses in Ms. Young's psychological and social ecology. He has little sense of her possible career goals, and professional interests, or the pressure she may be feeling. Instead, Chauvan seems to be relying on a stereotypic interpretation of her complaint, which may have little relevance to her immediate needs or symptoms. Likewise, Mr. Focus is unaware of the cultural pressures his client feels, and the impact these pressures may have on the current problem. Focus is deceived in part by the head nodding, a cultural response intended as a common courtesy, but interpreted by Focus as license to pursue irrelevant goals. Neither therapist shows much interest in eliciting specific goals or therapeutic direction from the client.

Another dilemma related to the client's frame of reference and goals is a tactic known as the ''bait-and-switch'' technique in psychotherapy (Williams, Note 1). This term refers to the unethical tactic sometimes used in retail sales, wherein a store may advertise a product at substantial savings to lure customers into the store. After the customer enters the store, a salesperson will attempt to make the sale product seem inferior and encourage the client to purchase a more expensive model of the product. Williams draws the analogy between this practice and certain types of long-term psychotherapy. He describes the following comments from one of his clients describing a previous therapist:

My physician was concerned that there might be a psychological cause for my high blood pressure, so he sent me to see a psychotherapist. I was eager to go because I had become desperate for some kind of relief, and the medicine I took had too many bad side-effects. Psychotherapy was an approach I hadn't even considered. I walked into the therapist's office for my first session.
He greeted me and asked me to sit down, and we sat there looking at each other for a while. Finally, he asked me about my sex life, which I said was fine.

We looked at each other some more, then he told me that the time was up. He expected to see me the following week, but I never went back. (Williams, Note 1, p. 5)

In this case, the client had gone to see the therapist for help with hypertension. The next thing he knew the topic of discussion was his sex life. In the client's view, the therapist had a certain agenda different from his own, and he expected the client to accept his view without serious question. If the client explicitly chose to discuss his sex life or any other issues on his own or because the therapist indicated some connection might exist between the topic and the presenting symptom, there would be no switch and no ethical problem. If the client decided to seek personal growth and exploration through treatment, there would also be no problem. Instead, however, the story implies that the pursuit of these other issues was a unilateral and undiscussed decision of the therapist, intended at least in part to extend the duration of contact with the client. Perhaps this was therapeutically indicated, but, in any case, it should have been discussed with the client. Williams notes that psychotherapy systems as diverse as psychoanalysis and Gestalt therapy incorporate rationales for such bait-and-switch tactics (e.g., "The problem is really unconscious and the patient is unaware of the real meanings," or "Anybody who goes to a therapist has something up his sleeve"), but that a theoretical rationale does not make use of the technique ethical. It is possible, of course, to retain one's theoretical integrity in any psychotherapy system, while requesting the client to participate actively in setting goals and following the treatment program.

> **Case 5–3:** Mary Slick, Ph.D., advertised a special "assessment package" and low-cost, "short-term treatment option" for children with behavior problems at a relatively low price. One consumer complained that when she took her child for the appointment she was encouraged to purchase "the complete battery" rather than the package advertised. The more elaborate procedure suggested was also considerably more expensive.

This case is more obviously unethical than the situation described by Williams. Dr. Slick advertised an attractive price and then attempted to switch the client to a more expensive arrangement after the person arrived at the office. Slick's inclusion of a "treatment option" as part of an assessment package also sounds suspiciously as though she has preordained the existence of a problem requiring treatment.

Conflicting Values in Psychotherapy

What happens when the goals and values of the client and therapist are at variance, or the result of treatment may be more than the client bargained for? One of the most fundamental dilemmas related to therapy goals is whether to encourage a client to rebel against a repressive environment or to attempt to adjust to it (Karasu, 1980). Issues related to abortion choice, sexual preference, religion, and family values are among the potential conflict areas. The therapist must be responsible for avoiding the imposition of his or her own values on the client.

> **Case 5–4:**   Helena Sistine, Ed.D., is a Catholic psychologist who holds deep traditional values. She works in the counseling service of a state university. Carl Quandry comes in for an initial appointment and wants to discuss the anxiety he is experiencing over several homosexual contacts he has had during the prior six months. Mr. Quandry reports: "I don't know what I'm supposed to be. I want to try and figure it out." Dr. Sistine realizes that her own feelings in opposition to homosexuality would make it difficult for her to work with Quandry objectively, especially if he should decide to continue having sexual relationships with other men. She listens carefully to his concerns and explains that she plans to refer him to a colleague at the counseling service who has had particular experience helping clients with similar issues.

Dr. Sistine has recognized her own value system's potential conflict with Quandry's need to make important life decisions according to his own values. She also recognizes that Quandry is in a highly vulnerable emotional state, so she does not expose her value system to him and does not attempt to engage him in a therapeutic dialogue. Instead, she collects the information needed to make an appropriate referral and presents the referral to the client in a positive manner to minimize the risk of his feeling rejected because of his problem.

There are other occasions, however, when such a resolution might not be possible. In such instances, therapy may solve some problems while creating new ones.

> **Case 5–5:**   Arnold Polite, age 14, is referred to Frank Facilit, Psy.D., because he is becoming increasingly depressed and socially withdrawn. Dr. Facilit finds Arnold to be somewhat inhibited by the close and at times intrusive ministrations of his parents, while struggling to develop a sense of adolescent autonomy. For several months, Facilit perceives good progress in his work with Arnold, but then he begins to receive telephone calls from Mr. and Mrs. Polite expressing concern that Arnold is becoming too assertive and too interested in people and activities apart from the family. They express the fear that Facilit's work with Arnold will alienate him from them.

In this instance, the progress of the client in treatment interacts with his relationship with his parents, and they may not care for the new behavior. As we will discuss later in this chapter under the heading of marital and family therapy, the best interests of one client may well be antithetical to the best interests of a co-client or close family member. Perhaps Dr. Facilit can work toward some accommodation by means of a family conference or other similar approach, but the possibility exists that this will not be satisfactory.

> **Case 5-6:** Sam Escape, age 23, moved from Boston to Chicago and entered psychotherapy with Sidney Silento, Ph.D. Shortly thereafter, Mr. Escape terminated contacts with his family in Boston. His parents and uncle, a psychiatrist, contacted an ethics committee to complain that Dr. Silento would not respond to inquiries about the location or welfare of the young man. Because Mr. Escape was an adult, the committee was reluctant to become involved; however, it seemed to members that the family was at least entitled to a response to their unanswered letters and phone calls. Dr. Silento ignored three letters from the committee, and he was sent a letter from the committee's legal counsel threatening him with sanctions for failure to respond to a duly constituted ethics panel. At this point, Dr. Silento replied apologetically, noting that he was preoccupied with his day-to-day therapeutic efforts and had a poor correspondence filing system. He reported that Mr. Escape was attempting to establish himself as an autonomous adult in Chicago, and he did not wish to contact his family nor did he authorize Dr. Silento to contact the family.

In this situation, Silento was certainly not unethical for failing to give information to the family, although he certainly could have responded to them with that fact, rather than simply ignoring their calls and letters. His rather lame excuse in failing to respond to the committee for several months was another matter. His procrastination only dragged out the case and caused the family considerable additional anxiety, while costing the psychological association a substantial sum in staff time and legal fees needed to evoke a simple explanation. It was unclear to what extent the treatment with Dr. Silento led to Escape's decision to avoid family contacts, although he was well within his rights to do so, and Dr. Silento was obligated to respect that decision, even if he felt sympathy for the family.

Consent to Treatment and the Right to Refuse

The matter of informed consent is discussed throughout this book, especially in relation to confidentiality (Chapter 3) and participation in research (Chapter 14). The preceding section, however, has implied that consent issues may be rather different in the context of psychotherapy. Psychotherapy unavoidably affects important belief systems and social relationships. This phenomenon is well illustrated in a case study of "Mary," a Christian Scientist with a socially-reinforced obsessive disorder (Cohen and Smith, 1976). In a discussion of the ethics of informed consent in this case, it is clear that Mary experienced some sense of divided loyalties related to her religious practices as a result of psychotherapy. As Coyne (1976) notes, "even the simplest intervention may have important repercussions for the client's belief system and social relationships" (p. 1015).

The consent-getting process for psychotherapists will usually involve a discussion of goals, expectations, procedures, and potential side-effects with clients (Hare-Mustin et al., 1979; Everstine et al., 1980; Noll, 1976, 1981). The need to disclose the limits of confidentiality in particular is discussed in Chapter 3. Clients might also reasonably expect to be warned about other foreseeable, though indirect, effects of treatment. Obviously no psychotherapist can anticipate every potential indirect effect of treatment, but a client who presents with marital complaints, for example, should be cautioned that therapy might lead to behavior or decisions that could result in the choice of divorce. Likewise, a client who presents with job-related complaints could be cautioned that he or she might choose to resign from work as a result of therapy. Such cautions are especially warranted when the therapist notes that the client has many issues that are being inadequately addressed and suspects that uncovering these issues (e.g., long repressed anger) might lead to distressing feelings.

Consider the married adult who enters individual psychotherapy hoping to overcome individual and interpersonal problems and to enhance the marriage. What if the result is eventually harmful to the marriage and a decision to dissolve it?

> **Case 5–7:** Tanya Wifely enters psychotherapy with Nina Peutic, Ph.D., complaining of depression, feelings of inadequacy, and an unsatisfactory sexual relationship with her spouse. As treatment progresses, Ms. Wifely becomes more self-assured, less depressed, and more active in initiating sexual activity at home. Her husband is ambivalent about the changes and increased sense of autonomy he sees in his wife. He begins to feel that she is observing and evaluating him during sexual relations, which leads him to become uncomfortable and increasingly frustrated. He begins to pressure his wife to terminate therapy, and he complains to an ethics committee when she in turn decides to separate from him.

We certainly do not have sufficient information to elucidate all of the psychodynamics operating in this couple's relationship, but treatment did change it. Perhaps Ms. Wifely experiences the changes as improvements. She certainly has the right to choose to separate from her spouse and to continue in treatment. We might wonder whether Dr. Peutic ever informed Ms. Wifely that her obligation as a psychotherapist was to Wifely's mental and emotional health, not to the marriage. One must wonder, however, whether things might have been different if Dr. Peutic had warned Ms. Wifely that changes might occur in the marriage as a result of her individual therapy.

A client who does not like the specifications and risk/benefit statement offered by the therapist can generally decide not to seek treatment or to seek alternative care, but some clients do not have such a choice. Those clients include patients confined in mental hospitals and minors brought for treatment by their parents or guardians. Several ethical issues related to special settings (e.g., child treatment centers and correctional institutions) are discussed in Chapter 12. It is important to recognize the rights and vulnerabilities of the hospitalized patient concerning ethics and psychotherapy.

In the case of *O'Connor v. Donaldson* (1975), the U.S. Supreme Court recognized for the first time a constitutional basis for a "right to treatment" for the nondangerous, mentally ill patient. This ruling essentially said that the state could not confine such patients unless treatment was provided. What happens, however, if the patient does not want the treatment? Numerous law suits asserting the right of mental patients to refuse treatment, especially those involving physical interventions (e.g., drugs, psychosurgery, and electroconvulsive shock therapy) have highlighted special ethical problems (Appelbaum and Gutheil, 1980; White and White, 1981). In particular, the right of the patient to refuse medication has been described ironically as the "psychiatrist's double bind" (Ford, 1980) and dramatically as the "right to rot" (Appelbaum and Gutheil, 1980).

As nonphysicians, psychologists are not trained to use somatic therapies and have therefore not been the object of such suits, although, as concerned professionals, they have been involved in the dialogue on the issues. One development predicated on the basis of these newly asserted rights to refuse medication and other somatic treatments is an increased demand for nonmedical treatment of psychological disorders, and hence a greater role for psychologists (White and White, 1981). There are instances in which institutionalized clients have asserted a right to refuse psychological treatment, but these cases have generally been technique-related (e.g., behavior modification) and are discussed later in this chapter.

Obtaining consent for treatment from a minor presents another set of issues. At the present time, only the Commonwealth of Virginia permits minors to consent independent of their parents to psychotherapeutic treatment. In some states, such services could conceivably be provided as adjuncts to a minor's right to seek birth control, venereal disease, or drug abuse treatment without parental consent. But usually a parent's permission would be needed in order to undertake psychotherapy with a minor client. When a child wishes to refuse treatment, no legal recourse exists under many circumstances, even if the proposed treatment involves inpatient confinement (Melton et al., 1983). The courts have tended to assume that the mental health professional contacted to hospitalize or to treat the child at the parent's request is an unbiased third party who can adequately assess what is best for the child. Some psychologists have argued that the best interests of parents are not necessarily those of their children, and that mental health professionals are not always able to function in the idealized, unbiased, third-party role imagined by the court (Koocher, 1983; Melton et al., 1983).

Case 5-8:   Jackie Fled, age 13, seeks an appointment at the Downtown Mental Health Center. Jackie is seen by Amos Goodheart, Ph.D., and tells him of many personal and family problems, including severe physical abuse at home. Jackie asks Dr. Goodheart not to discuss the case with "anyone, especially my folks." Dr. Goodheart discusses his options with Jackie, explaining that he cannot offer treatment to anyone under 18-years-old without parental consent. Goodheart also discusses his duty to report suspected child abuse to the state's department of child welfare. Jackie feels betrayed.

Some decisions are too difficult to expect children to make independently. Although many children under age 18 may be competent to consent to treatment in the intellectual and emotional sense, it is also evident that many are not (Grisso and Vierling, 1978). Dr. Goodheart recognized two important legal obligations and an additional ethical obligation. First, he recognized that he could not legally accept Jackie's request as a competent, informed consent to treatment with all that it implies (including responsibility to pay for services sought), although it did not occur to him to warn Jackie about the limits of confidentiality from the start of their session. Second, he recognized his obligation to report the case to authorities duly constituted to handle child abuse complaints. This may be a statutory obligation in some states, although it certainly would have been less than professionally responsible if he had sent Jackie home to additional potential abuse and done nothing. Finally, he recognized Jackie's rights as a person and as a client, taking the time to discuss his intended course of action to Jackie, thereby showing considerable respect for the child.

OBLIGATIONS OF THE THERAPIST

Although we have already discussed many obligations of the psychotherapist to the client, three special subareas of obligation also deserve highlighting. These areas include the following: respect for the client, even the difficult or obnoxious client; the obligation to terminate a relationship when it is clear that the client is not benefitting; and the question of malpractice. These three areas are frequently related to ethical complaints. In essence, few clients complain to ethics committees about a psychologist's failure to obtain treatment consent or to consider adequately their cultural value system. Many complaints evolve from cases related to particularly difficult clients, failure to terminate a nonbeneficial relationship, and malpractice.

The Exceptionally Difficult Client

The definition of this type of client is relative, since the client may prove difficult for one therapist, but not for another. There are some clients, however, who would be considered difficult by virtually any therapist: for example, the client who makes frequent suicidal threats, who is intimidating or dangerous, who fails to show for appointments and/or fails to pay bills, who is actively decompensating and acting-out, who is overdependent, telephoning with urgent concerns at all hours of the day and night, or who harasses the therapist's family.

> **Case 5−9:**   Robert Bumble, Ph.D., was licensed as a psychologist, without an examination, under the "grandparent" clause of his state's licensing law. He began treating a troubled young woman in an office at his home. Dr. Bumble failed to recognize signs of increasing paranoid decompensation in his client until she began to act-out destructively in his office. At that point, he attempted to refer her elsewhere, but she reacted with increased paranoia and rage. Dr. Bumble terminated the relationship, or so he thought. She took an apartment across the street from his home to spy on him, telephoned him at all hours of the day and night with various complaints and explicit threats, and filed ethical complaints against him.

> **Case 5−10:**   An ethics committee received a long, handwritten letter from Anna Crock, an anguished client of a public agency, complaining that the supervisor of her therapist, Ira Brash, Ph.D., had treated her in an unprofessional manner, creating considerable stress and depression. The therapist, a psychology intern who was apparently having severe difficulties with Ms. Crock, asked her to attend a joint meeting with Dr. Brash. Crock had seen the intern for 14 sessions, but had never met the supervisor. She complained that during the joint session Dr. Brash was extremely confrontative. The committee wrote to Dr. Brash asking for his account of these events. Brash gave a clinical description of Ms. Crock's "negative transference" to the intern. Ms. Crock allegedly treated the intern in a hostile manner, and she called him "stupid" and "a know-nothing." He indicated that the joint meeting was an attempt to "work through" the problem. He stated that the use of confrontative tactics was an effort to help Ms. Crock to release some feelings. He stated that he had to leave the joint meeting early, and he alleged that after his departure the intern berated Ms. Crock for her abusive behavior during the joint meeting and abruptly terminated her. Dr. Brash attempted to remedy this problem later in another meeting with Ms. Crock where, by her account, "He was a completely different person." Nevertheless, she was still quite angry.

In both of these cases, the psychologists appear to have seriously miscalculated how to handle their troubling clients. Dr. Bumble failed to realize that he was dealing with a client beyond his ability to treat, until matters had seriously deteriorated. When he finally recognized that the case had gone awry, there was little he could do. Although many of the client's bizarre accusations were unfounded, it was evident to the committee that Dr. Bumble had been practicing beyond his level of competence and, as a result, had contributed to the client's problems. Dr. Bumble ultimately had to seek police protection and a court restraining order in an effort to stop his ex-client's instrusive harassment.

The case of Ms. Crock, Dr. Brash, and the intern is problematic from several viewpoints. First, Ms. Crock had thought that treatment was progressing well for 14 weeks, while the intern and his supervisor believed that treatment was progressing poorly. Brash's attempt to handle a complicated clinical problem in a single session, which he had to leave prematurely, showed questionable judgment. His use of a confrontative style with Crock in the absence of a therapeutic contract, alliance, or even minimal rapport was also questionable in the committee's view. The committee also chastised Dr. Brash for attempting to shift some of the responsibility for the premature termination to the intern. As the supervisor, Brash could not escape ultimate responsibility. Poor communication, a difficult client, an attempt to move too quickly in therapy, and a botched termination—all combined in a manner that left the client feeling angry and hurt.

In working with difficult clients, psychologists must remain cognizant of their professional and personal limitations. Consequently, they must know enough not to accept clients they are not adequately prepared to treat, or they must know enough to help clients locate different services early in the relationship, rather than waiting until problems develop.

Some types of clients seem especially likely to evoke troubling feelings on the part of the therapist. The client who is verbally abusive, sarcastic, or who does not speak much during the session can certainly generate a number of unpleasant feelings on the therapist's part. Substance abusers, individuals with borderline personality styles, and mentally retarded clients will occasionally be referred elsewhere by some therapists. It is not unethical to refuse to treat a client who provokes troubling feelings or anger in the therapist. In fact, it is probably more appropriate to refer such clients to another therapist, rather than to try and treat them while struggling with strong countertransference issues. On the other hand, it is important to minimize the risk and discomfort to all clients. One should learn, therefore, to identify the types of clients one cannot or should not work with, while referring them appropriately and quickly without causing them personal discomfort or stress.

Case 5–11: Jack Fury was an angry 15-year-old who had been referred to Harold Packing, Ph.D., when his parents became concerned about antisocial behavior, including school vandalism. After the fourth session, Dr. Packing began an appointment with another client. They smelled smoke and discovered that a fire had been set in the waiting room. The fire was extinguished, and Dr. Packing called Jack and his parents in for a meeting. Jack acknowledged setting the fire, and when Packing expressed concern that he could have been killed in the blaze, Jack replied, "Everybody's got to go sometime." Dr. Packing was understandably angry and informed the Fury family that he was no longer willing to treat Jack.

Case 5–12: Serena Still contacted Patience McGraw, Ph.D., seeking psychotherapy as a means to overcome her shyness and difficulty in establishing new relationships. The sessions were characterized by long periods of silence. Dr. McGraw found herself unable to draw Ms. Still into conversation aside from the most superficial pleasantries. She tried several different approaches, including asking Ms. Still to write down her thoughts about events between sessions, as well as similar techniques, but Ms. Still remained quite taciturn and uncommunicative. After four such sessions, Dr. McGraw suggested that perhaps she should attempt to help Ms. Still find a therapist with whom she could communicate better, or that they should discontinue sessions until Ms. Still had some issues she wished to discuss.

In both of the previous cases, the therapists were clearly uncomfortable with the client's behavior. Dr. Packing was so angry at Jack Fury's fire-setting and subsequent attitude that he was unwilling to continue treating him. Presumably, he would be willing to refer the family elsewhere, giving the new therapist an appropriate warning about Jack's behavior. While some therapists might have been willing to continue working with Jack, Dr. Packing was not. He recognized these feelings and dealt with them promptly.

Dr. McGraw has a somewhat different problem. Her client's stated problem is shyness, and this is the manifest symptom that she has not been able to address in treatment sessions. Her best efforts to engage the client have been fruitless, and she is feeling somewhat frustrated. Certainly she should raise the problem directly with Ms. Still, while exploring other alternatives (e.g., a different therapist or a break in the treatment program), but she should do this as gently as possible, given the likelihood that this is a source of probable anxiety for the client. We shall address the matter of the client who is not benefitting from treatment in the following section of this chapter, but raise the problem of Ms. Still here because Dr. McGraw might have a tendency to become angry by her client's lack of participation and, as a result, fail to be fully sensitive to Ms. Still's fears.

Still another type of difficult client is the one whose behavior or problems tend to interact with the psychological issues of the therapist to cause special countertransference situations.

Case 5–13: Barbara Storm sought a consultation from Michael Splitz, Psy.D., shortly after her divorce. Splitz was also recently divorced, although he did not mention this fact to Ms. Storm. Her presenting complaint was that she had difficulty controlling her rage toward her exspouse. As Dr. Splitz listened to her vindictive attacks on her exhusband, he found himself tensing considerably and continually biting his lip. Minutes later, Ms. Storm screamed and fled out of the office. She wrote to an ethics committee complaining that Dr. Splitz was a vampire. The committee feared that they were dealing with an extremely disturbed complainant, but contacted Dr. Splitz, asking if he could provide any explanation for her perception.

Dr. Splitz recounted essentially the same story, noting that he had unconsciously bitten his lip until it began to bleed. He had not realized it until after Ms. Storm had left, when he looked in a mirror and saw the trickle of blood that ran from his lip to his shirt collar.

Except for the unfortunate stress the incident caused Ms. Storm, the scene might have been laughable. The point, however, is that psychologists must strive for sufficient self-awareness to recognize their anger toward clients, and then make every effort to avoid acting-out or otherwise harming the client unnecessarily. There are many appropriate ways to handle anger toward a client, ranging from direct overt expression (e.g., "I am annoyed that you kicked that hole in my office wall, and I am going to charge you the cost of repairing it.") to silent self-exploration (e.g., the client who stirs up countertransference feelings because of similarities to some "significant other" in the therapist's life). The client should always be considered vulnerable to harm relative to the therapist, and the psychologist is obligated not to use the power position inherent in the therapist-role to the client's detriment. If such problems occur more frequently than rarely in a psychologist's career, it is probable that the person is practicing beyond his or her competence, or the person has a personal problem that should be treated (see Chapter 9).

Failure to Terminate a Client Who Is Not Benefitting

Although this important obligation of the psychologist to the client is discussed in Chapter 9, it warrants additional comment with respect to psychotherapy. Ethical problems related to the duration of treatment are included in this category. In the previous case examples, we discussed premature termination. But what about the client who, by virtue of fostered dependency or other means, is encouraged to remain "in treatment" beyond the point of actually benefitting? Such judgments are complicated by various theoretical attitudes and orientations. Some therapists would agrue: "If you think you need therapy, then you probably do." Others might argue: "If you are sure you don't need it, then you definitely do."

We recognize such biases in many of our colleagues and could choose two colleagues on opposite ends of the continuum for a test. A person might be selected at random and sent to each for a consultation. One would probably find the person basically well adjusted, while the other would probably find the same person in need of treatment. One might presume that one or the other therapist is unethical, either for suggesting treatment where none is needed or for dismissing a person prematurely who is in need of help; neither assumption, however, is necessarily correct. If the psychologist presents the client with the reasons why treatment is or is not needed and proposes a specific goal-directed plan (Hare-Mustin et al., 1979), the client is in a position to make an informed choice. The therapist who sees emotional health may do so in the absence of symptoms, while the therapist recommending treatment may sense some unconscious issues or potential for improved functioning. These views can and should be shared with the client.

Ethical problems arise if the psychologist attempts to use the client's fears, insecurities, or dependency as a means of treatment when it is not needed. Consider the following examples:

Case 5—14: Justin Funk has been quarreling with his spouse about relationships with in-laws and decides to consult a psychologist, Tyrone Mull, Ph.D. A half-dozen sessions later, Mr. Funk believes that he has acquired several new insights into matters that upset him and several new ways of handling them. He is arguing less with his wife, thanks to Dr. Mull, and states his intention to terminate treatment. Mull acknowledges that progress has been made, but reminds Funk of many sources of stress in his past that have "not been fully worked through," hinting darkly that problems may recur.

Case 5—15: Brenda Schmooze has been in psychotherapy with Vivian Vain, Psy.D., for nearly five years. At the beginning of treatment, Ms. Schmooze was extremely unhappy with the hostile-dependent relationship she had developed with her intrusive mother. Schmooze had long since resolved those problems and was living independently, working in an office, and coping well in a general sense, although she remained an emotionally needy and lonely person. Her therapy sessions with Dr. Vain have usually entailed discussions of her activities mixed with praise for Dr. Vain's help. There has been minimal change in Schmooze's social or emotional status for nearly two years.

Mr. Funk believes that he has received something from psychotherapy, but Dr. Mull's remark suddenly makes him feel somewhat anxious. Has he really made progress? Will he experience a "pathological regression" if he drops treatment now? Will his marriage worsen? Dr. Mull seems to be using his power position (i.e., his reputed expert status) to hint that additional treatment is needed. This suggestion seems at variance with Funk's desires, but instead of outlining the basis of his impression and suggesting an alternative contract, Dr. Mull stirs Funk's insecurities in a diffuse and unethical manner.

Ms. Schmooze and Dr. Vain seem to have established a symbiotic relationship. Schmooze has acquired an attentive ear, and Vain an admiring client. Some might say: "What's wrong with that, if it's what Schmooze wants? She's an adult and free to make her own choice." Unfortunately, it seems that Dr. Vain may have replaced Ms. Schmooze's mother as a dependency object. Schmooze may not be able to recognize this, but Dr. Vain should be sensitive to the problem. Perhaps the relationship with Dr. Vain is preventing Ms.Schmooze from forming more adaptive friendships outside of treatment, for which she would not be paying. If Dr. Vain does not find treatment issues to raise with Ms. Schmooze, she is ethically obligated to help the client work toward termination.

Of course, legitimate doubts occasionally will arise regarding a client's therapeutic needs. When this problem occurs, client and therapist should discuss the issues, and the client should probably be referred for a consultation to another practitioner. This procedure is also often useful when a client and therapist disagree on other major treatment issues.

> **Case 5–16:** Ernst Angst had been in treatment with Donald Duration, Ed.D., intermittently during a three-year period. Angst had many longstanding neurotic conflicts, which he struggled with ambivalently. He began to question during his sessions with Dr. Duration whether therapy was helping him at all. Angst acknowledged that he wanted to work on the issues involved, but had mixed feelings about them. He suggested that perhaps someone else, instead of Dr. Duration, could help him more. Dr. Duration interpreted these comments to be a means of avoiding other issues in treatment, but he suggested that Angst should obtain a second opinion. He provided Angst with the names of several well-trained professionals in the community. Angst selected one and saw him for two sessions, after which both client and consultant decided that he should continue trying to address the difficult conflicts he felt with Dr. Duration, who knew him well and could help him focus on the work better than a new therapist could.

In this case, the client raised a legitimate issue, and the therapist had a contrary opinion. The therapist suggested a consultation in a nondefensive manner and assisted the client in obtaining it. In the end, the client returned to treatment with renewed motivation and reassured trust in his therapist.

Malpractice

We have chosen to discuss malpractice in the psychotherapy chapter, since most people tend to associate it with botched treatment. From the broader perspective, however, professional liability applies to all of one's professional service delivery activities. In a legal sense, three elements must be present before a malpractice action is possible. First, the psychologist must have a professional relationship with the party in question: that is, a psychologist/client relationship must have existed with a resulting duty to the client. Second, there must be some negligence or dereliction of that duty by the psychologist. Finally, some harm must have accrued to the client as a result of the negligence or dereliction of the duty. According to this definition, a successful prosecution for malpractice would necessarily imply that the behavior of the psychologist was unethical.

> **Case 5–17:** Luke Acher sought the services of Anna Sthesia, Psy.D., in response to her newspaper announcement about a new pain clinic she had opened. Mr. Acher gave a history of low back pain beginning several years earlier, and he expressed interest in the application of biofeedback techniques. He told Dr. Sthesia that he had

"been to everyone, chiropracters, orthopedists, hypnotists, and even tried acupuncture." The psychologist began to initiate biofeedback training. Several weeks later, Mr. Acher collapsed at work and was taken to a hospital where he was discovered to have a malignant tumor of the spine. The disease had metasticized widely and was too advanced for all but palliative care.

Case 5–18:   Regina Yahoo met Sonia Specula, Ph.D., at a cocktail party. After learning that Specula was a psychologist who specialized in work with children, Ms. Yahoo began telling her about threats that her 15-year-old daughter was making to run away from home. Dr. Specula casually mentioned that "lots of teenagers say things like that to annoy their parents, but never do it." Two days later Ms. Yahoo's daughter ran away from home and was hit by a truck and killed while attempting to hitchhike out of town.

Case 5–19:   Manual Kant was angry that after nine months in psychotherapy with Seymour Sherwood he still could not convince women to date him. For some reason, Kant did not understand why few women were willing to go out with him beyond the first date. Several had told him: "You need a lot of help!" Dr. Sherwood had agreed to work with Kant on this problem, but, as far as Kant could tell, the situation had not changed much.

All three of these clients attempted to sue the psychologist in question, but only one was successful. If you guessed that the client was Mr. Acher, then you probably understand the concept of malpractice. Acher was clearly a client of Dr. Sthesia's, and she clearly had an obligation to treat him reasonably. She neglected to check on his physical status or to send for reports from the other professionals he had alluded to, and she began to treat an important physical symptom (i.e., pain) without first ruling out a medical problem. By this negligent act, she contributed to a delay in forcing Mr. Acher to seek other treatment or proper evaluation, thus giving his cancer time to spread. Although it is not clear whether Mr. Acher could have been saved with early treatment, her behavior may have cost him the opportunity to find out.

Dr. Specula was not guilty of malpractice. Perhaps she should have been more cautious in the advice she gave, but it is clear that Ms. Yahoo was never truly a client of hers. The contact was casual, because it occurred at a social gathering, rather than at an office, no fees were charged or paid, and the relationship between the alleged advice and the injury sustained is not clear.

In the case of Dr. Sherwood and Mr. Kant, a psychologist/client relationship did indeed exist. We have no evidence of negligence, however, and no evidence that harm was sustained by the client. If Sherwood had promised results within a certain time span and these did not occur, he might be accused of misrepresentation or of misleading the client. But we have no evidence that any promises of specific results were made. It is also unclear whether the best psychotherapist in the world could have provided better help to Mr. Kant.

The greatest number of malpractice or professional liability insurance claims against psychologists derive from complaints about sexual matters, finances, or evaluation reports. Two other broad categories that result in complaints are negligence and serving as a member of certain governing bodies (e.g., as the member of a licensing board or ethics committee). In this latter instance, of course, the complaint will probably come from a colleague. A retrospective review of such claims against psychologists (Wright, 1981a) notes that two major causes of malpractice suits against psychologists concern sex and fees. Allegations of sexual misconduct are predictable sources of complaint, but malpractice suits are also frequently filed when a practitioner attempts to collect a debt (i.e., engages a collection agency or files suit). Wright also provides a readable and useful set of suggestions to follow when psychologists are notified that they are about to be sued (1981b).

MULTIPLE CLIENT THERAPIES

In marital, family, and group therapies the psychologist has more than one client. It is most unlikely that the best interests of one client in the treatment group will fully overlap with those of another. In certain groups, especially in marital and family work, the needs or wishes of one member are usually quite different from those of another. Group therapies also require different techniques and training than do individual psychotherapies.They raise numerous other ethical issues, including matters of confidentiality, social coercion, and similar problems. This section will attempt to highlight and discuss some of the most common ethical dilemmas associated with such therapies.

Marital and Family Therapy

Ethical guidelines concerning a therapist's responsibility to clients, confidentiality, informed consent, and client rights can certainly be ambiguous, even when only one psychologist is interacting with a single client. When a couple or multiple family members are involved in treatment, however, matters become even more complicated. Treatment will often involve a therapeutic obligation to several individuals whose needs are conflicting (Hines and Hare-Mustin, 1978; Hare-Mustin, 1980). Margolin (1982) cites several illustrations of such conflicts. She describes the mother who seeks treatment for her child so that he/she will be better behaved, which may ease pressure on the mother, while not helping her child. Margolin (1982) also cites the case of the wife whose goal is to surmount "fears of terminating her marriage," while her husband's goal is to "maintain the status quo" (p. 789).

A therapist in such situations must strive to ensure that improvement in the status of one family member does not occur at the expense of another. When such an outcome may be unavoidable (e.g., in the case of the couple whose treatment may result in the decision of one or both partners to seek a divorce), the psychologist should advise the couple of that potential outcome early in the course of treatment. In this type of situation, the therapist's personal values and therapeutic system are of critical importance (Hare-Mustin, 1978; Hines and Hare-Mustin, 1978; Hare-Mustin, 1980; L'Abate, 1982; Margolin, 1982).

> **Case 5—20:** Hugo Home, Psy.D., likes to consider himself a "gentleman of the old school" who holds the door open for women, tips his hat when passing them on the street, and is generally quite deferential to the "fair sex." In conducting family therapy, however, Dr. Home has a clear bias in favor of the woman in the wife-mother role. He believes that mothers of children under 12 should not work outside the home, and he frequently asks his female clients who seem depressed or irritable whether it is their "time of the month again." Dr. Home does not recognize how these biases might adversely affect the female partner in marital counseling when he offers that service.

> **Case 5—21:** Ramona Church, Ed.D., is a family therapist and a devout member of a religious group that eschews divorce under any circumstance. She continues to encourage her clients in marital therapy to work with her, "grow up," and "cease acting-out immature fantasies," even when both partners express some serious consideration of divorce. She will often tell clients who have worked with her for several months that they will have "failed in treatment" and that she will "have no more to do with" them, if they "choose divorce."

Both Dr. Home and Dr. Church have clear biases, and they seem either oblivious to the impact these biases may have, or they are self-righteously assertive of them. They fail to recognize fully the power and influence they wield as psychotherapists and their responsibility to clients as a result. Neither should be treating couples in marital therapy, or at least not without a clear warning from the outset about their biases. Dr. Church's threat to abandon any of her clients who stray from the lifestyle she prescribes is particularly dangerous. The vulnerable and insecure client will be especially prone to harm at the hands of such therapists. Hines and Hare-Mustin (1978) highlight the "myth of valueless thinking" and warn therapists to attend carefully to the impact that their own values and stereotypes may have on their work.

The APA Task Force's report on "Sex Bias and Sex-Role Stereotyping" (1975) found that family therapists are particularly vulnerable to certain biases. These biases include the assumption that remaining in a marriage represents the better adjustment for a woman, as well as a tendency to defer to the husband's needs over those of the wife. The same report noted the tendency to demonstrate less interest in, or sensitivity to, a woman's career as opposed to a man's, in addition to perpetuating the belief that child-rearing and children's problems are primarily in the woman's domain. The report also cited that therapists tend to hold a double standard in response to the extramarital affairs of a wife versus those of a husband.

Several authors have noted that the prevailing "therapeutic ideology" maintains that all people can and should benefit from therapy (Silber, 1976; Hines and Hare-Mustin, 1978). Some family therapists also insist that *all* members of the family must participate in treatment (Hines and Hare-Mustin, 1978; Hare-Mustin, 1980; Margolin, 1982). What does this do to a person's right to decline treatment? Must the reluctant adolescent or adult be pressured into attending sessions at the request of the psychotherapist? We know that some children as young as 14 are as competent as adults in making decisions about treatment (Grisso and Vierling, 1978), yet it is unclear how often such family members are offered a truly voluntary choice.

Case 5−22: Ronald McRigid, Ph.D., a family therapist, was consulted by Harold and Anita Hassol. The Hassols have three children ranging in age from 12 to 18. The youngest child has been acting-out and was recently arrested for destroying school property. The juvenile court judge recommended family counseling. The Hassol's oldest child has no interest in participating, but both parents and the two younger children (including the identified client) are willing to attend sessions. Dr. McRigid informs the Hassols that he will not treat them unless *everyone* attends every session.

Coercion of any reluctant family member to participate in treatment would be, of course, unethical. This does not preclude a therapist's urging that the resistant family member attend at least one trial session or attempting to address the underlying reasons for the refusal. The therapist who strongly believes that the *whole* family *must* be seen should not use coercion to drag in the reluctant member. Nor should such therapists permit that reluctant member from denying treatment to the family members who wish to have it. In such cases, the therapist should be willing to provide the names of other professionals in the community who might be willing to treat the group desiring it. When the client in question is a minor child, the therapist has a special duty to consider that client's needs as distinct from those of the parents (Koocher, 1976; Simmonds, 1976).

Still another issue that complicates marital and family therapy is the matter of confidentiality. Should a therapist tolerate keeping secrets or participate in the practice? Should parents be able to sign away a child's right to confidentiality (Hare-Mustin, 1980)? The concept and conditions of confidentiality are somewhat different in the family context than in those situations discussed in Chapter 3. Often couples may have difficulty establishing boundaries and privacy with respect to their own lives and their children's lives (Hines and Hare-Mustin, 1978; Margolin, 1982). Adult clients can and should be able to assert some privacy with respect to their marriage and to avoid burdening the children with information that is frightening, provocative, or simply beyond their ability to comprehend adequately. On the other hand, there are many attempts to maintain secrets that are manipulative and do not serve the general goals of treatment.

The most reasonable way of handling this matter ethically is to formulate a policy based on therapeutic goals and to define the policy for all concerned at the beginning of treatment. Some therapists may state at the beginning of therapy that they will keep no secrets. Others may be willing to accept information shared in confidence in order to help the person offering it determine whether it is appropriate for discussion with the entire group. Still another option would be to discuss the resistance to sharing the information with the member in question, with the goal of helping that person to share the information with the family, if indicated. Keeping secrets presents the added burden of recalling which secret came from whom, not to mention the need to recall what was "secret" and what was not. The therapist who does not consider these matters in advance and does not discuss them early with family clients is asking for serious ethical dilemmas within a short period of time.

Group Therapy

Psychotherapists may treat unrelated clients in groups for a variety of reasons, ranging from simple economy to specificity of program. For example, a group may consist of recently hospitalized mental patients, divorced males, bereaved parents, or handicapped children. In such groups, the identified clients gather together to address similar emotional or social problems in a common supportive context. Other groups, however, may focus on enhancing personal growth or self-awareness as opposed to addressing personal psychodynamics or psychopathology. Rogers (1970) offered a sample listing of group types, including T-groups, encounter groups, sensitivity groups, task-oriented groups, sensory awareness or body awareness groups, organizational development groups, team building groups, and Gestalt groups.

Group treatment has considerable potential for both good and harm. The influence and support of peers in the treatment process may facilitate gains that would be slow or unlikely in individual treatment. The group may also become a special therapeutic ecology within which special insights and awareness may develop. At the same time, however, there are significant hazards to group members when the group leader is not properly trained or unable to monitor adequately the experience for all members. The group therapist has considerably less control over the content and direction of the therapeutic session than does the individual therapist. As a result, there is greater potential for individuals in the group to have unfavorable or adverse experiences. Problems might include stresses resulting from confrontation, criticism, threats to confidentiality, or even development of a dependency on the group.

Our discussion will focus on two sets of related issues: first, groups intended as therapy experiences; and second, group programs intended as growth experiences. "Group programs" refer to short-term group experiences in which individual development or growth rather than psychopathology is the focus. We shall use the term group therapy in general to discuss treatment for people seeking help in response to specific emotional or psychological symptoms, usually during a period of months or years, rather than days or weeks, such as in the growth experience programs.

The APA's "Guidelines for Psychologists Conducting Growth Groups" (1973), which include several important points that can be categorized as general mandates, enable the psychologist leader to accomplish the following: provide informed consent; ensure that participation is fully voluntary; conduct proper screening of participants; and differentiate roles based on whether the group is intended to be therapeutic or educational. As these guidelines reveal, the psychologist leading the group is responsible for these obligations.

> **Case 5–23:**   The president of a small manufacturing company was so excited about the insights he acquired in a weekend marathon therapy session conducted by Grover Grouper, Ed.D., that he hired Grouper to conduct such a session for his executive staff and ordered them all to participate.
>
> **Case 5–24:**   Lena Lonely was a socially isolated freshman at a large state college. She joined an eight-week "encounter group" run by Vivian Speedo, Ph.D., at the college counseling center. Ms. Lonely hoped that the group experience would help to remedy her social isolation. Eight weeks later, when the group sessions ended, Lonely was disillusioned by her lack of accomplishment and in despair over what she perceived as her inadequacies. She dropped out of school.
>
> **Case 5–25:**   Fernando Frank, Psy.D., is a strong proponent of the "tell it like it is" school of therapy. In the first meeting with a new group, Dr. Frank focused attention on Jack Small, encouraging Small to reveal some intimate detail of his life to the group. After Mr. Small shared such a detail, Dr. Frank and the other group members focused on it and highlighted the personal inadequacies it implied. Small never returned to the group and was admitted to a mental hospital two weeks later, experiencing severe depression.

All three of these cases suggest inadequate preparation and follow-through by the psychologist in question. Dr. Grouper, for example, in agreeing to conduct the group, seems to have ignored the coercion involved in demanding that the staff attend. Both the nature and goals of the group are unclear. If it is intended as therapy, then the failure to screen potential participants for appropriateness and the enforced participation (or even voluntary participation) of people who work together raise serious questions regarding privacy and therapeutic merit. If the goals of the group are educative, Grouper still should screen participants carefully and ensure that no coercion, however subtle, is involved in their decision to attend. Parker (1976) reports the somewhat radical views of Schutz (1971) that each person in the group is solely responsible for himself or herself: "You have your choice. If you want to bow to pressure or resist it, go crazy, get physically injured, stay or leave or whatever, it's up to you." Parker correctly recognizes this philosophy as one that leads to high-risk groups and a dangerous laissez-faire leadership style. However trendy or attractive this philosophy may seem, it is dangerous and presents the potential of serious harm to clients.

Lieberman et al. (1973) list many participant vulnerability factors that therapists must consider in constructing and conducting groups. The factors include vulnerability to aggression, fragile self-esteem, excessive dependency needs, intense fears of rejection, withdrawal, transference to the group leader, internal conflicts aroused by group discussions, unreal expectations, and guardedness. In many ways, the group therapist's ethical burden is far greater than that of the individual therapist, since the psychologist conducting group therapy must consider the psychological ecology of the therapy or program as it affects different participants.

The matter of confidentiality and privileged communication in group psychotherapy is also an important issue. Although these issues were discussed in general in Chapter 3, the group context raises a new variable to the equation since, by definition, more than two people are in a position to disclose a confidence learned in the session (i.e., the therapist and at least one other client). As discussed in Chapter 3, privilege and confidentiality are two distinct concepts. The therapist should therefore advise clients of both concepts early in the group treatment process. In most jurisdictions, no statutory privilege extends to material disclosed in group sessions to client members of the group (Slovenko, 1977). Thus, clients must be cautioned about the lack of legal protections (i.e., privilege) regarding information disclosed. In addition, the therapist should encourage all group members to recognize and respect confidentiality regarding issues each member discusses during the course of treatment.

Slovenko (1977) notes that therapists tend to be far more concerned about issues of confidentiality than are members of the group. One wonders whether clients in group treatment are aware that gossip about sensitive material revealed in sessions could be communicated to others outside the group by their peers. As a result, clients might reasonably be expected to censor material about which they are particularly sensitive. Nevertheless, the pressures toward self-disclosure in group therapy or even experiential growth programs may be quite intense, and therapists should remember these issues as the group sessions proceed.

SPECIAL TECHNIQUES AND ISSUES

Included under the general heading of psychotherapy are a number of special issues or techniques that have attracted a sufficient number of ethics inquiries to warrant specific discussion. These issues include triage and intake procedures, as well as techniques associated with sex therapy, hypnosis, behavior modification, the use of psychological devices, and so-called coercive treatment techniques. Such issues and techniques often attract special ethical concerns: (1) because of the sensational nature of the context or style within which they are applied; and (2) because of the particular social concerns associated with the treatment issue (e.g., sexual practices and sex therapy, or civil rights and coercive treatment programs).

Triage and Intake

Triage, a concept frequently applied in medical emergency situations, refers to a priority assignment to certain patients waiting for treatment. For example, a patient who has stopped breathing or who is hemorrhaging will be seen immediately, even if other, less severely injured patients must wait for an extended time period in pain and discomfort. Likewise, a clinic with an extensive psychotherapy waiting list might place a suicidal client at the head of the line for treatment because of the urgent nature of the problem. Occasionally, however, clients are not informed of such priorities, even if reasonable; consequently, the client may suffer needlessly, rather than seek an alternative treatment. In some instances, the system of priorities or intake procedures themselves may be ethically questionable.

> **Case 5–26:**   Midtown Psychological Associates, Inc., is a private group practice consisting of several licensed psychologists. To keep all available appointment times filled, the secretary is instructed to maintain a waiting list of at least eight to ten clients. Potential clients seeking an appointment are told that they are being placed on a short waiting list and will be called for an appointment soon, even if there are no openings in the foreseeable future.
>
> **Case 5–27:**   The Central City Community Mental Health Center, which had a four week backlog for intake assessments, maintained a policy that only emergency cases could be taken out-of-order. Nicholas Bluster, the Mayor of Central City, telephoned

the psychologist who directed the CMHC seeking an immediate appointment for his adolescent son who "has been mouthing off at home." The psychologist placed Junior Bluster at the head of the list.

Both of these cases demonstrate an unethical prioritization system that is detrimental to some clients. In the case of Psychological Associates, the people waiting for appointments should be advised of the potential duration of their wait and offered the opportunity to be referred elsewhere. An indefinite hold on the waiting list could be reasonable if the potential clients were advised of the details and still chose to wait, but the situation described above is misleading. The director of the CMHC was clearly responding to political expediency. Perhaps Junior Bluster is in need of services and entitled to them; however, moving him ahead of others on the list is unethical, unless an emergency intervention is, in fact, required. The director could have met the political social demands of the situation in other appropriate ways, such as offering to give a referral elsewhere or providing personal time to assist the Blusters while not delaying services to other clients in need.

The therapist who always has time for clients he or she finds physically attractive but is "too busy" for others, or the agency that routinely transfers persons of certain ethnic minority heritage elsewhere reflect even more insidious priority systems. Intake and triage policies are important ethical issues and must be established sensitively in order to ensure quality intervention and service utilization (Levenson and Pope, 1981).

Sex Therapy

The use of the word "sex" tends to capture immediately the attention of an adult audience. In addition, when the term "sex therapy" is used, most mental health professionals envision only the most common presenting symptoms (i.e., impotence, premature ejaculation, anorgasmia, dyspareunia, vaginismus, and withdrawal from sexual activity). Various other problems, however, might also become the focus of "sex therapy." These problems include hysterical conversion reactions with a sexual focus, the paraphilias (e.g., exhibitionism, pedophilia, and voyeurism), gender dysphoria syndromes (e.g., transsexualism), physical developmental disorders (e.g., hypospasias), disease-related disorders, and problems resulting from medical side-effects, surgery, or traumatic injury to the sex organs (Meyer, 1976). Some clients may also present with varying degrees of concern about sexual functioning and homosexuality.

The American Association of Sex Educators, Counselors, and Therapists (AASECT) (1980) has developed a code of ethics and training guidelines for individuals practicing in this specialized field. As their code of ethics and the complexity of the social, psychological, anatomic, and physiological factors that may be involved in sexual problems suggest, special skills and ethical sensitivities are required in this field of practice. In addition, the style and substance of clinically appropriate sex therapy will often differ dramatically from other therapeutic activities. For example, Lowery and Lowery (1975) claim that the most ethical sex therapy is that "which cures the symptom and improves the marital relationship in the briefest time and at the least cost" (p. 229). They also specify that neither insight-oriented treatment nor sex with the client satisfies these criteria. Special credentials, therefore, are required for any practitioners who desire to practice treatment of sexual dysfunction (AASECT, 1980; Meyer, 1976).

Emotional reactions linked to the nature of the problems treated are not limited to the general public. A fascinating debate began in the professional literature with the publication of a study describing highly specific behaviorally oriented masturbation procedures for inorgasmic women (Zeiss et al., 1977). This study provoked the publication of a critique entitled, "Psychotherapy or Massage Parlor Technology?" (Bailey, 1978), which invoked ethical, moral, and philosophical (as well as social-psychological) reasoning. This paper was followed by another that described Bailey's view as being "antiscientific" (Wagner, 1978) and later by another critique noting that value-free therapy does not exist and enjoining the therapist to involve the client fully in goal-setting, while conducting the least intrusive treatment (Wilson, 1978).

Perhaps the most dramatic focus of concern in the practice of sex therapy involves the use of sexual surrogates: i.e., sexual partners used by mental health professionals to assist certain clients by engaging in a variety of social and sexual activities for a fee. The use of surrogates is far more than a prescription for prostitution (Jacobs et al., 1975). Although initially used by Masters and Johnson with a few single clients, the actual use of sex surrogates is today a more rare and atypical technique, with more attention directed toward other issues and techniques (Masters and Johnson, 1976). Nonetheless, some therapists may occasionally use surrogates, although this practice can lead to substantial ethical and legal complications.

In some states, a mental health professional who refers a client to a sex surrogate may be liable for criminal prosecution (Berkowitz, Note 2). Some state laws could lead to prosecution under prostitution statutes, antifornication laws, or even under rape charges, if some aspect of the relationship goes wrong or is brought to the attention of a zealous district attorney. Berkowitz also describes various potential civil liabilities or tort actions that are possible if one spouse objects to the other's use of a surrogate, or if the client contracts a venereal disease from the surrogate. In such cases, the referring practitioner may have a vicarious liability and may find his or her liability insurer unwilling to cover the resulting claim.

Case 5-28:   Lorna Loose worked as a receptionist and secretary to Cecil Thud, Ph.D. Dr. Thud approached her about acting as a sexual surrogate for some of his male clients. Ms. Loose agreed and allegedly so enjoyed the surrogate work that she began to offer such services on a freelance basis in addition to her work with Thud's clients. Subsequently, her exspouse sued for custody of their two children, citing her work as that of "a prostitute." Loose allegedly sought emotional and documentary support from Dr. Thud, and later claimed that he seduced her.

Case 5-29:   George Trotter, Psy.D., employed three female and one male assistants with masters degrees in counseling fields to work in his clinic. His specialization was sex therapy, and he would occasionally refer some of his clients to one of the assistants who acted as a sexual surrogate. Dr. Trotter reasoned that he was behaving appropriately because the surrogates were trained in counseling and were not the therapists of the specific clients in question. Ultimately, Dr. Trotter was prosecuted on prostitution charges, and fraud charges were filed by an insurance company claiming that Trotter had billed the sessions with his assistants as psychotherapy.

These rather dramatic cases are illustrative of the blurring of roles and values that often seems to occur when sexual surrogates are employed, as well as some of the complex problems that may develop. Dr. Thud denied ever having had sex with Ms. Loose, although he did acknowledge recruiting her as a sex surrogate, and he admitted that this role later caused her considerable personal difficulty. It caused him difficulty as well when she sued him and won a substantial award in a highly publicized trial. Dr. Trotter was, of course, ethically insensitive and careless in his conclusion that the use of his assistants, however willing, was not a conflict situation. His decision to bill these visits as compensatory services, when he had been given clear information that they were not covered by the insurance company, constituted evidence of fraud. Although the prostitution charges were ultimately dropped, a substantial amount of harmful publicity deeply troubled the more appropriate and conservative sex therapists in the community.

Sexual behavior is an emotionally charged, value-laden aspect of human life, and therapists working actively at altering such behavior must be appropriately cautious and sensitive to both community and professional standards. In such areas of practice, haphazard ethical practices and indiscretions are more likely to cause major problems for both the client and practitioner.

Behavior Modification Techniques

Similar to the use of sex therapy, the application of behavioral techniques—such as operant conditioning, classical conditioning, aversive therapies, and other types of physical interventions (e.g., physiological monitoring, biofeedback, stress management, etc.)—requires specialized, interdisciplinary training. This training may involve courses in anatomy and physiology, as well as the analysis of behavior and application of learning theory. In addition, an awareness of one's own limitations is also required, as illustrated by knowing when a medical consultation is indicated or when a certain instrumental procedure may edge toward the violation of a client's rights.

The application of behavioral techniques usually involves the assumption of a substantial degree of control over the client's environment. In general, this control occurs with the active involvement and consent of the client. In some instances, however, the client may be technically or literally incompetent to consent, such as in the case of mentally retarded or severely psychotic clients. When the client is incompetent to consent fully and powerful environmental controls are enforced, special substituted judgment procedures using independent advocates may be required (Koocher, 1976; 1983).

The mass media and public literature occasionally decry the application of behavioral techniques in schools, prisons, and other settings. Many people have requested, produced, or rebutted the need for specialized guidelines to be used in applying behavioral techniques (Davidson and Stuart, 1975; Geller et al., 1977; Thaw et al., 1978; Turkat and Forehand, 1980; Stolz, 1977). We find that behavioral therapies do not require more regulation *per se* than do other forms of treatment that are also subject to abuse. As Stolz notes,

> Behavioral clinicians, like other therapists, should be governed by the ethics code of their professions; also, the ethics of all intervention programs should be evaluated in terms of a number of critical issues.

Specific complaints regarding behavior therapies that ethics committees may encounter tend to illustrate this concept.

Case 5–30: Gordon Convert, Ed.D., agreed to treat Billy Prissy, age 5, whose parents were concerned about his "effeminate" behaviors. Dr. Convert devised a behavioral approach for implementation in the office and at home involving the differential reinforcement of toy choice, dress-up play, and various other activities of a stereotypical sex-role nature. When reports of this project were published in professional journals, a storm of protests resulted.

Case 5–31: Seymour Diversion, Ph.D., worked in a state hospital for children with emotional problems. He designed a specific program involving the use of aversive stimulation (e.g., brief application of an electric shock rod) as a means to interrupt self-injurious behavior in a head-banging child. The child had caused permanent damage in one eye and was in danger of losing the other as well. Less drastic means of interrupting the behavior had failed. A nurse at the hospital was outraged and informed local newspapers of how Dr. Diversion was "torturing" the child.

Case 5–32:   Thelma Splatter, Psy.D., designed an aversive treatment program to deal with severely retarded residents of a state school who were toileting in public on the grounds of the school or in corridors. The program involved an operant reward system, as well as a spray of icewater in the face administered from a small squirting bottle. Some of the attendants were inadequately trained in the rationale and application of the technique. One evening an attendant caught a male resident of the school smearing feces and pushed the man's face into a toilet bowl while flushing it several times. He reported that he did not have the spray bottle with him.

The case of Dr. Convert is typical of those complaints concerning the questions of client choice and goal setting in therapy. From the brief information given here, it is impossible to ascertain how appropriate or inappropriate the program was. The context and nature of decision making and treatment goal setting are critical (Stolz, 1978). These issues are well illustrated in a series of comments to a manuscript on alternatives to pain medication (Cook, 1975; Karoly, 1975; Goodstein, 1975). The original report focused on a 65-year-old man admitted to a psychiatric ward with symptoms of chronic abdominal pain and a self-induced drug habit to control the pain (Levendusky and Pankratz, 1975). He was successfully withdrawn from the drug using a treatment procedure that involved some deception and lacked fully informed consent. The ethical dilemma here is the matter of client involvement in making choices, rather than the technique itself.

Dr. Diversion was asked to respond to an ethics committee and did so with openness and in detail. Several less-invasive attempts to prevent the child from destroying his remaining eye by head banging had been unsuccessful. A special panel had been asked to review the case and approve the trial of aversive techniques independently of Dr. Diversion and the hospital. Dr. Diversion managed the program personally and noted that he had been prepared to discontinue the use of aversive stimuli promptly, if no benefit resulted to the child. The committee agreed that every appropriate precaution had been taken and that Diversion had behaved appropriately, given the severe nature of the child's self-injury.

Dr. Splatter's program may have been adequately conceptualized, but it was poorly implemented. The attendant clearly did not discriminate between the intended shock value of the icewater spray and the sadistic and punitive act of holding a person's face in the toilet. The unethical behavior was primarily Dr. Splatter's failure to supervise adequately the people charged with executing her treatment program. If she were unable to supervise adequately all of those participating in the program she designed, then she should have limited the scope of the program to those she could adequately supervise. Although the attendant was responsible for his own behavior, Dr. Splatter may have inadvertently provided a context within which the act seemed appropriate to him.

During a conversation hour at an APA meeting several years ago, B. F. Skinner was talking bemusedly about the controversy that seemed to focus on labels, rather than on practices. He noted that a school board had promulgated a threat to fire any personnel who used behavior modification. He then wondered aloud what would happen the next payday when the "reinforcements" were handed out in the form of paychecks. This example illustrates that the technique itself does not present the ethical problem, but the manner in which it is applied.

Unfortunately, not all psychologists who attempt to employ behavioral techniques are well trained in underlying learning theory. Confusion on the distinction between the concepts of "punishment" and "negative reinforcement" is only one example of a common problem. In other instances, aversive treatment protocols have occasionally been introduced without first trying less restrictive techniques.

Furthermore, psychologists should show careful concern for ethical problems inherent in the use of aversive stimuli with relatively powerless clients. These clients would include, for example, institutionalized, incarcerated, or incompetent individuals, as well as children or other people not fully able to assert their rights.

> **Case 5–33:** Marquis deSique, Ph.D., operated a private residential facility for emotionally disturbed and delinquent children. The parents of a ten-year-old boy filed ethics charges when they discovered multiple bruises and lacerations on their son's body during a visit. Dr. deSique explained that the boy required several beating sessions each week to "break his strong will" and permit more appropriate behavior to emerge. It was later discovered that all of the residents were routinely subjected to such sessions. In addition, Dr. deSique would also take nude photographs of them after the beatings.

This type of case causes sensitive, objective, and competent behavioral psychologists to become outraged, because Dr. deSique's "treatments" do not conform to standards of professional practice or ethics. The practices also have no basis in empirical data or learning theory. It seems more likely that deSique was satisfying some peculiar needs of his own at the expense of his vulnerable wards.

Psychological Devices

The report of the APA Task Force on "Psychologists' Use of Physical Interventions" (1981) lists more than a score of instruments and devices used by psychologists for clinical assessment and psychotherapy. These devices include various electrodes and monitors used in biofeedback training, as well as an assortment of color vision testers, dynamometers, audiometers, restraints, and even vibrators. Some of these devices are regulated by the United States Food and Drug Administration, and most require specialized training to use. Detailed suggestions for the use of such devices have been published by R. L. and R. K. Schwitzgebel (1970; 1978) and Fuller (1978). Psychotherapists have also been involved in discussing problems associated with the use of lie detectors (Lykken, 1974; Szucko, and Kleinmuntz, 1981), therapy by telephone (Grumet, 1979), and, more recently, suicide prevention by means of computer-mediated therapy (Barnett, 1982).

The use of technology in the future of psychotherapy will probably increase, and along with it ethical complaints of a related nature. The case of Dr. Anna Sthesia (*Case 5-17*) presented earlier in this chapter is a recent example. The basic caveat is that psychologists should recognize the boundaries of their competence, especially in attempting to use new technologies. They must avoid using unsafe or unproven devices, not to mention those that might prove dangerous to clients through electric shock or other hazards. Psychologists must also remember that they are not physicians and should never attempt treatment of problems with possible organic causes without a collaborative relationship with a qualified physician. In addition, federal law may govern the licensing and use of some instruments, and psychologists are obligated to keep themselves informed of these statutes and resulting obligations.

Coercive Therapies

As noted earlier in this chapter, psychotherapy has sometimes been considered a means of social control (Hurvitz, 1973) and has been compared in some ways with brainwashing (Dolliver, 1971; Gaylin, 1974). The use of "coercive persuasion," "deprogramming," and hypnotic suggestion techniques (Fromm, 1980; Kline, 1976) have all been discussed from the viewpoint of client manipulation. In essence, to what extent do certain psychological techniques permit the psychotherapist to either manipulate or control the client by force or threat? Earlier in this chapter, we discussed the right to refuse treatment, and we cite these issues only as examples of techniques that occasionally have been the object of complaints.

In general, it is unethical for a psychotherapist to coerce a client into treatment or to force certain goals or outcomes against the client's wishes. In Chapter 12, we discuss several special problem situations in this area (e.g., clients who are in involuntary institutions, such as prisons). The subtler aspects of coercion are often the most difficult to identify: for example, group pressure, guilt induction, introduction of cognitive dissonance, attempts at total environmental control, and the establishment of a trust relationship with the goal of effecting change in another person (Dolliver, 1971). It is critical that the psychotherapist attempt to remain aware of potentially coercive influences and to avoid them without first obtaining full participation, discussion, and choice by the client. The constant critical reexamination of the strategies and goals of treatment involving both client and therapist is the best means to achieve this goal.

UNTESTED OR FRINGE THERAPIES

Ethics complaints will occasionally develop in response to a new or unusual form of psychotherapy or allegedly therapeutic technique. Often these so-called treatments have questionable merit or are obviously dangerous. Although appropriate innovation and the development of new treatment strategies should exist in any scientific field, rigorous standards must be applied to avoid misleading or harming potential clients. No program of psychotherapy or psychotherapeutic technique should be undertaken without a firm theoretical foundation and scientific basis for anticipating client benefits. Such programs should be labeled as experimental, with appropriate informed consent required, and they should be discontinued at the first indication that any harm is accruing to the clients.

Examples of a few of the more questionable psychotherapeutic practices include "past lives therapy," "rage weekends," and "harassment therapy." Some people consider Scientology a type of fringe or unproven therapy as well. The work of Wilhelm Reich, which seems to have occasionally involved physical stimulation of clients to the point of orgasm (Reich, 1948), the body invasion technique of Rolfing (Leland, 1976), and the dramatic stresses of implosive therapy (Stampfl, 1975) are all examples of therapeutic ideas approaching the outer limit of acceptability. Of course, psychology as a science has not yet evolved sufficiently to guarantee precise evaluation of therapeutic results. Nevertheless, some obvious ethical problems do arise.

> **Case 5–34:**   Millard Brute, Ph.D., prepared an audio tape for experimental use in implosive desensitization of child abusers. The tape described with vivid imagery the successively escalating physical assault on a child, culminating in the dismemberment and cannibalization of the corpse. The tape was played for a professional audience, and one outraged participant filed an ethics complaint.

> **Case 5–35:**   Astrid Blaster, Psy.D., is a proponent of "harassment therapy." This therapy sometimes involved extended verbal attacks on some clients, and in other situations involved tying clients up and forcing them to struggle to get loose. When an ethics complaint was filed, Dr. Blaster explained her belief that it was necessary to be "harsh" on "the whimpering, dependent types."

> **Case 5–36:**   Gwendolyn Haughty, Ed.D., required her individual therapy clients to participate in group therapy sessions at her home on a biweekly basis. They were required to sit in a circle on floor pillows, while Dr. Haughty perched above them on a stool, clothed in a black leotard, and read to them from a book manuscript she was writing.

Dr. Brute informed the ethics committee that the tape was not an actual treatment tool, but rather an experimental project that he used for illustrative purposes with audiences composed of professionals only. Nonetheless, the committee noted the sensitive nature of the tape and advised Dr. Brute to be more considerate of his audience's sensitivities in the future. Certainly the intense nature of the implosive therapy regimen would require thorough discussion with any client prior to implementation. Some might question whether a substantial enough data base exists on which to predicate such treatment.

The theoretical rationales of Dr. Blaster and Dr. Haughty are vague and questionable at best. It is difficult to imagine that either one has advised the clients in question of the potential risks involved in the so-called treatments. It is also unclear whether any of their clients have been objectively apprised of more conventional and better proven treatments for their problems. Often it is the most egocentric and least competent practitioners who are brought to the attention of ethics committees via this sort of complaint.

SUMMARY GUIDELINES

1. Psychotherapists should strive to reach explicit understandings with their clients regarding the terms of the treatment contract, whether formal or informal. This agreement includes some mutual discussion about the goals of treatment and the means to achieve these goals.

2. Psychotherapists are obliged to consider carefully the unique needs and perspective of each client in formulating therapeutic plans.

3. A psychotherapist's personal beliefs, values, and attributes may limit his or her ability to treat certain types of clients. Therapists should strive for awareness of such characteristics and limit their practices appropriately.

4. In certain circumstances, clients have specific legal rights either to receive or to refuse treatment. Psychologists should be aware of these rights and respect the underlying principles, even if no specific laws are applicable.

5. Therapists should strive to recognize their own feelings with respect to each client, as well as the degree to which these feelings may interfere with therapy. If the client does not seem to be benefitting or if the client's behavior is provocative, the therapist should promptly consider alternative courses of action.

6. When the psychologist is treating more than one client at a time, such as in group or family therapy, the rights of all clients must be respected and balanced. Therapists should also be sensitive to their own values with respect to the family or group and attempt to facilitate the growth of all concerned within their own value systems.

7. The psychologist conducting group treatment or educational programs should carefully define and articulate the goals, methods, and purposes of each group for each participant in such a manner as to permit each potential client a fully informed choice about participation.

8. In the application of special therapeutic techniques, including (but not limited to) sex therapy, behavior modification, hypnosis, and the use of

psychological devices, psychologists must be certain that their training is adequate to use the technique in question.

9. When symptoms or techniques raise particular emotional or public policy questions, the psychotherapist should be sensitive to the issues and discuss these issues, along with their implications, with the client. Psychologists are also obliged to keep abreast of evolving standards and regulations governing the use of specialized techniques and devices.

10. Coercion is not an appropriate part of a psychotherapeutic program. To the extent that subtle coercive pressures enter into a therapeutic relationship, a psychologist should attempt to ensure that they are not used to the client's detriment.

11. Only well-validated approaches to treatment should be presented to clients. Experimental procedures must be described as such, and extreme caution should be used in the development of new modalities of treatment in order to minimize client risk.

REFERENCE NOTES

1. Williams, M. H. *The bait-and-switch tactic in psychotherapy*. Unpublished manuscript, available from the author at Department of Psychiatry, Kaiser-Permanente Medical Center, 900 Kiely Boulevard, Santa Clara, CA, 95051.

2. Berkowitz, S. R. *Opinion on potential legal liability with respect to the use of sexual surrogates for therapy*. Paper prepared for the Massachusetts Psychological Association by its legal counsel, October 1, 1980.

REFERENCES

American Association of Sex Educators, Counselors, and Therapists. *ASSECT Code of Ethics*. Washington, DC: ASSECT, 1980.

American Psychological Association. Guidelines for psychologists conducting growth groups. *American Psychologist*, 1973, *28*, 933.

American Psychological Association Task Force. *Report on Psychologists' Use of Physical Interventions*. Washington, DC: APA, 1981.

———. Report of the task force on sex bias and sex-role stereotyping in psychotherapeutic practice. *American Psychologist*, 1975, *30*, 1169–1175.

Applebaum, P. S., and Gutheil, T. G. Drug refusal: A study of psychiatric inpatients. *American Journal of Psychiatry*, 1980, *137*, 340–345.

Bailey, K. G. Psychotherapy or massage parlor technology? Comments on the Zeiss, Rosen, and Zeiss treatment procedure. *Journal of Consulting and Clincial Psychology*, 1978, *46*, 1502–1506.

Barnett, D. C. A suicide prevention incident involving use of the computer. *Professional Psychology*, 1982, *13*, 565–570.

Brodsky, A., and Hare-Mustin, R. T. *Women and Psychotherapy: An Assessment of Research and Practice.* New York: Guilford Press, 1980.

Cohen, R. J., and Smith, F. J. Socially reinforced obsessing: Etiology of a disorder in a Christian Scientist. *Journal of Consulting and Clinical Psychology,* 1976, 44, 142–144.

Cook, S. W. Comments on ethical considerations in "self-control" techniques as an alternative to pain medication. *Journal of Abnormal Psychology,* 1975, 84, 169–171.

Coyne, J. C. The place of informed consent in ethical dilemmas. *Journal of Consulting and Clinical Psychology,* 1976, 44, 1015–1017.

Davidson, G. C., and Stuart, R. B. Behavior therapy and civil liberties. *American Psychologist,* 1975, 30, 755–763.

———. Homosexuality: The ethical challenge. *Journal of Consulting and Clinical Psychology,* 1976, 44, 157–162.

Dolliver, R. H. Concerning the potential parallels between psychotherapy and brainwashing. *Psychotherapy: Theory, Research, and Practice,* 1971, 8, 170–173.

Everstine, L.; Everstine, D. S.; Heymann, G. M.; True, R. H.; Frey, D. H.; Johnson, H. G.; and Seiden, R. H. Privacy and confidentiality in psychotherapy. *American Psychologist,* 1980, 35, 828–840.

Eysenck, H. J. The effects of psychotherapy: An evaluation. *Journal of Consulting Psychology,* 1952, 16, 319–324.

Ford, M. D. The psychiatrist's double bind: The right to refuse medication. *American Journal of Psychiatry,* 1980, 137, 332–339.

Fromm, E. Values in hypnotherapy. *Psychotherapy: Theory, Research, and Practice,* 1980, 17, 425–430.

Fuller, G. D. Current status of biofeedback in clinical practice. *American Psychologist,* 1978, 33, 30–48.

Galinsky, M. J., and Schopler, J. H. Warning: Groups may be dangerous. *Social Work,* 1977, 22, 89–94.

Garfield, S. L. Psychotherapy: A 40-year appraisal. *American Psychologist,* 1981, 36, 174–183.

Gaylin, W. On the borders of persuasion: A psychoanalytic look at coercion. *Psychiatry,* 1974, 37, 1–9.

Geller, E. S.; Johnson, D. F.; Hamlin, P. H.; and Kennedy, T. D. Behavior modification in a prison: Issues, problems, and compromises. *Criminal Justice and Behavior,* 1977, 4, 11–43.

Glenn, C. Ethical issues in the practice of child psychotherapy. *Professional Psychology,* 1980, 11, 613–619.

Goodstein, L. D. Self-control and therapist-control: The medical model in behavioral clothing. *Journal of Abnormal Psychology,* 1975, 84, 178–180.

Grisso, T., and Vierling, L. Minors' consent to treatment: A developmental perspective. *Professional Psychology,* 1978, 9, 412–427.

Grumet, G. W. Telephone therapy: A review and case report. *American Journal of Orthopsychiatry,* 1979, 51, 574–585.

Hale, W. D. Responsibility and psychotherapy. *Psychotherapy: Theory, Research, and Practice,* 1976, 13, 298–302.

Hare-Mustin, R. T. Family therapy may be dangerous for your health. *Professional Psychology*, 1980, *11*, 935–938.

———. A feminist approach to family therapy. *Family Process*, 1978, *17*, 181–194.

———; Marecek, J.; Kaplan, A. G.; and Liss-Levenson, N. Rights of clients, responsibilities of therapists. *American Psychologist*, 1979, *34*, 3–16.

Hines, P. M., and Hare-Mustin, R. T. Ethical concerns in family therapy. *Professional Psychology*, 1978, *9*, 165–171.

Hurvitz, N. Marital problems following psychotherapy with one spouse. *Journal of Consulting Psychology*, 1967, *31*, 38–47.

———. Psychotherapy as a means of social control. *Journal of Consulting and Clinical Psychology*, 1973, *40*, 232–239.

Jacobs, M.; Thompson, L. A.; and Truxaw, P. The use of sexual surrogates in counseling. *The Counseling Psychologist*, 1975, *5*, 73–76.

Jones, A., and Seagull, A. Dimensions of the relationship between the black client and the white therapist: A theoretical overview. *American Psychologist*, 1977, *32*, 85–88.

Kanoti, G. A. Ethical implications in psychotherapy. *Journal of Religion and Health*, 1971, *10*, 180–191.

Karasu, T. B. The ethics of psychotherapy. *American Journal of Psychiatry*, 1980, *137*, 1502–1512.

Karoly, P. Ethical considerations in the application of self-control techniques. *Journal of Abnormal Psychology*, 1975, *84*, 175–177.

Kaschak, E. Therapist and client: Two views of the process and outcome of psychotherapy. *Professional Psychology*, 1978, *9*, 271–278.

Kline, M. V. Dangerous aspects of the practice of hypnosis and the need for legislative regulation. *The Clinical Psychologist*, 1976, *29*, 2–5.

Koocher, G. P. A bill of rights for children in psychotherapy. In G. P. Koocher (Ed.), *Children's Rights and the Mental Health Professions*. New York: Wiley, 1976.

———. Consent to psychotherapy. In G. B. Melton, G. P. Koocher, and M. Saks (Eds.), *Children's Competence to Consent*. New York: Plenum, 1983.

Korchin, S. J. Clinical psychology and minority problems. *American Psychologist*, 1980, *35*, 262–269.

L'Abate, L. *Values, Ethics, Legalities and the Family Therapist*. Rockville, Maryland: Aspen Systems Corporation, 1982.

Leland, J. "Invasion" of the body? *Psychotherapy: Theory, Research, and Practice*, 1976, *13*, 214–218.

Levendusky, P., and Pankratz, L. Self-control techniques as an alternative to pain medication. *Journal of Abnormal Psychology*, 1975, *84*, 165–168.

Levenson, H., and Pope, K. S. First encounters: Effects of intake procedures on patients, staff, and the organization. *Hospital and Community Psychiatry*, 1981, *32*, 482–485.

Lieberman, M. A.; Yalom, I. D.; and Miles, M. B. *Encounter Groups: First Facts*. New York: Basic Books, 1973.

Liss-Levinson, N.; Hare-Mustin, R. T.; Marecek, J.; and Kaplan, A. G. The therapist's role in assuring client rights. *Advocacy Now*, March 1980, pp. 16–20.

Lowery, T. S., and Lowery, T. P. Ethical considerations in sex therapy. *Journal of Marriage and Family Counseling*, 1975, *1*, 229–236.

Lykken, D. T. Psychology and the lie detector industry. *American Psychologist*, 1974, *29*, 725–739.

Margolin, G. Ethical and legal considerations in marital and family therapy. *American Psychologist*, 1982, *37*, 788–801.

Marshall, E. Psychotherapy faces test of worth. *Science*, 1980, *207*, 35–36.

Masters, W. H., and Johnson, V. E. Principles of the new sex therapy. *American Journal of Psychiatry*, 1976, *133*, 548–554.

Melton, G. B. Children's participation in treatment planning: Psychological and legal issues. *Professional Psychology*, 1981, *12*, 647–654.

——; Koocher, G. P.; and Saks, M. *Children's Competence to Consent*. New York: Plenum, 1983.

Meredith, R. L., and Riester, R. W. Psychotherapy, responsibility, and homosexuality: Clinical examination of socially deviant behavior. *Professional Psychology*, 1980, *11*, 174–193.

Meyer, J. K. Training and accreditation for the treatment of sexual disorders. *American Journal of Psychiatry*, 1976, *133*, 389–394.

Noll, J. O. Material risks and informed consent to psychotherapy. *American Psychologist*, 1981, *36*, 916–918.

——. The psychotherapist and informed consent. *American Journal of Psychiatry*, 1976, *133*, 1451–1453.

O'Connor v. Donaldson, 422 U.S. 575 (1975).

O'Leary, K. D., and Borkovec, T. D. Conceptual, methodological, and ethical problems of placebo groups in psychotherapy research. *American Psychologist*, 1978, *33*, 821–830.

Parker, R. S. Ethical and professional considerations concerning high risk groups. *The Journal of Clinical Issues in Psychology*, 1976, *7*, 4–19.

Pederson, P. B., and Marsella, A. J. The ethical crisis for cross-cultural counseling and therapy. *Professional Psychology*, 1982, *13*, 492–500.

Piper, W. E., and Wogan, M. Placebo effect in psychotherapy: An extension of earlier findings. *Journal of Consulting and Clinical Psychology*, 1970, *34*, 447.

Reich, W. *The Discovery of the Orgasm. Volume One: The Function of the Orgasm*. New York: Orgone Institute Press, 1948.

Rogers, C. *Carl Rogers on Encounter Groups*. New York: Harper and Row, 1970.

Schofield, W. *Psychotherapy: The Purchase of Friendship*. Englewood Cliffs, NJ: Prentice-Hall, 1964.

Schutz, W. C. *Here Comes Everybody*. New York: Harper and Row, 1971.

Schwitzgebel, R. K. Suggestions for the uses of psychological devices in accord with legal and ethical standards. *Professional Psychology*, 1978, *9*, 478–488.

Schwitzgebel, R. L. Behavior instrumentation and social technology. *American Psychologist*, 1970, *25*, 491–499.

Shapiro, A. K., and Struening, E. L. The use of placebos: A study of ethics and physicians' attitudes. *Psychiatry in Medicine*, 1973, *4*, 17–29.

Silber, D. E. Therapeutic ideology and the professional psychologist. *The Clinical Psychologist*, 1976, *24*, 3–5.

Simmonds, D. W. Children's rights and family dysfunction: "Daddy, why do I have to be the crazy one?" In G. P. Koocher (Ed.), *Children's Rights and the Mental Health Professions*. New York: Wiley, 1976.

Slovenko, R. Group psychotherapy: Privileged communication and confidentiality. *Journal of Psychiatry and the Law*, 1977, *5*, 405–466.

Stampfl, T. G. Implosive therapy: Staring down your nightmares. *Psychology Today*, February, 1975, 66–73.

Stolz, S. B. Ethics of social and educational interventions: Historical context and behavioral analysis. In A. C. Catania and T. A. Brigham (Eds.), *Handbook of Applied Behavior Analysis*. New York: Irvington, 1978.

———. Why no guidelines for behavior modification? *Journal of Applied Behavior Analysis*, 1977, *10*, 541–547.

Strupp, H. H. On failing one's patient. *Psychotherapy: Theory, Research, and Practice*, 1975, *12*, 39–41.

Szucko, J. J., and Kleinmuntz, B. Statistical versus clinical lie detection. *American Psychologist*, 1981, *36*, 488–496.

Thaw, J.; Thorne, G. D.; and Benjamin, E. Human rights, behavior modification, and the development of state policy. *Administration in Mental Health*, 1978, *5*, 112–119.

Turkat, I. D., and Forehand, R. Critical issues in behavior therapy. *Behavior Modification*, 1980, *4*, 445–464.

Wagner, N. N. Is masturbation still wrong? Comments on Bailey's comments. *Journal of Consulting and Clinical Psychology*, 1978, *46*, 1507–1509.

White, M. D., and White, C. A. Involuntarily committed patients' constitutional right to refuse treatment: A challenge to psychology. *American Psychologist*, 1981, *36*, 953–962.

Wilson, G. T. Ethical and professional issues in sex therapy: Comments on Bailey's "Psychotherapy of massage parlor technology?" *Journal of Consulting and Clinical Psychology*, 1978, *46*, 1510–1514.

Wright, R. H. Psychologists and professional liability (malpractice) insurance: A retrospective review. *American Psychologist*, 1981a, *36*, 1485–1493.

———. What to do until the malpractice lawyer comes: A survivor's manual. *American Psychologist*, 1981b, *36*, 1535–1541.

Zeiss, A. M.; Rosen, G. M.; and Zeiss, R. A. Orgasm during intercourse: A treatment strategy for women. *Journal of Consulting and Clinical Psychology*, 1977, *45*, 891–895.

Money Matters 6

When it is a question of money,
everyone is of the same religion.

Voltaire

If you are reading this chapter first, it is likely that you are either in private practice or want to be. To be successful, the independent practitioner must pay careful attention to a variety of details not usually discussed in graduate school. When finances are discussed during a psychologist's formal training, references to actual practices of billing and collection are rarely mentioned. Perhaps this omission is one reason why client complaints and ethical difficulties frequently arise in connection with charges for psychologists' services. Often the problems result from miscommunication, procedural ignorance, or naivete, rather than from avarice. Discussion of money matters in this chapter is divided broadly into five main categories: what to charge, fee-splitting, third-party relationships, fraud, and bill collecting.

WHAT TO CHARGE?

Determining the customary charges for one's services is a complicated task combining issues of economics, self-esteem, and various cultural and professional taboos. Regarding mental health services, the task is complicated by numerous subtle, as well as obvious, psychological and ethical values, regardless of whether one is a psychologist (Lovinger, 1978), a physician (DiBella, 1980), or a pastoral counselor (Houck and Moss, 1977).

Comparison of fees is further complicated by differences in procedures, length of sessions, and other variables. In 1980, *Psychotherapy Finances* notes that a single psychotherapy session might vary as much as 100% across the range of practitioners surveyed for single-session hourly rates. More recently, *Medical Economics* (1982) reported a median fee increase from $55 per session for an office visit to a psychiatrist in 1978 to $76 for a similar visit in 1982. Matters are further complicated by the issue of what constitutes a "therapy hour." A re-analysis of data from the Civilian Health and Medical Program of the Uniformed Services (CHAMPUS) conducted by the AAP (Association for the Advancement of Psychology, 1983) showed that a "session" could range from 20 to 120 minutes. Some practitioners offer their clients a 60-minute hour, while others conduct a treatment "hour" that may be 50, 45, or fewer minutes. Likewise, group or family therapy sessions might extend 90 minutes or more, thus making accurate comparisons difficult.

The most recent data (AAP, 1983) show that the typical fee paid under CHAMPUS for an out-patient treatment session of 45−60 minutes was $53.57 to psychiatrists and $52.51 to psychologists. Inpatient treatment hours were slightly different, averaging $56.85 and $51.29 respectively. An average 45 to 50 minute family therapy session cost $68.40 for psychiatrists and $65.55 for psychologists. These amounts reflect the fees allowed by the CHAMPUS insurance program, not the actual fees billed, which are generally higher.

Psychiatrists tend to have the highest fees, with some charging $120 or more per session, with psychologists second, and social workers, marriage counselors, and pastoral counselors closely tied for third place. Psychotherapeutic services also tend to show regional cost differences, with the East being the least expensive region (perhaps because it has the greatest per capita number of service providers), the West having the highest fees, and the South and Midwest falling in between (*Psychotherapy Finances*, 1980).

Some practitioners may offer a sliding-fee scale for clients who cannot afford to pay a customary charge. Other practitioners, however, maintain a high "usual rate," while providing many types of discounts: for example, a client who has been in treatment for an extended period of time may be offered a lower rate than a new client, or an individual who is being seen three hours per week may be given a lower hourly rate than will a person being seen once per week. The actual fee charged for services rendered is not as important from the ethical standpoint as the manner in which it is set, communicated, managed, and collected. By definition, however, many clients may be vulnerable to potential abuse because of emotional dependency, social naivete, psychosis, or other psychopathological conditions, and the psychologist should not take advantage of these factors.

Case 6−1: Arnold Avarice, Ph.D., was contacted by Sally Sibyl for treatment of her emotional problems, and he diagnosed her as having a multiple personality disorder. During the first two months of treatment, Dr. Avarice claimed to have treated

Ms. Sibyl an average of three hours per day (some days as many as five to six hours) at a rate of $100 per hour. Ms. Sibyl's wealthy family was billed approximately $12,000 for services during this time. When questioned, Dr. Avarice justified the frequency of his work with the client by noting: "I often had sessions with two or three different personalities the same day. She is a very disturbed woman requiring intensive work." Dr. Avarice offered to consider reducing his fee in exchange for the "exclusive rights to a book on her case story."

From the outset of a relationship with a new client, the psychologist should carefully explain the nature of services to be offered, the fees to be charged, the mode of payment to be used, and other financial arrangements that might reasonably be expected to influence the potential client's decision. The psychologist's doubts about the ability of the client to make a responsible decision must also be considered in the decision of whether to accept the client or to refer the person to another service. If an estimate of charges is given, it should be honored. Potential financial difficulties should be discussed openly and resolved at the outset of the relationship.

Occasionally clients complain to ethics committees about pressure to enter treatment at a higher fee than they can afford. Such practices include both "soft" and "hard-sell" pitches by therapists. An example of the low pressure pitch might be: "If you really want to get better, you will find a way to finance good therapy. It's an investment in yourself." A more high pressure pitch might be: "You can't afford *not* to see me. I have been very successful in solving your type of problem. " Aside from the implication of special skill explicit in both of these pitches, they subject the client to unethical pressure by playing on his or her insecurities.

There are many ways to address the issue of the client who cannot afford the services of a particular practitioner. Many psychologists are willing to provide a flexible fee schedule that varies as a function of client-income. The *Ethical Principles* also specify the expectation that psychologists render at least some "pro bono" services: i.e., professional activity undertaken at no charge in the public interest (*EP:* 6d). In addition, a variety of surveys have yielded self-reports suggesting that most psychologists do provide at least some services on this basis. Many psychologists will also offer a financially troubled client the opportunity to extend payment over a long period of time, but this is not helpful if the charges being incurred remain beyond the reasonable means of the client. This practice may also involve substantial administrative difficulties, however, since a special disclosure statement could technically be required under provisions of the Federal Truth-in-Lending Act. It is critical that the psychologist consider these issues early in the professional relationship and discuss them openly with the client in a realistic yet supportive fashion. If a client is unable to afford the services of the particular practitioner, the psychologist should be prepared to make a sensitive and appropriate referral. Consequently, psychologists should be

aware of hospitals, clinics, community mental health centers, training programs, and other resources offering services that might be more affordable
for the client with financial difficulties.

Furthermore, one is obligated to consider the client and community
agencies regarding treatment continuity and limited financial resources in
the community. A practice known as "creaming and dumping" illustrates a
refusal to fulfill this obligation.

> **Case 6–2:**   Roberta Poore consults Phil T. Lucre, Psy.D., a clinical psychologist, for
> treatment of longstanding difficulties with her parents and coworkers. After only one
> session, it is clear to Dr. Lucre that Poore will require at least several months of
> weekly psychotherapy to address her relationship problems effectively. Dr. Lucre's
> usual hourly rate is $60, and he does not have a policy of reducing his fee for clients
> who cannot afford it. Poore has health insurance coverage that provides a maximum
> of $500 per year in outpatient mental health benefits. Her salary is low, and she
> cannot afford more than $25 per week to pay for psychotherapy out-of-pocket. Dr.
> Lucre begins to work with her and sees her for nine sessions. As soon as her insurance
> coverage is exhausted, he refers her to the local community health center where she
> can be seen at a "reduced fee."

In this case, the psychologist has skimmed the "cream" or insurance
coverage and then "dumped" the patient in the lap of a community agency.
This practice is a disservice to the patient, whose therapeutic course is
disrupted, and it is a disservice to the community agency, which would have
benefitted from the insurance payments while providing continuity of care
when the coverage was exhausted. If the psychologist considers the treatment or evaluation plan early and discusses it with the client, including all
relevant financial aspects, the client would be in a position to express a
preference considering the continuity issue as well.

Although this case represents one type of abandonment of the client by
the therapist, what happens in the more general situation concerning the
client who cannot pay for services rendered? Should the practitioner terminate services in midcourse of treatment, or does that represent desertion of
the client as well? The ethical practitioner will attempt to avoid abandoning
clients with two specific strategies. The first is not contracting to provide
services without initially clarifying the costs to the client and reaching
agreement that they are affordable. The second is not misleading the client
into thinking that insurance or other such coverage will bear the full cost of
services, if it is clear that insurance benefits may expire before the needs for
service does. When treatment is in progress and a client becomes unemployed or otherwise can no longer pay for continued services, the practitioner should be especially sensitive to the client's needs. Although it may
eventually be necessary to either terminate care or transfer the client's care
elsewhere, neither action should be done abruptly or in the midst of a crisis
period in the client's life.

Changing one's fees in the course of service delivery can also pose ethical dilemmas. If a commitment is made to provide consultation or to conduct an assessment for a given fee, it should be honored. Likewise, a client who enters psychotherapy at an agreed-upon fee has a reasonable expectation that the fee will not be hiked excessively. After service has begun, the provider has an obligation to the client that must be considered. Aside from financial hardship issues, the psychologist may have special "leverage" with the client at this time.

Case 6–3:   Chuck Gelt begins psychotherapy with Helen Takem, Ed.D., expecting to pay $45 per session. After several weeks of treatment, Mr. Gelt has shared some intense and painful concerns with Dr. Takem. These emotional issues included ambivalence over relationships with Gelt's deceased parents from whom he had inherited substantial wealth. Dr. Takem pressed Gelt to contract with her for a minimum of 100 sessions at a cost of $100 per session. She argued that for this particularly affluent client the fee needed to be high for him to perceive the therapy as "valuable." The minimum contract for 100 sessions was needed, Dr. Takem argued, because Gelt was ambivalent and tended to "lack commitment."

In this case, the client's ambivalence may inhibit his ability to see the inappropriateness of the dramatic boost in fees. At the same time, the client may be reluctant to go through the emotional pain of sharing his concerns "from the beginning" with a new therapist. The emotional investment made by the client during the first few sessions may contribute to make him less able to act as an informed, reasoning consumer to his financial detriment (*EP*: 6a).

When a client has been in treatment for an extended period of time (e.g., six months to a year) and inflation or other costs of conducting a professional practice have risen, it is not unreasonable to adjust fees upward. This should, however, be done thoughtfully, reasonably, and with due consideration for each client's economic status and treatment needs. Some practitioners, for example, will raise fees for new clients, while maintaining "old clients" at the existing rate. The key point to consider ethically is whether the professional incurs added responsibility because of the power role she or he occupies relative to the client.

Similar issues will be discussed in Chapter 7 with respect to "free sessions" or "special bonus offers" used to attract clients. Clients may not realize the subtle emotional pressures that may accompany an initial consultation or "free visit." Although there is certainly nothing wrong with not charging a client under some circumstances, this should not be used as a lure to initiate a professional relationship through advertising or other communications.

Some practitioners require clients to pay certain fees in advance of rendering services as a type of retainer. Although this is an unusual practice, it is not unethical as long as the contingencies are mutually agreed on. The most common uses of such advance payments involve relationships in which the practitioner is asked to hold time available on short notice (such as in certain types of corporate consulting) or in which certain types of litigation are involved. A specific example might be when a psychologist agrees to undertake a child-custody evaluation and the two contesting parties each agree in advance to pay half of the fee. At least one of the parties will probably be unhappy with the outcome, and in such circumstances may refuse to pay for the services rendered because of displeasure with the findings. In such situations, it is not unusual for the practitioner to request a retainer or escrow payment prior to commencing work.

Payment for missed appointments is another source of occasional in-quiries to ethics committees. It is not unethical to charge a client for an appointment that is not kept or that is cancelled on short notice, but again the key issue is proper advance notification about this practice to the client. If a practitioner has a waiting list and could well use the vacant appointment time, it is frustrating and costly to have a client either cancel on short notice or not cancel at all but simply fail to keep the appointment. If the practitioner intends to charge the client in such instances, however, it is necessary to advise the client of this practice at the start of the relationship and to make the conditions explicit. (It is not usually permissible, however, to bill insur-ance companies for such missed appointments, as we will discuss later in this chapter.) In actual practice, it appears that few psychotherapists charge clients for a missed appointment unless the behavior is a recurrent problem.

Fees certainly do have substantial psychological impact on a number of levels and may often become a "therapeutic issue" (see, for example, Lovin-ger, 1978; Vasile and O'Loughlin, 1977). Lovinger (1978) notes that the *fee* is all that the client has to give, aside from coming to the psychologist's office. In essence, the client does not owe the practitioner gratitude, respect, consensus, or anything else, except a fee for services rendered. The fee may in that sense assume some special meaning via transference: in essence, the client may regard the fee in the same manner as some duty owed in a prior relationship. It may become a means for addressing the anger held in relation to a demanding parent or represent a penance to atone for some imagined wrong to a spouse. Lovinger, similar to Freud (who, according to Lovinger, viewed fees as an obvious matter of the therapist's livelihood), suggests that a direct and candid approach is the best means to begin a client–psychologist relationship. Raising the fee exponentially or without a meaningful economic rationale, however, is seldom, if ever, therapeutically defensible.

FEE-SPLITTING

In fee-splitting (a general practice often called a "kickback"), part of a sum received for a product or service is returned or paid out because of a prearranged agreement or coercion. As practiced in medicine or the mental health professions, the client is usually unaware of the arrangement. There is nearly universal agreement, however, that such practices are unethical, primarily because they may preclude a truly appropriate referral in the client's best interests, result in delivery of unneeded services, lead to increased costs of services, and, in general, exploit the relative ignorance of the client (*EP*: 6d). Unfortunately, fee-splitting may exist in rather complex and subtle forms that tend to mask the practice that is occurring.

> **Case 6−4:** Irving Slynapse, M.D., a prominent neurologist, agrees to refer a substantial number of his patients to Ester Choline, Ph.D., for neuropsychological assessment. Dr. Choline bills the client or insurance company and pays Slynapse 10% of all the money collected on clients he refers to her. Slynapse characterizes that 10% as a continuing charge for medical coverage and consultation; however, there are no regular appointments scheduled for consultation, and Choline never avails herself of that service.

> **Case 6−5:** Nick Proffit, Ed.D., P.C., has a large professional practice in which he supervises several master-level psychotherapists and rents office space to other doctoral-level clinicians. His secretary does all of the billing at a rate of $60 per session. The supervisees are paid 25% of the fees collected, and the renters are paid 40% of the fees collected. The clients are unaware of this distribution.

> **Case 6−6:** G. Ima Helper, Psy.D., is well known for her many "self-help" books and media appearances. Her public visibility results in many self-referrals by clients in the community. Dr. Helper refers such clients to Helper's Haven, her private clinic, where they are seen for $60 per session by M.A. level therapists who are paid $20 per session. The clients believe that their therapists either are supervised by or receive consultation from Dr. Helper. In fact, however, they are not even employees (i.e., salaried), but simply earn a fee for each session held and have nothing to do with Dr. Helper, who has little direct involvement with the clinic.

Each of the cases cited above shares a number of common, unethical features. First, the client is usually unaware of the proprietary relationship between the service provider and the person making the referral. Therefore the client would probably not realize that motives other than their own best interests were being considered. In each of the cases, one party is also being paid for services not rendered. In essence, Drs. Slynapse, Proffit, and Helper are being paid a commission to the detriment of the client. None of these clinicians has objectively weighed the needs of the individual client and considered these in making the referral. Some clients may, in fact, be referred for and charged for services that they do not really need.

The case of Dr. Helper also raises the basic question of what one must disclose to a client about arrangements among practitioners. Although Dr. Helper may well be exploiting the M.A. level therapists in her clinic, that is an issue addressed in Chapter 11. The issue in the current context is that clients should be told any aspects of the arrangement that might reasonably be expected to influence their decision about whether to use the services. In essence, they should be told that Dr. Helper will not participate in their treatment in any way. In all of the cases in which a *commission* is being paid to someone not rendering service, the client should also be advised. In this instance, we consider a commission to be any payment for a referral, rather then payment for services rendered.

Many practitioners work in group practices or collaborative arrangements in which certain costs (such as rent, secretarial services, utilities, answering services, etc.) are shared. Many other practitioners also have, or work as, assistants to other psychologists and are paid at less than the full rate billed to the client. These types of arrangements are not necessarily unethical, unless compensation is paid to some party simply for referring clients, or a percentage of gross income is charged against a clinician automatically, rather than for services legitimately provided. In the group practice previously described, for example, each practitioner might be asked to make a monthly payment for office expenses based on actual or reasonably estimated costs and their use of the services. This charge, which should be independent of the gross income of clients seen, should be based instead on an actual use paradigm. In the case of the assistant, it is more appropriate to pay him or her a salary or base compensation on actual gross income less actual costs. Costs might include a reasonable charge for supervision (when allowable by law), as well as for administration, consultation, or office services, but these must be based on a mutually acceptable set of real expenses and be open to renegotiation as time-demand shifts occur. In all cases, the practitioners must be free to make referrals to the "outside," when this seems to be in their clients' best interests. There should be no financial rewards or penalties to any party as the result of an "inside" or "outside" referral.

One subtle difficulty involved in group practice arrangements or in using assistants is the fair determination of costs versus service use. Considerable opportunity exists, of course, for inflation of expenses or other manipulations. This problem often occurs when one of the practitioners assumes a position of power by being either the senior party or licensed doctoral clinician employing individuals too junior for independent licensure who are thus dependent on the employment. In such situations, the practitioner should avoid even the appearance of abuse and should be fully open with his or her colleagues.

Another subtle difficulty is the tendency to refer clients to practitioners one knows well. This practice can be appropriate and responsible, if one tries to help each client obtain the services best suited for her or his needs. The person making the referral, however, should receive no financial benefit or gain from the referral. If the most suitable referral is to a colleague or employee, and some indirect benefit inevitably results (e.g., overhead costs in a group practice kept lower by virtue of more patients being seen), this referral can still be made. The client should be informed, however, that a relationship exists between the practitioners, and they should know why a referral is being made to that specific practitioner. Another alternative would be to offer the client a choice among practitioners, including at least one practitioner not linked to the referring party.

Special Business Agreements

Although not technically "fee-splitting," various special business agreements commonly practiced in the commercial world would be considered unethical in professional practice for reasons similar to the issues raised in this chapter. These agreements would include so-called "covenants not to compete" or contracts with "liquidated damages clauses." Consider, for example, the following case.

> **Case 6–7:**   Lester Workman, Ph.D., has spent ten years building a professional reputation and a busy private practice in a suburban community. He is beginning to attract more referrals than he is able to handle, but he is not sure whether the volume will be sufficient to warrant the addition of a full-time colleague to the practice. He hires Peter Partner, Ph.D., as a half-time salaried employee at a salary agreeable to both for a one-year contract. By the end of the year, Dr. Partner, who is young and energetic, has also begun to build a strong reputation in the community, and he wonders if he should consider starting an independent practice.

In the ideal situation, Dr. Workman and Dr. Partner will attempt to resolve matters according to their clients' best interests. If they are indeed to have separate practices in the same community, the choice of whom to consult should be the client's. Clients in midtreatment with Dr. Partner, for example, should reasonably expect to continue their relationship with him. Unfortunately, however, such changes often result in considerable acrimony between the practitioners, with clients trapped in the middle. Dr. Workman, for example, might avoid this potential outcome by constructing some reasonable professional plan with Dr. Partner to meet clients' needs.

Two types of advance planning for the termination of such relationships cause serious ethical problems. In the first type, Dr. Workman might have attempted to convince Dr. Partner to sign a contract that included a "covenant not to compete." Under such a clause, Partner would agree, for example, not to establish an independent practice or to work for any other practitioner within a 50-mile radius of Workman's office for a period of time after leaving the practice. While this might meet Workman's needs, it would deny clients their freedom to choose and it is clearly unethical. In some jurisdictions, laws have been enacted making such agreements among health care professionals illegal as well. Differences clearly exist between the obligations to a client who is psychologically vulnerable and the more usual circumstances in business and industry in which such covenants are used more appropriately.

The second type of problematic contractual element Dr. Workman might have considered would be a "liquidated damages" clause. Such a clause might have asked that Dr. Partner pay Dr. Workman financial "damages" for each client he takes with him, either at a flat-fee rate or as a percentage of future revenues. This is clearly a fee-splitting situation, and it would most probably be legally unenforceable, even if Partner had agreed to it initially.

The message inherent in this discussion is threefold. First, these issues should be raised and clarified prior to beginning the professional association. Second, the choice of therapist should ultimately rest with the client. Finally, professional colleagues must exercise great care and at times suffer potential economic disadvantage to avoid abusing the relative position of power and influence they have over the clients they serve. Psychologists should not profit unfairly at the expense of either clients or colleagues.

THIRD-PARTY RELATIONSHIPS

Mental health services are essentially paid for in one of three ways: directly by the client; in whole or in part by some health insurance company, health maintenance organization (HMO), or other employee benefit plan; or by public funds. In any case in which an agency or organization other than the practitioner and client is involved, we have a fiscal "third-party" relationship. These third parties, their reimbursement policies, and the regulations that govern these policies have a direct and powerful influence on practice and client care (Chodoff, 1978; Dorken, 1980; Dorken and Webb, 1976; Dujovne, 1980; Julius and Handal, 1980). Although one survey has indicated that at least half of all psychiatrists and one-third of all psychologists contracted to receive more than 60% of their income from third-party reimbursement (*Psychotherapy Finances*, 1980), it is also clear that the involvement of third parties in the client and provider relationship is not an unmitigated blessing (Meltzer, 1975).

Some critics claim that including psychotherapy in health insurance coverage creates several problems, such as the following: inequitable service to different income groups (Albee, 1977; Edwards et al., 1979); concern about threats to clients' confidentiality (Grossman, 1971; Jagim et al., 1978); concern about accountability and review criteria (Sharfstein et al., 1975; Stricker, 1979); expensive litigation (Kiesler and Pallak, 1980); and many intra- and inter-professional squabbles about who should be able to bill third parties for what services. In this book, the confidentiality problems are discussed in Chapter 3, and we shall minimize discussion of primarily political issues involved in insurance reimbursement in favor of a focus on the ethical problems that third-party relationships raise. In the pages that follow, the topics of "freedom-of-choice" (FOC) options, copayment dilemmas, and billing for services-not-covered will be discussed prior to a major discussion of fraud.

Freedom of Choice (FOC)

The freedom-of-choice (FOC) issue refers to legislation and regulations that permit clients the freedom to choose which providers of services they wish to use. As used in discussions of psychological services, FOC usually refers to whether the practitioner is authorized to bill a third party directly for services rendered to a client, or whether that practitioner must first obtain the approval or referral of another. For example, must a psychologist obtain a referral from a physician or obtain a physician's signature prior to billing for services rendered? Dorken and Webb (1980) provide a discussion of third-party reimbursement experience in the FOC context.

Psychologists have pressed the FOC concept as the right of the client, noting that certain psychologists are well trained to function as independent health service providers. Other arguments include the claim that the availability of psychologists improves consumer access to qualified care and increases competition among professional provider groups, resulting in cost benefits to consumers (Dorken and Webb, 1980). Failure to recognize licensed psychologists as independent providers has been viewed by some critics as restraint of trade. Now that all states have psychology licensing statutes, and other credentials exist to identify those psychologists trained to provide health services, it has been possible to enact FOC or so-called "direct recognition" laws in 38 states representing 87% of the U.S. population.

Legal questions regarding FOC issues do arise occasionally, but they are more often gray areas, as opposed to more clear-cut black and white problems. Complaints are frequently registered by unentitled or unrecognized providers who believe they have been excluded or discriminated against with respect to some FOC policy or regulation, including complaints against licensing or credentialing bodies, whose actions may be related to provider recognition under FOC laws.

Complaints may also derive from specific providers or provider groups against their colleagues. When social workers, family counselors, psychiatric nurses, or unlicensed psychologists have sought entitlement to be independent vendors for third-party payments, they have usually cited the same arguments (i.e., consumer's right to choose, increased competition tends to reduce fees, etc.). In general, the entitled practitioner groups tend to oppose direct reimbursement of unentitled groups for various economic and political reasons. Quality of care issues and cost containment are frequently cited as reasons for limiting the size of the practitioner pool to doctoral-level clinicians. Other critics occasionally argue that these reasons merely mask the desire to reduce competition for a limited supply of clients. Although this problem may indeed present some moral or ethical issues, the complexity of public policy on such matters and the usual absence of obviously malevolent individuals make pursuit of these problems as ethical matters difficult. They are more properly treated as professional standards problems.

Copayment Dilemmas

Many third-party benefit contracts require a copayment by the client who receives services. For example, in a 20% copayment contract, the insurance company or health services organization requires the client to pay one-fifth of the cost of services. If a psychologist's bill were $200, the client would pay $40 and the third party would pay $160. Copayment ratios vary widely from plan to plan. Some may require a fifty-fifty payment, while others may require the client to pay a still larger percentage of the bill.

One advantage to this type of plan is that it tends to lower the overall cost of mental health benefits to all policyholders by asking those who actually use the benefits to pay a greater share of the costs. Another advantage is that clients must provide some of their own funds from the start of service delivery, thereby potentially increasing their level of motivation in treatment.

Ethical problems develop in a number of ways, but most often arise when a psychologist waives the copayment portion of the client's bill. For example, a psychologist's normal fee is $60 per hour and the client has a health insurance policy with a 20% copayment obligation. This arrangement would normally mean that the client pays $12 per hour and the insurance company pays $48. Suppose, however, that the client asks the psychologist to bill the insurance company for $75 dollars per hour and to accept the payment as the full fee. The company would then pay $60 to the psychologist, assuming that the client would be billed $15.

In some cases, psychologists may tend to view this as a favor to the client, although it is clearly unethical in the sense that it misrepresents one's actual fees. In other cases, a client may not be able to afford the cost of the copayment required. In such cases, a psychologist may choose to reduce or waive part of the amount owed by the client, similar to a sliding-fee scale. In no case, however, should the cost of the sliding scale be passed on to the insurance company by raising the specific rates for that client. Many psychologists do provide some services on a low-cost or no-cost (*pro bono*) basis as suggested in the *Ethical Principles (EP:* 6d), but attempting to compensate for such reductions by increasing rates to some clients is not appropriate.

Services Not Covered

A common third-party problem with major ethical and legal implications relates to billing for services that are not covered under the third party's obligations. Because most third parties are health insurance companies, coverage is limited to treatments for illness or health-related problems. Usually one must assign a diagnosis to the client in order to secure payment. Some services provided by psychologists are not, strictly speaking, health or mental health services. For example, marriage counseling, educational testing, school consultation, vocational guidance, child custody evaluations, and various forensic functions may not be considered health services, and as such would not be covered by health insurance.

Some insurance carriers also specify certain types of procedures or treatments that are not "covered services." Such treatments or services might be considered ancillary, experimental, unproven, or simply health-promoting (e.g., weight control and smoking cessation), but not treatment for an illness. Attempts to conceal the actual nature of the service rendered or otherwise attempt to obtain compensation in the face of such restrictions may constitute fraud. Earlier in this chapter we discussed the practice of billing clients for missed appointments. Since this practice essentially bills for services that have not been rendered, virtually no third-party payer will cover such charges.

Exactly what is covered under a particular insurance policy is a matter of the specific contract language. A psychologist should check each contract for specific exclusions prior to initiating services for which the client will need insurance reimbursement to pay the bills. Some psychologists have found themselves in the position of negotiating one fee if the patient receives reimbursement and another fee if the service is not covered. This practice may lead to client resentment and may violate certain contracts between providers and insurance companies.

> **Case 6–8:** Becky and Barney Bicker have been separated for three months and have filed for divorce. They are contesting for the custody of their two children. Their respective attorneys, who suggest a psychological consultation to help the Bickers assess the best interests of the children, refer them to Bill Lesser, Ph.D. Lesser assures the Bickers that their Blue Shield policy will cover his fee and proceeds with the evaluation. He subsequently files an insurance claim for his services without noting that it was conducted primarily for resolution of a custody dispute. He assigns diagnosis of "childhood adjustment reaction" to their children for billing purposes.

> **Case 6–9:** Sven Gully, Ed.D., is a licensed psychologist who is skilled in the use of hypnosis and relaxation techniques. He offers a "quit smoking program" that regularly attracts clients. Clients often ask about costs and whether Gully will accept health insurance coverage for payment of his services. Gully knows that many companies will not cover hypnosis or will not pay for "health promoting" programs in the absence of actual illness. He completes billing forms listing his services simply as "psychotherapy," and he assigns "adjustment reaction" diagnoses to his clients.

Both psychologists described may be competent, caring professionals, but both are being unethical and flirting with fraud charges. Perhaps neither has carefully asked the third parties involved whether the services are indeed covered, and they are simply trying to expedite claim processing. On the other hand, both should recognize that the specific services rendered in both cases may not be considered related to mental health or treatment of a particular illness. What appears to be expedient and helpful to the client (i.e., making services less expensive) may be both illegal and tend to increase insurance costs for all policyholders. The more appropriate behavior would be to check with the third party for explicit advice, when in doubt, and then to inform clients early in the relationship whether coverage is indeed applicable. Dr. Lesser and Dr. Gully may believe that they are helping their clients, but they are technically engaged in a "white-collar" ethical violation that costs all consumers money.

FRAUD

As a legal concept, fraud refers to an act of intentional deception resulting in harm or injury to another. There are four basic elements to a fraudulent act. First, a false representation is made by one party who either knows it to be false or is ignorant of its truth; this may be done by misrepresentation, deception, concealment, or simply nondisclosure of some key fact. Second, the maker intends for that false representation to be relied on by another. Third, the recipient of the information is unaware of the intended deception. Finally, the recipient of the information is justified in relying on, or expecting, the truth from the communicator. The resulting injury may be financial, physical, or emotional.

Various unethical acts might be considered fraudulent, including deception in some research paradigms or educational settings, lies about one's training or qualifications, or inappropriate promotional advertising. In this chapter, however, the focus will be on fraud as a financial matter. *Cases 6−8* and *6−9*, for example, highlight one aspect of the problem in which no "victim" is easily identifiable—a situation that often arises in fraud cases. Because the offense often occurs in paper transactions, some offenders do not regard themselves as serious violators.

> **Case 6−10:**   Carla Dingle, Psy.D., was indicted for fraud by a Grand Jury and asked to explain her conduct to an ethics panel. She explained that she consulted at a private proprietary hospital on a fee-for-service basis whereby part of each charge went to her and part to the hospital for administrative costs. To simplify the billing process, Dr. Dingle signed several dozen blank claim forms and left them for the billing office secretary to complete. She described herself as absentminded and reported that she simply had not noticed whether insurance companies were paying her for services not rendered. She claimed that hospital administrators must have improperly added extra appointments to the billing sheets in order to inflate their income.

> **Case 6−11:**   Ernest Church, Ph.D., worked as a consulting psychologist of a nursing home run by a religious group. He offered his services free to the home as an act of religious devotion, and he submitted bills for his services to a government agency

turning over all money collected to the home. He was indicted for fraud when an audit disclosed that he had been paid for several thousand dollars' worth of services not rendered. Church had simply added two or more extra visits to the billing for each of the clients he was asked to evaluate. He was apologetic when confronted, but noted that the home was in need of funds and that the money did not come from any patients, all of whom were on government-sponsored insurance plans.

Neither Dr. Dingle's "absentmindedness" nor Dr. Church's well-intentioned diversion of federal funds is ethically tolerable. Dr. Dingle should not have provided signed blank forms, and she remains fully responsible for any acts she delegated to others. Her carelessness and failure to monitor her accounts accurately raise serious questions about her competence and awareness of professional practices. Dr. Church was obviously guilty of defrauding the government, despite his good intentions and rationalized sense of economic necessity. Perhaps neither seems as culpable as the greedy individual who deliberately swindles a neurotic senior citizen out of his or her life-savings, but the financial impact of fraud on third-party payers and those who underwrite their services is substantial.

It is wise, therefore, to retain duplicate copies of all insurance claims completed. Such a practice might help to prevent problems resulting from alterations made on the forms after they leave the psychologist's hands. In some cases, clients have been known to inflate listed charges, especially when insurance company procedures require the client (rather than the practitioner) to submit the form and reimburse the client directly.

Contractual Obligations

Some third parties seek to sign a contract with providers before agreeing to pay for their services. Blue Shield is an example of such a provider in many states. In the typical contract, a provider is asked to agree to accept the company's payment as specified in full for the service rendered to the subscriber or client. The provider also promises not to charge a policyholder more for any given service than would be charged to another client. In other words, the provider agrees to accept certain set fees determined by the company and agrees not to treat policyholders differently from nonpolicy holders. In this way, the company attempts to provide good, inexpensive coverage, while attempting to prevent its policyholders from being overcharged or treated in a discriminatory manner. The psychologist gains access to a client population, timely payment for services, and the ability to treat covered clients at less expense to them.

Contractual violations are occasionally the basis for complaints, and such violations, if intentional, are usually considered to be illegal and unethical. Two typical types of such contractual violations include the practices of "balance billing" and "hiking your profile."

> **Case 6–12:** Sam Moore, Ph.D., is treating a client whose Blue Shield policy provides payment for outpatient psychotherapy to a maximum of $500 per year. His usual charge is $50 per hour, but his contract obliges him to accept a $40 per-session payment from the company as full compensation for each session. After the $500 is exhausted, he may bill the client his usual fee. Dr. Moore decides to bill his client for the balance between the Blue Shield payment and his usual fee.

This is clearly a contract violation and an unethical act. Some practitioners have been known to attempt to avoid this issue by sending a bill marked "optional," or by telling the client: "You don't have to pay the difference, but I want you to know some of my clients do so voluntarily." This tactic may be a subtle contract violation, and it does seem an abuse of the practitioner's relative power position with respect to the client. Other practitioners similar to Dr. Moore have been known to accept the $40 payment until the coverage is exhausted and then increase their charge to $60 for a comparable number of sessions to recoup their "loss." This is also a contract violation because it results in the policyholder being treated differently from the nonpolicyholder. It is clearly of questionable ethical propriety both in terms of contract violation and in terms of a radical fee increase in mid-treatment.

> **Case 6–13:** I. B. Hire, Psy.D., knows that he will be paid only $40 per session by Blue Shield, and he abides by his obligation not to "balance bill" or otherwise subvert the client's coverage. He also knows that no matter what fee he lists on the insurance claim form—$40, $60, or $100—he will still be paid only $40, rather than the $50-per-hour he usually charges clients who pay out-of-pocket. Dr. Hire also knows that future increases in reimbursement by Blue Shield are based on his "billing profile," his usual charges for similar services noted on claim forms. He knows that future rates will be linked to this profile. As a result, he fills in his usual hourly rate at $100-per-hour on all of the claim forms, reasoning that he will eventually receive a fairer rate than if he allows the company to know that his usual fee is only $50.

Dr. Hire's behavior presents a more subtle form of contract violation. In some ways, it is actually fraud, since he is deliberately lying to the company to obtain some future gain. Dr. Hire would probably rationalize that he is hurting no one, since he will never bill the client more than his usual $50 when coverage is exhausted. He is, however, lying to the company and violating his agreement.

If Dr. Moore and Dr. Hire do not like the Blue Shield contract that is offered, they have the option not to sign it. Some clients would be lost, perhaps, but professional disagreements over fee contracts are not subject to individualized attempts at remedies, such as those previously described. The acts of Dr. Moore and Dr. Hire are illegal, given their contracts, as well as unethical.

BILL COLLECTING

Fee disputes are frequently the basis for legal complaints against psychologists (Cohen, 1979), in addition to many client-initiated ethical complaints. The creditor and debtor relationship in the psychologist−client relationship is similar to that in most other relationships concerning purchases of service. Inevitably some clients fall behind in paying for services or neglect to pay for them at all. Because clients have various reasons for consulting psychologists and different types of relationships are established, however, psychologists are obligated to consider these factors in formulating debt-collection strategies.

When a client remains in active treatment while incurring a debt, the matter should be dealt with frankly, including a discussion of the impact of the debt on treatment. In most cases, however, the problems that arise occur after delivery of formal service has terminated.

> **Case 6−14:** Cindy Late complained to an ethics committee that her former therapist, Lucy Tort, Ed.D., had taken her to small claims court to recover $400 in unpaid bills. Ms. Late reported that she had been emotionally stressed and publicly embarrassed by having to appear in court and to acknowledge that she had been treated by a psychologist. Dr. Tort advised the committee that Ms. Late had not responded to her bills or offers to work out an extended payment plan, noting that no confidential information was released and that the court was only informed that Ms. Late owed the money for services rendered.

Some psychologists would argue that disclosure of a client's status to the court violates a client's right to confidentiality, unless specific informed consent is first obtained (Faustman, 1982). Although that is an ethically considerate and conservative view, initiating a small claims action in particular instances, such as in Dr. Tort's situation, is probably not unethical. In 1978, the APA's Ethics Committee sought an option on the matter from its legal counsel. The Committee was advised that no rules or ethical principles prohibit a psychologist from releasing the name and address of a clinical client to a collection agency (or, presumably, small claims court) for nonpayment of fees. An unpaid bill constitutes a broken contract between the client and practitioner. The psychologist may pursue legal recourse as long as no confidential material, other than client status, is disclosed. While recognizing the difference between confidentiality and privileged communication (see Chapter 3), the attorney compared the psychologist−client relationship with the attorney–client relationship, noting that the name and address are not privileged; in essence, only the communications between client and practitioner are included in the confidential category (Fienberg, Note 1).

Collection agencies represent a different matter from the small claims court, however, since the collection agent acts as an agent of the psychologist. In such instances, the psychologist would be held responsible for the behavior of the collector. Although most states regulate the nature and frequency of contracts by collection agencies, the psychologist could be held responsible for any improper, abusive, invasive, or otherwise noxious collection activities initiated in her or his name. Most states regulate collection practices, whether an organization or individual practitioner is involved. In Massachusetts, for example, the Attorney General has promulgated sixteen pages of regulations on this issue.

One recent study found that 60.8% of the professional psychologists surveyed had used a collection agency, but of those using such agencies, only 48.9% reported informing their clients about the limits of confidentiality (Faustman, 1982).Faustman discusses a variety of collection practices and related problems, noting that "psychologists should use extreme caution in relying on external services for the collection of delinquent accounts" (p. 208).

Because psychologists are occasionally in a unique position to cause clients emotional pain, they should never take advantage of their professional status or relationship to collect a debt. While "ethics" may not be used as an excuse to deprive psychologists of their legal rights, mental health professionals should use caution in exercising those rights.

> **Case 6–15:**　Sara Caustic, Ph.D., was annoyed with Nellie Angst who had terminated treatment, without paying a bill for several months of therapy. Dr. Caustic continued to bill Ms.Angst monthly, and she began adding handwritten notes to the bill, stating, for example, "Don't hold me responsible for the resentment you have toward your mother."

In this instance, Dr. Caustic is inappropriately expressing her anger through using sensitive material gained in her professional capacity. Although it would not necessarily be inappropriate to give a client factual warning that some collection agency or court action might follow if a bill remained unpaid, threats of this type are unprofessional and not often effective. If emotional damage results from collection practices, a malpractice suit may result. In this sense, a psychologist may be obligated to assess the clinical risks associated with different debt-collection strategies. Debt collection should be businesslike and totally devoid of any psychological or clinical content.

Another way in which a psychologist may occasionally attempt to abuse a professional relationship to collect a debt involves the withholding of information.

> **Case 6–16:**   Nellie Angst was so distraught by the notes from Dr. Caustic (see *Case 6–15*) that she sought treatment again, but from a new therapist. She signed a "release of information," and the new therapist contacted Dr. Caustic to obtain data on the prior treatment progress. Dr. Caustic told the new therapist that she would not discuss the case or provide copies of any reports she had prepared until Angst paid her bill.

In this situation, Dr. Caustic is continuing to exercise her professional leverage irresponsibly. If she were being asked to undertake new work on behalf of Ms. Angst, she certainly would have the right to decline. On the other hand, she should not withhold material already prepared or refuse to communicate with a colleague about a vulnerable client, solely because of her own financial dispute with the client. In this instance, she is potentially harming the client and compounding her own unethical behavior.

SUMMARY GUIDELINES

1. Clients should be informed about fees, billing and collection practices, and other financial contingencies as a routine part of initiating the professional relationship. This information should also be repeated later in the relationship if necessary.
2. Psychologists should carefully consider the client's overall ability to afford services early in the relationship, and they should help the client to make a plan for obtaining the services that will be both clinically appropriate and financially feasible. Thus psychologists should be aware of referral sources in the community.
3. Psychologists should routinely perform some services at minimal or no fee as a *pro bono* service to the public.
4. Relationships involving kickbacks, fee-splitting, or payment of commissions for client referrals are unethical.
5. Psychologists should give careful attention to all contractual obligations, understand them, and abide by them.
6. Because psychologists may be held responsible for financial misrepresentations effected in their name by an employee or agent they have designated, they must choose employees with care and supervise them closely.
7. In all debt collection situations, psychologists must know the laws that apply in their jurisidiction and make every effort to behave in a cautious, business-like fashion. They must avoid using their special position or information gained through their professional role to collect debts from clients.

REFERENCE NOTE

1. Fienberg, L. D. Letter from the law firm of Arnold and Porter to Joseph R. Sanders, Administrative Officer for Ethics, American Psychological Association, January 24, 1978.

REFERENCES

Albee, G. W. Does including psychotherapy in health insurance represent a subsidy to the rich from the poor? *American Psychologist*, 1977, *32*, 719–721.

Association for the Advancement of Psychology. *Advance*, 1983, *9*, 6.

Chodoff, P. Psychiatry and the fiscal third party. *American Journal of Psychiatry*, 1978, *135*, 1141–1147.

DiBella, G. A. W. Mastering money issues that complicate treatment: The last taboo. *American Journal of Psychotherapy*, 1980, *24*, 510–522.

Dorken, H. National health insurance: Implications for mental health practitioners. *Professional Psychology*, 1980, *11*, 664–671.

———, and Webb, J. T. 1976 third-party reimbursement experience: An interstate comparison by insurance carrier. *American Psychologist*, 1980, *35*, 355–363.

Dujovne, B. E. Third party recognition of psychological services. *Professional Psychology*, 1980, *11*, 574–581.

Edwards, D. W.; Greene, L. R.; Abramowitz, S. I.; and Davidson, C. V. National health insurance, psychotherapy, and the poor. *American Psychologist*, 1979, *35*, 411–419.

Faustman, W. O. Legal and ethical issues in debt collection strategies of professional psychologists. *Professional Psychology*, 1982, *13*, 208–214.

Grossman, M. Insurance reports as a threat to confidentiality. *American Journal of Psychiatry*, 1971, *128*, 96–100.

Houck, J. B., and Moss, D. M. Pastoral psychotherapy, the fee-for-service model, and professional identity. *Journal of Religion and Health*, 1977, *16*, 172–182.

Jagim, R. D.; Wittman, W. D.; and Noll, J. O. Mental health professionals' attitudes toward confidentiality, privilege, and third-party disclosure. *Professional Psychology*, 1978, *9*, 458–466.

Julius, S. M., and Handal, P. J. Third-party payment and national health insurance: An update on psychology's efforts toward inclusion. *Professional Psychology*, 1980, *11*, 955–964.

Kiesler, C. A., and Pallak, M. S. The Virginia Blues. *American Psychologist*, 1980, *35*, 953–954.

Lovinger, R. J. Obstacles in psychotherapy: Setting a fee in the initial contact. *Professional Psychology*, 1978, *9*, 350–352.

Medical Economics. Psychiatry Fees. *Medical Economics*, October 11, 1982, pp. 232–233.

Meltzer, M. L. Insurance reimbursement: A mixed blessing. *American Psychologist*, 1975, *30*, 1150–1164.

Psychotherapy Finances. 1980 Survey Report. *Psychotherapy Finances*, 1980, *7*, 1–7.

Sharfstein, S. S.; Taube, C. A.; and Goldberg, I. D. Private psychiatry and accountability: A response to the APA Task Force Report on Private Practice. *American Journal of Psychiatry*, 1975, *132*, 43–47.

Stricker, G. Criteria for insurance review of psychological services. *Professional Psychology*, 1979, *10*, 118–122.

Vasile, R. G., and O'Loughlin, M. Initiation of fees in a nonpaying group. *Psychiatric Annals*, 1977, *7*, 77–84.

Psychologists in the Marketplace 7

*Advertising may be described as the science of
arresting the human intelligence long enough to get
money from it.*

Stephen Butler Leacock

The manner in which psychologists present themselves to the public has important ethical implications. Some type of advertising to announce one's services or product is certainly appropriate for educating and informing potential consumers. Some psychologists, however, occasionally use either confusing or frankly deceptive practices in presenting themselves to the public. Ethical violations range from the bizarre to the tacky; moreover, identifying specific clients as "victims" of such infractions is often difficult. Nevertheless, certain violations reflect quite unfavorably on the profession as a whole.

In this chapter, we will review the evolution of today's advertising patterns and attitudes among the professions and, in particular, among psychologists. We will also review both acceptable and unacceptable types of advertisements, while noting both subtle and obvious variations. We will include issues related to products (e.g., books and devices used by psychologists) as well as services offered to individuals, groups, and organizations. Related issues, including ethical problems with referral services, as well as ethics of the "lecture circuit" or "media circuit," will also be discussed (*EP*: 4).

HISTORICAL ISSUES

Historically, numerous professions have considered advertising of services or direct solicitation of clients to be declassé. Psychology professionals

175

in general preferred to view themselves as self-regulating, and they have rejected the notion that advertising would be meaningful to a client. To justify this view, they argued that an advertisement indicated neither skills nor competence, and one should instead rely on the referral of a presumably informed and knowing colleague. Certain types of advertising were considered distasteful or even misleading because they traded on public fears or ignorance related to the services being offered.

A set of "Guidelines for Telephone Directory Listings," published in the *American Psychologist*(APA, 1969), is typical of the attitudes held into the mid-1970s. Psychologists were requested to list only names, highest relevant degree, and some narrow indication of specialization if desired (e.g., "Practice Limited to Children" or "Psychological Consultant to Management"). Psychologists were advised that the type size and face should be uniform, but to avoid boldface type. Listing of multiple specializations was considered "a form of unwarranted self-aggrandizement." So-called "box ads" were to be avoided, as well as using listings in directories outside of the area where one maintained an office.

If a psychologist were opening a new practice two decades ago, a tasteful box notice, written in a formal tone, would have been inserted in the local newspaper: e.g., "Ronald J. MacDonald, Ph.D., announces the opening of his office for the practice of clinical psychology at 555 Main Street in Anytown, U.S.A. Office hours by appointment. 555−1212." This announcement would not have been repeated more than once or twice, although it was considered reasonable to send an "announcement" to colleagues in the community by mail. These views held sway within psychology and many other professions, until they began to be scrutinized by the Federal Trade Commission.

Federal Trade Commission Actions

The rising tide of consumerism in America during the 1960s and 1970s was an important factor in the decision of the Federal Trade Commission and the U.S. Department of Justice to instigate changes in the ways professional associations attempted to regulate their members (Koocher, 1977). In 1972, the Antitrust Division of the Justice Department initiated complaints against various professional associations, including the American Institute of Architects, the American Institute of Certified Public Accountants, and the National Society of Professional Engineers (Rose, Note 1). On June 6, 1975, the United States Supreme Court unanimously struck down the publication of fee schedules by bar associations, effectively terminating attempts to enforce a minimum fee schedule for lawyers (*Goldfarb* v. *Virginia State Bar*, 1975). The Goldfarb ruling (1975) specifies the following: (1) the professions do not enjoy some special form of antitrust exemption; and (2) at least some rules of these associations that directly eliminate competition may be illegal. The Federal Trade Commission actions were specifically concerned with ethical codes that had prohibitions against the following actions: (1) soliciting business by advertising or other means; (2) engaging in price competition; and (3) otherwise engaging in competitive practices. In the case of the medical societies, enforcing the existing ethical code was deemed to create de facto price interference and to frustrate the consumer's right to choose services in an unrestrained fashion (Koocher, 1977).

The government agencies did not intend that psychologists should necessarily adopt the market approaches of used car dealers and carnival barkers, but rather focused on bans against *all* advertising (Nannes, Note 2). Potential harm, which could result from hucksterism and abused advertising, was deemed a valid focus of specific tailored restrictions by professional associations.Claims to "professional dignity" and the imagined need for "uniformity" would no longer constitute a valid basis for limiting advertising by professionals.

The APA Ethics Committee decided to act prospectively, rather than waiting for a call from the Federal Trade Commission. The *Ethical Principles* adopted more recently by the APA suggest that advertising in general will be tolerated, as long as certain basic tenets are adhered to. When bills were introduced in Congress during the Reagan Administration to exempt the professions (including psychology) from the scrutiny of the Federal Trade Commission, they were actively opposed by organized psychology (Association for the Advancement of Psychology, 1982), suggesting a continuing strong consumer orientation among psychologists.

RESTRICTIONS ON ADVERTISEMENTS

The American Bar Association responded to the Goldfarb (1975) case with a proposed revision of their *Code of Professional Responsibility* aimed specifically at publicity and advertising (American Bar Association, 1976). That listing summarizes a variety of issues so well that we have adapted the code in this book for consideration by psychologists, as a detailed accompaniment to the principle on public statements in the APA ethics code. For simplicity, we have changed the word "lawyer" to "psychologist" in the following adaptation of the revised code proposed by the American Bar Association:

> A psychologist should not use or participate in the use of any form of public communication containing a false, fraudulent, misleading, deceptive, or unfair statement or claim. A "public communication" would include, but is not limited to, communication by means of television, radio, motion pictures, newspaper, book, professional journal, or directory. A false, fraudulent, misleading, deceptive, or unfair statement includes a claim that has the following

aspects: (1) contains a misrepresentation of fact; (2) is likely to mislead or deceive because it appears out of context or is only a partial disclosure of relevant facts; (3) contains a client's laudatory comments; (4) is intended to create false or unjustified expectations of favorable results; (5) implies that the psychologist has unusual abilities other than a factual statement of practice limitation or specialization; (6) relates fee information without disclosing all relevant variables; (7) is intended or is likely to appeal to a person's fears, insecurities, or similar emotions; and (8) contains any other representations that might deceive an ordinary, prudent person. In addition, the psychologist should not compensate or give anything of value to a representative of the media in return for professional publicity, unless the existence of such compensation is made known publicly. (*Adapted from*: American Bar Association, 1976, pp. 53–54.)

Interestingly, these procedures are remarkably similar to the points made independently in the *Ethical Principles* (*EP:* 4).

Citation of APA Membership Status

For many years, the APA prohibited mention of a psychologist's membership status in advertising. The rationale was that APA is a scientific and professional organization whose membership practices do not include evaluation of individual credentialing functions. Consequently, mentioning APA membership status would be meaningless to the public and might inappropriately imply APA approval of the psychologist in question. Others argued that APA membership did represent a type of credential. Since APA members are obligated to follow the *Ethical Principles* and since APA enforces these standards through an ethics committee, organizational membership does indeed represent a special qualification that should be called to public attention.

In apparent recognition of the latter viewpoint, the APA Ethics Committee voted in October 1978 to recommend that, should they wish, members be permitted to list their APA membership status in public advertising. The recommendation was adopted as official policy by the Council of Representatives in January 1979. The listing must not, however, suggest that APA membership status implies sponsorship of the psychologist's activities, competence, or specialized qualifications (*EP:* 4b).

Mention of Other Credentials

Various other credentials also exist in psychology, including membership in certain APA divisions that have special requirements, holding a diploma from a postdoctoral accrediting body (e.g., the American Board of Professional Psychology), listing in the *National Register of Health Service Providers in Psychology*, and mention of honorary degrees or other titles. Some controversy exists regarding whether membership or receipt of such recognition even constitutes a credential, since it is often granted in recognition of more valid indicators of professional accomplishments (Koocher, 1979). The general rule-of-thumb should be to list only those credentials that could reasonably be deemed meaningful to the consumer population (e.g., state licensure and earned degrees). Honorary degrees and degrees earned in fields other than psychology should not be listed when presenting oneself as a psychologist. An exception might be degrees acknowledged by the APA to be *equivalent* to a psychology degree, although technically granted in a related field. Degrees earned at institutions that are not regionally accredited or recognized by APA should also not be cited as psychology credentials.

Diplomate status presents a problem because of recent controversies related to specialty status within psychology. The American Board of Professional Psychology (incorporated and recognized by APA in 1947) grants advanced diplomas in recognition of "excellence" in the fields of clinical, counseling, school, and industrial and organizational psychology. An advanced degree, several years of postdoctoral experience, submission of a work sample, and a formal examination are required to earn the diploma. Subsequently, an American Board of Psychological Hypnosis was formed, which awards similar diplomas in clinical or experimental hypnosis, and this Board was also recognized by APA by virtue of listing its diplomates in the official APA directory. More recently, organizations have formed to grant diplomas in forensic psychology, family therapy, psychotherapy, and other specialties or subspecialty fields. APA has not yet recognized any of these newer boards officially for several reasons. First, some question exists concerning what consitutues a valid specialty area in psychology. Second, some of the organizations have had extensive *grandparenting* periods during which diplomas were granted with minimal review of credentials and questionable examinations, if any. Finally, questions have been raised about some of the organizations' procedures in conducting their activities. It is probably not unethical to cite a specialty diploma from an organization unrecognized by APA, but one must be factual in explaining its meaning to clients and others.

To indicate an earned degree from an accredited educational institution, it is most proper to use initials after the holder's name (i.e., John Jones, Ph.D., or Mary Smith, M.D.). Simply using the prefix "Doctor" invites confusion, since the doctorate may be in psychology, divinity, social work, law, or even medicine. In fact there are currently APA members who hold all of these degrees in addition to, or in some cases as equivalent to, a psychology doctorate. Occasionally individuals list themselves as "Ph.D. Cand." or "ABD," presumably to indicate that they are *Ph.D. candidates* or have completed *all but the dissertation*. This type of listing is deceptive and considered ethically inappropriate, since only earned degrees may be listed and potential admission to candidacy does not relate to an earned degree. One certainly should explain the precise nature of one's professional training and credentials directly to clients, but abbreviations that falsely imply actual degrees should not be used.

Similarly, one must strive for factual accuracy in mentioning any professional licenses. Most states have *generic* licensing laws, but a few states have different levels of psychology licensure. In states with generic laws, psychological practitioners are licensed as *psychologists*. Thus it would be inappropriate to list oneself as a *licensed clinical psychologist* or *licensed school psychologist* in such states. The best guide is to look carefully at the certificate or license itself and use only the specific title authorized. Some people may handle the situation by a listing such as the following: "Mary Roe, Psy.D., Licensed Psychologist, Practice Limited to Clinical Psychology." This listing would be both factually accurate and ethically appropriate.

Listing Affiliations

Many psychologists work in more than one agency or practice relationship. For example, a psychologist may be employed by a clinic or corporation full-time, while also conducting a part-time practice or consultation business. Many psychologists serve on boards and committees of corporations, professional organizations, and private agencies. When presenting this information to others, however, such affiliations should not be presented in a way that falsely suggests sponsorship by, or approval of, that organization or agency. In addition, it must also be made clear to clients whether the organization mentioned has any role in their relationship with the psychologist. Consider the following case, for example, of the "all purpose" psychologist:

> **Case 7-1:**   Robert Hartley received a letter from a psychology ethics committee after a neighbor complained of a six-foot-high sign he had erected on his lawn announcing his practice of psychology in four-inch letters. He replied to the committee on stationery that was even more interesting than the sign. The stationery was headed as follows: "Dr. Robert Hartley, Ph.D., Consulting Clinical Psychologist and Sexologist." Three-color printing ran down the side of the page listing the services that Hartley offered, including the following:

Psychotherapy
    Adults, Adolescents, and Children
    Individuals and Group
    Hypnosis
    Lay Analysis

Psychological Testing
  Neuropsychological Evaluation
  Personality Assessment
  Intellectual Evaluation
  Diagnostic Evaluation
  Vocational Evaluation
Counseling
  Sex and Divorce
  Marriage Enrichment Courses
Management Consulting
  Executive Leadership, Development, and Assessment
  Personnel Evaluations

Across the bottom of the page, the following institutions were listed: "The Mid-American Hypnosis Clinic, XYZ Learning Disabilities Center, Sex Counseling Institute, the Affective Education Foundation, and the Plainville Marriage Enrichment Center."

For Hartley to list himself with the prefix "Dr." and the suffix "Ph.D." is redundant and simply in poor taste. The six-foot sign and the three-color stationery were equally inappropriate. Moreover, an investigation revealed that Hartley's Ph.D. was in sociology and from a university that was not regionally accredited. He did hold a valid master's degree in psychology, but the context in which he listed his doctorate was inappropriate. The organizations listed across the stationery had only two things in common: they were all headquartered in his office, and he was the sole employee of each. When asked about his training relative to the services listed, Hartley proudly cited a long chain of briefly held jobs and workshops he had attended, covering virtually all of the services mentioned. The training, of course, was rather shallow in most of the areas mentioned, creating a substantial competency question (which will be discussed in detail in Chapter 9). Although Hartley's presentation-of-self was rather cloddish, and he was truly ignorant of his infractions, the potential for public deception in his style of performance is obvious.

Case 7–2: Roger Snob, Ed.D., was in full-time private practice, but volunteered a few hours a week to supervise a practicum student at State University. In exchange for his time, Dr. Snob was given a largely symbolic appointment as an Adjunct Professor at the university. He promptly had new stationery printed including his new title and used it for all of his professional correspondence.

Case 7–3: C. U. Infer, Psy.D., worked at the Northeast Mental Health Institute, a prestigious, nationally known facility, on a research project that lasted for two years. He was a licensed psychologist and was permitted to see private clients in his office at the Institute during hours when he was technically off-duty from the project. Many clients assumed that they were being treated by a clinical staff member of the Institute and under its auspices. When he moved away at the end of the project, several of his former clients were surprised to find that the Institute had no records of their treatment and could not easily provide continuity of care for them.

Dr. Snob's misrepresentation is one of pride and possibly ignorance. Although he cannot be accused of demonstrably harming any individual, he is attempting to trade on the reputation of the university to enhance his own status. In reality, his relationship to the university is rather remote and does not have actual relevance to most of his professional work. Dr. Infer, on the other hand, may mislead clients to their later detriment. He is also trading on the reputation of an agency, although his actual affiliation is quite different from the one clients may be led to believe. Some clients may have chosen to use his services in part because of the presumed coverage, back-up, or expertise represented by the Institute. It is inappropriate for Infer to remain silent. Rather, he is obligated to inform others of incorrect impressions or erroneous conclusions.

Testimonials

It is certainly gratifying when a client values one's services or has praise for one's professional efforts, but it is not appropriate to cite such laudatory comments in advertisements for professional services. Such statements may be taken out of context or reflect value judgments from which the public cannot reasonably be expected to draw valid generalizations.

One exception in which testimonials are acceptable in advertising includes book promotions, where excerpts from book reviews and adoption lists are sometimes used. The rationale for permitting specific use of testimonials in this exceptional circumstance is linked to the type of client involved and the presumption that the psychologist permitting the use of such material will do so fairly. Unlike the potential client who seeks the help of a psychologist in a period of emotional distress, it is assumed that the selection of a book can be made relatively dispassionately. The reader is more likely to evaluate testimonials from a critical standpoint than is the troubled client. Nevertheless, the psychologist who uses these testimonials must be assiduously careful not to take the comments out of context or to use them in a misleading fashion. If such quotes are used improperly, they will probably be detected eventually. In fact, permission should be sought prior to the use of such quotes, if they must be used at all.

In recent years, using nonflamboyant testimonial statements to advertise nonclinical products or services has become an acceptable practice in general. Continuing education courses or workshops and new test instruments being marketed to professional audiences are two examples.

Testimonials do not substitute for accuracy or replace factual descriptive advertisement content, and they should never be misleading. The professional community is presumed more likely to evaluate critically such endorsements.

Product Endorsements

Product endorsements by psychologists are not considered appropriate, especially when the psychologist is rewarded or compensated in some way for the endorsement. The rationale is twofold. First, if the product is psychological in nature (e.g., a relaxation tape, biofeedback apparatus, or assessment technique), its merit should stand on a foundation of empirical research, rather than on personal testimony. Second, if the product is not psychological in nature (e.g., a brand of toothpaste, pasta, or soft drink), the psychologist is using his or her professional stature in an irrelevant realm to endorse a product in a way that may be deceptive and misleading to the public. If a psychologist were to have a dual career, such as performing psychotherapy by day and announcing television commercials in the evening, the circumstances might theoretically be ethically appropriate, as long as the psychologist's role (i.e., by day) was not mentioned or otherwise employed as a means to influence the public to buy products in the evening.

As noted earlier, this principle especially holds true when the psychologist has played a major role in the development of a particular device, book, or other product. Often one may be blind to this type of difficulty when personal involvement is substantial. Nonetheless, every effort should be made to ensure that commercial products offered for public sale are presented in a professional, scientifically acceptable, and factually informative manner (EP: 4e). The use of due caution, scientific modesty, and avoidance of sensationalism or undocumented claims will help prevent such careless ethical infractions (EP: 4g).

Many illustrations of problems in this area will also be found in the following chapter (Chapter 8) under the topic of "self-help" books and similar products.

Tackiness

Occasionally psychologists will engage in advertising practices that, although not obviously unethical, hold the profession up to ridicule or are otherwise in poor taste. Certainly Dr. Hartley (Case 7−1) showed such tendencies with his tri-color stationery and lawn billboard, but other, more bizarre examples also exist.

Case 7–4: In anticipation of a lecture and workshop program by two psychologists who had written a self-help book for mass consumption, their publisher took out a full-page ad in a large metropolitan newspaper. The ad, describing the psychologists as "The Butch Cassidy and Sundance Kid of Psychology," included a detailed cartoon depicting the two in cowboy outfits, with guns drawn, charging over the "boot hill" of psychology with grave markers inscribed "Freud, Adler, and Jung." It is unclear whether the goal of the ad was to portray them as "straight shooters" or psychological "outlaws."

The psychologists were reportedly embarrassed by the ads, claiming that they had not been consulted. On the other hand, they had certainly not exercised much care in monitoring how their names were being used.

Case 7–5: Consider the following newspaper advertisement:
The name's Jack Lame,
Psychotherapy's the game.
Call for appointment:
Jack Lame, Ph.D.
555-1212

While not unethical per se, Dr. Lame is certainly not doing much to maintain a professional image or to demonstrate a sense of responsibility that would reassure clients and colleagues. Such advertisements imply a lack of sensitivity to or awareness of public reaction. Whether the author of such an ad could also be sensitive to the emotions and problems of others remains an open question.

CONTENTS OF ACCEPTABLE ADVERTISEMENTS

In general, it is appropriate to advertise in the print and broadcast media, as long as the tone and content of the advertisement is appropriate. Specific examples of unethical and inappropriate public statements and advertisements will be discussed later in this chapter, but the following samples illustrate acceptable advertisements.

Case 7–6: The following notice appreared weekly in a metropolitan newspaper:
Harrison Troll, Ph.D.
Licensed Psychologist
Ph.D. in Clinical Psychology, granted by Western State University, 1979
Specializing in the treatment of children and adolescents
Convenient office hours
Sliding-fee scale
Health insurance accepted
Family therapy available
24-hour answering service
Call 555–6666

Case 7-7: The following is the text of a radio announcement aired in a major metropolitan area: "Mary Okay, Ph.D., is a clinical psychologist specializing in marital therapy. She is opening her practice in Centerville at the Glenwood Mall, with ample free parking and convenient evening office hours. If you are having marital problems, she may be able to help. Call 555-2211 for an appointment."

Assuming that the facts are accurate and truthful and that Dr. Troll and Dr. Okay are indeed qualified to perform the services they list, there is nothing wrong with these notices. Any information that might be of interest to a consumer, including facility in speaking a foreign language, application of special techniques (e.g., behavioral treatment of obesity, relaxation training, parent consultation, or hypnosis for habit control), convenience of office location, availability of evening hours, or other facts would be permissible (*EP:* 4a). One must be careful not to mix facts that may be misleading, however. In Chapter 6, for example, the fact that some psychological services (e.g., child custody evaluations) are not covered by health insurance was raised. Therefore, if Dr. Troll noted that he specialized in child custody work, he should not simultaneously mention that he accepts health insurance. Likewise, if Dr. Troll cannot accept low-fee clients in his practice, he should drop the reference to a sliding-fee scale. Such matters can be discussed, of course, in a first session or telephone consultation, but to give a false impression in the advertisement is inappropriate even if the situation is later remedied without harm to the client.

If a psychologist intends to advertise, several precautionary steps should be taken. First, one should consult with colleagues to obtain informal advice about the nature and content of the plan, as well as a sense of community standards. Second, one should not delegate the details of the advertising to others, especially those with little understanding of psychological ethics. Third, one must proofread or carefully monitor the final product before it is distributed or broadcast. Finally, a psychologist should retain a copy of the advertisement, whether in print, film, or tape recording. He or she will then have documentation of exactly what was communicated if questions are asked later. This can be especially important if the broadcast media are used. We know of instances in which psychologists, anxious to take advantage of liberalized advertising policies, hired public relations firms. All were unhappy with the flashy packages created for them, but they had to pay the high fees anyway.

Yellow Pages Advertisements

Listing oneself in the classified pages of the telephone directory presents an interesting subset of problems. In part, these emanate from the fact that the telephone companies are interested in selling space and are relatively unwise in the ways of professional ethics. Little is known by way of scientific data about whether or not telephone directory advertising generates client referrals. For instance, if one were searching for a skilled surgeon or trial lawyer and relied solely on a box ad in the telephone directory, the consequences might indeed be unfortunate. Still, telephone directories are highly visible and attract the attention—and occasionally the ire—of colleagues, if not clients.

Some general suggestions should be considered when a psychologist does decide to list in the directory. First, the listing should be only under the heading *psychologist*. Occasionally individuals will want to list as *counselor*, *psychotherapist*. This is not unethical, but we believe that if one's primary identity is as a psychologist that should be the sole listing. Some psychologists do have advanced degrees in other disciplines and may be licensed to practice medicine, are members of the bar, or certified public accountants. In such cases, they may also list themselves under the appropriate respective headings in the classified directory. Second, he or she must be qualified to perform the services listed, if any, including holding licenses in the appropriate geographic areas. In some geographic areas, directories are subdivided in metropolitan and suburban volumes and occasionally state lines are involved (e.g., a psychologist living in Philadelphia may also have an office in southern New Jersey, or a Virginia psychologist may also treat clients in Maryland and in the District of Columbia). Third, while the psychologist may list in different directories, a bona fide office address should be listed that is reasonably convenient to the area served by the directory. Fourth, the other guidelines previously discussed also apply equally to telephone directory ads, with a special caution. Because a directory may have a relatively long shelf-life, any promises made in the advertisement (e.g., specific fees) may have to be honored for an extended period.

Some controversy exists about style matters in telephone directory listings. For example, should box advertisements be permitted; or, if directories have color capability, should psychologists be permitted to run multi-colored ads? Taste, rather than ethics, is the issue, as long as the ad is otherwise appropriate. In a debate among members of the APA ethics committee several years ago, one respected psychologist argued that, for the sake of homogeneity, only names, degrees, and telephone numbers should be permitted. A younger colleague replied that if homogeneity were the issue, why not simply require every psychologist who chooses to advertise in the directory to buy a full-page space?

Another controversy concerns individuals, who either are not psychologists or are not licensed as psychologists, listing themselves in directories as psychologists. In response to an official request from APA (Pallak, Note 3), the Director of Directory Services for American Telephone and Telegraph made two points. First, no evidence indicated that such inappropriate listings occur in a great number of cases. Second, dealing with this issue is the duty and responsibility of the state licensing authority, not the phone company. He also noted the following:

Should a licensing authority inform us that our directories contain the listing of a customer who requires a license but who is unlicensed, we will notify the customer at an appropriate time. If the customer has not by that time obtained a valid license and refuses to remove his/her listing or advertisement, we will advise the licensing authority. In any event, we cannot remove the representation unless ordered to do so by the customer, or by other appropriate legal action. (Hancharik, Note 4)

UNACCEPTABLE ADVERTISING

The range of unacceptable advertising is rather broad, encompassing misrepresentation, guarantees or promises of favorable outcome, appeals to client fears or vulnerability, claims to unique or "one of a kind" services, statements critical of competitive providers, and direct solicitation of individual clients (*EP*: 4b). Consider, for example, the following cases:

Case 7—8:   Martha Newly, Psy. D., a recently licensed psychologist, who attempted to establish her private practice quickly, took out a full page ad in the local newspaper to announce an "office open house," complete with a visit from "Psycho, the Crazy Clown," free balloons imprinted with her address and phone number, a "first session free" coupon, and a door prize of "twenty free sessions for you or the significant other of your choice."

Case 7—9:   The New Wave Underground Army kidnapped a bus full of school children and held them at gunpoint for several hours before the police were able to negotiate the children's release. Tym Lee Buck, Ph.D., drove to a shopping center parking lot where the children were to be reunited with their parents. He passed out handbills describing himself as an expert on hostage psychology. The material included the following: "It is a well-known fact that hostages can suffer serious emotional delayed reactions. Preventative psychotherapy for your child is a must." His address and phone number were also listed.

Case 7—10:   The advertisement read: " 'You'll just have to live with it!' Is that what you've been told? It's not true! New techniques available at the Southside Psychological Development Center will help you master your chronic problems, whether they be bad habits, chronic pain, or relationship problems. Don't delay, call today! 555—9999."

All of these cases have a common element that could be termed lack of a professional perspective, poor taste, or simply gross insensitivity. Each case also has several unique and difficult aspects. Dr. Newly represents a type of colleague who has been categorized as "a Green Menace" (Keith-Spiegel, Note 5). In essence, she is a relatively inexperienced psychologist in a huge hurry, making ethical blunders in an implusive effort to start her practice. Fortunately, such colleagues are usually amenable to constructive, educative approaches to their ethical misconduct. Psycho, the "Crazy Clown," certainly does little to enhance the image of the profession, while tending to make a mockery of people with emotional problems. In addition, the offer of free treatment sessions via a door prize belies the careful assessment and planning that should accompany any course of competently delivered psychological services. Finally, the "first session free" coupons create a problem akin to the *bait and switch* routines used by unscrupulous salespeople. In the *bait and switch* scam, the potential client, who is drawn into the store or potential sale by an attractive offer, is encouraged to switch to an item or service that is more profitable to the seller. In psychological service delivery, a first interview is often critical to the formation of a working rapport between psychologist and client. Often the client will share emotion-laden material and form an attachment to the psychologist, which may predispose the client to continue the relationship. In this sense, the offer of a free first session represents a type of bait with implications that the client will seldom recognize. There is nothing wrong with offering to waive the fee for a session. Many psychologists, however, will waive the fee, if they decide that they will not be able to work with a client after the first session; of course, this is quite different from using a no-fee-for-the-first-session advertisement used as bait to attract clients.

Dr. Buck is even more obnoxious in his behavior, since he is trading on the fears and vulnerabilities of people. He may be correct in anticipating psychological problems among the hostage children, but his presumption that virtually all will need "preventive psychotherapy" is ludicrous, and his style is offensive. He is also soliciting individual clients directly and personally, which is unethical for any psychologist to do, even when emotional appeals are not used. His behavior and the circumstances under which he approached the families actually seem to create a potential for increasing the psychological stress on the strained families.

The advertisement from the Southside Psychological Development Center seems folksy and well-meaning, but it also appears to promise or ensure the likelihood of a favorable outcome. Aside from the inherent misleading quality of its tone, the ad implies success with recalcitrant problems and suggests the application of some novel or unique technique not available elsewhere. In fact, the Center included a group of well-intentioned, but overzealous, psychologists trained in behavioral techniques. The comparative desirability of their services and the "new techniques" were more representative of their hopes, rather than documented scientific claims. The ad also has one additional flaw, because it did not name the individuals responsible for the operation. Qualified psychologists should not hide behind a corporate or group practice title, and it would be preferable (in fact, legally required in some states) for the names of the psychologists to be listed along with the name of the Center. The final problem with this ad is the implication that effective treatment will be available for virtually any problem at the Southside Center. This is the same type of problem evident in Dr. Hartley's (*Case 7–1*) situation, since the range of effective services offered at the center is actually more narrow than the advertisement implies.

Direct Solicitation

Besides the blatant behavior of Dr. Buck in *Case 7–9*, it is important to recognize why the solicitation of individual clients is proscribed. The central issue is the potential vulnerability of the client, relative to the psychologist. Vulnerability may include client insecurities, emotional problems, naivete, lack of information, or even awe of the professional. The psychologist's special expertise and knowledge are usually accorded a degree of respect or deference that may predispose clients to follow their advice and recommendations, even if this means changing longstanding patterns of behavior. Psychologists must recognize this social influence or power and consider its use carefully. Advice must be presented with due respect to the limitations of our scientific knowledge and the recognition of a client's freedom to choose a lifestyle or course of action. Recommendations must always be tailored to an understanding of the client and his or her unique life situation.

A direct solicitation may pit the expert's advantage directly against the potential client's insecurities and fears. It may capitalize on a client's ignorance or social naivete. Although, there is nothing wrong with a psychologist's announcing general availability to the community through advertising, the direct solicitation of individual clients has considerable potential for abuse and distress to the object of the pitch.

> **Case 7–11:** Max Pusher, M.D., a psychiatrist well known for his syndicated newspaper column, was invited to teach an extension course at Central State University, dealing with topics on anxiety, tension, and depression. A huge audience was attracted by his name and reputation. Dr. Pusher was accompanied by several assistants wearing colored armbands who distributed brochures about Dr. Pusher's private clinic and other private workshops he offered. In addition, some of the assistants approached selected students, saying: "You look troubled. Perhaps this material will be helpful to you."

This approach was clearly upsetting to many of the students approached, and it would certainly play upon the insecurities of others. This approach seems little more than an appeal to fear as a means to recruit clients in the guise of a public lecture.

Similar to the case of testimonials discussed earlier in this chapter, there are some tolerable exceptions to the general prohibition on solicitation of individual clients. These exceptions usually apply when the client is not an individual person, but an agency, business firm, or other organizational entity. Consider, for example, the following cases:

> **Case 7–12:** Edward Efficacy, Ph.D., an industrial and organizational psychologist, has developed a well-validated assessment center program (see Bray, 1976, 1977, for an explanation of assessment centers) to evaluate pharmacists. He pre-

pares a factually accurate descriptive brochure and mails it to potential employers of pharmacists and colleges of pharmacy, offering his consultative and evaluative services.

Case 7–13:   Karen Kinder, Psy.D., is trained as a school psychologist and has developed a kindergarten screening instrument with good reliability and predictive validity. She has appropriate information printed in pamphlet form and mails these brochures with cover letters offering to conduct training workshops to superintendents of schools and directors of special education in school systems throughout her locale.

While the clients approached by Dr. Efficacy and Dr. Kinder are indeed being contacted as individuals, they are not in the same relative position of vulnerability as an individual person. Employers, schools, or other organizations will usually be in a better position to know their own needs for such services, and the nature of the services offered are quite different from individual offers of psychotherapy. (For the sake of illustration, we are assuming that the programs and instruments used by Dr. Kinder and Dr. Efficacy are properly validated and reasonably useful. Issues related to assessment in general are relegated to Chapter 4 in this book.) Under some circumstances, therapeutic services might also be offered in this manner.

Case 7–14:   Ethyl Fluid, Ed.D., plans to approach various large corporations to encourage their purchase of alcoholism counseling services for their employees. She will offer to provide a team of properly trained clinicians to staff an in-house clinic at each company's plant. Employees would be seen on a self-referral basis, with appropriate confidentiality safeguards for counseling. Dr. Fluid cites advantages of the program to include convenience for employees and improved conditions of employment, with a possible reduction in alcohol-related work problems and absenteeism. She presents this plan in letters to presidents and personnel directors of the companies.

If Dr. Fluid observes other ethical obligations related to providing the treatment she proposes, this type of solicitation presents no problem. No outrageous claims are made, and each company is obviously free to evaluate its own need for the program, as well as other alternatives. Client freedom is assured, and no one is pressured individually.

WHAT POTENTIAL CLIENTS THINK

Minimal research has been done to document the impact of psychologists' advertising on potential clients, but the results of one particular study are interesting (Keith-Spiegel et al., Note 6). Keith-Spiegel et al. surveyed 164 California college students who had already completed at least one psychology course. The students, presented with 13 sets of five brief ads each, were asked to imagine that they needed psychological services either for themselves or for someone close to them. They were told to imagine that they were to consult a telephone directory and find the sets of five ads in question. Within each set, they were to indicate the rank order of their choices of whom to call first, after reading all five ads in the set. Within each set of ads, various factors were altered. For example: in some ads, the psychologist was listed as Dr. Jones, instead of J. Jones, Ph.D. Some listed professional affiliations (e.g., APA member); others listed all earned degrees (e.g., B.A., M.A., Ph.D.); still others included slogans (e.g., "the psychologist who cares") or offers (e.g., "no charge for first appointment").

In formulating the study, the investigators had been concerned that flashy, hard-sell, or gimmicky ads might be highly rated in contrast to more simple, professionally dignified ones. Although the data and analyses were not conclusive, the trends were both interesting and somewhat reassuring. Degrees definitely made a difference in the rankings: ads using a "Ph.D." ranked higher than those ads without it, although the suffix "M.A." was rated more impressive than the appellation "Dr." The dual listing of M.A. and Ph.D. was most favored, which suggests that the public is impressed with the number of degrees, but may not realize that most doctoral-level psychologists also have masters degrees or their equivalent.

Certification, licensure, and memberships in professional associations also tended to enhance selection potential. Personalized "grabber" lines (e.g., "the psychologist who cares"), however, did not have special appeal. Particular demographic variables, however, did seem influential. Responses to the sex, ethnicity of the name, and even the peculiarity of the psychologist's name were varied. For example, participants identifying themselves as Jewish on the questionnaire seemed more likely to choose a psychologist named Cohen or Goldstein, rather than one named Caldwell or Thomas. Women participants in general ranked women psychologists higher, while a peculiar name (e.g., Fabian Tuna) reduced the likelihood of a high ranking.

When fees were specified, a Ph.D. psychologist with a low fee was chosen most often, and an M.A. psychologist with a low fee was chosen rather than a Ph.D. psychologist with a very high fee. On the other hand, a doctoral-level psychologist was usually chosen rather than a masters-level psychologist when the M.A. person's fee was only slightly lower. Lowest ranking of all was the person listed with no degree, even though the fee was modest. Ads with additional descriptive or factual information tended to be selected over either less-detailed ads or ads that used lines with emotional appeal. In general, a conservative ad listing degree, license, specialty, and the phrase "reasonable rates" seemed to do the best. Such lines as "money-back guarantee" rated very low.

Ads offering a "free consultation" were extremely popular, but would be clearly unethical, as explained earlier in this chapter. The ethical issue is not the free service per se, but the promise of free service as an inducement to a professional relationship. Appeals to informality, such as "hangups are my business," did not do well, and visual illustrations or promises of effective results also did not impress the college student sample.

Except for the preference for the "free session" ads, the students seemed to select in accordance with currently ethical guidelines, even though these guidelines were not presented to the students. Factual detail and informational material had the most striking impact. Interestingly, diplomate status, as mentioned earlier in this chapter, did have a favorable impact when listed. No student queried had any idea what diplomate status entailed, but most thought that it "sounded good." It seems as though this segment of the general public has expectations regarding professional behavior in the marketplace that are consistent with ethical decorum.

GROWTH GROUPS AND EDUCATIONAL PROGRAMS

One type of psychological service that has often skirted the border between ethical and clearly unethical behavior in marketing issues are *growth* or *enrichment* seminars and workshops. When does a course or workshop become psychotherapy? Is there a difference between a seminar, which has a psychotherapeutic impact on an individual, and psychotherapy, which is conducted in the form of a seminar? Although psychotherapy and related ethical matters are discussed primarily in Chapter 5, psychologists in general are not permitted to solicit clients for therapy. May one then solicit clients for a psychotherapeutic course? Consider, for example, the following cases:

> **Case 7–15:**   The Happy Karma Institute under the direction of Harry Creeshna, Psy.D., frequently advertises seminars in "Personal Power and Creative Change" and "Relaxation Systems." Clients are solicited with direct mail advertising and told that the seminars teach "increasing harmony in interpersonal relationships, self-analysis, Sullivanian analysis, biofeedback, autogenics, deep muscle relaxation, and guided fantasy." Dr. Creeshna is described in the mailings as having been trained in psychological techniques and esoteric disciplines.

> **Case 7–16:**   Communication Associates, Inc., advertises a seminar entitled, "Introduction to Personal Growth." The format is described as lecture and experiential group participation, including "psychodrama, confrontation, gestalt, assertive, encounter-transactional analysis, and training" techniques. The ad appears weekly in a metropolitan newspaper.

> **Case 7–17:**   Psycho-Tron Laboratory Learning Systems, Inc., directed by Lester Clone, Ph.D., uses a business card with an optical illusion imprinted on it. Instructions on the card explain that viewing the illusion in a certain way is a sign of an inflexible problem-solving style requiring "cognitive reprogramming" that can be obtained through an individualized course at Psycho-Tron.

Giving didactic or explanatory lectures about therapeutic techniques is entirely different from applying techniques intended to achieve psychotherapeutic results in the context of a course or seminar. In fact, certain therapeutic techniques, such as group confrontations, can have a harmful impact on some individuals. Furthermore, individuals with serious somatic problems might seek psychologically based treatments, such as relaxation training, instead of first obtaining proper medical care. Without appropriate screening and follow-up, the eclectic seminar topics resemble random, indiscriminate episodes that play with legitimate therapy techniques. These seminars may be educational, but they are also potentially harmful if targeted at the lay public in a commercial venture. In addition, the promises or claims alluded to, especially in the ads from the Karma Institute and Psycho-Tron Laboratory, are inane and misrepresentational. Sullivanian analysis cannot be taught adequately in a few weeks of a group seminar, and "cognitive reprogramming" seems to be a vague term conjured up by an Orwellian psychologist. Communication Associates mention "training" in their ad, but they target it to the lay public. Whom are they intending to train for what? (Ethical problems associated with group enhancement programs in academic settings are discussed in Chapter 10.)

Those psychologists oriented toward group enhancement of the human potential should, of course, fully explore their goals. If these goals are therapeutic in nature, psychologists must use appropriate professional cautions and must not solicit individual clients. If their goals are educative, then the didactic nature of the course or seminar must be stressed, and it must be clear to all concerned that the program is not intended to be either therapy or therapeutic training. Insurance companies will not cover such non-health-related services, as discussed in the previous chapter.

REFERRAL SERVICES

In some parts of the country, professional associations operate a service in which callers can specify a needed type of psychological consultation or intervention and be given the names of potential providers. In some cases, similar services are offered by private practitioners, community agencies, or clinics. Consider, for example, the following operations:

Case 7–18:   The Northeast State Psychological Association offers a referral service to its members for the benefit of the public. It developed in response to frequent telephone inquiries from the public. Any members of the Association who are licensed, carry professional liability insurance, and have no ethical complaints pending against them may be listed. A file containing provider information, including the availability of a sliding-fee scale, foreign language skills, specialty training, and so forth, is maintained. When a person calls seeking a referral, a message is taken and referred to a doctoral-level psychologist who is hired as the coordinator of the service. The coordinator contacts the caller to establish the nature of the request and provides three names of psychologists whose skills, location, and availability fit the client's needs. No fees are charged to either party, and the service is paid for through general membership dues. Often the calls are requests for speakers or for general information, rather than for referral to a practitioner.

Case 7−19:   Psychotherapy Assistance is a psychotherapist-finding service run by three psychologists in a large metropolitan area. They attempt to match potential clients with psychotherapists on the basis of many factors, including fees charged, areas of specialization, treatment style, and so forth. Psychologists who wish to receive referrals are interviewed regarding their practice by the service operators. All psychologists must be appropriately licensed and carry liability insurance. Clients who phone the service are given a diagnostic interview and charged the usual and customary rate for that service. They are then given the names of two or more therapists recommended by the service, if psychotherapy is recommended. The only fees are those paid by the client.

Case 7−20:   Nadia Nerk is an unemployed real estate agent who has opened a storefront service known as "Shrink Finders." Clients pay Nerk a fee and are offered access to a set of videotaped interviews with psychotherapists, recorded in their offices. Clients may look through as many tapes as they wish and will then be given the names and addresses of any therapists whose tapes impress them. The therapists have paid Nerk $100 for making their tape and $10 per month to keep the tape "on file" in her office.

The three referral services listed all have one feature in common: namely, they provide clients with the names of psychologists. Presumably, they also advertise their services in telephone directories, the media, or elsewhere. Certainly the same advertising obligations that bind psychologists as individual or group practitioners should also bind the operators of such referral services.

The service run by the state psychological association (*Case 7−18*) does not charge any fees and is intended as a public service. Clients are advised that the service is not endorsing any particular provider, but rather is giving a list of qualified practitioners who seem to meet the client's stated needs. The rationale for listing only members may be supported on the basis that the organization can enforce only consumer ethical complaints on members. Clients unable to pay the usual practitioner fees are referred to those who offer a sliding-fee scale or to community clinics. The service is paid for through general association funds for public benefit.

Psychotherapy Assistance (*Case 7−19*) represents a fee-for-service matching program. A clinical service is rendered in the form of an evaluation, and referral is then made to practitioners who are presumably known to the referer. Supposedly the matching is more individualized and based on clinical judgments of psychologists, which is not possible under the more limited state association system. No fees are charged to the providers, which is appropriate unless the question of *fee-splitting* (see Chapter 6) is raised. Care must be taken, however, to be certain that any advertising undertaken is appropriate and responsible.

The Shrink-Finder (*Case 7–20*) service seems questionable for several reasons. The catchy name for the services and the videotaped interviews raise the potential that superficial data are being promulgated as the basis for formulating important decisions. No efforts are made to tailor the service to client needs or to otherwise introduce professional judgment or advice. Although no advertising has been presented for the service, one wonders what form advertising would take and how appropriate it might be. Most troubling, however, are the financial arrangements. Although the providers do not pay a commission to Ms. Nerk, they do pay a fee in consideration of receiving referrals (*EP*: 6d). This is clearly an ethical violation, as discussed in detail in Chapter 6.

While referral services can be helpful to both clients and the public in general, their operations determine their ethical propriety. Advertising and financial aspects of the operations may raise ethical problems. Any psychologists considering involvement with such a service should be quite careful about first exploring all of these issues. The legitimate economic needs of the practitioner should never take precedence over client needs.

OTHER PUBLIC STATEMENTS

Psychologists will often have the opportunity to be heard in public. Advertising is only one such avenue; another is the media, as addressed in Chapter 8. Other opportunities to influence the public occur while teaching, as discussed in Chapter 13, or while giving public lectures. Potential opportunities for misrepresentation, striving for personal gain, causing distress, or embarrassing the profession and one's colleagues abound. It is important to consider the impact of any public pronouncements made in the role of psychologist before presenting them.

Presentation-of-Self

It is always flattering to hear one's expertise celebrated in public, but it is also important to be represented accurately and objectively. Psychologists are trained as professionals with a scientific base of knowledge. It is just as important, therefore, for them to be honest and objective about the limitations of their knowledge as about their credentials. If introduced incorrectly or in a misleading manner, even if well intentioned, the psychologist has a duty to correct the misinformation promptly (*EP*: 4j).

Case 7−21:   Hank Puffery, Psy.D., held an adjunct academic appointment as an Assistant Professor in a large medical school. Several documents, including a lecture program and a grant application, listed his academic rank as Associate Professor or Professor. His failure to correct these inaccurate listings for several months ultimately led to the loss of his academic appointment on the basis of professional misrepresentation.

We do not know for certain whether Dr. Puffery's inaccurate listings were intentional or inadvertent, but his superiors at the medical school claimed that he did not correct the errors despite many opportunities to do so. Many other examples of presentation-of-self problems concerning the public appear in Chapter 8, but encounters with problems may also occur between psychologist and client alone.

Case 7−22:   After an evaluation by Roger Fallic, Ed.D., a competently trained sex-therapist, the client was informed that he could probably be helped with a treatment plan involving at least six months of office visits. This prediction, according to Dr. Fallic, was based on the normative patterns documented in his treatment of clients with similar problems. When the client balked at the $100 per hour fee, Dr. Fallic commented: "You really ought to come up with it somehow, since I'm the only one who can really help you in your current state."

Perhaps Fallic did have a good treatment plan for his client, which was well validated and potentially quite effective. The implication that no one else could provide effective treatment, however, is probably false. The high fee charged and the apparent unwillingness of Dr. Fallic to reduce it are not actually unethical, but the statement, with its grandiose implications and Dr. Fallic's apparent unwillingness to make a less costly referral, represent serious problems.

Embarrassing Others

It is not unethical to be a fool or an abrasive lout, but such behavior becomes embarrassing to the profession when the perpetrator is identified as a psychologist (see, for example, the case of Ditz Dervish in the next chapter— Case 8−5). At the same time, public comments presented in a sarcastic or offensive manner can easily exceed the bounds of ethical propriety. Chapter 11 deals with these issues concerning individual colleagues, but consider the following class action violations implied in these comments overheard in public lectures or meetings:

"Psychoanalysis really never helps anyone do anything except enhance the person's own narcissism."

"Social workers really aren't trained to do deep therapy and ought to be supervised by psychologists or psychiatrists for most direct service work."

Remark to a group of students in abnormal psychology: "Okay, what crazies did we read about this week? Any nominations for psychotic of the week based on people you know on campus?"

These overgeneralizations, offensive comments, casual demeaning of people with problems, and similar remarks tend to hurt the entire profession. The following chapter will pursue these matters in more detail, using the print and broadcast media as context. It is important to remember, however, that other public arenas are important as well. When lecturing, testifying before a legislative or judicial body, or making any statement for public consumption, one must consider the impact of one's words and style carefully, especially when the public is looking at a person identified as a *psychologist*.

SUMMARY GUIDELINES

1. Recent changes in the attitudes of professionals toward advertising now make certain types of advertising permissible, but advertisements must be firmly based on facts of meaningful and valid interest to the potential consumer.

2. One must be particularly careful when listing affiliations, degrees, and other data to ensure that the public is not misled, confused, or otherwise deceived.

3. Testimonials or quotes from *satisfied users* are usually prohibited and unethical.

4. The direct solicitation of individuals as clients is also usually prohibited, as opposed to mass solicitation through media advertising.

5. Psychologists who serve organizational or industrial clients may be entitled to some broader latitude than those who serve individuals, lay groups, and families; however, they too must use factual, validity-based criteria in their advertising claims.

6. Fees mentioned in advertisements must be honored for the reasonable duration of the announcement.

7. It is inappropriate in general to offer a *free* or *no charge* appointment in advance as an inducement to attract new clients.

8. Psychologists offering courses or seminars must carefully discriminate the difference between educational and therapeutic programs. These distinctions must be made clear to the potential participants (Boring, 1972). Programs intended as *educational* should not be billed as therapeutic, and when claims of therapeutic efficacy are made, they must be supported by valid data.

9. Referral services may be run in an ethically appropriate manner, but this requires careful attention to detail and ethical sensitivity.

10. Psychologists must carefully consider their style of presentation-of-self and their public statements, whether or not advertising is directly involved.

REFERENCE NOTES

1. Rose, J. Remarks prepared for delivery before the Antitrust Law Committee of the Bar Association of the District of Columbia's 12th Annual Symposium on Trade Association Law and Practice, Washington, D.C., February 24, 1976.

2. Nannes, J. M. Remarks before the Virginia Association of Professions, Annandale, Virginia, January 13, 1976.

3. Letter from Michael S. Pallak, Executive Office, American Psychological Association, to Edward Hancharik, Director of Directory Services, American Telephone and Telegraph Company, dated January 22, 1980.

4. Letter from Edward Hancharik, Director of Directory Services, American Telephone and Telegraph Company, to Michael S. Pallak, Executive Officer, American Psychological Association, dated February 1, 1980.

5. Keith-Spiegel, P. *Moral conundrums, shibboleths, and gordian knots: current issues in ethical standards for psychologists.* Presidential Address to the Western Psychological Association, Sacramento, California, 1982.

6. Keith-Spiegel, P.; Segar, P.; and Tomison, G. *What potential clients think of various modes of advertising.* Paper presented at the 8th Annual Meeting of the American Psychological Association, Toronto, 1978.

REFERENCES

American Bar Association. Legal profession is considering code amendments to permit restricted advertising by lawyers. *American Bar Association Journal*, 1976, 62, 53–54.

American Medical Association. Principles of medical ethics. In *Judicial Council Opinions and Reports*. Chicago: AMA, 1971.

American Psychological Association. Guidelines for telephone directory listings. *American Psychologist*, 1969, 24, 70–71.

Association for the Advancement of Psychology. FTC's jurisdiction over professions threatened. *Advance*, 1982, 8, 5.

Boring, F. H. An ethical perspective on growth groups. *APA Monitor*, 1972, 3, 3.

Bray, D. W. The assessment center method. In R. L. Craig (Ed.), *Training and Development Handbook*. New York: McGraw-Hill, 1976.

———. Current trends and future possibilities. In J. L. Moses and W. C. Byham (Eds.), *Applying the Assessment Center Method*. New York: Pergamon, 1977.

Goldfarb v. *Virginia State Bar*, 421 U.S. 773 (1975).

Koocher, G. P. Advertising for psychologists: Pride and prejudice or sense and sensibility? *Professional Psychology*, 1977, 8, 149–160.

———. Credentialing in psychology: Close encounters with competence? *American Psychologist*, 1979, 34, 696–702.

Psychology for Mass- Media Audiences

8

Cheap truth is like junk food. It comes in pretty packages, and you can place a take-out order, but it loses so much flavor by the time you get it home.

Clint Weyand, Surviving Popular Psychology *(1980)*

The impact of mass media increases as our society moves steadily toward an information/communication-based economy. Obviously the media provide the most efficient means whereby education about psychology can be provided to large public audiences. Unfortunately, what the public *thinks* it is learning about psychology is often distorted, trivialized, sensationalized, or inaccurate information. For example, homicidal multiple-personalities (usually erroneously referred to as schizophrenics) populate television dramas with such frequency that the uninformed viewer may develop the false impression that such diagnoses are relatively common occurrences. Psychotherapists are often portrayed as uncaring exploiters, incompetent boobs, or people capable of effecting "instant cures" by uttering just the right words that release the person from life-long torment. Experimental psychologists are usually absent from dramatic media fare except for an occasional portrayal of a researcher as a power-hungry mind-controller who seduces unsuspecting victims into his (sometimes her) gadget-and-drug-stocked laboratory. Research conducted by psychologists is typically cited on the basis of its "interest value," rather than on its quality, and it is often imparted as if far more information were discovered than is warranted by the actual data. Sometimes important findings are ridiculed.

Psychologists face a true quandary here. On the one hand, it is beneficial for society when psychologists are more actively involved in the media, thereby enabling people to receive more accurate information about human behavior. Nevertheless, the *Ethical Principles* tacitly acknowledge the tenu-

199

ous and sometimes contradictory state of our knowledge base by admonishing psychologists to avoid sensationalism, exaggeration, and superficiality when making public statements (*EP:* 4g). Unfortunately, media are geared to sensationalism and exaggeration and, considering the quick-paced format, usually present information superficially. Distinctions between facts and speculations are frequently obscured. What is one psychologist's opinion is often attributed as a consensus within the discipline.

Before launching into the clash between the different drummers to which psychologists and media professionals march and the resulting ethical quagmires, it is important to note that responsible and competent media representatives *do* exist and that many psychologists have been involved in media activities that are beyond reproach. Our purpose in this chapter, however, is to focus on the dark side of the love-hate relationship between psychology and the media, but not to deny the value and potential of the media and the role of psychology in it. We further believe that the solutions to the perplexing ethical questions, which surface when psychologists merge with the media, must be effected in constructive ways. We must seek to improve what we do, rather than institute harsh restrictions. Censorship has often been justified in the name of righteousness, yet the resulting restriction on the free-flow of ideas would undermine the essence of the ethical standards of the profession (*EP:* Preamble).

This chapter explores problems sometimes encountered when psychologists interact with journalists or media interviewers, in addition to exploring ethical issues associated with advice-giving via the media, including "radio therapy" and "self-help" books.

INTERACTING WITH JOURNALISTS

Feeling flattered when a reporter or writer expresses interest in your work or ideas is natural. Not all interactions with journalists, however, prove satisfying. In our informal discussions with psychologists, we consistently observed that those who have had several experiences with journalists told at least one "horror story." Some examples include the following:

> My simple study comparing how groups of psychiatric patients participating in a large drug study responded to cartoons before and after the treatment period was headlined in a newspaper as "Psychologist discovers pill to improve your sense of humor."

> I was interviewed for almost two hours. The reporter used all my good stuff without crediting me and only quoted me on two offhanded jokes I made. He came off sounding well-informed, and I came off as an ass.

I couldn't believe what I saw in print. I was quoted out of context in such a way that the effect was to portray me as holding views to which I am diametrically opposed.

My 20-year commitment to basic research has never drawn the attention of a single journalist, despite the many articles, papers, and books I have contributed. Then last year a student and I did a quick, brief survey on cheating behavior on campus and every reporter in town called. I worry about the criteria used to determine what the public learns about our discipline.

Occasionally a printed article written by a journalist about a psychologist has been brought to the attention of an ethics committee. In the majority of instances, the psychologists involved have been able to defend themselves by affixing the blame on irresponsible or incompetent journalism. As the following case indicates, insult is added to injury when psychologists endure collegial criticism and an ethics inquiry procedure.

Case 8–1:   An article in a local newspaper quoted psychologist Adolf Blunt, Ph.D., as having said: "No responsible psychologist can deny that minority ethnic heritage is the major cause of violent crime." Dr. Blunt was outraged over how he had been subjected to numerous criticisms from colleagues and others on the basis of a "mish-mash of a misquote that totally distorted my comment." He noted that the quotation was based on an extended conversation with the reporter, during which he presented data showing that acts of violent street crime were proportionately higher in some areas where certain ethnic minority groups were concentrated, and that this fact cannot be denied. He said he then discussed numerous possible explanations, none of which had racist connotations.

From time to time, an ethics complaint is sustained based on information supplied by a psychologist to a journalist.

Case 8–2:   Starr Mouth, Ph.D., was interviewed about his celebrity clients in a popular movie magazine. He identified his clients by name and revealed some personal and interpretive material about them. His response to an ethics committee inquiry was that his clients would welcome the publicity because the information was not particularly unflattering. The ethics committee reminded him of his own professional responsibility and strongly admonished him to keep information shared in confidence to himself and leave the promotion of famous clients to the press agents.

Psychologists cannot ensure that the final reports about them will reflect their ethicality and integrity. The following suggestions are proposed to increase the likelihood of an acceptable final product and responsible public education about psychologists and psychology.

1. Find out the purpose of the story, how the journalist is approaching it, and the publication in which the story will appear. If the approach sounds exploitative or extremely superficial, or if the outlet is known for its questionable quality, consider waiting for another opportunity to share yourself with the public.

2. If possible, give the journalist a written statement. Many psychologists have reported obtaining far better results when brief, but clearly stated, material is available. It is often quoted directly, thereby reducing error rate in the final product.

3. Be sure that the journalist is aware of your interest in ensuring that the story is accurate. Invite the journalist to call you back if any questions arise. This procedure is especially important if the topic is controversial or easily misinterpreted. Editorial review of the final story is sometimes offered, but rarely at the request of interviewees, since this is viewed by journalists as infringement on the "freedom of the press."

4. If you are contacted to comment on an area in which you have insufficient knowledge or experience, politely refuse comment. Sometimes reporters may push anyway because their deadline panic renders any psychologist's view acceptable, but be firm. If possible, refer the reporter to a more appropriate person. Most reporters are grateful for good leads (and their phone numbers). The Public Information Office at APA is always a constructive referral.

5. If, after the interview, you realize that you may have made a significant error or neglected to mention something important, call back to offer these additional comments.

6. Remember that a 20-minute interview may be collapsed into a few words by the time it is printed. Your most salient or dramatic remarks will be extracted. If you make a major or controversial assertion or claim and then qualify it at length, only the major assertion may reach the public. Avoid becoming so comfortable with the interviewer that you make irresponsible or offhanded comments. These remarks are always fair game for print as well, and the effect can be humiliating.

7. Remember that you cannot speak for the profession as a whole. Embarrassment and ethics complaints can be avoided by refraining from making statements beginning with, for example, "Psychologists believe," unless hard data exist to verify such unanimity.

8. If a question strikes you as too difficult to answer, or if you do not have an answer, say so. The journalist may print your reluctance or ignorance, but that may be far preferable to quotes of remarks you offer under such circumstances.

9. If the topic is sensitive and controversial, inform journalists of this fact and suggest colleagues to be contacted who can balance the report. Journalists may already be aware of the diversity, but it doesn't hurt to help ensure that the public receives a more complete view.

10. Stories are often constructed about a newsworthy topic that has psychological overtones. Psychologists may be contacted to comment on psychological

ramifications of being held hostage, the impact of video games on children's development, and so on. Often no solid data exist on which to base a comment. In these cases, be modest by suggesting possibilities, rather than by providing what could be interpreted as definitive answers or explanations.

11. Sometimes journalists are interested in "psychological evaluations" of *specific* newsworthy individuals the psychologist has never met. Commentary is often irresponsible and erroneous and should therefore be avoided. If the psychologist has had professional contact with the individual (including deceased people), confidentiality becomes a critical issue and should not be compromised. Even if the individual consents to or requests a psychologist to make public statements, professional judgment may dictate that such information should not be shared with journalists.

12. If you are embarrassed or dissatisfied with the final product, let the journalist know about it. Frame remarks in a constructive way that may help educate the journalist. Angry letters are easy to dismiss!

"LIVE" RADIO AND TELEVISION GUEST APPEARANCES

Psychologists are often called to be interviewed in person on radio or television. This format can produce frustrations, such as being cut-off before the point is fully made, being asked stupid or inappropriate questions, or being repeatedly referred to as a psychiatrist. Sometimes, however, the psychologist bears full responsibility, as the following cases reveal.

Case 8–3:   Buff Showit, Ph.D., was interviewed about his book on hot-tub group therapy. He asserted that his technique was more useful in relieving tensions and dissolving "ghosts haunting us from the past" than "all of the rest of psychiatry and psychology combined," and that the technique promised relief from any emotional disturbance, no matter how serious.

Case 8–4:   Flamba Gambit, Ed.D, made regular appearances on local radio programs discussing various aspects of psychology. Her authoritative manner could be easily interpreted as implying knowledge based on scientific findings, although this was rarely the case. One of several complaints about her was an assertion that women who were raped "unconsciously wanted it," and that her research indicated that this was due to "a childhood fantasy of being simultaneously loved and punished by Daddy for being a good and bad little girl." Inquiry revealed that the "research" cited was no more than her opinion based on several of her clients who had been raped.

Case 8–5:   Ditz Dervish, Ph.D., was a regular guest on a local daytime television entertainment hour. He would literally twirl onto the stage, make unusual noises, and roll his eyes. His long hair was styled in such a way that it stood straight up. He dressed conventionally, except for a wide, flowered tie that flapped as he jumped around. He delivered a monologue of nonsensical psychological jabber that was apparently meant to be amusing. Some psychologists assumed he was an actor panning psychology and were surprised to learn that he had indeed earned a legitimate doctorate. Nevertheless, he was not a member of any professional association, and he was not licensed by the state, so his behavior could not be dealt with by his peers.

Case 8–6:   Rem Voltic, Ph.D., a noted psychologist and expert on sleep, was invited to appear as a guest on a television "magazine format" show devoting a segment to "The Bedroom." Models were to show the latest sleep wear; bed-time snacks were to be demonstrated by the resident chef; and a bedroom set was rigged at the studio in which the production would be staged. When Dr. Voltic arrived at the studio, the production staff manager asked him to report to "wardrobe" for a pajama fitting. Dr. Voltic refused to appear on the show under such conditions. He argued that he had agreed to participate as a professional person and that he should dress as he would when performing in a professional capacity.

Showit could produce no data to substantiate his excessive claims about hot-tub therapy and was thus guilty of making irresponsible statements about the validity of his work, in addition to demeaning his own profession and a related profession in the process. Gambit's statements about her rape "research" were highly misleading, irresponsible, and possibly caused certain listeners psychological harm. Dervish's actions were outrageous, but also irreproachable, because of his lack of association with the profession. Fortunately for psychology, the show was ultimately cancelled. Voltic, in stark contrast to the other three, escaped probable criticism by refusing to put the lure of the limelight above his professional identity.

POPULAR WORKS WRITTEN BY PSYCHOLOGISTS

Books and articles written for the "trade" or mass markets, which attempt to impart information about psychological concepts or phenomena (as opposed to "self-help" books, which will be considered in a separate section), pose few ethical concerns when done conscientiously and objectively. (Ethical issues involving scholarly works, such as textbooks and articles contributed to periodicals intended for a professional readership, are considered in Chapter 13.) Occasionally other professionals, usually colleagues whose work was referenced or who were quoted, will complain to an ethics committee that they were misrepresented or characterized in a way that caused embarrassment.

Case 8–7:   Dunn Damage, Ph.D., claimed that a magazine article written by Leonardo Barracuda, Ph.D., which evaluated Damage's theories on the antecedents of depression, caused considerable humiliation. Dr. Barracuda allegedly quoted Dr. Damage as saying, "All other theories are incorrect because they are untestable." Dr. Damage, however, claimed he said that "Many theories must be interpreted tentatively because they have not been subjected to research verification."

Occasionally more perplexing cases arise, such as the following:

Case 8–8: Psychologist Gustav Slammen, Ph.D., wrote a popular article for a women's magazine on the psychological effects of being mugged and robbed on the streets. Based on his literature review and some interviews with victims, he asserted that people who resisted their attackers had a better chance of foiling the robbery attempts, recovered more quickly from the emotional impact, and maintained self-esteem better than did nonresisters. He concluded by encouraging readers to resist assaults vigorously if they were ever placed in such an unfortunate situation. A research psychologist charged Dr. Slammen with irresponsible journalism. The complainant did not dispute the facts as far as they went. She noted, however, that research also supports the fact that victims who resist also run a much greater risk of being hurt or killed than do nonresisters and that readers should have been informed of this peril. The researcher claimed that Dr. Slammen knew this fact because her work was lavishly cited in his article.

Case 8–9: Grass Roots, Psy.D., wrote an article on rape and published it in a magazine characterized in general as "hard-core pornography." A psychologist-reader complained that the profession was demeaned by the contribution and that accompanying simulated rape photographs probably titilated more than they educated. The quality of the article was not an issue because it was judged to be well written and accurate. Dr. Roots responded that he chose this outlet because the target readership would not be likely to obtain this important information from any other source. Dr. Roots explained that he contributed the article without pay as proof of his altruistic motivation. Furthermore, the addition of photos was done by the publisher without his knowledge.

Barracuda was sloppy, and the effect was judged to be unfair to his colleague. Slammen's omission was more serious and was judged to be possibly harmful to readers. Actions by Roots were exonerated, because the committee was impressed with his rationale and sincerity, but the general issue is still a complicated one. Under some circumstances, the choice of topic, the mode of presentation, and the nature of publication outlets might be causes for ethical concern.

OFFERING INDIVIDUAL ADVICE THROUGH THE MEDIA

One of the most heated contemporary debates concerning ethical issues has been waged over "media psychologists" who offer advice to troubled and conflicted individuals on radio and, more recently, on television shows. Almost every major urban area has at least one "doctor," who is not always a psychologist or even a related mental health professional, doing a call-in-your-problem program.

Reactions within the profession are undocumented in any large-scale systematic fashion, although a recent survey of about 200 clinical psychologists revealed more positive than negative views (Keith-Spiegel, Bouhoust-sos, and Goodchilds, Note 1). Informal indications reveal extremes in both positive and negative directions. Some critics believe that this phenomenon has done more good for psychology than has any previous movement. Others decry it as vulgarized, "fortune-cookie psychology," embarrassing to the profession as a whole and blatantly *unethical*. Ironically, this debate has been among the few within our discipline to receive wide and consistent coverage by the media.

Until recently, the American Psychological Association prohibited the offering of psychological services or products for the purpose of diagnosing, treating, or giving personal advice to individuals through mass media outlets. However, in 1981, the APA altered its ethics code in a way that has prompted approval, outrage, controversy, and confusion. Although individual diagnostic and therapeutic services are still confined to the context of a professional relationship, personal advice given through public lectures, newspaper and magazine articles, mail, and broadcast media is allowed, as long as the psychologist uses current, relevant data and exercises a high level of professional judgment (*EP*: 4k).

It would be inaccurate to conclude that the APA was bending to pressure when the code was liberalized to permit psychologists to be media advice-givers. The phenomenon was beginning to mushroom, and whether APA members were involved or not would be irrelevant to the development of such programming. To retain opportunities for input and guidance, however, the national association determined that the ethics code required some alteration, since such involvement could occur most effectively through its members. (Remember that APA has no jurisdiction over nonmembers.) In addition, the drafters of the new code decided to assume that such activities could potentially be conducted in a professional manner with positive results.

Problems with the new code are obvious, even to its drafters. First, although diagnostic and therapeutic services are distinguished from personal advice, it remains unclear whether these concepts can be easily separated or whether workable operational definitions can be developed. For example, if a media psychologist tells a caller, "You have an affective disorder known as major depressive episode," a diagnosis has obviously been offered. But what happens if the psychologist merely says, "You sound depressed to me"? To many, psychodiagnostic terms are part of our everyday labels for feeling states. Separating "personal advice" from "psychotherapy" is even more problematic. The drafters of the code had a general notion that advice implied the offering of alternative suggestions regarding how one might approach or solve a problem (including offering the idea of seeking psychotherapy services). Statements of psychodynamic interpretations (e.g., "It sounds to me that you are purposely failing in your own marriage as a way of getting back at your mother," or, "People like you who overact are trying to compensate for the love you did not get as a child") are not seen as falling under the definition of "personal advice."

The second problem relates to the admonishment to use current and relevant data. Although it can be surmised that this phrase is a request to use empirically based findings when presenting information, critics are quick to note that media psychologists are typically not researchers by practice or by training and that anyone can locate an isolated finding to support even a ridiculous point. The third problem relates to the admonition to exercise the highest level of professional judgment. The drafters of the revision meant that media psychologists should take their activities seriously and refrain from exploiting callers or the format. Critics, however, note that such a call for excellence is impossible to translate to formats that are inherently exploitative and demanding of professional judgments based on minimal or incomplete information. This is an awkward loophole that was partially opened. The committee's attempts may ultimately not have satisfactory results, in which case the APA may later revise its code again.

The ethical implications of media advice-giving by psychologists extend beyond whether the ethics code specifically allows or disallows the activity. *How* it is done raises ethical and professional questions about social responsibility, competence, participant welfare, conflict-of-interest, and whether psychologists are using their knowledge and skills for the promotion of human welfare.

Social Responsibility

It is not difficult to create a number of arguments favoring the socially responsible and public service aspects of media-advice programming. Educating large audiences about psychological concepts, research findings, and mental health resources would, if done properly, be beneficial to the public as well as to the profession itself. Media psychotherapists may help fill the gap created by the steady crumbling of traditional social support systems, such as extended families, the neighborhood police, or doctors who make house calls. They are available to those who may not have anywhere else to start. Most supporters note that referral rosters are maintained to assist participants in locating additional assistance if they need it. Audiences learn that problems and conflicts are not unsharable and not unsolvable. Many who feel isolated, uniquely troubled, or attach a stigma to needing help may benefit from learning that others have similar conflicts and concerns, and they may even be motivated to seek needed services. The public images of psychologists may be altered for the better, since media advice-givers are seen as self-confident, easy-to-relate-to human beings. Finally, the "services" offered are all free to callers and listeners.

Counter-arguments, however, can be leveled against claims that media-advice programs are ethical because they promote social welfare. Despite the potential for educating the public, critics claim that psychologists who give media advice are hired *not* for their expertise as educators and scholars, but for qualities more aligned with media criteria, such as voice, verbal facility, and engaging or charismatic personality characteristics. Furthermore, no individual psychologist has sufficient expertise to respond intelligently and thoroughly to the diversity of topics encountered in this format. Yet the public may well assume, sometimes with explicit encouragement, that the psychologist is an expert on all things psychological. The format itself, with its rapid pace and focus on drawing out the details of the problems of the individuals seeking advice, hampers less dramatic education and information dissemination. Moreover, research findings or other basic information are often transmitted so quickly that the material is either misleading or meaningless, or it is blatantly erroneous. Witness, for example, the following unfortunate example involving the media advice-giver's lack of knowledge or confusion about a potent antipsychotic agent:

> I think you are overreacting to what the doctor is telling you about your son's
> problems. He's receiving Mellaril which is a mild and commonly used
> mood elevator. Mellaril would not be used for a serious psychiatric disorder.
> Your son is probably just depressed and your worrying will just make
> things worse. Explore your own guilt, then relax.

Critics of media advice-giving disagree with the argument that the image of the psychologist may be a vast improvement by describing the number of glib, bubbly, fast-paced, know-it-all advice-givers currently on the air. Regarding the argument that this format is available to everyone who may need it, critics note that more people may call in than can be put on the air. The selective screening criteria employed in deciding which calls to air also raises additional concerns. Rejecting drunks and referring obviously psychotic people or those in intense crisis elsewhere are understandable omissions from mass audience fare. Nevertheless, sometimes the elderly, people who don't speak clearly, those who have an "uninteresting" problem, or people with the same problem aired during the previous hour, and anyone who is of the sex that would unbalance the representation desired at a particular point in the program are also excluded. Restricting callers-on-the-air to younger, verbally fluent people with the "right" problem and gender for the moment mutes the "social service" argument advanced in favor of this type of programming. This bias may also restrict the alleged impetus for listeners or watchers to seek help, because they do not see people like themselves revealed in these programs. Furthermore, the fast pace of these programs may trivialize human misery.

Moreover, rather than encouraging the seeking of needed services, the opposite could possibly happen. Some listeners and viewers may become "radio-therapy junkies" and not seek more appropriate assistance. Little is known about the "referral" process and how it actually works. What criteria are used to devise it? How extensive are the lists? How available, geographically and/or financially, are the referrals to callers?

To the assertion that the media-advice programs offer amelioration without cost, critics might respond that this type of advice is worth exactly what one paid for it.

Competence and Participant Welfare

Most of the psychologists who participate in the media as advice-givers appear to be "properly" trained to deliver psychotherapeutic services in traditional settings. Thus the questions of competency concern whether the psychologist can do the job competently, based on the nature of the radio-therapy format used. Defenders say they can. They have noted that the call-in format resembles brief crisis intervention or "hotline" services that have existed free from major ethical debate for years. The radio personalities claim that the telephone is a particularly useful therapeutic context for people who are ambivalent, shy, or have poor emotional control, because it permits closeness without the caller having to leave his or her own safe space. Contact can be made without making any kind of a commitment, and it can be terminated with the push of a button. It has been argued that despite the short duration of any single episode, the media psychologist can cut through the murk and reach the heart of the problem without major difficulty. Most people have numerous problems and are anxious for advice, support, and encouragement. The ones asking for help also assist the passive audience members by serving as their proxy. Consequently many people may benefit from the advice given to only one person.

Critics, however, level numerous rebuttals against these presumptions and argue that "fast-food therapy" can lead to drastic misperceptions about the psychotherapeutic process and may be harmful to the individual participants and the audience. It can be asserted that, considering the circumstances, the advice is probably defective, since it is based on minimal and incomplete information given by a complete stranger. Consequently, the interpretations and guidance may not only be inappropriate, but also contraindicated. The secondhand advice taken by an audience member may be even less applicable than that given to the principal participant. Harm could result, particularly for vulnerable or "brittle" people with no other ongoing support systems, those advised to make some major life changes, those hit with an interpretation they are not prepared to handle, or those who try the advice and find that it fails to ameliorate the problem. Errors will not be corrected the way they can be when made in the context of an ongoing, psychotherapy relationship. No formal provisions for monitoring or follow-up are provided, which leaves the participants on their own or, more forcefully stated, abandoned. Audience members and participants may be led to believe that fast, snap answers can solve even serious personal or interpersonal problems. The "chin-up" encouragement may merely be a quick and gratuitous way of disposing of a participant's tribulations or anxieties, while giving the impression of sympathy and understanding. Sometimes callers are berated for their position. Regarding the "hot-line" analogy, critics quickly note that crisis telephone services focus exclusively on the caller's needs, and the conversation can last for hours if necessary.

Whether media advice-givers can be held responsible for catastrophic results, if a person follows the advice offered, has yet to be fully tested in the courts. A large part of the issue will concern whether the parties constitute a doctor-patient relationship. Media psychologists have argued against this definition, since they were voluntarily contacted and no money exchanged hands. It can be countered that people seek medical and psychotherapeutic services voluntarily and that the lack of monetary exchange for services does not obviate professional responsibility or liability. It is probably only a matter of time before the malpractice implications of this activity are discussed in court.

Most media advice-givers counter these criticisms by arguing that they do not *do* psychotherapy when they are on the air. Various terms, such as "giving information," "educating," "practicing community psychology," and so on, have been used by advice-givers to characterize their media activity. Critics would certainly agree that the media advice-giving psychologists do not do *real* psychotherapy or anything closely resembling it. Yet they remain concerned that what media advice-givers say they do are euphemisms for an attempt to practice their therapy skills under a set of artificial and improper circumstances.

Media personalities may even underestimate their own power to affect people's lives, since research has revealed that people can form intense relationships with "celebrities" and model their own lives and attributes after them (Caughey, 1978). John Hinkley's obsession with actress Jody Foster, for example, had ultimately tragic consequences. This phenomenon concerns critics who believe that audiences may take the pronouncements of media advice-givers far more seriously than is warranted.

Dual Roles and Conflicts of Interest

Ethical standards admonish psychologists to keep the welfare of the clients being served as the top priority and to refrain from engaging in activities that pose conflicts of interest or roles that may compromise the quality of their professional judgment, standards, and behavior (see Chapter 10). Is it possible, however, for a call-in psychologist to uphold these ethical standards when participating in a commercial media venture? As employees in a "nonprofessional" business, media advice-givers are under the control of the station management. Even those working without pay, as some do, may buckle under pressure if strong personal needs are satisfied by participating in media activities. Several psychologists once employed by the media resisted attempts to conform to the management's priorities and found themselves promptly out of jobs.

Media management personnel rather unabashedly spell out their priorities. The goal is to attract and retain large audiences so that advertisers will buy time for their messages, and the station can make a profit. Serious conflicts emerge when ordinary commercial practices clash with the ethical standards of the profession of psychology. Can the welfare of the participants and the listening public be upheld? Critics argue that it cannot. "Show-biz" standards pertain in maintaining a quick turnover of calls, fast-paced and up-beat dialogue, and high interest or entertainment value achieved primarily through encouraging sharing of any sordid details and making snappy, absorbing commentary. The audience must not become bored, because their minds might wander or they might switch stations. Goleman (1981) recounted his experiences while auditioning as the host of a therapy-format television show. The media staff person referred to the possible participants as "Problems," admonished him to smile frequently, to draw out the "Problem's problem," to keep things moving, and to wrap-up quickly. Goleman wondered what he and the "Problems" were doing there.

Is it true that callers' pain and personal agonies are exploited as a cheap source of entertainment and profit? Some media psychologists themselves have compared their activity to "*real* soap opera," which is a tacit admission that they have abandoned their role as professionals in favor of roles as performers, while "real people" are solicited to be merely grist for the entertainment mill.

Concerns must also be raised about the dual role conflicts *within* the psychologists who participate in this media format. Do these people define themselves as psychologists or as celebrities? These two roles have inherent contradictions. Celebrities must focus on how they connect with their admirers and how to behave to attract more admirers. Critics contend that psychologists may use this format primarily as a way to display their savoir-faire and to enhance their own self-esteem, leaving the goal of helping people somewhat lower on the totem pole.

Privacy, Confidentiality, and Informed Consent

Modern technology has effected the eradication of the "funny little telephone voice" of previous eras. People now sound on the phone similar to the way they do in person. Television takes the process two steps further by retaining both the actual voice and revealing the physical appearance of people.

Concern has been expressed that the privacy and confidentiality of radio call-in advice seekers are not fully protected, especially if they are quite specific about their situation, and they are unprotected altogether by television advice programs. The veiled attempts to honor rights to confidentiality by using first names, and not necessarily the *real* names, may be useless when audience members personally know the participants. Furthermore, third parties, such as spouses or employers, may be embarrassed whenever participants are identifiable.

Whereas it can be argued that the primary participants voluntarily seek this medium for advice and are even willing to wait in line for it, we are concerned that they may not fully understand the potential risks that could accrue as a result of making their problems public. At the time, participants may be focusing only on the excitement and fun of being on radio or television, or they may be hurting in a way that precludes looking further down the road. Their consent may be *voluntary* but not truly *informed* (see Chapters 3 and 14). Third parties, such as family members, who may also be exposed were denied both the voluntary and informed aspects of consent.

Respecting Other Professionals and Their Orientations

The ethics code admonishes psychologists to respect other mental health professionals and their approaches and to exercise considerable caution when approached by an individual who is receiving psychotherapeutic services from another professional (*EP*: 7b). Some media psychologists dispensing advice deserve criticism for violating these ethical principles in the course of either expressing their opinions or offering their recommendations. Examples of actual demeaning of other professionals or their orientation include the following:

> Social workers have no understanding of individual personality dynamics.
>
> I do not believe that a psychoanalytic approach is useful or appropriate for most people.

Examples of interfering with ongoing therapeutic relationships include the following:

> It sounds to me like your therapist isn't doing a very good job.
>
> Judging from what I'm hearing you say, you might be better off terminating with your present female therapist and switching to a male therapist who may have a better understanding of your feelings.

Advice to Individuals Offered in Writing

The nonpsychologist twins, Ann Landers and Abigail Van Buren, are not first, but they are certainly the most famous people to use the news column advice-to-the-troubled formats. Psychologists have also moved into this realm, ranging from writing columns for high-circulation national magazines to local throwaway newspapers. A number of the same ethical conflicts evident in call-in radio and television programs applies in this situation as well. Additional problems include the lack of back-and-forth clarification, since this medium uses a single stimulus and a single response to it; moreover, making more appropriate referrals is impossible when the letter-writers do not include full names and return addresses. Some ethical dilemmas are diminished by this format, however. The psychologist can take time to respond thoughtfully and consult the relevant literature and/or others with special expertise. Also confidentiality can be guaranteed more easily. Some ethics complaints, illustrated in the following cases, have been leveled specifically at this format.

> **Case 8–10:** A psychologist complained that the advice column in a local paper by Tack Gross, Ph.D., was used to entertain readers at the expense of the troubled correspondents. For example, an elderly woman expressed frustration over having sexual desires but no sex partner. Dr. Gross suggested that she either hang around the Senior Citizen's Center at night or start a cucumber patch.

> **Case 8–11:** Several psychologists complained that Quick Curer, Ph.D., who contributed a column to a magazine, was dispensing trite solutions to difficult psychological problems. For example, readers were told that shedding neurotic patterns, such as chronic depression, is accomplished by making a decision to change. They felt that Dr. Curer was not only setting readers up for failure, but was also trivializing psychological knowledge as well.

An ethics committee responded poorly to Dr. Gross' brand of humor and censured him for demeaning the correspondents and the profession of psychology. Dr. Curer was also censured for his superficial approach to dealing with emotional disorders.

Critics might argue that this format is best left to the witty and sensitive journalists who do not present their qualifications as psychology experts. This solution avoids misrepresenting psychology and psychotherapy to the public.

Solutions to the Ethical Dilemmas of Media Advice-Giving: Conceivable or Cosmetic?

Considering the combined, huge, regular audiences of the four dozen or so media advice-givers who are trained as psychologists, the *potential* number of complaints that ethics committees might receive is astronomical. In fact, ethics committees have *not* received numerous complaints. This might indicate pervasive acceptance by and satisfaction with psychologists who participate in these programs, or lack of knowledge of ethics codes and action recourses available to callers or listeners who were upset with what they experienced. As illustrated in the following cases, however, some letters from listeners and callers questioning specific incidents have resulted in ethics committee investigations:

> **Case 8-12:** A caller complained to an ethics committee that Grace Goodtalk, Ed.D., treated her shamefully during an "on-air" advice session. The caller claimed she was berated as being "immature and silly" because she called for advice on how to clear up an argument with a friend. When the caller protested that her problem was serious to her and that she wanted help rather than ridicule, she claimed that Dr. Goodtalk abruptly cut her off. The caller claimed that this incident caused her considerable and prolonged mental stress. She noted that if this is "what psychologists do to people who hurt," she didn't understand why anyone would consult one.

Inquiry revealed that Dr. Goodtalk defended her comments as appropriate for that caller and added, "I don't need psychology. Psychology needs me." Her indignant letter of resignation from the professional organization was accepted.

> **Case 8-13:** A listener wrote to an ethics committee complaining about how Mike Flap, Ph.D., handled a repeat caller during his radio advice show. The caller, who was on the show several times, complained of headaches, which she felt were due to intense stress. Dr. Flap gave suggestions during each call regarding how she could learn to relax and minimize environmental factors contributing to the tension. About three months after the initial call, the woman called in and informed Dr. Flap that a neurologist had located a brain tumor that was probably causing the intense headaches. The listener-complainant was extremely concerned that Dr. Flap had behaved irresponsibly by encouraging the woman to continue calling in updated reports on how his advice was working, thus contributing to the delay in locating the true reason for the headaches—a cause Dr. Flap could not possibly assess himself.

Inquiry by an ethics committee revealed that Dr. Flap had insisted that verification be made "off-air," after the first call, that the woman was under the close supervision of a physician. The ethics committee concluded that the psychologist should have made the listening audience aware of the fact that he had known about, and supported, medical intervention; moreover, he should state "on-air" that a radio-advice format should never be the sole source of advice about a physical complaint.

Many media psychologists themselves have joined the ranks of the critics and have proposed that a set of guidelines are required to clarify the ethical conflicts and assist psychologists in the actual practice of public advice-giving. Improvements could obviously be effected, while requiring station managers' cooperation, and specific psychologists could make tailor-made reformations.

A few suggestions that might be included in a set of guidelines are as follows:

1. Media psychologists should carefully assess their areas of training and experience and refrain from handling topics beyond their competence. Bringing in expert guests or presenting prepared special reports are alternative ways of responsibly broadening the menu.

2. Media psychologists should avoid offering suggestions that require radical life changes or decisions.

3. All potential participants should be screened by a competent person, preferably a crisis intervention specialist. Persons not suitable for media exposure because their difficulties are not appropriate for the format should be given referrals to agencies or individual professionals in their localities. This function should receive sufficient support to allow the screener enough time to spend with each caller and sufficient resources to maintain a comprehensive and constantly updated referral roster. People who ask for assistance through correspondence to the psychologist should be answered by the psychologist or a staff member. Referral lists should be offered to correspondents.

4. Callers selected to participate should be informed, in advance, of some of the risks that might accrue as a result of exposing one's personal problems in this forum. If, after contemplating these risks, participants choose not to pursue the activity further, they should be offered information about alternative forms of assistance.

5. Resources should be provided so that persons in crisis, whether or not they went on the air, are followed up to ensure that more direct intervention was obtained.

6. Media psychologists should maintain a crew of peer monitors who regularly listen and make suggestions for improvement or change.

7. Participants should not be asked to wait for prolonged periods of time before talking to the psychologist, and distressed callers should never be "put on hold" while a commercial or other message is run.

8. Tapes should not be re-run later (e.g., on holidays) without the consent of the participants.

9. Media psychologists should never read commercials or news stories. If the psychologists find a given advertisement or sponsor inappropriate, this objection should ideally be respected by the station management.

10. Media psychologists should not maintain private practices or they should not allude to having private practices on the air or in any promotional program messages.

11. Media psychologists should make frequent disclaimers about misperceptions that the public might have about the show format (e.g., distinguishing the media episodes from traditional psychotherapy).

12. Media psychologists should never belittle participants or make jokes at their expense.

13. Media psychologists should phrase their comments in such a way that the audience realizes they are reflecting from personal training and experience, but not speaking for an entire discipline, through using such phrases as the following: "Not all psychologists would agree with me. . . " and, "It is my own, personal opinion that. . . . "

14. Media psychologists should not criticize the competence of other mental health workers based on a participant's narrative, nor should orientations other than one's own be denigrated unless clear and reasonable evidence suggests that such orientations are dangerous or fraudulent.

Some people believe that guidelines will not solve many problems until the commercial aspects of this format are removed. Quality programs of this nature may be possible only on educational (i.e., public, noncommercial) radio and television. Managements would be either unwilling or unable to finance the vast off-air services suggested. Furthermore, it is presumed that many media psychologists would find the limitations and restrictions unacceptable, although we believe that unless psychologists are allowed to be fully professional in their media activities, they should refuse to participate. Finally, those who would voluntarily submit to the guidelines and vigorously encourage the media managements to comply are probably those who pose the fewest problems without them. The recently formed Association for Media Psychology hopes to prove the pessimists wrong by becoming a constructive force, in both the profession and the media industry, to ensure quality and regard for ethical practices and to sponsor research on the impact of media psychology on the public.

SELF-ADMINISTERED THERAPEUTIC PROGRAMS

Among the public's longstanding favorite forms of "mass psychology" are self-help books and articles and, more recently, audio tapes and "kits." Hard financial times, stressful living conditions, and desire for self-reliance are among the contemporary factors that perpetuate the considerable success of self-help industry products.

Increasing numbers of psychologists, including some exceptionally prominent ones, have been entering the do-it-yourself-psychology market. A few examples of the "how to" topics contributed by psychologists include the following: improvement of self-concept, self-confidence, social assertiveness, parenting skills, physical fitness and sexual functioning; control of smoking, weight, stress, phobias, and anger; and coping with depression, guilt, shyness, insomnia, anxiety, problem children, loss of love, and divorce.

In this section, we will focus on books and other products marketed to the public that possess the following characteristics: (1) presented as an effective alternative to procedures directed by a therapist; (2) totally self-administered by the individual consumer; and (3) obtained without the necessity of contract or consultation with a professional (e.g., bookstores or mail order).

Although numerous ethical concerns surround the involvement of psychologists in the creation of such programs, even the critics agree that such involvement has positive features (Rosen, 1976; 1977). By their training and experience, psychologists are capable of creating self-administered programs that may prove beneficial to many people for a fraction of the cost of long-term, professional services. (It is difficult, of course, to compare self-help products and direct professional services on a strictly cost-effectiveness basis. If a book that costs ten dollars provides minimal help and direct services costing four-hundred dollars provide enormous help, what can be said about cost-effectiveness *per se?*)

Indeed, psychologists can properly evaluate and validate their programs and can be explicit about cautions and shortcomings. Experts in a given field, however, can offer their knowledge to people who would not normally have direct access to them. Such products do not have most of the inherent limitations of the direct-advice formats considered in the previous section. Authors can use time and care in creating the programs to ensure their quality. Thus it is difficult to argue that psychologists should refrain from introjecting better material into an already established self-help market gorged with potboilers embroidered with hype-lines and psycho-babble. To the extent that it *is* possible to offer the public sound, effective programs that do not require professional intervention, it would be socially irresponsible to restrict unduly or to discourage psychologists from making such contributions.

Ethical Concerns about Self-Help Programs

Despite the positive potential associated with the involvement of psychologists in this vast self-help market, a number of ethical questions have been raised regarding how it is currently being done. Some of these concerns are similar to the criticisms raised about media advice-giving. Consumers are often given instructions on how to solve difficult problems or on how to manage their lives, but no support system is available to sustain them through the procedure, to correct errors, to clarify misunderstood text statements or directions, to caution against counter-indications for particular consumers, or to alleviate any negative consequences resulting from following, or from failing to follow, the program.

These products are typically written and advertised in ways that are geared to sell as many copies as possible. The result is often inappropriate flamboyance, superficiality, and generalizations not warranted by available evidence—all of which are cautioned against by the ethics code (*EP*: 4g). Extravagant claims that may cause unrealistic expectations of favorable results are often promoted in the text, the title, or the promotional materials supplied by the publishers or their agents. Such claims (see Chapter 7) are specifically prohibited in the ethics code (*EP*: 4b).

Sometimes it is discovered that the psychologist was not directly involved in what, at first, appeared to be an ethical impropriety. Nevertheless, psychologists are obligated to correct misrepresentations of themselves by others (*EP*: 4j).

> **Case 8–14:**   Several psychologists complained that Tip Banana, Ph.D., a respected expert in sexual dysfunction, had made absurd and outrageous effectiveness claims for his book on the cover and in advertisements, such as: "Your sex life will be totally fulfilled after reading this book," and, "Guaranteed to make you the lover of the year."

During questioning by an ethics committee, Dr. Banana expressed his own horror concerning the way his book had been promoted. He noted that no such comments were found in the content of the book and that these indiscretions had been committed by the publisher without his permission or awareness. He supplied a letter he had sent to the publisher expressing his anger and disappointment.

This now-familiar clash between business promotional standards and ethical standards of the profession is one area of particular concern to critics of self-help products. The situation is even further exacerbated when either the content or promotional material suggests that more direct services are unnecessary or a waste of money. This tactic, which is not uncommon, may preclude consumers for whom the product was not beneficial from seeking more appropriate alternatives.

> **Case 8–15:**   The promotional advertisement and content of a do-it-yourself psychotherapy book promises to save the reader thousands of dollars, because it will be unnecessary to consult "paid advisors." The book promises "relief within two weeks from guilt, anxiety, and depression" and assures that anyone can follow the easy-to-understand program. No data are presented to support any of the benefits that are guaranteed to the readers.

> **Case 8–16:**   A self-management sex-therapy program book claims to be unique, proven successful, and to provide a program that would cost several hundreds of dollars if the individual were to be treated in a clinic. In fact, the program had

never been evaluated, nor were the techniques described unprecedented ideas or applications.

Consumers may jump from one self-help product to another for a "$7.95 fix," as they appear to do with diet books, but miss the underlying causes of dissatisfaction or pathology for a prolonged period of time. Or they may consider themselves to be failures and give up altogether. Since the book was written by an "expert," consumers may be more likely to fault themselves rather than the faulty product.

By purchasing self-help products, the consumer has at least tentatively "diagnosed" himself or herself as needing a particular type of assistance. Products typically require either general self-diagnoses, such as "social inadequacy" or "dissatisfaction with life," to *specific* self-diagnoses, such as being phobic, depressed, shy, or sexually inadequate. Critics of the self-help industry are concerned about how the creators of these products leave the diagnosis to the consumer. Few products recognize or attempt to caution the consumer to avoid the dangers of misdiagnosis. People may be falsely convinced that they have a particular problem that renders a program unnecessary and may perpetuate inappropriate self-labels. Or consumers may have a different problem for which a self-help program or *any* psychological approach is ineffective or even counter-indicated (Barrera, Rosen, and Glasgow, 1981).

Perhaps the most serious ethical conflict in the self-help book and products business is in the area of predistribution evaluation. Before selling consumers instructions on how to deal with life in general or with specific problems, a socially and ethically responsible psychologist should have obtained evidence that his or her program or advice has, in fact, proven to be beneficial and effective. The *Ethical Principles* admonish psychologists to base statements on scientifically acceptable findings and techniques and to recognize the limits and uncertainties of such evidence (*EP*: 1a).

Unfortunately, most self-help programs contributed by psychologists have not been subjected to any systematic evaluation prior to being marketed. Glasgow and Rosen (1979) have calculated the ratio of programs with some pretesting evaluations to those with no such groundwork and found that the trend is, proportionately, toward increasing numbers of *unevaluated* products being marketed to the public. Yet the claims of such untested, self-administered therapies often are neither cautious nor modest.

Even those books claiming to be based on assessed programs have often been inappropriately or incompletely evaluated. Others are based on extensive, therapist-assisted evaluations (i.e., the clients used the program as it appears in the product, but were simultaneously supervised by a professional). Evaluations of the efficacy of books or products used by themselves are virtually nonexistent. Since even therapist-assisted evaluations some-times reveal discouraging levels of positive results, particularly in the instruction compliance level of clients and long-term maintenance of beneficial effects, consumers acting in a totally self-administered context may be purchasing materials that will be either ineffective or unlikely to be used at all (Rosen, 1976; 1981).

It is possible to evaluate a self-help product for efficacy *prior* to marketing it to the public. But this procedure requires time and considerable hard work. An adequate evaluation requires the consideration of many variables, such as expectancy for improvement, format and length, levels of task difficulty, involvement and role of significant others, reading level, long-term gains, and so on. See Glasgow and Rosen (1978; 1979) for a discussion of possible methodologies. Psychologists who may be lured by the potential fame and profits to be acquired from creating self-help market products for a public that is apparently not aware of or concerned about thorough evaluations are unlikely to conclude the demanding task of assessing the value of what they are offering.

On occasion, programs have been evaluated *after* their publication and have been found to be useless or even to have produced additional negative consequences (e.g., Matson and Ollendick, 1977). Rosen (Note 2) has suggested that self-help programs proven to be ineffective and/or harmful *after* publication should be removed from the market. This extreme action can certainly be defended on ethical grounds. If psychologists learn that their programs do not work or have negative consequences in a large percentage of trials, then they must wrestle with the ethic that admonishes psychologists to accept responsibility for the consequences of their acts and to make every effort to ensure that their services are used appropriately (*EP:* 1 preamble). If an analogy can be drawn between a consumer of one's self-administered therapy techniques and a client in a professional relationship, the mandate to terminate a professional relationship when it appears that the consumer is not benefitting from it applies as well (*EP:* 6e).

Could Guidelines Be Developed?

Although a consensus resulting in strict guidelines would probably be impossible to develop, several minimal criteria have been suggested. Webb (1981) has offered the following guidelines for self-help books:

1. The authors are expert in the behavior domain of the book.
2. The advice is judiciously derived from a sound data base.
3. The advice has been validated.
4. The book does not offer what it cannot deliver.
5. The advisee is given appropriate warnings when *not* to engage in the program.
6. The advice is organized into a program that the advisee can systematically follow.

7. The advisee is given criteria by which appropriate progress can be evaluated.

8. The advisee is appropriately warned of placebo effects (p. 192).

As Webb (1981) asserts, "If the book does not meet minimum standards of the first five criteria, I question the morality of such books and, in the case of a professional, the ethics of them" (p. 192). *The Report of the APA Task Force on Self-Help Therapies,* chaired by Gerald Rosen, proposed the creation of a set of guidelines to assist psychologists in developing responsible, high-quality, self-help programs. Included would be providing consumers, at the onset, with information about the extent of evaluation the program has undergone, the conditions under which evaluation occurred, recommended uses of the program and the readability level. The Task Force also recommended the creation of a set of guidelines and sample contracts to assist psychologists in their negotiations with publishers as one way of ensuring that the work will be properly promoted. A short pamphlet to educate the public about the self-help market was also proposed. Following through with these proposals would be an important step in ameliorating many ethical conflicts (APA, 1978).

SUMMARY GUIDELINES

1. While committing themselves to assisting the public in understanding psychological knowledge, psychologists strive to ensure accuracy, maintain due caution and modesty, and exhibit a high level of professional responsibility. Exaggeration, superficiality, and sensationalism should be vigorously avoided.

2. Psychologists must recognize their responsibilities to media consumers who may unequivocally accept their public statements by virtue of their presumed expertise.

3. Recognizing the limits of one's knowledge and experience is especially critical in media activities, since a large number of people can be misled or misinformed by incorrect or incomplete public statements.

4. When offering public statements via the media intended to ameliorate a particular problem, considerable caution must be exercised. Such advice should ideally have a scientifically based foundation. Information should not be presented as factual, unless a reasonable data base exists.

5. Psychologists should avoid public statements that purport to speak for the entire profession because such unanimity probably does not exist on any issue.

6. Media goals and purposes are likely to be different from those of individual psychologists and the tenets of the *Ethical Principles.* Such an awareness may assist in detecting those instances where caution is appropriate.

7. Public statements by psychologists should never be made for entertainment or ego-gratification purposes at the expense of others.

REFERENCE NOTES

1. Keith-Spiegel, P.; Bouhoutsos, J.; and Goodchilds, J. *Can media psychology be ethical?* American Psychological Association meetings, Los Angeles, California, 1983.
2. Rosen, G. M. *Symposium on nonprescription psychotherapies.* American Psychological Association meetings, Toronto, Canada, 1977.

REFERENCES

American Psychological Association. *Report of the Task Force on Self-help Therapies.* Washington, DC: APA, 1978.

Barrera, M.; Rosen, G. M.; and Glasgow, R. E. "Rights," risks and responsibilities in the use of self-help psychotherapy. In G. T. Hannah, W. P. Christian, and H. B. Clark (Eds.), *Preservation of Client Rights.* New York: MacMillan, 1981.

Caughey, J. L. Media mentors. *Psychology Today*, September, 1978, pp. 44–49.

Glasgow, R. E., and Rosen, G. M. Behavioral bibliotherapy: A review of self-help behavior therapy manuals. *Psychological Bulletin*, 1978, *85*, 1–23.

———. Self-help behavior therapy manuals: Recent developments and clinical usage. *Clinical Behavior Therapy Review*, 1979, *1*, 1–20.

Goleman, D. Will the next problem sign in, please! *Psychology Today*, December, 1981, 31–38.

Matson, J. L., and Ollendick, T. H. Issues in toilet training normal children. *Behavioral Therapy*, 1977, *8*, 549–553.

Rosen, G. M. The development and use of nonprescription behavior therapies. *American Psychologist*, 1976, *31*, 139–141.

———. Nonprescription behavior therapies and other self-help treatments: A reply to Goldiamond. *American Psychologist*, 1977, *32*, 178–179.

———. Guidelines for the review of do-it-yourself treatment books. *Contemporary Psychology*, 1981, *26*, 189–191.

Webb, W. B. How to or not how to. *Contemporary Psychology*, 1981, *26*, 192–193.

Weyand, C. *Surviving Popular Psychology.* Northridge, CA: Being Books, 1980.

Knowing Thyself: Competence and Weakness 9

*There is nothing more dangerous
than ignorance being practiced.*

Johann Wolfgang von Goethe

The quotation from *Faust* stands as a warning to psychologists who believe that they know everything about their specialized field. This chapter emphasizes recognizing one's limitations and the way inadequacies can affect one's ethical behavior. Truly competent psychologists recognize their limitations and weaknesses, as well as their strengths and skills (*EP*: 2 preamble). When psychologists become blind to their areas of weakness or inadequacy, clients may be hurt and the public is at risk. The ultimate problems related to competence in psychology involve matters of knowing when to terminate services and dealing with the "sick doctor" (*EP*: 2f and 6e). The ability to explore one's own motives and relationships insightfully is not easily taught and never perfected, yet these skills are among the most critical to the effective ethical functioning of the psychologist.

Before exploring the problems of the incompetent or troubled psychologist, it is important to understand basic ethical problems associated with training, credentialing, and maintaining competence at the postgraduate level, in addition to recognizing problem relationships when they develop. Although standards and credentials in psychology are topics of some controversy, it is critical that psychologists recognize the boundaries of their competence and the limitations of their techniques.

CONCEPTUAL ISSUES

The American Psychological Association and other organized groups of psychologists have long struggled with the problem of defining professional competence and incompetence. These efforts have taken many forms, including development of ethical codes, standards of practice, Professional Standards Review Committees (PSRCs), third-party-payer quality assurance programs, state licensing or certification boards, and other types of credentialing bodies (e.g., the American Board of Professional Psychology). Despite these efforts, however, none of the structures has been effective in detecting and then adjudicating incompetent professional behavior, or even routinely enforcing sanctions against those professionals deemed incompetent (Claiborn, 1982). The difficulty often relates to a general presumption of competence, similar to the dictum that one is "innocent until proven guilty." In addition, it has also been difficult to obtain a consensus on a definition of competence. In fact, incompetence is often difficult to prove, especially when one is bound by the constraints of *due process* and the need to accumulate substantial evidence in each case.

Standards of Practice

The APA has promulgated two documents that represent significant and comprehensive attempts to codify general standards of practice in psychology (APA, 1977; 1981). In part, these documents are designed to define minimum levels of competent professional practices and procedures, both in general (APA, 1977) and in the specialties of clinical, counseling, industrial/organizational, and school psychology (APA, 1981). These documents constitute suggested guidelines, rather than enforceable rules, such as those specified in the *Ethical Principles*. The documents outline policies and procedures for the conduct of one's practice, but APA does not require its members to follow these guidelines as a condition of membership in the same manner that adherence to the ethical code is obligatory.

Part of the difficulty involves controversy about what constitutes a specialty, subspecialty, or particular area of expertise in the practice of psychology. Clinical, counseling, industrial/organizational, and school psychology have traditionally been recognized as specialties, but many special areas of expertise also exist within each of these headings. For example, an industrial psychologist competent in human-factors engineering may not be qualified to consult on personnel selection; a clinical psychologist well trained in psychotherapy and assessment may lack the forensic knowledge to evaluate a defendant's competence to stand trial; and a counseling psychologist with many years of experience as a psychotherapist to adults may be untrained in work with children. What constitutes the basic qualification needed to practice personnel consultation, forensic evaluations, or child psychotherapy? Are these specialties or subspecialties, or are they merely special types of competence or skills? Psychology currently has no answer to these questions, and in virtually all cases, individual psychologists are expected to know and practice within their own areas of competence. Consider the case of Dr. Robert Hartley, discussed in Chapter 7 (*Case 7−1*), as well as the following cases.

> **Case 9−1:** Charlotte Hasty, Ph.D., has practiced individual psychodynamic psychotherapy with adult clients for ten years. After attending a continuing education program (half-day workshop) on family therapy, Dr. Hasty begins to conduct family therapy sessions for some of her clients while reading books in the field during her spare time.
>
> **Case 9−2:** Carl Klutzkind, Psy.D., has been treating a woman with many adjustment problems in the wake of a separation and impending divorce. After he has worked with the client for six months, he is asked by her attorney if he is willing to testify in support of her having custody of her seven-year-old child, as part of the divorce proceedings. Dr. Klutzkind agrees and offers many opinions about the adjustment of the woman and her child in court. An ethical complaint is subsequently filed against him, noting that he is not trained in child work, he never actually interviewed the child, and was generally negligent in offering an opinion. Although the child was in treatment with another psychologist, Klutzkind had never sought information from that colleague or from the child's father. Klutzkind obviously knew little about either child-custody work or even clinical assessment of children.

In these two cases, the psychologists have failed to recognize the boundaries of formal training. Although no clear professional standards now exist to define expertise in family therapy or child-custody work, it is reasonably clear that more expertise than either Dr. Hasty or Dr. Klutzkind had is required. In Dr. Hasty's case, we cannot say for certain whether anyone was actually hurt or helped, nor would the lack of training be discovered under normal circumstances. She does not see anything wrong with applying this new *technique*, since she is an "experienced therapist." Dr. Klutzkind failed to prepare adequately for the role he agreed to perform, which he was not equipped by training to undertake. Perhaps his concern for his client, his desire to expound on his views in court, or simple ignorance led him into trouble. His behavior clearly had a potentially hurtful impact on all the parties in the case. Dr. Hartley, discussed in Chapter 7, was sincere, but superficial, in assessing his training and experience. When no formal standards exist for particular practices or techniques, the practitioner must be prudent and conservative in assessing whether additional training is required. In such circumstances, it is best to consult colleagues who are widely regarded as experts in the particular area for their guidance regarding adequacy of both training and practice standards.

Competence-related issues pervade many chapters in this book. Competence issues related to psychodiagnostic assessment and testing were specifically addressed in Chapter 4. Similarly, issues related to competence as a psychotherapist are implied in Chapter 5. This chapter, however, discusses matters of competence and weakness in general, especially as they relate to the psychologist's personal development and professional behavior.

Other Conceptualizations of Competence

In theory, ethical codes, PSRCs, third-party quality assurance (QA) or utilization review (UR) programs, and credentialing processes in psychology all contribute to the recognition and maintenance of professional competence by psychologists. Credentials are discussed later in this chapter, but the remaining structures noted above have not been very effective in ensuring competence.

Ethical codes, for example, are general in nature and give too few specifics to permit an easy identification of incompetent practice. Periodic formal reports by the APA ethics committee, usually published in either June or December issues of the *American Psychologist*, attempt to define incompetence and other unethical behavior through examples. Detection of infractions must rely on complaints by someone. The most severe punishment available is expulsion from the organization. Although this is not a minor penalty, since colleagues are notified of the action, this will not necessarily interrupt the practice of the offender, but may terminate the psychologist's access to malpractice insurance coverage.

PSRCs are limited by their roles as arbitrators. They will usually not function well unless both parties (i.e., the psychologist and the complainant) agree to participate, and this is not always the case. In any event, the decisions of a PSRC are often considered merely *advisory*.

Third-party payers were discussed in Chapter 6, and their quality assurance and utilization review (QA/UR) efforts are potentially the most powerful tools for altering the behavior of practitioners, since they have the power to control payments and may actually terminate provider status in the face of abuses. Such utilization review programs, however, are still in their infancy, and there is little evidence to suggest that the *peer judgments* used to enforce QA/UR monitoring have any significant validity as measures of the quality of service or competence of the providers (Claiborn, 1982).

In one of the few published papers exploring conceptualizations of competent practice, Peterson and Bry (1980) studied appraisals of 126 Psy.D. students in psychology by 102 faculty members and field supervisors. After rating students with whom they had worked, faculty and supervisors were asked to describe the dominant characteristics of "outstanding" and "incompetent" trainees. The quality most frequently mentioned for outstanding students was "high intelligence," while the most common characteristic for incompetent trainees was "lack of knowledge." When a rating scale composed of the 28 most commonly used terms was used by supervisors to rate students in the subsequent year, four factors emerged as central to the conceptualization of competence: i.e., professional responsibility, interpersonal warmth, intelligence, and experience. The data also suggested that behaviorally oriented supervisors gave somewhat less weight to warmth in evaluating competence than did eclectic or psychodynamically oriented supervisors.

One other problem to remember in conceptualizing competence is the range or variability of skills among psychologists, whether they be practitioners, academics, or consultants to industry. The point is well summarized by Hogan (1977) who notes, with respect to the regulation of psychotherapy, that there is a substantial difference between adequate and superior competence. Within each pool of credentialed practitioners, for example, some candidates barely passed, while others markedly exceeded, the admission criteria. By definition, not everyone can be above average. It is certainly desirable to be exceptionally competent, but it is not unethical to practice in an area in which one's competence is simply "adequate," assuming we know what adequate means.

TRAINING ISSUES

Various controversies have evolved regarding the training of psychological practitioners. These controversies have involved questions about how psychological practitioners should be trained and how psychologists who were not trained as practitioners should be retrained if they wish to become human-service providers. Various training conferences have been held, often referred to by the meeting's geographic site, yielding the *Boulder* or *Vail* (Colorado) training models or the *Virginia Beach* (Watson et al., 1981) recommendations. We do not intend to explore the question of whether a *scientist-practitioner* training model is ideal or whether a *professional-school* program is most appropriate for modern practitioners. Rather, we are concerned about ethical issues in the conduct of training. Are psychologists adequately trained for the jobs they intend to perform? Are the techniques used to train them ethically defensible? Are students evaluated in an ethically appropriate manner? Is the institution providing the training competent to do so? These are the substantive ethical problems linked to psychologists' training.

Ingredients of the Program

Recognizing that psychologists who act as human-service practitioners assume considerable responsibility, the APA has developed a thoughtful and detailed accreditation system (Committee on Accreditation, 1980). This system provides a means for evaluating academic and internship programs purporting to train psychological practitioners. Coursework in at least four substantive areas (i.e., biological bases of behavior, cognitive-affective bases of behavior, social bases of behavior, and individual behavior) must be provided. Nevertheless, considerable latitude is permitted within categories. For example, it is possible for a program fully approved by APA in clinical psychology to graduate doctoral students who have never treated a child, studied human development, or learned projective testing. Some programs send students on internships who have acquired experience in several practica and dozens of client assessments, while other programs believe that students who may have seen as few as three or four assessment and treatment cases in practica are ready to start their internship.

The variability across different programs is not necessarily negative, as long as its graduates are aware of their competence and limitations. The recent graduate of a doctoral program who recognizes a training inadequacy can remedy it in many ways. The clinical psychology graduate who has had little experience with children, for example, can take coursework in child development and seek postdoctoral training at a facility serving children and families. The more substantial problems occur with psychologists who wish to change specialties, such as the social, experimental, or developmental psychology graduate who wishes to do human-service work. The number of such individuals are increasing as funding in academia and research areas evaporates. Such shifts are occasionally permitted by *generic* state licensing laws, as discussed in the following section.

APA policy, adopted by the Council of Representatives, maintains that an internship or applied training as such is insufficient for the professional "re-tread," a term sometimes applied to those who wish to convert to clinical work. The policy maintains that these individuals must also complete any coursework that would be equivalent to the desired degree but is missing from their own academic records. It is preferable that this coursework be taken in a programmatic, sequential, and carefully monitored program, rather than in a cluster of casually collected courses. Some universities offer special one- or two-year programs aimed at retraining such individuals. There are also psychologists who choose a "back door" route, seeking internships or training in applied settings without accompanying coursework. The APA can attempt to discipline approved training sites that accept such individuals, but licensing or credentialing bodies are not bound, or necessarily influenced, by APA criteria. Training may also occur in settings that are not APA-approved. Consider the following case examples that describe specialized services to children:

> **Case 9-3:** George Grownup, Ph.D., completed a degree in clinical psychology from a program fully accredited by the APA. He took all of his practica, field work, and internship training at settings treating adults (i.e., a college counseling center and Veterans Administration Hospital). Although he has not taken courses in child development, he now wants to do work with children, so he begins to add child clients to his practice after reading a few books about developmental psychology and child treatment.

> **Case 9-4:** D. Vella Pmental, Ph.D., completed her degree in human development within a psychology department. She has worked for two years as a researcher in a family violence study and in a program assessing the cognitive development of infants with Down's Syndrome. She has decided that she would like to be able to do more clinical forms of work, including personality assessment and psychotherapy with the types of patients she has been studying. Dr. Pmental volunteers more than a dozen hours per week for three years at a local teaching hospital with an APA-approved internship program. She sees patients under close supervision, while attending didactic seminars and taking courses in personality assessment at a local university.

Dr. Grownup is a well-trained adult clinician, whose attempt to prepare himself to work with children is glaringly superficial, and certainly exceeds his trained competencies, although he does not seem to realize it. Dr. Pmental is certainly better trained to work with children than is Dr. Grownup, but she has not technically sought formal "re-treading." She has gone further and is considerably more cautious than Dr. Grownup in attempting to ensure her own competence in the activities she hopes to practice. Although her behavior may technically violate an APA *policy* or *professional standard*, it is not necessarily unethical. As long as she limits her ultimate practice to the areas in which she is well trained, her behavior would be considered appropriate.

Student Evaluations

The APA *Accreditation Handbook* (Committee on Accreditation, 1980) stresses the special responsibility of faculty to assess continually the progress of each student and to keep the students advised of these assessments. Students who either exhibit long-term, serious problems or who do not function effectively in academic and/or interpersonal spheres should be counseled early. If necessary, they should be advised of career alternatives or, after appropriate due process procedures, dropped from the program. Each program should have specific procedures to assess routinely the progress and competence of students, advise them of the outcome, and to delineate appropriate sequences of action and alternative outcomes. These procedures should be explicit, written, and available to all students and faculty. Graduate students terminated from degree programs represent an occasional source of ethics complaints against faculty raising competency issues.

> **Case 9—5:**   Michael Mello left his urban west-coast home to attend graduate school at a rural midwestern university. At the end of his third semester, he received a written notice that he was being terminated as "personally unsuited" to continue in the school's counseling psychology doctoral program. Mello filed ethics complaints against the director of the training and department chair, complaining that he had never previously been advised of problems, his grades were excellent, and he had been denied due process.

> **Case 9—6:**   Liz Militant also traveled across the country to attend graduate school in psychology. After three years in the program with satisfactory grades, she took her comprehensive examinations and failed. In a hurry to take an internship for which she had been accepted, Ms. Militant again attempted the exams and failed. As a result of failing twice, she was terminated as a degree candidate in accordance with department regulations. Ms. Militant filed an ethics complaint against several faculty members, noting that the grading of the exams she failed was highly subjective, and other psychologists to whom she had shown her answers thought they were well done. She went on to claim that her strong feminist views and ethnic heritage had been a source of friction between her and several faculty members for her three years at the school, and she attributed her failures to contamination by these factors in the subjective grading of her exams.

These two cases had several elements in common when they came before an ethics committee at approximately the same time. They involved students with cultural values different from those of the majority of the faculty and community within which they were training. Inquiry by the ethics committee revealed that both schools lacked formal procedures for student grievances and that both students were "surprised" by the efforts to dismiss them. Mello claimed he had no warning prior to the written notice that he was deemed to have serious problems. Although he may have been given ambiguous messages, he had never been counseled or warned that dismissal was possible. Militant had sensed friction with several faculty members, but she had received good evaluations from her field placement supervisors and satisfactory or better grades in all courses. While she had known about the rule that two failures terminated candidacy, she had expected to pass; in addition, she believed that she was entitled to an appeal.

Although the universities and students involved believed they had valid reasons for criticizing one another's behavior, the students were obviously the more vulnerable parties and had been subjected to communication problems. Mediation by the ethics committee led to Mello's being awarded a master's degree for work completed, and he was able to transfer to another university. Militant's university agreed to ask a panel of psychologists suggested by the ethics committee from universities in neighboring states to evaluate her exam answers independently and to be guided by their judgments. Most of the acrimony generated in these episodes might have been prevented if the universities involved had developed more specific procedures for monitoring the progress of students and had given them feedback about their competence.

The students mentioned in *Cases 9−5* and *9−6* were not, however, clearly impaired, such as the students described in the following cases.

Case 9−7: In 1975, Jane Doe entered New York University's Medical School. Prior to her admission, she had had a long history of emotional problems, including numerous involuntary hospitalizations, which were never revealed to the school. During her first year her condition "flared up" again, and she began behaving in a "bizarre and self destructive manner," including at least one alleged suicide attempt in a laboratory on campus. She was later encouraged to take a leave of absence, sought voluntary hospitalization, and was released with a "guarded" prognosis. The medical school later denied her readmission after an examining psychiatrist deemed her emotionally "unfit to resume her medical education" (*Doe* v. *New York University*, 1981; *Mental Disability Law Reporter*, 1981).

Case 9−8: Irwin Flamer was enrolled as a graduate student in clinical psychology at Middle State University. After a series of 12 arson fires in the psychology building, Flamer was discovered to be the culprit and sentenced to a term in prison. After his parole, he reapplied to complete his degree. He was a "straight A" student and had nearly completed a master's degree prior to his arrest.

Case 9−9: Emma Petuous was enrolled as a graduate student at the Manhattan School of Professional Psychology, where she earned respectable but not outstanding grades. Some of the practica supervisors noted that she tended to be impulsive and somewhat "emotionally immature," although she was also able to function quite well in a number of professional circumstances. After receiving an unsatisfactory "C" grade in her statistics course, Ms. Petuous prepared a batch of handbills characterizing the instructor as "sexist, idiotic, an anal personality, a perverse intellectual" and a variety of other unflattering terms. She placed the handbills on bulletin boards around the school building, and she also inserted them in student and faculty mailboxes.

As the citations indicate, the Jane Doe case is indeed drawn directly from case law. A New York federal court issued a preliminary injunction ordering the medical school to readmit Ms. Doe as an "otherwise qualified" person under federal antidiscrimination legislation. The court found that she would "more likely than not" be able to complete her education, despite her psychiatric history, based in part on the fact that she had earned a master's degree in public health at Harvard and had held down a stressful job without deterioration during the years of litigation (*Mental Disability Law Reporter*, 1981). Mr. Flamer and Ms. Petuous represent disguised cases of variable "pathology." They presented focal symptoms that must be considered in light of the emotional context, their other behavior, and their professional goals. One cannot say without more information whether the behavior cited is grounds for termination from the program, instead of some less drastic and more rehabilitative approach. The most difficult case is that of the student who seems personally unsuited to the field in which he or she is pursuing a psychology degree, but whose problems are more diffuse and less easily documented.

The key point to remember is that psychologists who operate training programs hold a dual responsibility—one toward the public and potential clients, and the other toward the student. Although it requires time and careful "due process" to advise students of their perceived difficulties, to suggest remedies, and to assist them in exploring other alternatives, these are responsibilities that must be assumed by psychologists who direct academic and field-training programs.

The Incompetent Institution

Although many people are aware that it is possible to purchase phony diplomas by mail, few realize that the diploma-mill industry flourishes in this country and abroad. Certificates or transcripts based on flimsy correspondence courses or no coursework at all can easily be used to mislead and defraud the uninformed consumer (Daly and Keith-Spiegel, Note 1). Often such institutions provide diplomas that are larger and more decorative than those from accredited schools, and the names of these diploma mills sound quite impressive. Sometimes the names of legitimate institutions of higher learning are used as well.

In one announcement, the mail-order inquirer is informed that the institution has no formal or rigid academic requirements and no courses of study. The sole qualification for the degree is the completion of the application form and payment of the required fee. In another advertisement, a company offers a "make your own diploma kit," as well as offering degree certificates from the bachelor's through the Ph.D. level in any field from a variety of nonexistent institutions. (For a complete description of diploma mills operating in the United States and other countries, see Bear, 1981.)

The rules and regulations relative to awarding degrees vary from state to state, and there are few regulations with any impact on the sale of such "credentials" through the mail. Thus many opportunities exist for deception. There are also no national standards for accreditation, and a school that may be state accredited in California might not be recognized in New York (Bear, 1980). The watchword in determining a degree's professional validity is *regional accreditation*. The following commonly used terms *do not equal accreditation*: "licensed, recognized, authorized, approved, or chartered."

Those terms may differ in legal meaning from state to state and may have no relevant meaning at all. Many poor quality schools or bogus degree programs will claim accreditation, but often by a spurious or unrecognized body. The U.S. Office of Education and its Council on Post-Secondary Accreditation (COPA) are the bodies that recognize accrediting associations, and for colleges or universities there are only six regional accrediting associations—the Middle States, North Central, Northwest, Southeastern, Western, and New England Associations of Schools and Colleges (Bear, 1980).

As noted in the case of Dr. Hartley (*Case 7−1*), only earned degrees from regionally accredited universities and colleges may be cited by APA members when discussing their credentials. Although it is not unethical to purchase or hold a phony degree, any misleading or deceptive use of the degree as a psychologist would be unethical. This includes hanging or posting the degree in a location where a client or member of the public might be mistakenly influenced by it.

CREDENTIALING ISSUES

Credentials presumably exist as a tangible indicator of accomplishment in a given field with implications for gauging the competence of the holder. In psychology there are at least three different levels of credentials, distinguished by their intrinsic characteristics and the data on the basis of which they are awarded. These have been referred to as *primary, secondary,* and *tertiary credentials* (Koocher, 1979). As one moves from the primary toward the tertiary level, one moves further away from the data most relevant for predicting potential competence. The need to develop valid measures of entry-level and continued professional competence is widely acknowledged, but the predictive validity of current levels of credentials is highly variable (Bernstein and Lecomte, 1981).

Primary credentials are those that are earned over time by direct contact with trained instructors. They are based on longitudinal samples of the practitioner's behavior with person-to-person supervision and through direct observation by senior colleagues. Objective and subjective evaluations of progress are made by multiple evaluators as training progresses in a stepwise fashion. Examples of such credentials include graduate training programs, supervised practica, internships, and specialized postdoctoral training. The credential is not a generic one; instead, the person develops expertise in the particular matters and activities studied.

Secondary credentials use primary credentials as prerequisites, but also incorporate other elements in determining qualifications. Such credentials include statutory licensing and certification, as well as recognition by specialized certification boards (e.g., American Board of Professional Psychology). One must first complete the appropriate training and degree programs (i.e., have the appropriate primary credentials) in order to be considered for a secondary level credential. Next, some sample of the psychologist's professional behavior is sought (except in the instance of certain grandparent clauses). The sample is usually cross-sectional in nature and may consist of a multiple choice, essay, or oral exam, submission of a work sample, direct observation of a session with a client, or a combination of these. Some of the examination models used may be extensive, as well as representative of the practice domain the psychologist intends to enter, but others are notoriously inappropriate (Carsten, 1978; Greenberg, 1978). An example of the latter type would include using a multiple-choice, pencil-and-paper instrument to predict competence in delivery of psychotherapy. No validity data exist to justify such predictions.

In the absence of detailed knowledge of the candidate's background and behavior over time, the grantors of secondary credentials usually require the approval or endorsement by colleagues chosen by the candidate. In general, secondary credentials place heavy reliance on the honor system, and the credential granted is often generic in nature. The psychologist is supposed to recognize, acknowledge, and abide by her or his own limitations; there is little exploration of these undertaken by the grantor of the credential (Hogan, 1979; Koocher, 1979).

Tertiary credentials in psychology are relatively recent developments, although the factors leading to their development are essentially the same as those for other credentials. What distinguishes this third-level credential from the other two is that no behavioral sample, first-person contact, or substantial individual scrutiny intrinsic to the credential itself is considered. Rather, they are based solely on evidence that primary and secondary credentials have been obtained. In essence, they simply attest to the fact that the psychologist holds primary and secondary credentials. Membership in certain APA divisions and listing in the *National Register of Health Service Providers in Psychology* are examples of tertiary credentials.

In Chapter 7, we discussed the listing of various credentials in advertising or presentations-of-oneself in a professional manner to the public. We also cited preliminary data indicating that the public may not necessarily understand the meaning or underpinnings of certain credentials, and these credentials may sound more impressive than is justified. Certainly in terms of content validity, criterion-related validity, or predictive validity in which professional competence is an issue, tertiary credentials are relatively worthless and secondary credentials may be suspect for reasons that are discussed in the following pages (Koocher, 1979). Primary credentials are worthwhile, as long as they are accurately represented and understood by the holder. How does this become an ethics issue? Consider the following case.

Case 9−10: Narcissa Schmit, Ed.D., served as a field placement supervisor for the Central States School of Professional Psychology, and she was appointed to be adjunct assistant professor at the school. Her role consisted of volunteering two hours per week of supervision. She was also listed in the *National Register of Health Service Providers in Psychology* by virtue of her degree, state license, and two years of experience working in a health-care setting. Next to her diplomas and licenses in her waiting room were framed copies of a letter confirming her "faculty" status and a "certificate of inclusion" in the *Register*. She also chose to list those credentials in a published announcement of her practice.

Dr. Schmit's behavior falls in that grey area between the unethical and the acceptable in professional behavior. The uninformed member of the general public has no idea what the *Register* listing signifies and could misinterpret it as an additional credential or as a testimony to Dr. Schmit's competence. The reference to faculty status could also be misleading and could represent a deceptive attempt to boost her prestige by implication of a university affiliation that has little or no bearing on her practice. Depending on how these affiliations are presented, Dr. Schmit could be behaving unethically if the misrepresentation is deemed substantive. It would be better, however, not to present these accomplishments and affiliations as credentials, which they are not.

Licensing

Licensing of the professions has rarely been sought by the public. More often, licensing has been sought by professionals as a legal means to obtain recognition by the state, although protection of the public is usually cited as the paramount rationale (Gross, 1978; Shimberg, 1981). The relationship between licensing and the competence of practitioners is at best speculative and based on unverified assumptions (Bernstein and Lecomte, 1981; Gross, 1978; Hogan, 1979; and Koocher, 1979). In fact, the evidence tends to refute the claim that licensing protects the public, while suggesting it may have some potentially adverse effects (Danish and Smyer, 1981; Gross, 1978).

Aside from questions of validity of the examinations on which licensure is based, as noted earlier (Bernstein and Lecomte, 1981; Carsten, 1978; Greenberg, 1978), Hogan (1979) has demonstrated how, in the case of psychotherapy, licensure has failed to protect the public adequately. Except for the most populous states, licensing boards are often so overworked and underfunded that disciplinary enforcement is nearly impossible except in the most flagrant cases of abuse or misconduct. Considering the time-consuming task of investigating complaints with due process to the accused, while also screening applications, conducting examinations, drafting regulations, and attending to the other duties of the board, minimal time remains to worry about such idealistic matters as checking the competence of practitioners who have *not* been complained about.

In most states the psychology license is a *generic* one: that is, one is licensed only as a psychologist. In the application the candidate may have been asked to specify and document areas of expertise (e.g., clinical psychology, school psychology, industrial consultation), but there is seldom any monitoring after licensing unless a complaint is filed or suspicions are aroused. Some would argue that such monitoring is necessary because psychology is a broad field, but others call the field too broad. In 1975, a Federal District Court noted that there was no single "corpus of knowledge" that must be mastered in order to consider oneself a psychologist (*Berger* v. *Board of Psychologist Examiners*, 1975). Thus the courts ordered that Mr. Berger, an accountant with no formal training in psychology, be admitted to the licensing examination in the District of Columbia. Mr. Berger did not pass the exam, although that may have been due to chance rather than to incompetence. Although this is a rather severe indictment of psychology (and one that has not held up in other court decisions), it does cast doubt on the adequacy of the examination procedure.

Generic licensure creates a public information problem, since many people tend to assume that a *licensed psychologist* is synonymous with a *clinical psychologist* (Greenberg, 1982). Greenberg (1982) argues for strict regulation of title use and public education to help overcome this problem. The assumption of the ethics code is that this could be unnecessary because the psychologist should recognize his or her limitations and act in a responsible, informing manner toward the public. Wiens and Menne (1981) dismiss the need for specialized licensure with a medical analogy (i.e., any physician is qualified to make an initial evaluation or appraisal and follow it with an appropriate referral). Unfortunately, many psychologists do not seem to know either their own competency limits or when to make a referral to someone else.

Perhaps the greatest single problem with licensing statutes for psychology is their variability from state to state. Even states that use the same examination procedure may employ different cut-off scores. An individual, who is deemed qualified to sit for the licensing examination in one state, may be denied entry to the examination in a neighboring state. In addition to the Ph.D., Ed.D., M.A., and M.S. degrees, psychologists have listed the following earned degrees in reporting their qualifications for recognition as health-service providers (Wellner, 1978):

C.A.G.S.	D.M.S.P.	D.S.Sc.	M.C.P.
D.A.G.S	D.M.H.	Ed.S.	M.Ed.
D.Min.	D.P.A.	J.D.	M.L.

M.L.H.	M.P.S.	M.S.S.W.	P.D.
M.P.A.	M.S.Ed.	M.Sc.	Th.D.
M.P.H.			

In addition to Departments of Psychology, the following academic departments were listed as granting related degrees (Wellner, 1978):

Philosophy	Education	Special Education
Guidance Counseling	Child Study	Social and Human Relations
Home and Family Life	Law	Health and Physical Education
Anthropology	Religion	Political Science
General Studies	Rehabilitation	American Civilization
Speech Pathology		Educational Research and Measurement

The major fields within these departments in which degrees were granted are even more diverse. In part, this diversity results because many state licensing laws recognize degrees in psychology or, "a closely related field," and some state boards perceive "close relations" between many fields.

Attempts to address this problem have taken two thrusts. The first was a model state licensing law proposed by the APA's Committee on State Legislation (COSL); however, the APA Council of Representatives declined to adopt this model, and it was withdrawn in part because of pending "sunset" legislation (i.e., elimination of the state's licensing function). Furthermore, an APA task force is developing a way to identify those programs offering degrees in psychology. This procedure may help solidify the nature of degrees preferred by would-be psychologists. Programs seeking designation as granting "psychology" degrees would submit their curricula, degree requirements, and faculty credentials for evaluation in accordance with accepted professional standards.

The Master's Degree

The APA recognizes the doctorate as the basic professional degree in psychology, and the master's degree is usually regarded as a way-station or interim level of training. There are subareas of psychology (primarily school psychology) in which the majority of practitioners across the nation are at the master's level. Since many of these master's level practitioners are women and/or older individuals, sexism and ageism have been attributed as the bases for refusing to recognize these degrees as full credentials. Concern about the proliferation of masters' programs designed to produce people to intervene with emotionally disturbed children and adults, as well as the production of a large number of terminal master's degrees in clinical psychology, would be typical complaints (Centor and Stang, 1976).

As an ethical issue, the master's degree problem is usually irrelevant. Little, if any, data suggest that a relationship exists between competence and level of degree. A study by Stevens et al. (1979), for example, found that master's level clinicians are viewed as competent professionals with an important role in the community mental-health-center system. Professional standards sometimes seem to dictate that master's level clinicians must be supervised by psychologists with doctorates, while ignoring the irony that a psychologist with a master's degree and twenty years of experience could be told that she or he required supervision by a recently licensed Ph.D. with two years of experience. The key ethical issues, regardless of degree, are threefold. First, the psychologist must function in accordance with the appropriate legal regulations stipulated for the practice of psychology in his or her state. Second, the psychologist must be competent in the relevant area of practice. Third, the psychologist must be sensitive enough to her or his own individual skills and weaknesses to seek supervision and/or consultation or to refer clients elsewhere when necessary.

The Student in Transition

Students in psychology are obligated to abide by ethical principles, just as are other psychologists. At times, however, some advanced students find themselves caught in an interesting bind when they attempt a professional transition. Consider the following case example:

> Case 9–11:   Karen Quandry, M.S.W., has four years of experience as a clinical social worker and is licensed as an "independent clinical social worker" in her state. She decides to enter the Applied Institute of Professional Psychology, a fully accredited and approved program near her home, to study for the Psy.D. degree in clinical psychology. While going to school to train as a psychologist, Ms. Quandry is supporting herself by practicing psychotherapy part-time in her home office, just as she had done for the past two or three years. She joins the state psychological association and is called to account for "practicing without a license."

Ms. Quandry acknowledges that she is not licensed as a psychologist, although technically she is a "psychology student," and she has identified herself with psychology by joining a professional association. At the same time, she is trained in social work and psychotherapy through that program. She is licensed to practice as a social worker and has been practicing legally. Although she is not qualified for licensure as a psychologist, and thus cannot practice as a psychologist, no evidence indicates that she is not competent to practice as a social worker. A person with two valid professional identities is not required to surrender one, while developing the second. As long as Ms. Quandry is not leading the public or her clients to believe that she is a psychologist and as long as she practices within her areas of social work competency, she is not behaving unethically. Technically, Ms. Quandry cannot consider herself a psychologist nor announce herself to be a psychologist to the public, until she meets appropriate professional and statutory standards for the profession. One must, however, discriminate between professional titles and professional functions for which one has appropriate training.

MAINTAINING COMPETENCE

Estimates indicate that the half-life of a doctoral degree in psychology, as a measure of competence, is about 10−12 years (Dubin, 1972): that is, using the analogy of radioactive decay, about a decade after receipt of the doctorate, half of the knowledge that went into that training is obsolete. In other fields, such as medicine and law, the turnover may be even more rapid (Jensen, 1979) because of advances in the basic sciences and changing legal decisions, respectively. Jensen (1979) poses the interesting question of how one can retain any modicum of professional competence over a 30-year career. He also notes that rapidly advancing technology in many fields can also reduce the half-life time dramatically. The 1941 engineering graduate's training had a half-life of 12 years, but by 1971 the new graduate could expect only a 5-year half-life. Similarly, it is not surprising to find analogies in psychology considering the impact on psychological practice and research of the introduction of modern computers in such areas as automated testing, improved actuarial prediction, biofeedback, artificial intelligence, and all types of simulation programs.

Various strategies have been advanced to ensure that professionals strive to maintain competence, including mandated continuing education, recertification requirements, and professional development models (Jensen, 1979; Regan and Small, 1971; Small, 1975, 1978). Many states now require practitioners to complete certain amounts and types of continuing education coursework to maintain a professional license. No states or certifying bodies, however, have deemed it appropriate to require formal reexamination or recertification of licensed holders or diplomates.

Part of the difficulty in implementing plans to monitor practitioner competence is a definitional problem. What constitutes a meritorious step toward maintaining one's competence? Is attending a workshop commensurate with teaching one? Is writing an article for a respected journal a sign of continuing competence? Will taking or retaking a multiple-choice examination prove anything? Before we can suggest a method for maintaining professional capabilities, we must define criteria that are linked to continuing competence (Jensen, 1979). Professional skills, competently executed on a daily basis, will certainly enhance competence, but experience alone does not immunize a person against making errors. It seems unlikely that a comprehensive solution to the problem of maintaining competence over time will be found in the near future. The most appropriate course of action for a psychologist is to strive for a constant awareness of her or his own limitations, recognize that these limitations can increase over time when formal training has ended, and seek constructive remedies by both formal and informal means to keep skills current (*EP*: 2c).

> **Case 9—12:** Nardell Slo, Ed.D., conducted a cognitive evaluation of an adult client using the Wechsler Adult Intelligence Scale (WAIS) more than two years after the revised form (WAIS-R) had been published. After being questioned on this point, he noted: "They're about the same, and the new kit is too expensive."

> **Case 9—13:** I. P. Freely, Psy.D., continued to recommend long-term individual psychotherapy for child-clients with secondary reactive enuresis, despite substantial evidence that certain behavioral treatments for this problem can be highly effective in a relatively brief period of time. When this fact was called to his attention, he seemed surprised and sought information in the professional literature.

Dr. Slo and Dr. Freely are in the same category as the college professor who has not bothered to update course notes in several years. Both are delivering substandard service to their clients. Slo uses some disturbing and inaccurate rationalizations for his actions, while Freely is simply ignorant of treatment innovations. At least Freely seems willing to learn about the area in which he lacks expertise, although the apparent apathy implied by the fact that he did not do so sooner is worrisome. Slo's resistance suggests a more serious problem, blending ignorance with arrogance. Clients who rely on the expertise of these practitioners will not receive the most efficient and effective treatments. Even if some new technique (e.g., the behavioral treatment of enuresis) presents problems from Freely's professional and theoretical perspective, he has a responsibility to be aware of the development and to advise clients of alternative treatments and choices when discussing his recommendations with them.

THE SICK DOCTOR

When personal problems begin to interfere with professional activities, the psychologist becomes a serious danger to clients. More has been written about the impaired physician than about the impaired psychologist (see, for example, the April and May, 1975 issues of *Psychiatric Opinion*, or Green et al., 1978), but perhaps that is because physicians' access to drugs makes them more visible. Many other facets also pertain to the problem, however, including consideration of some types of psychological practice as "high risk" or "burnout prone" occupations (Freudenberger, 1975; Freudenberger and Robbins, 1979; Koocher, 1980). Another facet is a psychologist's failure to recognize when a client is not improving or is deteriorating while in the psychologist's care. Most dramatic, however, are the instances in which the psychologist, because of addiction, emotional disturbance, or other problem-induced inadequacy, begins to harm clients and presents a danger to the public.

These cases can be especially painful for members of ethics committees, since the ethics inquiry itself often places additional stress on the troubled colleague. When the case is severe in terms of public impact, the ultimate sanction available to such a committee is expulsion from the professional organization. At the same time, however, expelling a member places that person beyond the rehabilitative influence of the committee. Formal rehabilitation programs for the impaired psychologist are rare, although not unheard of (Larson, 1981), and increasing attention is being devoted to this problem. The difficulty in handling such impaired practitioners is well summarized by Annas (1978). According to Annas, a conference of physicians agreed that an emotionally impaired airline pilot should be grounded immediately and, before being permitted to fly again, required to submit to carefully monitored treatment until beneficial results could be documented. Not surprisingly, a group of pilots believed that impaired physicians should immediately cease practicing and abstain from practicing permanently unless successfully treated and rehabilitated. Some pilots argued that at least they have co-pilots present in the cockpit. Needless to say, some physicians find this type of turnabout unfair play.

Burnout

Burnout has been described in general as emotional exhaustion resulting from excessive demands on energy, strength, and personal resources in the work setting (Freudenberger, 1975). It may involve a loss of concern for the people with whom one is working, as well as a loss of positive feelings, sympathy, and respect for one's clients (Maslach, 1978). Another major component, however, is that of aversion to the client at times, mixed with elements of genuine malice (Maltsberger and Buie, 1974). Important client factors related to staff burnout include the client's prognosis, the degree of personal relevance the client's problems have for the psychologist, and the client's reactions to the psychologist (Maslach, 1978).

Helplessness and emotional loss have long been recognized as causal components of depression (Seligman, 1975) and as powerful components of countertransference stress (Adler, 1972; Maltsberger and Buie, 1974). These stresses can arouse substantial anger in the therapist. The anger appears to have two distinct components: *aversion* and *malice*. Societal and professional values mediate against direct expressions of malice or sadism toward one's clients. The aversion component of countertransference stress may be more subtle and, as a result, more insidious. The psychotherapist may experience aversion in relation to the client both directly and unconsciously. A schedule suddenly becomes "too crowded for an appointment this week." A troubled client who gripes, "I don't need any help," is permitted to withdraw emotionally instead of being engaged in dialogue. These events are especially likely when the therapist is feeling helplessness and associated guilt because the client is not progressing satisfactorily or is continuing to manifest signs of difficulty (e.g., suicidal ideation, addiction problems, or life-threatening illness).

If efforts to assert control over one's own emotional issues and the client's distress fail, perceived helplessness may result (Seligman, 1975). People experiencing this reaction no longer believe that their actions are related to their outcomes. Both patient and therapist may begin to feel that they will suffer regardless of their own behavior. In such circumstances, a therapist may defend against experiencing strong emotion by using detachment (Maslach, 1978). While some have suggested that a style of "detached concern" is an appropriate means of relating to clients (Lief and Fox, 1963), there are clear dangers inherent in this response. Clients may experience such detachment as a lack of concern or unresponsiveness.

> **Case 9–14:**   George Sarcoma, Ph.D., worked as a clinical psychologist at a cancer treatment facility. This was his full-time job for several years. He was a caring and sensitive clinician who made himself available "on call" for extended service hours. After both the death of a client with whom he had been particularly close and a disruption in his marriage, Dr. Sarcoma's performance began to fall off. He failed to respond to messages from colleagues and clients, occasionally missed appointments without notice, and became somewhat aloof and detached from his clients. Ultimately, he was fired from his job, but went on to perform well in another setting.

> **Case 9–15:**   Susan Skipper, Ed.D., was an educational psychologist in a large urban public school system. She was overworked and unappreciated by clients and administrators who often made unreasonable demands on her time. Dr. Skipper was not able to set limits on her work situation, and she began to dread going to work each day. She applied for a job in another part of the country and resigned her position to take the new job, giving less than adequate notice, and leaving several uncompleted student evaluations behind.

Dr. Sarcoma and Dr. Skipper were both *burned out*. This occurred as an interaction of their jobs, personal life events, the stressful client problems they handled regularly, and a variety of other factors. Any psychologist who spends most of his or her day listening to the problems of others is a potential victim. Both Sarcoma and Skipper became victims of learned helplessness and depression, and both hurt their clients as a result. Sarcoma's avoidance and detachment may not have yielded identifiable injury to his clients; however, it is likely that a few clients suffered as a result. While Dr. Skipper's abrupt departure has elements of vengeful retaliation against her unappreciating employer, it may well have hurt a number of her clients whose reports went unfinished or who had to wait for her replacement.

Similar to handling many potential ethical problems, the best way to deal with burnout is through prevention. Employers must be aware of impending problems among their employees, and psychologists who begin to see symptoms of burnout in colleagues or sense it in themselves should implement early intervention (Koocher, 1980).

The Troubled Psychologist

Whether the impaired psychologist works in research, teaching, or clinical practice does not seem to affect the incidence of pathology. Although the variety of resulting ethical infractions seems endless, many people, including the psychologist involved, are hurt in the end. Consider, for example, the following cases.

Case 9–16: Martha Ottenbee, Ph.D., was charged with overbilling clients. Apparently she was an extremely disorganized and absentminded psychologist. Her records were often incomprehensible. She was totally inept at managing her practice, although she seemed basically goodhearted. She was slightly frantic and easily distracted when asked to explain her behavior to the ethics committee.

Case 9–17: Kurt Mores, Psy.D., was convicted in state court of "fornication," after a female client complained that she had been emotionally harmed as a result of having sex with him. At an ethics committee hearing, Dr. Mores admitted to having had intercourse with a dozen of his female clients in the past few years. He added that extreme pressure within his marriage had caused considerable anxiety, loss of self-esteem, and feelings of sexual inadequacy for him. He told the committee, referring to his sexual activity with clients, "It was good for them, it was good for me, and I didn't charge them for that part of the session." He also expressed the belief that, "It's okay to violate the ethical code as long as you think about it carefully first and talk it over with colleagues."

Case 9–18: Paul Pious, Ph.D., is a nationally known psychologist and author in the field of moral development. He is working on a major teaching program for application in public schools, when his life begins to become unglued. He is involved in a stressful divorce and is publicly listed in a newspaper as a "tax delinquent." He finds himself becoming increasingly suspicious about the motives of people he works with. When a school teacher raises objections to the teaching program, Dr. Pious calls the school superintendent and reports that the teacher, a member of the gay community, is engaging in sexual relationships with high school students. An investigation reveals no support for the allegations, and Dr. Pious acknowledges lying to protect his project. He is subsequently admitted to a mental hospital for treatment.

Case 9–19: Lester Lapse, Ed.D., appeared before an ethics committee, after the committee received a complaint that he had plagiarized an entire article from a professional journal and had submitted it to another journal, listing himself as the sole author. At the committee hearing, Dr. Lapse appeared despondent. He described many pressures in his life and admitted that he must have plagiarized the article, although he had no conscious memory of having done so. He actually believed that he had conducted the study himself, although there was no evidence that he had done so, and the article he submitted was identical to the prior publication by another psychologist.

Dr. Ottenby's incompetence in managing the business aspects of her practice causes one to wonder what she is like as a clinician. Dr. Mores seems to have a unique moral outlook, with minimum insight into problems caused by his conduct and few, if any, regrets. Dr. Pious finds himself in a desperate situation and adopts a distorted moral standard that permits him to lie and nearly ruin the career of an innocent party. Dr. Lapse, like Dr. Pious, seems to have a mental illness defense for his admittedly unethical conduct.

Some cases, such as the following one, present competency problems that are especially frightening:

Case 9–20: Two clients had almost died while in treatment with Flip Grando, Ph.D. At an ethics hearing investigating the case, Dr. Grando explained these unfortunate occurrences as the result of "insufficient faith" on the part of the clients. Dr. Grando's therapy technique involved locking the client in an air-tight box for an extended period of time since, according to Grando, he had been given the special power to convert the client's own carbon dioxide into a healant for all psychological and physical ailments. Dr. Grando's whole demeanor suggested emotional disorder.

How should each of these cases be handled? Certainly no single remedy or rehabilitation applies to all of these cases. Should one even bother to try and rehabilitate the psychologists mentioned? Is mental illness a proper defense against a charge of ethical misconduct? Will Dr. Mores' arrogant attitude justify a harsher sanction than that given to Dr. Lapse and Dr. Pious, who acknowledge their weaknesses? Should the committee investigating Dr. Ottenby's slipshod business practices seek to investigate her clinical skills, which have not been specifically addressed in the complaint? Will Dr. Grando eventually cause a person's death?

These are complex questions that demand additional data before they can be adequately addressed, but such is the nature of these complaints. In general, we would reply that rehabilitation should be the paramount goal, except when the behavior itself is sufficiently objectionable to warrant more strictly punitive action. Mental illness is certainly an issue that psychologists will want to consider, but it does not justify ethical misconduct (*EP*: 2f). Many psychologists with serious emotional problems are able to seek treatment without committing ethical misconduct. An interesting paper on the claim of mental illness as a defense by lawyers brought before the bar association on charges of misconduct (Skoler and Klein, 1979) suggests similar reasoning. Skoler and Klein (1979) conclude that while bar association discipline committees and courts will consider mental illness to be a mitigating factor, it will seldom be a fully adequate protection.

We have observed that the impaired psychologist is most typically a professionally isolated individual. Consequently, those psychologists who strive to maintain regular professional interactions with colleagues may be less susceptible to burnout and decompensation, or they may simply have such problems called to their attention constructively prior to committing serious ethical infractions.

The psychologist who recognizes the problems of such behavior and is committed to address the problems constructively could probably be rehabilitated. At the same time, one must be careful about broadening an ethics inquiry to include aspects of a psychologist's professional life that are not in question. If personal impairment or mental illness is suspected, however, a broad inquiry may be necessary in the public interest. This inquiry is especially necessary if the psychologist claims emotional problems as a defense. Such a claim implies that the psychologist would be willing to cooperate in a comprehensive rehabilitative plan.

Rarely does a psychologist spontaneously admit that personal distress is impairing his or her judgment. Even more rare is the psychologist willing to make these judgment errors public. A sensitive paper by Kovacs (1974) describes such events and their consequences for himself and one particular client. (This paper is certainly worth reading by anyone who would like to see the subtle encroachments of poor judgment in eroding a therapeutic relationship.)

An important potential remedy for the troubled colleague might involve the formation of support networks through professional associations at the state and local levels. Such groups might offer supportive consultation, as well as referrals to colleagues willing to treat disturbed peers. Mutual support groups for psychologists working in particularly stressful settings, as well as checklists or guides to the warning signs of professional burnout, are other possible aids.

THE CLIENT WHO DOES NOT IMPROVE

The APA ethical code clearly indicates that a psychologist should seek to terminate a relationship with a client, if the client is not benefitting from it. This termination may involve transferring the client to another practitioner who may be able to treat the client more effectively, or it may mean simply advising the client that services are no longer needed. Consider, for example, the following cases:

> **Case 9-21:** Ida Demeaner had been in psychotherapy with Manny Continua, Psy.D., weekly for six years. She had successfully dealt with the issues that had first brought her to treatment, but had become quite dependent on her sessions with Dr. Continua. While there had been no real change in Ms. Demeaner's emotional status for at least four years (aside from the increasing attachment to him), Dr. Continua made little effort to move toward termination. His philosophy is as follows: "If the client thinks she needs to see me, then she does."

> **Case 9-22:** Nemo Creep initially entered psychotherapy with Harold Narrow, Ph.D., for treatment of his growing anger at his employer. It became evident to Dr. Narrow that Mr. Creep was becoming increasingly paranoid and troubled. Dr. Narrow tried to suggest hospitalization to Creep several times, but each time Creep refused to consider the idea. Narrow continued to treat him and ultimately became the object of Creep's paranoid anger.

> **Case 9-23:** Ivan Snidely, Ph.D., is an industrial/organizational psychologist who was hired to assist a major corporation improve employee morale and reduce product defects in a large factory. According to effectiveness data Snidely collected himself, it was evident that his efforts were not meeting with success. Nonetheless, he chose to ignore the data, tell the company that a longer trial period was needed, and continued to supply the ineffective services at a high fee for several additional months before the company cancelled its contract with him.

Dr. Continua has a conceptualization of psychotherapy that suggests the potential for endless psychotherapy. Although it is not possible to state categorically that diminishing returns begin at a certain point, or that all treatment beyond "X" sessions is useless, Continua may well be mistreating his client. He may have fostered her dependency and actually be perpetuating her "need" for treatment. Ideally, he should periodically evaluate his work with her critically and refer her for a consultation with another therapist if he has doubts about the necessity for continued treatment. This presumes, of course, that he does not have an emotional blind spot that prevents him from recognizing her situation.

Dr. Narrow has failed to recognize that a case is beyond his capability to treat. When it became clear that Mr. Creep needed more intensive (i.e., inpatient care) treatment, but was refusing to consider it, Dr. Narrow could have taken a number of steps to help Creep. One step, for example, would have been to decline to treat Creep any longer unless Creep sought appropriate care for himself. If Creep's behavior presented a danger or warranted a commitment for involuntary hospitalization, Dr. Narrow would be responsible for considering those options (see Chapter 3 for related case material).

Dr. Snidely may be greedy or simply blind to his own inadequacy, but that is no excuse for his ignoring the data. If he had no alternative plan, he should not have continued to provide services that he knew to be ineffective. The failure to reassess treatment plans in the face of continued client problems or the failure of the intervention is inexcusable.

A NOTE ABOUT TEACHING AND RESEARCH PSYCHOLOGISTS

In this chapter we have been highlighting psychologists who perform clinical and related services, because the discipline has almost exclusively confined its attention to competency evaluation in these areas. Teaching and researching require no formal training or licensing, despite the fact that most professionals who engage in such work have earned advanced degrees or are in the process of earning them.

Nevertheless, competency issues concerning teaching and research activities also involve ethical problems. As revealed in Chapters 13 and 14, for example, many of the case examples involve competency deficits that have harmed both students and research participants.

SUMMARY GUIDELINES

1. Official APA documents describing standards of practice and standards for providers of psychological services carry neither the weight nor the enforcement mandate of the *Ethical Principles*, but they can be useful in assessing competent practice behaviors.

2. Many subareas, specialty interests, or unusual techniques require expertise for which no generally accepted, practice criteria exist. In those situations, psychologists should consult with experienced practitioners in that subarea, specialty, or technique in order to assess appropriate levels of training before undertaking to practice themselves.

3. There is no comprehensive consensus on coursework or training ingredients for all types of degrees in psychology; the holders of many types of psychology degrees (i.e., Ph.D., Ed.D., or Psy.D.) may be equally well qualified to perform certain tasks. Ultimately, however, it is each psychologist's personal responsibility to ensure that she or he is practicing within the range of activity appropriate to her or his training.

4. Psychologists administering training programs should recognize dual responsibilities—one set to their students, and another set to the public who will be studied, counseled, or otherwise served by the students.

5. Students in psychology training programs should be able to expect timely evaluations of their developing competence and status. Each program should have a formal evaluation system with routine means of feedback, progress assessment, and appeal.

6. Many institutions or organizations exist that grant degrees of a questionable or totally bogus nature. Psychologists should not associate themselves with such institutions and should not behave in any way that implies that the credentials granted by such programs suggest competence in the field.

7. Generic licensing laws and the variety of validly earned degrees that are held by people licensed as psychologists in various states present the potential for considerable ambiguity. Psychologists should behave in ways that make the nature of their training and credentials explicit, recognizing that some credentials have little relationship to competence or little meaning to the public at large. Consumer questions should be answered frankly, honestly, and with appropriate factual information.

8. Students or master-level psychologists may well be competent to perform a number of sophisticated psychological functions, but they must abide by all appropriate statutes and professional standards.

9. Psychologists should realize the potential for burnout or exhaustion in certain types of job settings. They should counsel colleagues who are distressed or seek help themselves as needed to avoid causing distress, inconvenience, or harm to the clients they serve.

10. When a client does not show progress or seems to be worsening despite a psychologist's interventions, that psychologist should seek consultation and/or appropriate means to terminate the ineffective relationship.

11. The distressed or impaired psychologist should refrain from practicing to the extent that his or her impairment bears on ability to perform work with competence and responsibility. If in doubt, the psychologist should consult with colleagues who are familiar with her or his skills and problems.

REFERENCE NOTE

1. Daly, J., and Keith-Spiegel, P. Diploma Mills and Consumer Awareness: or, "Where Did Your Psychologist Go To School?" Paper presented to the Western Psychological Association, Sacramento, California, 1982.

REFERENCES

Adler, G. Helplessness in the helpers. *British Journal of Psychology*, 1972, *45*, 315–326.

American Psychological Association. Specialty guidelines for the delivery of services. *American Psychologist*, 1981, *36*, 640–681.

————. *Standards for Providers of Psychological Services*. Washington, DC: APA, 1977.

Annas, G. Who to call when the doctor is sick. *Hastings Center Report*, December 1978, pp. 18–20.

Bear, J. B. *The Alternative Guide to College Degrees and Non-Traditional Higher Education*. New York: Stonesong Press, 1980.

————. *Bear's Guide to Non-traditional College Degrees* (7th ed.). Mendocino, CA.: Bear's Guides, 1981.

Berger v. Board of Psychologist Examiners, 521 F 2d 1056 (1975).

Bernard, J. L. Due process in dropping the unsuitable clinical student. *Professional Psychology*, 1975, *6*, 275–278.

Bernstein, B. L., and Lecomte, C. Licensure in psychology: Alternative directions. *Professional Psychology*, 1981, *12*, 200–208.

Carsten, A. A. A public perspective on scoring the licensing exam. *Professional Psychology*, 1978, *9*, 531–532.

Centor, A., and Stang, D. Masters level programs in areas of clinical psychology. *Council of Representatives Agenda*, Item No. 16S–1. Washington, DC: APA, September 1976.

Claiborn, W. L. The problem of professional incompetence. *Professional Psychology*, 1982, *13*, 153–158.

Committee on Accreditation, American Psychological Association. *Accreditation Handbook*. Washington, DC: APA, 1980.

Danish, S. J., and Smyer, M. A. Unintended consequences of requiring a license to help. *American Psychologist*, 1981, *36*, 13–21.

Doe v. New York University, No. 77 Civ.6285 (GLG) (S.D.N.Y. Sept. 25, 1981).

Dubin, S. S. Obsolescence or lifelong education: A choice for the professional. *American Psychologist*, 1972, *27*, 486–496.

Freudenberger, H. J. Staff burn-out. *Journal of Social Issues*, 1974, *30*, 159–165.

————. The staff burn-out syndrome in alternative institutions. *Psychotherapy: Theory, Research, and Practice*, 1975, *12*, 73–81.

————, and Robbins, R. The hazards of being a psychoanalyst. *The Psychoanalytic Review*, 1979, *66*, 275–296.

Green, R. C.; Carroll, C. J.; and Buxton, W. D. *The Care and Management of the Sick and Incompetent Physician*. Springfield, Ill.: Thomas, 1978.

Greenberg, M. D. The examination of professional practice in psychology (EPPP). *American Psychologist*, 1978, *33*, 88–89.

————. "Specialty" licenses in psychology. *American Psychologist*, 1982, *37*, 102.

Gross, J. S. The myth of professional licensing. *American Psychologist*, 1978, *33*, 1009–1016.

Hogan, D. B. *The Regulation of Psychotherapists* (Vol. 1–4). Cambridge, MA: Ballinger, 1979.

Jensen, R. E. Competent professional service in psychology: The real issue behind continuing education. *Professional Psychology*, 1979, *10*, 381–389.

Koocher, G. P. Credentialing in psychology: Close encounters with competence? *American Psychologist*, 1979, *34*, 696–702.

———. Pediatric cancer: Psychosocial problems and the high costs of helping. *Journal of Clinical Child Psychology*, 1980, *9*, 2–5.

Kovacs, A. L. The valley of the shadow. *Psychotherapy: Theory, Research and Practice*, 1974, *11*, 376–382.

Larson, C. Psychologists ponder ways to help troubled colleagues. *APA Monitor*, August/September, 1981, p. 16 and p. 50.

Lief, H. I., and Fox, R. C. Training for "detached concern" in medical students. In H. I. Lief, V. F. Lief, and N. R. Lief (Eds.), *The Psychological Basis of Medical Practice*. New York: Harper and Row, 1963.

Maltsberger, T., and Buie, D. H. Countertransference hate in the treatment of suicidal patients. *Archives of General Psychiatry*, 1974, *30*, 625–633.

Maslach, C. The client role in staff burn-out. *Journal of Social Issues*, 1978, *34*, 111–124.

Mental Disability Law Reporter, 1981, *5*, 409–410.

Peterson, D. R., and Bry, B. H. Dimensions of perceived competence in professional psychology. *Professional Psychology*, 1980, *11*, 965–971.

Regan, P. F., and Small, S. M. Toward a continuum of formal and continuing education. *American Journal of Psychiatry*, 1971, *128*, 99–101.

Seligman, M. E. P. *Helplessness: On Depression, Development, and Death*. San Francisco: Freeman, 1975.

Shimberg, B. Testing for licensure and certification. *American Psychologist*, 1981, *10*, 1138–1146.

Skoler, D. L., and Klein, R. Mentally troubled lawyers: Client protection and bar discipline. *Mental Disability Law Reporter*, 1979, *2*, 131–143.

Small, S. M. Focus: Continuing certification in psychiatry. *Journal of Psychiatric Education*, 1978, *2*, 4–14.

———. Recertification for psychiatrists: The time to act is now. *American Journal of Psychiatry*, 1975, *132*, 291–292.

Stevens, J.; Yock, T.; and Perlman, B. Comparing master's clinical training with professional responsibilities in community mental health centers. *Professional Psychology*, 1979, *10*, 20–27.

Watson, N.; Caddy, G. R.; Johnson, J. H.; and Rimm, D. C. Standards in the education of professional psychologists: The resolutions of the conference at Virginia Beach. *American Psychologist*, 1981, *5*, 514–519.

Wellner, A. M. *Education and Credentiality in Psychology*. Washington, DC: APA, May 1978.

Wiens, A. N., and Menne, J. W. On disposing of "straw people": Or an attempt to clarify statutory recognition and educational requirements for psychologists. *American Psychologist*, 1981, *36*, 390–395.

Dual-Role Relationships and Conflicts of Interest

10

Whatever houses I may visit, I will come for the benefit of the sick, remaining free of all intentional injustice, of all mischief, and in particular of sexual relations with both female and male persons, be they free or slaves.

The Hippocratic Oath
(c. *400 BC*)

The vast majority of psychologists work in the context of relationships. Psychologists often hold an advantage of power over the people with whom they work, especially when they are psychotherapy clients or students. They occupy a position of trust and are expected to advocate the welfare of those who depend on them.

When psychologists place their own needs and goals above those of consumers or when they lose sight of the fiduciary nature of their professional relationships, exploitation, faulty professional judgment, and harm to consumers can result. Ironically, the psychologists are often harmed as well. The *Ethical Principles* (*EP*: 6a) recognize the perils of relating to consumers on other than a professional level and counsel psychologists to remain continually aware of their own needs and their potentially influential position. The code admonishes psychologists to make every effort to avoid exploiting trust and dependency. Blending the professional role with another is to be shunned whenever professional judgment may be compromised or impaired.

This chapter will explore sexualizing professional relationships, which is clearly an unethical as well as unsound professional practice, as well as a host of other dual-role relationships and conflict-of-interest situations that often present more complex and subtle dilemmas. We must candidly note, however, that dual-role conflicts *not* involving sexual intimacies cannot always be avoided. Psychologists and their clients, students, or supervisees typically live in the same community and may share many similar interests that may result in the crossing of paths outside of a professional setting. Social networks in a given community are also complex and can result in coincidences, such as learning that a client has just become the leader of your son's Boy Scout troop or that a friend's daughter has enrolled in your course. If we argued that *no* dual roles are permitted, we would be forced to advocate that psychologists live as hermits. Rather, our purpose is to sensitize readers to the potential dangers and conflicts inherent in such roles so that possible consequences can be minimized to the greatest extent possible.

SEXUALLY INTIMATE BEHAVIOR WITH PSYCHOTHERAPY CLIENTS

The express prohibition against sexual intimacies in the 2500-year-old Hippocratic Oath was not duplicated by the American Psychological Association until a few years ago. The psychotherapy literature has acknowledged transference of feelings among clients and therapists, but erotic *contact* has gone virtually unmentioned until relatively recent times. Feminism, consumerism, and a growing admission by psychologists that such contact does occur are among the factors accounting for increasing concern about psychotherapists who would take sexual advantage of their clients. Charges of sexual exploitation against psychotherapists are increasing, no doubt resulting from media publicity and a forceful denouncement of client-therapist sex from within the profession.

Although the number of complaints are increasing, whether the *actual incidence* of sexual relationships with clients is also accelerating cannot be verified. According to some critics, a general climate of permissive sexuality and relaxed standards of "therapeutic decorum" have blurred the role boundaries between therapists and clients (Barnhouse, 1978; Zelen, 1979, Note 1; Len and Fisher, 1978). Serban (1981) asserts that for current "new-wave" therapies, the relationships between doctor and patient are so flexible that they border on improvisation. Others contend that the problem has always existed, but that the victims felt too powerless to protest or, if they did, were discounted as delusional, fantasizing and struggling with their transference neuroses (Schwendinger and Schwendinger, 1974; Barnhouse, 1978; and Kelly, 1979). A fascinating letter written by Sigmund Freud in 1931 to his disciple, Sandor Ferenczi, reveals that the issue was brewing more than fifty years ago. Ferenczi suggested that showing physical affection to patients might assist in neutralizing early emotional deprivation and shared his ideas with his mentor. Freud responded:

> You have not made a secret of the fact that you kiss your patients and let them kiss you. . . . Now I am assuredly not one of those who from prudishness or from consideration of bourgeoise convention would condemn little

erotic gratifications of this kind. . . . But that does not alter the fact. . . that with us a kiss signifies a certain erotic intimacy. . . . Now picture what will be the result of publishing your technique. . . . A number of independent thinkers will say to themselves: Why stop at a kiss? Certainly one gets further when one adopts "pawing" as well, which after all doesn't make a baby. And then bolder ones will come along who will go further, to peeping and showing—and soon we shall have accepted in the technique of analysis the whole repertoire of demiviergerie and petting parties, resulting in an enormous interest in psychoanalysis among both analysts and patients. (Jones, 1957, 163–164, cited in Marmor, 1972.)

Freud's letter raises questions that still cannot be definitively answered: Where is the line that demarcates non-erotic touching from erotic contact or sexual intimacy? Does touching patients lead to sexual intercourse? The general definition of erotic contact offered by Holroyd and Brodsky (1977, 1980) includes behavior that is primarily intended to arouse or satisfy sexual desires. Intercourse or other forms of contact with the genitals would probably receive consensus as constituting "sexual intimacies." But kissing, embracing, and hand-on contact can vary from the tenderly wholesome to the imprudently impassioned. Interpretations lie both in the intent of the perpetrator and the reaction of the recipient, which may or may not be congruent. The situational context is also a large part of the criterion. A vigorous and warm embrace upon learning that an anxious client successfully passed the bar exam would probably be viewed and experienced by both parties differently than would that same embrace given without referential cause. The following case illustrates how differing perceptions of touch can lead to ethical problems:

> **Case 10–1:**   Janet Demure complained that her therapist, Ram Rush, Ph.D., behaved in a sexually provocative manner, which caused her considerable stress and embarrassment. He allegedly put his arm around her often, massaged her back and shoulders, and leered at her. Dr. Rush vehemently denied any improper intentions. He said he touched most of his clients in this manner and intended to communicate warmth and acceptance toward them. He noted that Demure seemed uneasy, but expected this would "quickly pass as it did with several others who were not used to physical expressions."

This case illustrates the necessity for remaining sensitive to individual clients and their needs, a sensitivity that may require an alteration in one's usual approach. It also raises the question of how the degree of harm is related to the extent of sexual activity. No evidence exists to prove that sexual intercourse with clients causes more overall damage than is caused by provocative verbalizations or suggestive fondling. After boundaries have been crossed, trust has been compromised and the impact of even more minor sexual advances may be extensive.

Incidence

Estimating the frequency of any type of ethical infraction is difficult, but surveys have attempted to sample professional attitudes and practices toward sexual intercourse and both erotic and non-erotic touching of clients. Holroyd and Brodsky (1977) surveyed 1,000 licensed psychologists and found that, of the 657 who responded, 5.5% of the male therapists and 0.6% of the female therapists reported having had sexual intercourse with their clients. An additional 2.6% of the males and 0.3% of the females reported having had sexual intercourse with exclients within three months after termination of the therapy relationship. The male psychiatrist subsample in a survey conducted by Kardener, Fuller, and Mensh (1973) revealed a similar incidence pattern (5%) for sexual intimacies with patients, which was lower than patterns found among other medical specialties. These findings indicate a lower incidence than predicted by Butler and Zelen (1977), who estimated that one in five therapists have been sexually intimate with patients. Nevertheless, Forer's unpublished survey conducted in 1968 reported that 17% of his sample of male private practice therapists admitted to having had sexual relationships with clients as compared to *no* such sexual experiences reported by female private practice therapists or male therapists working in institutional settings (Forer, 1981, Note 2).

Erotic touching (*excluding* intercourse) was reported by 9.0% of male and 1.0% of female therapists by Holroyd and Brodsky (1977). Approximately half of the therapists in the Holroyd and Brodsky survey thought that *non-erotic* contact, such as hugging, kissing, or affectionate touching, might be beneficial to both male and female clients under certain conditions, and 27% reported engaging in this type of contact. The emotionally or socially immature (e.g., children or schizophrenics) and the distressed or depressed were most frequently mentioned as the types of clients who might particularly benefit from non-erotic touching. Circumstances most frequently mentioned for appropriate use of non-erotic touching included expressions of emotional support, reassurance, and initial greeting or closing of sessions.

Risks to Clients and Therapists

The available data cannot be considered totally representative, since they consist primarily of accounts by clients who complained, who sought additional therapy, or who responded to advertisements requesting information from those who had experienced sexual contact with their therapists. However, for most clients assessed from these populations, the sexual experiences were harmful (Chesler, 1972; Seagull, 1972, Note 3; Belote, 1974, Note 4; Butler, 1975, Note 5; Taylor and Wagner, 1976; D'Addario, 1977; Keith-Spiegel, 1977, Note 6; Zelen, 1979, Note 1; Bouhoutsos et al., 1981). Common consequences for the clients include distrust of members of the opposite sex and of psychotherapy, depression, sexual relationship impairment, anger, devastation, rejection, and feelings of being exploited and abandoned. Hospitalizations and suicides have been traced to sexual encounters with therapists as the triggering incidents. Once a therapy relationship becomes sexualized, treatment frequently ends abruptly or is affected adversely.

Surveys of psychologists (Holroyd and Brodsky, 1977) and psychiatrists (Kardener et al., 1973) reveal that the vast majority do not believe that erotic contact or sexual intercourse with clients could be beneficial. Such behavior has been compared to rape or incest (Masters and Johnson, 1976; Barnhouse, 1978), and it creates "therapeutic orphans" whose caretakers have failed in their role (Kardener, 1974). Such behavior has been widely regarded as an abuse of trust and power and as desertion of the professional role and fiduciary duty. The therapy in a sexualized relationship has been described as detrimental, since the therapist's objectivity is destroyed.

Whereas consequences to clients from engaging in sexual intimacies with their therapists can be shattering, many of the psychologists involved have not fared much better. Some people erroneously assume that psychologists who engage in sexual intimacies with clients are risking very little, since psychotherapy is conducted in the absence of witnesses. If a client complains, one can simply deny the accusation, citing "fantasy," "craziness," or "transference problem" as the basis for the charges. Does this work? In one sense it does. Perhaps half of the sexual intimacy cases result in the "he-said, she-said" category because the differing stories cannot be substantiated by either party. Ethics committees usually cannot sustain such charges. *But* the psychologist is not exonerated since the victory is by default. If another charge is subsequently filed against the same therapist, the scale becomes tipped against the psychologist, because ethics committees do not destroy files containing serious charges when the psychologist was not explicitly judged innocent, and a case may be reopened at any time if new evidence suggests that an earlier conclusion could have been in error.

Such psychologists will find no contemporary sources of support for their actions or grounds for defense since sexual intimacies with clients are unethical under *any* circumstances, even when actively solicited by the client. Malpractice insurance will not pay when courts have awarded damages to clients who are judged to have been sexually exploited. Clients have a number of options for redress in addition to ethics committees, including criminal law statutes, tort actions (including malpractice), and licensing boards. A. A. Stone (1976) and Hays (1980) provide detailed accounts of legal remedies available to clients who claim that sexual improprieties were committed by their therapists. Clients also have additional support systems, including expert witnesses, subsequent therapists who are prepared to testify regarding the damage the previous sexualized therapy caused, and the APA ethics code itself, which is a favorite "witness for the prosecution."

Regardless of the outcome of an ethics inquiry or legal action, the accused psychologists often suffer an impugned reputation, and sometimes loss of job and spouse. In general, engaging in sexual intimacies with clients is a dangerous, unprofessional, and grossly unethical activity that harms both the clients and therapists.

Characteristics of Psychologists Who Engage in Sexual Relations with Clients

Stereotypes of sexually exploitative psychologists as dashing, debonair, and self-assured, do not reflect the current information available about characteristics of therapists who sexualize relationships with clients. The actual descriptions more closely fit those of psychologists who are impaired or troubled (see Chapter 9).

Although data cannot be collected with the rigor demanded by the traditional scientific method, what information is available indicates that therapists who engage in sexual intimacies with clients have one or more personal problems, including the following: vulnerability; fear of intimacy; crises in their own personal sex or love relationships; feelings of failure as professionals or as persons; high needs for love or affection or positive regard; poor impulse control; isolation from peer support; and depression (Dahlberg, 1970; Marmor, 1972; Butler and Zelen, 1977; Keith-Spiegel, 1977, Note 5; Forer, 1981, Note 2). Data also suggest the most common offender is a male in his 40s or 50s (Chesler, 1972; Dahlberg, 1970; Belote, 1974, Note 4; and Butler and Zelen, 1977). The fact that clients involved tend to be younger females suggests that sexually exploitative psychologists may view such women as easy sources of "as-if" intimacy, or as a means to recapture waning youth and virility (Keith-Spiegel, 1981, Note 7).

Case 10−2: Samuel Sorry, Ph.D., explained to an ethics committee that his sexual relationship with a young and vulnerable client was prompted primarily by a series of rapidly accelerating crises in his own personal life. His wife of twenty-five years had left him for another man, his son abused drugs, and his father had recently died. He was feeling alone, abandoned, and saw himself as a failure. His young client was trusting and complimentary. He saw her as a way to reestablish his self-esteem and feelings of adequacy and potency.

Case 10−3: Mid Crises, Ed.D., became increasingly depressed after his fiftieth birthday. He had not achieved the success he had aimed for and believed it was now too late. He was feeling old and unattractive. A young client began tentatively to express her deep and adoring feelings for him. He reported finding the situation irresistible and compelling. They commenced a sexual relationship. The client ultimately felt confused and unfulfilled in the relationship and contacted an ethics committee.

Such therapeutic rationalizations as rescuing clients from their sexual difficulties or using erotic behavior to facilitate the development of trust are difficult to accept when one considers the fact that the targets for such "therapy" are *not* randomly spread across the whole range—young and old, beautiful and plain—of female clients (Kardener et al., 1973; M. H. Stone, 1976)

The question of why female therapists are less likely to engage in sexual intimacies with clients has been debated in the absence of solid data. Perhaps female sex roles have allowed women, rather than men, to learn and practice a broader spectrum of techniques for providing love and nuturance. Perhaps the cultural conditioning of women to refrain from taking the sexual initiative has also taught them better control of sexual impulses, as well as techniques for resisting sexual advances (Marmor, 1972). Dahlberg (1970), who admits that his concept may be unfair, suggests that because therapists tend to be older people, and because men do not usually find older women as sexually attractive as younger women may find older men, relationships between male clients and female therapists may not entail the type of dynamics that can lead to sexual contact.

No instance of a male client pressing charges of sexual exploitation against a female therapist has ever been brought to our attention, although a small number of female therapists have admitted to engaging in sexual intimacies with clients on anonymous survey responses. We do not know how male clients were affected by such experiences, nor why, if any were psychologically harmed, they do not choose to complain to ethics committees. Only two males, to our knowledge, have submitted a formal complaint of sexual misconduct against their therapists, but the therapists were also male. Moreover, in the handful of cases known to us involving complaints of sexual intimacies against female psychotherapists, the complainants were either female clients or wives of male clients alleging that the therapist engaged in sexual intimacies with their husbands.

Offender Profiles

Based on our analysis of more than a hundred cases of sexual misconduct, we will illustrate four general types: "the seducer," "the sexperts," "the hit-and-runner," and "the love bitten."

The Seducer. The smooth, Svengali type who deftly manipulates his clients into sexual liaisons and continues to sustain that level of "service" indefinitely is *not* a common offender profile brought to the attention of ethics committees. Perhaps most psychotherapists who possess the skills of an exciting lover do not need to exploit clients to fulfill their needs.

Case 10–4:   Several student clients at a university counseling center complained that Jack Rabbit, Ph.D., first gained their trust and then took sexual advantage of them. The students claimed that they had located almost another dozen women who could tell the same story. One described his office as "the hutch with a revolving trap door."

Case 10−5:   A client complained that Sam Svelt, Psy.D., always behaved as the perfect gentleman in a "Prince Charming" sort of way. She admitted to being beguiled by him and did not realize how her own personal problems were being exacerbated until well after a sexual relationship was established.

Occasionally clients have complained that they were attacked without warning by their therapists, although this offender-profile variation is also rare:

Case 10−6:   A client complained that during the second therapy session Mel Sprint, Psy.D., whom she had personally characterized as soft-spoken and mild-mannered, bolted from his chair and started pulling at her clothing.

The Sexpert. A fairly small percentage of offenders have attempted to justify their sexual involvement with clients on various therapeutic grounds, such as the following:

Case 10−7:   Sid Lust, Ph.D., lost his license based on multiple complaints by clients about his therapy techniques. The women were routinely told that although his method might seem unusual, he could guarantee that their emotional and sexual lives would vastly improve. He would first ask his clients to disrobe and then fondle their breasts and genitals murmuring all the while how this would "set them free."

Case 10−8:   Barney Best, Ed.D., convinced Marcia Trust that a psychotherapist was the perfect person with whom to have a sexual affair since no one else could better understand her needs and desires or could be as trusted. When Marcia found Best to be a mediocre lover and felt the psychotherapy was now confusing and somewhat frightening, she contacted an ethics committee.

The Hit-and-Runner. The most prevalent offender group brought to the attention of ethics committees is composed of psychologists who became sexually involved with clients and then, for various reasons, attempted to extricate themselves from the sexual aspects of the relationship.

The sexualization of these therapy relationships typically started tentatively and involved some back-and-forth attraction signals in the form of non-erotic hugging, mildly flirtatious remarks, or suggestive joking. The first sign of deterioration, after the relationship becomes more actively sexualized, usually occurs when the client expresses a wish to extend the relationship and deepen the commitment between the two of them. At this point, most therapists (especially those who are married) reacted with some form of distancing. Whether a response to fear, guilt, belated-moralistic stirrings, or disinterest, such withdrawal is experienced by the clients as rejection and abandonment. At this point, the now-angry clients often contact an ethics committee.

Case 10−9: Ho Hum, Ph.D., found Dulce Swing a diversion from his predictable and unexciting personal life. Even though she was his psychotherapy client, it did not seem to pose any dangers at the time. Dulce dated many men and seemed fun-loving and fancy-free. After a while, Dulce wanted to be taken to a nice restaurant or to Las Vegas for a weekend because, as she explained, "I'm beginning to feel like the mistress you are ashamed of." Dr. Hum began to panic because he could not get away very often nor could he risk detection. He told Dulce that they would have to stop seeing each other because their behavior could hurt people. He assured Dulce that he would be happy to continue as her psychotherapist. She was insulted and charged Dr. Hum with emotional and financial exploitation.

Case 10−10: Tim Scare, Psy.D., became concerned when his client, with whom he had intercourse on several occasions, began to call him frequently at home "just to say hello." He had not predicted the increasing informality in the relationship, nor did he welcome it. He suggested to his client that therapy be terminated. She asked if that meant that they would then be "just lovers." When he responded that this was not his desire either, the client felt hurt and abandoned.

Case 10−11: Willie Nip, Ph.D., realized too late that his outwardly affectionate and sometimes erotic kissing and touching of a client he found particularly attractive was not acceptable professional behavior. However, when he discontinued the behavior, the client felt that he no longer cared about her and was punishing her. He tried to assure her that this was not so, but she contacted an ethics committee charging that Dr. Nip's rejection and now cold manner had worsened her mental state.

The Love-Bitten. Occasionally, psychologists who enter sexually intimate relationships with clients explained their involvement as due to *genuine* love feelings towards their clients.

Case 10−12: Elmer Smitten, Ph.D., was attracted to Luna Fond from the minute she walked in the door. He recalled wanting to reach out and hold her, to take care of her. He thought about Luna constantly and anxiously anticipated the sessions with her. If Luna cancelled an appointment, he was disappointed and depressed for days. The first social meeting occurred under conditions similar to the type that "love-sick" adolescents contrive. He called to ask if she would mind changing her 10:00 A.M. appointment to 11:00 A.M. At the end of the session, he would then mention that he had not eaten all day and would casually ask Luna to join him at the deli across the street for a sandwich. He noted that he should have realized the pending danger, when he found himself mentally rehearsing the lunch situation many times. Luna accepted lunch. There were more lunches, then dinners, and finally sexual activity. Smitten maintained that if he were free, he would have committed himself fully to this woman. She was everything he did not have in his life. Soon the guilt about having an affair with a married man began to gnaw at Luna. Dr. Smitten began to feel pressured and frequent spats occurred. Luna terminated both the "therapy" and the personal relationship, consulted another psychologist, and contacted an ethics committee, charging Dr. Smitten with exacerbating her emotional problems. In the meantime, Smitten continued to pursue Luna and begged for her return. He continued writing her love letters even after the ethics committee investigation had been initiated.

This type of offender evokes more feelings of compassion than the others, perhaps because the theme of "star-crossed lovers" seems tragic, rather than malevolent. Loving a client, however, does not excuse a psychologist from professional responsibility.

Preventing Accusations and Occurrence

How can innocent psychologists protect themselves against *unwarranted* claims of sexual impropriety, since the impact of being accused, regardless of outcome, can be potentially devastating? It is difficult to believe that anyone would be so enraged that he or she would unjustly risk harming a psychologist's professional and personal life. Assuming it is possible, however, the following precautions might be considered:

1. Before attempting any form of non-erotic touching or verbal compliment that could be considered flirtatious or suggestive, thoroughly know your client's psychological functioning. Some clients may remain unsuited to these types of displays for the duration of therapy.

2. If uneasy feelings about attraction dynamics are perceived as emanating from a client, consult a trusted, sensitive, and preferably experienced colleague about the proper course of action with this particular client.

3. If a client is open and direct about erotic feelings or a desire for a sexual relationship, deal with these impulses in a way that protects the client's self-esteem. Taylor and Wagner (1976) suggest that the therapist express a feeling of flattery followed by a firm declaration that such behavior cannot ever occur between them because it is both a serious ethical violation and potentially harmful. Then the therapeutic issues surrounding the attractions can be handled.

4. The truly fearful might consider some practical safeguards, including the following:
   a. Conduct therapy in a group-practice setting where other people are always around.
   b. Furnish the office tastefully but businesslike. Avoid decor and furniture that suggest a too-cozy ambience.
   c. Avoid offering therapy sessions in other than a traditional, professional setting.

Obsession over forestalling such a threat can lead to absurd considerations, such as one person who considered moving his practice to a window showcase. Recognition of signs, both in the client and in oneself, and dealing with these feelings immediately and objectively is the best protection for any therapist.

If a therapist senses an attraction toward a client, it should not be ignored. In many cases, the act of sexual intimacy was a culmination of a lengthy process that started with vague, uneasy feelings of excitement, but progressed in tidy, rationalized steps. The therapist must monitor his or her own attraction feelings from the start and assess whether these feelings are having any impact on the quality of professional judgment. Dr. Smitten (*Case 10–12*), for example, recognized retrospectively that he had begun to counsel Ms. Fond to refrain from dating men for his *own* reasons long before he began seeing her socially himself. Whether these attractions should ever be discussed with clients is a matter of debate within the therapeutic community. The therapist should discuss the feelings with someone, preferably a sensitive and experienced colleague, whom the psychologist trusts and respects. In those instances in which the therapist cannot control his or her feelings, termination and referral are recommended as a way to protect both parties from possible harm.

The question often arises whether, after terminating therapy, the two people are "ethically free" to commence a relationship. This problem is tricky on ethical grounds and raises questions about protection of the client's welfare. Ethics committees have indeed pursued cases known informally as the, "You're cured; your place or mine?" type.

Case 10–13: Tom Anxious, Ph.D., was sexually attracted to his client, Sue Reddy. The vibes indicated that she felt the same way toward him. Although Sue's treatment issues were far from resolved, Dr. Anxious terminated her without recommending further treatment and asked her out to dinner. Their sexual relationship was brief and unsatisfying to both. She eventually charged Anxious with exacerbating her problems, taking advantage of her vulnerability, and then abandoning her. Because the termination was handled improperly, the ethics committee processed the case despite the fact that Sue was not formally a client when the sexual intimacies occurred.

If termination is done more judiciously, usually involving a referral to another therapist and sometimes a meeting among the three parties to settle and clarify the transition, can the first therapist and client then pursue a sexual relationship? At this point, the therapist may be technically off an "ethics hook," but we recommend that he (or she) *very* carefully assess the situation further before proceeding. Questions, such as the following, should be honestly explored, perhaps with the assistance of a counselor:

1. How would such a relationship affect the client's life and my own? (Psychologists committed to another relationship should be especially concerned about this issue.)

2. How much time has passed since termination? (The shorter the time period, the more the therapist should be careful.)

3. Was the termination mutually agreed on and similar to client terminations not involving sexual attraction? Was a termination plan agreed on (e.g., limited to six sessions) in advance? Or was it a cover-up or ploy to enter into another type of relationship?

4. What type of therapy was involved? Certain therapy relationships, used for the purpose of working on a specific behavioral problem (such as smoking), or for vocational counseling, and so forth, may pose fewer complications than deep, uncovering, insight-oriented therapy relationships.

5. What is the client's current level of autonomy? After termination, would the client be able to function independently without therapy so that the client-therapist role was no longer required?

6. Why am I so attracted to this client? Is this a person I would have pursued if I had met her (or him) in another context? Or am I attracted primarily for reasons that are inherent in a therapeutic relationship, such as a need to rescue, a need to control, or a need to be admired and depended on?

7. If I enter into an intimate nontherapeutic relationship, will I be able to abdicate my position of power and authority and share my own limitations and vulnerabilities with this person?

8. What is it that I want from this relationship? Do my needs correspond to the needs of a person who once trusted and depended on me for help? Or could I be another source of disappointment or unhappiness in this person's life?

9. Why is this person attracted to me? When I am no longer the therapist, will she (or he) continue to find me attractive, or will I probably fail to meet exaggerated expectations?

Some people have suggested that a "cooling off" period, perhaps for several months, should be agreed to by both parties to ensure the mutual desire to meet on a new level. We encourage psychologists to be as cautious and as conservative as they can possibly be in such situations.

Another type of prevention, requiring thought and widespread implementation, involves teaching graduate students about such issues as sex-bias in therapy, consequences of sexualized therapy for clients and psychologists, and ways of handling erotic feelings and attractions toward clients (American Psychological Association, 1975; Abramowitz, 1976; Edelwich and Brodsky, 1982). Holroyd (1984) suggests that training curricula confront the reality that a psychotherapist will find some clients attractive and that it is still possible to function effectively without acting out any fantasies and needs. Students should also learn that one does not *have* to respond to a seductive client. Schultz and McGrath (1978) studied students' management of sexual feelings and provocations and found that many of them experienced high levels of anxiety and feelings of inadequacy when encountering such phenomena either in themselves or in their clients. To assist students in understanding and dealing with such eventualities, these authors developed a series of staged video scenes depicting various sexually laden incidents that might occur in the course of conducting therapy. Unfortunately, not all instructors are so creative, and later in this chapter we will discuss an unfortunate model of professional behavior provided by some professors and supervisors.

Professional and public education about the dangers of sexualized therapy also requires upgrading. Practicing psychologists must remain sensitized to the issues, and they should learn more about the "warning signs." They must also strive to keep their professional identity and judgment at a high level, even in the face of their own personal conflicts.

The public should be consistently advised, preferably by professional groups themselves, that the seductive practitioner is not to be tolerated and that sexualization of psychotherapy runs counter to their own best interests.

We know little about the rehabilitation of psychologists who have engaged in sexual misconduct with clients. Rehabilitation potential is probably strongly related to the type of offender. Those who suffer from character disorders would probably not be successful candidates, whereas those who became aware of their improprieties and experienced remorse and a willingness to cease their sexual acting-out and explore their own motives may be more amenable to change. Butler and Zelen (1977) report discouraging data. Despite the fears, conflicts, and guilt reported by 95% of their offender sample, most continued their sexual acting-out. Psychotherapy was sought by only 40% of their sample. These data, however, were collected before the *Ethical Principles* were revised explicitly to forbid sexual intimacies. Raised consciousness and pressure from within the profession may have resulted in increased motivation among offenders to rehabilitate.

Ethics committees sometimes include supervision or referral for therapy among their sanctions. The penalty for violating the code by engaging in sexual intimacies with clients often includes either expulsion from the APA or a forced resignation with the stipulation that membership may be reinstated, usually after five years, if the psychologist can give evidence of rehabilitation. At this time, however, professional associations have not provided clear guidelines nor have they developed programs to assist the psychologists in proving themselves ethically restored.

Sexual Intimacies with Students and Supervisees

Male professors conducting sexual liaisons with young female students is as durable an academic stereotype as ivy, football, tower clocks, caps and gowns, and founder statues. Aristides (1975) describes the allure of the professor as "the man with the most knowledge in the room where knowledge is the only business of the hour, a figure of authority, confidence, intellectual grace—an object, if he does his work even half-well, of love" (p. 361). Professors, who are aging, are surrounded by a perpetual bevy of attractive young people who treat them with respect, deference, and even a touch of awe. Indeed, we all know of cases in which such relationships ended in marriage and sometimes accord such culminations "Cinderella status."

Gossip regarding the incidence of sexual relationships with students has been replaced in recent times by research data. Students have begun to complain about unwanted sexual advances, organized attempts to curb sexual harassment on campuses have been established, and public sanctions have increasingly been imposed on sexually exploitative professors. (The more general issue of sexual harassment, not necessarily involving actual sexual intimacies, is examined in Chapter 11.)

A nationwide survey of psychologists by Pope, Levenson, and Schover (1979) revealed that 10% of the respondents reported having had sexual contact, as students, with their educators, and 13% reported entering into sexual relationships, as educators, with their own students. Gender differences were significant, mirroring both the "academic image" and the sex difference trends in client-therapist sexual encounters: that is, 16.5% of the women and 3% of the men reported sexual contact with their educators when they were students, and 19% of the men, compared with 8% of the women, reported sexual contact with their students. Moreover, as psychotherapists, 12% of the males and 3% of the females reported sexual contact with their clients, which is a slightly higher percentage for both sexes than those revealed from other recent surveys of therapists. In addition, student–educator sexual relationships appear to be on the increase since 25% of the recent female graduates reported having had sexual contact with their educators, compared to 5% among those who had earned their degrees more than 21 years before the survey was conducted. These findings not only suggest that the incidence of sexual relationships among psychologists and their students are more prevalent than those between clients and therapists and that this pattern is increasing, but that a "modeling effect" may be operating as well.

Prohibitions against sexual encounters between professors or supervisors and their students or trainees are not *explicitly* stated in the *Ethical Principles*. Some psychologists have attempted to include "students" along with the express prohibition against sexual intimacies with psychotherapy clients (*EP*: 6a). Why that inclusion has not been effected is somewhat complicated. Part of the problem is the inherent difficulty in reaching agreement concerning what constitutes student status. A large campus-wide survey revealed that professors overwhelmingly agreed that sexual relationships with students *currently enrolled* in a professor's class were both improper and unethical. The overwhelming majority also believed that sexual relationships with adult students in academic departments other than that of the professor were the business of the parties involved and that any risks incurred were strictly personal ones. In the gray area—i.e., students in the department but not currently enrolled in the professor's class or under his/her supervision—more widely divergent views prevailed. A survey of upper division and graduate students in a psychology department (Gerard, Note 8) revealed a similar pattern to that of the survey of professors described above. Some students objected vigorously to extending the ban on sexual intimacies to psychology educators. Rather than objecting that such behavior was inappropriate, however, most students objected to being classified on a par with psychotherapy clients. As one student explained, "I would resent being viewed by the APA as an unstable, immature person with no rights to my own decision making and no respect for my personal judgment. I am a competent, adult woman, and what I do in my private life is no one's business but my own."

On the surface, it may appear that those who are concerned about the ethics and impact of sexual relationships between psychology educators and their adult students are paternalistic moralists who are intruding in matters that should not concern them. On the other hand, it should be recognized that students and educators may not be in touch with their own vulnerable positions when their relationships sexualize. If the *affaire de coeur* goes amiss, the effects must be reckoned with in both the private and professional realms. Emotional fallout can include grief, embarrassment, fear, bitterness, and a desire for vengeance. When these feelings are superimposed on the academic role, serious consequences for students, professors, or both can ensue.

Case 10–14:   Dexter Yentz, Ph.D., had been having frequent sexual liaisons with one of his graduate assistants, Mary Switch, for almost a year. Then Mary met a young man whom she wanted to date exclusively. When she told Professor Yentz that she would not be seeing him anymore, he became furious and expressed his intention to get even. She was abruptly relieved of her assistantship. She heard rumors that Dr. Yentz was telling other faculty that she was fired for gross incompetence and was not really "graduate school material." When she confronted Yentz, he allegedly told her that this was only the beginning. He had status and clout in the field and if she chose to stay in psychology, she would find it uncomfortable both now and in the future.

Case 10–15:   Cloris Push, Ed.D., made numerous suggestive remarks to her student, Sam Shun, and implied that the closer their personal relationship, the more likely Sam's path to successful completion of his degree program would be facilitated. Although Sam was not attracted to Professor Push, he feared that rejecting her advances and desire for intimate relations would endanger the quality of her academic evaluations of him.

Case 10–16:   Selma Long greatly admired psychology professor, Irving Idol, Ph.D., and took advantage of opportunities to interact with him. Although she did not aspire to an affair with him, he began to suggest more intimate liaisons. Selma felt that if she did not comply he might not like her anymore. But as the relationship continued, Selma fell in love with Dr. Idol. She envisioned a life with him both as a co-worker and as love partner. When she verbalized her fantasies, Dr. Idol became firm and rejecting. He told her that she had misunderstood his motives, and he had no such long-range intentions. He suggested they not see each other anymore. Selma was so abashed and hurt that she could not face him at school. She dropped out of the degree program.

Case 10–17: After an affair between Gary Gozlin, Ph.D., and Paula Sad had ended, Paula filed charges against Professor Gozlin for sexual harassment and exploitation. She also contacted the local papers who ran the story. She was joined by several other students who felt harassed and exploited by Gozlin. Ultimately, Dr. Gozlin lost his wife and job.

In these cases, we see the results of revenge, as well as the effects of coercion, abandonment, and hindsight gone awry, but the superimposition of the professional role heaped additional consequences or pressures on the parties.

Even educators who are not opposed to sexual intimacies with students must ask themselves: "What are these students learning?" It seems to us that they are learning it is acceptable for psychologists to gratify their own needs under whatever circumstances they choose, with minimal regard for maintaining objectivity and clarity in professional relationships with those over whom they have substantial power, influence, and responsibility. An ironic combination of findings in the Pope et al. (1979) research was that only 2% of the psychologists believed that sexual relationships with students could be beneficial, despite the fact that five times that percentage had engaged in such relations with their own students. We must also reiterate that sexual intimacy may compromise the process of assigning fair and valid evaluations, regardless of the motivation (Pope et al., 1980). Thus sexual intimacies with students undermine the obligation to evaluate students fairly and accurately.

Support systems for students harmed by their educators are increasing. University redress channels are readily available, and ethics committees are receiving more complaints from students who are exploited sexually or otherwise. The ethics code provides protection for students suffering such damage. Dual-role relationships are proscribed, and sexual intimacies with students over whom one has influence constitutes a dual role. Other parts of the code admonish psychologists who supervise professionals in training to honor the obligation to facilitate professional development and not to exploit trainees in any manner. Although the code does not ban sexual intimacies with students outright, aggrieved students or supervisees have sufficient avenues of recourse in the *Ethical Principles* (*EP*: 7c and 7d).

Unfortunately, students still remain more vulnerable than they may fully appreciate. Many may be too frightened to complain because of their inherently weaker position. They may fear risking their professional futures, as in the case of Dr. Yentz and Mary Switch (*Case 10–14*). Although a psychotherapy client could be harmed by a therapist, her career would rarely be at stake. Students risk damage to themselves in both personal and career terms. Professors are more vulnerable than therapists in the sense that psychotherapy clients are usually "on their own" when pressing a formal charge of exploitation, since they do not have access to their clients' identities in seeking corroboration of the offender's behavior pattern. Students, on the other hand, have ready access to each other, leaving the exploitative educator open to "group charges," with a considerably greater possibility of exposure and censure.

OTHER DUAL-ROLE RELATIONSHIPS AND CONFLICT-OF-INTEREST SITUATIONS

Role conflicts without sexual aspects have not received the attention they deserve in the ethics literature, perhaps because the role superimpositions are often not inherently controversial or riddled with moral overtones. The *Ethical Principles* are not explicit about *nonsexual* dual roles. The general message implicit in the ethics code is that psychologists who enter into a professional, fiduciary relationship with a client must hold that relationship paramount. When a prior relationship (e.g., a close friendship) exists, superimposing a professional relationship may be inappropriate. If an opportunity to enter another level of relationship arises after a professional relationship is already established, it should probably be rejected. It is probably impossible to create clear guidelines for psychologists with regard to dual-role relationships not involving sexual intimacy, since each situation presents unique features that must be considered. Our goal is to sensitize readers to the possible conflicts and potential damage of one's actions so that professional judgment may be exercised prior to risking a blending of roles.

We have already discussed how the term "sexual intimacies" poses some definitional confusions. These problems are minor compared to the operational definition problems in other dual-role and conflict-of-interest situations. For example, what differentiates a "close friend" from "acquaintance?" When is a "client" no longer a client? Who is a "student" or an "employee"? Psychologists differ in their definitions and practices. Some psychologists, for example, would define an appropriate psychotherapy relationship as commencing with someone they have never met before. A client is "forever" since that individual may wish to renew the professional relationship even after a termination. A former student one has taught or supervised may also be "forever," since she or he may require an evaluation by the professor long after leaving academia. An employee can be anyone who works in the same organization, regardless of the line of supervision or authority.

It is unlikely that a psychologist who takes a cautious approach would ever have to cope with an ethics inquiry involving dual-role or conflict-of-interest issues. Strict definitions, however, are sometimes unrealistic or inappropriate.

Among the various multiple roles or conflict-of-interest situations a psychologist might conceivably encounter with consumers, the following eleven have been selected for discussion: entering into professional relationships with close friends and family members; entering into professional relationships with employees; socializing with clients and students; "small world" hazards; accepting "significant other" referrals; the perils of propinquity; service bartering; peer co-counseling; accepting gifts and favors; "affective-experiential" academic coursework; and "in-situ" therapy.

Entering into Professional Relationships with Close Friends and Family Members

Psychologists, including those with no clinical training, must resign themselves to frequent requests for advice and information from friends and relatives on matters ranging from a child's poor report card to a grandmother's memory gaps. When the issues require more than casual comment, psychologists may be tempted to take on good friends or relatives as clients in a professional or quasi-professional role. Frequently, the psychologist reasons as follows: "I will do my best since these people are important to me." The psychologist has already obtained considerable first-hand knowledge of such people that might facilitate the therapy process. The psychologists might offer such clients low rates or see them in a professional capacity at no charge.

Despite these seeming advantages to client/friends or client/family members, such relationships should be strictly avoided. Friendship, family, and psychotherapy relationships are complex and intimate. Parties in intimate relationships are vulnerable to harm since they place trust in others who mean a great deal to them. But the differences in function and purpose between these types of intimate relationships are significant. Friendships ideally involve a satisfaction of mutual needs and are not necessarily goal-directed, while professional relationships are focused on serving the needs of the client and are directed toward specific therapeutic ends. Friendships and family relationships are geared toward longevity, whereas professional relationships should be concentrated on specific goals and terminated once achieved. When these two types of relationships are superimposed, the potential for adverse consequences to all concerned is substantially heightened.

Case 10-18:   S. R. Mod, Ph.D., agreed to give his best friend's daughter a series of behavioral therapy sessions to control her nailbiting. He explained to her father that some aversive conditioning was involved, but the father's enthusiasm remained undaunted. When the girl complained about the procedures, the father stormed over to Dr. Mod's house demanding to know what was going on. When Mod noted that all of this had been described to him prior to the session, the friend retorted: "Well, I certainly didn't think you would do anything painful to your best friend's daughter. I guess I don't know you well after all."

Case 10-19:   Stella Stern, Psy.D., agreed, after many requests, to work on a professional basis with the weight problem of her good friend, Zoftig Bluto. Progress was slow, and most of the weight would return shortly after it was lost. Dr. Stern became impatient because Bluto did not seem to be taking the program seriously and avoided facing deeper issues. Bluto became angry with Dr. Stern's irritation as well as the lack of progress. She expressed disappointment in Dr. Stern whom she believed would be able to help her quickly and effortlessly since, as she explained, "I am one of her closest friends."

Case 10-20:   An intellectual assessment of Billy was recommended by the boy's school. Billy's father, Paul Proud, asked his brother, Peter Proud, Ph.D., to do it. The results revealed some low performance areas and a full scale I Q score of 97. Paul was very upset with his psychologist/brother for not "making the boy look good to the school."

Case 10-21:   Murray X. Plode, Ed.D., accepted the seventeen-year-old daughter of his sister as a client. During the course of therapy, the girl revealed that she had been sexually abused by her father (the therapist's brother-in-law). Dr. Plode went directly to the parents' home, threatened the father with police action in front of the entire family, and asked his brother-in-law to pack his things and leave his sister's house immediately. The father, who denied ever sexually molesting his daughter, complained to an ethics committee that the therapist had violated his rights and destroyed his family. Plode responded that this was a personal family matter, and, therefore, no one else's business.

These cases show common pathways of faulty expectations, mixed allegiances, and misinterpretations of motives leading to disappointment, anger, and sometimes a total collapse of relationships. Dr. Mod's friend did not *hear* what he was attempting to convey in his role as a psychologist. Dr. Stern's friend could not get into the professional role, but expected results anyway. Dr. Proud's brother assumed that Dr. Proud would fudge results for him. Dr. Plode could not separate his own dual roles from each other, resulting in extremely improper actions for a psychologist.

Psychologists are free to be completely human in their friendship and family interactions, and to experience all of the attendant joys and heartaches. To some extent, their psychological expertise might be helpful in alleviating difficulties that arise within such relationships by offering emotional support, information, or casual suggestions. When the problems become more serious, however, the prudent course of action is to refer to other professionals who can deal with the problems and individuals involved in an objective fashion.

Entering into Professional Relationships with Employees

Another closely related issue involves forming a dual-role relationship with employees or close associates at one's work place. The same types of misunderstandings resulting from role blending can occur at work. In the case of employees or supervisees, the elements of power, control, and influence are even more marked than among friends or family members, since a "double-power base" accrues to the psychologist.

> **Case 10–22:** Jan Job worked as a records clerk for a large community mental-health agency. She was supervised by Helmut Honcho, Ph.D. Jan was experiencing personal problems and asked Dr. Honcho if she could be a client. He agreed. Jan would later bring an ethics complaint against Honcho, charging him with blocking her promotion based on assessments of her as a client rather than as an employee.

In such instances, it may be impossible to unravel the true bases for any job-related decision making. Whether valid or not, the employee/client may interpret any unpleasant feelings about what happens on the job as linked to therapy, or vice-versa. Trust is compromised either way.

Socializing with Clients and Students

Critics of psychotherapy have referred to it as, among other things, "purchased friendship" (Schofield, 1964). Supporters contend that it is precisely the differences between psychotherapy and friendship that account for its effectiveness. Despite the psychoanalytic tradition of formality, however, it is currently acceptable in most circles for psychotherapists to behave as feeling human beings, rather than as "therapy machines." The stiff, professorial model is crumbling as well. Criticism is seldom leveled toward professors who have adopted a relaxed and warm teaching style, and they are often popular among students. In this instance, we explore the ethical issues that emerge when psychology practitioners and teachers move into a *nonsexual* social/friendship role with current consumers of their services.

A small-scale survey on socialization with ongoing psychotherapy clients (Tallman, 1981, Note 9) revealed that about one-third of the thirty-eight psychotherapist respondents had formed social relationships with selected clients (usually including their respective spouses) on occasion. Interestingly, these respondents were all males, even though half the sample was female. Role blending was justified on various therapeutic grounds, such as providing additional support and facilitation of rapport. Some offered no therapeutic justifications, stating simply that socializing occurred with clients with whom it was enjoyable to be. In more than half of these instances, the friendships persisted after the professional relationship terminated. Another third of the sample of psychologists (mostly women) indicated that they had, on occasion, attended "special events" in clients' lives, such as a wedding or Bar Mitzvah. They added that these were single and isolated episodes, attended for the meaning-value to the client rather than as a vehicle for two-way socializing. The final third of the sample held to a strict policy of no client contact outside of the professional setting. This group believed that risks, including ethical ones, were too likely. For example, new sets of needs may develop for both therapists and clients, and these may interfere with or contaminate the therapy process. Clients may be unsure of the boundaries of social relationships and experience anxiety or confusion. The therapists' capacity to function as an objective party may deteriorate. Dependencies may be reinforced. The roles are incongruent in the areas of power and trust. Finally, since people do not have to pay their friends for support and caring, the meaning of "friend" becomes perverted in this instance.

Case 10−23:   Soon after Patty Pal began counseling with Richard Chum, Ed.D., Patty asked Dr. Chum and his wife to spend the weekend at their family beach house. The outing was enjoyable for all parties. During therapy, however, Patty became increasingly reluctant to talk about her problems and insisted that things were going quite well. Other social interactions among the foursome continued to occur on weekends. Chum finally confronted Patty during therapy with his impression that "nothing was moving." It was at that point that Patty admitted that she was experiencing numerous pressures and problems. But she felt that if she were honest about them in therapy, Chum might choose not to socialize with her and her husband anymore.

Case 10−24:   Jack Ace, Ph.D., and his client King Stud shared an affinity for poker. They started playing with some of Stud's other friends on Wednesday nights. One evening Dr. Ace was the big winner and Stud was the big loser. Right after that evening, Stud began to cancel both appointments and games. When Dr. Ace confronted him, he said he did not feel "right" about their relationship anymore. He could not be specific, but did recognize that when Dr. Ace won several hundred dollars from him he "saw him differently." Dr. Ace seemed "dangerous" somehow, rather than helpful.

The above examples did not involve clients who pressed formal ethics charges against the psychologists, but such cases do exist. In these instances, clients felt exploited or duped and abandoned.

Case 10–25:   Buddy Flash had been seeing Will Crony, Psy.D., in treatment for two years. They had also invited each other to their homes. Buddy gave especially elegant parties and several important people, including entertainment celebrities, were usually in attendance. During one of these parties, Buddy and Dr. Crony had an argument over what, to Crony, was a minor matter. However, Buddy abruptly terminated therapy and wrote to an ethics committee complaining that Dr. Crony had kept him as a client in order to exploit his social status and take advantage of his hospitality.

Case 10–26:   Raphael Baroque, professional artist, complained that Duo Face, Ph.D., did not follow through with her promises and had exacerbated his insecurity and low self-concept. Baroque had seen Dr. Face in psychotherapy for more than a year, during which time she praised his art work, accompanied him to art shows, and promised to introduce him to some of her gallery contacts. Baroque reported that he began to feel so good about himself and his talent that he terminated therapy, fully expecting that the mutual interest in his art career would continue. However, Dr. Face did not return his calls. When he did reach her, she was evasive and said she would get back to him, but never did. Baroque became depressed and his self-esteem dropped. He felt tricked. When contacted by an ethics committee, Dr. Face explained that she was always "unconditionally supportive" to her clients. But since Baroque was no longer a client, she had no further obligations to him.

While psychologists and their clients must actively and willfully make specific arrangements to alter the professional relationship, professors and students often do not. Indeed, encouragement of both groups to attend simultaneously many activities outside of the classroom are commonplace. Because the professor-student relationship does not involve the type of trust and emotional intimacy characteristic of psychotherapy relationships, such socializing on a casual basis does not raise much concern. Nonetheless, responsibilities toward students and the power of professors to influence them and their life opportunities are forceful enough to warrant caution.

Case 10–27:   Marsha Scholar, Ph.D., was popular among the students and socialized with many of them. She was shocked to learn that charges had been leveled against her by a student who claimed she had given her a low grade because her husband had insulted Professor Scholar at a party. Scholar claimed she did not even recall the incident and had graded the student objectively and fairly.

Case 10–28:   Several students complained to the university administration that Gregarious Buch, M.A., was nice to the students he liked and froze out the students he disliked. They also charged that "liked" students received grading advantages. Professor Buch responded that he may have seemed friendlier to some students than to others because he knew some much better than others. In essence, he socialized with the more assertive ones that sought out his company for coffee, parties, dinners, and so forth. An analysis of his grading procedure revealed that the "friend" students did not receive higher marks as a group than the "nonfriend" students.

Professors are probably wise to limit their social contacts with students to casual contact or to social events associated with the university (such as departmental parties) until the student graduates. Those who wish to form closer relationships with current students should carefully assess the risks and be aware of the misunderstandings that might arise.

When can more intimate social friendships be formed with people who were clients and students without the danger of dual-role complications? As noted earlier, conservative critics say "never," even after the therapy and student relationships have terminated, since an exclient may wish to reenter therapy and an exstudent may require letters of recommendation years after the professional relationship has been concluded. Others believe that this view is too conservative and denies opportunities for what could be productive, satisfying, long-term friendships for all concerned. We suggest that the most prudent course of action is to wait until the professional relationship terminates "naturally" (i.e., a therapeutic relationship should not be abruptly ended because the parties involved want to be friends). In the case of therapy clients, future treatment, if needed, should be with someone else. Both students and faculty should understand that requests for future letters of recommendation should mention the fact that the exprofessor (or exsupervisor) and exstudent are now friends. In most cases, this is not to the student's disadvantage. Although such a recommendation could be viewed as biased, it may also be perceived as a positive sign that a professor thought so well of a student that he or she chose to maintain the relationship. The primary risk that cannot be predicted in advance is the possibility that the exprofessor/exstudent friendship could go awry, in which case the student could lose a reference resource. One method of protection from this unfortunate possibility is to place a letter in the student's file at the university *before* a social relationship ensues. That letter can stand on its own merits, regardless of the friendship pattern, for the exstudent's lifetime.

Small-World Hazards

Psychologists working in small, isolated communities must adapt to the realities of bumping into clients or students beyond the context of professional settings, while coping as best they can with other perplexing role mixings. One psychologist, for example, reported the special care that had to be taken to ensure that he and his client, the only sixth-grade teacher in town, could avoid difficulties that might arise due to the presence of the psychologist's twelve-year-old son in her class. Another small-town psychologist noted the difficulties in scheduling neighbors to avoid having them run into each other in the waiting room. Another psychologist required guidance from an ethics committee when the alcoholic and abusive husband of a client yelled profanities at him at every opportunity—in the barbershop, bowling alley, restaurant, park, market, and even as they passed each other in their cars!

Psychologists working in huge, metropolitan settings can also experience small-world hazards, often in unexpected ways. A psychologist might learn that his client is his wife's best friend's secret lover or is his daughter's boss. Such discoveries emerging during the course of psychotherapy can often be handled by staunchly maintaining the professional role without regard for the coincidences that link the therapist and client in other ways. Other situations, however, can become more complicated:

Case 10–29: Sid Fifer consulted Ron Wrung, Ph.D., when Sid's offensive and antisocial behavior caused increasing trouble on the job and at home. During the early course of therapy, it was casually revealed that Sid and the therapist's wife worked for the same large company, though in different departments. Several weeks later, Sid was fired. He charged that Dr. Wrung told his wife stories about him, which she, in turn, shared with the company boss. Wrung vehemently denied sharing material about Sid or any other client with his wife or anyone else.

Case 10–30: During the beginning of the second session, Kin Tribe, Ph.D., and his client Clip N. Split learned that Split had been briefly married years before to a distant cousin of Tribe. Split had deserted the cousin two weeks after the wedding and had taken all of their gifts and other possessions with him. The therapy sessions continued without any further discussion of the historical connection. Split ultimately complained that Tribe punished him for what he had done by being cold and abrupt and for failing to provide competent services. Tribe was astonished by the ethics charge. He replied that he barely knew his cousin and that she was not an issue at all. Rather, he focused on Split's current problems, which revealed continued flight from responsibility.

Dr. Wrung was apparently a casualty of the type of circumstances that could be neither predicted nor prevented. But Dr. Tribe encountered warnings early in the course of the professional relationship that should have been addressed directly.

It is most likely that psychologists will be judged culpable when a "small-world hazard" was known in advance *and when alternatives were clearly available,* but the psychologists undertook a professional relationship anyway, and charges of exploitation, prejudice, or harm resulted.

Case 10–31: Ginger Nailbrain, the daughter of the divorced boyfriend of Linda Pleasemore, Ph.D., was encouraged to enroll in Dr. Pleasemore's section of an introductory psychology course. Pleasemore thought this experience would bring the daughter and herself closer and help solidify the relationship with the father. Half-way through the semester, the relationship between Pleasemore and Ginger's father dissolved. Ginger's final course grade was a "D." Ginger and her father filed complaints with the university and a state ethics committee charging that Dr. Pleasemore was expressing vengeance toward the father by assigning the daughter a poor grade.

Pleasemore's professional judgment was faulty on several grounds. She was not only agreeing to a dual-role relationship, but was also using a professional relationship as a vehicle for developing a personal relationship to her own advantage. Even if the relationship had worked and the girl had received a high mark, the ethical issues would remain unchanged (though also probably uncontested).

Accepting "Significant Other" Referrals

Word-of-mouth is a primary means by which new clients for all types of psychological services are generated. However, when a satisfied consumer recommends a psychologist to a close friend or close relation, care must be taken to assess adequately the potential for conflict of interest, unauthorized passing of information shared in confidence, and compromises in the quality of professional judgment.

> **Case 10–32:**   Dum Tweedle was pleased with his individual therapy progress and asked Janis Divide, Ph.D., to see also his wife Dee in individual therapy. Dum eventually pressed ethics charges against Dr. Divide for contributing to the failure of their marriage, a process that began at the time Dee entered therapy. He contended that Dr. Divide encouraged Dee to change in ways that were detrimental to him and to their relationship. Dr. Divide contended that it was her responsibility to facilitate growth in each party as individuals, a responsibility she felt she had upheld.

> **Case 10–33:**   Tuff Juggle, Ed.D., accepted Jane Amiga as a client with full knowledge that she and Sandy Chaver, an ongoing client, were best friends and that many aspects of the friendship were serious treatment issues for Sandy. He reasoned that he could compartmentalize them sufficiently and that both women would benefit from the fact that he knew them both. One day he slipped and shared something significant that Jane had told him with Sandy. Jane brought ethics charges against Juggle for breach of confidentiality and disregard for client welfare.

Dr. Divide ignored the "third client"—namely, the relationship between husband and wife—and attempted the improbable task of treating close relations as though they were unconnected entities. Dr. Juggle's case involved a less engrossing relationship between the two clients, but a red flag (i.e., the friendship was an emotional issue) was known to him in advance, which should have provided sufficient warning. Juggle's "slip" of information to the wrong party is an ever-present danger when consulting people who know each other well enough to share some of the same material during individual sessions. Even the sharpest of memories may fail under such circumstances, and the results can be harmful to both clients.

The "significant other" referral problem is not necessarily confined to *direct* referral from an ongoing client, as is illustrated in the following case:

Case 10−34: Buck Bank introduced his business competitor to Bart Mercantile, Ph.D., an industrial psychologist who consulted with Bank's firm on personnel management and evaluation matters. The competitor hired Dr. Mercantile to perform similar services for his firm. Bank brought legal action against Dr. Mercantile, charging that he used his inside knowledge to the detriment of Bank's operation and gave the competitor a substantial edge in the marketplace.

Industrial clients may differ from individual psychotherapy clients in many respects. But it is still incumbent on the psychologist to avoid even the appearance of "two-timing."

The Perils of Propinquity

In addition to business generated by referrals from satisfied customers, another ready source of potential client contacts is found through one's circle of acquaintances. A member of the psychologist's athletic club or church congregation may request the psychologist's professional services. Not allowing acquaintances to be potential clients would in general be unacceptable to consumers as well as to psychologists. This section illustrates the necessary cautions that should be heeded before taking on clients who base their contact for services on the fact that they "know you slightly" from someplace else.

Case 10−35: Feline Breed, Ph.D., spent much of her time outside her professional role raising pedigree cats. Most of her weekends were devoted to traveling the cat-show circuit. Many of her therapy clients were "cat people" whom she had met through her hobby contacts. The small-talk before and after the therapy sessions was usually devoted to discussions about cats. Interest in purchasing kittens that she raised was often expressed, and she did sell them to clients. In more than one instance, the sale of kittens to clients caused difficulties. Once, for example, the therapy process was not proceeding as the client wished, and the client accused Dr. Breed of "using" him as a way of selling high-priced cats and not really caring about his problems. In another instance, a woman client was upset because Dr. Breed sold her an animal that had never won a single prize. The client assumed that if the therapist raised such defective cats, then the trustworthiness of her therapy skills should be questioned as well.

In this instance, the task, which Dr. Breed did not accomplish, concerned suppressing the former acquaintance role when engaging in the professional role. This suppression can usually be done without untoward consequences if the continuation of the former acquaintance role does not require more than minimal energy or contact and does not involve a conflict-of-interest situation.

An example of a more delicate propinquity peril involves delivering private-practice therapy services to students in the university where one also teaches. Here the acquaintance role involves contact that may actively continue, and the nature of that contact may well include evaluations and other responsibilities that extend a powerful influence on the student. In short, both facets of the dual-role relationship are (or could be) intense, and the potential dangers of role blurring could ensue. For example, the student, as a paying client, might expect special favors at school. Or the psychologist may view and evaluate the student's academic performance differently, depending on therapy issues.

The *Ethical Principles* (*EP*: 6a) admonish psychologists to avoid client/ student dual roles. But, as we have seen, the definition of "student" is not clear-cut. Privately counseling students, who are not and who are never likely to be in one's academic department, poses no dual-role conflicts in most cases. A few university departments have policies on this matter and allow psychology faculty members to see psychology students in their private practices off-campus, but require a stipulation between the two that the professor will not serve the student in any academic evaluation capacity for the duration of the student's tenure at the university. Although this policy defuses the potential for dual-role conflicts, the student may be disadvantaged by the restriction. We strongly recommend the conservative course of action in the spirit of protection for all concerned: i.e., refer students and supervisees from one's department to the university's counseling center or to another practitioner in the community.

The following case illustrates how other situations can arise to tear at loyalties and muddle the guideposts on which to base judgments:

Case 10−36: Ian Shaky, a doctoral student in a clinical psychology program, was experiencing serious depression. He asked one of his professors to see him privately. The professor agreed. Several weeks later, Shaky made a serious suicidal gesture. The professor told the program director about it. Shaky was then asked to leave the program until he could pull his life together. Shaky brought ethics charges against the professor for violating the confidentiality provisions of the therapy relationship. The professor claimed he was not acting unethically because the student/client was "in clear danger" to himself.

The dual-role nature of Shaky's therapy relationship complicates the provision to disclose information to others in cases involving imminent danger, a judgment that is difficult to make even under simpler conditions (see Chapter 3).

Service Bartering

Trading a service for a service or product has a nostalgic attraction. Psychologists may even enter into service-bartering agreements as a humanitarian gesture to people who require services but who do not have cash to pay for them. Because the services psychologists offer usually involve trust, sensitive evaluations, social influence, and the creation of some dependencies, the potential for untoward consequences are always present in such relationships.

We have heard of situations in which forms of bartering occurred with mutually satisfactory results. A gifted seamstress was offered the job of making clothes for a psychologist in exchange for psychotherapy. The client was happy because she needed psychotherapy and had plenty of time available to sew. The therapist's elation was summarized by her remark: "I am the best-dressed Ph.D. in town." These two people were lucky. What if the dresses did not fit properly or were not made to the therapist's satisfaction? What if the client became displeased with the therapy process and began to feel like a one-person garment sweatshop? These "what ifs" are neither silly nor idle speculations, if one considers actual incidents of bartering gone awry.

Case 10–37: Kurt Court, Esq., and Leonard Dump, Ph.D., met at a cocktail party. Mr. Court's law practice was suffering because of his debilitating personal problems. Dr. Dump was about to embark on a bitter divorce proceeding. They hit upon the idea of swapping professional services. Dr. Dump would see Mr. Court as a psychotherapy client, and Mr. Court would represent Dr. Dump in the divorce proceeding. Mr. Court proved to be a difficult and more disturbed client than Dr. Dump had anticipated. Furthermore, Court's representation of Dump was erratic and the likelihood of a favorable outcome looked bleak. Yet Mr. Court brought ethics charges against Dr. Dump. Court charged that the therapy he received was inferior and that Dump spent most of the time expressing anger and berating him for not getting better.

Case 10–38: Decora Shod, Ph.D., was seeing a client who owned a furniture manufacturing outlet. Dr. Shod mentioned that she was in the process of redecorating her home. The client offered to allow Dr. Shod to select furniture from his warehouse at his cost if Dr. Shod would see him at a greatly reduced rate. The client reasoned that they would both benefit since Dr. Shod would still be receiving more for far less than she could in retail outlets, and the client could also save some money. During the therapy, Shod increasingly confronted the client in areas where she felt the client was being self-destructive and defensive. The client reacted negatively to the therapeutic techniques and contacted an ethics committee, charging Dr. Shod with attempting to lock him into unnecessary treatment until her home was completely refurnished.

Case 10–39: Lex Icon, Ed.D., offered to tutor Trillion Typos, a student in the graduate department who was having trouble in one of her courses, in exchange for typing his book manuscript. Dr. Icon had taken Typos' report of her skill level at face value, but later found it to be totally unacceptable. Dr. Icon gave her a few tutoring sessions anyway, but terminated the typing arrangement. Typos received an "F" in the course and charged Dr. Icon with failing to follow through with his agreement to help her and with telling the professor that she was incompetent, thus contributing to the failing grade.

All three cases illustrate not only the destructive results that can occur when the follow-through phase of bartering reaches snags and results in unhappy consumers, but also the vulnerability of the psychologists. Court's impatience, Shod's confrontations, and Icon's dissatisfaction may all have been appropriate under simpler circumstances. Because of the complexity in each situation, however, the actions of all three psychologists were perceived as being retaliatory or self-serving.

Bartering psychologists are also vulnerable to exploitation charges if the values of the psychologists' time and skills are set at a higher rate than those of the clients.

Case 10−40:   Elmo Brush agreed to paint the house of Peel Schuff, Ph.D., in exchange for psychotherapy for Brush's teenage daughter. Dr. Schuff saw the girl for six sessions and terminated her therapy. Brush complained that his end of the bargain would have brought him $900 in a conventional deal. Thus it was as though he had paid $150 a session for the services of a person who normally charged $50 a session. Dr. Schuff argued that he had satisfactorily resolved the daughter's problems and the deal was valid because task was traded for task, not dollar value for dollar value.

Case 10−41:   X. Ploit, Ph.D., offered financially strapped and unemployed Penn Ledger the opportunity to do his bookkeeping in return for psychotherapy. Dr. Ploit charged $60 an hour and credited Ledger at a rate of $5 an hour, which meant that Ledger worked twelve hours for every one therapy session received. Ledger complained to Dr. Ploit that the amount of time he was spending on the books precluded entering into full-time employment. Dr. Ploit simply responded that Ledger could choose to terminate at this point and reenter the therapy at such a time that he could afford to pay the full fee.

The ethical complexities of Dr. Schuff's case could have been avoided if he had hired Brush outright to paint his house. The "contact" resulting in a client for Dr. Schuff poses no ethical dilemmas, and Dr. Schuff could have then been paid for his services with Mr. Brush's income from the painting job. As illustrated in this case, trading a one-shot service with a known estimate, based on Brush's own professional experience, with a service that cannot be cost-estimated in advance is problematical. Brush's daughter may have required 50 sessions, or $2,500, if Schuff had been collecting his usual fees, and thus the psychologist would have taken a monetary loss.

Dr. Ploit's case is more complicated. He was figuring the amount of an ongoing service at far below the going rate for a skilled bookkeeper. The bartering contract may well have contributed to the client's difficulties since he was hampered in his search for better employment. When the bookkeeper-client complained, he interrupted the agreement, which may not have been in the best therapeutic interests of the client.

Some psychologists, recognizing the potential complications of one-on-one bartering, have proposed loosely affiliated groups of psychologists and client pools permitting the psychologists to receive services from somebody else's client, and so on. The administration of such systems rapidly becomes cumbersome, and redress procedures for incompetence, whether the shoddy service was performed by either client or therapist, remain unresolved. Commercial "bartering contractors'" business may be acceptable, as long as the service or products received are from people other than the clients serviced by the psychotherapist.

We live in an era geared toward placing a monetary value on just about everything. Considering additional questions about income tax evasion, we recommend using the customary exchange system and to make referrals or other special arrangements (as discussed in Chapter 6) for clients who may not be able to afford one's services.

Peer Co-counseling

Trading psychotherapy *for* psychotherapy is a service bartering system that presents enough unusual complicating factors to warrant its own discussion. Peer co-counseling has several special features that may appear engaging to some. The psychologist-client should not feel the stigma or powerlessness associated with being a patient because each will be therapist to the other. Some who have participated in the arrangement report it to be beneficial both as a personal and as a professional growth experience.

However, this dual role of therapist-client/client-therapist has inherent risks that could lead to disappointment, resentment, and ethical complications. What happens when one psychotherapist-client improves to the point where continued participation is unnecessary, but the other requires considerably more therapy time? What happens when one psychotherapist-client views the other as so troubled that his or her competence and trust is questioned? What happens when one psychotherapist-client believes he or she is doing better work as a therapist and the other is lazy or is perceived as delivering shoddy therapy? These are only a few of the possible eventualities that could negatively affect peer co-counseling. Ethical issues related to competence and termination indicators would be involved in all of these instances if the relationship were of a traditional nature. However, because this is a nontraditional set-up, ethics charges are rarely pressed when the relationship collapses.

> **Case 10–42:** Four female psychologists decided to create a leaderless peer-counseling group to explore their mutual adjustment reactions to divorce. Alka Lewd, Ph.D., began to create disorder in the group because of her heavy drinking and promiscuity to which the other three could neither relate nor handle. They asked Dr. Lewd to resign from the group and seek individual psychotherapy. Dr. Lewd brought ethics charges against the other three for abandonment and lack of concern for her welfare.

Case 10−43:   Teena Yin, Ph.D., and Foster Yang, M.A., agreed that counseling each other would be "kicks." The therapy relationship sexualized. When Teena learned that Foster was dating another woman, she charged Foster with taking sexual advantage of her as his client.

Ethics committees encounter obfuscation when attempting to process complaints arising from peer co-counseling. For example, since Lewd was also a "therapist," she could be technically countercharged with incompetence. Yin could also be technically countercharged with having sexual relationships with her "client."

Peer co-counseling is currently "trendy" and will no doubt continue despite warnings of possible results. Those who choose to engage in this practice are cautioned to discuss fully the pitfalls and to agree on contingencies should they arise. Better yet, psychologists who respect and care about each other's welfare and growth should consider the simple, but sometimes not-so-obvious, option of just becoming closer friends.

Accepting Gifts and Favors

Psychologists who serve consumers as therapists or as teachers are often appreciated for jobs well done. Sometimes clients or students express their gratitude beyond a verbal expression of thanks. Accepting small material tokens, such as homemade cookies or an inexpensive gift, typically poses no real ethical problem. Some psychologists with whom we have talked refuse any gift as a matter of principle, but most believe that to refuse small gifts would constitute a rejection or insult to the detriment of the client or student.

When a gift is no longer "small," or when it constitutes a therapeutic issue or potential manipulation, the issue cannot always be easily discerned. It is clear from several cases that the lines can be crossed, and ethical or other adverse consequences can ensue.

Case 10−44:   Rich Porsche gave his recently licensed therapist, Grad Freshly, Ph.D., a new car for Christmas accompanied by a card stating: "To the only man who ever helped me." Dr. Freshly was flattered and excited. He convinced himself that his services were worth the bonus since Rich had churned through many previous therapists with disappointing results. As a more seasoned therapist might have predicted, Rich soon began to find fault with Dr. Freshly and brought both ethics charges and a legal suit against him for "manipulating him into giving expensive gifts."

Case 10−45:   A graduate student gave Bic Smoke, Ph.D., a silver lighter engraved with his initials on the last day of class. When the student got a "C" in the course, she was irate and went to the professor to complain. He shared his grading procedure with her, but she was still dissatisfied and went to the Department Chair and the

Dean. Smoke wrote an ethics committee describing what he now saw as a bribe attempt and asked for guidance. He noted that he was uncomfortable with such a valuable gift, but since it was already engraved he didn't know what else to do but to accept it.

Case 10-46:   Suzie Pepper brought Newton Callow, M.A., coquettish little gifts almost every session from the beginning of their counseling relationship. These consisted of handkerchiefs hand-embroidered with tiny nude women, T-shirts imprinted with sayings such as "Therapists Do It In Groups," original poems imbedded with *double-entendres*, and a fancy bottle with a label reading "Chemical That Makes Therapists Irresistible to Clients." Suzie ultimately pressed ethics charges against Mr. Callow for abruptly terminating and abandoning her after promising that he would "be there to make her happy." During the inquiry, Mr. Callow stated that he initially found Suzie to be a "fun client," whom he thought needed massive support to help boost her self-esteem. As therapy progressed, he became increasingly uneasy with her little gifts and her flirtatious style. What was, at first, amusing and flattering began to be excessively demanding. She became more than he felt he could handle. When he suggested referring her to another therapist, she became livid and stalked out of the session, allegedly threatening him with reprisal for "leading her on."

These three cases illustrate naivete and inexperience, which are the common denominators among psychologists who accept gifts and favors beyond the realm of small "one-time" or "special occasion" tokens. Regardless of other dynamics, a very valuable gift (e.g., Porsche's car) should be refused. A person in a vulnerable situation, such as a client or student, can always charge exploitation later, and such a charge may well have substance despite the rationalizations of the psychologists. Dr. Smoke's touchy situation, given the fact that the lighter was engraved and therefore inappropriate to give to someone else and unacceptable for a refund, might have been handled by telling the student to keep it until after she graduated and then give it to him if she still wanted to. Although this may not be the ideal resolution, it at least defuses attempts at manipulation. Callow was naive and probably coping with unfulfilled needs of his own, which blurred his professional vision substantially.

Experience and a strong professional identity appear to be the key ingredients in dealing appropriately with offers of gifts and favors and the probable motivation for them on a case-by-case basis. Until one reaches a level of professional comfort, a very conservative course of action may be in everyone's best interests.

Gifts and (usually) favors should never, of course, be requested from either clients or students by psychologists. Unfortunately, cases involving the direct solicitation of gifts and favors have been reported to ethics committees. One psychotherapist asked to borrow large sums of money from his wealthy clients, and then he went bankrupt leaving them all unpaid. Another required members of her therapy groups to bring her little gifts every session as symbols of their commitment. Another routinely asked his influential clients to make arrangements to introduce him to their friends and associates as a way of generating more business.

When small, situationally based favors or requests by psychologists are involved, the picture greys a little. It may not be inappropriate for a professor to ask a student to drive him to the auto repair shop to pick up a car or for a psychotherapist to change an appointment time to accommodate a special need. However, the most prudent course of action is to avail oneself of alternatives whenever possible. Any favor requiring more than a minor inconvenience to a consumer should not be requested under any circumstances, except for a major crisis. The psychologist who had a heart attack in the presence of his client in an otherwise deserted building, requiring the client to assume rather major responsibilities for a short time, is the exceptional case.

"Affective-Experiential" Academic Coursework

It may surprise many readers to learn that a common type of academic course, the "experiential" group format wherein students are encouraged to explore and to share their own feelings and conflicts, can pose explosive episodes leading to complicated dual-role overtones. These courses, sporting various names, such as "sensitivity seminar" or "applied group dynamics," are often quite popular among students. Judging from the paucity of ethics complaints received about them, it is probable that they usually run a satisfactory course. But when complaints arise, they are typically volatile, and the inherent dual roles of student/quasi-client and professor/quasi-therapist are usually at the base of the predicaments.

> **Case 10−47:**   Lettit Hangout enjoyed speaking out during her sensitivity training class. She revealed many areas of personal discontent during the sessions and assumed that by doing so she was "being a good student." She began to notice, however, that the professor was becoming more distant. Her major professor then began making vague suggestions that she choose another line of academic study. The other students began to withdraw from her as well. She brought ethics charges against the sensitivity class professor for explicitly encouraging her to reveal her problems, which resulted in endangering her academic reputation and alienating her from her peers and other professors.

> **Case 10−48:**   Tim Orous brought ethics charges against Morris Tellall, Ph.D., when he received a "D" in "Group Experience 463." The class was required as part of his degree program. His grade was a reflection of his silence throughout the quarter, although he had told the professor early in the term that he did not feel comfortable participating in the discussions. Tim asserted that it was inappropriate to require students to reveal personal, nonacademic information and then to jeopardize the student's academic status for noncompliance.

It may be valuable to expose students to experiences that may assist them in their interactions with people, provide feedback in areas requiring modification, and facilitate the self-examination process, especially when the students are aspiring service providers to troubled people. Those students who may someday do group process work themselves may also benefit from participating in this course model. As Salvendy (1980) noted regarding criteria for quality group psychotherapy training, "program designers have to be aware of the risk involved in a predominantly didactic set-up [and] the avoidance of an affective engagement can have deleterious effects on the learning process." It can also be asserted that attempts to separate intellect from affect in the education process in general, and for people in psychotherapy training in particular, are not only impossible but contraindicated if an overall goal of training is to enhance the students' ability to function in life outside academia. However, concern has been expressed about the ethical risks of blending elements of therapeutic treatment with academic coursework (Bass, 1977; Lakin, 1969; Sherrer and Sherrer, 1972) and the need for guidelines (American College Personnel Association, 1972; Caple, 1976). It has also been argued that educational institutions do not have the responsibility or *prima facie* legal authority to engage in quasi-healing arts (Sherrer and Sherrer, 1972).

We suggest a consideration of the following precautions that may preclude untoward consequences for "affective" learning experiences, particularly if such courses are a requirement for a degree program:

1. Students should be informed at the beginning of the course what is required, the justification for such requirements, and some of the possible negative effects that might be experienced. The leader should make time available on a regular basis for individual discussions with students who may be experiencing difficulties with the class.

2. If after considering the information, a student decides not to continue, the leader should assist the student in entering an alternative class. If the course is part of a degree requirement, the student and the leader should devise substitute experience. This might consist of entering an off-campus group and writing a paper about that experience.

3. Hiring a psychologist from off-campus to lead this type of course has advantages. The psychologist is separated from the ongoing training pipeline to an extent that greatly softens the dual-role conflicts that might be experienced by both students and regular, ongoing faculty.

4. Grading criteria must be carefully established and, to the greatest extent possible, consideration of the nature of the students' problems or willingness to share them should be avoided. Some programs offer such courses, but they are on a "credit only" basis. Others grade students only on written assignments.

5. Student-selection criteria and screening are encouraged. Students found to be highly disturbed should be excused or removed from the class experience and placed in an alternative situation.

Some programs allow or require students to enter individual psychotherapy for academic credit as part of an applied program. Again, benefits to the students and, hopefully, to their future clients may accrue. However, using regular faculty and members in the program to provide these services is not recommended, even if payment is not involved. When individual psychotherapy is required as an experience in an academic program, the model that appears to be used by most programs is the generation of a list of competent therapists in the community who will consult with students, often at a reduced fee and sometimes at no cost. If students may avail themselves of university counseling centers to fulfill an academic requirement, and if the counseling-service psychologist is also involved in teaching or evaluation responsibilities with the academic department, special safeguards must be instituted to defuse any dual-role conflicts.

"In-Situ" Therapy

Sometimes therapeutic goals are better achieved by stepping outside of the office setting. "Action-oriented" therapies, including crises modalities, may often involve ecological involvements with clients. A psychologist might accompany his "airplane phobia group" on a flight from Los Angeles to San Francisco. A stress reduction group may meet in a serene resort atmosphere for a special weekend retreat. Nevertheless, excursions beyond traditional settings require special forethought in case charges of exploitation with dual-role or conflict-of-interest overtones subsequently result.

Case 10–49:   Homa Cloister feared crowds. Her therapist, Rip Vivo, M.A., suggested that they go out to dinner at busy restaurants after each therapy session as a way of conditioning her to feel more comfortable around people. He did not charge an additional fee for the after-hour activity but did require her to pay for the food, drinks, and gratuity. Homa later charged that Dr. Vivo exploited her by disguising a free meal ticket as psychotherapy.

Case 10–50:   Stuffy Short complained of sexual inhibition to his therapist, X. Flick, Ed.D. Dr. Flick suggested that Stuffy accompany him to local "adult theatres" to view sexually explicit movies as a way of desensitizing his fears. Stuffy ultimately charged Dr. Flick with satisfying his own "perverted needs" by forcing Stuffy to be exposed to "disgusting and unsettling experiences, which made the sexual problems worse."

Case 10–51:   Several marathon encounter group members charged that the therapist associated with the Touchie-Feelie Clinic conducted their weekend retreats in a mountain resort in a way that facilitated oppressive and promiscuous behavior among the participants. They believed that various exercises encouraged and stimulated some members to become obnoxious and pressure others into sexual activities after the group sessions terminated. They found the experience to more closely resemble a "single's bar" than a legitimate and safe therapy setting.

Such inimical results clearly reveal that decisions to venture away from a strictly professional setting must be based on the following: (1) the therapist's careful self-assessment of motivations and needs; (2) a treatment plan that clearly justifies the arrangement as the more effective setting for facilitating therapeutic goals; and (3) adequate client understanding of the proposed experience, preparation, and consent to participate in it.

Other Role Conflicts

We have focused on dual-role conflicts wherein the psychologist directly occupied one of the roles. However, situations often arise that squeeze psychologists between two other entities. For example, the demands of an agency employing the psychologist may conflict, in the psychologist's opinion, with the needs and welfare of the agency's clients. Government policy, legal requirements, or the welfare and safety of society in general may, in some instances, clash with the psychologist's judgments regarding what might be in the best interests of an individual consumer. The identifications of priorities and loyalties can cause acute stress and dilemmas. Often psychologists are not in an objective position when making such decisions since the more powerful of the conflict sources, such as the law or the psychologist's employer, may issue sanctions against the psychologist if his or her actions do not favor their position. Psychologists have sometimes been cited for contempt of court and/or have lost their jobs in such instances. Nevertheless, psychologists who comply with the more powerful of the conflict sources, despite a personal conviction that in so doing they harmed or shortchanged the less powerful conflict source, may be left with feelings of self-disgust, guilt, and weakness. Throughout this book, these types of conflicts are illustrated in the context of specific settings and conditions under which they are likely to arise (see especially Chapters 12 and 15).

SUMMARY GUIDELINES

1. Psychologists should avoid dual-role relationships and conflict-of-interest situations with clients or students, especially when the dynamics of the psycholoigsts' role are characterized by power, trust, dependencies, or influence.
2. Sexually intimate behavior with clients is considered to be a serious ethical violation and may also carry legal consequences. Sexual intimacies with

students over whom one has (or may have) evaluative responsibilities is discouraged since unsuccessful relationship outcomes have resulted in serious consequences for students and psychologists.

3. Psychologists should remain aware of not only the harm dual-role relationships may cause consumers of professional services but to themselves as well. Psychologists have sometimes faced disapproval for even the appearance of dual-role conflicts. Thus it is wise to avoid giving the impression of dual-role or conflict-of-interest improprieties even if psychologists believe that they have clearly separated their dual roles.

4. Sometimes dual-role overlaps are difficult to avoid, such as for psychologists who work in small communities. When alternatives are very limited, thus necessitating role-blending, psychologists should be especially sensitive to possible complications and should attempt to minimize them.

5. Service bartering, including mutual co-counseling, should be avoided since the possibility of misunderstandings, disappointment, or exploitation is substantially heightened.

6. Psychologists should avoid accepting gifts and favors from consumers of their services unless they are small tokens or gestures of appreciation. Complaints of exploitation may arise if the consumers are later disappointed with the services or if their motives were manipulative.

7. Academic course work that includes a heavy affective or quasi-therapeutic component, such as sensitivity training seminars, should include safeguards to protect students.

8. In-situ therapy—that is, therapeutic sessions conducted in other than a traditional office surrounding—should be carefully planned prior to inception. Therapeutic goal justification and careful preparation of clients are among the factors to be considered.

9. When faced with a decision regarding whether to risk role blending, psychologists should carefully assess their own motives and discuss all relevant aspects, including potential conflicts and consequences with the other parties involved, prior to reaching a final conclusion.

REFERENCE NOTES

1. Zelen, S. L. *Sexual Abuse of Women by Therapists*. Paper delivered at Applied Research Conference, University of California, Davis, California, February 1979.

2. Forer, B. R. *Sources of Distortion in the Therapeutic Relationship*. Paper presented at the American Psychological Association meeting, Los Angeles, California, August 1981.

3. Seagull, A. A. *Should a Therapist Have Intercourse with Patients?* Paper presented at the American Psychological Association meeting, Hawaii, September 1972.

4. Belot, B. *Sexual Intimacy between Female Clients and Male Psychotherapists: Maso-chistic Sabotage.* Unpublished doctoral dissertation, California School of Professional Psychology, San Francisco, California, 1974.

5. Butler, S. *Sexual Contact between Therapists and Patients.* Unpublished doctoral dissertation, California School of Professional Psychology, Los Angeles, California, 1975.

6. Keith-Spiegel, P. *Sex with Clients: Ten Reasons Why It Is a Very Stupid Thing to Do.* Paper presented at the American Psychological Association meeting, Washington, DC, September 1977.

7. Keith-Spiegel, P. *Sex and Love between Therapist and Client.* Paper presented at the Western Psychological Association meeting, Los Angeles, California, 1981.

8. Gerard, S. *Attitudes of Students towards Sexual Relationships between Students and Professors.* Paper presented at the Western Psychological Association meetings, Los Angeles, California, April 1981.

9. Tallman, G. *Therapist-client Social Relationships.* Unpublished manuscript. California State University, Northridge, California, 1981.

REFERENCES

Abramowitz, S. E., and Abramowitz, C. V. Sex role psychodynamics in psychotherapy supervision. *American Journal of Psychotherapy*, 1976, 30, 583–592.

American College Personnel Association. A proposed statement for ACPA regarding the use of group experiences in higher education. *Journal of College Student Personnel*, January 1972, 90–95.

American Psychological Association. Report on sex-bias and sex-role stereotyping in psychotherapeutic practice. *American Psychologist*, 1975, 30, 1169–1175.

Aristides. Life and letters: Sex and the professors. *American Scholar*, 1975, 44, 357–363.

Barnhouse, R. T. Sex between patient and therapist. *Journal of the American Academy of Psychoanalysis*, 1978, 6, 533–546.

Bass, S. J. Ethical practices in sensitivity training for prospective professional psychologists. *Catalog of Selected Documents in Psychology*, May, 1977, pp. 47–48.

Bouhoutsos, J.; Holroyd, J.; Lerman, H.; Forer, B.; and Greenburg, M. Sexual intimacy between psychotherapists and patients. *Professional Psychology*, 1983, 14, 185–196.

Butler, S., and Zelen, S. L. Sexual intimacies between therapists and patients. *Psychotherapy: Theory, Research and Practice*, 1977, 14, 139–145.

Caple, R. B. The use of group procedures in higher education: A position statement by ACPA. *Journal of College Student Personnel*, 1976, 17, 161–168.

Chesler, P. *Women and Madness.* New York: Doubleday, 1972.

D'Addario, L. Sexual relationships between female clients and male therapists. Unpublished doctoral dissertation, California School of Professional Psychology, San Diego, 1977.

Dahlberg, C. C. Sexual contact between patient and therapist. *Contemporary Psychoanalysis*, 1970, *6*, 107–124.

Edelwich, J., and Brodsky, A. *Sexual Dilemmas for the Helping Professional*. New York: Brunner/Mazel, 1982.

Hays, J. R. Sexual contact between psychotherapist and patient: Legal remedies. *Psychological Reports*, 1980, *47*, 1247–1254.

Holroyd, J. C. Erotic contact as an instance of sex-biased therapy. In J. Murray and P. R. Abramson (Eds.) *The Handbook of Bias in Psychotherapy*. New York: Praeger Press, 1984.

———, and Brodsky, A. Does touching patients lead to sexual intercourse? *Professional Psychology*, 1980, *11*, 807–811.

———, and Brodsky, A. M. Psychologists' attitudes and practices regarding erotic and nonerotic physical contact with patients. *American Psychologist*, 1977, *32*, 843–849.

Jones, E. *Life and Work of Sigmund Freud*. Vol. 3. New York: Basic Books, 1957.

Kardener, S. H. Sex and the physician-patient relationship. *American Journal of Psychiatry*, 1974, *131*, 1134–1136.

———; Fuller, M.; and Mensh, I. A survey of physicians' attitudes and practices regarding erotic and nonerotic contact with patients. *American Journal of Psychiatry*, 1973, *130*, 1077–1081.

Kelly, J. Sexual abusive doctors: How women are betrayed by the men they trust most. *Ladies Home Journal*, June 1979, *55*, 179–182.

Lakin, M. Some ethical issues in sensitivity training. *American Psychologist*, 1969, *24*, 923–928.

Len, M., and Fisher, J. Clinician's attitudes toward and use of four body contact or sexual techniques with clients. *Journal of Sex Research*, 1978, *14*, 40–49.

Marmor, J. Sexual acting-out in psychotherapy. *American Journal of Psychoanalysis*, 1972, *22*, 3–8.

Masters, W. H., and Johnson, V. E. Principles of the new sex therapy. *American Journal of Psychiatry*, 1976, *133*, 548–554.

Pope, K. S.; Levenson, H.; and Schover, L. R. Sexual intimacy in psychology training. *American Psychologist*, 1979, *34*, 682–689.

Pope, K. S.; Schover, L. R.; and Levenson, H. Sexual behavior between clinical supervisors and trainees: Implications for professional standards. *Professional Psychology*, 1980, *11*, 157–162.

Salvendy, J. T. Group psychotherapy training. *Canadian Journal of Psychiatry*, 1980, *25*, 394–402.

Schofield, W. *Psychotherapy: The purchase of friendship*. Englewood Cliffs, N.J.: Prentice-Hall, 1964.

Schultz, L. G., and McGrath, J. Developing seduction management skills through the use of video vignettes. *Journal of Humanics*, 1978, *5*, 70–78.

Schwendinger, J. R., and Schwendinger, H. Rape myths in legal, theoretical, and everyday practice. *Crime and Social Justice*, 1974, *1*, 18–26.

Serban, G. Sexual activity in therapy: Legal and ethical issues. *American Journal of Psychotherapy*, 1981, *35*, 76–85.

Sherrer, C. W., and Sherrer, M. S. Professional or legal standards for academic psychologists and counselors. *Journal of Law-Education*, 1972, *1*, 289–302.

Stone, A. A. The legal implications of sexual activity between psychiatrists and patient. *American Journal of Psychiatry*, 1976, *133*, 1138–1141.

Stone, M. H. Boundary violations between therapist and patient. *Psychiatric Annals*, 1976, *6*, 8–21.

Taylor, B. J., and Wagner, N. N. Sex between therapist and clients: A review and analysis. *Professional Psychology*, 1976, *7*, 593–601.

Relationships with Colleagues, Cohorts, and Collaborators

11

*It is easier to love humanity
than to love one's neighbor.*

Eric Hoffer

A substantial percentage of complaints to ethics committees about psychologists derives from their colleagues, students, or employees. This fact should not be surprising, since they are the people most likely to be aware of the *Ethical Principles* and most likely (aside from clients) to observe directly the behavior of the psychologist in question. An intriguing aspect of such complaints, however, is the intensity or vindictiveness with which they are sometimes pursued. The focus of this chapter is on intra- and interprofessional relationships with colleagues, as well as the ethical conduct expected of psychologists with respect to their students and employees.

People trained as psychologists often find themselves functioning in roles that are not directly related to psychology. For example, many psychologists serve as agency administrators, university presidents or deans, directors of foundations, and other such posts far afield from more traditional psychological activity. When challenged on a matter related to the *Ethical Principles* some of these individuals argue that since they are not functioning as psychologists in their current role, they do not need to follow the code. This problem often develops in the context of complaints by colleagues or subordinates related to lack of supervision or inadequate feedback. In such cases, ethics committees in general assert that psychologists are bound to the code in all of their professional work, regardless of the specific role they occupy.

PEER AND INTERPROFESSIONAL RELATIONSHIPS

A psychologist's general relationships with peers and other professionals should ideally be governed by a climate of cooperation and mutual respect (*EP*: 7). The professional "best interests" of psychologists and psychology are not congruent with those of psychiatry, social work, or psychiatric nursing. Despite a common focus on human emotional problems, human nature will always result in professional disagreements based on politics, economics, territoriality, and other such issues. The goals and views of some psychologists are not synonymous with those of others. Nonetheless, recognition of valid competencies and client interests should prevail in interprofessional relationships (*EP*: 7a). We shall discuss the general issue of cooperation, with specific attention given to concepts related to inquiries about referrals, peer evaluation, public criticism, and risk factors that are related to professional relationship disputes.

Cooperation

Passive-aggressive behavior often escalates when colleagues are angry at each other. Consider the following case examples:

> **Case 11–1:**   Gloria Seeker, Ph.D., proposed a research project to be carried out at a state institution near her university. The project had first to be approved by the facility's Human Subjects Protection Committee, headed by Tyrone Plod, Ph.D., the chief psychologist. Seeker filed an ethics complaint alleging that Plod had procrastinated for several months in the consideration of her study, despite the fact that it posed no substantial risk to the population involved. She accused Plod of professional jealousy and hence inaction. Dr. Plod replied that he was very busy performing his duties as chief psychologist, and he could not give high priority to the request of a psychologist outside the agency.

> **Case 11–2:**   Rodney Freeman had terminated psychotherapy with Stefan Witholden, Psy.D., one year ago. Mr. Freeman decided to reenter therapy with another practitioner, and he signed a release-of-information form authorizing the new therapist to contact Dr. Witholden for information. When no report or records were forthcoming, the new therapist tried to contact Witholden several times and was finally told: "I don't have any materials that would be useful to you."

> **Case 11–3:**   Flora Thorn, Ed.D., was contacted by a peer review panel, and she was asked to supply a treatment plan summary and other related information on several clients whose cases were being reviewed. She ignored the requests for several months until an ethics inquiry was filed. She then apologized for overlooking the request and supplied the necessary information.

Each of these cases implies a certain measure of psychologist passivity or lack of prompt cooperation. Although it was not clear whether Dr. Plod was intentionally thwarting Dr. Seeker's project, it was evident that he gave her request a very low priority. At the very least, Dr. Seeker was entitled to know what position the committee might take and whether it represented an official policy of the state facility. If Dr. Plod were truly unable to perform his assigned duties on the committee expeditiously, then he should have stepped down from that position in favor of someone who could act in a more timely fashion. If evidence existed that Dr. Plod treated Dr. Seeker unfairly, given institutional policy or relative favoritism to others, his behavior would be clearly unethical.

The example involving Dr. Witholden is not an uncommon occurrence. At times, a former therapist may be angry at a client's decision to switch, even after an appropriate termination. At other times, a practitioner may fail to cooperate because of some anger about or disapproval of the choice of the new therapist. Did Mr. Freeman, for example, choose a psychiatrist or a social worker as his new therapist? In any case, Witholden's reluctance to share information with the new therapist at the client's request is potentially harmful to the client and is unethical (*EP*: 6).

Dr. Thorn represents another category of cooperation problem that often troubles ethics panels, peer review boards, and other colleagues. She may be a procrastinator who simply assumes that the burdensome request for information will disappear if she ignores it. Or she may simply assign a low priority to responding to such requests. Her inaction becomes an ethical violation as the duration of noncooperation increases and the resulting difficulty caused to her colleagues is magnified.

Interference with Ongoing Relationships

What happens, however, if some help is sought, but to offer it fully might damage an ongoing relationship? The most common types of concern raised in this category involve "pirating" clients or seeing clients who are involved in a relationship with another professional at the time (*EP*: 7b).

> **Case 11–4:** Suppose that Sidney Switch was still in active treatment with a psychologist, but sought an appointment with Roberto Resque, Ph.D.? Switch tells Dr. Resque that he feels his current psychologist is not helping him, and he would like to change therapists and be treated by Resque. What are Resque's obligations and duties?

Switch certainly has the right, of course, to choose the person from whom he will receive services. It would not, however, be appropriate for Dr. Resque to begin treatment, while ignoring the other, active professional relationship. Ideally, Resque would suggest that Switch discuss his dissatisfaction directly with his current therapist. If Switch balks at this suggestion,

Resque should seek his authorization to contact the therapist and confer with him about the case. If Switch refuses to permit this, Resque should probably decline to offer him services. It could well be that Switch is attempting to conceal some issues, or he is simply acting-out in some way against his current therapist. One could argue that a psychologist should not deny treatment to a client in need, but it is difficult to treat adequately a client who wishes to conceal something about a prior psychotherapy experience. It would be best for Resque not to become involved, unless it is ethically possible for him to do so in an open manner. Potential exceptions to this strategy are discussed later in this chapter with respect to discovering ethical misconduct on the part of colleagues.

Not all ongoing relationships involve psychotherapy, however, and these other relationships can yield equally troubling dilemmas.

> **Case 11−5:** Tanya Trainee is a psychology intern at a community mental-health center where Lorna Doone, Ed.D., surpervises her psychotherapy cases. Ms. Trainee disagrees with several of the recommendations Dr. Doone has given her regarding some of her cases, so she approaches her testing supervisor, Mack Beth, Psy.D., for his suggestions on the cases.

> **Case 11−6:** Clarence Farrow, a young attorney, contacts Jack Forensic, Ph.D., for some advice regarding another psychologist. Apparently, the psychologist in question, Marvin Turkey, Ph.D., was appearing as an expert witness against one of Farrow's clients and made some statements under oath that Farrow had reason to question. Dr. Forensic looked up Dr. Turkey's credentials in the *APA Directory* and noted that they did not include the type of experiences usually associated with the type of expertise claimed. He suggested several questions that Farrow could ask Turkey in order to establish or challenge his credibility. Dr. Forensic also provided Farrow with several publications that tended to refute the claims asserted by Dr. Turkey in his testimony. Dr. Turkey later telephoned Dr. Forensic and angrily claimed that Farrow had embarrassed him in public by using the information Dr. Forensic had supplied.

Ms. Trainee appears to be isolating aspects of her relationship with Dr. Doone, which, for some reason, are unsatisfactory to her. Dr. Beth must realize that he is being approached by Ms. Trainee on several issues for which another supervisor has been designated. He should explain this to Ms. Trainee, while suggesting that she discuss differences directly with her supervisor or with the person designated as director of the training program. Offering supervisory consultation without the knowledge of Dr. Doone could potentially create more serious collegial anger, even if that were not Ms. Trainee's goal. If Ms. Trainee has serious questions regarding the nature of Dr. Doone's supervision or competence, and if Doone is unresponsive to a direct discussion with her, she should then consult with other colleagues in the setting for advice on how to proceed.

Dr. Forensic owed no specific duty to Dr. Turkey. It seems that Dr. Forensic was asked for consultative advice by a third party, Attorney Farrow, and provided him with factual material (e.g., articles and information from a directory). If the material supplied to Farrow was used to embarrass Dr. Turkey, this outcome was probably justified: that is, if Dr. Turkey were as competent as claimed, he should neither have been upset about answering direct questions about his credentials nor about responding to questions raised in the published scientific literature. These are standard procedures in establishing the qualification of "expert" witnesses. If Dr. Forensic offered gossip or a biased presentation of facts, an ethical problem would indeed exist; however, he owed no duty of protection to Dr. Turkey.

If a request for a consultation changes into something more, however, complications could result, as illustrated in the following case examples:

Case 11–7:   Fritz Couch, M.D., is a psychoanalyst who has been treating Hester Pymm in analysis for three years. Pymm has been blocking in her free associations for several weeks, and Dr. Couch wonders about the possibility of an impending thought disturbance. He refers Ms. Pymm to Ursula Norms, Ph.D., for psychodiagnostic testing. During the course of the psychological assessment, Ms. Pymm tells Dr. Norms that she is increasingly frustrated with the lack of progress she is making in her treatment with Dr. Couch and asks whether Norms would be willing to treat her.

Case 11–8:   Gladys Prudent, Psy.D., is concerned about the persistent depression exhibited by her client, Phoebe Downer. Dr. Prudent believes that perhaps an antidepressant medication would be useful to Ms. Downer in resolving what appears to be an endogenous depression. Thus Dr. Prudent refers Ms. Downer to Ingrid Pill, M.D., for a medical consultation. Ms. Downer is impressed when Dr. Pill expresses the belief that medication could offer her some relief, and she asks Dr. Pill to begin managing her case completely, expressing the willingness to terminate therapy with Dr. Prudent.

Both of these cases illustrate situations that are not uncommon. The therapists recognize some potential limitations in their ability to diagnose adequately or to treat a specific problem alone, and they seek specific consultations from qualified colleagues. The clients are having problems that may make them feel frustrated, depressed, or troubled. The consultants have been imbued with some positive aura by the clients who request treatment. Certainly clients have the right to free choice, even if the choice might not be viewed as being in their best interests by their therapists. The idealized consultants may be benefitting only from a contrast effect, and it is unlikely that anyone knows the client as well as the referring therapist does.

In both cases, the ideal course of action would be similar. The consultants should refer the clients back to their therapists with the recommendation that they discuss this issue directly. In Ms. Pymm's situation, this might require "working through the negative transference," while for Ms. Downer it might require talking about the frustrations of a prolonged depressive reaction. Ultimately, the clients may choose to terminate with the therapists and seek treatment from the consultants or elsewhere, but the consultants should not encourage this practice, while recognizing the unusual nature of their limited relationships with the clients. Assuming that the client has authorized the consultant to communicate with the referring therapist, it might also be wise for Norms and Pill to inform Couch and Prudent, respectively, of their clients' concerns, because these concerns may be impeding the progress of treatment.

Making a Referral

The hazards of making consultation referrals are well illustrated in the preceding two cases, but they also exemplify the importance of knowing when to seek advice from a colleague with a different set of competencies. What about other requests for referrals, however? What about the client who seeks a referral for a friend in a neighboring state or the colleague who asks for a suggestion regarding a specialized type of consultant? The person asking for the referral has the right to expect that the psychologist making the referral will offer the best advice available, regardless of personal or financial interests.

Although *Cases 6–4* and *6–5* in our chapter regarding money matters illustrate *inappropriate* referrals concerning fee-splitting arrangements, psychologists still can, of course, make referrals to colleagues with whom they are very familiar or have close working relationships. The key factor should be the best interests of the client, including the client's needs, wishes, geographic location, finances, and similar considerations. The following cases illustrate appropriate referral behavior.

> **Case 11–9:**   Gene Defer, Psy.D., works in a group practice with several other mental-health professionals. He conducts an intake interview with a new female client in her mid-30s, who expresses a preference for a female therapist during the session. Two women work with Dr. Defer in the group practice, and he describes both in terms of ages and special clinical interests to the client, suggesting that she might choose to have an appointment with one of them.

> **Case 11–10:**   Ronda Reffer, Ed.D., is telephoned by a client who asks her to assist in locating a psychologist to evaluate a relative in a distant state. Dr. Reffer does not know anyone in that geographic area, but uses a professional directory to provide the client with the names and addresses of several appropriately licensed practitioners in that general vicinity.

The behavior of both psychologists in these two cases is ethically appropriate. Dr. Defer has no specific financial interest in his referral to another member of the same practice group. Although he may derive some diffuse benefit by keeping the client within the group, the client did initially consult that particular group. Presumably she also understands that Dr. Defer and his female colleagues are part of a group that works in close association. Dr. Defer is also being responsive to the client's stated preference for a female therapist, and he has presented some additional data regarding options within the group so that the client has a measure of choice.

Ideally, Dr. Reffer would try to suggest a colleague or two with whom she was well acquainted to ensure appropriately satisfying the client's needs. In this case, she knows no one in the area and knows relatively little about the client's specific needs. By using the directory to locate colleagues and by ensuring that she provides only names of licensed colleagues, she is offering at least some minimal assurance regarding the quality of the practitioners. One presumes that these practitioners will have the ethical sensitivity to make additional local referrals, in case the client contacts them and requires services that they are not equipped to offer. Dr. Reffer, however, should offer appropriate warnings to her client (i.e., "Please tell your relative that I do not know these practitioners personally; however, they are fully licensed."). If a psychologist does not feel comfortable making such a referral, he or she could refer the client to a state psychological association for guidance.

Remember, however, that part of the psychologist's reputation and professional responsibility is affected by any referral that is made. One should not make a referral for a client that one would be unwilling to accept either personally or for a member of one's own family.

Professional Etiquette

Colleagues both inside and outside of the field of psychology deserve to be treated with respect and equanimity, even if one is legitimately annoyed with them. The tossing of impolite barbs can often result in an escalating professional feud, in addition to ethics complaints concerning issues that should have been resolved informally between the particular colleagues early in the dispute.

> **Case 11–11:**   Horace Right, Ph.D., is asked by a journal editor to review a manuscript by Lester Wrong, Ph.D., with whom Right has long held substantial theoretical disagreements. Right drafts a scathing review of the paper based primarily on the theoretical disagreements, but including such comments as, "Dr. Wrong continues to cling to obsolete ideas in a narrow-minded and idiotic fashion."

> **Case 11–12:**   Dr. Right (*Case 11-11*) also teaches a course at a local university. During the semester, he frequently attacks the work of Dr. Wrong, describing it as trivial, poorly prepared, and useless.

Case 11–13:   Manfred Potz, Ph.D., and his colleague Stefan Blitz, Ph.D., have known each other personally and professionally for many years. After an unfortunate personal dispute leads to a dissolution of their friendship, Dr. Potz complains to an ethics committee that Dr. Blitz is telling other professionals that Dr. Potz is a Nazi and a homosexual.

Certainly personal motives, including anger, jealousy, competitiveness, and inflated views of one's self-importance, may contribute to anger toward one's colleagues. Such anger should not, however, be expressed in an unprofessional manner. In the case of Dr. Right, the theoretical disagreements with Dr. Wrong have been inappropriately personalized. If Dr. Right is not prepared to offer a critique in a rational and dispassionate manner, he should consider telling the editor: "I am too personally angry with Dr. Wrong to give this paper a fair reading. You should find another reviewer." The adjectives "narrow-minded" and "idiotic" have no place in an ethically formulated scholarly review. Hopefully, the editor will recognize this fact, even if Dr. Right does not, and thus disregard emotionally based criticisms.

Dr. Right's classroom attacks are also inappropriate. Such public statements are not in keeping with the scientific foundations of psychology. Ideally, Right could outline Wrong's arguments or points and then contrast them with his own in a scholarly fashion. In the case of legitimate scholarly differences, the ideal means of presenting the dispute is through articles and comments in peer-reviewed professional publications in which complete citation and documentation of claims are possible under the critical eye of scholarly peers. Examples of this type of scholarly disagreement were summarized in Chapter 5 (e.g., the comments of Bailey, 1978 on Zeiss et al.; and the comments of Cook, 1975 on Levendusky and Pankratz). Right's attacks on Wrong were again too personalized and lacked the appropriate scholarly support to validate them for presentation in educational formats. (See Chapter 13 for additional discussions of classroom presentations.)

The controversy between Dr. Potz and Dr. Blitz unfortunately occurs all too frequently. When friendships dissolve, personal enmity can turn to rage, which is acted-out inappropriately in professional contexts. Dr Potz's sexual preference and political affiliations are not appropriate topics of gossip among professional colleagues. Colleagues cannot assess the validity of such personal criticisms with respect to professional competence, nor can they ascertain the veracity of Blitz's verbal assault. If Blitz has some factual basis for criticizing Potz (e.g., if he recently discovered that Potz formerly worked as a Nazi concentration camp guard and has lied about this fact), then he should bring this evidence to appropriate authorities. Gossip and rumor-spreading are not appropriate ethical behaviors.

Another area of professional etiquette, which has often been ignored by writers on ethics in psychology, concerns political activity in psychological associations or organizations. Active campaigning for elective office with colleagues endorsing or campaigning on behalf of one another is not un-usual in some professional organizations (Koocher et al., 1982). Sometimes the campaigning can be downright foul.

Case 11–14:   Kirby Urban, Ph.D., and Roscoe Rural, Ed.D., were both nominated for office in a national psychological organization. Both were invited to submit with their ballots statements reflecting their qualifications and positions on major issues. Neither had access to the other's statement until the ballots were mailed, at which time Dr. Rural became outraged. Apparently, Dr. Urban had cited some direct quotations from a paper written by Rural and used these to contrast his own position. Rural believed that the statements were unfairly cited out of context and noted that the goal of providing candidates' statements was to offer a positive basis for selection rather than a unilateral attack. He filed ethics charges for uncolleagial behavior against Urban, including a verbal tirade of his own, and he sought to void the election, which he lost.

The ethics committee receiving the complaint was troubled by the vin-dictive claims and counterclaims being tossed about by two respected senior colleagues. There was some truth to each set of claims. Rural had indeed been quoted accurately, yet in an inappropriate, misleading context. Rural certainly would have framed his statement differently, if he had anticipated this problem. Urban claimed that the difference between him and Rural was distinct on the matters in question and that he wanted the electorate to understand this distinction clearly. The ethics committee could not sustain an ethics complaint, but ended the case by chiding both senior colleagues to behave with more composure and balance when such competitions arose in the future.

Risk Factors

A number of factors may create situations in which colleagues are at special risk for incurring each other's ire, including spreading any type of gossip, personal arrogance or narcissism, and a hostile or critical personality style. In addition, the competition for scarce resources, such as tenure, promo-tion, or salary increases in the face of limited options, is also likely to stir dissatisfaction if the perception of bias appears to be operating in the decision-making process. Failure to fulfill obligations made to one's peers is also a potential risk for later complaints of an ethical nature. These failures may range from the intellectually sublime (e.g., the psychologist who switched topics of a scheduled invited address at the last minute, thereby angering many who had traveled substantial distances to hear a talk on the original topic) to the absurd (e.g., the psychologist who sued a colleague with whom she had allegedly had a prior love affair, claiming that he had talked her into having an abortion and then reneged on a promise to re-impregnate her).

Psychologists are just as human as any other group of people, and ethics complaints cannot serve as a means to overhaul irritable personalities, reform prejudiced people, or enforce social agreements between consenting adult colleagues. Nevertheless, we should still treat our colleagues with the same respect and professionalism accorded to our clients.

THE VINDICTIVE COLLEAGUE

Special mention must be made concerning colleagues who are so angered by real or perceived wrongs that they either act-out in a manner that is clearly unethical or seek redress through ethics committees for problems that are not, strictly speaking, ethical in nature.

> **Case 11–15:**   Rea Venge, Ph.D., gathered strong circumstantial evidence that her colleague and professional rival at South Central University had stolen the sole copy of her unprocessed raw research data. Dr. Venge was later seen setting her colleague's experimental rats loose in the university's botanical gardens.

> **Case 11–16:**   Ralph Romeo, Ed.D., and Jane Juliet, Ph.D., were fellow faculty members at the Farnsworth Institute of Psychology. They developed a sexual relationship and subsequently Romeo contracted genital herpes from Juliet. He filed an ethics complaint against her, asserting that he had asked specifically whether she had any venereal disease prior to their sexual intimacy and had been assured by her that she did not.

In the case of Dr. Venge, we see a possible ethical violation by a colleague who provoked Dr. Venge to commit a violation of her own in retaliation. While her anger may be understandable, the resulting act is not appropriate professional behavior and only compounds the situation. The case of Dr. Romeo and Dr. Juliet is interesting from several viewpoints. First, it illustrates that underlying an ethics complaint filed by one colleague about another may well be numerous emotional issues that cannot be addressed through an ethics inquiry. Second, it illustrates the problem of attempting to address personal or interpersonal difficulties in the context of an ethics complaint. The ethics committee contacted Romeo, acknowledged his distress at contracting the illness, but noted that the infectious relationship was not a professional one and was hence beyond the purview of the committee.

The ethical-code violator in this category sincerely believes that he or she has been wronged or attacked by another, and thus responds with either an impulsive reaction or (in rare cases) a well-plotted form of retaliation. These actions often lead to future feelings of remorse, but sometimes only after considerable damage has been done. The acts themselves often have a childish quality to them, with the angry colleague looking toward the ethics committee as a parent figure who will redress the perceived wrong. Unfortunately, because the players are adults acting in a professional capacity, the consequences of their actions cannot be easily discounted.

MONITORING THE CONDUCT OF COLLEAGUES

The Ethical Principles of Psychologists enjoin those who encounter ethical problems with colleagues to address them first by informal consultation, and later by formal complaint to appropriate bodies as necessary (*EP:* 7g). Although this procedure is discussed in additional detail in Chapters 1, 2, and 9, the aspect of informal consultation deserves special comment with respect to collegial relations. Raising concerns with colleagues about their ethical conduct will often evoke a hostile or angry response. This problem occurs most often when a critical tone is used, although it is even possible when an educative stance is taken. The colleague's reaction may also be related to the nature and seriousness of the alleged infraction.

Case 11—17: Errol Esteem, Psy.D., was elected to serve as a member of the Commission on Special Activities of a national psychological organization. He listed this membership on his professional stationery below his name and doctoral degree. When a colleague noted that this listing was inappropriate since it was an activity unrelated to his actual professional practice, Dr. Esteem ordered some new stationery.

In this case, the colleague's comment was presented in a nonadversarial fashion, and was accepted; thus it never led to an unnecessary ethical inquiry.

Case 11—18: Shelby Merrit, Ed.D., was angry at the behavior of a colleague, Sheila Dunit, Ed.D. Dr. Merrit told Dr. Dunit that she had brought ethics charges against her and that Dr. Dunit had been found guilty. The first time the ethics committee even heard of the case was when Dunit sent a letter asking why she had not been given a chance to tell her side of the story. An embarrassed Dr. Merrit later acknowledged that she had called the secretary of the committee for informal advice regarding the particular issue, and she had misrepresented the resulting feedback to Dunit, who had never even been named in the conversation.

This case involved an ethical violation by Dr. Merrit, who was so enmeshed in the situation that she actually lied to Dr. Dunit about what had transpired. Whatever objective value Dr. Merrit's issue might have had was not sufficient to warrant such outright prevarication.

Occasionally, a serious ethical infraction is discovered, but the psychologist who makes the discovery must withhold the information in order to protect a client. These situations often involve allegations of sexual misconduct.

> **Case 11–19:**   Sonia Victim sought psychotherapy with Anita Rule, Ph.D. Ms. Victim told Dr. Rule that she had recently decided to terminate her "psychotherapeutic" relationship with Peter Grossout, Ph.D., who had convinced her that she should engage in a variety of sexual activities with him as a means to "overcome the adverse psychological influence of her father in her life." Ms. Victim told Dr. Rule that she was feeling increasingly depressed and worthless after her encounters with Dr. Grossout. Dr. Rule inquired whether Ms. Victim might wish to pursue a complaint against Dr. Grossout, but discovered that the client only wanted to forget those events and begin treatment with Dr. Rule for other concerns.

Dr. Rule would probably want Dr. Grossout called to account for the allegations made by Ms. Victim. If Victim's accusations are true, then Dr. Grossout's future clients may be at risk for such sexual predation. On the other hand, Victim's disclosures were offered in confidence and cannot be disclosed without the client's consent. The client's relative vulnerability and the emotional cost of pursuing a complaint against Grossout may well be too high a price to pay. While Rule can certainly provide her new client with information regarding the fact that the behavior described was unethical and that means for pressing a formal ethics complaint exist, she should not attempt to force her client to press charges. Dr. Rule cannot initiate a complaint herself, since that would violate her client's confidence. Moreover, Ms. Victim might not want Dr. Rule to contact Dr. Grossout about her case. (In this type of situation, a psychologist might accept a new case without consulting a colleague who had been serving the same client in the recent past.)

Perhaps the client will ultimately develop sufficient personal resources to make an appropriate complaint, or perhaps the offending psychologist will be reported to a disciplinary panel by some other route. Another interesting suggestion might be for Dr. Rule to contact Dr. Grossout and ask about his views on sexual relationships with clients, without mentioning a specific context or any particular individuals. This tactic might precipitate an attack of anxiety in Grossout with rehabilitative impact, while protecting the distressed client.

RELATIONSHIPS WITH EMPLOYEES, SUPERVISEES, AND STUDENTS

A psychologist's relationships with employees, supervisees, and students are characterized by similar ethical duties and responsibilities due to clients. The supervising or employing psychologist, who is in a power relationship with respect to those who work for him or her, must recognize the special obligations accompanying this circumstance. Students are even more similar to clients, since the psychologist is hired expressly to provide a service (i.e., teaching) for them. Students, supervisees, and employees have the same rights to privacy, respect, dignity, and due process that should be accorded to others in the more traditional client roles.

Because it is difficult to characterize broadly all potential problems in relating to employees, supervisees, and students, we will begin by discussing particular ethical problems within each category and then examine two special issues: letters of reference and sexual harassment.

Students

The obligations of faculty members to their students are increasingly being brought to the attention of courts and other adjudicatory panels as students become more aware of their rights within the educational system (Sherrer and Sherrer, 1972). Some of these issues are raised elsewhere in this book (especially in Chapters 9 and 13). In this chapter, we are particularly concerned with the quality of the relationship between psychologist and student. Consider the following case examples:

> **Case 11–20:** Helmut Grudge, Ph.D., responded to negative comments made about him by a graduate student to other students by entering "unflattering data" into the student's academic evaluation file. After a lengthy investigation, the "data" were proven to be completely without substance.

> **Case 11–21:** Millard Ire, Ed.D., became enraged at the incompetent performance of a student research assistant and knocked the student to the ground with such force that the student required medical attention.

> **Case 11–22:** Walter Woozie, Psy.D., was annoyed by the persistent questioning by a student in his abnormal psychology class. When she challenged one of his pronouncements, he embarrassed her by commenting: "It's too bad that you haven't managed to work out your hatred for your father by this point in your life." The student fled the class in tears.

In each of these cases, the psychologist has abused a student. Drs. Grudge and Woozie did so by exercising their relative power positions over the student, while Dr. Ire used brute force in a moment of impulsive anger. In some ways, Ire's offense was the least unethical, since it was at least direct, although clearly inappropriate and harmful. The student could as well have been an employee or another colleague. One must wonder whether Ire is an impaired psychologist who needs treatment for his quick, assaultive anger.

Dr. Grudge and Dr. Woozie are more insidious in their unethical behavior. Dr. Grudge simply lied, but did so in a way that took unfair advantage of his power position and placed a substantial burden on the student in terms of disproving his false allegations. Dr. Woozie used his classroom platform to embarrass a student publicly. He may have had an accurate clinical insight about the woman who was annoying to him, but he abused his clinical skills by offering an "interpretation" outside of a therapeutic relationship with the primary intention of retaliation. Unfortunately, "bruised egos" are often the initiating factor in such exchanges.

> **Case 11−23:**   Bob Choice, Ph.D., had recently been divorced by his wife. When he discovered that he and a graduate student working in his lab were both dating the same woman, he terminated the student's access to lab equipment. Dr. Choice became increasingly paranoid and subsequently accused the student of turning poisonous spiders loose in his office, although no such spiders were ever found.

When a teacher becomes emotionally unbalanced, a student is placed at a greater disadvantage than a client normally would be. Both a student and a client can be hurt by a vengeful or troubled psychologist who acts-out in unethical ways; however, a client normally has more degrees of freedom. The client can "fire" the psychologist and seek services elsewhere, but the student cannot extricate himself or herself from the relationship so easily and runs the risk of a poor grade or similar travail. In some situations, the faculty member might even cause long-range career problems for the student. At times, students may be set-up in manipulations they did not create.

> **Case 11−24:**   Angela Sturm, Ph.D., and Portia Drang, Ph.D., were intensely rivalrous faculty members at Northwest Central University. Drang filed an ethics complaint against Sturm, charging that she had convinced a graduate student to develop a dissertation aimed at discrediting theories and research published by Drang.

Students may, of course, select their own advisors and dissertation sponsors, but they are influenced by these faculty members. While the freedom to pursue any area of valid scientific inquiry should be available to everyone, psychologists should do their best not to drag students into personal quarrels. In this instance, Dr. Sturm was not behaving unethically in attempting to interest a student in a dissertation topic, but she may well have been jeopardizing that student's welfare by incorporating him into her dispute with Drang. Because psychological research should ideally seek scientific truth, initiating studies based on an intent to discredit, rather than explore, lacks ethical propriety.

Supervisees

Supervisees are a special subset of students who are at an advanced point in their training, whether it be clinically or academically oriented. These relationships are somewhat more delicate than the usual teacher/student relationship because the supervisee role usually involves an enhanced degree of responsibility. On the one hand, supervisees may be colleagues serving clients for whom the supervisor also holds a measure of responsibility. On the other hand, the supervisee may also be viewed as the client of the supervisor. Timely feedback, or lack thereof, is probably at the root of most ethical complaints developing from such relationships. This phenomenon is especially true when supervisees are abruptly notified that they will be terminated or are given an unfavorable rating. Routine feedback sessions should be included in all supervisory relationships (*EP*: 7c), and when serious criticisms are discussed with supervisees, they should invariably be placed in writing as well as being followed or accompanied by a dialogue about expected changes. This is not a one-way process, and although supervisees are usually considered "one down" in any hierarchical structure, they should routinely communicate professional concerns with supervisory colleagues both orally and in writing.

When a client is receiving services from a psychologist who is also being supervised, the client has the right to know this fact. The client should be told explicitly that aspects of the case will be shared with the supervisor. Indeed, many clients would be pleased to know that the psychologist serving them has consulted a senior colleague. This information should not be brought to a client's attention at a sensitive moment, however, and it is best presented factually as part of the initial contract formed between client and psychologist. Consider the following examples of problems in relationships with supervisees:

Case 11–25:   At the end of a twelve-month clinical internship, Sheldon Lout is shocked to read an evaluation by his supervisor describing him as insensitive and rude in his relationships with colleagues. He is afraid that these comments will hurt his chances of completing a degree and asserts that they are unethical, since he heard nothing about them earlier.

Case 11–26:   Amy Shy arrives at the mental health center for her weekly appointment with the psychology intern who has been treating her, and she is met by Solomon Foot, Ph.D., the intern's supervisor. Dr. Foot explains that the intern broke her leg skiing the weekend before and will not be back at the clinic for four to six weeks. He offers to provide interim services for Ms. Shy, since he is familiar with her case through his supervision of the intern. Ms. Shy is embarrassed that he seems to know "personal things" about her and files an ethics complaint.

Case 11–27:   Lee Trainee, who is in the final stages of completing his doctorate, approaches Marcus Slip, Ph.D., to arrange for special supervision. Apparently, Trainee wants to see several private clients at his home, and he contracts with Dr. Slip to supervise him on that work. Dr. Slip agrees and is paid by Trainee for several hours of supervision time. Several months later, several women complain that they were sexually molested by Trainee in the guise of "therapy." Trainee flees the state and complaints are subsequently directed toward Dr. Slip for inadequately supervising Trainee. Dr. Slip is very upset, claiming that Trainee never told him about the sexual activities or even the specific names of the clients involved.

The common problems inherent in all three of these cases concern the adequacy of supervision and communication of the supervisory relationship to clients. One could argue that Mr. Lout, if he were truly insensitive, might not have heeded supervisory criticism. Nonetheless, he was certainly entitled to timely feedback and would be correct in asserting that it is inappropriate to say nothing about a trainee's shortcomings until the final evaluation. This behavior, if true, permitted Lout no opportunity to remediate the problem.

Dr. Foot appeared to have Amy Shy's best interests at heart, although she was certainly distressed by his awareness of details in her case. It is unclear whether the trainee failed to inform Ms. Shy that a supervisor was involved in her case, or whether Dr. Foot's introduction was a bit too abrupt for her to tolerate. This case does not necessarily represent unethical behavior, but it does reveal the difficulty a sensitive client may face if supervisory relationships are not carefully articulated.

The case of Mr. Trainee and Dr. Slip illustrates the importance of recognizing the supervisor's responsibilities. Dr. Slip, for example, may have extended more trust than was warranted to Mr. Trainee in agreeing to provide supervision. Although it is possible that Trainee either lied or selectively reported material to Dr. Slip, it also appears that Slip may have failed to monitor Trainee's work in adequate detail. It is also possible that several state regulations may have been violated, if the physical presence of the supervisor at the site of service delivery is required, or if payment for supervision is prohibited.

Clear understanding of the contract between both supervisees and supervisors regarding the nature of their relationship, mutual expectations, frequency of contact, feedback format and intervals, and other similar contingencies is essential. Although these arrangements do not have to be formal or written ones, they should be explicitly and thoughtfully executed. Such arrangements are not only the obligation of the supervisor (Scofield and Scofield, 1978), but are also usually desired by the supervisees themselves (Nelson, 1978).

Employees

As agents of the psychologist who hires them, employees and their behavior fall under the purview of the ethics code. A psychologist is responsible for training and monitoring the behavior of employees with respect to any duties delegated to them. A psychologist should not employ persons who cannot conform to standards of behavior required in dealing with their clients. Employees who either handle confidential records or do billing, for example, should understand the ethical issues involved in these duties and be reliable in carrying out these functions. They must also be prepared to handle various other situations that might not arise in different work settings.

Case 11–28: An anonymous caller to a psychologist's office reaches the secretary and explains that she is afraid that she is about to abuse her child. She refuses to give her name, but wants to talk to someone. The psychologist is not available.

Case 11–29: After beginning work as a secretary to a group of psychologists, a young man discovers that several acquaintances of his from the same small town are clients of the group. He is routinely asked to type reports and notes about people who are personally known to him.

Both situations demonstrate the care and training required in the selection and hiring of employees. We have chosen two examples typical of a clinical practice, but they are equally valid for academic or business settings, regarding the need to safeguard confidential materials and to handle clients (or students) appropriately.

If the anonymous caller in *Case 11-28* does not receive some professional help, problems could result. In this case, the secretary could refer the caller to the local child abuse hotline (if one exists) or to another agency in which a telephone response might be available (e.g., community mental health center, hospital emergency room, or crisis center). Abrupt termination or failure to refer such a call could have serious consequences. The psychologist should train employees to handle these situations, for example, by providing such callers with information on referral resources.

Although it is possible to respect the privacy and confidences of personal acquaintences in many situations, a psychologist should assess this ability and sensitivity in potential employees prior to hiring. This procedure is especially important in those communities (e.g., small towns or universities) where social circles may result in many possible overlaps. The new secretary mentioned in *Case 11-29* may be capable of adequately handling the situation, but the psychologists hiring him are ultimately responsible for his behavior and should take special precautions to protect the clients' privacy if needed. Precautions might include, for example, placing files in secure locations or discussing potential confidentiality concerns with the client in question.

Letters of Reference

Letters of reference or endorsement are often sought by colleagues, supervisees, and employees. In general, these letters should be composed on the assumption that they will eventually be seen by the person about whom they are written. Some letters are accompanied by the pledge of confidentiality, but one can never guarantee confidentiality after the letter leaves the office. In addition, the letter should contain the type of information that one would want to receive on the candidate (i.e., for graduate school, employment, promotion, etc.) if the situation were reversed. Finally, if one cannot in good conscience write a favorable evaluation, this problem should be discussed with the candidate so that another reference choice could be considered.

Some critics may view the latter two points as being contradictory: that is, if the candidate in question has personal flaws and you were considering that person for a position, would you want to know about them? Our answer would be: of course, if the candidate is also aware of them. Some candidates may disagree with particular points in a letter of reference written by a supervisor, employer, or colleague, but will not be able to address them in an interview without having been told about the problems. The situation could arise of being damned without knowing either the reason or the accuser and having no chance to reply.

If it is not possible to write a glowing letter, it is always possible to send a factual confirmation letter (e.g., "Dr. Jones was employed at this facility in the role of staff psychologist for two years."). While the candidate may not be pleased by a refusal to send a note of praise, he or she will be gratified by the opportunity to find a person more favorably disposed to write the recommendation.

Considerable disagreement exists among professors regarding what is and what is not appropriate for inclusion in letters of reference (Mebane, Note 1). Although Mebane's study focused on letters written for graduate school applicants, a similar diversity of views would probably be prevalent among other psychologists writing other types of references. In Mebane's survey, approximately half of the professors sampled expressed a primary allegiance to the student, while others viewed their primary duty as one to the graduate school, the profession, or to society in general. In addition to the general lack of consensus Mebane found, conventional wisdom on the meaning of such letters is highly variable. Some colleagues find a letter that is "too uniformly positive" unconvincing, while others may regard a letter with "strengths and weaknesses" primarily in terms of the weaknesses.

It is not easy to know what to do when telephoned by a prospective employer for "informal" comments about an applicant, especially if you have not been consulted in advance about the use of your name as a reference. Advanced consultation would permit you to forewarn the applicant, if you cannot give a wholehearted endorsement. We would caution that it is unwise to say something about a colleague in private that might ultimately be repeated to the candidate and attributed to you, unless you are willing to have the candidate know your opinions.

A mild ethical abuse, but one that is all too common, is the agreed-upon reference that is never sent. In short, the faculty member agrees to write a letter, but never does it. The student may not discover the omission until it is too late. Students may be reluctant to nag the faculty member to send the letter, but they also run the risk of missing deadlines if they do not. If in doubt, the student should check with the potential recipient or alert the letter-writer that the deadline is approaching.

It would obviously be prudent for anyone seeking a reference or endorsement to approach colleagues, supervisors, or employers prior to using their names. Asking whether they feel they could write a strong letter of reference in relation to a particular position is a fair question. If hesitancy or reluctance is sensed, alternate recommenders should be approached.

Sexual and Gender Harassment

In the past, women's passive endurance of uninvited expressions of sexual interest and sexually oriented remarks in the workplace or academia was expected. Recipients who responded negatively to such remarks or behavior risked sanctions, especially if they were in a disadvantageous power relationship with the initiators. Today, such acts have increasingly been recognized as "harassment" and as forms of sex discrimination, thus gaining civil rights credibility through Title VIII of the Civil Rights Act of 1964 and Title IX of the Education Amendment of 1972 (Middleton, 1980). A specific reference to sexual harassment, as well as a stern admonition to refrain from initiating it, appear for the first time in the 1981 revision of the *Ethical Principles* (*EP*: 7d). (Sexually intimate behavior with psychotherapy clients, students, and trainees is discussed in detail in Chapter 10. Harassment in the form of sex-biased therapy with female clients is briefly discussed in Chapter 5.)

Most of the writings (and the case material we present here) are primarily concerned with how sexual and gender harassment have been used to degrade and oppress women both as individuals and as a class (Goodman, 1978; Farley, 1978; Polansky, 1980). As women gain positions of authority, however, they may increasingly find that their own behavior or remarks (even when intended to be playful) will increase their vulnerability to charges of sexual or gender harassment.

Clearly agreed on specifications of what behaviors or verbalizations constitute sexual or gender harassment are difficult to obtain. Except for the more extreme vituperations or lewd acts, definitions are determined in large measure by the motivations of the perpetrator, interpretation by the recipient, the nature of the relationship between the parties involved, and the context in which the incident occurred. Surveys have also revealed sex differences in perceptions of what constitutes harassment, with men tending to view many behaviors as either less serious or less inappropriate than do women (Gutek et al., 1980; Johnson and Tangri, Note 2).

We have adapted the following definition of sexual harassment from the definition issued by the Equal Employment Opportunity Commission (1980): Unwelcome sexual advances, requests for sexual favors, and other verbal or physical conduct of a sexual nature that force submission as either an explicit or implicit condition of employment or academic standing or that have the purpose or effect of substantially interfering with an individual's work or academic performance or create an intimidating, hostile, or offensive work or learning environment.

> **Case 11-30:**   Professor Jerry Built, Ph.D., often told his technical equipment supervisee, Gena Dynograph, that allocations, which were usually issued as a normal part of her work responsibilities, would be given only if she were "nice to him." When supplies were not forthcoming, he would say that they would be made available "when she treated him nicer." According to Ms. Dynograph, "being nice" meant complimenting Dr. Built on his appearance and acting mildly flirtatious. She resented feeling forced to perform in this manner in order to fulfill her required job functions.

> **Case 11-31:**   Each time he brought his secretary, Ann Scribe, a task, Sherman Tactile, Ph.D., habitually placed his hand on her lower back for a prolonged period of time. When Ms. Scribe tried to turn her body or to stand farther away, Dr. Tactile would either alter his own position so that he could resume his touching, or he would say: "Come back here so I can explain this to you." Or: "Why are you such a distant and unfriendly person?" Ms. Scribe brought charges against Dr. Tactile when he fired her on grounds of an "uncooperative attitude."

> **Case 11-32:**   During an office hour, Leroy Lust, Ed.D., told Nora Nubile, a student in his class, that he was interested in seeing her on a personal basis. When Ms. Nubile inquired what this remark meant, Dr. Lust allegedly laughed and said: "I want to get into your pants." When Ms. Nubile retorted that she found such a suggestion highly inappropriate, Dr. Lust warned that if she mentioned this conversation to anyone, she would "not be at all happy with her course grade."

> **Case 11-33:**   Dexter Swinish, Psy.D., was known for making suggestive remarks to his female trainees. Dr. Swinish approached Sandra Firm and said: "Hey, want to get it on with me this weekend?" Ms. Firm replied: "Go sit on your thumb." Dr. Swinish reportedly avoided her after that and, at the end of the term, entered unflattering and undocumented comments into her evaluation file.

These cases illustrate how demands for sexually oriented favors, as well as reprisals for rejecting these demands, can interfere with job and academic status of particular individuals. The intimidations, however, can also be more diffuse as illustrated by the following case:

Case 11-34: Professor Tim Traditional, Ph.D., announced to his classes that he was a "dirty old man who likes to flirt with the ladies." He then noted that if anyone found this small pleasure a burden, they should drop his course because he was "too old to keep up with this women's liberation nonsense."

In this instance, female students as a class were explicitly identified as potential targets; moreover, the message implied that they were unworthy of the contemporary mores favoring equality and respect between the sexes.

Dr. Traditional's stance has elements of "gender harassment," which need not involve direct references to sexuality. Gender harassment has been defined as comments or behavior directed at one sex but not the other (Fuller, 1979). Not all gender-related behavior can be reasonably defined as harassing, but it does result when the behavior causes discomfort or humiliation (e.g., referring to all women as "cutie" or "honey") or is used as a means of power containment (e.g., counseling only female students to avoid certain academic goals).

Case 11-35: Macho Mann, Ph.D., told Zena Freeman, after she requested assistance with problems she was having understanding the course content, that women did not belong in this particular course because they were not suited to the field. He refused to respond to her specific questions. Rather, he continued to refer to the unsuitability of women in general in his course and cited her difficulties in comprehension as evidence.

Case 11-36: Marsha Torpid experienced some difficulty adapting to a new word processor in the psychology clinic where she worked as the receptionist. The director, Roger Rough, Psy.D., was irritated by her errors and berated her with such comments as the following: "This is woman's work, and you aren't much of a woman at it." Or: "Stop acting as if the damn thing is about to rape you." Ms. Torpid felt that such comments were so intimidating and they caused her so much resentment that they interfered with her progress in mastering the task. When Dr. Rough gave her an unsatisfactory job performance evaluation, she complained that his harassment was primarily responsible for blocking her potential.

Case 11-37: Gilly Bloom complained that Wag Rogue, Ph.D., made jokes at her expense during class. She alleged that he would tease her about such things as her clothing, fingernail polish, hair style and big purse. Professor Rogue was surprised by her formal complaint. He thought her customary shy, giggling responses were indications that she enjoyed his "gentle chiding."

Although none of the above examples involved direct sexual solicitations, the effect was obviously intended to keep the women in a subordinate position through exclusion or ridicule. In all cases, the women's work or academic experiences were made uncomfortable for them, which, in turn, had implications for their ability to transact their primary roles as employees or students.

Sexual harassment and sex discrimination are appallingly prevalent practices (MacKinnon, 1979; Johnson and Tangri, 1981, Note 2; Kelber, 1975); thus legal sanctions and grievance procedures are becoming increasingly formalized and utilized (Weisel, 1977; Munich, 1978; MacKinnon, 1979; Pendergrass, 1979; Seymour, 1979; Polansky, 1980). How can men and women, however, establish criteria for judging whether their verbal comments or behavior constitute sexual harassment? Traditional attitudes die hard, and males, who may be unaware of the impact of their ingrained personal styles, will be vulnerable to censure unless they begin raising their consciousnesses. Women who are in the process of becoming comfortable with more direct expressions of their feelings, including the replacement of coyness and indirect expressions of sexual interest for more direct approaches, may find that this newly developed honesty may have serious consequences when displayed under certain conditions. Ironically, one of the largest monetary awards issued in such a case in a federal court was given to a male supervisee (*Time*, 1982).

THE DIFFICULT ASSOCIATE

The troublesome client is discussed as a special problem in Chapter 5. In this section, however, we focus on the student, employee, or colleague whose behavior or interpersonal relations are particularly difficult. To some extent, these issues are discussed in Chapter 9 in the context of the troubled colleague; in addition, several of the case examples cited earlier in this chapter also illustrate the problems of the difficult colleague. Certain types of situations and individuals, however, present particular risks. Thus recognizing and dealing with these hazards can often minimize ethical problems.

Risky Situations

The most risky situations regarding collegial conflict are those in which an individual is being evaluated in a pass/fail system. In these situations, the person being assessed is under substantial personal stress. The evaluator's failure to recognize and respond sensitively presents a serious hazard. Such situations include doctoral examinations, tenure decisions, annual salary reviews, or simply grading a term paper.

Another type of high risk situation occurs when the parties have failed to communicate adequately their expectations for role performance. The absence of specific outcome goals and timely feedback often characterize these situations. One or both parties will often assume erroneously that the other's needs and goals are fully congruent with their own.

Case 11–38: George Faraway, Ph.D., hired Timothy Toil, Ph.D., a recent graduate of his department, to conduct a research project in rural Ecuador for a twelve-month period. Communications between the small towns in which the data were being collected and the university were difficult. Dr. Faraway visited Ecuador once shortly after Dr. Toil had arrived, and he seemed satisfied with the progress of the project. Near the end of the project, an earthquake damaged some equipment, and Toil became ill for two weeks. He returned to the United States with the data collection incomplete. Faraway was angry that his study was not finished and refused to pay Toil until he returned to finish the data collection. Toil filed an ethics complaint.

In this instance, a difficult work environment was complicated by poor communication and misunderstanding of roles and responsibilities. Toil was prepared to do the best he could under the circumstances for twelve months. Faraway expected a completed project, although he was not in regular contact with Toil, and he was not able to monitor the complex program from his distant university office. Their agreements were based primarily on personal understandings, rather than on written contracts. When distance and nature intervened, the friendly agreement deteriorated.

Still another type of high-risk situation is the dispute for which there is no resolution format. In essence, when no formal mechanism exists to process a complaint or to resolve a dispute, or when such disputes are ignored, a special risk situation develops.

Case 11–39: William Bicker, Ed.D., Frank Fracas, Psy.D., and Mildred Brawl, Ph.D., work together in a group-practice arrangement. They share the cost of office space, utilities, and a receptionist's salary. As time goes on, it is clear that each engages in some behavior that is annoying to the other two. Because they were all such "good friends" when entering the arrangement, no contractual contingencies for handling disputes were drafted. Each is a strong-willed individual, and eventually at least one person threatens another with an ethics charge.

How can three, highly educated individuals find themselves in this type of situation? It happens frequently enough for us to suggest that any business arrangements among colleagues should include formal contractual agreements specifying both operational contingencies and details on dispute resolution (e.g., agreement to use binding arbitration), even if they are all "good friends."

Risky Individuals

Several types of people are difficult to work with. At the same time, such people may be perfectly happy with themselves despite this difficulty. In several of the cases described previously, however, one person's behavior could negatively affect everyone concerned.

Individuals who are emotionally labile or unstable certainly present some risk. Perhaps arrogance, narcissism, or a critical personality style may also contribute to such problems. We could continue listing various, unwholesome personality traits (e.g., procrastination, impulsivity, hostility, etc.), but the point is clear. Considering human nature, every risky situation can include one or more risky individuals. How, then, can one avoid a clash?

> **Case 11–40:** Bernice Dweezel, Ph.D., is a distinguished psychologist whose research is world renowned. Unfortunately, she is also rather egotistical and demanding. Students who are willing to tolerate criticism and pontification often benefit from working with her, but not everyone is able to tolerate her behavior. The faculty respect her scholarly work and appreciate the way her professional reputation enhances the status of their department, although few of them would choose to socialize with her away from the university. Each year there are several incidents involving tirades directed at students or colleagues by Dr. Dweezel.

Dr. Dweezel may be an obnoxious individual by many standards, and she may border on behaving unethically when she is inconsiderate to students and colleagues. Unfortunately, she may have little insight into the nature of this problem and no motivation to change her personal style. In any case, an ethics complaint would probably not evoke a positive change in her behavior. The more serious danger will occur if, or when, Dr. Dweezel encounters a hostile student or colleague more inclined to act-out than argue on an intellectual plane. One might caution others about the hazards of working with her, or counsel avoiding her entirely. Others might attempt some collegial consultation with gentle references to a need for treatment. Unfortunately, however, people like Dr. Dweezel will always exist in the world, and ethics codes may have minimal use in handling them.

Dealing with the Difficult Associate

Rules and procedures are the most powerful tools available to handle the difficult associate in a risky situation. Having an explicit set of guidelines and standards can provide a giant step toward avoiding conflict and reducing stress for everyone concerned. The use of formal procedures not only enhances communication, but also cools passions by drawing out a decision in a deliberative fashion (Clark, 1974). Due process provides emotional insulation as well as procedural safeguards.

Although one cannot restructure personality to suit circumstances, it is possible to minimize risk in risky situations by imposing structure and enhancing communication. Evaluations, for example, should always be presented thoughtfully and empathically, with the evaluator listening as well as informing. At the same time, it is often advisable to repeat material in writing since oral communications may be forgotten or tempered by intervening variables.

These suggestions may seem contrary to the concept of resolving disputes informally by mutual agreement. Indeed, that mechanism is preferable; however, if communication is already complicated, or difficult, a more formal approach may be needed. Ironically, the ethics complaints that result from such circumstances are rarely ethics matters. More often they represent interpersonal conflicts that have escalated to the point of ethical name-calling. By then, it is too late for a simple resolution.

When the difficult associate is a superior or supervisor, rather than a peer or subordinate, similar fundamental principles apply in terms of the ideal course of action. Unfortunately, in many situations management tends to support management, without a full examination of the issues. Raising an objection, however valid, may be regarded as "rocking the boat" or being disloyal. Formal, written grievance procedures can be helpful, if they exist; however, one must be sensitive to the potential hazards in deciding a course of action. An ethics complaint has minimal value in resolving personality clashes and conflicts.

SUMMARY GUIDELINES

1. Colleagues should always try to cooperate on a professional level when a client's best interests are at stake, despite any personal antipathy they may feel toward each other.

2. Services should not be delivered in a manner that interferes with a client's preexisting or ongoing relationship with another professional. The ultimate choice of where to seek any service belongs to the client.

3. One should always attempt to offer respect and courtesy in relationships with other professionals, even if one is legitimately annoyed with one's colleague.

4. Colleagues should attempt to resolve disputes informally whenever possible, and they should attempt to prevent disputes by clarifying mutual expectations at the outset of any collaborative arrangement.

5. Students, supervisees, and employees are at an inherent disadvantage in any disagreement with their instructor, supervisor, or employer, respectively. This fact should be recognized with respect to the obligation to treat these individuals with courtesy, fairness, and dignity.

6. A psychologist should exercise caution in training and monitoring the behavior of employees and supervisees to ensure their conformity with ethical practice.

7. In preparing letters of reference, it is wise to be honest and direct, discussing with the person requesting it the type of letter one could, in good conscience, write.

8. Psychologists should familiarize themselves with the issue of both subtle and more obvious forms of sexual and gender harassment. In addition, they should make efforts to educate colleagues regarding the inappropriateness of such behavior when they observe it in others.

9. When placed in a decision-making role with respect to a student, supervisee, or colleague (e.g., grading, promotion, or tenure), one should recognize the stress on that individual and afford appropriate consideration and due process to each.

10. In handling the troubled or troubling student, employee, or colleague, it is usually best to operate using standard rules and procedures, while attempting to avoid being victimized by an angry emotional response.

REFERENCE NOTES

1. Mebane, D. L. *Ethical issues in writing recommendation letters*. Paper presented at the Annual Meeting of the Western Psychological Association, San Francisco, California, April 1983.

2. Johnson, L. B., and Tangri, S. S. *Results of the National Survey of Federal Workers by the U.S. Merit Systems Protection Board*. Paper presented at the American Psychological Association, Los Angeles, California, August 1981.

REFERENCES

Bailey, K. G. Psychotherapy or massage parlor technology? Comments on the Zeiss, Rosen, and Zeiss treatment procedure. *Journal of Consulting and Clinical Psychology*, 1978, 46, 1502–1506.

Clark, R. D. Tenure and the moderation of conflict. In R. H. Peairs (Ed.), *Avoiding conflict in faculty personnel practices*. San Francisco: Jossey-Bass, 1974.

Cook, S. W. Comments on ethical considerations in "self-control" techniques as an alternative to pain medication. *Journal of Abnormal Psychology*, 1975, 84, 169–171.

Equal Employment Opportunity Commission. Sex discrimination harassment. *Federal Register*, April 11, 1980.

Farley, L. *Sexual Shake-down: The Sexual Harassment of Women on the Job*. New York: McGraw-Hill, 1978.

Fuller, M. M. *Sexual Harassment—How to Recognize and Deal with It*. Annapolis, MD: Eastport Litho, 1979.

Goodman, J. L. Sexual demands on the job. *Civil Liberties Review*, 1978, 4, 55–58.

Gutek, B. A.; Nakamura, C. Y.; Gahart, M.; Handschumacher, I.; and Russel, D. Sexuality and the workplace. *Basic and Applied Social Psychology*, 1980, 1, 244–265.

Kelber, M. The UN's dirty little secret. *Ms.*, 1975, 6, 51.

Koocher, G. P.; Sobel, S. B.; and Hare-Mustin, R. T. Making of the president 1982: On campaigning for office in a learned society. *The Clinical Psychologist*, 1982, *35*, 1–9.

MacKinnon, C. A. *Sexual Harassment of Working Women: A Case of Sex Discrimination*. New Haven, CT: Yale University Press, 1979.

Middleton, L. Sexual harassment by professors: An increasingly visible problem. *Chronicle of Higher Education*, 1980, *1*, 4.

Munich, A. Seduction in academe. *Psychology Today*, 1978, *11*, 82–84.

Nelson, G. L. Psychotherapy supervision from the trainee's point of view: A survey of preferences. *Professional Psychology*, 1978, *9*, 539–550.

Pendergrass, V. E. *Women Winning: A Handbook for Action against Sex Discrimination*. Chicago: Nelson-Hall, 1979.

Polansky, E. Sexual harassment at the workplace. *Human Rights*, 1980, *8*, 14–19, 46–47.

Scofield, M. E., and Scofield, B. J. Ethical concerns in clinical practice supervision. *Journal of Applied Rehabilitation Counseling*, 1978, *9*, 27–29.

Seymour, W. C. Sexual harassment: Finding a cause of action under Title VII. *Labor Law Journal*, 1979, *30*, 139–156.

Sherrer, C. W., and Sherrer, M. S. Professional or legal standards for academic psychologists and counselors. *Journal of Law and Education*, 1972, *1*, 289–302.

Time Magazine. Role reversal: Man wins office sex suit. August 2, 1982, p. 19.

Weisel, K. Title VII: Legal protection against sexual harassment. *Washington Law Review*, 1977, *53*, 123–144.

Ethical Dilemmas in Special Work Settings 12

New occasions teach new duties.

James Russell Lowell

The ethical pressures from within the workplace may range from subtle erosion of professional values to overwhelming emotional distress. Some settings in which psychologists work seem especially likely to evoke ethical quandaries. Examples of such settings include the military, government agencies, medical centers, prisons, and schools. In these workplaces, psychologists may expect to encounter clients with rather specialized needs. Client needs may, in fact, be incongruent with other demands of the agency or institution placing the psychologist in an ethical predicament. Private practices also represent a unique type of work settings, as do academic and psychological research laboratories (although these latter two categories are addressed in Chapters 13 and 14).

The courtroom and criminal justice system will be used as an example of a specialized newly emerging work setting for psychologists in this chapter. These contexts provide a particularly useful example because of the increasingly important roles psychologists are playing in the forensic arena, contrasted with the relative lack of training most psychologists receive to prepare them for working there. The temptation to work in an area with special demands when one is not fully trained to do so often has the most dramatic consequences in such settings.

In categorizing the types of difficulties that are linked to specialized work settings, there are three distinct areas of focus. First are the nature and demands of the agency, organization, or special context within which the psychologist's services are rendered. Second are issues related to the particular nature of the clients and their problems. Third are the special skills or competencies needed by the psychologists who wish to work with these clients. It is important to clarify and conceptualize all of these areas.

WHO IS THE CLIENT?

A major monograph entitled "Who Is the Client?" (Monahan, 1980) developed from the work of the American Psychological Association's Task Force on the "Role of Psychology in the Criminal Justice System." Despite the "criminal justice" focus, the edited collection of papers has important generic value for helping psychologists to recognize the complex nature of many different types of client relationships. In particular, psychologists must always be conscious of who the client is, and they should be prepared to define carefully client relationships concerning confidentiality, responsibility, and other critical ethical issues.

Many employment situations have varying categories of clients and distinct client need hierarchies. It is critical that the psychologist carefully consider and conceptualize these situations, since the needs of the different components may often compete or be mutually exclusive. For example, a psychologist could be requested to provide direct services for a person, while they are employed by an organization that is a government branch. In those circumstances, the psychologist might owe professional duties to all three entities (i.e., the individual client, the specific agency or organization, and government or society as a whole), although the specifics and clarity of the lines of obligation will obviously have great potential variability. In such situations, the psychologist should clarify the nature of the ethical obligations due to each party, inform all concerned about the ethical constraints, if any, and take whatever actions are necessary to ensure appropriate respect for the client(s) (*EP*: 1, 6).

WHAT SKILLS ARE NEEDED?

The issue of competence assessment and recognition of limitations by psychologists is addressed in Chapter 9, and difficulties inherent in evaluating competence, especially regarding new or emerging areas of practice or psychological expertise, are also discussed in that chapter. In this chapter, it is important to recognize a more subtle issue in assessing one's own skills: namely, evaluating the ability to perform with appropriate sensitivity and expertise in a special context. In essence, one may be quite competent at psychodiagnostic assessment and psychotherapy in general practice, but these talents will not necessarily transfer directly to performing treatment in a prison or to conducting psychological assessments to aid in the selection of a corporate executive.

The transfer or generalizability of training across situations or populations can be quite variable, and the psychologist who fails to recognize and compensate for this fact may encounter serious ethical problems. There are times when enthusiasm, necessity, or poor judgment may propel a psychologist into a new professional arena; thus, without a clear and thoughtful assessment of the situational demands, the risk of an ethical violation is substantially potentiated. Caution is the primary way to avoid these types of problems, but the following pages highlight some of the more subtle aspects of specialized skills required at certain work sites.

ORGANIZATIONAL DEMANDS

Individual psychologists are accountable for upholding the *Ethical Principles*, but organizations are not accountable in the same manner. There are times when a psychologist/employee may be asked or told to behave in an ethically inappropriate manner as a function of the employing organization's needs. Monahan and his colleagues (1980) provide a cogent example by citing the case of a client of a psychologist in private practice who reveals racist attitudes or behavior in the course of treatment. These attitudes may or may not be relevant to the treatment program, but the issue is clearly a confidential matter between client and therapist. If, on the other hand, the psychologist is consulting to a law enforcement agency and discovers a pattern of racist organizational policies or discrimination it would not *always* be unethical to keep this confidential. It would, however, be unethical for the psychologist to cooperate in establishing, maintaining, or implementing such policies. In this situation, the psychologist must balance an obligation to protect the individual client's confidentiality with the obligation to disclose important information to a client organization (*EP*: 3c).

What if the psychologist described above chose to inform the agency's employer (e.g., the legislative or executive body supervising the agency) about the racist policies? What if the psychologist took the story to the press? As discussed in Chapter 3, it is permissible to violate a confidence in the case of clear and imminent danger, but racist behavior does not usually meet that test. Certainly there are circumstances when "whistle-blowing" behavior is appropriate ethical behavior, although the matter is not a simple one to identify. As Monahan and his colleagues (Monahan, 1980) explain:

> We are not suggesting that psychologists should avoid serving in imperfect organizations, only that the perennial debate concerning whether it is better to work from inside to achieve gradual change or to leave the organization and apply pressure from the outside for reform . . . is common to all organizational structures. (p. 3)

Consequently, what is right for the psychologist's work with an individual client may be wrong for work with a client organization or employing agency, and vice versa. The differentiation of obligations and the linkage of these obligations to broader issues of human welfare are important ethical questions that require thoughtful analysis, while often lacking clear answers (*EP*: 6c).

SAMPLE SETTINGS

Government Employment

The government employs psychologists on many levels and in all branches. Psychologists serve at the municipal, state, and federal level with roles in the legislative, judicial, and executive branches. Later in this chapter we shall specifically discuss some subsets of governmental agencies (i.e., the military, schools, community agencies, and the criminal justice system) in detail. First, however, it is worth considering government services as a whole. Government settings involve an important degree of public trust, while at the same time being subject to a high degree of political pressure. Functioning as a public servant/psychologist can be both rewarding and frustrating (see, for example, Shakow, 1968), especially at the level of integrating professional judgment with policymaking (Boling and Dempsey, 1981).

> **Case 12–1:** Sam Uncle, Ph.D., a psychologist working as a clinician at a federally operated hospital, was instructed to provide access to case records in a manner that seemed contrary to the *Ethical Principles*. This was called to the attention of the supervisor who replied, "Those ethical principles do not apply to federal employees at this facility."

> **Case 12–2:** A government agency planned to administer hallucinogenic drugs to unwitting individuals and observe the resulting behavioral changes. Two psychologists were recruited to participate in the project by a clandestine government agency, and they cooperated in the conduction of the project.

> **Case 12–3:** A municipal government hired Maxine Datum, Ed.D., to explore the question of whether racist attitudes among certain officials influenced hiring practices. Dr. Datum's study and analysis of the personnel system confirmed the presence of active racial discrimination. The officials ordered Dr. Datum to keep these findings confidential and several months later they had done nothing to alter personnel practices.

These three situations illustrate the range and complexity of issues that may occur in government service. In the first case, Dr. Uncle was informed that the agency employees are not bound by the *Ethical Principles*.

That is not true. All psychologists who pledge to uphold the *Ethical Principles* are bound by the principles in all contexts of their work as psychologists (*EP*: 1d). The supervisor in this particular case was actually misinterpreting federal policy; however, situations may arise in which employers will demand that their psychologist/employees behave contrary to the dictates of ethical standards. Each psychologist must consider how best to handle the individual situations as they occur, but the basic principles are not waived for any employer, government or otherwise.

In the case of the covert administration of hallucinogenic drugs to uninformed individuals who had not consented to participate in an experiment of this type, the psychologists engaged in unethical complicity. Their assertion that national security was at issue and the notation that they had not actually administered the drugs were not salient to the ethics panel that investigated the case.

The case of the municipal personnel research adds a new wrinkle to the role of the psychologist. Presumably the city in question was the client, and the government officials who hired Dr. Datum have a right to control the data collected on their behalf, similar to an individual's right to confidentiality. One could argue that the public interest would best be served by making the data public, but would that produce the socially desirable change? Suppose the municipal officials tell Datum that they will use the information to "bring about appropriate change in our own way"? Does Datum have a right or a duty to challenge this? Can one draw an analogy to the racist client in therapy, who listens to the therapist interpret the racist behavior but desires to adhere to the same attitudes? These questions are not easily answered, but they lead to an important issue in ethical behavior. The psychologist must assume the burden of articulating the nature and expectations of his or her professional role (*EP*: 1b). When the psychologist works for a government agency, it is no less important to explore these issues in order to assess the degrees of freedom and ethical comfort one may expect to enjoy in the job.

In the next several pages we shall explore specific ethical issues that relate to particular components of government: namely, the military, schools, and community agencies.

The Military

Given that psychologists are supposed to be dedicated to advancing the cause of human welfare, should they work for the military, the Central Intelligence Agency, or similar governmental units? The question is not as simple as it might seem, since a military or espionage force is certainly necessary and since behavioral sciences certainly have much to contribute to the military, as is the case in any other complex human organization (Allen et al., 1982). At the same time, many psychologists might feel concern about the contribution of psychology to Pentagon activities.

A paper on military psychology published during the Vietnam era (Crawford, 1970) evoked the following stinging response: "The chief goal of military psychology is the transformation of human beings into more efficient murder machines" (Saks, 1970, p. 876). This in turn brought forth a series of rebuttals (Kelley, 1971; Leuba, 1971) and considerable acrimony. While that debate may have been more a function of the times than of ethics issues, some would express similar concerns today—on both sides of the issue.

For purposes of this chapter, we delineate two distinct aspects of military psychology. One is the work of the civilian employee or military personnel in research, and the other is the role of military personnel in the delivery of psychological services. Most ethical decision making is precisely analogous to that involved in the work of the research or industrial/organizational psychologist or the clinician in general, but there are special subtleties and matters of relative emphasis that necessitate critical ethical review.

Allen et al. (1982) describe a variety of roles psychologists perform for the military in the nonclinical realm. These can be described as personnel functions (e.g., selection, assessment, classification, and retention of military personnel), training (e.g., leadership development, skill acquisition, teaching, and effectiveness enhancement), human performance research (e.g., human factors engineering, job design, information processing, and decision-making studies), development of specialized training (e.g., simulators and assessment centers), and health-related research (e.g., sleep deprivation, fatigue, and physical fitness studies).

Although the goal of such research may be to enhance the ability to destroy an enemy before being destroyed, any moral decision about whether to participate in such programs is primarily a matter of personal conscience. The constraints on such research or training programs are essentially the same as those in nonmilitary settings (i.e., informed consent of participants, appropriate respect for the rights of the individual, etc.). It is evident that much of the research conducted on behalf of the military will have beneficial civilian applications (e.g., flight simulators designed for the military can also be adapted to train civilian pilots or physical fitness research done for the military may be generalized for the public at large, as in the widely marketed Canadian Air Force Exercise Program).

When a military psychologist is functioning as a provider of clinical or counseling services, some special ethical dilemmas do occasionally arise, as illustrated in the following situations.

Case 12–4:   Captain Henry B. Trayed filed a complaint with an ethics committee against a military psychologist at his base hospital. Captain Trayed stated that the psychologist had indicated that information received in the context of treatment would be held in confidence. The psychologist had informed Captain Trayed's superiors of his extreme depression and other psychopathological symptoms resulting in considerable career sanctions. The psychologist responded to the committee's inquiry by noting that Captain Trayed knew that the base hospital treatment setting operated differently from those "on the outside."

Case 12−5: Major Mary Militia, Ph.D., serving as a commissioned officer in a branch of the U.S. military, was ordered to report to her superiors any military personnel seeking services at the base hospitals whom she considered to be at risk for decompensation or who were engaging in homosexual activities.

Confidentiality issues are a key source of concern in mental health service delivery to military personnel by military personnel. On the one hand, individuals in sensitive defense-related positions could be especially dangerous when attempting to perform their duties in emotionally troubled states. At the same time, such individuals should have the same rights to privacy and confidentiality so important to effective general psychotherapeutic care (as discussed in Chapter 3). One way to deal with the issue is to inform clients from the outset of the professional relationship and to explain any limitations it places on their confidentiality. The military client could be advised in the first session that certain types of problems must be reported, thus providing the option for the individual in question to seek treatment off-base or from civilian personnel, if appropriate. Such referral obviously is not possible on shipboard or in a battle zone, but the client can and should be advised of the limits of the professional relationship (if any) from the start (*EP*: 5 preamble).

The question of whether sexual preference has any bearing on job performance in the military or elsewhere has been the subject of considerable litigation. A psychologist may find himself or herself in the position of having to help enforce such criteria, while having personal reservations about the validity of the criteria. The options are essentially twofold: The psychologist may decide not to participate in the system at all and may seek employment elsewhere, or the psychologist may seek to work for change in the system from within. In any case, once again, the client is entitled to advance warning that certain types of disclosures may have specific consequences.

Case 12−6: A psychologist in the community became concerned when he learned that a female client, whose husband was a military officer, was taking medication prescribed by a psychologist working at the base hospital. Psychologists are not typically trained in, nor authorized to prescribe, medication.

The psychologist who was accused of prescribing medication without a medical degree had indeed done so, but not unethically. In addition to his psychology degree, this individual was trained as a physician's assistant in mental health and was authorized under military regulations to prescribe medication, under specific circumstances, for military personnel and their dependents under treatment at military facilities. In this instance, the psychologist was practicing within his sphere of competence in full compliance with military regulations appropriate to the care of the client in question. Although this particular type of service is unusual for psychologists, who are not usually trained to prescribe medication nor authorized to do so under state laws, it was appropriate in the context and in accordance with the provider's competence in this instance.

Cases involving the intelligence or espionage community are by definition not often in the public eye, but occasional cases have called attention to the work of psychologists in such agencies.

> **Case 12–7:**   Carl Covert, Ph.D., worked on the staff of a defense-related federal agency and was assigned to a project drafting interrogation protocols for enemy prisoners. His job was to assist in applying psychological principles likely to place emotional pressures to divulge information on the subjects of interrogation. In one "experiment" Dr. Covert was assigned to monitor the effectiveness of hallucinogenic drugs in breaking down the resistance of an American soldier. Several years later the soldier would charge that he had never knowingly volunteered for such an experiment and was harmed psychologically by his unknowing participation.

> **Case 12–8:**   Cassandra Troy, Ph.D., also works in a defense-related intelligence service. Her job is to study the behavior and writings of world leaders and to prepare personality profiles for secret applications by other branches of government. She attempts to predict how individuals might respond in different sets of circumstances and is often asked to provide confidential briefings to state and defense department negotiators prior to their meetings with these leaders.

Dr. Covert and Dr. Troy are in some sense responsible primarily to their governmental client, although the immediate impact of their work certainly affects other people. One might argue that their work is a special category and in the national interest. To the extent that Dr. Covert was actually involved in the experiment as claimed by the soldier, he was guilty of participating in the unethical abuse of a research participant (i.e., an unwilling one). Assuming, however, that his work does not otherwise involve violations of international conventions on the treatment of prisoners, it may not be unethical. If her work is accurately able to predict behavior, Dr. Troy may be giving her employer some very useful data. Her work is not unethical per se, although she would certainly want to present appropriate scientific caveats regarding its predictive validity to those who may rely on the briefings to the exclusion of other factors.

Schools

Schools may be public or private, day or residential, but most American children are required by law to attend school and hence are subject to the powerful influence of the school as a socialization agent. Much of the recent controversy in the practice of school psychology involves issues of competence, credentials, and professional control. Many psychologists who practice in school settings are subdoctoral in academic training, and APA has often asserted that the doctorate is the entry-level professional degree. Questions of competence and qualifications are discussed in Chapter 9; however, the reader may be interested in the specifics of school psychology that are uniquely affected in this area of controversy. A section of the December 1982 issue of *Professional Psychology* is devoted to papers focusing on this matter, and the lead article for that section (Bardon, 1982) summarizes the issues well. We shall not rehash the regulatory disputes here, but we will instead focus on more specific types of ethical dilemmas in the schools.

Important issues of special ethical concern that have been highlighted in school settings (O'Leary and O'Leary, 1977) include the following: informed consent, privacy, determination of classroom goals, legitimacy of rewards and aversive controls in the classroom, and the use of "time-out" as a potential type of abuse (Gast and Nelson, 1977a; 1977b). The role of the psychologist in privacy and confidentiality matters (Trachtman, 1974) and the role of a psychologist as "whistle-blower" (Bersoff, 1981) are all important issues that we will briefly discuss.

There are also special problems for school psychologists at the interface of ethics and the law. At times, laws bearing on mental health and educational issues may conflict. For example, the Buckley Amendment, P.L. 94-142, as well as related state laws, give parents control over whether their child receives evaluations or special services, as well as access to the relevant records. Suppose that the state also gives minors the right to independent access to drug counseling, venereal disease information, abortion advice, and/or psychotherapy? Which set of laws does the school psychologist obey? The *Ethical Principles* instruct us to "work toward a resolution of the conflict" (*EP*: 3d), but it would be wisest to anticipate such conflicts and work toward their resolution prospectively rather than reactively.

Case 12−9: International Psychometric Services was in the process of developing specialized norms on its high-school level achievement tests for use in classification work by the military. They offered school systems the opportunity to have the senior class evaluated on the instrument free of charge in order to establish an improved normative base. They also added some additional questions regarding "attitudes toward the military" to the instrument. These included such questions as, "Have you registered for the draft?" Schools were offered the service only if they would require all of their high school seniors to take the test. The director of psychological services at the Lakeville Unified School District accepted the offer.

Case 12−10: Jonathan Swift, Ph.D., gave a lecture on the use of "time-out" interventions to teachers and administrators at the Centerville Public Schools, where he was employed as a school psychologist. Several weeks later he discovered that a school principal had interpreted his talk as license to lock misbehaving children in a darkened closet for an hour at a time.

Case 12−11:   At the Farnsworth Elementary School, teachers have full access to a child's cumulative school record. Material of a personal nature entered in these records occasionally became a topic of conversation in the teacher's lounge. When school psychologist Sylvia Caution learned of this practice, she decided that she would no longer record any of her clinical observations in the record.

Case 12−12:   Andrew Rigor, Ed.D., was frequently asked to assess "special needs children" in his role as a psychologist for the South Suburbia School system. When the special education budget began to show signs of strain, Dr. Rigor was informed by his superintendent to do shorter evaluations, produce briefer reports, and refrain from recommending additional services or evaluation needs for the children he evaluated. The superintendent explained that these steps were needed to keep costs in line.

These four cases are all quite different and raise a sampling of the issues confronted regularly by school psychologists in a fashion somewhat exaggerated for emphasis. In *Case 12−9* we see the issue of informed consent and privacy with respect to testing. In particular, one wonders whether the answers to questions irrelevant to school functioning (i.e., draft registration information) would be provided to the military along with the student's name. If the student is required to take a test by the school, it would be an invasion of privacy to compel answers to such questions. It appears that the director of psychological services should carefully examine the manner in which the test information will be used before signing up for the program. In addition the students should not be required to take the examination or otherwise provide personal data without appropriate informed consent relative to the nature of data to be collected, purpose of the program, and information regarding who will have access to it. We would assert the school is not justified in waiving these important personal rights of the students.

Regarding actual case law on this type of situation, however, at least one federal district court decision seems relevant. In the case of *Merriken v. Cressman*, the American Civil Liberties Union represented the mother of a student who objected to an ill-conceived program intended to predict which junior high school students in Norristown, Pennsylvania might become drug or alcohol abusers. A "consent" form asking whether parents objected to the program was sent home including the assumption that parental consent was granted if no objections were raised (Bersoff, 1983). Although many constitutional issues were raised by Mrs. Merriken on behalf of her son, the court specifically addressed the invasion of family privacy rights, finding in their favor. As the court noted, "the children are never given the opportunity to consent to the invasion of their privacy; only the opportunity to refuse consent by returning a blank questionnaire" (p. 919). The court also criticized the lack of "candor and honesty" on the part of the school system comparing the so-called consent letter to a Book-of-the-Month Club solicitation (Bersoff, 1983). The question of the child's privacy rights above and beyond those asserted by his parent on his behalf were not clarified in this case; however, we would encourage colleagues to extend respect for privacy to children as well as to adult clients.

When Dr. Swift gave his lecture on "time-out" practices, he never thought that it would be so rapidly misinterpreted and abused. Although the school principal was probably responsible for the problem behavior, it is also clear that Swift should have used warnings and cautions in an effort to avoid being misunderstood. Ideally Dr. Swift could have helped to formulate a system-wide policy on the use of such techniques and arranged for appropriate training or supervision of those authorized to use isolative or aversive strategies. As the expert presenting the information, Dr. Swift had the additional responsibility of presenting appropriate limitations or otherwise alerting the participants at the lecture on appropriate constraints.

The case of the school record system highlights a variety of issues discussed in Chapter 3 and considered specifically in the school confidentiality context by Trachtman (1972, 1974). Ms. Caution's response seems a bit overreactive, however. As discussed earlier (Chapter 3), it is possible to consider record entries with a balance of utility and the "need to know." The teachers may not need to know that Johnny Smith was born prior to his parents' marriage, but it would clearly help Johnny if teachers could be alerted to his tendency to withdraw socially when stressed. In the former instance, the data add nothing to assist Johnny's educational progress, but in the latter case the information might help a teacher reach out to him more effectively in the classroom. Ms. Caution should take some professional initiative in educating her colleagues about more appropriate treatment of confidential information, or she could take steps to limit access to records, if that is needed.

The case of Dr. Rigor is especially endemic to school systems increasingly under pressure to keep costs down, while also obligated under Public Law 94-142 (Education for all Handicapped Children Act) to meet the needs of special students. It is also relevant to other nonschool institutions where nonpsychologist administrators may attempt to limit or modify professional standards in order to meet institutional needs. In a case similar in some ways to Dr. Rigor's, although considerably more complex, the APA filed an amicus brief in support of a school psychologist under such pressures (Bersoff, 1981).

Ideally Dr. Rigor should vigorously resist any attempt to do less than a fully professional job on his assigned cases. He should be willing to consider reasonable administrative needs consistent with professional standards, but should not be willing to compromise his integrity by providing less than adequate services (or violate legal obligations to report genuine student needs) in order to comply with administrative fiat. The difficulty, of course, is sorting out the appropriateness of each position and balancing one's integrity with threats of job loss or other retaliation. There may be some circumstances in which the psychologist will have to choose between a job and conscience, but often a reasonable attempt at accommodation and a careful explanation of professional standards will produce less drastic solutions.

Community Agencies

A community agency for purposes of this discussion may be a state funded community mental health center, a nonprofit community run clinic, a municipal hospital, or some other similar type of service delivery system. These facilities are at once important community service resources and politically reactive organizations by their very nature. Such agencies often have competing demands placed on them by various interests, and psychologists working in these agencies are likewise subject to multiple and occasionally conflicting demands. At times, these become significant ethical issues.

Joseph and Peele (1975) illustrate the particular problems presented by the fact that professionals in such settings serve both the community and their individual clients. The following two cases are adapted from their presentation.

> **Case 12–13:**　Dale is a 14-year-old boy who was referred to a community agency by his mother and school because of his unmanageable, hostile, and aggressive behavior. The assessment indicated that collateral treatment for both Dale and his mother would be needed if success were to be achieved. Although she initially agreed to the plan, Dale's mother refused to keep appointments. She did not respond to information that Dale would be discharged from the program if she refused to participate. Ultimately Dale was discharged because his mother would not cooperate in the treatment plan.

> **Case 12–14:**　Mrs. Wilder was admitted to the inpatient service of a community mental health center for treatment of severe depression. Because she had abused her children, a protective services agency was involved in her case. After a few weeks her depression had improved sufficiently to warrant her discharge to outpatient treatment. Afraid that she would again harm her children, the protective service agency urged the mental health center to delay her discharge.

Joseph and Peele note that the staff in both cases are caught between two conflicting sets of duties. In Dale's case, they had begun serving the young client, but soon realized that they could not be effective in their available modes of therapy without the support and involvement of his mother. When she refused to participate, they were effectively using a treatment slot in a manner that was nonproductive. If Dale is retained on the clinic's rolls, he would be occupying a slot that others in the community might use more effectively. When Dale's mother broke her initial participation contract, the clinic's obligation to Dale was likewise ended.

In Mrs. Wilder's case, a similar situation existed in terms of the allocation of scarce resources and effective cost control in community agencies. The task of the mental health center was to provide the most effective and least restrictive treatment to their client, Mrs. Wilder. Since she no longer required inpatient care, she should not be kept hospitalized to serve the needs or concerns of another social agency, however laudable. The children's protective services should provide necessary care for the children regardless of their mother's hospital status.

Other creative solutions might, of course, have been possible in the cases of Dale and Mrs. Wilder; nevertheless, professionals may often be caught between their appropriate concern for individual clients and concern for the community. Bureaucratic demands in such social welfare agencies can be overwhelming at times, and legislation intended to improve services may result in unrealistic expectations and frustrations. Sharfstein and Wolfe (1982) cite the example of a community mental health center regulation that required a wide range of services to be operational within a limited amount of time for centers to receive continued funding. The rules were relatively inflexible and did not consider start-up costs, redundant services in the community, components of desirable services, or adequacy of service levels.

It is not surprising that some studies of agency workers and administrators suggest that the supremacy of agency needs over individual client needs is modal. As governmental funds evaporate and caps are placed on medicaid reimbursement or other subsidies, clinics and mental health centers will be under continuing pressure to take instructions from the bureaucracy on how to contain costs and serve clients. This will place a substantial pressure on the value system of practitioners in community settings (Bloom and Parad, 1977). Individual long-term psychotherapy may be rejected as a service option in place of more readily reimbursable and cost-efficient modes of treatment. The only question is whether clients' needs will be subordinated to their detriment (*EP*: 3b). When the survival of the agency (or one's job) is at stake, considerable intellectualization and rationalization are possible.

It is clear that community mental health work and service in public social welfare agencies force psychologists in those settings to examine their values and motivations closely. Perlman (1977) notes that ethical issues evolving from the mental health worker's decisions and actions cannot be avoided. He attempts to elaborate the *Ethical Principles* to apply in the context of community participation, continuity of services, politics, planning, services to minority groups, and other critical issues. He succeeds well at this difficult task and provides a solid ethical context in this complex set of work settings.

Private Practice Settings

To many, the private practice of a professional psychologist represents glamor, freedom, and a life of ease. At least that is the fantasy or myth of the private practitioner's lot (Lewin, 1974; Taylor, 1978). As one practitioner explained, "The portrayal of our work is as a luxury for the self-indulgent . . . we all 'know' of the psychologist working a 35-hour week at $60 per hour . . . [treating only] . . . movie stars, successful writers, and the wives of corporate executives, with maybe a sprinkling of high level bureaucrats" (Taylor, 1978, p. 70). We "know" such people are "out there," although we never seem to meet them.

The realities of private practice are far less alluring and in many ways more taxing than the practice of psychology at an agency, clinic, or hospital. True, the private practitioner is his or her own boss, but that must be balanced with overhead costs, employee relations (e.g., receptionist, answering service, etc.), backup coverage, billing, and a host of other mundane but necessary chores. In addition, professional loneliness or isolation can afflict the private practitioner, especially when the practice is a solo one.

Little has been written on the ethical problems faced by the private practitioner, although a number of the examples cited throughout this volume certainly apply. The most difficult problem in the ethical sense is probably related to the fact that the private practitioner must be both a professional and an entrepreneur in order to survive, but these needs are not always congruent. In addition, the absence of peer collaborators may lead to less social comparison of a professional nature and a resulting failure to think carefully about the manner in which one practices or manages cases.

The private practitioner may have a secretary or other employees requiring careful supervision, but generally does not have the luxury of paid vacations or sick-days, and is far more susceptible to the vicissitudes of working with the emotionally troubled (e.g., the client who does not pay bills or the "no show" client). The material in this volume dealing with psychotherapy, advertising of services, and employee relations will all be highly relevant to the private practitioner. There are also some unique problems that may occasionally occur.

Case 12–15: Napoleon Solo, Psy.D., practiced psychotherapy on his own in a private office. An automobile accident disabled him for a period of three months, during which time no coverage was available for any of his clients.

Case 12–16: An attractive young lady appeared in the office of Robert Taylor, Ph.D. She became increasingly uneasy with the surroundings and the direction his questions were taking. Finally she interrupted and made the red-faced confession that she had thought she was at the gynecologist's office.

Dr. Solo hopefully had the foresight to take out adequate disability insurance to cover his needs during the recovery period. He apparently did not consider any means of providing back-up for his clients, however, and was clearly in no position to do this easily from his hospital bed. Depending on the clients' individual needs, this could be a rather serious ethical oversight.

Dr. Taylor's rather humorous example (Taylor, 1978) illustrates that the private practitioner never knows precisely what to expect when a prospective client comes through his/her door. The psychologist must be prepared to evaluate and recognize that he or she may not be the type of person the client is really looking for or needs, and then must be prepared to make appropriate referrals as needed.

Business and Industry

Psychologists are often involved as participants in or as consultants to businesses or industries. Roles might include management consulting, personnel selection, organizational research, human factors applications, program evaluation, training, consumer psychology and advertising applications, public relations services, marketing studies, or even applying clinical skills to enhance the functioning of an organization and its executives (Levinson, 1968). The ethical difficulties psychologists face in such settings derive both from the special demands or needs of the particular role and from the fact that the ethics of psychology and the ethics of business are not usually congruent (*EP*: 1 preamble).

A key issue concerns the basic question: "Who is the client?" This point is raised over and over again in papers on the ethics of the industrial or organizational psychologist (London and Bray, 1980; Mirvis and Seashore, 1979; Purcell et al., 1974). The notion of seduction of the psychologist by the pressures of the industry or the marketplace with resulting severe role conflicts is hardly a new issue (APA Task Force on the Practice of Psychology in Industry, 1971). Most ethical complaints from business settings concern responsibility-to-client, assessment, and advertising issues. Often one senses that the psychologist in the business world about whom a complaint is received may have become a servant of power or may have lost some focus on human values to those of productivity and the company.

Case 12–17: Harry Driver has been a member of the management team at Western Tool and Die Corporation for the past six years. He is being considered for promotion to the chief operating officer position in the company, and he is told that he will be sent to the company psychologist for an evaluation as part of the selection process. Driver knows that he can refuse to take the evaluation, but he probably would not be considered for the promotion in that case. He is concerned about what type of personal information about him might be transmitted to others in the company.

Case 12−18: Because of declining sales linked to an economic recession, the Paragon Steel Corporation will lay off several hundred workers. The company wants to attempt a modification of its union contract and base the layoffs on employee productivity rather than seniority, as the union's contract specifies. The company's managers ask their corporate psychologist to prepare a detailed memorandum citing research data to support their position. They are not interested in contrary data, and, in fact, they would prefer that contradictory data not be mentioned. They also want a detailed plan for assessing the productivity of their workers to fit these specified needs.

Case 12−19: Bozo Pharmaceutical Industries sell over-the-counter "natural food" diet aids. They have developed a new diet based on seaweed extracts known as "Kelp Power." A consumer psychologist is approached as a consultant to assist in devising a marketing survey and advertising plan. The psychologist is offered a substantial fee, plus a bonus based on the ultimate effectiveness of the program in boosting sales. When the psychologist asks about data on the product to incorporate in the project, she discovers that there is no evidence that the product is really helpful in dieting. It is not harmful, but there are no documented benefits.

Case 12−20: Manny Jobs, Psy.D., is an industrial psychologist assigned to work on a job enrichment program aimed at improving the quality of life and, hence, quality of work among assembly-line workers at Amalgamated Motors. After a careful job analysis, many hours of interviews, and considerable effort, Dr. Jobs produces a report with many potentially useful suggestions. Management thanks him and shelves the report, which was regarded as "ahead of its time." Dr. Jobs is frustrated that his efforts and the potential benefits are being ignored and toys with the idea of leaking the report to union negotiators prior to the next round of contract talks.

The case involving Mr. Driver is not at all uncommon. These issues were discussed briefly in Chapter 4 and in more detail by London and Bray (1980). The psychologist involved will hopefully recognize the vulnerability of Mr. Driver as well as the legitimate needs and rights of Western Tool and Die. The company has a right to screen its applicants using reliable and valid assessment tools. Driver knows that he has the right to refuse participation, just as the company has the right to pass him over should he do so. One assumes that the psychologist will be willing to discuss these issues with Driver, including the nature of the assessment, type of report to be rendered, and circulation of the report (*EP*: 8a). Driver may, for example, fear that some personality inadequacy may be revealed and broadcast widely when, in fact, no personality assessment tools are to be used. Driver also has a right to know in advance whether he will have access to the report, test data, debriefing, and so forth. In summary, Driver has the right to full informed consent regarding the nature of the planned evaluation before he decides whether to participate. Hopefully the psychologist will recognize this and provide Driver with ample information to assist him in making the decision.

The Paragon Steel Case raises the problem of using research as an influence strategy (Purcell et al., 1974), but does so in a manner that implies a one-sided bias. Many business executives firmly believe that "corporate self-interest is inexorably involved in the well-being of the society," or, as Charles Wilson explains, "What's good for GM is good for the country" (Purcell et al., 1974, p. 441). Many businesses find nothing wrong in asserting their best interests via whatever legal means are available based on the rationale that they are ultimately helping society and the economy. Intellectual or scientific honesty is not necessary for economic success, and total scientific honesty might not be good for the company in some instances. If we assume that data do exist to support the company's position that productivity can be validly assessed and that laying off employees who fail on that assessment is desirable, is the psychologist behaving ethically in applying it? The answer is probably yes, *as long as meaningful contrary data are not concealed or ignored* (*EP* 1a and c).

What about overlooking misleading public statements as long as the lies are benign? That is the question raised by the Bozo Pharmaceutical case. A successful marketing plan must make the public believe that Kelp Power can help them diet. The psychologist might argue that no one will be hurt and that the placebo effect might help some people diet. Is that a sufficient ethical basis for assisting in the promotion of an ineffective product? We would argue that providing support for this product's marketing is unethical (*EP*: 4e), although this would be a difficult ethics case to prove. The psychologist would have little public visibility and an ethics complaint would most likely not occur as an idea to the parties who had first-hand knowledge of the activity.

The Amalgamated Motors case presents another set of complex conflicting needs. Amalgamated needs information and ideas, but it is not necessarily ready to act on them. Dr. Jobs is angry that his work has seemingly been wasted, although he has been paid and his client, the company, seems satisfied. Does he have the right to violate his client's right of confidentiality by revealing information to the unions? Dr. Jobs might argue "society's interests are at stake," but he is obligated to respect the proprietary rights of his employer as long as it is possible to do so and still maintain standards of ethical practice (London and Bray, 1980).

Medical Settings

It will come as no surprise to the hundreds of psychologists at work in medical settings that psychologists and physicians do not always speak the same language. A degree of mutual education and, implicitly, a willingness to be educated, is required for the psychologist who plans to work in such settings. One must, for example, acquire a new lexicon of terminology, a knowledge of physical illnesses and their treatments, and an understanding of how medical hospitals (as distinct from mental hospitals, community mental health centers, or college counseling services) are run.

Psychologists in medical settings must also be keenly aware of their own expertise and its limitations. Some physicians are too willing to see physical complaints as "psychological" and some psychologists are all too eager to concur. Although the following case is unusual, it provides an important illustration.

> **Case 12–21:**   Teri was referred to a major pediatric teaching hospital for the treatment of anorexia nervosa. She had always been petite and slender, but seemed unusually thin to her father just prior to her fourteenth birthday. She was medically evaluated at a large hospital near her home and sent off for treatment of her anorexia to the other hospital. She was again evaluated, diagnosed as anorexic, and admitted to the "psychosomatic unit" for treatment. Her parents were divorced. Her father was an unemployed business executive, and her mother was reported to be a narcotic addict living in another state. At the end of two months of treatment, Teri was still malnourished and was making "no progress" in treatment. Intravenous feeding was contemplated in the face of her progressive weight loss, and she was prepared for transfer to another hospital ward so that a venous feeding line could be implanted. It was at that time that a senior pediatrician asked, "Has she ever been evaluated for Crohn's disease?" Several weeks later Teri was discharged from the hospital minus a segment of her intestine and on anti-inflammatory medication. She continues to do well in response to the treatment for her Crohn's disease.

Teri had been worked up twice by physicians who were outstanding in their field, and her care was continually supervised by physicians who were slow to diagnose her physical illness and had referred her for what was essentially a psychological treatment program. Crohn's disease is not easy to diagnose, but neither are numerous medical problems that seem to manifest themselves primarily through "psychological" symptomatology. (Crohn's disease is a chronic "regional enteritis" or inflammation of the small intestine. Anorexia and weight loss are not uncommon symptoms.) The point is that a close collaborative collegial relationship is needed in dealing with such patients, including well-integrated psychological and medical care (*EP*: 7a).

There are times when psychologists working in medical settings will be employed under the supervision of physicians (for example, in departments of psychiatry or pediatrics). At other times, they may be administratively organized in a separate department (for example, medical psychology). Wherever they work, psychologists must be careful not to surrender their professional integrity or standards.

> **Case 12–22:**   Bertram Botch, M.D., was the Chief of Neurology at a pediatric hospital and often chaired interdisciplinary case conferences. Reporting on her

assessment of a low-functioning, mentally retarded child, Melissa Meek, Ph.D., presented her detailed findings in descriptive terms. Dr. Botch listened to her presentation and asked for the child's IQ. When Dr. Meek replied that the instruments used were developmental indices that did not yield IQ scores, Dr. Botch demanded that she compute an IQ for him to use in his report.

Case 12–23: After sitting in on some lectures that Ralph Worthy, Psy.D., was giving to a group of medical students regarding projective testing, the Chief of Medicine asked him to establish a workshop on the topic for medical residents. The Chief told Worthy that he thought it would be a good idea to teach the residents how to use "those tests," and he assumed that it could be done in "a half-dozen meetings or so."

Hopefully Drs. Meek and Worthy will not yield to the pressures described. Dr. Meek could politely but firmly attempt to educate Dr. Botch regarding the fact that an IQ score is not appropriate in the given situation. She can perhaps find other terms useful and meaningfully appropriate for his report, but she should not be coerced or bullied into contriving the digits he seems to want. Likewise, Dr. Worthy will hopefully attempt to educate his Chief regarding the nature of personality assessment and the inappropriateness of thinking that six lectures will enable anyone to use such techniques competently. He might explain that knowledge of personality theory, abnormal behavior, psychotherapeutic interventions, and psychometrics are all required to use these tools effectively (*EP:* 8f).

These situations are, of course, generalizable to any context in which one's employer may not understand psychological theory and practice, or in which a cooperative team effort is required for effective and successful work. The psychologist, however, must again take the lead in defining the appropriate role for his or her services. The psychologist must also be prepared to recognize and stand by appropriate professional standards.

The Criminal Justice System

We began this chapter with reference to the APA Task Force Report on the ethics of psychological intervention in the criminal justice system (Monahan, 1980), and we will soon be discussing the role of psychologists in the courtroom. It seems appropriate, however, to dwell at least briefly on the role of psychologists more broadly within the criminal justice system, including their work with criminal defendants, prison populations, and police agencies.

In each of these contexts, the critical element in successfully negotiating the complex ethical relationships is identifying obligations to clients. Thus the psychologist must carefully consider who the client is, and then spend sufficient time and energy clarifying the accompanying obligations, roles, expectations, and work conditions. When ethical duties are explicitly detailed in advance, a violation is much less likely, in part because the psychologist has anticipated potential problems, and in part because the client has been appropriately cautioned.

The following three examples represent classic ethical problems for the psychologist in the criminal justice system. They are modified from material presented in the Monahan (1980) and Vetter and Rieber (1980) volumes.

> **Case 12—24:** Roberta Reason, Ph.D., often participates in the evaluation of criminal defendants as part of court-ordered determinations of their competence to stand trial. Defendants are usually forced to meet with her unaccompanied by their lawyers. When she begins to interview a woman charged with the beating death of an infant, the defendant complains, "If I don't talk to you they'll say I'm not cooperating and I'll be in trouble. If I do talk to you, I'll be losing my Fifth Amendment rights."

> **Case 12—25:** Andrew Penal, Ed.D., works at the Stateville Prison Colony as a correctional psychologist. During an individual treatment session, a new inmate reports that an escape attempt is about to take place. After this revelation, the client begs, "Please don't tell anyone about this. If the other cons find out I snitched, they'll kill me."

> **Case 12—26:** George Cops, Psy. D., is a special consultant to the Center City Police Department. He is available on retainer to provide therapeutic intervention to police officers under pressure from job-related stress, and especially to assist officers with their feelings after they have been involved in shootings where a suspect is killed. A new police chief has been appointed recently and asks Dr. Cops to provide comments for the personnel files of the officers he has counseled.

The defendant who confronts Dr. Reason is quite correct in her assumptions about the risks of her cooperation or noncooperation. Hopefully Dr. Reason has thought through her role sufficiently to guide the defendant. Dr. Reason might explain as follows: "My job is to help determine whether you are able to understand the charges against you, their potential consequences, and whether or not you can cooperate in your own defense. You may choose not to answer some of my questions if you wish, but I shall try to focus them on matters relative to your ability to assist your lawyer at the trial, rather than on your guilt or innocence." Dr. Reason must clearly delineate for herself and the defendant her role and responsibilities, and she must do her best to avoid an undue invasion of privacy or placing her client at inappropriate legal risk (*EP:* 3c and 6b).

Dr. Reason should also consult carefully with the defense attorney and judge to ensure that proper protective orders are issued limiting access to her reports. Most courts that have considered the problem have held that the Fifth and Sixth Amendments prohibit admission as evidence of information obtained during a competency evaluation. The problem, however, is that a prosecutor might use such information as a lead in investigating or planning the conduct of the case. This would be ethically troublesome.

Dr. Penal is in a very difficult situation. As noted in our chapter on confidentiality (Chapter 3), he might be obligated to warn certain potential victims, but he must also protect the rights and welfare of his client. Brodsky (1980) reports a full range of conflicting views on what Dr. Penal should do, varying from upholding absolute confidentiality to the opinion that there is no such thing as confidentiality in a prison setting. The prison setting is by definition one in which the client will often test the therapist, particularly to determine whether trust is possible. There are also wide variations in reasons why inmates would seek treatment or consultation, ranging from the traditional (i.e., "I need psychological help") to the pragmatically self-serving (i.e., "It will look good when I come up for parole to have therapy on my record here"). Although we do not know enough about the context to determine Dr. Penal's options, we can outline the steps he should have considered prior to this situation.

Dr. Penal should have clarified with prison authorities what his legal and professional obligations would be, relative to their expectations. If they expect him to report all infractions of the rules, for example, he would need to evaluate his willingness to work in that context. When beginning work with inmates, Dr. Penal should also have clarified with each of them the limits of his role and the nature of their relationship. For example, will he honor every confidence, which confidences can he not respect, will inmates have the right to ask him not to speak to the parole board or to clear with them in advance what he would say? These are just a few sample questions that should routinely be answered. While the psychologist should never surrender professional standards to the work site, each client is entitled to know the special constraints on, or parameters of, the professional relationship prior to entering it (*EP*: 5 preamble).

Dr. Cops will hopefully advise the new chief of police that he must respect the confidentiality of the police whom he was asked to treat as therapy clients. If the chief wished personnel selection advice or other consultation, that should not come from the same person expected to provide an uncritical therapeutic role. We have not raised the more complex situation regarding what Dr. Cops should do if an officer he is counseling appears to be at some nonspecific, but real, risk for future behavior problems. The point at which Cops becomes responsible to report a "clear and immediate danger" is an important ethical problem he will have to address for himself. Clearly these are issues that Dr. Cops will have to think through and resolve with the police department prior to accepting the job.

THE PSYCHOLOGIST IN THE COURTROOM

We are devoting a substantial portion of this chapter to consideration of the psychologist as a player in the legal system for two reasons. First, psychologists are playing an increasingly important role as expert witnesses or consultants in legal matters. This is well illustrated by the growing number of books on psychology and the law, the creation of an APA division on that topic, and the emergence of journals, such as *Law and Psychology*. Even journals more broadly concerned with the practice of psychology have included special issues on psychology and the law (e.g., the August 1978 issue of *Professional Psychology*, Volume 9, Number 3). Second, the legal arena is paradigmatic of a special work setting replete with ethical dilemmas for psychologists. The logic of jurisprudence assumes, for example, that truth may best be revealed when two parties confront each other with passionate debate on the merits of their respective cases. In contrast, the rules of science assume that a single party employing rigorous scientific methods can test and eliminate erroneous conclusions (Anderten et al., 1980).

Anderten and her colleagues also note that the law requires decisions based on available evidence be made regardless of residual ambiguities. Science, and psychology in particular, do not require that all problems investigated have a clear conclusion. Scientists must endure ambiguity with nearly infinite patience to avoid conclusions based on inadequate data. These differences highlight key sources of potentially ethical conflicts.

In addition, the courtrooom can be a very seductive place for the psychologist. Imagine a setting in which you are asked to play a role in assessing truth and justice—central values of American society. Surrounded by the trappings of power, you are placed at center stage in the witness box, recognized as an "expert" in the eyes of the court, and carefully questioned about your *opinions* (a luxury not usually extended to nonexperts). All concerned hang on your every word and a stenographer dutifully records it all for posterity. These are weighty matters you are asked about, and the fate of others may well turn on what you have to say. Will the temptation to provide answers and have your advice taken cause you to forget, even for a moment, the scientific underpinnings and caveats that necessarily accompany psychological "facts"? How can the skills of the psychologist be most fairly and ethically applied in the courtroom and other legal contexts? The question is obviously rhetorical, but the ethical dilemmas are quite serious.

Training Issues

Most graduate training programs do not prepare psychologists for participation in the forensic arena (Poythress, 1979). Most psychologists are unfamiliar with the adversary system and with legal tests and concepts, such as levels of proof, competence to stand trial, criminal responsibility, or legal definitions of insanity. Even well-trained psychologists will often confuse psychological concepts (e.g., psychosis) with legal ones (e.g., insanity). Even when the psychologist understands the legal concepts and questions, the usual training in psychological assessment often doesn't help in answering these questions (Poythress, 1979). Few of the standard instruments used in psychological test batteries have, for example, content or construct validity bearing on competence issues or the prediction of dangerousness.

> **Case 12–27:**   Hasty Injuria, Ph.D., was approached by an attorney to do a pretrial evaluation of his client who had been charged with assault and battery. Injuria administered the WAIS-R, Thematic Apperception Test, Rorschach Inkblots, Minnesota Multiphasic Personality Inventory, and the House-Tree-Person drawing. When placed on the witness stand, Dr. Injuria was asked about the defendant's propensity to commit violent acts against others, and about his criminal responsibility at the time of the alleged assault. Although Injuria had no information regarding the defendant's history (devoid of violent acts) and was unfamiliar with the concept of criminal responsibility, he testified that the defendant was schizophrenic and therefore clearly both dangerous and not responsible.

Not only did Dr. Injuria misunderstand the legal concepts in question, he was also not in a position to address the questions on the basis of solid knowledge. He did not, for example, consider one of the most consistent predictors of dangerous behavior (i.e., prior dangerous behavior) and made the erroneous assumption that being schizophrenic absolves one of responsibility for one's acts and indicates dangerousness. In this case, the psychologist made the major mistake of falling back on an old and successful assessment behavior (i.e., his standard clinical test battery) without recognizing his involvement in a special setting with unique requirements that he was not qualified to address. In his ignorance, Injuria may well have caused serious problems for his "client."

A more basic question that is being debated among psychologists and attorneys is the question of what kinds of opinions *if any* by mental health professionals are sufficiently reliable and valid to warrant admissibility (see, for example, Morse, 1982; Poythress, 1982). In addition to the question of whether courts should admit such opinions is the issue of the limits that ethics must place on the expression of opinions. This is especially true when psychologists are requested to give "informed speculation" (Bonnie and Slobogin, 1980) on matters defined in law rather than in behavioral science. For example, it is clearly unethical to provide an ultimate-issue opinion without also giving the caveat that such opinions are legal judgments, not based on psychological expertise. The ultimate issue of whether a defendant was "insane" is not a psychological question, since the concept of insanity is a legal, rather than a psychological, one. Too frequently, psychologists will neglect such cautions in their testimony and may even be encouraged to do so by attorneys and judges (Poythress, 1982).

Poythress (1979) describes several curricula for psychologists interested in forensic work, including topical introductions (e.g., philosophical issues, terminology, application of psychological skills to legal problems, and ethical issues); topical seminars (e.g., criminal law, civil law, child/juvenile law); and supervised practica or field placements. Such formal training is obviously a necessity for those who would be forensic "experts"(*EP*: 2c).

The Use of Research Data

The extent to which psychologists called to testify as expert witnesses can fall back on scientific data has been a topic of recent interest (Loftus and Monahan, 1980; Tanke and Tanke, 1979). Although expert psychological testimony based on empirical data has been used in cases dealing with jury size, eyewitness identification, prediction of dangerousness, adequacy of warning labels, and child custody, to name a few (Loftus and Monahan, 1980), judges and juries are not always influenced by these presentations. Some interesting questions have been raised regarding the nature in which such research is presented. Are the findings valid and generalizable to the situation in question? Are there legitimate differences in interpretation of the data, and, if so, must the psychologist testifying present both sides? How should psychologists testifying deal with the probabilistic nature of some research findings? What role should the psychologist's personal values play in the decision to testify or not in certain cases?

> **Case 12–28:**   Helena Scruples, Ph.D., is very knowledgeable regarding research in eyewitness identification. Her research tends to show the unreliability of such identifications. She is sought as an expert witness by the defense in a rape case. Dr. Scruples is sympathetic with the woman who was raped and knows that it is difficult to convict men charged with rape. If she agrees to help the defense, she may well be reducing the defendant's chance of being convicted.

> **Case 12–29:**   Herman Beastly is accused of raping and murdering an adolescent babysitter. Evidence strongly indicates that he is guilty and can be sentenced to death based on a state law that permits capital punishment for criminals likely to commit repeated violent crimes. John Qualm, Psy.D., is considered an expert on the prediction of dangerousness, and he has published reports highlighting the difficulty in making such predictions reliably. He is asked to testify by the defense in the hope that his opinions may save Beastly from execution.

Both of these cases represent major clashes in personal value systems. Both Dr. Scruples and Dr. Qualm may be repulsed by their "client's" behavior. At the same time, each defendant is entitled to have the data exposed. Although it is probably true that the defendant has a right to present the relevant scientific data, a psychologist is not obligated to testify in such a case. In similar situations, Loftus has rationalized that her testimony could help to prevent the conviction of an innocent man (Loftus and

Monahan, 1980). Monahan reports testifying for the defense in a case similar to Dr. Qualm's because, although repulsed by the defendant, he is morally opposed to the death penalty (Loftus and Monahan, 1980).

The extent to which an expert witness is obligated to present "both sides" when discussing psychological research or theory is also a complex matter. Wolfgang (1974) and Rivlin (1973), for example, make cases for the legitimacy of the expert scientist as an adversary. They assert that a balanced objective presentation of research or theory is not needed in expert testimony. According to Loftus and Monahan (1980), on the other hand, an oath to "tell the whole truth and nothing but the truth" is violated if the "whole truth" is not told. They also note that opposing counsel may always ask the witness: "Do you know of any studies which show the opposite result?" (p. 279). We would not argue in favor of universal discussion of all possible interpretations of a data set, but we strongly agree with the assertion that the "whole truth" is a necessity for the psychologist acting as an expert witness.

Hypnosis in the Courtroom

Hypnosis has been used increasingly in forensic settings by psychologists and others. An article published in *Science* (Kolata, 1980) summarized the issue succinctly: "Researchers fear misuse by police and warn that a hypnotic state is no guarantor of truth." While the intense concentration that characterizes hypnosis often enables individuals to recall events or details in striking fashion, many individuals may respond with embellishments to subtle suggestions of the examiners. Some hypnotic subjects may "confabulate" or inject new elements into their reports of events following a hypnotic session. These confabulations may be based on conscious or unconscious motivations (Kolata, 1980).

Case 12–30:   Theodore Trance, Ed.D., consulted with the police investigating a double homicide. He hypnotized and interrogated a woman who claimed to be an eyewitness to the murders, but recalled little of what happened. During the hypnotic sessions the woman emotionally recalled being forced to shoot the two victims by two male companions. Her testimony resulted in conviction of the two for murder. Subsequently it became clear that the two were innocent and that the woman had substantial motivation to wish them punished for reasons of her own.

It seems that Dr. Trance had failed to investigate fully the background and motivation of the woman he was asked to hypnotize. At the time of the trial, there were also allegations that Dr. Trance may have conducted his questioning of the witness in a suggestive manner; however, tapes of his sessions with the woman had somehow been erased. No information was provided to the jury regarding the potential for confabulation by individuals using hypnotic techniques to "enhance" memory for purposes of testimony.

As a result of cases such as this one, many jurisdictions now prohibit information uncovered through hypnosis from being admitted as evidence at a trial. Psychologists have long recognized the fact that hypnosis interacts significantly with suggestibility, and Dr. Trance's role in applying it with few caveats and cautions raises serious ethical problems.

Child Custody

Although most mental health professionals agree that matters of child custody should be predicated on the best interests of the child, that is occasionally the only point of agreement. Some writers have asserted that "Family loyalty is . . . on biological hereditary kinship" (Boszhormenyi-Nagy and Spark, 1973, p. 42). Others argue that biological ties are far less important than psychological ones based on "a continuing, day-to-day basis . . . [which] . . . fulfills the child's psychological needs for a parent, as well as the child's physical needs" (Goldstein, Freud, and Solnit, 1979, p. 98).

What will happen as a result of custody decisions is a difficult matter to predict. Unfortunately, however, one may reliably predict that a contested custody situation will have an adverse effect on the children. Great stresses are applied simply in terms of prolonging the period of uncertainty and instability in the lives of children, subjecting them to the whims of the legal system, and casting them as pawns in the struggle between sets of angry combatants for custody. Into this void rides (or are tossed) too many unwary would-be Solomons ready to share their psychological wisdom with the courts in resolving these agonizing cases, although no research base exists on which to support opinions about custody (Clingempeel and Reppucci, 1982).

Too often psychologists agree to assist in performing child-custody evaluations with little understanding of statutes governing child custody, adversarial proceedings, data useful in making such decisions (Ochroch, Note 1), or their own values and attitudes that might contribute to biased outcomes (Hare-Mustin, 1976). At times, the custodial struggles clearly harm a child rather than attending to his or her best interests (Schwartz, 1983).

There are times, however, when psychological testimony or participation, except in actual courtroom appearance, is relevant and constructive (Woody, 1977a, 1977b). Ideally the psychologist should function as an advocate for the child or a neutral expert, preferably appointed by the court to avoid being cast as the advocate of one contesting party or the other (Fredericks, 1976). This will not always work, however, and at times full adversarial proceedings with experts on both sides result. It is not our purpose to provide a "how to do it" manual here, but rather to highlight some potential ethical problems that can arise to the detriment of all concerned in these situations.

Case 12—31: Helen Testee, Ph.D., agreed to undertake a child-custody evaluation. During the course of her assessment, she administered psychological tests to both parents, including the MMPI and the Rorschach Inkblots. The mother, who was a foreign national, had an elevated L-scale score on the MMPI and was "evasive" on the Rorschach inquiry. As a result, Dr. Testee concluded that she was a pathological liar and recommended against her having custody.

Case 12—32: Jack Balance, Psy.D., undertook a child-custody evaluation at the request of the child's father. He met the father and the child for assessment purposes, but the mother subsequently declined to participate. At the trial, Dr. Balance testified only with respect to the child-father relationship, but the mother's attorney attempted to discredit the presentation since she had not been involved.

Case 12—33: Sam and Sylvia Splitter were in the middle of a bitter divorce and child-custody dispute. Each sought and found a mental-health professional willing to advocate on their behalf at the custody hearing. Both professionals testified in support of "their client" based on interviews with the one parent and children. Neither professional had sought contact with the other parent or the other professional prior to the hearing, and each testimony dramatically contradicted the other.

Case 12—34: Cynthia Oops, Psy.D., conducted a careful evaluation of both parents and two children involved in a custody dispute. She had been recruited by one parent, but her participation was seemingly agreed to by the other. When Dr. Oops completed her report prior to the hearing, the parent who was not favored asserted her right of confidentiality and demanded that the report be kept out of court. Dr. Oops had not obtained a signed waiver from the parties.

Dr. Testee had made several rather serious errors. First, she seems to be basing her evaluation on two instruments that have never been validated for use in child-custody work (i.e., the Rorschach and MMPI). Her use of the MMPI on a foreign national raises additional validity questions, and her conclusion based on two isolated test findings that have many alternative interpretations is highly suspect. One wonders if Dr. Testee ever bothered to interview the child or observe parent-child interactions.

Dr. Balance would have been better advised to confirm the willingness of all parties to cooperate in advance. This might have been accomplished through personal contact or by court order, if necessary. He was certainly being ethical in commenting only on his actual contacts (i.e., the adequacy of the child-father relationship), while refraining from any comments about the parent who declined to participate. The attempt to discredit his testimony is unfortunate, but not a matter of psychological ethics.

The Splitters have successfully "split" their experts and established a so-called "battle of the shrinks." Nothing does more to discredit the mental health professions in public than do adversarial confrontations by "experts" with pieces of data. Although the Splitters may have established this situation, the mental-health professionals involved were foolish to agree to participate. They could have insisted on access to all appropriate data and the right to interview the other spouse as a prerequisite for agreeing to do the evaluation. One cannot help but wonder whether their contradictory testimony evolved from information that their clients kept from them.

Dr. Oops had positive intentions, but she should have spelled out the parameters of her role from the outset. Each of her clients (i.e., the two parents and the children) should have been given a clear understanding of her obligations to each, especially since their needs and wishes were mutually exclusive in some areas. In particular, she should have secured written waivers from all concerned in order to share her findings with all concerned and with the court. Now the status of one claim of confidentiality is unclear, and it will have to be resolved by the judge. It is not possible to predict the outcome based on the information presented, but the problem was avoidable.

Although the case of Dr.Oops seems to be a routine confidentiality problem, a slight variation yields a rather commonly noted problem of a more complex nature. Suppose Dr.Oops had provided marriage counseling to both parents prior to their decision to divorce, and she is subsequently subpoenaed by one to testify in a child-custody dispute? In such situations, a legitimate duty of confidentiality to both parties might exist, even if Dr. Oops believes that she has some basis on which to offer an opinion to the courts. Ideally Dr.Oops should avoid such a role by discussing the potential problem early (if it appears that a couple in treatment may divorce) or by suggesting that expert testimony be sought from another practitioner who does not have a preexisting relationship with the clients.

While we certainly did not exhaust the range of ethical problems that psychologists may encounter in legal settings, we hope we did illustrate several key points. First, to be expert witnesses, psychologists must give serious consideration both to the nature of their expertise and to the manner in which they present their psychological knowledge to the courts. Second, providing services in a forensic context demands special training and knowledge not usually part of a psychologist's training. This form of competence is not acquired lightly, and the caveats discussed generically in Chapter 9 (i.e., knowing one's own competences and weaknesses) are particularly important in these settings. Finally, the adversarial system establishes conflicts that are quite alien to the work of most psychologists. Special foresight and caution are required to perform professional services in this context.

SUMMARY GUIDELINES

1. Psychologists entering a new work setting for the first time should familiarize themselves with the special needs and demands of the job. This includes

consulting with colleagues about the ethical pressures and problems unique to that type of work setting.

2. In complex service delivery or consultation systems, the usual psychologist-client relationship may be blurred. It is appropriate that the psychologist take the lead in defining his or her role and obligations to each level of client served. In addition, the psychologist should clarify expectations with all relevant parties from the outset of the professional contact.

3. A psychologist is *never* exempted from any portion of the *Ethical Principles* by virtue of an employer's dictum.

4. The matter of whether to work for reform within an unethical institution or whether to "blow the whistle" in public is often a matter of personal judgment. A psychologist should not, however, cooperate as a party to unethical behavior. In addition, a psychologist must carefully consider any duty of confidentiality owed to a client (including a client organization) before making public disclosures about that client.

5. When a special work setting demands special qualifications or competencies, psychologists should be exceptionally careful that they meet these standards prior to working in that context. Consultation with colleagues experienced in the specialized setting is often the best way to make that assessment.

REFERENCE NOTE

1. Ochroch, R. *Ethical pitfalls in child custody evaluations*. Paper presented at the Annual Meeting of the American Psychological Association, Washington, DC, August, 1982.

REFERENCES

Allen, J. P.; Chatelier, P.; Clark, H. J.; and Sorenson, R. Behavioral science in the military: Research trends for the eighties. *Professional Psychology*, 1982, *13*, 918–929.

Anderten, P.; Staulcup, V.; and Grisso, T. On being ethical in legal places. *Professional Psychology*, 1980, *11*, 764–773.

APA Task Force in the Practice of Psychology in Industry. Effective practice of psychology in industry. *American Psychologist*, 1971, *26*, 974–991.

Bardon, J. I. School psychology's dilemma: A proposal for its resolution. *Professional Psychology*, 1982, *13*, 955–968.

Bersoff, D. N. The Brief for Amici Curiae in the matter of Forrest versus Ambach. *Academic Psychology Bulletin*, 1981, *3*, 133–162.

———. Children as participants in psychoeducational assessment. In Melton, G. B., Koocher, G. P., and Saks, M. J. (Eds.), *Children's Competence to Consent*. New York: Plenum, 1983.

Bloom, B. L., and Parad, H. J. Values of community mental health center staff. *Professional Psychology*, 1977, *8*, 33–47.

Boling, T. E., and Dempsey, J. Ethical dilemmas in government: Designing an organizational response. *Public Personnel Management Journal*, 1981, *11*, 11–19.

Bonnie, R., and Slobogin, C. The role of mental health professionals in the criminal process: The case for "informed speculation." *Virginia Law Review*, 1980, *66*, 427–522.

Boszhormenyi-Nagy, I. B., and Spark, G. *Invisible Loyalties*. New York: Harper and Row, 1973.

Brodsky, S. L. Ethical issues for psychologists in corrections. In Monahan, J. (Ed.), *Who is the Client: The Ethics of Psychological Intervention in the Criminal Justice System*. Washington, DC: APA, 1980.

Clingempeel, W.G , and Reppucci, N. D. Joint custody after divorce: Major issues and goals for research. *Psychological Bulletin*, 1982, *91*, 102–127.

Crawford, M. P. Military psychology and general psychology. *American Psychologist*, 1970, *25*, 328–336.

Fredericks, M. U. Custody battles: Mental health professionals in the courtroom. In Koocher, G. P. (Ed.), *Children's Rights and the Mental Health Professions*. New York: Wiley, 1976.

Gast, D. L., and Nelson, C. M. Time out in the classroom: Implications for special education. *Exceptional Children*, 1977a, *43*, 461–464.

———. Legal and ethical considerations for the use of time-out in special education settings. *Journal of Special Education*, 1977b, *11*, 457–467.

Goldstein, J.; Freud, A.; and Solnit, A. J. *Beyond the Best Interests of the Child*. New York: Free Press, 1979.

Hare-Mustin, R. T. The biased professional in divorce litigation. *Psychology of Women Quarterly*, 1976, *1*, 216–222.

Joseph, D. I., and Peele, R. Ethical issues in community psychiatry. *Hospital and Community Psychiatry*, 1975, *26*, 295–299.

Kelley, C. R. In defense of military psychology. *American Psychologist*, 1971, *26*, 514–515.

Kolata, G. B. Forensic use of hypnosis on the increase. *Science*, 1980, *208*, 1443–1444.

Leuba, C. Military are essential. *American Psychologist*, 1971, *26*, 515.

Levinson, H. *The Exceptional Executive: A Psychological Conception*. Cambridge, MA: Harvard University Press, 1968.

Lewin, M. H. Diaries of the private practitioner: Secrets revealed. *Professional Psychology*, 1974, *5*, 234–236.

Loftus, E., and Monahan, J. Trial by data: Psychological research as legal evidence. *American Psychologist*, 1980, *35*, 270–283.

London, M., and Bray, D. W. Ethical issues in testing and evaluation for personnel decisions. *American Psychologist*, 1980, *35*, 890–901.

Merriken v. *Cressman* 364 F. Supp. 913 (E.D. Pa., 1973).

Mirvis, P. H., and Seashore, S.E. Being ethical in organizational research. *American Psychologist*, 1979, *34*, 766–780.

Monahan, J. (Ed.). *Who Is the Client? The Ethics of Psychological Intervention in the Criminal Justice System*. Washington, DC: APA, 1980.

Morse, S. J. Reforming expert testimony: An open response from the tower (and the trenches). *Law and Human Behavior*, 1982, *6*, 45−47.

O'Leary, S. G., and O'Leary, K. D. Ethical issues of behavior modification research in schools. *Psychology in the Schools*, 1977, *14*, 299−307.

Perlman, B. Ethical concerns in community mental health. *American Journal of Community Psychology*, 1977, *5*, 45−57.

Poythress, N. G. A proposal for training in forensic psychology. *American Psychologist*, 1979, *34*, 612−621.

───. Concerning reform in expert testimony: An open letter from a practicing psychologist. *Law and Human Behavior*, 1982, *6*, 39−43.

Purcell, T. V.; Albright, L. E.; Grant, D. L.; Lockwood, H. C.; Schein, V. E.; and Freidlander, F. What are the social responsibilities for psychologists in industry? A symposium. *Personnel Psychology*, 1974, *27*, 435−453.

Rivlin, A. Forensic social science. *Harvard Educational Review*, 1973, *43*, 61−75.

Saks, M. J. On Meredith Crawford's "Military Psychology." *American Psychologist*, 1970, *25*, 876.

Schwartz, L. L. Contested adoption cases: Grounds for conflict between psychology and the law. *Professional Psychology*, 1983, *14*, 444−456.

Shakow, D. On the rewards (and, alas, frustrations) of public service. *American Psychologist*, 1968, *23*, 87−96.

Sharfstein, S. S., and Wolfe, J. C. The community mental health centers program: Expectations and realities. *Hospital and Community Psychiatry*, 1982, *29*, 46−49.

Tanke, E. D., and Tanke, T. J. Getting off a slippery slope: Social science in the judicial process. *American Psychologist*, 1979, *34*, 1130−1138.

Taylor, R. E. Demythologizing private practice. *Professional Psychology*, 1978, *9*, 68−70.

Trachtman, G. M. Pupils, parents, privacy, and the school psychologist. *American Psychologist*, 1972, *27*, 37−45.

───. Ethical issues in school psychology. *The School Psychology Digest*, 1974, *3*, 4−15.

Vetter, H. J., and Rieber, R. W. (Eds.). *The Psychological Foundations of Criminal Justice, Volume II*. New York: John Jay Press, 1980.

Wolfgang, M. E. The social scientist in court. *Journal of Criminal Law and Criminology*, 1974, *65*, 239−247.

Woody, R. H. Behavioral sciences criteria in child custody determinations. *Journal of Marriage and Family Counseling*, 1977a, *3*, 11−18.

───. Psychologists in child custody. In Sales, B. D. (Ed.), *Psychology in the Legal Process*. New York: Spectrum, 1977b.

Scholarly Publishing and Teaching 13

Your manuscript is both good and original, but the part that is good is not original, and the part that is original is not good.

Samuel Johnson

Scholarly writers and psychologists teaching in academic settings have traditionally claimed vast freedom to pursue knowledge and to impart what they have learned or discovered without censure or restrictions. The preamble of the *Ethical Principles* supports both the freedom of inquiry and of communication and the rights of psychologists to demand them. The only qualifier is that psychologists also accept the responsibility such freedoms imply, and this responsibility is defined as upholding the tenets of the ethics code.

Many scholarly writers and academic psychologists with whom we have spoken have expressed surprise, and sometimes indignant astonishment, after learning that the recent revisions of the APA ethics code contain numerous specific references to responsibilities of psychologists as teachers and as authors. They believed that the ethics code was devised primarily to protect consumers of psychotherapy services and research participants, perhaps because earlier versions of the code focused on these issues.

As a result of the "new consumerism," civil rights advances, a creeping reluctance to accept the pronouncements of "experts" as infallible, and increasing commitment to excellence within the discipline of psychology, the sanctuaries of "academic freedom" and "literary license" have been tempered by a call to responsibility and accountability from both within and outside the profession.

SCHOLARLY PUBLISHING ISSUES AND ABUSES

Published works are the means through which knowledge is shared and advanced as well as the currency for status in the scientific and professional community. This section explores the following: ethical aspects of assigning publication credits; plagiarism and unfair use; ethical questions regarding "author assisted" projects; forged and fudged published research data; and the ethical responsibilities of publishing gatekeepers, such as journal editors. Writing on controversial topics with sociopolitical overtones is briefly considered in Chapter 15.

Publication Credit Assignments

Mutiple-authored scientific works are increasing in frequency (Price, 1963; Garfield, 1978). Many might assume that decisions concerning who deserves authorship credit on joint projects, and in what order the names should be placed, is a reasonably straightforward procedure. The same forthright process would seem to operate when citing footnote acknowledgments for those who were helpful, though not in a major or critical way. Bitter disputes concerning assignments of publication credit, however, are the most prevalent type of complaints to ethics committees from the academic-scientific sector of psychology.

The *Ethical Principles* are somewhat general regarding assignment of publication credit (*EP*: 7f). Authorship credits are to be assigned to contributors in proportion to their professional contributions, with the person making the principal contribution listed first. Minor professional contributions or extensive nonprofessional assistance (e.g., typing a complicated manuscript or helpful ideas offered by a colleague) may be acknowledged in a footnote or in an introductory statement. All contributors to an edited work should be acknowledged and named with the organizer or editor listed as such. The brevity of the code leaves key terms, such as "professional contribution" and "minor contribution," undefined, and psychologists often vehemently disagree with one another's interpretations. The nature of the "principal" contribution has also been debated. In joint effort research, in which *different* people made each contribution, who is the "principal contributor"? Is it the one who generated the hypothesis and design? The one who wrote the material for publication? The one who established the procedure and collected the data? Or the one who analyzed the data? Spiegel and Keith-Spiegel (1970) found modal trends ordering "principal contribution" as they are listed above, but no firm consensus level agreement among their 769 respondents was reached.

Readers might wonder, at this point, why matters such as whose name appears as first author or whether one receives a footnote or an authorship are so important. A complex set of factors are operating, such as the need for publication credits to advance one's career (e.g., to gain entrance into graduate school, obtain a job, or earn a promotion where publication output is required), to gain status and recognition among one's peers, and to accord "psychic reward" to compensate for the low or nonexistent monetary rewards associated with conducting research or writing for scholarly outlets. Senior (first-named) authors are assumed to be primarily responsible for the existence and content of the work, although this is not always the case. Junior authors have become upset when individuals, usually people with the power and authority over them, take the senior authorship for themselves when they allegedly were far less involved in the project than were the junior or secondary authors. Sometimes people complain that they received a footnote or no credit when a junior authorship was warranted. Others have asserted that psychologists have "bullied" their way into junior and sometimes senior authorship positions on work done primarily by others, except for some editorial comment. Sometimes ethics committees agree that junior people have been disadvantaged by more powerful psychologists; at other times, honest differences in the meaning of, and value placed on, a contribution are at issue.

An increasingly frequent theme involves charges by graduate students that their dissertation supervisors insist on being listed as co-authors on any published version of the student's project. Students argue that their supervising professors have the duty to facilitate their professional development and that assisting them with their projects constitutes a teaching obligation. The professors respond that their contributions to the student projects were of significant magnitude and that co-authorships were warranted. Here are instances where, on the surface, both arguments can be substantiated by the *Ethical Principles* (*EP*: 7c and 7f).

Case 13−1: A major magazine approached Lucky Byte, Ph.D., about her doctoral dissertation on the effects of home computer technology on children, and asked if she would write up a short version for which she would be paid $500. When Byte told her thesis supervisor, Leonard Grab, Ph.D., he insisted on being involved in the write-up and to share half of the payment. Dr. Grab claimed that the dissertation would have never been completed without his help and guidance and therefore he deserved credit and payment for this commercial venture.

Case 13−2: A student completed her doctoral dissertation under the supervision of Jack Pervasive, Ph.D. Dr. Pervasive provided laboratory space, equipment, and research animals. Pervasive approved the design and read drafts of the work as it progressed. After completion, Pervasive wanted it published with his name as senior author. The student was upset since she felt Dr. Pervasive pressured her into doing things his way in the first place and contacted an ethics committee for an opinion.

In these two cases, ethics committees decided that the supervisor's demands were covetous and that neither could justify the level of recognition demanded.

We suspect that the recent increase of doctoral student complaints reflects changes in the assertiveness level of contemporary students, as well as changing views of roles among professors. Perhaps there was a time when professors would serve as mentors to students and expect no more than an acknowledgment in the preface and a footnote in any subsequent published version. In 1970, for example, the attitudes of the large sample of psychologists in the Spiegel and Keith-Spiegel publication credit study (1970) generally expressed generousness and responsibility toward students without expectations of authorship credit on students' projects. The modal respondent agreed that students might *offer* authorship to professors who were exceptionally helpful. Research support and student assistant funds, however, have steadily withered in recent years, while competition for jobs and promotions has increased. These factors may have led to a revised perception of almost-fully-trained, but still subordinate and primarily powerless, graduate students as one solution to the disappearing-resource problem. The potential for exploitation of graduate students is heightened during "hard times" and recent complaints have resulted in a policy statement issued by the APA Ethics Committee (Note 1).

1. Only second authorship is acceptable for the dissertation supervisor.

2. Second authorship may be considered *obligatory* if the supervisor designates the primary variables or makes major interpretative contributions or provides the data base.

3. Second authorship is a courtesy if the supervisor designates the general area of concern or is substantially involved in the development of the design and measurement procedures or substantially contributes to the write-up of the published report.

4. Second authorship is *not* acceptable if the supervisor provides only encouragement, physical facilities, financial support, critiques, or editorial contributions.

5. In all instances, agreements should be reviewed before the writing for publication is undertaken and at the time of submission. If disagreements arise, they should be resolved by a third party using these guidelines.

Let us look at a few other patterns that arise regarding publication credit disputes: namely, obtaining authorships by virtue of power in the organization; the unfulfilled commitment; and the role of time spent on a project in the assignment of credits.

Case 13–3:   Holden Power, Ph.D., insists that all research projects carried out by psychologists he supervises in his hospital psychology service department bear his name as the last-listed author. He argues that this is fair and appropriate since he arranges for the staff time to spend on research activity and is administratively in charge of all departmental activities, including research. The psychology staff resented the forced inclusion of a person who contributes nothing substantive to the research and who often does not even read the manuscript prior to submission for publication.

Case 13—4:   Chuck Ham, Ph.D., and Marvin Eggs, M.A., started off on a collaborative writing project and fleshed out the outline and half of a very rough draft together. Then Eggs became busy with other things and did not follow through with his agreed on obligations. Ham finished the project himself and published it as sole author. Eggs complained to an ethics committee that his contribution was more than sufficient to warrant a junior authorship. Ham disagreed by declaring that if he had not completed the rough material and had not made it into something publishable, the whole project would have been scrapped.

Case 13—5:   Don Tedious, B.A., was hired by Jim Longitudinal, Ph.D., to collect data for a long-term study. Don Tedious worked for three years at an agreed on hourly rate, testing participants, scoring the measures, and placing the raw data on computer discs. After publication, Tedious was upset because he was not listed as an author. He argued that he had put in far more time than anyone else had and therefore deserved at least a junior position in the authorship credits. Dr. Longitudinal argued that a footnote credit was proper because Tedious was paid to perform supervised, routine procedures.

The *Ethical Principles* implicitly disallow credit when no direct contributions to the project were made. In the Spiegel and Keith-Spiegel (1970) survey, respondents rejected status as consideration by overwhelmingly agreeing that all contributors, including paid or volunteer personnel at the subdoctoral level, be given equal consideration when authorship credit is assigned. They further agreed that it is unethical to give a co-authorship to someone of higher status in one's organization unless she or he makes a substantial contribution to the project. Dr. Power's policy was seen as unethical. Dr. Ham was not acting unethically in completing the project, assuming that Mr. Eggs was indeed shirking his commitment, but since some groundwork had been completed, it would have been appropriate for Ham to have acknowledged Eggs' contributions during the earlier stages of the project in a footnote. Offering no acknowledgment of Mr. Eggs' contribution whatsoever does not reflect the final product properly and, in this sense, Ham was acting unethically. Dr. Longitudinal acted properly in acknowledging Tedious in a footnote, not because he was *paid* to do his duties, but rather because of the nature of the work he performed. The vast majority of the Spiegel and Keith-Spiegel (1970) sample agreed that the types of functions performed by Don Tedious would earn either footnote credit or no acknowledgment whatsoever. Time spent on a project, *per se*, is not a significant factor.

The case of Tedious versus Dr. Longitudinal also illustrates the wisdom of reaching agreements *before* the research or writing collaboration begins about what each person can expect in terms of credit. The agreement should allow for alterations in case participants' actual contributions deviate from it. But, in our experience, many of the bitter disputes might have been avoided if the parties had decided ahead of time on who would receive what type of credit for doing what.

Plagiarism, Fair Use, and Citation Attribution

Writers who had tremendous subsequent influence, such as Charles Darwin (Eiseley, 1979) and Ellen G. White, the founder of the Seventh-Day Adventists (Rea, 1982), have posthumously faced serious challenges to the originality of their words. Best-selling authors, such as Alex Haley (*Roots*, 1976) and Gail Sheehy (*Passages*, 1976), have agreed to settlements sharing their financial gains with others whose prior writings were "suspiciously similar." Unfortunately, psychology has been plagued with occasional discoveries of the same nature, and these tend to be in our more recent history (Seashore, 1978).

Copying the original work of others without proper permission or citation attribution is often experienced as "psychic robbery" by the victims, producing the same kind of rage expressed by those who arrive home to find the TV set and stereo missing. When plagiarizers reap financial rewards or recognition from passing someone else's words off as their own, the insult is still greater. Readers are also mislead and, in a sense, defrauded. Plagiarism and unfair use of previously published material are among the more serious ethical infractions a psychologist can commit.

Once a work has been copyrighted, protection is offered to writers through federal copyright infringement statutes (17 U.S.C.C. 101–180, 1978). Copyright protection is extended to original literary and other types of works, including factual, reference, or instructional materials, that can be reproduced or copied. To meet the "originality test," authors must have created the work by their own skill, labor, and judgment without directly copying or evasively imitating the words of others. Copyright bars the use of the arrangement of words or the particular expression of the idea, but does not bar the use of intellectual conceptions since there is no exclusive right to "an idea." The three basic elements of infringement are as follows: (1) access to the original work (defined as showing that the author had a reasonable opportunity of access to the complainant's work); (2) substantial similarities between the two works; and (3) copying of another's original work by the accused author (requiring evidence that the original material was used as a model by the accused author). Unintentionality is not a defense of copyright infringement, although it may affect the judged extent of liability. The amount of the original work copied is also a factor in determining infringement liability although many factors, such as the extent to which the copied material will supersede the original work or interfere with its sale, are taken into consideration on a case-by-case basis (adapted from Bersoff, Note 2).

"Fair use" is defined as the freedom to use copyrighted material in a reasonable manner without the consent of the copyright owners. Scholarly writings often quote *short* sections of works by others (properly cited) without permission. This is typically acceptable unless, for example, the market value of the original work is impaired as a result, or when it can be demonstrated that copying was done to avoid the effort of creating independent work (adapted from Bersoff, Note 2).

The ethics code includes a statement that reflects copyright infringement concepts: "Psychologists take credit only for work they have actually done" (*EP*: 1a). Reference to fair use appears in the following sentence: "Acknowledgment through specific citations is made for unpublished as well as published material that has directly influenced the research or writing" (*EP*: 7f).

Cases brought to ethics committees range from blatant infractions to ambiguous and unclear situations. Obvious cases of plagiarism, in which large amounts of material were copied verbatim, are the easiest for ethics committees to process since the evidence is concrete and overwhelming. Ambiguous cases, however, are difficult to adjudicate. Interestingly, the primary source of discovery of major acts of plagiarism is neither by the public nor by psychologists, but by psychology graduate students who are in the process of researching for their own projects or theses.

Case 13–6:   In the course of accessing the literature for her own doctoral dissertation, a graduate student found that the 1978 dissertation of Rep Lica, "Ph.D.," was almost identical in wording and contained the same data and analysis as that of Dr. Paula Primary's, dated 1972. She showed the two documents to her supervisor who wrote to an ethics committee. Lica could not dispute the facts, but offered the defense that he was under extreme pressure to finish his degree and was receiving no support or assistance from his committee.

Case 13–7:   Multy Lingual, Ed.D., was discovered, in the course of a visiting foreign student's library research, to have lifted two articles from foreign language journals and then to have published them, word-for-word, in American journals under his own name. Further investigation revealed that Dr. Lingual had been translating the work of scholars from three countries into English and publishing them as his own work for more than a decade.

In these instances, the overlap was so substantial that ethics committees were able to reach swift decisions. The penalties imposed in such instances are often heavy ones, although sometimes committees have allowed respondents to make restitution and then imposed a lesser penalty.

Less clear-cut cases involve complaints alleging plagiarism or unfair use based on brief or occasionally similar passages, heavy paraphrasing, or unattributed idea models.

Case 13—8:   Tick Off, Ph.D., complained to an ethics committee that Sam Likeness, M.A., used a number of his previously published ideas, including a few similar sentences, in Likeness' article on signal detection theory without crediting Dr. Off. The committee noted the similarity in ideas and an occasional resemblance in wording. Likeness, however, adamantly denied using or even having read Off's work, provided other articles (which were cited in Likeness' paper) as his primary sources, and asserted that the occasional wording similarities were strictly co-incidental.

Case 13—9:   Sol First, Ph.D., complained that Moon Second, Ph.D., had used his idea without permission from a previous, but unpublished, paper on the nature of transference. Second claimed she had never even heard of First. The committee read the two papers and found the idea, but not the material itself, similar.

In these situations, the ethics committees were faced with far more difficult decisions, which is common when "fair use," rather than plagiarism is the primary issue. Writers or researchers working in similar areas certainly cull notions from each other and even similar ways of expressing their thoughts, which render complaints based on similar, but not identical, written material difficult or impossible to unravel. Remember that ideas, *per se*, are not legally protected. Mr. Likeness probably had access to Dr. Off's work since it was available in published form, but the basic ideas also appeared elsewhere and were cited by Likeness. The word overlap was minimal and could have been coincidental. Dr. Second's case was more easily defended, because the paper had never been published, and it was less likely that Second had access to it; in addition, the two texts were quite dissimilar.

Let us consider two other, more perplexing cases that involved some convoluted sets of circumstances between literature access and final publication.

Case 13—10:   Ann Tecedent, Ed.D., was shocked to see chunks of her previously published journal article appearing in another journal under the name of Jack Next, Ph.D. Many other colleagues had also brought the incident to Dr. Tecedent's attention since both periodicals were major ones in the same specialty area. Dr. Tecedent contacted an ethics committee charging plagiarism. The investigation revealed a complicated chain of events. Dr. Next had assigned the literature review gathering phase to his graduate assistant who, in turn, assigned the initial library research to two undergraduate assistants. These assistants copied down information, often verbatim, from the literature and passed them onto the graduate assistant who, after finding the material "well-written," passed the notes virtually unchanged to Dr. Next. Dr. Next also found the notes "well-written," and incorporated them directly into his manuscript.

Case 13–11: Chris Nip, Ph.D., charged Cross Tuck, Ph.D., with plagiarism. Dr. Nip produced a copy of his 1970 physiological psychology textbook and a copy of Dr. Tuck's 1980 text annotating some 30 paragraphs that were either identical to or too similar to be coincidental. During the inquiry, Tuck presented an unexpected defense. It seems that a 1975 revision of the original Nip text was co-authored by Nip and Tuck, but the two authors had since squabbled and were no longer in contact with each other. Tuck documented that the 30 paragraphs appeared in the 1975 text as well. Tuck argued that he could not be criticized for copying from a book he had co-authored and on which he held copyright privileges.

Dr. Next was exonerated from the more serious ethics charge of intentional plagiarism, but was directed to explain the situation to the original author and to the journal staff (which printed an explanation in a subsequent issue). He was reprimanded by the ethics committee for lax supervision and scholarship. The most rasping consequence to Dr. Next, however, was acute embarrassment. Dr. Tuck may have had a technical legal right to reuse material originally written by Nip, but the ethical propriety of its use is questionable.

A number of unfortunate factors may account for an increase in actual or suspected cases of plagiarism or unfair use. Pressures to publish or to complete theses in departments that lack careful supervising mentors may account for part of the increase. The growing stockpile of written material in our field allows malintentioned psychologists to risk a lower probability of detection as well as the possibility for innocent psychologists to publish something that might appear suspiciously similar to another person's work. Publishers of both books and journal articles, faced with their own space and financial limitations, increasingly admonish authors to "write tightly," which often makes it difficult or impossible to cite every source of every idea. But the rules of thumb remain: Do not copy the work of others and pass it off as your own; and, if you use a *small* section of someone else's work in your own, credit it properly.

Finally, we raise the question of "verbal plagiarism," which has never, to our knowledge, come before an ethics committee. Psychologists, especially those who teach, are often requested to give lectures. Other sources are typically consulted during the preparation phase for the talk. It is our position, and perhaps also implicit in the *Ethical Principles*, that when one draws significantly from another source, that source should be credited in the verbal presentation.

"Author Assisted" Publications

At some point along the continuum between original work and unauthorized copying, claiming credit for unoriginal work becomes technically legal, but remains ethically questionable. Ghost-written works, for example, pose no legal problems as long as a valid contract is honored between the "ghost" and the author-of-record. But is it *ethical* for psychologists to let readers believe that they originated a work that, in fact, someone else was paid to create for them?

We will confine our discussion to a form of author-assisted writing known as "managed projects," a major focus of ethical questions. Managed books can be created in several specific ways, but the underlying communality is that the publisher retains major control over the creation, development, and finalization of the manuscript and, in a sense, becomes the primary author (Whitten, 1976). Many individuals (either on the staff of the publishing house, freelance writers, junior level psychologists, or advanced students) are typically involved in accessing material and drafting chapters to fill in the master plan devised by the publishing company. The author-of-record whose name appears on the book spine, cover, and title page may have varying degrees of writing and editorial involvement. In many cases this involvement has been extremely minimal, such as serving as a reviewer of a final manuscript written by others.

Although managed texts comprise a relatively new publishing innovation, and they still account for a minority of the textbooks on the market, publishers are attracted to this format for a number of reasons. The tight control they retain enables the final product to resemble closely the original plan, keeps production on schedule, and is far more cost-effective than the traditional single-authored textbook project. Scholarly works are often poorly written or written at a level beyond the intended use. Academics, who tend to be the textbook writers, must write in their spare time, which often means that the project proceeds on a sporadic basis. Scholarly writers often miss agreed-on deadlines, and a large proportion of contracted-for works are never completed.

The managed text technique, however, presents profound ethical issues (McKeachie, 1976). Let us first consider quality. Most managed texts involve heavy culling of already published textbook formats, focusing on those that have already achieved success in the marketplace. Indeed, the resemblance has occasionally been so marked that legal actions against the authors-of-record of the subsequent (and competing) managed text projects have resulted. In one instance, the psychology textbook was ordered removed from the market by the courts (Haupt, 1976). The question also remains whether innovative and sound works can be created in this mechanistic manner. The result may be lavishly packaged and interesting to read, but not necessarily academically sound (McKeachie, quoted in Haupt, 1976). It may be a paraphrase of scholarship rather than scholarship itself (Owen, quoted in Haupt, 1976). A related moral issue is that the recombined and paraphrased nature of some managed textbooks excludes those responsible for the original scholarship from recognition and financial reward.

Another ethical issue relates to the false impressions the buyer or text adopter may have concerning how the book was created and who was responsible for the content. When a single author's name appears in the acknowledgments, it is assumed that this individual created the book by original thinking and hard labor. But this individual may have actually written very little, if any, of the material appearing in the book. Such attributions certainly mislead consumers, regardless of the quality of the work, and violate the spirit of the *Ethical Principles*, which admonish psychologists to take credit only for work they have actually done and to credit authors according to the extent of their contributions. For managed text publishers, as well as for psychologists who participate with them, clear information regarding how the book was developed should be prominently displayed to avoid misrepresentation. Thus a long list of authors (including any nonpsychologists) might be included with a statement in the preface that notes the specific nature of each contribution.

Psychologists who choose to participate in managed text projects should remain aware of the potential ethical liabilities. Book publishers are not subject to the provisions of our ethical code, although APA has attempted to exert pressure by excluding advertisements from its sponsored publications for books known to be "managed" but not fully identified as such. Ultimately it is the psychologist who will face the brunt of peer sanctions if complaints subsequently arise. Because the psychologist does not have primary control over the project, however, his or her ability to monitor any ethical matters is greatly diminished.

> **Case 13–12:**   Pur Blind, Ed.D., was brought up on ethics charges for "authoring" a textbook that contained numerous passages that closely resembled those of a previously written, competing text. Dr. Blind responded that he did not actually author the book, but received a flat fee and primary authorship credit for final editorial review.

> **Case 13–13:**   Several text authors banded together to complain about the irresponsible scholarship of Polly Parrot, Ph.D. They plotted out how parts of their respective previously published books could be combined together, resulting in a mosaic that was Dr. Parrot's book. Parrot responded that she did not actually write any of the chapters but did help with the organization of topics to be covered and the editing of the final drafts. She placed the blame on others over whom she had no control.

Ethics committees were not persuaded by the excuses either psychologist offered. Because both appeared as authors-of-record, they were held responsible for their own level of involvement in products of dubious quality or originality.

Writers routinely use many forms of assistance. Paying someone to help access and/or distill the literature for information to be included in the book typically poses no ethical problems, although an occasional assistant has complained that the agreed on payment or recognition was not forthcoming. Most scholarly authors (who are rarely trained as writers) must suffer the "blue pencil/pink query slip" attack on their manuscripts by professional copy editors who are trained to turn ungrammatical pieces into readable material. No ethical questions are typically raised here because copy editors alter form rather than meaning. A few complaints have arisen when psychologist-authors charged psychologist-editors with "mutilating" their work or publishing a vastly altered version without first sharing it with the individual to whom it was attributed. Sometimes it seemed that the disputed editing truly improved the work, but bruised the author's ego in the process. Other times it appeared that the editing was unnecessarily heavy-handed. In any event, it is wise to insist that editors always work out changes with the author *before* publication. Finally, pairing psychology scholars with professional journalists for the purpose of creating textbooks is no longer uncommon. If all authors are fully and saliently credited, no ethical questions arise.

Forged and Fudged Data-Based Publications

Similar to plagiarism, creating fraudulent data is considered among scientists and scholars to be one of the most dire ethical violations. However, the longer term impact of reporting fraudulent data is far *more* serious than mimicking others since the false information is absorbed into and then contaminates the knowledge stockpile. Application of the implications of fradulent findings may ultimately harm the well-being of others. For example, the ramifications of Sir Cyril Burt's research (described more fully in the proceeding section) extended beyond the realm of academic debate since the British school tiers system was largely based on Burt's belief in fixed intelligence (Diener and Crandall, 1978).

Three basic varieties of concocting fraudulent data can be defined: (1) "dry lab" or forged findings that are simply "invented" without any actual data collecting; (2) tampered, "fudged," "doctored," "smoothed," or "cooked" data that are based on data actually collected but altered to approach more closely the desired or expected outcome; and (3) selected or "trimmed" data that are actually collected but edited to delete discrepant or unwanted information from the final analysis. Invalid findings may also result in a variety of more subtly malintentioned or inadvertent ways through inappropriate design, poor sampling procedures, misused statistical tests, and so on.

The discovery of fraudulent data reporting practices is not confined to recent times. Ptolemy, Gregor Mendel, and Isaac Newton have been suspected of fudging a little to align reality more closely to their theories. The Piltdown Man, discovered in England in 1912, earned a significant place in paleontology until 1953, when the remains were discovered to be a sophisticated hoax accomplished by combining modern human and ape bones. Unfortunately, numerous instances of fraudulent research have scandalized science during the past decade, many uncovered at the most prestigious and respected universities and institutes.

Cornell University: A young biochemist, while a graduate student working with eminent specialists in the field, seemed destined for major honors for his breakthrough work in carcinogenesis. It was later discovered that the work was based on "doctored" cellular matter. (Golden, 1981)

University of California at Los Angeles: Other researchers expressed incredulity upon repeatedly being unable to replicate the findings by a UCLA investigator of the existence of an enzyme defect associated with a rare nerve disease. Subsequently, an assistant in the UCLA laboratory became concerned that the published data did not reflect the complete set of data collected. The paper was retracted from a major journal attributing the reason to an error in calculation. (Jacobs, 1982)

Sloan Kettering Institute for Cancer Research: A young dermatologist had reported findings of successful skin transplants that could not be replicated by others. Under pressure, he had darkened skin sections of two mice with ink in an ill-fated and quickly unmasked attempt to falsify success. (Hixon, 1976)

Massachusetts General Hospital/Harvard University: A research scientist claimed to have successfully grown four cell lines of Hodgkins' disease in culture dishes. Most of these cells turned out to be owl monkey rather than human cells. The circumstances under which the cells were contaminated are not known for sure, but it is documented that the scientist was informed that the cells were defective by an outside source and that the investigator delayed sharing this discovery with those who had been supplied with his samples. The same investigator is reported to have been caught by a laboratory assistant faking data entries on a biochemical experiment. (Hilts, 1981)

Boston University Medical Center: Data on cancer patient charts were altered to make it appear that an experimental group was progressing much better than it actually was, and a tumor was "invented" for a research patient that had none. (Altman, 1980; Roark, 1980; Hilts, 1981)

Yale University: A young associate of a prominent medical researcher was discovered to have both plagiarized and altered data on a study of anorexia nervosa published under the authorship of both men. Numerous other papers on insulin binding, authored by other colleagues with the associate, were published in major journals and later discovered to be questionable when the associate could not produce the original data and notes during an investigation. (Broad, 1980; Hunt, 1981)

Harvard Medical School: A young medical researcher, heralded as one of the most prolific and brilliant men in his field, destined for a prominent place in science, unabashedly concocted data in the presence of several stunned witnesses. A deeper inquiry into the researcher's previous studies revealed that a considerable amount of "original data" was inexplicably missing, casting doubt on the veracity of his earlier work as well. (Broad, 1982)

Two recent and publicized discoveries in psychology have brought some discredit to our field. Sir Cyril Burt, one of the most distinguished figures in British psychology, has posthumously been exposed for publishing implausible and fictitious data in his classic identical twin research, which supported his theory of the inherited nature of intelligence (Kamin, 1974; Wade, 1976; Evans, 1976; McAskie, 1978). Defenders (e.g., Jensen, 1974; 1978) attempt to discount the discrepancies as mere carelessness, but others (Hearnshaw, 1979; Eysenck, 1980) describe additional incidents that suggest that Burt committed more errors in his publications than can be attributed to nonchalance. More recently, the scandal at the Institute for Parapsychology, headed by the late Joseph B. Rhine, may have eroded what legitimacy the much beleaguered study of extrasensory perception had achieved through the efforts of its sincere and generally respected founder. In a frank article, an obviously shaken Rhine outlined how his chosen successor, a young medical doctor, was discovered by co-workers to have fabricated data for an investigation of precognition in rats (Rhine, 1974b). Ironically, Rhine had published an article just three months earlier on the problems of deceptive practices by parapsychology researchers and outlined safety measures that should be taken (Rhine, 1974a).

The themes that recur in many of these and other instances of unmasked data fraud include the following: lax supervision of the data gathering and analysis procedures; and, in the perpetrators, excessive ambition and competitiveness, intense pressure to produce findings, and previous records of prolific writing. We do not imply that any researcher fitting one or all of these descriptions or operating under these conditions should be identified as a suspicious character. All these factors are relatively common among scientists and their work settings. The emerging portrait does, however, reveal the circumstances under which decisions to abandon ethical, scientific practice may germinate.

Why would scientists engage in such practices when the chance for discovery is always present and the result is a swiftly destroyed career? Pressure to produce probably accounts for some of the motivation. A researcher who "publishes first," thus establishing "discovery" of a finding, also establishes a priority for allocation of shrinking grant funds. A project failing to produce significant findings may be judged as unattractive for publication, which may then weaken the likelihood of additional funding to pursue the same line of inquiry. Nevertheless, one must also have lost a sense of scientific responsibility. It is unlikely that a person who is dedicated to uncovering the *real* answers to difficult questions would ever falsify data.

Discovery of data fraud results in many ways, often starting with an uneasy feeling in laboratory assistants or colleagues who find a published piece of work improbable. The merely suspicious, however, begin to check further, and their investigations may reveal more clear evidence of data mismanagement. In the case of the Rhine laboratory scandal, assistants installed duplicate recording devices and surreptitiously observed Rhine's successor altering the data. The Yale incident might not have been detected except that a tenacious colleague cried "foul," when an unpublished manuscript bearing a striking resemblance to her own was produced by the Yale team, and she discovered that her manuscript had been sent to a member of that team several months earlier for editorial review.

After formal investigations commenced, raw data and laboratory notes were often not available or were reportedly destroyed. Data, when available, were often "too neat" and neither reflect the pattern of other previous findings nor the findings of subsequent replication attempts. Laboratory directors are often at a loss to explain the discrepancies because they were spread thin across several projects or administrative duties and relied on the trustworthiness of summary reports prepared by their staffs. It is clear that the reputations of some very prominent researchers have been tainted as a result of the unethical behavior of their subordinates.

Most of the research programs involved in these scandals were heavily funded by the government. Consequently, the National Institutes of Health are now attempting to introject additional safeguards and stronger sanctions, such as precluding future funding for any investigator caught cheating. NIH spokespersons admit, however, that safeguards and sanctions will be difficult to implement. By their nature, scientists would probably rebel at overly strict accountability procedures, such as keeping daily logs of events, data entries, and personnel activities. Turning research laboratories into "scientific police states" would probably erode the spirit of sound, scientific inquiry.

The government is also concerned about the delays that have occurred between the discovery of improper acts and the reporting of them. Such resistances may be understandable from the institution's vantage point since massive ramifications for all concerned are likely, including the endangering of future support on which most large research programs are dependent. But white-washes and coverups merely exacerbate the overall consequences. One notable researcher was forced to resign from a subsequent high-level position because of poor judgment in not being more forceful in investigating the improprieties of one of his subordinates. Delays in exposure also harm unaware researchers trying to build on fraudulent data-based findings. One investigator claimed that two years of his life were wasted attempting to pursue work based on what were later proven to be bogus data.

The vast majority of the contemporary data scandals have resulted from biomedical research laboratories. No one knows for sure whether the incidence is higher in this field than in the social and behavioral sciences, or whether it is simply easier to detect fraud in biomedicine. The latter interpretation could, unfortunately, be valid since most research conducted in the social and behavioral sciences (except, perhaps, in such specialties as physiological psychology) do not necessitate chemical analyses, tissue cultures, or similar "hard" documentation. Psychological research data often involve numerical scores from questionnaires, assessments, or performance measures. The research participants are long gone, taking their anonymous identities with them. Such data are relatively easy to generate, fudge, or trim. We hope that psychology researchers are motivated by the responsible quest for truth, but it is disquieting to note that the same "publish-or-perish" pressures exist in our field and that research has revealed that some psychology students do fabricate data (e.g., Azrin et al., 1961).

Experiences of ethics committees are not too helpful in estimating the incidence of fraudulent data publication among psychologists. Incidents brought to the attention of ethics committees are quite rare, hopefully indicating that the actual rate is also low. Most of the cases of clear guilt involve plagiarized data; that is, the psychologist simply copied someone else's statistical findings and took credit for them. The few incidences involving charges of falsified data have been difficult to adjudicate.

> **Case 13—14:** Golda Brick, Ph.D., was accused by a colleague of analyzing and reporting data that were different from those actually gathered in the laboratory. Brick's concerned graduate student had brought the evidence to the colleague asking for guidance. After viewing the graduate assistant's data sheets and the reported results, it was very apparent that the two did not jibe.

> **Case 13—15:** Hocum Bunk, Ph.D., was charged by several members of his academic department with presenting data findings at a professional meeting that were based on experimental trials never actually run. The colleagues based their suspicions on the fact that an analysis of the student "research pool" records did not reveal any record of Bunk's conducting a study during the last year, although he stated he ran it during that time period and used students as participants. Furthermore, the room shared by several faculty members allegedly used to collect the data, showed no signs of use by Dr. Bunk. He never signed up for it, was never seen in it, and his experimental device had "never changed position and was accumulating dust."

Dr. Brick denied any wrongdoing, explaining instead that she did not use the data that the student assistant had collected, but rather data she collected by herself on weekends. Dr. Bunk alleged that he did not use the "student research pool" because he conscripted students directly and ran them through a similar device he had in his office. Neither psychologist could produce their original data, both claiming that they threw it away after completing their statistical analysis. Although the defenses were judged to be insufficient to convince the ethics committees that no wrongdoing had occurred, neither the complainants nor the committees could *conclusively* prove the stories false. Sound evidence is required to sustain such a serious violation. The ethics committees did not exonerate the respondents, but did declare that insufficient evidence precluded further action.

Errors in alleged scientific advances, whether based on honest or deceitful practices, are assumed to be eventually self-correcting through replication. However, the scientific community does not support replication research. Journals are more likely to use their limited space for the reporting of "new findings." Thus there is little motivation for researchers to spend time and effort replicating someone else's work. Furthermore, most large-scale projects (as many of those associated with fraudulent practices were) are far too expensive and complicated to even attempt to replicate. The peer-review system may be useful in discovering fraudulent data-based findings, but it is far from fail-safe. Peers typically do not have the time to review carefully raw data and analyses, when they are evaluating results for publication, even if the submission of raw data with the manuscript was a requirement. In one instance, for example, it took a fraud investigation expert three full weeks to uncover the improprieties in the data collection and analysis materials. Communicating instances of fradulent findings to the scientific community is encouraged, but retractions are cumbersome to effect and may be largely unnoticed.

Even if such discoveries are discounted as honest errors due to human fraility, what stock is the public to place in scientists' work? The public's distrust, which is sure to ensue as the media exposes suspicious scientific findings regularly and prominently, could have disastrous consequences for everyone. Scientists are as dependent on the public for continued support as society is on their work (Hunt, 1981). Although part of the problem is a system of scientific rewards that implicitly encourages dishonest practices, researchers in psychology and other fields must remain true to higher level reasons for undertaking research activity in the first place.

Responsibilities of Publishing Gatekeepers

Since publication quality and integrity are critical to the growth of a discipline, and since "getting published" is often essential to one's professional status, it is not surprising that criticisms of decisions by acquisition editors, journal editors, and manuscript referees abound. Some publishers are faulted for emphasizing "big name" authors, production gimmicks, and large adoption markets. Journal editors and reviewers have been variously faulted for the following: favoritism toward and biases against certain topics or theoretical approaches; shoddy or deficient evaluations; and inclinations to reject manuscripts reporting negative or equivocal findings, replications, or work in an area for which rigorous methodology does not yet exist (Sterling, 1959; Brackbill and Korten, 1970; Smith, 1970; Walster and Cleary, 1970; Bowen, Perloff, and Jacoby, 1972; McKeachie, 1976; Gordon, 1977.)

Peters and Ceci (1982) tested the capriciousness of the reviewing process of twelve prestigious psychology journals by *resubmitting* cosmetically altered (including author and affiliation changes) *previously* published articles to each respective journal. Surprisingly, only three articles were detected as resubmissions, and eight of the nine remaining articles were rejected for publication in the same journals that had published them only a short time earlier! The authors confirmed that the rejection rates and editorial policies of the journals had not been subsequently altered.

Ethics complaints against psychologists who serve as publishing gatekeepers are quite rare, possibly because disgruntled would-be-published-authors realize that ethics committees are neither in a position to referee disputes of this nature nor to dictate what is published. When complaints arise, they are usually along the lines illustrated in the following cases:

Case 13−16:   Big Bust, Ph.D., complained that Simon Noshow, Ph.D., editor of the *Journal of Psychoscience*, routinely published invited addresses delivered to the Psychoscience Society's annual meeting. Dr. Bust was asked to submit a manuscript version of his invited address. Dr. Bust submitted it, but nine months passed, and he heard nothing. He wrote Dr. Noshow again and received a letter back from Edy New, Ed.D., who informed Bust that she was now the journal editor and had decided not to publish Bust's address. Dr. Bust complained to an ethics committee that Dr. Noshow's inaction ruined his opportunity to publish in the journal and delayed submission to other publication outlets. Dr. Noshow's actions, according to Dr. Bust, were not in accord with responsibilities that professionals have toward one another.

Case 13−17:   Harold Fester, Ph.D., was outraged by an article, appearing in *The Significant Statistician*, that objected to Fester's previous work. According to Dr. Fester, the critique was based on faulty calculations that resulted in erroneous conclusions. He wrote to Latin Square, Ph.D., the journal editor, requesting space for a blasting rejoinder. Fester complained to an ethics committee that Dr. Square's decision not to publish the reply would result in an unfair loss of professional status.

Although ethics committees expressed compassion for the plights of Dr. Bust and Dr. Fester, the decisions in both cases were to refer the psychologists back to the parties involved. Dr. Bust was encouraged to send the invitation letter from the ex-editor to the new editor and request reconsideration. This proved to be successful, and the address was ultimately published. Apparently the ex-editor had left his records in such disarray that the incoming editor did not realize that an implicit agreement between the two had existed. Dr. Fester was encouraged to mute his salty rejoinder and rework his substantive points into a brief article format. This was also acceptable to the editor.

ETHICAL RESPONSIBILITIES OF TEACHERS OF PSYCHOLOGY

The *Ethical Principles* note that the primary obligation of a teaching psychologist is to help others acquire knowledge and skill (*EP*: 1e). The code admonishes psychologists to protect the welfare of all who seek their services (*EP*: 6 preamble).

Writings dealing with the ethics of instruction are virtually nonexistent (Redlich and Pope, 1980; Cahn, 1983), and publications about ethical implications of professors' job functions are scanty (e.g., Peairs, 1974; Deutch, 1979; Cole, 1981.) Some may argue that no need exists for such a literature because those who attain the level of knowledge that bestows upon them the status of being called to share it with others require no additional qualifiers. Yet we have never met an individual who has not been able to express dissatisfaction with the competence of, or treatment received by, one or more educators. The neglect of the ethics of instruction probably results from many other factors, some of which are most unfortunate. One reason may be that institutions of higher education require proficiency (typically defined as the earning of an advanced degree, and including perhaps publishing record) in a particular subject matter. Ability to communicate to students and possessing a concern for students' welfare are important attributes that are not easily assessed at the time professors are hired. Another reason may be the assumption that any unethical or other type of dispute will be handled at the source since instructors work within the structure of an organization that presumably has formalized check-and-balance mechanisms. Even when such channels are functioning in a way that allows students fair hearings and due process, only the most assertive may use them. Most students feel relatively powerless and inadequate and may either be discouraged from seeking redress for grievances or routinely place the blame for their discontent on themselves. A "silent pact" may sometimes implicitly exist between students and professors in which professors do less-than-adequate jobs and require less-than-adequate student performances, leaving everyone involved free to do "better things with their time." Academic freedom may be misinterpreted to mean the right to do whatever one pleases, rather than the freedom to communicate. Finally, teaching psychologists (compared to most other service-providing psychologists) are salaried and deal with "captive audiences." Such a situation may be conducive to focusing on issues in which the teaching psychologists are the aggrieved parties (e.g., too many students, too little money, or too few resources to do the job well), while neglecting the ethical issues relevant to the consumers of their services.

Hard economic times coupled with no-growth or declining university enrollments have led to funding cutbacks for most academic departments. Shrinking resources invariably lead to competition among faculty for equipment, travel funds, laboratory space, and promotions. Shortages lead to stress, which may reveal itself in low morale and/or explosive bickering and dissension among faculty members. Students may indirectly reap the consequences because their education is sometimes controlled by unmotivated, burned-out, unhappy, or irritated professors. In addition, professors who find it difficult, for whatever reason, to publish in scholarly journals are often forced to publish anyway, since their promotions or retentions depend on it. The ironic result is that energy is diverted from teaching students, while, at the same time, uninspired, shoddy, or trivial work is churned into the knowledge stockpile.

This section describes and illustrates several specific ethical issues that arise in the didactic process: teaching skills and course preparation; lecturing on sensitive or controversial issues; questionable teaching techniques and assignments; evaluation of student performance; ethical issues relating to catalog and other course description material; and textbook adoption practices. Related issues are also discussed in other sections of this book: for instance, discussing confidential case material in the classroom is presented in Chapter 3; interpersonal and social relationships with students are discussed in Chapters 10 and 11; and ethical implications of "experiential-affective" courses, such as sensitivity training, are discussed in Chapter 10.

Teaching Skills and Course Preparation

Psychologists are admonished by the ethics code to provide services and use techniques only in those areas for which they are qualified by training and experience. As teachers, "psychologists perform duties on the basis of careful preparation so that their instruction is accurate, current, and scholarly" and "maintain high standards of scholarship by presenting psychological information objectively [and] fully" (EP: 1e). Most students probably do not realize that psychology professors who are ill-prepared or who exclusively cite older work and theories on a topic, when more recently recognized work and theories are also readily available, are violating the ethics code. The accuracy, objectivity, and completeness of the information taught are not qualities that student consumers can easily assess since, by definition, they do not know the topic area well enough to make such judgments. Upholding these mandates, then, requires a personal commitment by psychologists who teach.

Whereas the complaints received about psychology educators are most often associated with disputed performance evaluations and offensive interpersonal styles, occasional complaints about teaching skill and course preparation are reported to ethics committees. Probably most student complaints, however, are processed at the department or university level.

> **Case 13—18:** Daze Fluster, Ed.D., was charged with incompetence by a student who expressed outrage over the quality of education he was receiving from Dr. Fluster, and the department's apparent unwillingness to remedy the situation. The student claimed that Dr. Fluster always arrived late, spent most of the time flipping through a tangled mass of papers from his briefcase, had no apparent agenda for each class session, and simply rambled in an unconnected fashion about the course topic. The student asserted that because he was spending both money and valuable time pursuing his education, he was entitled to a better course.

> **Case 13—19:** Mala Droit, Ph.D., joked on the first day of class that she "did not know anything about statistics," but since no one else was available to teach the course, she was asked to do it. The students were upset about this deficiency, because the course was a prerequisite for understanding the content of future required courses. They approached the department chair with a demand for a qualified statistics teacher and were told that they should feel lucky that the class was offered at all. The most tenacious of the group, consisting of graduate-school aspirants, wrote an ethics committee charging Dr. Droit and the department chair with insensitivity and disregard for their legitimate academic needs.

Ethics committees are not in an advantageous position to resolve such disputes directly, even though the allegations, if true, would violate the spirit of the *Ethical Principles*. In such instances, committees typically take an "educative" stance by informing the psychologist of the complaint, discussing the complaint as it relates to the provisions of the code, and requesting a response.

The definition and evaluation of effective and competent teaching has been a raging controversy for years (see Haefele, 1980). Recent law suits against teachers for "malpractice" attest to the lengths to which some dissatisfied customers are willing to go when they believe that they (or their children) received shoddy educational experiences (Newell, 1977). During difficult financial times, more students are attending school at some personal sacrifice or because they need to learn something new in order to be competitive in the marketplace. These students may not sit still when their educational needs are not satisfied. Thus attending to teaching quality also protects against charges of incompetence or irresponsibility.

Lecturing on Sensitive or Controversial Issues

Although it is probably impossible for professors to objectify completely their presentation and selection of course materials, psychologists are admonished by the ethics code to remain aware of the influence of their own personal biases and values. In addition, "when dealing with topics that may give offense, [psychologists] recognize and respect the diverse attitudes that students may have toward such materials" (*EP*: 3a).

With today's widely diverse student population and the inherently sensitive or controversial nature of many psychological topics, upholding these ethical mandates becomes somewhat of a challenge.

> **Case 13−20:** Chip Straight complained that Lenny Open, Ph.D., offended him by discussing homosexuality in class and showing a film that depicted people of the same sex embracing and kissing each other. He believed such discussions should be "confined to the gutter where they belong and not in an institution of higher learning."

> **Case 13−21:** Murray Green, Ph.D., was complained against by Chaim Gold for making derisive statements about Jews. Dr. Green allegedly listed a number of traits sometimes attributed to Jewish people, such as large noses, pushiness, and ruthlessness in business practices.

These two cases illustrate how a professor might offend a particularly sensitive student. During an inquiry, Dr. Open produced materials indicating that the topic was relevant to the course content, based on scholarly writings, and balanced in terms of varying views people have about homosexuality. The movie was an educational film, owned by the university, and highly rated for its sensitivity to the issues. In addition, Dr. Open had informed the students on the first day of class that a number of controversial issues would be discussed during the semester, and that students who felt uncomfortable about any of these topics should feel free to speak with him about them or, if very uncomfortable, consider dropping out of the course. Chip had chosen neither to drop the course nor to speak with Dr. Open. Dr. Green, who noted he was Jewish himself and was thus particularly surprised by Gold's rendition of the class presentation, explained that he was discussing stereotyping in his social psychology course. He used the list of characteristics sometimes attributed to Jews as a way of concretely illustrating stereotypes, and the list was clearly presented as such. After the list was read, a discussion of the dangers, inaccuracies, and functions of stereotyping had ensued. In these two cases, the complaints were not pursued any further.

The next two cases are particularly problematic regarding the professors' choice of contexts in which to couch their value judgments.

> **Case 13−22:** Libby Now complained that Gude Olboy, M.A., derided the goals of the women's liberation movement by stating that sufficient research existed to demonstrate that women's brains, physical bodies, and lack of aggressive tendencies precluded the possibility of success in endeavors currently dominated by

men. He cited, as "definitive proof," the fact that if women had been endowed with qualities similar to those of men, they would have "achieved equality during a much earlier phase of human evolution."

Case 13–23: Con Right complained that his professor, Rad Left, Ph.D., was highly selective in his choice of topics and data interpretation in his course on social issues. Mr. Right claimed that value judgments were imparted as facts and that students received a highly biased perspective on various topics, such as abortion, child-rearing, and conservative politics. He did not dispute Dr. Left's right to offer his perspective, but he did object to the lack of coverage and/or derision of data or views contrary to his own.

These cases reveal how the judgments of professors may not only offend students, but also compromise the quality of the educational process. Neither professor disputed the student-complainant's perceptions. Both asserted that it was their right to teach the facts as they saw them. Each objected to the student-complainants as people: Mr. Right was viewed as an "ultra conservative, close-minded snit"; and Ms. Now was called a "man-hater." The ethics committee showed the professors how their own rigid values surfaced in their "defenses," and then admonished both professors to be more diligent in their teaching responsibilities, including objectivity and a balanced presentation when contradictory or conflicting facts and values pertain.

Based on an analysis of many cases and complaints about sensitive and controversial lectures and topics, we suggest the following guidelines that may lower the incidence of offensiveness to some students, without compromising the rights of professors to express themselves in a responsible manner.

1. Inform students at the onset of the course if considerable sensitive or controversial material will be covered. This allows students to make a voluntary, informed decision about whether to remain in the course. If exceptionally sensitive material will be covered on a particular day, the professor might consider informing the students of that fact during the prior meeting. For example, an explicit movie on child abuse may be too painful for some students to watch, so they might be given the opportunity to skip that session.

2. When expressing one's own opinion or interpretations, identify them as such. Offering other points of view, in as objective a fashion as possible, is encouraged.

3. Attempt to stick as closely as possible to a scientific data base, if one exists, when discussing sensitive or controversial topics. If the information base is rooted only in opinion, present the full range rather than only one. A professor can always state why he or she *personally* disagrees with other opinions, but all should be aired so that students do not accept opinion as fact.

4. Allow students an opportunity to express their views without penalty, censure, or ridicule.

5. Ensure that students are offered opportunities to discuss in private any feelings they might have about sensitive or controversial material presented in class.

6. Ensure that presentation of sensitive and controversial material is justified on pedagogical grounds directly related to the course. Sometimes criticism is based on the fact that the material was added for "effect" or "shock value" and such complaints have even made their way through the legal system (Sherrer and Sherrer, 1972). The American Association of University Professors' principles on Academic Freedom and Tenure (1974) also warns against persistently introjecting controversial matter that has no relation to the subject at hand into the classroom.

Questionable Teaching Techniques and Assignments

Somewhat aligned with the issues previously discussed are teaching techniques or unusual assignments that may raise questions of an ethical nature. Each professor has his or her own style, based primarily on personality characteristics. Some professors are deeply involved with innovations or assignments geared to motivate students to become more involved in the learning process. While we have no desire to regiment teaching style or to stunt innovation, it is worthwhile to note how an ethical controversy may arise.

Case 13–24:   John Nice complained about the teaching style of Flam Boyant, Ph.D. Nice was offended by his frequent use of profanity in the classroom. He felt that it was not only "unprofessional," but served as a poor role model for other students and trivialized the knowledge being imparted. Nice supplied letters from other students attesting to the consistent use of "four-letter words," which were used to describe just about everything Dr. Boyant talked about.

Case 13–25:   Riley Blatent, Ph.D., faced university sanctions when students complained about required assignments for a course on contemporary alternative life styles. These included visits to swinging singles and gay bars, nudist camps, and "sex shops." The students contended that such assignments were not in keeping with standards of scholarly, academic requirements.

Case 13–26:   Bob Tail, Ph.D., caused a flurry of complaints when he showed slides of male and female genitalia in his physiological psychology class and then declared that the last slide of the series was a photo of his own penis.

In all three cases, the respondents argued that their methods were used to "gain attention" or to "bring a sense of reality" to the learning process. However, sanctions were upheld in each instance on the grounds that such techniques could not be justified on pedagogical grounds.

In an era when it may appear that "anything goes," academics may mistake this image as "relevance" and hence a viable style that all students would welcome and enjoy. They may not be sensitive to the fact that our pluralistic society is composed of many who do not share an acceptance of unbridled verbal or sexual expression. Furthermore, many others may find such expressions acceptable in private, but not appropriate for assimilation into educational curricula.

Evaluations of Student Performance

Student complaints to ethics committees are few in number, but may be increasing. The usual student disputes concern grades or other aspects of academic evaluations. The *Ethical Principles* do not refer specifically to assigning grades and mention evaluations only in the sense that they should be "timely" (*EP*: 7c). Although the general thrust of the code mandates fairness and concern for the welfare of all consumers, which implicitly extends to the evaluation of students, the omission of specific references to grading and evaluations of students was not an oversight because it would be very difficult to assess such cases. Institutions of higher learning have redress channels for students who believe their evaluations were unfair, and these seem the more appropriate and practical student resource. However, ethics committees have intervened on occasion when timeliness was an issue or when the case seemed to extend beyond a disputed grade in a particular course and all university-based channels had been exhausted.

> **Case 13–27:** Tim Anxious, the spokesman for an entire class of students, complained that Milton Strike, M.A., had withheld grades for the whole class for four months after the course had ended. At the time of the complaint, the grades were still unissued. Mr. Strike, a part-time instructor at the private college, claimed that the administration had not paid him his salary and he would turn in the grade roster upon receipt of a check.

> **Case 13–28:** Sookey Judge received a poor evaluation from her clinical supervisor, Robert Dilatory, Ph.D., during the last term of the program. She complained that the supervisor had not filed earlier evaluations that could have warned her of her shortcomings and given her an opportunity to remedy them. She also complained that her attempts to meet with Dr. Dilatory about some of the problems she was experiencing with her internship assignment were met with excuses, such as, "I am too busy today; maybe next week."

Mr. Strike was admonished by an ethics committee to issue grades immediately since holding the students' evaluations hostage was inappropriate and unethical. Dr. Dilatory responded to a committee inquiry that he had refrained from issuing early, negative evaluations and from meeting with the student because, "It looked like Ms. Judge was improving at the time." The committee found the excuse unacceptable and noted that the ethics code implies that evaluative feedback must be issued at such time as substantive information of an evaluative nature presents itself. To withhold for seven months feedback in areas where improvement is required was unfair to Ms. Judge and did not fulfill the ethical obligation, stated explicitly in the code, to facilitate the professional development of professionals in training.

On rare occasions, ethics committees have intervened when a student has documented that negligent or prejudicial evaluations have jeopardized an academic career. In such instances, the student typically has support from other faculty members and/or university officials who corroborate the student's position. Not unsurprisingly, such instances typically involve departments embroiled in bitter factional disputes or controversies. The grievance machinery has broken down, and the student appears to have received insufficient due process.

The fact that ethics committees do not respond, except under unusual and extreme circumstances, to grading and evaluation disputes does *not* mean that profound ethical issues are not therefore inherent in the assessment of students. Indeed, academic performance ratings are assumed to differentiate among the bright, mediocre, and dumb. Given the meaning of such labels in our culture, these blessings and stigmas may be among the most significant assessments that can be made about people. In this context, academic psychologists should be held accountable for their judgments. To assess students using invalid or biased criteria constitutes infliction of harm and is therfore unethical. Psychological assessments (see Chapter 4) emerge as more relevant for ethics committee scrutiny *not* because they are more important than academic assessments, but because the "rules" of their construction, administration, and interpretation have been formalized. Academic psychologists enjoy forms of anonymity that shield them from easy professional scrutiny. They are one discipline among a multitude of disciplines in their work setting. Furthermore, their assessments are based on information and assignments unique to the educational experience they offer to students. The criteria applied to standardized psychological assessments could not be applied. Neither of these factors, however, excuses academic psychologists from their personal and ethical obligations to invest considerable effort in educating and evaluating students appropriately and fairly.

Ethical Issues Related to Catalogs and Other Course Description Material

The educational program parallel to advertisements for psychotherapy services (see Chapter 7) are course descriptions included in catalogs or other promotional materials. The *Ethical Principles* are rather explicit in this situation. They mandate that catalog descriptions and course outlines contain accurate information, the bases for evaluation, and the nature of course experiences. Any eligibility requirements, fee information, and qualifications of instructors should be included in program announcements (*EP*: 4h).

Ethics cases involving disputes concerning university catalog descriptions are virtually nonexistent, probably because such descriptions are usually brief and very general. Even if a consumer were dissatisfied, an ethics committee is an unlikely choice of redress. But complaints have been filed by consumers of commercial educational programs, such as weekend workshops, on the basis of discrepancies between the promotional description of the program and the experience itself.

> **Case 13–29:** Dean Smart, Psy.D., paid $180 to attend a one-day professional workshop on schizophrenia. The promotional flyer listed several of the most prominent experts as among the speakers and specifically stressed that "brand new and unpublished material" would be shared with the audience. However, two of the five speakers did not appear and were replaced by "local talent." The three experts did not present new material, but rather cited material directly from their own published books, which Smart had already read. Smart request a refund from Org Deal, Ph.D., the psychologist in charge of arranging the program, but was refused. Dr. Smart then complained to an ethics committee.

> **Case 13–30:** Two women attended the first session of a six-week program on hypnosis. The basis of their decision was the promotional material listing the course name, "Deep Relaxation Hypnosis Techniques," followed by the phrase, "as taught by," then a list of three very prominent experts in clinical hypnosis in bold print. Other information followed, and on the bottom line, the small print read "Group Leader: Hip Mesmer, Psy.D." When the women arrived at the hotel conference room, only Dr. Mesmer was there. They waited for the three experts to show, but they never did. When they complained to Mesmer after the session, he explained that the ad did not say the three experts would *actually* teach the course, but that "as taught by" meant that he, Mesmer, would use their techniques. The women asked for a refund, received it after a long hassle, and wrote an ethics committee charging Mesmer with unfair advertising.

After reviewing the two educational experience advertisements, the ethics committees agreed that the consumers had based their decision to attend on misleading information. Dr. Mesmer was admonished to cease-and-desist from his promotional approach, because even though the information could be interpreted as technically accurate, the phraseology and print size differences could easily confuse consumers. Dr. Deal pleaded that the problem was beyond his control since two of the speakers backed out after the promotional materials were mailed and that speakers were clearly instructed to include their latest thinking. Nevertheless, Dr. Deal was reminded that the basis of the decision to buy was disparate from what consumers actually received and that those who were dissatisfied should receive due consideration.

Textbook Adoption Practices

Teaching psychologists have the obligation to select required readings with care, and the selection should be based strictly on the merits of the material's content. A situation that reaches ethics committees on occasion involves exposés of professors who selected required readings for personal gain. One psychology professor allegedly told a book sales representative that he would adopt the company's text for his classes if the company agreed to a one-dollar kickback on each copy purchased by his students. In another instance, a professor agreed to adopt a particular company's book after being offered a relatively large sum of money for providing the company with a three-page review of the book. Such practices are ethically reprehensible because they exploit students who assume that professors respect their learning interests.

A tangential issue that has generated debate is the practice by some teaching psychologists of selling still marketable, unsolicited, or unwanted "courtesy" textbooks supplied by book publishers to used textbook vendors. Those defending this avenue of disposal as a legitimate way to earn a few extra dollars contend that they have incurred no obligation and the property is theirs to do with as they please. Those more in tune with the increased costs passed on to students when a large number of "freebie resales" are introjected into the text market, which is unfair to the authors who receive no reward for their efforts from such sales, decry such resale practices. We recommend returning unwanted courtesy copies to the publisher sales representatives or donating them to a worthy institution or individual as small but helpful ways to help keep textbook costs down.

SUMMARY GUIDELINES

1. Psychologists should take credit on publications only for work they have actually contributed.
2. In collaborative research projects, early discussions of authorship credit expectations and assignments are encouraged.
3. Psychologists must be careful to attribute material originated by others when used in their own published work.
4. Despite pressure to publish research in some work settings, psychologists must remain sensitive to their responsibility and to the integrity of science and its methods by reporting data accurately and fully.

5. Psychologists who serve as publishing gatekeepers through editorial or reviewer positions should remain cognizant of their special influence and strive to perform their duties in an unbiased and competent manner.

6. Course materials should be carefully prepared and include recent, important work in the topic being taught. Textbooks and other required readings should be carefully selected on the basis of merit.

7. When lecturing on sensitive or controversial material, the professor should prepare the students in advance, the presentation should be objective and well-balanced, and the choice of content should be pedagogically justifiable. Professors should not present their own values or opinions in a way that could be mistaken for established fact.

8. Psychology teachers should strive to grade students fairly.

9. Descriptions of academic courses or other educational programs should accurately reflect the experience students will receive and the obligations they will incur.

REFERENCE NOTES

1. American Psychological Association Ethics Committee. *Authorship guidelines for dissertation supervision*, February 19, 1983.

2. Bersoff, D. N. Memo by APA General Counsel, requested by the Committee on Scientific and Professional Ethics and Conduct to clarify federal statutes related to copyright and the fair use doctrine, dated February 21, 1980.

REFERENCES

Altman, L. K. The doctor's world: How honest is medical research? *New York Times*, August 5, 1980, p. C-3.

American Association of University Professors. Academic freedom and tenure: 1940 statement of principles and interpretive comments. *AAUP Bulletin*, Summer, 1974, 269–272.

Azrin, N. H.; Holz, W.; Ulrich, R.; and Groldiamond, I. The control of the content of conversation through reinforcement. *Journal of the Experimental Analysis of Behavior*, 1961, 4, 25–30.

Bowen, D. D.; Perloff, R.; and Jacoby, J. Improving manuscript evaluations procedures. *American Psychologist*, 1972, 27, 221–225.

Brackbill, Y., and Korten, F. Journal reviewing practices: Authors' and APA members' suggestions for revision. *American Psychologist*, 1970, 25, 937–940.

Broad, W. J. Harvard delays in reporting fraud. *Science*, 1982, 215, 478–482.

———. Imbroglio at Yale (II): A top job lost. *Science*, 1980, 210, 171–173.

Cahn, S. M. The ethical thicket of academic autonomy. *Chronicle of Higher Education*, Feb. 2, 1983, p. 64.

Cole, D. L. Teaching tomorrow's psychology students: Who pays the piper? *American Psychologist*, 1981, *36*, 506–513.

Deutch, M. Education and distributive justice: Some reflections on grading systems. *American Psychologist*, 1979, 34, 391–401.

Diener, E., and Crandall, R. *Ethics in Social and Behavioral Research*. Chicago: University of Chicago Press, 1978.

Eisley, L. C. Darwin and the Mysterious Mr. X: New Light on the Evolutionists. New York: Dutton, 1979.

Evans, P. The Burt affair—Sleuthing in science. *APA Monitor*, 1976, 7, 1, 4.

Eysenck, H. J. Sir Cyril Burt: Prominence versus personality. *Psychological Reports*, 1980, *46*, 893–894.

Garfield, E. The ethics of scientific publication. *Current Contents*, 1978, *40*, 5–12.

Golden, F. Fudging data for fun and profit. *Time Magazine*, Dec. 7, 1981, p. 83.

Gordon, M. Evaluating the evalutors. *New Scientist*, Feb., 1977, pp. 342–343.

Haefele, D. L. How to evaluate thee, teacher—Let me count the ways. *Phi Beta Kappan*, January 1980, 349–352.

Haley, A. *Roots*. Garden City, NY: Doubleday, 1976.

Haupt, A. Managed books. *APA Monitor*, July 1976, 7, 13.

Hearnshaw, L. S. *Cyril Burt, Psychologist*. New York: Random House, 1979.

Hilts, P. J. Science confronted with "crime wave" of researchers faking data in experiments. *Los Angeles Times*, March 4, 1981, 1A, 6–7.

Hixon, J. *The Patchwork Mouse*. New York: Doubleday, 1976.

Hunt, M. A fraud that shook the world of science. *New York Times Magazine*, Nov. 1, 1981.

Jacobs, P. UCLA medical researcher's methods come under fire. *Los Angeles Times*, March 26, 1982, II, 1, 6.

Jensen, A. R. Kinship correlations reported by Sir Cyril Burt. *Behavior Genetics*, 1974, 4, 1–28.

———. Sir Cyril Burt in perspective. *American Psychologist*, 1978, *33*, 499–503.

Kamin, L. J. *The science and politics of IQ*. Potomac, MD: Lawrence Erlbaum, 1974.

McAskie, M. Kinship data: A critique of Jensen's analysis. *American Psychologist*, 1978, *33*, 496–498.

McKeachie, W. J. Textbooks: Problems of publishers and professors. *Teaching of Psychology*, 1976, *3*, 29–30.

Newell, R. C. Teacher malpractice: A new threat to education. *American Educator*, Summer, 1977, 2–6.

Peairs, R. H. What graduate students ought to know about the teaching business— But we seem afraid to tell them. In R. H. Peairs (Ed.), *Avoiding Conflict in Faculty Personnel Practices*. San Francisco: Jossey-Bass, 1974.

Peters, D. P., and Ceci, S. J. Peer review practices of psychological journals: The fate of published articles, submitted again. *The Behavioral and Brain Sciences*, 1982, *5*, 187–195.

Price, D. J. *Little Science, Big Science*. New York: Columbia University Press, 1963.

Rea, W. T. *The White Lie*. Turlock, CA: M and R Publications, 1982.

Redlich, F., and Pope, K. S. *Ethics of Mental Health Training*, 1980, *168*, 709–714.

Rhine, J.B. Comments: "Security versus deception in para-psychology." *Journal of Parapsychology*, 1974a, *38*, 99–121.

———. Comments: "A new case of experimenter unreliability," 1974b, *38*, 215–225.

Roark, A. C. Scientists question profession's standards amid accusations of fraudulent research. *Chronicle of Higher Education*, Sept. 2, 1980, p. 5.

Seashore, S. Plagiarism, credit assignment, and ownership of data. *Professional Psychology*, 1978, 719–722.

Sheehy, G. *Passages: Predictable Crises of Adult Life*. New York: Dutton, 1976.

Sherrer, C. W., and Sherrer, M. S. Professional or legal standards for academic psychologists and counselors. *Journal of Law and Education*, 1972, *1*, 289–302.

Smith, N. E. Replication study: A neglected aspect of psychological research. *American Psychologist*, 1970, *25*, 970–975.

Spiegel, D., and Keith-Spiegel, P. Assignment of publication credits: Ethics and practices of psychologists. *American Psychologist*, 1970, *25*, 738–747.

Sterling, T. C. Publication decisions and their possible effects of interference drawn from tests of significance—or vice versa. *Journal of the American Statistical Association*, 1959, *54*, 30–34.

Wade, N. IQ and heredity: Suspicion of fraud beclouds classic experiment, *Science*, 1976, *194*, 916–918.

Walster, G. W., and Cleary, T. A. A proposal for a new editorial policy in the social sciences. *American Statistician*, 1970, *24*, 16–19.

Whitten, P. *Analysis of the development and interaction of two innovations in educational publishing: The "managed" book and the "structured" book*. Unpublished doctoral dissertation, Harvard University, 1976.

Wolff, W. M. Publication problems in psychology and an explicit evaluation scheme for manuscripts. *American Psychologist*, 1973, *28*, 257–261.

Research Issues 14

A human being in perfection ought to always pre-serve a calm and peaceful mind, and never to allow passion or a transitory desire to disturb his tranquility. I do not think that the pursuit of knowledge is an exception to this rule. If the study to which you apply yourself has a tendency to weaken your affec-tions, and to destroy your taste for those simpler pleasures in which no alloy can possibly mix, then that study is certainly unlawful, that is to say, not benefitting the human mind.

Mary Shelly (Frankenstein, 1831)

More has been written about the ethics of social and behavioral research than all other topics in this book combined. The surge of interest in research ethics did not develop from nowhere. Consciousnesses were jolted when scientists learned of the Nazis' use of "Jews and other ethnic minorities as human sacrifices to a science gone insane" (Pattullo, 1980, p. 2), and then broadened with revelations of questionable and risky procedures used on human beings without their voluntary and informed consent in other coun-tries including the United States (see Beecher, 1966; Pappworth, 1967; Bar-ber, 1976; Swazey, 1978).

The federal government has been creating guidelines and policies for social and behavioral research for approximately two decades. (See, as examples, Ley, 1970; Wulff, 1979; Wax and Cassell 1979; Novick, 1981; Department of Health and Human Services, 1983.) Institutional review boards (IRBs) have also been established at each site that anticipates or receives federal research funds to educate scientists and to ensure that research is reviewed for ethical as well as scientific soundness. (See, for example, Curran, 1969; Nobel, 1974; Gray, 1975 and 1978; Chalkley, 1977; Gray, Cooke, and Tannenbaum, 1978; Gray and Cooke, 1980; Tanke and Tanke, 1982.)

The APA *Ethical Principles* make numerous references to research throughout the code (e.g., *EP*: 1a, b; 3d; 7e) and two of the ten major prin-ciples are concerned exclusively with research activity. Principle 9 covers research conducted with human participants, and Principle 10 deals with nonhuman participants.

Despite the fervor of activity, interest, and generation of policies related to research, ethics committees receive few complaints relating to research activities. The ideal explanation is that most research psychologists are ethical and sensitive professionals. But other possibilities surely exist. It has been demonstrated that research participants often view the issues that cause social and behavioral scientists considerable ethical concern as benign or acceptable (Wilson and Donnerstein, 1976; Sullivan and Deiker, 1973; Collins, Kuhn, and King, 1979). It may be that upset participants do not realize that they have been mistreated or are unaware of the mechanisms for pressing a complaint. Moreover, complaints may be expressed at the research institution or taken directly to the researchers themselves. Legal action is seldom taken, perhaps because ethical guidelines for research activity derive primarily in ethics codes and federal policy rather than from civil or criminal law (Swazey, 1978).

This chapter briefly explores some of the major ethical concerns that arise in social and behavioral research, including the following: investigator competency and responsibility, informed consent, risk and benefit assessment, coercion to participate, deception, privacy and confidentiality, special problems encountered in field research, and animal research. (For more detailed information on these and other topics, see Beecher, 1970; Katz, 1972; APA, 1973; Barber, Lally, Makarushka, and Sullivan, 1973; Bower and de Gasparis, 1978; Diener and Crandall, 1978; APA, 1982.)

INVESTIGATOR COMPETENCY, VALUES, AND RESPONSIBILITY

The images of "scientist" range from modern-day superheros to downright unsavory characters. The public is impressed with the dazzling technological advances and medical breakthroughs and may well expect the same gains from social and behavioral researchers, including solutions to our many psychosocial ills (see Chapter 15). Other stereotypes are far less charitable. Science fiction often promotes the image of the deranged genius who performs dastardly experiments on unwilling participants, creating mindless or controllable monsters. Sometimes the scientist is portrayed as cold and ultra-objective, without any compassion or concern. Another image is the impassioned, zealous experimenter whose disregard for the rights of participants is not so much from maliciousness as it is a casuality of obsession. Finally, there is the arrogant, paternalistic stereotype of investigators who fail to relate with participants because they are viewed as incapable of comprehending the complexities of science. In all of these unfortunate images, we find research participants viewed quite literally as *subjects*, a term defined as a person or thing under the control, influence, and

authority of another. The more recent adoption of the term "research participant," though more cumbersome than "subject," suggests a negotiated
role between equals (Keith-Spiegel, 1983).

Although the negative images are surely unfair as stereotypes, competencies and personal characteristics and values of researchers have critical
ethical implications. We have already explored the ethical problems that
arise when psychotherapists and teaching psychologists combine professional roles with self-serving motives. The same situations can threaten the
welfare of research participants as well as the integrity of science when
investigators focus too heavily on their own reputations, on publication
pressures, and on rushing to obtain funding and priority findings (see
Chapter 13). Examples of the forms such personal motives might take
include exposing participants to excessively risky procedures, using samples of convenience in a trivial manner, and designing or executing research
carelessly or hurriedly (Lewis et al., 1969).

Competency to Conduct Research

Researchers are in a unique situation compared to other types of psychologists. Although most research psychologists have had extensive training,
they are part of an enterprise that is unregulated in the·sense that *anyone* can
conduct research and attempt to publish it. Because researchers are not
required to attain certain degrees or to pass exams or to obtain other proof of
competence, peer and self-regulation of quality and ethical research practices are especially critical.

The scientific merit of a research design has been widely acknowledged
as a competence issue, but not always considered as an ethical issue with
potential consequences for participants and the knowledge-base of the
discipline. No meaningful information can result from poorly designed
studies or improperly analyzed or interpreted data (Mitchell, 1964; Edsall,
1969; Rutstein, 1969). Using human beings or animals in a flawed project
cannot be justified on any grounds. At best, the participants' efforts are
wasted and, at worst, they could be harmed. In addition, the scientific
enterprise has been failed as well.

> **Case 14-1:** Correy Lation, Ed.D., published a book about the early predictors of
> aggressive behavior patterns. Through interviews with men imprisoned for violent
> crimes, he noted that the main characteristics shared among the convicts were
> inabilities to spell or to read well as children. He concluded that a powerful predictor
> of antisocial and aggressive behavior was poor grade-school performance, espe-
> cially in the areas of reading and writing.

Much is wrong with this "research" design. The use of people who were
caught and convicted biases the sample in several ways. No control group of

people with the same general backgrounds but who were *not* violent was included. Finally, a causal inference was unwarranted. However, this case illustrates the dangers of poor research design beyond the competency issue. The general public is unlikely to judge design quality and may focus only on the conclusions. Stress and fear may well be induced among readers with children who are having problems with school achievement and, almost as problematical, some teachers may believe they have found a bizarre excuse for their inability to teach. Thus publicizing poorly formulated studies under the guise of *research* may cause widespread harm. Given recent statistical developments and vast computer capabilities, we suggest that a highly competent methodologist be consulted at the onset of a research project by those who feel weak or behind in these areas as an *ethical* as well as a scientific quality requirement.

Even the most competent of investigators face many serious dilemmas when designing their projects. Unfortunately, scientific merit and ethical matters are sometimes at odds, requiring some measure of one to be sacrificed to comply with the other. Examples include the following: fully informed and voluntary consent, which may weaken scientific validity (Rosenthal and Rosnow, 1975); the intrusion into the privacy of vulnerable people in long-term follow-up studies designed to evaluate and improve treatment techniques (Nelson and Grunebaum, 1972; Showstack et al., 1978); the requirement of base-line data requiring the withholding of treatment in single-subject designs to test the effects of treatment on self-injurious behavior patterns (Noonan and Bickel, 1981); balanced placebo designs requiring the misinforming of participants in order to reduce the effects of expectancies (Rohsenow and Marlatt, 1981); and the denial of potentially valuable treatment or programs to participants in a control group when a "true experimental design," involving randomized assignment of participants, is used (Weinstein, 1974; McLean, 1980). With sensitive and thorough advanced planning, the ethical problems can be minimized. Conner (1982), for example, makes a surprisingly good case for the use of the random assignment of clients in social program experiments, especially when the assignment to experimental and control groups is done equitably, when participants are informed in advance that they may be assigned to a control group, when the status quo is maintained (that is, no already available resources are removed from control group members), when the experimental program is not already *known* to be beneficial, and when the availability of participants exceeds the resources available to experimental group participants.

Values and the Search for Truth

Do values, besides objectivity and pursuit of knowledge, play a part in science? The traditional view of the scientist as one who uses unbiased techniques to search for objective truth is highly questionable. Research psychologists are likely to choose study topics according to their own interests and values, to use theory and methods that are currently the most popular, and to analyze data in ways that are unlikely to yield unexpected findings. Other influences may include a desire to prove a point, conforming to the demands of funding sources (which themselves reflect values in their priorities), the impact of training or discipline on how a research problem is perceived or studied, and personal needs for status and attention (Diener and Crandall, 1978). It has even been asserted that social and behavioral researchers' explanations and interpretations of findings are based as much on values and ideology as on the data (Albee, 1982). The intense debate concerning racial differences and genetic determination of intelligence is a case in point. (For examples of proponents of racial/genetically-based determinants of intelligence, see Jensen, 1969 and 1972; Shockley, 1971a and 1971b; Hernstein, 1973. For examples of their critics, see Chomsky, 1972; Kamin, 1974; Lappe, 1974; Williams, 1974; Hirsch, 1975 and 1981.)

The *Ethical Principles* do not mandate that values be excised from consideration by research psychologists. On the contrary, psychologists are admonished to use the knowledge they generate to promote human welfare (*EP*: Preamble and 9 preamble), which is in itself a value statement. However, psychologists must be objective in the application of their skills, must minimize the possibility that their findings may be misleading, must never suppress disconfirming data, to report the limitations of their data, and must acknowledge alternative hypotheses or explanations for the results of their investigations. The code notes that these matters be *especially* attended to whenever "their work touches on social policy or could conceivably be detrimental to persons in specific age, sex, ethnic, socioeconomic, or other social groups" (*EP*: 1a). Finally, psychologists are responsible for seeking ethical advice whenever scientific and human values may conflict in such a way as to compromise the spirit of any provision of the *Ethical Principles* (*EP*: 9a).

Responsibilities Toward Vulnerable Study Populations

Ethical standards related to the conduct of research with human beings are easiest to apply to participants who are fully functioning, competent, free agents with well developed senses of autonomy and established, reliable personal and financial resources. The researcher's role is to approach these people in good faith for their assistance and, if they agree to participate, to cause them no harm. Many research populations of interest to social and behavioral scientists, however, are restricted or vulnerable in ways that do not allow for large measures of self-determination (Lasagna, 1969).

When research populations are legally incompetent, consent to participate must be granted by someone (a "proxy") in addition to the participants
themselves. Psychotics, a population frequently studied by social and behavioral scientists, require special consent requirements (Stanley and
Stanley, 1981). However, minors comprise the population receiving the
most attention with regard to proxy consent. Legally, the researcher is
required to obtain consent from the parents or legal guardians, but that
procedure does not settle the ethical questions. Children, especially older
ones, are not without capacity to reason or to know what they want to do.
How much their wishes to participate should be taken into account has been
debated, eventually leading to the recommendation that the verbal child's
assent be obtained along with parental proxy consent (National Commission
for the Protection of Human Subjects of Biomedical and Behavioral Research, 1977) and that only rare exceptions involving likely and needed
benefit be allowed to override a child's wishes. (For further details on the
array of ethical issues in researching minors, see Lowe, 1970; Curran, 1974;
Lowe, Alexander, and Mishkin, 1974; Keith-Spiegel, 1976, 1983; Ferguson,
1978; Frankel, 1978; Grisso and Vierling, 1978).

Other populations require special safeguards because they may be vulnerable to exploitation due to their restrictive environments. Competent
but lonely or bored individuals residing in convalescent homes, for example, may be willing to engage in almost any research project in return for
some attention. Considerable concern has been expressed about research
that has been conducted on prisoners, a group that cannot be said to have
freedom of choice. Attitudes towards this population may not be compassionate and could translate into a justification for relaxing the ethical standards observed for others (Capron, 1973; Mitford, 1973; Rubin, 1976; Branson, 1977; Swan, 1979).

False beliefs mistakenly presumed to be objective or theoretical about a
study population's characteristics may influence investigators' perceptions
of the morality of research questions and experimental procedures. For
example, if a developmental psychologist subscribes to the theory that
children are tough and resilient, he or she may be willing to subject them to
experimental procedures that the investigator who believes that children are
highly vulnerable and fragile would be unwilling even to consider (Keith-
Spiegel,1976).

Another prevalent false belief is to assume that all members of a social
group are alike. As a consequence, the research may be designed so that it
fails to consider important factors that differentiate among members of the
population. Levin (1982), for example, discusses research on the elderly and
the ethical implications of failing to consider social class, ethnicity, race, and
sex as critical factors contributing to the understanding of old people.

Conscious or unconscious biases against a study population may affect
the research question or risks to which the participants are exposed in a way

that may cause harm to the participants themselves or perpetuate or create unfair or inaccurate generalizations about the entire study population. To the extent that researchers, most of whom are white and middle-class, see their study target population as "not like me," potential harm to participants exists unless special sensitivities are cultivated and maintained. To the extent that the study population is perceived of as inferior, more serious ethical errors are likely since such persons may be viewed as mere objects and "not quite human." Besides the aforementioned prisoners, other social categories that may be vulnerable to value biases include minority ethnic heritage groups, the poor, gays, women, and others who may be considered "deviant" (Rainwater and Pittman, 1967; Nikelly, 1971; Gray, 1971; X(Clarke), 1973; Allen, Heckel, and Garcia, 1980). Sometimes biases affecting the research may result not from assigning one's own values to the study population, but from ignorance about the cultural values and traditions of the group under investigation (Gray, 1972; Price-Williams, 1975).

Social scientists, however, rarely study people more powerful than themselves. Informal opinion seems to be that either powerful people avoid being studied or that they resist being studied using traditional techniques. For example, Mirvis and Seashore (1982) illustrate the frequent obstacles confronted when attempting to research organizations in the private sector.

CONSENT TO PARTICIPATE

The obligation to a fair and clear agreement with research participants is a primary ethical requirement. The concept and practice of informed consent originated as a protection for physicians against malpractice charges. The requirement of consent to participate in research as a protection for those participating was first stated clearly in the *Nuremburg Code* (first published in the United States in the *Journal of the American Medical Association* in 1946). Adopted as a judicial summary at the war trials of 23 Nazi physicians being indicted for crimes against humanity, the code clearly outlines the consent requirement for investigators to follow:

> The voluntary consent of the human subject is absolutely essential. This means that the person involved should have legal capacity to give consent; should be so situated as to be able to exercise free power of choice, without the intervention of any element of force, fraud, deceit, duress, overreaching, or other ulterior form of constraint or coercion; and should have sufficient knowledge and comprehension of the elements of the subject matter involved as to enable him to make an understanding and enlightened decision. The latter element requires that before the acceptance of an affirmative decision by the experimental subject there should be made known to him the nature, duration, and purpose of the experiment; the method and means by which it is to be conducted; all inconveniences and hazards reasonably to

be expected; and the effects upon his health or person which may possibly come from his participation in the experiment. The duty and responsibility for ascertaining the quality of the consent rests upon each individual who initiates, directs, or engages in the experiment. It is a personal duty and responsibility which may not be delegated to another with impunity.

Although never used as a legal precedent, the Nuremberg Code is the basis from which subsequent codes and policies were developed. The focus is currently on respecting participants' right to self-determination and autonomy by ensuring that research participation was entered into *voluntarily*, *knowingly*, and *intelligently*.

Factors complicating the voluntary and informed consent ideal arise all too easily. As we shall discuss later, "voluntariness" may often be manipulated, as when powerful incentives are offered, or the condition in which participants find themselves may preclude truly free choice (as when an employer requests an employee to complete a research questionnaire).

For a participant to understand what he or she is agreeing to do, information must be provided by the researcher and the participant must have the capacity to comprehend and evaluate it. Unfortunately, it has been documented that many legally competent adults had minimal understanding of what they agreed to (Martin, Arnold, Zimmerman, and Richard, 1968; Resnick and Schwartz, 1973; Gray, 1975; Cassileth, 1980). Furthermore, if the information offered is *too* detailed or technical, willingness to participate may decrease (Epstein and Lasagna, 1969; Berscheid, Dermer, and Libman, 1973). Many consent forms have been found to be lacking important elements (such as statements of risks or the right to withdraw) and are constructed or stated in ways that make them difficult for the average person to read (Tannenbaum and Cooke, 1976). (See Veatch, 1976, and Grunder, 1978, for helpful suggestions for improving consent forms.)

Finally, the use of deception (discussed more fully in an upcoming section) precludes obtaining fully informed consent. The use of deception is allowable under the *Ethical Principles*, though with reservation and requirements for special safeguards. The dilemma here is that the discipline of psychology cannot mandate voluntary and informed consent on the one hand, and allow the use of deceptive techniques on the other. Instead, an attempt is made to reconcile the inherent conflicts, which, in our opinion, emerge as an ambiguous stance. Specifically, the *Ethical Principles* (*EP*: 9d) state that *except* for "minimal risk" research (allowing here, for example, for naturalistic observations in public settings when the participants are not aware that their behavior is being studied), the investigator is to establish a "clear and fair agreement" with the research participants prior to data collection. Obligations and responsibilities of both investigators and participants are clarified during this phase and the investigator must honor all commitments. The investigator also informs participants of all aspects of the research that may reasonably influence willingness to become involved and answers any questions. It continues: *"Failure to make full disclosure prior to obtaining informed consent requires additional safeguards to protect the welfare and dignity of the research participants."* How one accomplishes this is left unclear. The elaboration of the research guidelines (APA, 1982) is not particularly helpful either, since this document raises the issues, asks profound questions but does not answer them, notes that psychologists differ markedly in their opinion on these matters without taking sides, and usually ends by suggesting that one should consult with others when in doubt.

VOLUNTARINESS, COERCION, AND ENTICEMENTS

Ethical research requires that participation be voluntary. However, "voluntariness" is an attribute that can be manipulated in both subtle and blatant ways.

Attracting Consent

It seems simple enough to assert that consent be obtained without exercising coercion, duress, pressure, or undue enticement or influence. Many complex factors, however, make it difficult to ensure *total* voluntariness.

It has been argued that *some* element of coercion is involved in any investigator-participant transaction. Simply being approached with a request by a person perceived as having some prestige and authority may be persuasive, especially if the researcher is enthusiastic and likeable or if the potential participant is vulnerable, deferent, needy for attention, desperate for a solution to a personal matter that relates to the subject under investigation, or is an inmate, student, or employee of the organization sponsoring the research.

The *explicit* offer of rewards, monetary or otherwise, is a controversial matter. Offering to pay participants a small amount of money to offset inconvenience and transportation costs is not considered coercive. The matter becomes more complicated, however, when the reimbursements or rewards are potentially great enough to sway participants to consent to participation for which they would not otherwise have agreed.

Case 14–2: Edward Noharm, Ph.D., complained to a university sponsor that a research project design involved tactics that were excessively enticing. In order to obtain a control group for a hospitalized experimental treatment group, the investigators approached parents in a low-income neighborhood and offered them several hundred dollars if they would allow their babies to undergo periodical laboratory tests, some of which involved considerable discomfort. Dr. Noharm argued that the control group children could in no way benefit from the study and that the offer to financially limited parents of such a large sum constituted a persuasion that could override concern for their children's welfare and best interests.

Case 14–3:   Mimi Dogood, Psy.D., complained to a state legislature that prisoners were being subjected to poorly designed, dangerous experimentation procedures in return for three dollars a day. Ironically, the prisoners objected to her intervention by noting that the money was sufficient to keep them supplied with cigarettes, candy, and other small items that made a big difference in the quality of their daily lives.

Both cases illustrate how people of limited means or opportunities may accept attractive enticements or even rewards that others with easy access to the free-enterprise system would see as trivial. The *Ethical Principles* do not directly address the issue of enticements to participate although the issue is briefly discussed in the context of "coercion" in the elaboration of Principle 9 of the code (APA, 1982). The APA document specifies that when participants have very strong needs resulting in little potential for rejecting incentives related to those needs, an investigator should never offer such incentives without first obtaining ethical advice from consultants. This advice could maintain the potential for abuse, however, depending on the sensitivity and wisdom of those one consults.

We ran into an unusual appeal that essentially turned participation into a sweepstakes.

Case 14–4:   A survey form sent to a large sample of students at a university for the purpose of assessing student needs and interests also advertised cash prize drawings from completed survey forms: "To add a note of fun—and, frankly, because we want to encourage your response, we have developed an incentive contest. First prize will be $50; second prize will be $25; and third prize will be $15."

Although this particular survey did not request any sensitive information, and it did take precautions to separate the participants' identity from the data, and it was conducted for the ultimate benefit of the respondents and their peers, such practices are *not* recommended for general research use.

A more subtle form of coercion has been described by Freedman and Fraser (1966) as the "foot-in-the-door" technique. These authors experimentally confirmed that participants were more likely to comply with a larger request if they had previously complied to a small request. The case below illustrates this phenomenon more concretely.

Case 14–5:   Hester Twostep, Ph.D., recruited participants to complete a brief questionnaire on attitudes toward contemporary sexual mores. After completion, Dr. Twostep told the participants that she would appreciate their cooperation in filling out a lengthy questionnaire about their own sexual practices. The participants were not informed of the second phase prior to taking the short, less-sensitive questionnaire. Several participants later expressed that they felt uncomfortable and "trapped."

Another common form of more subtle coercion involves appeals to the participants' sense of altruism. These can range from the researcher's personal pleas for help to suggestions that cooperation will benefit humankind or advance science. Noncompliance may be experienced as indicating selfishness. To the extent that investigators genuinely need participants and are sincere in their beliefs that their studies are valuable efforts, some level of altruistic appeal is unavoidable and perhaps not inappropriate as long as undue social pressure is not involved (Ferguson, 1978). It has been found that both adults and children are quite capable of refusing strong altruistic appeals to induce participation in painful or upsetting procedures (Keith-Spiegel and Maas, Note 1).

Social pressure can be powerful, however, as the following case illustrates.

Case 14−6:   Betty Roundup, Ph.D., asked her students to do her a favor by staying after class for a few minutes to fill out a research questionnaire on male-female relationships. She added that this task was voluntary, but when Skip Busy began to leave, she said, "Well, I'm certainly glad that the *rest* of you are willing to help me out." Skip sat back down, but was embarrassed and felt he had jeopardized his standing with the professor.

Skip's rights were clearly violated in this case (*EP:* 9d and f). Dr. Roundup's initial tactic is questionable in the first place. She has power over the participants in her professorial role, and they may feel pressured to comply. Then Dr. Roundup proceeded to sabotage her own statement of voluntariness by publicly humiliating the individual who desired to exercise this option.

The researcher must be careful not to create motives or needs artificially through coercive maneuvers such as suggesting that declining to participate is a sign of weakness or immaturity (APA, 1982). Similarly, participants may discount any potential risks in the hope of securing needed benefits, or they may think that needed services are contingent on participation in research. Any such misconceptions should be corrected. To hold treatment services that would otherwise be available as "ransom" constitutes unethical coercion.

Case 14−7:   When the baby of Mazy Duped convulsed, a researcher with the hospital plan in which Mazy's infant was enrolled approached her and indicated that the baby required a follow-up EEG to ensure that no brain damage had occurred. The anxious mother appeared with the baby at the follow-up appointment at which time she was told that the EEG was the first phase of a longitudinal research program on infants who had sustained convulsions. Mazy indicated that she did not want her baby to be studied, but that she did want the EEG results because she had been told that these might offer some significant information about the infant's condition. The researcher told her that unless she cooperated in the study, the EEG would not be run. Mazy reluctantly signed the research consent form, but remained uncomfortable with her decision and resented being forced to comply with the additional requirements of the study, which she did not fully understand.

Psychology's Human "Fruit Flies"

Almost 40 years ago, Quinn McNemar (1946) referred to psychology as "largely the science of the behavior of sophomores" (p. 333). College students do comprise the majority of psychology research participants and large proportions of these are recruited through "subject pools" (Rosenthal and Rosnow, 1969; Menges, 1973). Typically participants are offered some credit in their introductory psychology courses and thereby create a convenient, inexpensive study population (Rubenstein, 1982). Although the use of college recruits has been debated on grounds of methodological and other biases (Cox and Sipprelle, 1971; Oakes, 1972), concerns about coercion and related forms of exploitation have been raised, especially if alternative ways of satisfying course requirements are not offered or are noxious or excessively time-consuming, if students receive no worthwhile feedback, and if no readily accessible complaint resource is provided (Diener and Crandall, 1978). It should be noted, however, that surveys have generally shown positive ratings of experiences by subject pool participants (Britton, 1979; Leak, 1981). Still, it has been recommended that ethical use of student subject pools requires the following: (1) that credit be "extra," that is, added *after* the course performance grade has been computed giving the students the possibility of enhancing their grades rather than jeopardizing them in any way, and (2) that considerable attention and effort be placed into ensuring that the students gain some educational value (e.g., through feedback or a discussion of the studies).

The American Psychological Association (APA, 1982) offers several additional guidelines for subject pools although, curiously, APA waivers on several important issues. For example, instead of arguing against the inappropriateness of giving students lower grades and/or an "incomplete" grade on the basis of their research participation assignment, the APA document merely notes that some critics think such practices are inappropriate. APA holds that students must be fully informed of any penalties imposed for failure to complete the requirement or for nonappearance after agreeing to take part in a study. It is our belief that these practices run contrary to the basic ethical premises of voluntariness and freedom to withdraw at any time.

Freedom to Withdraw

Freedom from undue persuasion to participate does not end at the start of the experiment (APA, 1982; *EP*: 9f). Investigators must remain sensitive to participants' needs and to cues that withdrawal from the experiment is being contemplated because, after participants agree to take part in a study, the demand characteristics of the situation enhance the perceived power of the investigator, increase the participants' compliance, and alter the meaning attached to the task (Kelman, 1972; Orne, 1962).

Despite the disappointments that investigators undoubtedly experience when occasionally participants change their minds midcourse (*especially* if it occurs well into a complicated or longitudinal study), the right to withdraw, with rare exceptions, should be honored and should be made explicit during the initial consent phase. Withdrawal privilege may be overridden when the participant is legally or mentally incompetent and the experimental intervention may provide significant benefit to the person's health and welfare, if it is available *only* in a research context, and other alternatives have been exhausted or are unavailable (National Commission for the Protection of Human Subjects in Biomedical and Behavioral Research, 1977).

The wise investigator, whose goal is to obtain useful and valid data, will not only refrain from the use of coercion to gain consent, but will also be alert to signs of discomfort and anxiousness during the data collection. For example, children rarely specifically request permission to withdraw, but behavioral indicators (e.g., passivity, off-task activity, excessive yawning, random responses, and hand and foot dancing) and spontaneous comments (e.g., frequently asking, "When will we be done?" and responding repeatedly to age-appropriate questions with, "I don't know") suggest that the investigator initiate an inquiry concerning the child's wishes (Keith-Speigel, 1983).

Occasionally, participants may request that their data be withdrawn *after* it has been collected. Although this issue is not addressed in the *Ethical Principles*, APA (1982) has confirmed that data withdrawal be offered and honored during the debriefing session if deceptive techniques were used. However, if genuine informed consent was given, the experimenter is under no special obligation to provide this opportunity at the close of the data collection sessions.

ASSESSING BENEFITS AND RISKS

Potential Benefits

The potential benefits of a research project are virtually impossible to estimate. By definition, an experimental procedure is conducted to provide answers to heretofore unanswered questions. If a procedure or technique were *known* to be beneficial to participants, it would not be necessary to conduct research on that population. As Pryce (1978) explains, "It is not sufficient to say that a beneficial result is intended, since this glosses over the element of doubt which is always present in any procedure which is new and experimental, however good the theoretical reasons may be for expecting a beneficial outcome" (p. 366).

Ironically, despite the inherent impossibility of accurately predicting benefits, the assessment of potential benefit is a critical factor in judging the ethicality of research, especially if the participants are simultaneously placed at risk as a result of their participation.

Benefit assessment for biomedical research, as opposed to social and behavioral research, is often easier to reckon with. This is especially true in therapeutic research involving a potential remedy for an "incurable" disease when all known ameliorative treatments have been attempted and have failed to improve the condition of the study population. In social and behavioral research, the concept of benefit may exist primarily in the eye of the beholder since perceptions regarding what is "good" or "bad" for people vary according to one's theoretical or value system as opposed to the widely held agreement that "physically healthy" is better than "sick." For example, a psychologist may study ways to enhance children's assertiveness, figuring that early training in "asking for what you want" will provide young people with coping skills that will serve them well, increase independence, and elevate self-concept. A critic might argue that "assertive children" would be perceived by adults as bratty, selfish, demanding, and disrespectful and that to encourage youngsters to be assertive, given our present expectations for appropriate child behavior, would actually put them at risk in their homes and in the traditional school system.

The "benefit" test has also been debated regarding *who* or *what* may be the recipient. Some argue that the benefit test should be applied strictly to the research participants: that is, as a result of participation, some benefit might reasonably be expected to accrue directly. Others would say that it is not necessary to expect that benefits may be experienced by the participants of a given investigation, but that some likelihood exists for the possibility that the results may be useful in the conduct of future studies that may eventually provide beneficial findings. Indeed science is a continuous and evolving process, and important findings can often be traced to the end of a chain of individual studies, with some tributary links leading to dead-ends. Others hold that society is the acceptable beneficiary rather than the actual participants. Finally, there are those who believe that the benefit test is inappropriate altogether since the process of knowledge accumulation is in itself valuable regardless of whether anyone, including society, benefits directly or indirectly from it.

Some social and behavioral scientists have described the concept of benefit in yet another way. Here the definition applies not so much to the research outcome, but to the *experience* of participation. Bower and de Gasparis (1978) assert that benefit can accrue to the participants in the forms of feeling good about contributing to science, enjoying the experimental procedure, and/or learning something new and interesting through discussions and feedback from investigators.

Assessing Risks

The *Ethical Principles* do not dwell on the specifics of how to assess benefits and make only vague references to them (e.g., research psychologists are to consider how best to contribute to psychology and human welfare). The focus is on risks although, as we will see in the next section, the acceptability of risk levels varies with judgments of potential for benefit.

Three of the *Ethical Principles* under the main section dealing with research on human beings are concerned with risk: the responsibility to assess its potential (*EP*: 9b); the requirement to protect participants from physical or mental discomfort or to gain fully informed consent if its potential reasonably exist (*EP*: 9g); and the requirement to detect and alleviate any negative consequences that may have arisen as a result of participation (*EP*: 9i).

Risks involved in psychological research, however, are usually trivial compared to those in biomedical research (Reynolds, 1972; APA, 1982). Among the more serious risks that may be present in social and behavioral research are invasion of privacy, breach of confidentiality, stress and discomfort, loss of self-esteem, negative reactions to being deceived, reactions to being induced to commit reprehensible acts, and a host of "collective risks" wherein harm to the participants or others may result upon publication and interpretation of the findings (Reiss, 1976; Bower and de Gasparis, 1978; Diener and Crandall, 1978; APA, 1982). The next case illustrates harm caused by subjecting a person to risk in social and behavioral research.

Case 14-8:   Diane Crushed, a college sophomore, complained that Mike Deflate, Ph.D., caused her considerable stress as a result of her participation in his study. She had agreed to take a "life-goals inventory" and a "graduate school potential test" one week and to be interviewed the following week. After completing the tests during the first session, Dr. Deflate "scored" them and informed Ms. Crush that she was not graduate school material and should consider alternatives. Because she had the singular ambition to be an English professor, the incident made her extremely depressed. She even considered dropping out of school during the next week, but did show up for the scheduled interview. After assessing the impact of the first session, Dr. Deflate informed her that the "life-goals inventory" was a legitimate measure, but that the other "test" was not meaningful and that he had never really scored it at all. He explained that he was interested in assessing how the strength and clarity of life goals would be affected by "encouraging" and "discouraging" evaluations and she was part of the latter sample. He assured her that her goals should remain as they were before and that this experiment was irrelevant in assessing her potential for success. However, Ms. Crushed was not entirely disabused in the sense that the process of self-doubt had been put into motion and did not markedly abate, even by the time she entered an ethics complaint three months later.

Ms. Crushed had been placed at risk in several ways. The experiment itself involved deception and delayed "debriefing" (*EP*: 9e). Her self-esteem was purposely deflated. To use Holmes's (1976) system of analysis, Ms. Crushed was eventually "dehoaxed" but *not* effectively "desensitized." She was a sensitive person and possibly more vulnerable to harm than were other participants. In his defense, Dr. Deflate noted that no other student in that sample complained. Rather, they often simply accepted his explanation, occasionally expressing some relief. Of course, it may well have been that others were as upset as Ms. Crushed, but were not assertive or resourceful enough to complain. In any event, an ethics committee expressed concern that the manipulation was excessive and judged that the study was not important enough to justify it. The delay of one week greatly exacerbated the effect of the deceptive tactic. Furthermore, the committee argued that a creative design, *not* involving manipulated deception or risk of harm, could have been devised to answer the research question. For example, students could have been given the life-goals inventory and then interviewed upon receiving *genuine* positive or negative performance evaluations based on their academic work. This may not be as powerful a manipulation and most certainly would have required more planning and effort on the part of the investigator. However, the serious ethical problems would be avoided.

Predicting risk occurrence may be especially difficult in social and behavioral sciences because of the seemingly infinite variety of ways people respond to psychological phenomena. What one may find frightening or stressful, another may experience as exciting or pleasurably novel. Being asked to touch a live snake or view a pornographic movie are two such examples. Prescreening of potential participants and careful monitoring during the study trials should be used whenever a question exists. The wise investigator will also prepare for the possibility that the most seemingly benign request may cause discomfort to sensitive participants.

Case 14−9: Cresti Fallen participated in a student's research project as part of her introductory psychology course requirement. The student researcher asked Cresti to categorize brief selections of popular music according to the emotional reactions each evoked. When the student researcher played one particular song, Cresti broke down in uncontrollable tears. The inexperienced researcher terminated the session and, in an attempt to be helpful, suggested that Cresti go see a psychotherapist because she "needed help badly." This only intensified Cresti's discomfort, and she bolted from the research cubicle. No follow-up intervention was attempted. The following week, Cresti complained to the department chair about the project and the "insulting" comment made by the student researcher. She also explained that the song that had elicited such a strong emotional reaction was *the* song between her and her ex-boyfriend who had dropped her for another woman two days before she participated in the study.

There was no way the student researcher could have anticipated that Cresti or any other participant might react in this way. However, the researcher's handling of the matter was rather crude and only complicated the problem. It is worth noting here that much research is conducted by undergraduates as part of their training. Even though their efforts are unlikely to be published, leading us to sometimes think of such exercises as not being *real* research, human participants are involved and deserve the *same* treatment and protection provided in any other experimental effort. Ideally, all students who collect data should undergo training in dealing with upset participants and a supervisor should be close at hand. Even if a student researcher mishandles a participant, despite any good intentions, the incident should be reported *immediately* to the supervisor and ameliorative intervention steps taken.

Another complicating problem relative to risk assessment is that many contemplated techniques or study approaches have never been tried before and pretesting with animals or less vulnerable participants (i.e., free-agent, competent adults) may not be feasible. The degree of risk under these conditions may simply be unknown. In general, the conservative ethical stance is to assume the possibility of risk and to respond to the guidelines for consent acquisition accordingly.

Study populations who are easily identifiable and/or already vulnerable or oppressed are especially vulnerable to a risk known as "social injury." An ever-present concern is that the results or the way they are interpreted will lead to humiliation, harm, or justification for continued or further discrimination.

Risk/Benefit Analysis and Risk Minimization

Despite the difficulties inherent in adequately defining and predicting risks and benefits, ethical guidelines typically request that one be balanced against another in order to determine the acceptability of a research proposal. Diener and Crandall (1978), for example, state that the cost/benefit analysis can be viewed as a modern restatement of the moral proposition that the end justifies the means. In general, the level of acceptable risk can be greater if the research is intended to be "therapeutic," especially if the participants require some form of intervention and it is available only in the research context.

The investigator must consider whether any negative effects are warranted by the importance of the research (APA, 1982). Yet it is a difficult question to decide how the cost to individual participants can be weighed against benefits to them, psychological science, or society.

Certainly, a critical step in making such decisions involves risk minimization. A variety of strategies have been proposed. Many occur during the design phase. Levine (1975) outlines several dimensions along which the intensity of harm may vary: likelihood of risk occurrence, severity, duration, reversibility of effects, and potential for early detection. Diener and Crandall (1978) add yet another: the degree of similarity and potential for occurrence to the risks of everyday life. The closer a design falls to the "safe" end of each continuum, the fewer the ethical problems. Zeisel (1970) formulated several design techniques that may be useful in reducing risk occurrence. These techniques include keeping the number of people exposed to risky treatment at a minimum, making the experimental treatment the one that is expected to have favorable results, and using sequential designs (e.g., the "play-the-winner" design), and computed baseline designs whenever possible. Usually subjecting a control group to a "best-known" treatment is more ethical than is using a no treatment or placebo design.

Active solicitation of consultation during the design planning phase is an important type of risk minimization. It is suggested that colleagues who are not "just like you" and representatives of the study population itself may provide especially useful information. However, collegial review cannot be used to diffuse the ultimate responsibility of the investigator (APA, 1982).

Consideration of alternative procedures, even if they are more cumbersome and less powerful, should also be an integral part of the design phase. Sometimes animals may be appropriate. Or less vulnerable human participants (e.g, free-agent, competent adults) would often be more appropriate than using children or some other vulnerable population. Sometimes populations already in the risky state of study interest (e.g., depressed people or those functioning under high stress) may be available. If consent is not obtained in a coercive manner and if the participants' condition is not unnecessarily prolonged due to research design requirements, ethical problems are minimized. Cook (1976) adds a final wise criterion for minimizing risk during the design phase. He suggests that investigators should be willing to submit their own family members to the procedures they design for use on others.

Once the study design is complete, additional steps to minimize risk should be taken prior to full-scale data collection. Role-playing sessions or small-scale pilot studies may assist the investigator in learning more about the risk effects and how they are evaluated. Farr and Seaver (1975), for example, present some interesting data on participants' perceptions of stress and physical discomfort levels while contemplating subjection to various experimental procedures. Attempts to screen out individuals for whom risks would be high is another important consideration.

During the data collection phase, other safeguards can also be instituted. Safety precautions may include careful monitoring of the functioning of any apparatus, careful observation of individual participants for signs of adverse reactions, continued assurance of freedom to end participation at any point, available back-up resources (perhaps a clinical psychologist) for instances involving distraught participants, and post-session interviews (Diener and Crandall, 1978; APA, 1982).

Removing Negative Consequences

Removing or ameliorating known or unintended and unforeseen negative consequences that may arise as a result of research-related participation is a responsibility of the investigator (*EP*: 9i). Monetary compensation mechanisms have been proposed (Silverstein, 1974; President's Commission for the study of Ethical Problems in Medicine and Biomedical and Behavioral Research, 1982) and "malresearch insurance" may become increasingly desirable and available.

Post-experimental checks, as well as long-term follow-up studies, may be required to ensure that any consequences are indeed removed. Whenever vulnerable populations are used, special safeguards must be instituted to ensure that no harm befell the participants. It is also implied that the investigator incurs special responsibility to control group members. When appropriate, they are exposed to a treatment of known benefit instead of no treatment. However, if the experimental treatment proved efficacious, efforts should be made to offer it to control group members (APA, 1982).

DECEPTION AND CONCEALMENT

The most profound ethical dilemmas in social and behavioral research on humans involve misinforming participants about the nature or purpose of the study during the consent phase ("deception") and/or omitting information that might reasonably be expected to alter the consent decision ("concealment"). When either technique is used, consent is "uneducated."

Deception techniques range markedly from outright lies or concealment of risks to mild or ambiguous forms. Sieber (1982c) has created a taxonomy of seven varieties of deception, which include self-deception, third-person deception, offering false information, offering no information, and forewarning (informed consent about the deception to be used, consent to be deceived, and obtaining waivers to inform). Each has its own potential for harms and wrongs to participants, although the nature of the actual experiment is an important determinant of whether these problems will materialize. For example, the offering of no information means that the participants do not even know they are being observed for research purposes. Yet *what* behavior is being observed in *what* setting for *what* purpose are critical factors in assessing the appropriateness of the technique. Public behavior in the context where one expects to be observed is quite different from behavior carried out in a private setting with the assumption that no one is watching (Sieber, 1982d).

Deception, however, may often be unintentional. For example, despite an investigator's sincere desire to disclose all aspects of a study purpose, some aspects may remain unexplained and/or the information offered may not be fully understood by the participants. It is the *intentional* use of deception that we are concerned with here.

The Ethical Principles state that when psychologists fail to make full disclosures prior to obtaining consent, additional safeguards are required to protect the welfare and dignity of the research participants (*EP*: 9d). In addition, the code affirms that methodological requirements may make deception or concealment necessary, which carries the additional responsibilities to determine if the use of such techniques can be justified by the study's prospective value, to determine if any alternative, nondeceptive procedures exist to reach the same goals and to provide the participants with a sufficient explanation as soon as possible (*EP*: 9e).

Deception is often treated as an embarrassing relative within psychology— not something we are proud of, but what can you do when it is part of the family? The arguments favoring its continued use often revolve around the assertion that a considerable amount of useful, valid knowledge could never be accumulated if the participants had foreknowledge of the purpose of the study and/or its procedures (Smith, 1981; Baron, 1982). That psychological research uses deception regularly has been confirmed by Stricker (1967) and Menges (1973), with both authors finding that about 19% of published research intentionally used deception techniques.

Despite the allowance of deception in psychological research, the moral acceptability continues to be questioned among many in the professional community. Critics argue that deception, by definition, compromises the consent agreement, which means the following: that condoning such procedures condones lying; that the public increasingly sees social scientists as a manipulative, exploitative, suspicious group and loses trust in the profession as a result; that the assumption of the efficacy of deceptive practices has not been adequately tested and that other serious methodological shortcomings abound, which contaminate the validity of findings; that such techniques provide a quick, noncreative, and undesirable short-cut to more careful, clever, and ultimately higher level moral and scientific experimentation; and that degradation, embarrassment, anger, disillusionment, and other harms and wrongs are ever-present dangers to "duped" participants (Baumrind, 1976; Kelman, 1967; Stricker, 1967; Stricker, Messick, and Jackson, 1969; Seeman, 1969; Cook et al., 1970; Warwick, 1975; Weinrach and Ivey, 1975).

Although ethics committees receive very few research-related complaints, when they do surface they are most likely to involve negative reactions to being misled or deceived. The next case is typical.

Case 14–10: Tillie Testy was outraged concerning a research study unwittingly conducted on her and her classmates by her professor, Henry Sneak, Ed.D. The students had been told that they would be taking a multiple-choice test on a given day that would cover certain text readings. On exam day, another person entered the room, explained that Dr. Sneak was ill and had been unable to prepare the test, so an essay question would be substituted. The person wrote a question, unrelated to the assigned readings, on the board. After ten minutes, Dr. Sneak entered the room and explained that he was doing a study on the effects of confusion and stress and asked the students to fill out a brief questionnaire. He then handed out the *real* exams and told the students to "carry on." Ms. Testy was upset not only because she was deceived, but also because she was forced to attempt to function on an exam that would actually be graded immediately following what were, for her, some acutely tense moments.

An ethics committee agreed that expecting students to perform on an exam that would be evaluated for a grade right after a disruptive incident manufactured by the professor to fulfill his own needs was unfair to his students. Further concerns were expressed by the committee in this instance because the study was judged to be poorly conceived and unlikely to contribute any new or useful knowledge.

Psychologists are obligated to "come clean" with their participants in a timely fashion after data collection (*EP*: 9h and i). The procedures for doing this are described by various names, some distinguished by the nature of the investigatory procedures used, which include "post-investigation clarification," "dehoaxing," "desensitization," "disabusing," and, most commonly, "debriefing." The goal of the clarification procedure is to correct any misconceptions or supply any information purposely withheld in a sensitive and educational manner so that the participants can understand and accept the reasons offered, including the requirement for deception, and they can feel satisfied with the experience.

However, this procedure may in and of itself cause harm, particularly if the participants were chosen for inclusion in the first place because of some deficit or if their performance under pretenses revealed behavior that was, in retrospect, embarrassing. Baumrind (1976) speaks of debriefing as "inflicted insight," which may, of course, not always be welcomed! Sieber (1982e) notes that a thorough debriefing may be unnecessary or even harmful when the behavior under investigation is socially perceived as negative and when that behavior is typical of the subject. In this instance, very general information about the study may be offered. Debriefing may be withheld when a deception study is of long duration or when the deception would reflect so badly on the scientist or science that it is deemed best to keep participants ignorant. However, in these last two instances, the circumstances for deceiving and not debriefing are extremely difficult to justify on ethical grounds (Sieber, 1982e).

We know little about the effectiveness of debriefing, and we may inappropriately rely on it as a ameliorative step (Walster et al., 1967; Ring, Wallston,and Corey, 1970; Geller, 1982). In short, debriefing must be done with great care and sensitivity, because it is an extremely complicated and delicate procedure (Holmes, 1976; Mills, 1976; Tesch, 1977; Sieber, 1982e) lest reactions, such as those revealed in the following case, ensue.

Case 14–11:   Morty Fide complained to an ethics committee that he was disillusioned and angered by an experience associated with participation in a study conducted by Bambi Boozle, Ph.D. After he engaged in what he thought was a simple activity-preference questionnaire and line-length estimate task with several other participants, he was told that he had been selected into the "high femininity" group on the basis of his questionnaire score and that the other "participants" were actually stooges attempting to influence his judgments of line length. Morty stated that the explanation was perfunctory and that his expressions of concern about the femininity classification and a desire for more information about the study purpose were met with, "I'm too busy to go into that now."

Dr. Boozle caused more harm to the participant during the debriefing than if she had kept Morty uninformed. However, leaving the participant blissfully in the dark is not an acceptable alternative. Dr. Boozle should have been available to Morty for as long as he reasonably required an explanation, and she should have been more delicate in her explanation approach. Morty should have been offered an opportunity to have the data based on his participation withdrawn, as is required during the debriefing stage. In other words, one asks at *this* point for the voluntary and informed consent to use data already collected.

The next case illustrates a far better attempt to ameliorate the damages caused by deception and a more firmly grounded research endeavor.

Case 14–12:   Amy Bushed was outraged to learn that the purpose of a study was not to evaluate her ratings of the film she was shown, but rather to observe her reactions to a young man's crude and forceful attempts to convince a disinterested and protesting young woman to leave the theater with him and go for a ride. Although she said and did nothing, Amy was very upset by the young man's behavior and concerned about the young woman's welfare. When Amy learned that the entire incident was staged just so others could observe her reaction, her guilt over her non-involvement turned to rage and insult. The committee also learned that the investigator and his assistant spent more than an hour with Amy, attempting to explain why the study had to be done that way and why the information would be useful and important. They also reassured her that her response was not uncommon and that she should not feel badly about herself.

The committee did not sustain an ethics charge in this case because the procedures had undergone intensive scrutiny prior to data collection and attempts, including follow-ups, were made to ameliorate Amy's reactions. The study was also judged to be of great importance since it dealt with a topic of social significance. Many young women are forcefully abducted in front of witnesses who do not get involved. The researchers were interested in discovering the characteristics of people and situational contexts that differentiated "helpers" from "nonhelpers" and to perhaps apply them in some way. Yet, regardless of the absence of findings by an ethics committee, it must not be forgotten that a human participant remained emotionally upset for an extended period of time as a result of her willingness to contribute to scientific discovery.

A number of alternatives to deceptive techniques have been proposed, mostly involving some form of forewarning, role enactment, or simulation (see Forward, Canter, and Kirsch, 1976; Cooper, 1976; Diener and Crandall, 1978; Geller, 1982). We encourage serious consideration of every possible alternative to the use of deception techniques since the ethical pitfalls and potential for wronging or harming participants, *particularly* if the study invades privacy or involves behavior that may not be socially acceptable, are ever present.

RESEARCH OUTSIDE THE LABORATORY

The bulk of the discussions in this chapter apply to work conducted in a traditional laboratory setting. It must be at least briefly noted that a substantial amount of social and behavioral science data are collected "in the streets." In these instances, some laboratory setting ethics do not translate well to community or field settings, and new ethical dilemmas not relevant to traditional research settings present themselves.

Despite the thorny ethical problems inherent in much of the outside-of-the-laboratory research, it has been argued that laboratory settings are susceptible to numerous artifacts that reduce the validity of the findings (Wilson and Donnerstein, 1976) and that many important varieties of behavior are not amenable to observation in laboratory situations. Thus we again face the dilemma of scientific validity versus the ethics of the procedures used to gain and advance knowledge.

Unobtrusive Observation and Nonreactive Study Methods

Social psychologists often use "non-reactive methods" wherein the participants are not aware that they are being observed, thus precluding any advance voluntary and informed consent contracts. Sometimes the participants are simply observed in given settings (e.g., a rock concert) without involvement of any experimental manipulation. Sometimes the context is contrived (e.g., observing people's reactions to an unusual object placed on the sidewalk by the experimenters). At other times, the participants are deceived and their reactions observed (e.g., a confederate of the experimenter poses as an obnoxious store customer, while another confederate observes the salesperson's reaction). The *Ethical Principles* (*EP*: 9d) leave the door a crack open for such research by noting that consent is mandatory, "except for minimal-risk research." Yet the question remains whether such research always falls under the definition of "minimal risk" since invasion of privacy and deception are often involved, and both are typically considered sufficient conditions to constitute risk. Opinions regarding the ethicality and legality of nonreactive methods vary markedly among social scientists, legal scholars, and the public (Silverman, 1975; Nash, 1975; Wilson and Donnerstein, 1976). Since it is usually impossible to assess whether harm befell any of the participants, due to the fact that their actual identities are rarely discernible precluding follow-up assessment, nonreactive study techniques will likely continue to be debated regarding their ethical acceptability (see Erikson, 1967; Denzin, 1968; Brandt, 1972; Redlich, 1973; Sechrest, 1976; Schwartz and Gottlieb, 1980, 1981).

Ethical problems are minimized if nonobtrusive observations of public behavior are made in such a way that the data cannot be linked directly to those being observed. Technological advances allowing for visual and/or audio recordings of people's behavior using portable and easily concealed equipment complicate the ethical problems because a permanent record results, which heightens the potential for identification of the unwitting participants. When the participants perceive themselves to be in a private setting (e.g., in a public bathroom or in their own homes), additional ethical issues arise when experimenters intrude themselves surreptitiously into these environments (APA, 1982). As examples, see Koocher's (1977) criticisms of the Middlemist et al. (1976) study involving the effects of confederate "crowding" in an university lavatory on urination flow; Warwick's (1973) and Sieber's (1982a) concerns about Humphreys' (1970) classic "tearoom trade" study involving the author's observations of homosexual contacts in public restrooms while serving as a volunteer "watchqueen"; and Cook's (1975) ethical analysis of the West, Gunn, and Chernicky (1975) "ubiquitous Watergate" study involving attempts to induce participants to agree to commit burglary.

Ethnographic Fieldwork

Fieldwork is no longer confined to anthropological investigations of exotic cultures. Study populations, such as the dying, draft dodgers, hospital wards, political party workers, and so on, have been increasingly interesting to other varieties of social scientists including psychologists (Sieber, 1982a). Significant differences exist between fieldwork studies and laboratory research raising some special ethical concerns. To some extent, the investigators' power is reduced since they are operating on the turf of the host population and must rely on its members (the informants) for accurate data. The host group may well have agendas of expectancies for gain or advocacy from the fieldworker and these must be clearly understood by the investigator. There are no research designs or measurements in the usual sense, placing a heavy responsibility to engage in sensitive, compassionate, yet objective accumulation of information and to ensure that the host group has not been harmed as a result of being observed and studied. "Informed consent" may not be so much at issue as establishing clearly understood reciprocity agreements. When covert observation is used, additional ethical dilemmas accrue. Many have eschewed the use of misleading a host population believing it to be exploitative. Others suggest that the understanding of populations of considerable interest, such as organized crime members (Chambliss, 1975), could not be studied by other than deceptive means. (For excellent discussions of the ethics of fieldwork, see Appel, 1971; Cassell, 1982; Wax, 1982; Glazer, 1982; Johnson, 1982.)

Primary Prevention Research and Programming

Primary prevention/intervention programming differs from the above types of nonlaboratory based research in that benefit to the participants in the "treatment" group is *always* intended. In general, people judged to be "at risk" for some potential maladjustment are recruited to participate in a program designed to reduce their risk level so that the maladjustment will not ultimately manifest itself. "At risk" populations that have been studied include children with schizophrenic parents, recently divorced people, preschoolers from disadvantaged homes, parents fitting patterns indicating that they might be susceptible to abusing their children, and people functioning under high stress conditions. Educational, psychotherapeutic, and coping-building skill training are among the interventions frequently used.

Such research activity is often regarded as exceptionally humanistic since it attempts to discover ways to minimize human suffering by intervening *prior* to evolvement of full-scale maladjustment or damage. It is also viewed as cost-effective and expedient because it conforms to the old saying, "An ounce of prevention is worth a pound of cure."

However, several profound ethical issues lurk just below the surface, and investigators in this line of work should be ever cognizant of them. Questions of ethics arise from a number of sources including research ethicists, social activists, and members of the target study populations themselves (Keith-Spiegel, Note 2). For example, ideologies frequently enter into attempts to define *what* should be prevented. Political and social value implications abound whenever things are done to large groups (Kessler and Albee, 1975). Problems can arise whenever the values of the researchers are at variance with the cultural values and traditions of the target groups, especially since most are underprivileged or vulnerable in other ways. Since the participants, by definition, have *not* presented diagnosable symptomatology relative to the purpose of the intervention, two additional issues arise. First, risk-level assignment is an imprecise art and the potential for harm is present whenever those decisions were made inappropriately. Following directly from risk-level assignment is the process of "labeling" participants as "at risk" for something *not yet manifested*, and the label may carry stigma or other consequences that may limit their access to opportunity and growth (Hobbs, 1975; Stanley and Stanley, 1981). Another dilemma involves intruding into people's private lives to "treat" them for a condition they do not yet have. We must remember that even the fluoridation of water, vaccination requirements, and built-in seat-belts have been resisted by many on the grounds that personal freedom of choice is simultaneously denied (Kessler and Albee, 1975).

Because the definition of primary prevention is elusive, leading Cowan (1977) to describe it as a "glittering, diffuse, abstract term," and the desirable outcomes (dependent variables) are often vague (such as "security," "adjustment," and "well-being"), the scientific design aspects are even more problematic than were discussed in an earlier section of this chapter. Finally, primary prevention programming research is more likely than most other types of research to create dependencies. Researchers must be careful not to dump the participants, as soon as data are collected, leaving them as resourceless (or more so) than before.

Our examples of outside-of-the-laboratory research techniques are hardly exhaustive. (For more information on other techniques, including survey research, see Sieber, 1982a and 1982b.)

PRIVACY AND CONFIDENTIALITY ISSUES IN RESEARCH

The psychologists' responsibilities to maintain confidentiality and the conditions under which information shared in confidence can be disclosed to others were discussed in Chapter 3, though primarily in the context of psychotherapy practice. Numerous parallels between client-therapist and participant-researcher relationships relative to the maintenance of confidentiality are appropriate since the general *Ethical Principles* pertaining to confidentiality (*EP*: 5) do not exclude research-related conduct. However, striking differences between the two professional activities create additional dilemmas for the research psychologist. Psychotherapy clients usually present themselves for care and realize they are receiving psychotherapeutic services. Research participants are usually actively sought out and, as we have seen, do not always know or understand that they are being studied. Psychotherapists are performing a service and the process of therapy is in itself the goal of the activity. Data collection, on the other hand, is the means by which an end is to be achieved—namely the dissemination of the aggregate findings to the profession and the public-at-large. The therapist, because of the intimate and ongoing nature of the relationship, usually has a good sense of what information would be damaging to a client should it be known to others. The researcher, however, typically lacks such knowledge because the relationship is more formal, superficial, and narrowly confined to a specific study purpose. In general, then, the psychotherapist holds the interests and welfare of each individual as primary, whereas the researcher additionally contends with interests in gaining knowledge and the public's right to access to and use of it.

The *Ethical Principles* do address confidentiality related specifically to research activity. Information obtained about a research participant during the course of the investigation must remain confidential unless an agreement to the contrary has been negotiated in advance. Furthermore, if a possibility exists that others may obtain access to information, these facts should be made known in advance to the participants, including any plans for protecting their confidentiality (*EP*: 9j). Ethics committees occasionally receive complaints related to participant confidentiality or, as in the case presented below, privacy invasion related to research activity.

Case 14–13:   Tab Cross, Ed.D., a psychologist working at a university counseling center, administered a large number of personality inventories to students in the Educational Psychology department. He requested that the participants write in their names, but promised that identities would be held in the strictest confidence and would be destroyed immediately as soon as code numbers were assigned. A colleague wrote an ethics committee expressing concern that Dr. Cross then accessed the university Counseling Center files and separated the inventories into "has sought therapy" and who "has not sought therapy" piles from which he developed an article on personality characteristic differences between the two groups. The colleague argued that the psychologist entered confidential files for a purpose unrelated to Counseling Center business and that participants were not sufficiently informed of the study purpose nor was consent obtained to access their files.

Despite the fact that individual identities were not disclosed by the investigator to anyone else, the ethics committee agreed with the complainant that Dr. Cross committed an ethical violation by not informing the participants of his intent to access confidential counseling center records and gaining their consent to do so.

Case 14–14: Toni Alumni questioned the potential for privacy invasion by Nate Snoop, Ph.D. Dr. Snoop sent surveys to graduates of the university at which he held a full-time teaching position. Information about their relationships with their mentors when they were students was requested, including sensitive questions related to their professors' political ideology, attitudes toward campus administration, and knowledge of their private lives. Although anonymity was stressed and actual names of mentors were not requested, demographic data about the mentors (sex, department, rank, age, and teaching specialty) were solicited, which Toni believed would be sufficient to glean the actual identities of the mentors who the alumni were asked to characterize. Toni approached an ethics committee with concerns that the survey could potentially damage Dr. Snoop's colleagues should he choose to misuse it.

Dr. Snoop denied any intent to misuse the information and asserted that detailed demographic data were necessary to gain the desired knowledge about student-mentor relationships. However, the ethics committee agreed that Dr. Snoop overemphasized the anonymity he could actually promise the respondents' mentors and that the "third parties" about whom private information was being requested were completely unprotected since the university was very small and the mentors were not even aware that their privacy was being invaded. Alternative techniques were suggested to Dr. Snoop that would allow him to study the phenomenon in which he was interested without the attendant risks, such as using a number of universities so that questionnaires could not be linked to any specific department and/or removing some of the more delicate questions about which a non-participating third party "has the right to be left alone."

Case 14–15: Tushi See wrote an ethics committee after being repeatedly recognized as "the nude in Dr. Horn's experiment" by her fellow students. She explained that Blatherskite Horn, Ph.D., had approached her in the library several months previously asking her if she would be interested in being his temporary research assistant. He further explained that he was researching pupil dilation reaction to slide projected stimuli including unclothed human bodies. He asked if she would pose for the female nude slide, and Ms. See agreed, though she claimed she was not informed that her classmates would be viewing it.

Although one might question Ms. See's astuteness, Dr. Horn should certainly have realized that he was requesting a student to participate in an inappropriate activity that would also probably cause her embarrassment later on. Although Dr. Horn's defense was that he did obtain the young woman's consent to take and use the photograph, his act was seen as ill-advised. It was also noted that photos of nude females are hardly so unavailable that one needs to produce them personally!

Protecting the privacy and maintaining the confidentiality of data are *usually* routine procedures in social and behavioral research: that is, the investigator takes simple precautions to ensure that no one has access to identifying information. In most cases, the task of the researcher is far simpler than that of the mental health professional since actual identities are not necessary to keep on file, or they may not be necessary to record at all. Furthermore, the nature of the information obtained is often not inherently intriguing to anyone except the researchers: for example, how a particular person performs on a memory task.

Researchers, however, may often promise confidentiality without a full understanding of the disclosures that could possibly occur later. For example, lists of participants can sometimes be accessed by others and unauthorized follow-up studies or analyses for purposes other than the original one consented to by the participant could be run. Many techniques have been developed to limit the possibility for identification by others besides the obvious one of recording data anonymously in the first place, or to eliminate the usefulness of already collected data for other purposes (see Boruch, 1971, 1972; Boruch and Cecil, 1982).

Another complication, which can occur on occasion, involves the collection of highly sensitive information that may be of considerable interest to others, including legal authorities. Examples include research on drug users, draft evaders, or welfare recipients who are "cheating." Most researchers do not consider the possibility that their data could be subpoenaed, and yet this has occurred in several instances (Carroll, 1973; Wolfgang, 1981; Knerr, 1982). Although the investigator may prevail in maintaining the confidentiality of data, even if pressured by the authorities to identify participants, legal protections remain muddled and not fully understood. Researchers who can anticipate possible problems of this nature must first carefully assess whether their project should be implemented and, if so, should take advantage of techniques that will assist in protecting their participants and themselves (Kershaw and Small, 1972; Holden, 1975; Culliton, 1976; Knerr, 1982; see also Chapter 3).

Concerns about privacy invasion have drastically increased as technological advances allow for sophisticated surveillance, as well as link-ups and access among computer storage banks (Schwitzgebel, 1967; Goldberg, 1970; Miller, 1971; Kelley and Weston, 1975). APA (1982) suggests that psychologists may not wish to contribute information to data banks if confidentiality cannot be safeguarded or when individuals who have access to them are untrained or unmotivated to interpret the information accurately.

Pressures to reveal information about the identity of or information about the entire participating group, rather than any specific individual, can cause dilemmas whenever the investigator promised the participants that their affiliations would not appear in any public statements or publications. For example, workers or students may be told in advance that they will be characterized as "employees of a large corporation" or "students in a small western college." These promises must be fulfilled (Gibbons, 1975) despite occasional pressures to later be specific. If a publication involves detailed and sensitive information about individuals who may be known to some readers or aggregate data on a narrow population, such as a small political organization, the participants should be fully informed in advance and first given consent to the planned mode of publication and again give consent *after* they have viewed the final report (APA, 1982).

The following case illustrates how promises made to participants to keep their affiliation confidential can lead to unanticipated pressures later on.

Case 14-16:   Tite Lips, Ph.D., published a study on the relatively high incidence of homosexuality among males in a major athletic sport. The journal editor contacted Dr. Lips because many inquiries had been received demanding to know *what* sport was involved, likely reflecting homophobic concerns of those people who need to believe that their favorite sport is composed of athletes they consider to be "real males." The editor told Dr. Lips that by withholding the identity of the specific sport category, all categories were being "unfairly stereotyped." Dr. Lips sought counsel from an ethics committee because he had promised his participants, as a condition of gaining their cooperation, that he would never reveal the specific sport category.

Although some may choose to argue that Dr. Lips did not need to include that provision at the onset, this is irrelevant under the circumstances. Dr. Lips was ethically obligated to remain firm in his noncompliance with the editor's request (*EP*: 9d).

Finally, does one share information without consent when it may be judged that a given participant is in danger to him- or herself? For example, a research participant may indicate that he sells drugs to school children or intends to commit suicide even when gleaning information about such activities or intents were not integral features of the study purpose. Researchers, who may well not have had any clinical training, may feel especially inadequate to make a decision. As we have already seen in Chapter 3, it is difficult to decide what to do when such situations arise in psychotherapy settings. The researchers' obligations are even more ambiguous. APA (1982) acknowledges that such dilemmas may occasionally arise and notes that the obligation to disclose such information derives from more general ethical principles (see *EP*: 5 preamble) than from the principles limited to scientific research activity. It is advised that the investigator should inform the participant of a decision to disclose information to others (APA, 1982) despite the fact that the legal obligations of scientific investigators in such instances is not clear.

For additional information on the privacy invasion and confidentiality of *survey* respondents, see Conrad (1967), Byrant and Hansen (1976), Turner (1982), and Hartley (1982). For more detailed discussions of privacy and confidentiality related to social and behavioral science research, see Shils (1959), Ruebhausen and Brim (1966), Committee on Federal Evaluation Research (1975), and Bond (1978).

RESEARCH WITH ANIMALS

Although, as previously noted, the professional literature on research ethics is vast, very little of it deals with animal experimentation although we are beginning to see a vigorous upward trend (see, as examples, Bowd, 1980a and 1980b; Gallup and Suarez, 1980; Drewett and Kani, 1981; Shapiro, 1983). Although the public has expressed far less concern than have researchers themselves about ethical issues involved in experimenting with human beings, quite the opposite appears to be true when those research participants are not human. A number of vigorous, well-organized efforts from the public sector have expressed concern and even outrage. These range from groups that are not "anti-research," but dedicated to the improved care and welfare of laboratory animals, to groups that are opposed to most or all research conducted on animals regardless of its merit or potential for benefit. The more radical organizations often refer to scientists who use animals in their work as barbaric sadists who contribute nothing of value. Social and behavioral scientists are especially easy targets because their research findings and applications to date are not perceived of as being valuable as compared to the stunning advances made possible by biomedical animal research (Ryder, 1975; Singer, 1975; Pratt, 1976).

The Animal Research War

It is probably not difficult to understand why such a public furor over animal research has evolved. Whereas animals have been exploited by humans from the beginning of time for food, clothing, labor, sport, and pleasure, it is obvious that they have also been adored and cherished, sometimes with a zeal that exceeds that extended to other humans. Their vulnerable status also arouses sympathy whenever it is believed they are being treated unfairly or abusively.

Needless to say, researchers using animals take poorly to being characterized as torturers and insensitive brutes, and to having their work often publicized in biased, incomplete, and inaccurate ways. They tend to discount the radical animal activists as misguided and uninformed, and they make much of the contradictions and inconsistencies to be found in the anti-animal research groups' logic and targets. Some examples of comments we've heard from researchers include the following:

> Those vivisectionists care only about cuddly and cute animals. If they care so much about nonhumans in general as they claim to, why aren't they marching for rats, cockroaches, flies, gophers, and all of the other "creatures of God" the public spends millions on every year to try to wipe out?

I bet most animal rights activists eat meat, fish, or foul, have leather goods or a piece of fur on something, or wear cosmetics. [The FDA requires cosmetics to be tested for irritation. Animals, usually rabbits, are used for testing purposes and may be blinded in the process.] They are such hypocrites.

Have these people ever stopped to realize that their beloved pets are subjected to restraints to run free, mate, and explore, as is their nature? Why don't they pay more attention to saving the lives of the millions of cats and dogs that are exterminated every year because nobody wanted them, and get off our backs? We use few animals in science, by comparison, and do it for a beneficial purpose. Why us?

These people are either stupid or too rigid to accept proven facts. Research studies with animals were the keys to polio, diphtheria, hepatitis, immunization, and to the development of antibiotics, insulin, arthritis medication, chemotherapy agents, hypertension control medication, joint replacement techniques, kidney dialysis, heart surgery, and organ transplants, to name a few. And yet they either deny that these facts are true or insist that such research should not have been done in the first place or should have been done on prisoners or on the mentally retarded. I think they hate people.

How can one accept the eating of animals for the betterment of mankind but censure research on them for the betterment of mankind? It doesn't make sense to me.

Although such points may cause those who oppose animal research to fumble for a response, we do not take the position that the best defense is an offense for two reasons. First, Congress has taken an increasing interest in animal research and its critics as is evidenced by considerable animal research-related legislation, passed or pending, which renders verbal attacks a useless exercise. (See National Institutes of Health, 1984, for the most recent laboratory animal welfare provisions promulgated by the government.) More important, the expressed concerns are sometimes very well taken and it behooves psychology researchers, *independently of any external pressure*, to assess carefully the use of animals in research and to strive to improve the quality of care, treatment, and experimental procedures in ways that reduce these concerns.

Professional Guidelines and Attitudes Regarding Animal Use

Despite the paucity of writings on animal research ethics emanating from within the field of psychology, it is important to note that the APA has not ignored the care and welfare of animals used for research purposes. Although an ethics principle devoted exclusively to animal experimentation was not included in the *Ethical Principles* until 1981, this principle is heavily adapted from a much earlier APA policy statement (APA, 1968), which was to be posted in all psychology laboratories using animals, including the name of the appropriate designee to which abuses were to be promptly reported. Another early APA policy (Committee for the Use of Animals in School Science Behavior Projects, 1972) outlined guidelines for the use of animals in schools.

Basically, Principle *10* admonishes research psychologists to ensure the welfare of animals and to treat them humanely; to follow laws and regulations governing the acquisition, treatment, and care and disposal of animals; to maintain competence in their own knowledge of the species involved and to ensure that assistants are also well trained in these regards; to minimize discomfort; and to terminate animals, when that is necessary, rapidly and painlessly. When animals are subjected to pain or privation, the investigator must carefully consider alternatives first. If discomfort cannot be avoided, the study goal must be justified by its prospective scientific, educational, or applied value. Surgical procedures must involve appropriate anesthesia, and techniques to avoid infection and to minimize pain must be applied afterwards.

Obvious differences exist between animal and human research participants, and many of the ethical issues revolve around the exercise of the almost absolute power investigators hold over animal participants. Consent requirements and privacy invasion become, of course, irrelevant. Researchers determine the conditions under which nonhuman participants must live, including what and how much they eat and what they experience, for an indeterminant period. Allowable risks are considerably greater and even include the termination of the animals' lives. The risks, however, must still be justified and balanced against potential benefits as with research using human beings. Conflicts arise in the same ways as those we have discussed earlier: Differences in opinion and attitude pertain in areas of acceptable risk level (especially those involving pain and discomfort), appropriate beneficiaries of the knowledge obtained, and participant welfare and rights.

Because of the prevalent acceptability of confining animals to controlled living conditions, animals have many practical advantages over the use of human participants in research. It is easier to gather them together to ensure that comparison groups have had similar control or manipulated experiences or genetic endowment, and to study changes for long periods of time due to easy access and shorter life spans. However, it is not enough to justify animal research projects *solely* because of practical advantages (Shapiro, 1984).

The scientific "attitude" toward animals stems from Cartesian philosophy, which holds that organisms are mechanical systems. What differentiates human and nonhuman forms is the human possession of a "soul." Although the origination of this notion has been greatly obscured, the underlying viewpoint became a major justification for both the usefulness of animal study and the basis for acceptable differences in the ways animals could be perceived and treated. This resulted, according to Bowd (1980a), in the perception of animals as "complex lab tools."

Although no one in the scientific community argues about the existence of a soul (or lack thereof) anymore, the assumption that animals are mere "automatons" without significant feelings or awareness has come under increasing scrutiny within the scientific community itself. For example, Fraser (1975) argued that since ethology recognizes motivation in animals, it must also recognize that animals experience a broad range of emotions and feelings. Neurological studies have demonstrated continuities between human and animal brain functions and structures, suggesting that it is unreasonable to deny that animals possess some psychological features people ascribe to themselves (Solomon, 1982). The earlier strict criteria for "consciousness" (that is, the ability to reflect, and the possession of some concept of "selfhood") may well have set too high, and far too narrow, a standard, which rendered the animal mind and what it experiences as negligible (Soloman, 1982). Thus mentalistic and "anthropomorphic" views of animals are not nearly so taboo as they were in the heyday of behaviorism.

Such trends in thinking must almost, by definition, lead to a sharpening and reevaluation of not only theories about animal behavior and experience, but also about the ethical implications of researching them and the ways they are cared for between experimental trials. Even staunch defenders of animal research acknowledge that laboratory procedures and treatments can be improved (e.g., Keehn, 1979).

Alternatives to Animal Use in Research

No one (neither the supporters nor the critics of animal research) debates the worthwhileness of discovering valid alternatives to the use of whole, live animals in research. Current alternatives being developed include math models, isolated organs, tissue and cell cultures, mechanical models, computer simulations, chemical assays, anthropomorphic "dummies," simulated tissue and body fluids, and increased use of lower organisms (Holden, 1982). Unfortunately, however, the critics of animal research seem to assume that such technologies are currently developed to the point where whole, live animal research can be abandoned altogether. This is hardly the case. In some cases, alternatives will require substantial use of animals to refine them to the point of usefulness. For some others, the methodologies are still in their infancy and will not serve as valid substitutes for many years. These alternatives will probably lead to an eventual reduction in the use of animals in research but will never completely preclude altogether the necessity of using them (Holden, 1982).

Most of the developing alternatives are far more suited to biomedical research than to social and behavioral research requirements. Behavioral scientists often require fully functioning whole animals. As Drewett and Kani (1981) remarked, "If one is to study the behavior of an animal, one has to have an animal" (p. 177). It is impossible to glean much general information about behavior from tissue or cell cultures or even from very simple animals (such as sponges). This is not to say, however, that psychologists cannot actively pursue other alternatives. Using the fewest possible number of animals is one example. Already there is evidence of a steady reduction of animal use in research, perhaps partially due to the rising costs of procuring, feeding, and housing them (Gallup and Suarez, 1980; Goodman, 1982; Holden, 1982). Using fewer numbers of animals for classroom demonstration purposes is another way to reduce animal use. The current availability and relatively low cost of video equipment may be especially useful in these regards, and it is highly recommended for classroom demonstrations whenever an animal is put at some discomfort (e.g., a learning sequence using aversive conditioning). The tape made on a single animal can be reused for years.

Care and Study Method Alternatives

Alternatives for behavioral scientists also include ways that the lives of the experimental animals can be enhanced and/or their discomfort minimized by using the least intrusive procedures. Lea (1979) presents a variety of ways in which one can view alternatives in behavioral animal studies. First, one must consider if it is possible to do the study on humans instead. He notes that practicality and ethics are common reasons for a negative response. Assuming that animals emerge as the only appropriate population, he offers several ideas. For example, Lea suggested substituting recording for stimulation, and stimulation for lesion techniques, whenever possible. The goal is to minimize to the greatest extent damage done to the brain. He also suggests reducing unnecessary degrees of deprivation. Water deprivation should be used only when thirst is the specific interest since depriving an animal of water does more harm than depriving it of food. He also notes that depriving a rat of food for six hours will get rats working for a reward almost as well as a 23-hours food deprivation period. Or, as Lea suggests, avoid food deprivation altogether by using a preferred food, not in the normal well-balanced laboratory diet, as a reward. Sucrose for rats is one example. One can sometimes take the experiment to the animal's living quarters so that it works for its food as and when it wants. Such "free behavior" situations have advantages in that they allow for a more naturalistic evaluation of an animal's motivation and capabilities. Lea further suggests that one should consider avoiding punishment in avoidance tasks and use rewards instead. If aversion training must be used, he recommends considering alternatives to electric shock, such as loud noises, bright lights, or species-specific threat behaviors, since these cause less trauma and may be equally effective. Finally, Lea notes that researchers must thoroughly know the nature of the species they use. Researchers should have extensively studied how the species live in a natural environment and have an understanding of what causes distress. Lea's examples of alternatives apply best to researchers studying learning in animals, and he is quick to note that physiological psychologists may not be able to avoid more painful procedures. He reasons that this situation may be partially redeemed because medical application of findings is more direct in physiological studies.

Studying animal behavior in a *natural* habitat may cause practical problems but has both scientific and ethical advantages. Laboratory studies have been criticized because they deprive the opportunities of animals to exercise their true capacities and to engage in their normal, instinctual lives (Drewett and Kani, 1981). When animals are studied under conditions that are, for them, abnormal, the validity of scientific findings about their capacities may be distorted or blatantly in error. Some animals, usually rodents, have been used in laboratory work for so long that they may be more adapted to dependent, laboratory life than to the outside world. Lockard (1968) describes the history of the Albino rat in behavioral research, then suggests that psychologists might be making generalizations about animal behavior on an unnatural and nonrepresentative species. Beilharz (1982) describes possible techniques for genetically adapting animals to animal husbandry systems rather than adapting the systems to the animals. However, Van Rooijen (1983) warns that although rapid genetic alteration is a worthy goal, it may be unrealistic and subject much suffering to those who could not survive the procedure. He further warns that scientists must be careful when attempting these techniques so that they do not select animals that may no longer be in harmony with themselves: that is, "fitness" and "welfare" may not coincide, since many animals can be disturbed but they nevertheless stay alive and breed successfully.

Pain and Suffering

The animal research debate rises to its highest pitch concerning the issues of pain and suffering that animals may experience during the course of their lives in the laboratory.

Within psychology, the trials of psychologist Edward Taub, which began in 1981, have generated considerable publicity. Full accounts of the case read like a high adventure story and, in the end, one can still interpret the meaning of it all depending on what one wants to see. Briefly, for our purposes here, Dr. Taub was originally charged with 119 misdemeanor counts based on Maryland's animal cruelty statutes after a volunteer in the laboratory organized support from his animal rights' group culminating in a police raid that confiscated 17 monkeys. Although the care the animals were receiving was the only matter at legal issue, Taub's research program involving learned disuse of limbs in deafferented monkeys was highlighted in the negative publicity and characterized as cruel and worthless. Taub was eventually exonerated on all but a single count involving the care of one specific monkey although his NIH grant was suspended. Critics of his work continued to object to his laboratory setting conditions (and produced photos that his supporters claimed were "staged") and study purpose and value, while his supporters, which included scientific organizations such as the APA, insisted that Taub was railroaded and demeaned unfairly by a deceitful volunteer who had a preestablished agenda to discredit Taub and his research program. (See *Science*, Oct. 2, 9, and Dec. 11, 1981 for additional details on this case.)

Although humans can never know for certain what animals experience or feel, Gallistel (1981) notes that charges by animal research critics that scientists fail to recognize pain in animals is ridiculous, since if that were so, researchers would not take the care that they do to reduce pain during experimental surgery. No one—not even the most avid proponents of research using animals—advocates or condones "unnecessary pain or suffering." Yet, of course, the conflict quickly arises due to the lack of agreement or guidelines regarding what "unnecessary" means. This is not an easy criteria to operationalize and varies with the perceived potential benefits to be gained. For example, studies on the effects of aversive stimulation are justified by those who conduct them on the grounds that they contribute to knowledge about learning processes in general, and that this work has had important implications for ameliorating human problems, such as the development of behavior modification therapy techniques. Critics, however, have noted that aversive stimulation work on animals has been replicated to the point of overkill (Drewett and Kani, 1981) and that the human applications, although derived from early animal work, *could* have been developed by using humans in ethically conceived and implemented research (Shapiro, 1983). Shapiro contends that regardless of our historical roots, from now on we must evaluate whether using animals is the *most* effective way, the *only* way, or just *a* way of gaining important knowledge.

At this point in time, the only clearly stated, evolving principle relative to pain and suffering in animal experimentation involves the admonishment against the use of muscle paralyzing agents (such as curare) during experimental surgery. These agents immobilize the animal but do not render it unconscious. The editor of the journal, *Pain*, is unwilling to publish any article that involved subjecting animals to situations where they could not indicate or arrest the onset of pain (Drewett and Kani, 1981). Some large research facilities, such as the laboratories at the University of Southern

California, prohibit outright the use of muscle relaxants or paralytics without anesthetics during surgical procedures.

Finally, Zola, Sechzer, Sieber, and Griffin (1984) discuss the increasing recognition that the inducement of animal suffering usually reflects a low standard of scientific technique. That is, research using animals who have been traumatized yields invalid results unless the purpose of the research is specifically to study the reaction of a particular form of trauma.

A Call to Reason

It is unfortunate that the issue of animal use in research has become heated and polarized. We believe that if the dust were allowed to settle and the concerns were thoughtfully reviewed, we would find that researchers and many animal welfare advocates would find that their goals are not, and never were, disparate. Many animal welfare advocates would agree that the banning of animal research altogether would not solve the problems animals have on this planet (including the ones they create for each other "in the wild"), nor would halting research benefit anyone, including animals themselves. And few scientists would argue that *all* animal studies, facilities, and teaching demonstrations are acceptable, worthwhile, and not in need of reform.

A recently established independent organization, Psychologists for the Ethical Treatment of Animals (PsyETA), will hopefully emerge as a constructive moderate force within psychology. Several major goals of the organization include the following: improvement of the care standards and conditions for animals in psychological research; encouragement of the revisions of educational curricula to include ethical considerations in the treatment of animals; promotion of research, teaching, and theory that will contribute to animal welfare; development of reformed and revised procedures involving animals, including the reduction of the number of animals used; and maintenance of liaisons with scientific and animal welfare groups.

SUMMARY GUIDELINES

1. Research psychologists should fully familiarize themselves with the various extant policies governing research activity. In determining the ethicality of research, however, psychologists must additionally assess the design, procedures, and experiences to which the participants will be subjected with special attention paid to any value biases that may impact on the participants' welfare, meaningfulness of the data, and the interpretation of results.

2. Concern for the participants' welfare is paramount. Whenever wrongs or harms to participants are likely, research psychologists have special obligations to search for alternative study methods or even to refrain from conduct-

ing the research. If participants become upset during the course of collecting data or afterwards, it is the psychologists' responsibility to institute ameliorative procedures.

3. Consent from participants should be voluntary and informed. In those cases where participants cannot give meaningful or legal consent, or when deception is believed to be justified, psychologists are obligated to take safeguards to protect the welfare of participants. If deception is used, the participants must be adequately informed of this fact and given the justification for using such methods directly after the study trial. Stressing the participants' freedom to withdraw at any time, including the explicitly offered right to withdraw data when deception is used, is an important feature of ethical research. In cases where participants remain unaware of being observed, data should be gathered and disseminated in such a way that maintains anonymity.

4. Research psychologists must actively maintain their own competencies, including methods of study design and analysis, and must use participants in a way that maintains the integrity, as well as the ethics, of scientific endeavor.

5. Means of ensuring confidentiality must be implemented. Research psychologists must be aware of any potential access of participant identities and must inform them of any such possibilities during the consent acquisition phase.

6. When conflicts arise between "risks versus potential benefits," "scientific versus ethical considerations," and "participants rights and welfare versus society's rights or needs to know," research psychologists must carefully assess these dilemmas and proceed in ways that minimize the potential for wrongs or harms to participants.

7. Psychologists must treat their animal research participants with humane care and respect. Alternatives should be explored when pain or uncomfortable procedures are involved. If alternatives are not feasible, psychologists are under special obligation to assess the potential value and meaning of their work.

REFERENCE NOTES

1. Keith-Spiegel, P., and Maas, T. *Consent to research: Are there developmental differences?* Paper presented at the Annual Meeting of the American Psychological Association, Los Angeles, California, August, 1981.

2. Keith-Spiegel, P. *Ethics and primary prevention.* Organization paper for the conference sponsored by NIMH, Pacific Palisades, California, 1983.

REFERENCES

Albee, G. W. The politics of nature and nurture. *Journal of Community Psychology*, 1982, *10*, 1–36.

Allen, S. A; Heckel, R. V.; and Garcia, S. J. The black researcher: A view from inside the goldfish bowl. *American Psychologist*, 1980, *35*, 767–771.

American Psychological Association. *Ethical principles in the conduct of research with human participants*. Washington, DC: APA, 1973.

———. *Principles for the care and use of animals*. Washington, DC: APA, 1968.

Appel, G. N. Three cases dealing with dilemmas and ethical conflicts in anthropological inquiry. *Human Organization*, 1971, *30*, 97–101.

Barber, B. The ethics of experimentation with human subjects. *Scientific American*, 1976, *234*, 25–31.

———; Lally, J. J.; Makarushka, J. L.; and Sullivan, D. *Research on human subjects: Problems of social control in medical experimentation*. New York: Russell Sage Foundation, 1973.

Baron, R. A. The "costs of deception" revisited: An openly optimistic rejoinder. *IRB: A review of human subjects research*, 1981, *3*, 8–10.

Baumrind, D. *Nature and definition of informed consent in research involving deception*. Background paper prepared for the National Commission for the Protection of Human Subjects of Biomedical and Behavioral Research. Washington, DC: Department of Health, Education, and Welfare, 1976.

Beecher, H. K. Ethics and clinical research. *New England Journal of Medicine*, 1966, *274*, 1354–1360.

———. *Research and the individual*. Boston: Little, Brown, 1970.

Beilharz, R. G. Genetic adaptation in relation to animal welfare. *International Journal for the Study of Animal Problems*, 1982, *3*, 177–184.

Berscheid, E. R. S.; Dermer, M.; and Libman, M. Anticipating informed consent— An empirical approach. *American Psychologist*, 1973, *28*, 913–925.

Bond, K. Confidentiality and the protection of human subjects in social science research: A report on recent developments. *American Sociologist*, 1978, *13*, 144–152.

Boruch, R. F. Assuring confidentiality of responses in social research: A note on strategies. *American Sociologist*, 1971, *6*, 308–311.

———. Strategies for eliciting and merging confidential social research data. *Policy Sciences*, 1972, *3*, 275–297.

———, and Cecil, J. S. Statistical strategies for preserving privacy in direct inquiry. In J. E. Sieber (Ed.), *The ethics of social research: Surveys and experiments*. New York: Springer-Verlag, 1982.

Bowd, A. D. Ethical reservations about psychological research with animals. *Psychological Record*, 1980, *30*, 201–210.

———. Ethics and animal experimentation. *American Psychologist*, 1980b, *35*, 224–225.

Bower, R. T., and de Gasparis, P. *Ethics in social research*. New York: Praeger, 1978.

Brandt, R. M. *Studying behavior in natural settings*. New York: Holt, Rinehart, and Winston, 1972.

Branson, R. Prison research: National Commission says "No, unless. . ." *Hastings Center Report*, 1977, *7*, 15–21.

Britton, B. K. Ethical and educational aspects of participating as a subject in psychology experiments. *Teaching of Psychology*, 1979, *6*, 195–198.

Bryant, E. C., and Hansen, M. H. Invasion of privacy and surveys: A growing dilemma. In H. W. Sinaiko and L. H. Broedling (Eds.), *Perspectives on attitudes assessment: Surveys and their alternatives.* Champaign, Il: Pendleton, 1976.

Capron, A. M. Medical research in prisons. *Hastings Center Report*, 1973, *3*, 4–6.

Carroll, J. D. Confidentiality of social science research sources and data: The Popkin case. *PS*, 1973, *6*.

Cassell, J. Harms, benefits, wrongs, and rights in fieldwork. In J. Sieber (Ed.), *The ethics of social research: Fieldwork, regulation, and publication.* New York: Springer-Verlag, 1982.

Cassileth, B. R. Informed consent—Why are its goals imperfectly realized? *New England Journal of Medicine*, 1980, *302*, 896–900.

Chalkley, D. T. Federal constraints: Earned or unearned? *American Journal of Psychiatry*, 1977, *134*, 911–913.

Chambliss, W. On the paucity of original research on organized crime: A footnote to Galliher and Cain. *American Sociologist*, 1975, *10*, 36–39.

Chomsky, N. The fallacy of Richard Herrnstein's IQ. *Social Policy*, May/June, 1972, pp. 19–25.

Collins, F. L.; Kuhn, I. F.; and King, G. D. Variables affecting subjects' ethical ratings of proposed experiments. *Psychological Reports*, 1979, *44*, 155–164.

Committee on Federal Evaluation Research. *Protecting individual privacy in evaluation research.* Washington, DC: National Academy of Sciences, 1975.

Committee for the Use of Animals in School Science Behavior Projects. Guidelines for the use of animals in school science behavior projects. *American Psychologist*, 1972, *27*, 337.

Conner, R. F. Random assignment of clients in social experimentation. In J. E. Sieber (Ed.), *The ethics of social research: Surveys and experiments.* New York: Springer-Verlag, 1982.

Conrad, H. S. Clearance of questionnaires with respect to "invasion of privacy," public sensitivities, ethical standards, etc. *American Psychologist*, 1967, *22*, 356–359.

Cook, S. W. A comment on the ethical issues involved in West, Gunn, and Chernicky's "Ubiquitous Watergate: An attributional analysis." *Journal of Personality and Social Psychology*, 1975, *32*, 66–68.

———. Ethical issues in the conduct of research in social relations. In C. Selitz et al. (Eds.), *Research Methods in Social Relations.* New York: Holt, Rinehart, and Winston, 1976.

Cook, T. D.; Bean, R. B.; Calder, B. J.; Frey, R.; Krovetz, M. L.; and Reisman, S. R. Demand characteristics and three conceptions of the frequently deceived subject. *Journal of Personality and Social Psychology*, 1970, *14*, 185–194.

Cooper, J. Deception and role playing: On telling the good guys from the bad guys. *American Psychologist*, 1976, *31*, 605–610.

Cowan, E. Baby-steps toward primary prevention. *American Journal of Community Psychology*, 1977, *5*, 1–22.

Cox, D. E., and Sipprelle, C. N. Coercion in participation as a research subject. *American Psychologist*, 1971, *26*, 726—731.

Culliton, B. Confidentiality: Court declares researcher can protect sources. *Science*, 1976, *193*, 465—467.

Curran, W. J. Government regulations of the use of human subjects in medical research: The approach of two federal agencies. *Daedalus*, 1969, *98*, 542—594.

———. Ethical and legal considerations in high risk studies of schizophrenia. *Schizophrenia Bulletin*, 1974, *10*, 74—92.

Denzin, N. On the ethics of disguised observation. *Social Problems*, 1968, *15*, 502—504.

Department of Health and Human Services. *Protection of human subjects* (Code of Federal Regulations 45 CFR 46). Washington, DC: DHHS, March 8, 1983.

Diener, E., and Crandall, R. *Ethics in social and behavioral research*. Chicago: University of Chicago Press, 1978.

Drewett, R., and Kani, W. Animal experimentation in the behavioral sciences. In D. Sperlinger (Ed.), *Animals in research*. New York: Wiley, 1981.

Edsall, G. A positive approach to the problem of human experimentation, *Daedalus*, 1969, *98*, 463—479.

Epstein, L. C., and Lasagna, L. Obtaining informed consent: Form or substance. *Archives of Internal Medicine*, 1969, *123*, 682—688.

Erikson, K. A comment on disguised observation in sociology. *Social Problems*, 1967, *14*, 366—373.

Farr, J. L., and Seaver, W. B. Stress and discomfort in psychological research: Subject perceptions of experimental procedures. *American Psychologist*, 1975, *30*, 770—773.

Ferguson, L. R. The competence and freedom of children to make choices regarding participation in research: A statement. *Journal of Social Issues*, 1978, *34*, 114—121.

Forward, J.; Canter, R.; and Kirsch, N. Role-enactment and deception methodologies: Alternative paradigms. *American Psychologist*, 1976, *31*, 595—604.

Frankel, M. S. Social, legal, and political responses to ethical issues in the use of children as experimental subjects. *Journal of Social Issues*, 1978, *34*, 101—113.

Fraser, A. Ethology and ethics. *Applied animal ethology*, 1975, *1*, 211—212.

Freedman, J. L., and Fraser, S. C. Compliance without pressure: The foot-in-the-door technique. *Journal of Personality and Social Psychology*, 1966, *2*, 195—202.

Gallistel, C. R. Bell, Magendie, and the proposals to restrict the use of animals in neurobehavioral research. *American Psychologist*, 1981, *36*, 357—360.

Gallup, G. G., and Suarez, S. On the use of animals in psychological research. *Psychological Record*, 1980, *30*, 211—218.

Geller, D. M. Alternatives to deception: Why, what, and how? In J. E. Sieber (Ed.), *The ethics of social research: Surveys and experiments*. New York: Springer-Verlag, 1982.

Gibbons, D. C. Unidentified research sites and fictitious names. *American Sociologist*, 1975, *10*, 32—36.

Glazer, M. The threat of the stranger: Vulnerability, reciprocity, and fieldwork. In J. Sieber. (Ed.), *The ethics of social research: Fieldwork, regulation and publication*. New York: Springer-Verlag, 1982.

Goldberg, E. M. Urban information systems and invasion of privacy. *Urban Affairs Quarterly*, 1970, 5, 249–264.

Goodman, W. Of mice, monkeys, and men. *Newsweek*, August 9, 1982, p. 61.

Gray, B. H. An assessment of institutional review committees in human experimentation. *Medical Care*, 1975, 13, 318–328.

———. *Human subjects in medical experimentation*. New York: Wiley, 1975.

———. The functions of human subjects review committees. *American Journal of Psychiatry*, 1977, 134, 907–910.

———, and Cooke, R. A. The impact of institutional review boards on research. *Hastings Center Report*, Feb. 1980, 36–41.

———; Cooke, R. A.; and Tannenbaum, A. S. Research involving human subjects. *Science*, 1978, 201, 1094–1101.

Gray, S. W. Ethical issues in research in early childhood intervention. *Children*, 1971, 18, 83–89.

Grisso, T., and Vierling, L. Minor's consent to treatment: A developmental perspective. *Professional Psychology*, 1978, 9, 412–427.

Grunder, T. M. Two formulas for determining the readability of subject consent forms. *American Psychologist*, 1978, 33, 773–774.

Hartley, S. F. Sampling strategies and the threat to privacy. In J. Sieber (Ed.), *The ethics of social research: Surveys and experiments*. New York: Springer-Verlag, 1982.

Herrnstein, R. J. IQ in the Meritocracy. Boston: Atlantic/Little Brown, 1973.

Hirsch, J. Jensenism: The bankruptcy of "science" without scholarship. *Educational Theory*, 1975, 25, 3–28.

———. To "unfrock the charlatans." *Sage Race and Relations Abstracts*, 1981, 6, 1–66.

Hobbs, N. *The future of children*. San Francisco: Jossey-Bass, 1975.

———. Privacy: Congressional efforts are coming to fruition. *Science*, 1975, 188, 713–715.

Holden, C. New focus on replacing animals in the lab. *Science*, 1982, 215, 35–38.

Holmes, D. S. Debriefing after psychological experiments. *American Psychologist*, 1976, 31, 858–875.

Humphreys, L. *Tearoom trade: Impersonal sex in public places*. Chicago: Aldine, 1970.

Jensen, A. R. How much can we boost IQ and scholastic achievement? *Harvard Educational Review*, 1969, 39, 1–123.

———. The ethical issues. *The Humanist*, Jan./Feb., 1972, pp. 5–6.

Johnson, C. G. Risks in the publication of fieldwork. In J. Sieber (Ed.), *The ethics of social research: Fieldwork, regulation and publication*. New York: Springer-Verlag, 1982.

Kamin, L.J. *The science and politics of IQ*. Potomac, MD: Erlbaum, 1974.

Katz, J. *Experimentation with human beings.* New York: Russell Sage Foundation, 1972.

Keehn, J. D. In defense of experiments with animals. *Bulletin of the British Psychological Society*, 1977, *30*, 404–405.

Keith-Spiegel, P. Children's rights as participants in research. In G.P. Koocher (Ed.), *Children's rights and the mental health professions.* New York: Wiley, 1976.

————. Children and consent to participate in research. In G. B. Melton, G. P. Koocher, and M. J. Saks (Eds.), *Children's competence to consent.* New York: Plenum, 1983.

Kelley, V. R., and Weston, H. B. Computers, costs, and civil liberties. *Social Work*, 1975, *20*, 15–19.

Kelman, H. C. Human use of human subjects: The problem of deception in social psychological experiments. *Psychological Bulletin*, 1967, *67*, 1–11.

————. The rights of the subject in social research: An analysis in terms of relative power and legitimacy. *American Psychologist*, 1972, *27*, 989–1016.

Kershaw, D. N., and Small, J. C. Data confidentiality and privacy: Lessons from the New Jersey Negative Income Tax experiment. *Public Policy*, 1972, *20*, 257–280.

Kessler, M., and Albee, G. W. Primary prevention. *Annual Review of Psychology*, 1975, *26*, 557–591.

Koocher, G. P. Bathroom behavior and human dignity. *Journal of Personality and Social Psychology*, 1977, *35*, 120–121.

Knerr, C. R. What to do before and after a subpoena of data arrives. In J. E. Sieber (Ed.), *The ethics of social research: Surveys and experiments.* New York: Springer-Verlag, 1982.

Lappe, M. Censoring the hereditarians. *Commonwealth*, 1974, *C* (8), 183–185.

Lasagna, L. Special subjects in human experimentation. *Daedalus*, 1969, *98*, 449–462.

Lea, S. E. G. Alternatives to the use of painful stimuli in physiological psychology and the study of animal behavior. *ATLA Abstracts*, 1979, *7*, 20–21.

Leak, G. K. Student perception of coercion and value from participation in psychological research. *Teaching of Psychology*, 1981, *8*, 147–149.

Levine, E. K. Old people are not all alike: Social class, ethnicity/race, and sex are bases for important differences. In J. E. Sieber (Ed.), *The ethics of social research: Surveys and experiments.* New York: Springer-Verlag, 1982.

Levine, R. J. *The role of assessment of risk-benefit criteria in the determination of the appropriateness of research involving human subjects.* Background paper prepared for the National Commission for the Protection of Human Subjects of Biomedical and Behavioral Research. Washington, DC: Department of Health, Education, and Welfare, 1975.

Lewis, M.; McCollum, A. T.; Schwartz, A.H.; and Grunt, J. A. Informed consent in pediatric research. *Children*, 1969, *16*, 143–148.

Ley, H. L. Federal Law and patient consent. *Annals of the New York Academy of Sciences*, 1970, *169*, 546–572.

Lockard, R. B. The albino rat: A defensible choice or a bad habit? *American Psychologist*, 1968, *23*, 734–742.

Lowe, C. U. Pediatrics: Proper utilization of children as research subjects. *Annals of the New York Academy of Sciences*, 1970, *169*, 337–343.

Lowe, C. U.; Alexander, D.; and Mishkin, B. Non-therapeutic research on children: An ethical dilemma. *Pediatrics*, 1974, *84*, 468—472.

McLean, P. D. The effect of informed consent on the acceptance of random treatment assignment in a clinical population. *Behavior Therapy*, 1980, *11*, 129—133.

McNemar, Q. Opinion-attitude methodology. *Psychological Bulletin*, 1946, *43*, 289—374.

Martin, D. C.; Arnold, J. D.; Zimmerman, T. F.; and Richard, R. H. Human subjects in clinical research—A report on three studies. *New England Journal of Medicine*, 1968, *279*, 1426—1431.

Menges, R. J. Openness and honesty vs. coercion and deception in psychological research. *American Psychologist*, 1973, *28*, 1030—1034.

Middlemist, R. D.; Knowles, E. S.; and Matter, C. F. Personal space invasions in the lavatory: Suggestive evidence for arousal. *Journal of Personality and Social Psychology*, 1976, *33*, 541—546.

Miller, A. R. *The assault on privacy.* Ann Arbor: University of Michigan Press, 1971.

Mills, J. A procedure for explaining experiments involving deception. *Personality and Social Psychology Bulletin*, 1976, *2*, 3—13.

Mirvis, P. H., and Seashore, S. Creating ethical relationships in organizational research. In J. E. Sieber (Ed.), *The ethics of social research: Surveys and experiments.* New York: Springer-Verlag, 1982.

Mitchell, R. G. The child and experimental medicine. *British Medical Journal* 1964, *1*, 722—726.

Mitford, J. Experiments behind bars. *The Atlantic*, Jan. 1973, pp. 64—73.

Nash, M. M. "Nonreactric methods and the law": Additional comments on legal liability in behavior research. *American Psychologist*, 1975, *30*, 777—780.

National Commission for the Protection of Human Subjects of Biomedical and Behavioral Research. *Research involving children.* (Publication No. 0577-004). Washington, DC: Department of Health, Education, and Welfare, 1977.

National Institutes of Health. Laboratory animal welfare. *NIH Guide*, 1984, *13*, 1—27.

Nelson, S. H., and Grunebaum, H. Ethical issues in psychiatric follow-up studies. *American Journal of Psychiatry*, 1972, *128*, 1358—1362.

Nikelly, A. G. Ethical issues in research on student protest. *American Psychologist*, 1971, *26*, 475—478.

Nobel, J. H. Peer review: Quality control of applied social science. *Science* 1974, *185*, 916—921.

Noonan, M. J., and Bickel, W. K. The ethics of experimental design. *Mental Retardation*, 1981, *19*, 271—274.

Novick, M. R. Federal guidelines and professional standards. *American Psychologist*, 1981, *36*, 1035—1046.

Oakes, W. External validity, and the use of real people as subjects. *American Psychologist*, 1972, *27*, 959—962.

Orne, M. T. On the social psychology of the psychology experiment: With particular reference to demand characteristics and their implications. *American Psychologist*, 1962, *17*, 776—783.

Pappworth, M. H. *Human guinea pigs.* Boston: Beacon Press, 1967.

Pattullo, E. L. Who risks what in social research? *IRB: A review of human subjects research*, 1980, 2, 1–4.

Pratt, D. *Painful experiments on animals*. New York: Argus Archives, 1976.

President's Commission for the Study of Ethical Problems in Medicine and Biomedical and Behavioral Research. *Compensating research injuries*. Washington, DC: U.S. Government Printing Office, 1982.

Price-Williams, D. R. *Explorations in cross-cultural psychology*. San Francisco, CA.: Chandler and Sharp, 1975.

Rainwater, L., and Pittman, D. J. Ethical problems in studying a politically deviant community. *Social Problems*, 1967, 14, 357–365.

Redlich, F. Ethical aspects of clinical observations of behavior. *Journal of Nervous and Mental Disease*, 1973, 157, 313–319.

Reid, L. D. Rats are frequently subjects of choice. *American Psychologist*, 1969, 24, 956–958.

Reiss, A. J. *Selected issues in informed consent and confidentiality with special reference to behavioral/social science research/inquiry*. Background paper prepared for the National Commission for the Protection of Human Subjects of Biomedical and Behavioral Research. Washington, DC: Department of Health, Education, and Welfare, 1976.

Resnick, J. H., and Schwartz, T. Ethical standards as an independent variable in psychological research. *American Psychologist*, 1973, 28, 134–139.

Reynolds, P. D. On the protection of human subjects and social science. *International Social Science Journal*, 1972, 24, 693–719.

Ring, K.; Wallston, K.; and Corey, M. Mode of debriefing as a factor affecting subjective reaction to a Milgram-type obedience experiment: An ethical inquiry. *Journal of Representative Research in Social Psychology*, 1970, 1, 67–88.

Rohsenow, D. J., and Marlatt, G. A. The balanced placebo design: Methodological consideration. *Addictive Behaviors*, 1981, 6, 107–122.

Rosenthal, R., and Rosnow, R. L. (Eds.). *Artifact in behavioral research*. New York: Academic Press, 1969.

———, and Rosnow, R. L. (Eds.). *The volunteer subject*. New York: Wiley, 1975.

Ross, M. W. Ethics of animal experimentation. *Australian Psychologist*, 1978, 13, 375–378.

Rubenstein, C. Psychology's fruit flies. *Psychology Today*, 1982, 16, 83–84.

Rubin, J. S. Breaking into prison: Conducting a medical research project. *American Journal of Psychiatry*, 1976, 133, 230–232.

Ruebhausen, O. M., and Brim, O. G. Privacy and behavioral research. *American Psychologist*, 1966, 21, 423–437.

Rutstein, D. R. The ethical design of human experiments. *Daedalus*, 1969, 98, 523–541.

Ryder, R. *Victims of science: The use of animals in research*. London: Davis-Poynter, 1975.

Schwartz, S. H., and Gottlieb, A. Participation in a bystander intervention experiment and subsequent everyday helping: Ethical considerations. *Journal of Experimental Social Psychology*, 1980, *16*, 161–171.

———, and Gottlieb, A. Participants' postexperimental reactions and the ethics of bystander research. *Journal of Experimental Social Psychology*, 1981, *17*, 396–407.

Schwitzgebel, R. K. Electronic innovation in the behavioral sciences. *American Psychologist*, 1967, *22*, 364–370.

Sechrest, L. Another look at unobtrusive measures: An alternative to what? In H. W. Sinaiko and L. H. Broedling (Eds.), *Perspectives on attitudes assessment: Surveys and their alternatives*. Champaign, IL: Pendleton, 1976.

Seeman, J. Deception in psychological research. *American Psychologist*, 1969, *24*, 1025–1028.

Shapiro, K. Psychology and its animal subjects. *International Journal for the Study of Animal Problems*, 1983, *4*, 188–191.

———. Response to APA's "Why animals?" *Psychology in Maine*, 1984, *1*, 1–2.

Shils, E. Social inquiry and the autonomy of the individual. In D. Lerner (Ed.), *The human meaning of the social sciences*. New York: Meridian, 1959.

Shockley, W. Negro IQ Deficit: Failure of a "malicious coincidence" model warrants new research proposals. *Review of Educational Research*, 1971a, *41*, 227–248.

———. Models, mathematics, and the moral obligation to diagnose the origin of Negro IQ deficits. *Review of Educational Research*, 1971b, *41*, 369–377.

Showstack, J. A.; Hargreaves, W. A.; Glick, I. D.; and O'Brien, R. S. Psychiatric follow-up studies. *Journal of Nervous and Mental Disease*, 1978, *166*, 34–43.

Sieber, J. E. (Ed.). *The ethics of social research: Surveys and experiments*. New York: Springer-Verlag, 1982a.

———. *The ethics of social research: Fieldwork, regulation, and publication*. New York: Springer-Verlag, 1982b.

———. Deception in social research I: Kinds of deception and the wrongs they may involve. *IRB: A review of human subjects research*, 1982c, *4*, 1–6.

———. Deception in social research II: Evaluating the potential for harm or wrong. *IRB: A review of human subjects research*, 1982d, *5*, 1–6.

———. Deception in social research III: The nature and limits of debriefing. *IRB: A review of human subjects research*, 1982e, *6*, 1–4.

Silverman, I. Nonreactive methods and the law. *American Psychologist*, 1975, *30*, 764–769.

Silverstein, A. J. Compensating those injured through experimentation. *Federal Bar Journal*, 1974, *33*, 322–330.

Singer, P. *Animal liberation*. New York: Avon, 1975.

Smith, C. P. How (un)acceptable is research involving deception? *IRB: A review of human subjects research*, 1981, *3*, 1–4.

Solomon, R. C. Has not an animal organs, dimensions, senses, affections, passions? *Psychology Today*, March 1982, pp. 36–45.

Stanley, B. H., and Stanley, M. Psychiatric patients in research: Protecting their autonomy. *Comprehensive Psychiatry*, 1981, *22*, 420–427.

Striker, L. J. The true deceiver. *Psychological Bulletin*, 1967, *68*, 13–20.

———; Messick, S.; and Jackson, D. N. Evaluating deception in psychological research. *Psychological Bulletin*, 1969, *71*, 343–351.

Sullivan, D. S., and Deiker, T. E. Subject-experimenter perceptions of ethical issues in human research. *American Psychologist*, 1973, *28*, 587–591.

Swan, L. A. Research and experimentation in prisons. *Journal of Black Psychology*, 1979, *6*, 47–51.

Swazey, J. P. Protecting the "animal of necessity": Limits to inquiry in clinical investigation. *Daedalus*, 1978, *107*, 129–145.

Tanke, E. D., and Tanke, T. J. Regulation and education: The role of the institutional review board in social science research. In J. Sieber (Ed.), *The ethics of social research: Fieldwork, regulation, and publication*. New York: Springer-Verlag, 1982.

Tannenbaum, A. S., and Cooke, R. A. *Research involving children*. Background paper prepared for the National Commission for the Protection of Human Subjects in Biomedical and Behavioral Research. Washington, DC: U.S. Department of Health, Education, and Welfare, 1976.

Tesch, F. E. Debriefing research participants: Though this be method there is madness to it. *Journal of Personality and Social Psychology*, 1977, *35*, 217–224.

Turner, A. G. What subjects of survey research believe about confidentiality. In J. Sieber (Ed.), *The ethics of social research: Surveys and experiments*. New York: Springer-Verlag, 1982.

Van Rooijen, J. Genetic adaptation and welfare. *International Journal for the Study of Animal Problems*, 1983, *4*, 191–197.

Veatch, R. *Three theories of informed consent: Philosophical foundations and policy considerations*. Paper prepared for the National Commission for the Protection of Human Subjects of Biomedical and Behavioral Research. Washington, DC: Department of Health, Education, and Welfare, 1976.

Walster, E.; Bercheid, E.; Abrahams, D.; and Aronson, V. Effectiveness of debriefing following deception experiments. *Journal of Personality and Social Psychology*, 1967, *6*, 371–380.

Warwick, D. P. Tearoom trade: Means and ends in social research. *Hastings Center Studies*, 1973, *1*, 27–38.

———. Deceptive research: Social scientists ought to stop lying. *Psychology Today*, 1975, *10*, 38–40.

Wax, M. L. Research reciprocity rather than informed consent in fieldwork. In J. Sieber (Ed.), *The ethics of social research: Fieldwork, regulation and publication*. New York: Springer-Verlag, 1982.

———, and Cassell, J. (Eds.). *Federal regulation: Ethical issues and social research*. Boulder, CO: Westview Press, 1979.

Weinrach, S. G., and Ivey, A. E. Science, psychology, and deception. *Bulletin of the British Psychological Society*, 1975, *28*, 263–267.

Weinstein, M. C. Allocation of subjects in medical experiments. *New England Journal of Medicine*, 1974, *291*, 1278–1285.

West, S. G.; Gunn, S. P.; and Chernicky, P. Ubiquitous Watergate: An attributional analysis. *Journal of Personality and Social Psychology*, 1975, *32*, 55−65.

Williams, R. L. The silent mugging of the Black community. *Psychology Today*, May 1974, pp. 32−41, 101.

Wilson, D. W., and Donnerstein, E. Legal and ethical aspects of nonreactive social psychological research: An excursion into the public mind. *American Psychologist*, 1976, *31*, 765−773.

Wolfgang, M. E. Confidentiality in criminological research and other ethical issues. *Journal of Criminal Law and Criminology*, 1981, *72*, 345−361.

Wulff, K. M. (Ed.). *Regulation of scientific inquiry: Societal concerns with research.* Washington, DC: American Association for the Advancement of Science, 1979.

X(Clarke), C. (Ed.). The white researcher in black society. *Journal of Social Issues*, 1973, *29*, 1−137.

Zeisel, H. Reducing the hazards of human experiments through modifications in research design. *Annals of the New York Academy of Sciences*, 1970, *169*, 475−486.

Zola, J. C., Sechzer, J. A.; Sieber, J. E., and Griffin, A. Animal experimentation: Issues for the 1980s. *Science, Technology, and Human Values*, 1984, *9*, 40−50.

Psychology and the Public Trust 15

All professions are conspiracies against the laity.

George Bernard Shaw

Each preceding chapter has echoed the call to professional conduct that respects and protects those whose lives are touched by the work of psychologists. Our final chapter overviews ways the *general public*, as opposed to individual consumers, gains or loses trust in psychologists and psychology. Indeed, one of the reasons professions have ethics codes and ethics committees to enforce them is to gain and maintain the trust of the public.

The *Ethical Principles* abound with calls to socially responsible action and conduct. Psychologists are mandated to strive for the preservation and protection of fundamental human rights and to use their knowledge for the promotion of human welfare (*EP*: Preamble, 9 preamble, 10 preamble). The code stresses the special demands on psychologists to be cautious and conscientious when their work touches on social policy and violates or diminishes the civil rights of consumers, or when it may be construed to be detrimental to specific age, sex, ethnic, socioeconomic, or other groups (*EP*: 1a and 3c). It is also noted that psychologists bear a heavy social responsibility because their recommendations and professional actions may alter the lives of others (*EP*: 1f).

In addition, psychologists must remain alert to personal, social, organizational, or political situations that might lead to abuse or to a misuse of their influence (*EP*: 1f and 6a). Psychologists must not engage in or condone practices that are inhumane or that result in illegal or unjustifiable actions (*EP*: 3b) and, while adhering to the law, they must also remain involved in the development of legal and quasi-legal regulations that best serve the

433

public interest and work to change existing regulations that are not beneficial to the public (*EP*: 3d).

THE PUBLIC IMAGE OF PSYCHOLOGY

The public's image of psychologists and psychology is a mysterious and
confused one. Factors contributing to this impression include the often
inferior quality of information about psychology to which the public is
exposed (see Chapter 8), the inherently complex nature of psychology and
its many subspecialties, the still-emerging empirical data base of the subject
matters of the discipline, and our lack of sustained effort to educate the
general public about who we are and what we do. Considerable overlap
between the subject interest of psychology and other disciplines (such as
medicine, sociology, anthropology, biology, education, political science,
and economics), as well as similarities among the services offered by an
array of mental health specialists, clouds the identity of psychology to a
considerable extent. Thumin and Zebelman (1967) note that it is no wonder
that psychology is a muddled field in the public's mind since, "in addition to
working with the mentally ill [psychologists] run rats in mazes, assist in
designing aircraft, evaluate industrial applicants, conduct opinion polls,
and so on, ad infinitum" (p. 282).

Psychologists often experience identity crises after discovering that it
may be easier to communicate and share interests with people from other
disciplines than with some people within their own. For example, a clinical
psychologist working in a community mental health agency and a physiological psychologist working in a research laboratory may have more to say
to a social worker and a biologist, respectively, than to each other.

Since the 1960s, both psychology and psychiatry have increasingly
emphasized the family, as well as social, political, and economic factors, as
possible causes of mental illness. Suddenly, mental health professionals
were forced to question the efficacy of alleviating emotional disorders
through 50-minute, weekly talk sessions with one person at a time. Should
their professional role change, and, if so, how? Many have become involved
in social and political action with a goal toward ameliorating or preventing
the conditions in society that spawn maladaptive behavior. Whereas such
activities are virtually always well meaning, the goals are often grandiosely
asserted. The public expects results and then responds with cynicism when
they were not immediately forthcoming. Speaking specifically about psychiatry, Bourne (1978) has asserted that, "psychiatrists were seen as people
who promised too much and as naive idealists, who in the final analysis
failed to deliver" (p. 174).

Indeed, human nature and social problems are now often discussed by
the public in psychological terms (Back, 1973), which may reinforce the
layperson's high expectations for behavioral scientists and mental health

professionals to try and set the world straight. Behavioral scientists are often expected to provide the answers to complex social problems. While not discounting the useful findings that have emerged and may be applied to the alleviation of human suffering, the *big answers* the public expects, especially when their tax dollars are funding the attempts, have not appeared. Despite assertions (usually emanating from *within* the profession) that crime, environmental pollution, violence, family disintegration, substance abuse, overpopulation, and prejudice are basically psychological phenomena, the world remains overcrowded, dirty, unsafe, and unjust.

A general suspicion of the value of professionals has characterized our recent past (Lerner, 1975). Most citizens (75%, according to a recent Roper poll) regard professionals as overpaid. Books for popular consumption, written specifically about professions, are usually scathing indictments of the self-serving motives, incompetency, and even cover-ups perpetrated among colleagues. Most prominently displayed news items about individual professionals, including psychologists, tend to focus on those who flagrantly violated their responsibilities or maliciously committed reprehensible acts.

Positive public images of individual psychologists or of the profession as a whole are more rare. The recent acquisition of the popular magazine, *Psychology Today*, by the American Psychological Association may prove to be a useful vehicle for balance, though critics are concerned about the Association's ability to keep such a costly business venture afloat. Even here, a public trust controversy has arisen. Liquor and cigarette advertisements are a major source of funding for magazines, and already many socially conscious psychologists are outraged that a publication owned by the APA carries glossy enticements to engage in behavior well documented as harmful.

We should quickly note that public wariness about psychology and psychologists is not necessarily all bad. Professional arrogance and elitism have often translated into the assumption that consumers are ignorant and unaware of what is good for them. As Palmer (1981) notes regarding medical practice, it was once thought best not to let patients know what ailed them and safest if the prescriptions were written in a language patients could not understand. Contemporary concern about professionals may indicate a healthy trend—namely, that those who seek professional services see themselves as having the capacity to understand, the right to any information associated with the services being purchased, and entitlement to accountability for service quality.

"GOOD EGGS"

Psychologists who maintain their competencies, remain fair and sensitive in their dealings with consumers, and respect the ethical standards of the profession contribute to the preservation of public trust. Psychologists who, in addition, give of themselves to alleviate the suffering of those of limited financial means, who educate consumers about their rights, or participate in activities that will benefit others enhance the public trust and bestow honor on the profession.

A self-report survey of APA members revealed that 96% of the 900 respondents indicated that they engaged in one or more forms of public interest activity during the preceding year (Good, Simon, and Coursey, 1981). The most frequent (67%) was the provision of professional services without compensation, an activity explicitly encouraged in the *Ethical Principles* (*EP*: 6d). Other activities reported by a large number of respondents included the following: encouragement of one's agency, organization, or institution to evaluate the effectiveness of its programs, policies, or services (59%); taking additional training to maintain competence in the face of changing social developments (56%); development or modifications of a program or service technique designed to meet the needs of individuals or changing social conditions (48%); preparation of a verbal or written contract that included what the client could expect from the psychologist and what the psychologist expected from the client (48%); evaluation of the effectiveness of one's work (47%); and service on an advisory body to a governmental unit or on a board or a committee of a nonprofit service agency or community affairs group (44%).

The cases below illustrate some individual "good eggs." Unfortunately, such people typically do not receive the public (or even professional) recognition they deserve, whereas the "bad eggs," discussed in the next section, may become instantly notorious.

Case 15–1: Ernest Freebie, Ph.D., maintains a private practice specializing in psychotherapy with adolescents. He donates his Wednesdays to a community youth center where he provides counseling and assists the staff with program development.

Case 15–2: Marshall Advocate, Ed.D., works in a school for developmentally disabled adults. He is active in community education programs aimed at reducing the stigma associated with mental retardation and advancing the rights and opportunities for this population. He regularly consults with potential employers of developmentally disabled persons and is available to policy makers for input regarding legislation relevant to the developmentally disabled and their families.

Case 15–3: Ada Class, M. A., a retired school psychologist, volunteers as a consultant to the local Board of Education on matters of immediate concern, such as the impact of busing, corporal punishment, school violence, and mainstreaming. Ms. Class prepares background papers and conducts interviews for the Board to assist it with decision making.

Case 15–4: Emmett Contact, Ph.D., volunteers as a trainer one day a week and back-up resource two evenings a week for a community hotline. He also developed a community resource manual to assist the telephone volunteers in making appropriate referrals.

Some may doubt the public interest activities of some psychologists, suspecting that they are only contrived vehicles for self-serving motives.

Case 15−5:   Eli Jabber, Psy. D., is available for speaking to community groups in a variety of psychological topics. In the course of his talks, he makes references to his private practice and displays a small stack of business cards on the corner of the speaker's table.

Case 15−6:   Dee Fecund, Ph.D., routinely seeks grant funding for studies relevant to whatever social problem is associated with available monies. These have ranged from violence against children to teenage alcoholism and old age depression. A few colleagues have referred to her as a "grant chaser." Other colleagues counter that her critics are simply envious of her ability to generate funding.

Whether these psychologists deserve praise for their activities probably depends less on their motives, which may include personal gain, and more on the quality and benefits of what they actually do. If Dr. Jabber's talks are based on sound psychological knowledge and his reference to his own practice fits naturally with the material (e.g., used as an illustration), one cannot fault Dr. Jabber's educative contributions. If, however, Dr. Jabber's speeches are extremely superficial and the self-references are geared toward manipulating the audiences' vulnerabilities and selling his own services, the "public interest value" of Jabber's activities could most certainly be called into question. Dr. Fecund's position is somewhat similar. As long as she produces sound proposals and is equipped to follow through with competent work, the fact that her program of research is diverse does not mean that her interest in researching social issues is not genuine.

Examples of activities that most psychologists and others would consider to be socially responsible, public interest activities include advocating vulnerable populations that elicit public sympathy (e.g., abused children and the dying), providing research data or other forms of assistance to policy-makers in areas with widespread popular appeal (e.g., promoting quality, but cost-effective, mental health programs and preventing drug abuse in teenagers), and educating consumers about psychology, its various specialties, and how to assess whether members of the profession are delivering quality services. (See, for example, Mental Health Law Project, 1973; Noll, 1974; Simon, 1975; Ennis and Emery, 1978; Morrison, 1978, 1979; Hare-Mustin, Marecek, Kaplan, and Liss-Levinson, 1979; Hannah, Christian, and Clark, 1981.) Assisting the public in formulating accurate and nonstigmatizing views of people who have emotional disorders is another worthy cause about which psychologists have special expertise and responsibility (e.g., Sarbin and Mancuso, 1970; Morrison, 1980).

"BAD EGGS"

How psychologists can reduce the public trust and tarnish the image of the profession can be illustrated in two ways. First, individual psychologists can engage in conduct or activities that violate the law and/or professional standards that *attract public attention*. Each display of a piece of "dirty linen" takes a toll on the image of the profession. Second, the public trust is compromised whenever the profession itself is perceived of as ineffective, self-protective, neglectful, or trite due to the actions (or inactions) of larger collections of psychologists or professional inattention.

Publicized Cases of Individual Misconduct

Although psychologists, *as private citizens*, have the right to formulate their own moral and ethical standards, any act that may compromise the fulfillment of professional responsibilities or reflect negatively on psychology or psychologists by reducing the public trust violates the *Ethical Principles* (*EP*: 3 preamble).

The first series of cases presented illustrate breaches of *both* legal and ethical requirements by individuals, in the course of their *professional* activity, which resulted in widespread publicity.

> **Case 15−7:**   Ann Ergetic, Ph.D., was referred to an ethics committee by an insurance carrier indicating that their audit had revealed that Dr. Ergetic had billed their company for 120 hours of psychotherapy during a single 7-day period (17 hours of psychotherapy a day on the average). Although the clients failed to substantiate that many of the sessions actually took place, Dr. Ergetic insisted that the patients' recollections were in error and that "she enjoyed doing psychotherapy and did not require much sleep."

> **Case 15−8:**   Dick Imposter, Ph.D., used the name and qualifications of a psychiatrist from another state and accepted a position as a staff psychiatrist in a mental health clinic. When Dr. Imposter became concerned that his true identity might be discovered, he traveled to the authentic psychiatrist's office and attempted to murder him.

> **Case 15−9:**   A mother complained to the police and an ethics committee that Phil Pedo, Ph.D., had molested her young daughter during a counseling session. While bathing her daughter after the session, the mother noticed that the child's genital area was reddened. When questioned, the girl said that it must have happened during the "secret game" that she and Dr. Pedo had played; Dr. Pedo would take off her panties and have her sit on his face. The mother entered into legal action against Dr. Pedo.

Although these cases involve serious ethical and legal violations that could have been presented in previous chapters, they were selected for presentation here because each attracted considerable attention through media exposure. To the extent that the public generalizes its attitudes about psychologists from such accounts, psychologists would be viewed as potentially fraudulent, exploitative, perverted, and even violent.

Although the matter of ethics committees' investigating the commission of crimes or highly questionable activities *unrelated to one's professional identification as a psychologist* has been debated (see Chapter 2), it is clear that the public image of psychology is compromised when such acts are publicized. The next two cases are illustrative.

> **Case 15–10:** A young boy was seriously injured by hit-and-run driver, Hooch Jagger, Ph.D. A heavily intoxicated Jagger was quickly apprehended. Newspaper accounts highlighted the facts that Jagger had six previous arrests for drunk driving and that he was a psychologist who taught at the local university.

Whether Dr. Jagger's irresponsible drinking/driving behavior compromised his ability to teach students is not known, nor is it at issue here. However, along with Jagger himself, both his department and the discipline probably suffered some loss in reputation.

> **Case 15–11:** The discovery that a group of people in the United States arranged for the selling of arms to an unfriendly nation revealed that Billy Bazooka, Ed.D., was among the defendants. News accounts prominently revealed Dr. Bazooka's vocation as a psychologist.

Again, the same question pertains regarding whether Dr. Bazooka's competence to deliver psychological services was in anyway affected by his illegal gun-running activity. Yet, no doubt, his nonprofessional escapade was embarrassing and cast shame on his peers and on the name of psychology.

Illegal activity is not a necessary ingredient to the decline of public trust. As the next case illustrates, publicized acts of exploitation by a psychologist may not violate any laws, but may smear the image of psychology nevertheless.

> **Case 15–12:** Fasty Buck, Ph.D., was treating Persona Galore for a dissociative disorder. Dr. Buck discovered more than a dozen "personalities" within Miss Galore and persuaded the client to sign over exclusive book and movie rights to Miss Galore's story. Dr. Buck also arranged press conferences for herself and Miss Galore, and charged the client her usual hourly rate for the time spent promoting the forthcoming book. Galore eventually charged Dr. Buck with exploiting her unusual condition. She noted that the psychotherapy sessions had become less concerned with psychotherapy and more concerned with getting sordid, publishable materials, and, as a result, her condition was worsening.

Unfortunately, the public trust in psychology and psychologists may sometimes be compromised despite the fact that the psychologists themselves were innocent of any legal or ethical wrongdoing. Although psychologists are admonished to do whatever is within their power to ensure that their work or services will not be misused by others (*EP* 1: preamble, a, and f), such control is not always possible as the next two cases illustrate.

> **Case 15–13:** Edna Scholarly, Ph.D., a prominent research psychologist, wrote to an ethics committee expressing concern about an incident coming to her attention. She had received a letter from a distraught mother blaming her for having lost her child in a custody dispute. The mother had also contacted a newspaper who ran "her story." Further inquiry revealed that the father's attorney had used Dr. Scholarly's paper dealing with the effects of working mothers on child development as a "cheap" expert witness, and that certain comments taken out-of-context and embellished inappropriately, were persuasive to the court. Dr. Scholarly believed that her work had been used in an unethical manner and sought counsel for any possible redress.

> **Case 15–14:** Quick Whip, a journalist advocating the use of harsh physical punishment of children's wrongdoings, cited a number of prominent psychologists' works to bolster his argument that corporal punishment (including use of electric shock devices) is not only an effective means of eliminating unwanted behavior, but will also improve overall emotional status. The psychologists' research and techniques were grossly misrepresented and taken out of the context for which they would even be considered for application. The cited psychologists were outraged over how they had unwittingly been used to promote child-rearing techniques they considered to be extremely harmful for everyday use with normal children.

Shirking of Professional Responsibility to the Public

Aside from the misdeeds of individual psychologists that tarnish our image, the public may have negative associations toward psychology in more general ways. Some of these views are rooted in distortions and untruths that are difficult to overcome (e.g., "Only very crazy people consult psychologists," "All psychologists can read your mind," and "Psychologists can control your behavior"). As we have noted, the media are not very helpful in overcoming many of these less-than-accurate or unfavorable characterizations (see Chapter 8). Vocal nonpsychologist critics, such as Senator Proxmire (Miller, 1976; Shaffer, 1977), have no doubt taken some toll on the public's image of what research psychologists do.

Other contributors to the public's negative image of psychology occur whenever guild-protective interests or convenience supercede a concern for the welfare of consumers. For example, Lantz and Lenahan (1973) provide a stinging, tongue-in-cheek description of the mental health professional, most likely found in a social service system serving lower socioeconomic groups, who, regardless of the client's problems, insists that the responsibility belongs elsewhere and refers them on down the line. *Referral-Fatigue Therapy* (RFT) is, these authors assert, rapidly gaining adherents.

> On the surface it might appear that the RF Therapist does nothing, but this is truly not the case. The RF Therapist does a great deal. At the very least, the RF Therapist dictates lengthy memoranda about why he is unable to help and arranges for his clients to see other RF Therapists. The superior RF Therapist is even more active: he might also study the problem, develop job opportunities for other RF Therapists, and draw upon a large repertoire of therapeutic styles to help his clients understand his own and his agency's limitations. Any impression the RF Therapist may give of not helping his client is also inaccurate. To begin with, as any sensitive observer can testify, the clients of RF Therapists seldom return. What could be a more resounding demonstration that a therapy works than this?. . . A well-trained RF Therapist. . . realizes that after a certain amount of therapeutic runaround the client begins to believe that (1) "This is fatiguing," and (2) "I'd better do it myself or it won't get done." Obviously, this type of therapy promotes client autonomy. (Lantz and Lenahan, 1973, pp. 239–240).

Even the widespread use of psychological jargon that has been perpetuated by psychologists ("I'm into high energy," "I know that space," "I'm going to get my head together") has been criticized as causing public harm. Rather than facilitating understanding and communication, such "pop" jargon may convey nothing of significance and even block, conceal, or inhibit understanding (Rosen, 1977; Hallenstein, 1978). Hallenstein concludes that there is no room for irresponsible language in psychology, especially when the ethical charge of the profession is to increase people's understanding of themselves and others. The technical language, including research terminology, has also been criticized for being overly complicated, thus contributing to a lack of understanding about what professionals do (Newman,1975).

As a final example of a more general way that the public trust may be eroded, we note that the competitiveness that often characterizes the relationship between psychology and its "sister" professions (such as psychiatry, social work, and marriage and family counseling) often degenerates into mutual backbiting and less-than-responsible allegations about competencies and qualifications. For a public that does not have these disciplines clearly identified in the first place, the effect may be to downgrade the value of all of them.

"SCRAMBLED EGGS"

Many of the subject matters of psychology are controversial or sensitive, because values, attitudes, vulnerabilities, and human frailties and foibles fall into its domain. It should come as no surprise that many well-meaning public activities of psychologists are evaluated variously by others, depending on whose ox is being gored. Differences in opinion include conflicts over what approaches are acceptable to achieve a humane goal as well as whether certain goals are themselves "good" or in the best public interest.

Examples of some psychologists' causes that call forth praise from some and outrage from others (including other psychologists), depending on the evaluators' own attitudes and values, could fill volumes. A few examples include advocating decriminalization of marijuana use, abortion on demand, aversive conditioning technique use on psychotic children, diagnostic labelling, and the absolute right to refuse treatment. Sometimes the side taken is primarily a matter of basic belief systems that are highly resistant to change, even in the face of solid data in support of the opposing viewpoint. For example, those who see homosexuality as evil or unnatural are unlikely to accept any argument favoring acceptance of homosexuals as healthy, valuable members of society who also happen to prefer those of their own sex as sexual partners. At other times, it is one's own perspective of longer range consequences that determines a position. For example, those advocating the development of quality daycare programs for young children point to the fact that many families require two working parents to survive financially and that the current needs of preschool children cannot be ignored. Critics argue that the support of widespread child care facilities only serves to reinforce the already disintegrating family system.

A "scrambled" image also persists whenever one accepted ethic is pitted against another, and it is almost impossible to act in accordance with both simultaneously. For example, according people the right to autonomy and self-determination is echoed throughout the *Ethical Principles*, but conflicts can easily arise. Some psychologists have been actively involved in the "deprogramming" of cult members. The goal is to "free" individuals who may have been lured into an indoctrination process requiring the acceptance of rigid beliefs and life styles. Yet to engage in similar tactics to "rescue" such people raises questions about the extent to which one can use coercion for someone else's "own good." Similarly, the case of the woman who died on the streets in a cardboard box, after refusing efforts to provide her with protective care, has caused considerable debate concerning the responsibilities of society, acting through its mental health professionals and policies, to intervene forcefully into people's lives (Hopper, 1982; Kittrie, 1982). Robinson (1974) has developed an ethical rationale for involuntary therapeutic intervention, but the issue remains extremely complex.

Finally, we note the muddled issue of the involvement of psychologists and their research findings in matters of public policy. The *Ethical Principles* implicitly encourage psychologists to remain active in ways that will improve the lives of others, including the alteration or formulation of laws and policies (e.g., *EP*: Preamble, and 3d). However, psychologists and ethicists are typically not attuned either to the political and bureaucratic worlds of constituencies, interests groups, and power blocs or to the tactics used to scramble for limited resources (Jonsen and Butler, 1975). Concern has been expressed that involvement in policy matters may pose threats to the integrity of the scientific process and that data from social and behavioral sciences may be used primarily to maintain the powerful forces that control policy decisions rather than for the benefit of all (Chinoy, 1970; Lasswell, 1970; Carey, 1977). It has even been asserted that psychology may be losing its credibility due to increasing political activity by psychologists. Baron (1981) suggests that government funding has been drastically cut for social and behavioral science research primarily because of the perception that the findings of such research are almost *predictable* from the political views of the investigators.

It is hardly our purpose to provide the "right" answers to "scrambled egg" issues. Rather, we are simply noting that the level of public trust in psychology will continue to vary depending on how its members' views coincide or clash with those held by psychologists individually or collectively (i.e., through position statements that professional associations take on various matters of social concern) on issues about which values, opinion, theory, and evidence conflict. Despite the fact that the public trust may remain divided or confused in the process, this condition will remain as a necessary by-product of a democratic society that permits free speech and diverse beliefs. (See Rubinstein and Slife, 1984, for an intriguing selection of clashing views on controversial psychological issues.)

RISKS OF SOCIAL RESPONSIBILITY

Whenever people devote themselves to a cause they consider to be humane and right, at least a small measure of appreciation or recognition from others is probably expected. As we have just seen, well-meaning psychologists have faced criticism from those whose values or priorities differ from their own. Sometimes they have been labeled as troublemakers or as embarrassments to the profession. Although such outcomes should be anticipated by anyone advocating a controversial position, the backlash may be experienced as very painful.

Perhaps the riskiest form of action taken on behalf of the public and its welfare involves "whistle-blowing." In its typical and better-known form, the whistle-blower holds an "insider" position (often one of some authority) as a government, agency, business, or institution employee. Unethical, illegal, or socially deleterious practices within the work setting have caused the whistle-blower considerable concern because of the belief that these have caused, or will cause, harm to others. Typically, the whistle-blower had unsuccessfully attempted to remediate the situation through established channels within the organization. The employer's stone-walling, delays, excuses, or unresponsiveness eventually lead to sharing information with some outside source in the hope that the practice would be eliminated by external pressure or fiat.

The inherent risks in whistle-blowing are numerous, including loss of employment or, failing that, demotion or transfer, often to some undesirable location or position. If the individual remains within the organization, he or she may be "chilled out" socially, even by those thought to be friends. Those known to be potential informants may have difficulty finding other employment. *Most* disconcerting is the possibility that the action itself may amount to an exercise in futility if the information shared is ignored by the outside contact or suspended indefinitely in bureaucratic red tape. The highly publicized case of Karen Silkwood (Rashke, 1981) suggests that whistle-blowers may even risk being "eliminated." Nader, Petkas, and Blackwell (1972) offer many accounts of whistle-blowers, most of whom suffered loss of status and personal distress as a result of their decision to risk their own security in order to protect the public.

Throughout the years, psychology ethics committees have received a number of inquiries from psychologists who are concerned about practices at their places of employment, which they have construed as violations of the *Ethical Principles*, or employer mandates that require psychologists to violate the *Ethical Principles* as a condition of employment. One psychologist complained that he was instructed to use assessment techniques he considered to be extremely inappropriate for the purpose at hand, resulting in the misclassification of hundreds of job applicants. Another reported that the deaths of several mental hospital patients went unreported and that the deceased were, instead, listed as "AWOL." Another opposed the hiring practices at his university, which he claimed were blatantly sexist and racist as evidenced by remarks and decisions made during closed recruitment meetings. Yet another protested that confidential patient records were, in fact, available for viewing by anyone including other patients, since they were stored openly on shelves in the busy reception area of a mental health clinic. Most inquiries to psychology ethics committees do not involve matters of national significance as typify the better-known whistle-blowers such as Daniel Ellsberg or A. Ernest Fitzgerald. But the rights or welfare of some people were believed to be jeopardized.

A detailed portrait of a psychologist whistle-blower is presented by Simon (1978). (Although Simon's article reveals the actual identities of all of the parties involved, our adaptation refers to the psychologist as "Dr. Jack Provet.")

Case 15-15: Jack Provet, Ph.D., was promoted to the position of Unit Chief, a position usually held by an M.D., at a large Veterans Administration psychiatric facility. The building housing Dr. Provet's 200 patients was condemned because of structural damages. Instead of relocating the patients, the Medical Chief of Staff ordered Provet to discharge them immediately. Provet protested the orders on the grounds that many were not prepared for community living and, for the others, some time was necessary to make adequate plans to facilitate their chances for a successful transition. Dr. Provet was relieved of his position on-the-spot and assigned to a low-status duty, supervised by a social worker, in a Quonset hut on the periphery of the grounds. The veteran patients called the media and staged a protest in support of Dr. Provet. Reporters were also present to witness Provet clearing out his desk. Provet shortly received transfer orders to a small, rural VA facility in another state and, when the transfer was refused on grounds that seniority policy was violated, Provet was fired.

The *Ethical Principles* implicitly encourage responsible whistle-blowing. Psychologists are admonished not to permit the misuse of their skills by others (*EP*: Preamble), and are reminded that even though they may be members of governmental or other organizational bodies, they still remain accountable to the highest standards of their profession (*EP*: 3b). The code falls just short of *mandating* psychologists to "blow the whistle," leaving the ultimate decision to the individual while providing a faint green go-ahead. Specifically, the code states, "Where the demands of an organization require psychologists to violate these *Ethical Principles*, psychologists clarify the nature of the conflict between the demands of these principles. They inform all parties of psychologists' ethical responsibilities *and take appropriate action*" (emphasis added).

Unfortunatley, APA is not a sure-fire source of support for psychologists who upset a powerful organization in the course of upholding the standards APA promulgates. Ethics committees can do little more than clarify the psychologists' responsibilities to their profession. APA has established a defense fund (dependent on member contributions) for the purpose of assisting psychologists who face various sorts of adversities. But the Association is not well equipped to be responsive to members or to offer resources in a timely manner. Dr. Provet, for example, faced detached and passive processing of his request for assistance from APA's Committee on Academic Freedom and Conditions of Employment, which led Simon (1978) to hypothesize that the Association feared supporting a member who blew the whistle on the VA since, by doing so, the VA support of the clinical internship program might be jeopardized. Rather, it was a union (American Federation of Government Employees) that provided immediate and sustained support resulting in Dr. Provet's ultimate reinstatement and back pay restitution.

Nader and his colleagues (1972) admit that no tried and true formula for safe and effective whistle-blowing exist. However, they have provided a list of questions to assist the would-be whistle-blower with decision making and strategy.

1. Is my knowledge of the matter complete and accurate?
2. What are the objectionable practices, and what public interest do they harm?
3. How far should I, and can I go inside the organization with my concern or objection?
4. Will I be violating any rules by contacting outside parties and, if so, is whistle-blowing nevertheless justified?
5. Will I be violating any laws or ethical duties by *not* contacting external parties?
6. Once I have decided to act, what is the best way to blow the whistle— anonymously, overtly, by resignation prior to speaking out, or in some other way?
7. What will be the likely responses from various sources—inside and outside the organization—to the whistle-blowing action?
8. What is expected to be achieved by whistle-blowing in this particular situation? (p. 6).

Answering these questions thoughtfully and conscientiously, particularly with a careful awareness of one's owns values and needs and capacity for objectivity, is critical since whistle-blowing is not always done for the right reasons. Such activity could even carry drastic consequences for others while protecting no one. The unlamented activity of Senator Joseph McCarthy is a well-known case in point.

Ideally, an ethic of whistle-blowing could be implemented that could be practically applied in many contexts without fear of retribution. As Nader et al. (1972) note, the fabric for such an ethic already exists.

> Indeed, the basic status of a citizen in a democracy underscores the themes implicit in a form of professional and individual responsibility that places responsibility to society over that to an illegal or negligent or unjust organizational policy or activity. These themes touch on the right of free speech, the right to information, the citizen's right to participate in important public decisions, and the individual's obligation to avoid complicity in harmful, fraudulent, or corrupt activities. (p. 7)

Yet, as whistle-blowing now stands, it involves risk and the potential for considerable self-sacrifice. We suspect that many may rationalize inaction, or turn one's eyes aside, or engage in some form of procrastination that suspends action indefinitely (Sabini and Silver, 1982). Yet personal consequences are likely to ensue. As Nader and his associates (1972) explain, "Silence in the face of abuses may also be evaluated in terms of the toll it takes on the individuals who in doing so subvert their own consciousnesses" (p. 2). Despite the risks, the Good et. al. (1981) survey revealed that 135 of their 990 respondents indicated that they had blown the whistle after exhausting channels of redress at least once during the preceding year. Unfortunately, the survey required no detail about the nature of these activities. But the results may indicate that quiet, unpublicized action may be taking place on a larger scale than one might estimate.

THE LAST WORD: PSYCHOLOGISTS HAVE RIGHTS TOO!

The ethical responsibilities of psychologists to consumers, society, and each other may sometimes feel overwhelming and draining. It is, then, important not to lose sight of the rights psychologists must demand for themselves. By doing so, psychologists not only exercise their freedoms as citizens and their prerogatives to lead fulfilling and productive lives, but also enhance the possibilities of maintaining competent, sensitive, and ethical professional lives. We cannot expect adequate performances from psychologists who are overworked, who function in surroundings or under dictates that preclude optimum exercise of their skills, who are discouraged or barred from engaging in certain lawful activities as private citizens by their employers, who are required as a condition of employment to perform duties for which they are not trained or which may harm or violate the rights of others, or who are subjected to personal danger in their professional work setting. The following cases, gleaned from inquiries made to ethics committees by psychologists who believed that their personal and/or professional rights were denied to them, indicate the typical adverse conditions under which some psychologists have been pressured to function.

Case 15−16: Irwin Squeezed, Ed.D., contacted an ethics committee for assistance when the director of the university counseling center, Orville Posh, Ph.D., made drastic changes in office arrangements. Counseling offices were being converted to a conference room for the director. Dr. Squeezed was assigned to conduct private counseling sessions with students in a 6 by 6 foot windowless cubicle used for test storage. After protesting these working conditions, Dr. Posh allegedly told Dr. Squeezed to "quit fretting or go into private practice."

Case 15−17: The company president where Nuke Nobomb, Ph.D., worked as an industrial-organizational psychologist ordered Dr. Nobomb to remove himself from after-hour involvement in a community group promoting nuclear disarmament. The boss noted that the company's reputation was "solid, traditional, pro-defense, and American" and that this image was in favor with the current administration. Despite Dr. Nobomb's insistence that the group was "composed of concerned middle-class parents who are as American as anyone else," the president remained firm in his view.

Case 15−18: Recently licensed Tina Terror, Psy.D., accepted a community agency position as a counselor. She complained to her supervisor that one of her assigned clients, Snarlie Hulk, ridiculed her for her small stature and little-girl appearance and frightened her with such comments as, "I could snap you in two with one hand if I wanted." She asked her supervisor if Hulk could be reassigned because she was not sufficiently experienced to handle this type of client and that she was sure Hulk was not benefitting from her attempts to treat him. Dr. Terror noted that she felt comfortable and competent to deal with all of her other assigned clients. The supervisor ordered Dr. Terror to continue with Hulk saying, "You'll never learn unless you jump right in." Dr. Terror continued and Hulk's taunting and threats of bodily harm accelerated. The supervisor continued to refuse to reassign him to another therapist.

Case 15–19:   Sluff Fillit, Ph.D., the chair of a university psychology department, assigned Corpus Callosum, Ph.D., to teach a section of the personal adjustment course because Dr. Callosum's advanced neurophysiology class failed to meet the minimum enrollment requirement. Dr. Callosum objected because he had never taught the personal adjustment course and had no background whatsoever in personality theory or clinical psychology, except for two courses taken as an undergraduate. Dr. Fillit insisted that he give it a try since the course was fully enrolled and would generate considerable credit for the department. He added, "The students are all lower division, so they won't even notice that you don't know what you're talking about."

Occasionally, more bizarre situations are reported to the ethics committee.

Case 15–20:   Although Lionel Daunt, Ph.D., had initiated termination of his position as an assistant to Crone Warlock, Psy.D., he believed that the "goings on at Warlock's weekend marathons should be exposed." Warlock allegedly demanded that his assistants renounce their religious beliefs and actively practice his brand of voodooism. This involved chantings, burning of certain herbs in seashells, and an occasional sacrifice of a live reptile. These ceremonies, often accompanied by the use of drugs supplied by Warlock, were woven into the "therapy" weekends. Assistants were asked to swear loyalty and total allegiance to Warlock and to renounce all "nonbelievers."

We conclude our book with a brief overview of the rights that all psychologists should be free to enjoy. We have adapted some of our points from the APA's "Guidelines for Conditions of Employment of Psychologists" (APA, 1972).

1. Whereas psychologists are responsible to their employers for the functions and obligations they have committed to perform, their free-time activities should not be dictated by the primary employer as long as conflict of interest is not involved. Psychologists are free to engage in lawful non-job-relevant activities without threats to their employment status (*EP:* 3 Preamble).

2. Psychologists may practice their profession within the law free from duress or interference from other professions or groups. (See Annas, Glantz, and Katz, 1981, for a readable account of the rights of health professionals.)

3. Psychologists have the right to work in decent physical environments, allowing for both optimum performance of the psychologists and the privacy and comfort of clients.

4. Psychologists have the right to practice in safe surroundings. When the possibility for bodily harm or danger exists, it is the employer's responsibility to institute safeguards.

5. Psychologists have the right to practice within their areas of competence and to refuse pressures to perform inappropriate, harmful, or unethical services. Psychologists may limit their practices to a specific type of client or condition where such subspecialties are recognized. In specific instances, psychologists may terminate or withhold services when it can be reasonably argued that to do otherwise would constitute an ineffective professional relationship.

6. Psychologists have the right to protest conditions of employment, such as unreasonable case-loads or poor working conditions, whenever the welfare of consumers may be compromised.

7. Psychologists have the right to demand freedom of inquiry and communication, although they must also accept the responsibility these freedoms require (*EP*: Preamble)

8. Psychologists who are supervised by other psychologists have a right to timely evaluative feedback and to constructive consultation and experience opportunities (*EP*: 7c).

9. Psychologists have a right to credit for work they have accomplished (*EP*: 7f) and the right to redress when others have exploited them (*EP*: 1a, 3b, and others).

10. Psychologists have a right to fair compensation for professional services rendered, and to engage in appropriate action when compensation is withheld (see Chapter 6).

11. Psychologists have the right as well as the obligation to refuse to participate in professional, research, or educational activities that endanger human welfare.

REFERENCES

American Psychological Association. Guidelines for conditions of employment of psychologists. *American Psychologist*, 1972, 27, 331–334.

Annas, G. J.; Glantz, L. H.; and Katz, B. F. *The rights of doctors, nurses, and allied health professionals.* Cambridge, MA: Ballinger, 1981.

Back, K. W. The psychiatrist: Healer, prophet, both or neither? *Social Science and Medicine*, 1973, 7, 831–838.

Baron, R. A. The spring of our discontent: Some observations on the less-than-shocking view that science and politics don't mix. *APA Division 7 Newsletter*, Fall, 1981, 28–33.

Bourne, P. G. The psychiatrist's responsibility and the public trust. *American Journal of Psychiatry*, 1978, 135, 174–177.

Carey, A. The Lysenko syndrome in Western social science. *Australian Psychologist*, 1977, *12*, 27–38.

Chinoy, E. *Knowledge and action: The role of sociology*. Northampton, MA.: Smith College Press, 1970.

Ennis, B., and Emery, R. *The rights of mental patients*. New York: Avon, 1978.

Good, P.; Simon, G. C.; and Coursey, R. D. Public interest activities of APA members. *American Psychologist*, 1981, *36*, 963–971.

Hallenstein, C. B. Ethical problems of psychological jargon. *Professional Psychology*, 1978, *9*, 111–116.

Hannah, G. T.; Christian, W. P.; and Clark, H. B. (Eds.) *Preservation of client rights: A handbook for practitioners providing therapeutic, educational, and rehabilitative services*. New York: Free Press, 1981.

Hare-Mustin, R. T.; Marecek, J.; Kaplan, A. G.; and Liss-Levinson, N. Rights of clients, responsibilities of therapists. *American Psychologist*, 1979, *34*, 3–16.

Hopper, K. Commentary—The woman who died in a box. *Hastings Center Report*, 1982, *12*, 18–19.

Jonsen, A. R., and Butler, L. H. Public ethics and policy making. *Hastings Center Report 5*, August 1975, pp. 19–31.

Kittrie, N. N. Commentary—The woman who died in a box. *Hastings Center Report*, 1982, *12*, 19.

Lantz, J. E., and Lenahan, B. Referral-Fatigue Therapy. *Social Work*, 1973, *21*, 239–241.

Lasswell, H. D. Must science serve political power? *American Psychologist*, 1970, *25*, 117–123.

Lerner, M. Watergating on main street: The shame of the professions. *SR*, Nov. 1975, pp. 10–12.

Mental Health Law Project. *Basic rights of the mentally handicapped*. Washington, DC: Mental Health Law Project, 1973.

Miller, J. The Proxmire effect. *Human Behavior*, Sept. 1976, pp. 57–59.

Morrison, J. K. The client as consumer and evaluator of community mental health services. *American Journal of Community Psychology*, 1978, *6*, 147–155.

———. A consumer-oriented approach to psychotherapy. *Psychotherapy: Theory, Research and Practice*, 1979, *16*, 381–384.

———. The public's current beliefs about mental illness: Serious obstacles to effective community psychology. *American Journal of Community Psychology*, 1980, *8*, 697–707.

Nader, R.; Petkas, P.; and Blackwell, K. (Eds.). *Whistle Blowing*. New York: Bantam, 1972.

Newman, E. *Strictly speaking*. New York: Warner, 1975.

Noll, J. O. Needed—A bill of rights for clients. *Professional Psychology*, 1974, *5*, 3–12.

Palmer, R. E. A moron shortage. *New York Times*, Feb. 3, 1981, p. 6.

Rashke, R. *The Killing of Karen Silkwood*. New York: Houghton Mifflin, 1981.

Robinson, D. N. Harm, offense, and nuisance: Some first steps in the establishment of an ethics of treatment. *American Psychologist*, 1974, *29*, 233–238.

Rosen, R. D. *Psychobabble*. New York: Atheneum,, 1977.

Rubinstein, J., and Slife, B. D. *Taking sides: Clashing views on controversial issues.* Guilford, CT: Duskin, 1984.

Sabini, J, and Silver, M. *Moralities of everyday life*. London: Oxford University Press, 1982.

Sarbin, T. R., and Mancuso, J. C. Failure of a moral enterprise: Attitudes of the public toward mental illness. *Journal of Consulting and Clinical Psychology*, 1970, *35*, 159–173.

Shaffer, L. S. The golden fleece: Anti-intellectualism and social science. *American Psychologist*, 1977, 814–823.

Simon, G. C. Psychology and the "treatment rights movement." *Professional Psychology*, 1975, *6*, 243–251.

———. The psychologist as whistle blower: A case study. *Professional psychology*, 1978, *9*, 322–340.

Thumin, F. J., and Zebelman, M. Psychology versus psychology: A study of public image. *American Psychologist*, 1967, *22*, 282–286.

Appendix

ETHICAL PRINCIPLES OF PSYCHOLOGISTS*

PREAMBLE

Psychologists respect the dignity and worth of the individual and strive for the preservation and protection of fundamental human rights. They are committed to increasing knowledge of human behavior and of people's understanding of themselves and others and to the utilization of such

* This version of the Ethical Principles of Psychologists (formerly entitled Ethical Standards of Psychologists) was adopted by the American Psychological Association's Council of Representatives on January 24, 1981. The revised Ethical Principles contain both substantive and grammatical changes in each of the nine ethical principles constituting the Ethical Standards of Psychologists previously adopted by the Council of Representatives in 1979, plus a new tenth principle entitled Care and Use of Animals. Inquiries concerning the Ethical Principles of Psychologists should be addressed to the Administrative Officer for Ethics, American Psychological Association, 1200 Seventeenth Street, N. W., Washington, D.C. 20036.

These revised Ethical Principles apply to psychologists, to students of psychology, and to others who do work of a psychological nature under the supervision of a psychologist. They are also intended for the guidance of nonmembers of the Association who are engaged in psychological research or practice.

Any complaints of unethical conduct filed after January 24, 1981, shall be governed by this 1981 revision. However, conduct (a) complained about after January 24, 1981, but which occurred prior to that date, and (b) not considered unethical under prior versions of the principles but considered unethical under the 1981 revision, shall not be deemed a violation of ethical principles. Any complaints pending as of January 24, 1981, shall be governed either by the 1979 or by the 1981 version of the Ethical Principles, at the sound discretion of the Committee on Scientific and Professional Ethics and Conduct.

knowledge for the promotion of human welfare. While pursuing these objectives, they make every effort to protect the welfare of those who seek their services and of the research participants that may be the object of study. They use their skills only for purposes consistent with these values and do not knowingly permit their misuse by others. While demanding for themselves freedom of inquiry and communication, psychologists accept the responsibility this freedom requires: competence, objectivity in the application of skills, and concern for the best interests of clients, colleagues, students, research participants, and society. In the pursuit of these ideals, psychologists subscribe to principles in the following areas: 1. Responsibility, 2. Competence, 3. Moral and Legal Standards, 4. Public Statements, 5. Confidentiality, 6. Welfare of the Consumer, 7. Professional Relationships, 8. Assessment Techniques, 9. Research With Human Participants, and 10. Care and Use of Animals.

Acceptance of membership in the American Psychological Association commits the member to adherence to these principles.

Psychologists cooperate with duly constituted committees of the American Psychological Association, in particular, the Committee on Scientific and Professional Ethics and Conduct, by responding to inquiries promptly and completely. Members also respond promptly and completely to inquiries from duly constituted state association ethics committees and professional standards review committees.

Principle 1

RESPONSIBILITY

In providing services, psychologists maintain the highest standards of their profession. They accept responsibility for the consequences of their acts and make every effort to ensure that their services are used appropriately.

a. As scientists, psychologists accept responsibility for the selection of their research topics and the methods used in investigation, analysis, and reporting. They plan their research in ways to minimize the possibility that their findings will be misleading. They provide thorough discussion of the limitations of their data, especially where their work touches on social policy or might be construed to the detriment of persons in specific age, sex, ethnic, socioeconomic, or other social groups. In publishing reports of their work, they never suppress disconfirming data, and they acknowledge the existence of alternative hypotheses and explanations of their findings. Psychologists take credit only for work they have actually done.

b. Psychologists clarify in advance with all appropriate persons and agencies the expectations for sharing and utilizing research data. They avoid relationships that may limit their objectivity or create a conflict of interest. Interference with the milieu in which data are collected is kept to a minimum.

c. Psychologists have the responsibility to attempt to prevent distortion, misuse, or suppression of psychological findings by the institution or agency of which they are employees.

d. As members of governmental or other organizational bodies, psychologists remain accountable as individuals to the highest standards of their profession.

e. As teachers, psychologists recognize their primary obligation to help others acquire knowledge and skill. They maintain high standards of scholarship by presenting psychological information objectively, fully, and accurately.

f. As practitioners, psychologists know that they bear a heavy social responsibility because their recommendations and professional actions may alter the lives of others. They are alert to personal, social, organizational, financial, or political situations and pressures that might lead to misuse of their influence.

Principle 2

COMPETENCE

The maintenance of high standards of competence is a responsibility shared by all psychologists in the interest of the public and the profession as a whole. Psychologists recognize the boundaries of their competence and the limitations of their techniques. They only provide services and only use techniques for which they are qualified by training and experience. In those areas in which recognized standards do not yet exist, psychologists take whatever precautions are necessary to protect the welfare of their clients. They maintain knowledge of current scientific and professional information related to the services they render.

a. Psychologists accurately represent their competence, education, training, and experience. They claim as evidence of educational qualifications only those degrees obtained from institutions acceptable under the Bylaws and Rules of Council of the American Psychological Association.

b. As teachers, psychologists perform their duties on the basis of careful preparation so that their instruction is accurate, current, and scholarly.

c. Psychologists recognize the need for continuing education and are open to new procedures and changes in expectations and values over time.

d. Psychologists recognize differences among people, such as those that may be associated with age, sex, socioeconomic, and ethnic backgrounds. When necessary, they obtain training, experience, or counsel to assure competent service or research relating to such persons.

e. Psychologists responsible for decisions involving individuals or policies based on test results have an understanding of psychological or educational measurement, validation problems, and test research.

f. Psychologists recognize that personal problems and conflicts may interfere with professional effectiveness. Accordingly, they refrain from undertaking any activity in which their personal problems are likely to lead to inadequate performance or harm to a client, colleague, student, or research participant. If engaged in such activity when they become aware of their personal problems, they seek competent professional assistance to determine whether they should suspend, terminate, or limit the scope of their professional and/or scientific activities.

Principle 3

MORAL AND LEGAL STANDARDS

Psychologists' moral and ethical standards of behavior are a personal matter to the same degree as they are for any other citizen, except as these may compromise the fulfillment of their professional responsibilities or reduce the public trust in psychology and psychologists. Regarding their own behavior, psychologists are sensitive to prevailing community standards and to the possible impact that conformity to or deviation from these standards may have upon the quality of their performance as psychologists. Psychologists are also aware of the possible impact of their public behavior upon the ability of colleagues to perform their professional duties.

a. As teachers, psychologists are aware of the fact that their personal values may affect the selection and presentation of instructional materials. When dealing with topics that may give offense, they recognize and respect the diverse attitudes that students may have toward such materials.

b. As employees or employers, psychologists do not engage in or condone practices that are inhumane or that result in illegal or unjustifiable actions. Such practices include, but are not limited to, those based on considerations of race, handicap, age, gender, sexual preference, religion, or national origin in hiring, promotion, or training.

c. In their professional roles, psychologists avoid any action that will violate or diminish the legal and civil rights of clients or of others who may be affected by their actions.

d. As practitioners and researchers, psychologists act in accord with Association standards and guidelines related to practice and to the conduct of research with human beings and animals. In the ordinary course of events, psychologists adhere to relevant governmental laws and institutional regulations. When federal, state, provincial, organizational, or institutional laws, regulations, or practices are in conflict with Association standards and guidelines, psychologists make known their commitment to Association standards and guidelines and, wherever possible, work toward a resolution of the conflict. Both practitioners and researchers are concerned with the development of such legal and quasi-legal regulations as best serve the public interest, and they work toward changing existing regulations that are not beneficial to the public interest.

Principle 4

PUBLIC STATEMENTS

Public statements, announcements of services, advertising, and promotional activities of psychologists serve the purpose of helping the public make informed judgments and choices. Psychologists represent accurately and objectively their professional qualifications, affiliations, and functions, as well as those of the institutions or organizations with which they or the statements may be associated. In public statements providing psychological information or professional opinions or providing information about the availability of psychological products, publications, and services, psychologists base their statements on scientifically acceptable psychological findings and techniques with full recognition of the limits and uncertainties of such evidence.

a. When announcing or advertising professional services, psychologists may list the following information to describe the provider and services provided: name, highest relevant academic degree earned from a regionally accredited institution, date, type, and level of certification or licensure, diplomate status, APA membership status, address, telephone number, office hours, a brief listing of the type of psychological services offered, an appropriate presentation of fee information, foreign languages spoken, and policy with regard to third-party payments. Additional relevant or important consumer information may be included if not prohibited by other sections of these Ethical Principles.

b. In announcing or advertising the availability of psychological products, publications, or services, psychologists do not present their affiliation with any organization in a manner that falsely implies sponsorship or certification by that organization. In particular and for example, psychologists do not state APA membership or fellow status in a way to suggest that such status implies specialized professional competence or qualifications. Public statements include, but are not limited to, communication by means of periodical, book, list, directory, television, radio, or motion picture. They do not contain (i) a false, fraudulent, misleading, deceptive, or unfair statement; (ii) a misinterpretation of fact or a statement likely to mislead or deceive because in context it makes only a partial disclosure of relevant facts; (iii) a testimonial from a patient regarding the quality of a psychologists' services or products;

(iv) a statement intended or likely to create false or unjustified expectations of favorable results; (v) a statement implying unusual, unique, or one-of-a-kind abilities; (vi) a statement intended or likely to appeal to a client's fears, anxieties, or emotions concerning the possible results of failure to obtain the offered services, (vii) a statement concerning the comparative desirability of offered services; (viii) a statement of direct solicitation of individual clients.

c. Psychologists do not compensate or give anything of value to a representative of the press, radio, television, or other communication medium in anticipation of or in return for professional publicity in a news item. A paid advertisement must be identified as such, unless it is apparent from the context that it is a paid advertisement. If communicated to the public by use of radio or television, an advertisement is prerecorded and approved for broadcast by the psychologist, and a recording of the actual transmission is retained by the psychologist.

d. Announcements or advertisements of "personal growth groups," clinics, and agencies give a clear statement of purpose and a clear description of the experiences to be provided. The education, training, and experience of the staff members are appropriately specified.

e. Psychologists associated with the development or promotion of psychological devices, books, or other products offered for commercial sale make reasonable efforts to ensure that announcements and advertisements are presented in a professional, scientifically acceptable, and factually informative manner.

f. Psychologists do not participate for personal gain in commercial announcements or advertisements recommending to the public the purchase or use of proprietary or single-source products or services when that participation is based solely upon their identification as psychologists.

g. Psychologists present the science of psychology and offer their services, products, and publications fairly and accurately, avoiding misrepresentation through sensationalism, exaggeration, or superficiality. Psychologists are guided by the primary obligation to aid the public in developing informed judgments, opinions, and choices.

h. As teachers, psychologists ensure that statements in catalogs and course outlines are accurate and not misleading, particularly in terms of subject matter to be covered, bases for evaluating progress, and the nature of course experiences. Announcements, brochures, or advertisements describing workshops, seminars, or other educational programs accurately describe the audience for which the program is intended as well as eligibility requirements, educational objectives, and nature of the materials to be covered. These announcements also accurately represent the education, training, and experience of the psychologists presenting the programs and any fees involved.

i. Public announcements or advertisements soliciting research participants in which clinical services or other professional services are offered as an inducement make clear the nature of the services as well as the costs and other obligations to be accepted by participants in the research.

j. A psychologist accepts the obligation to correct others who represent the psychologist's professional qualifications, or associations with products or services, in a manner incompatible with these guidelines.

k. Individual diagnostic and therapeutic services are provided only in the context of a professional psychological relationship. When personal advice is given by means of public lectures or demonstrations, newspaper or magazine articles, radio or television programs, mail, or similar media, the psychologist utilizes the most current relevant data and exercises the highest level of professional judgment.

l. Products that are described or presented by means of public lectures or demonstrations, newspaper or magazine articles, radio or television programs, or similar media meet the same recognized standards as exist for products used in the context of a professional relationship.

Principle 5

CONFIDENTIALITY

Psychologists have a primary obligation to respect the confidentiality of information obtained from persons in the course of their work as psychologists. They reveal such information to others only with the consent of the person or the person's legal representative, except in those unusual circumstances in which not to do so would result in clear danger to the person or to others. Where appropriate, psychologists inform their clients of the legal limits of confidentiality.

a. Information obtained in clinical or consulting relationships, or evaluative data concerning children, students, employees, and others, is discussed only for professional purposes and only with persons clearly concerned with the case. Written and oral reports present only data germane to the purposes of the evaluation, and every effort is made to avoid undue invasion of privacy.

b. Psychologists who present personal information obtained during the course of professional work in writings, lectures, or other public forums either obtain adequate prior consent to do so or adequately disguise all identifying information.

c. Psychologists make provisions for maintaining confidentiality in the storage and disposal of records.

d. When working with minors or other persons who are unable to give voluntary, informed consent, psychologists take special care to protect these persons' best interests.

Principle 6

WELFARE OF THE CONSUMER

Psychologists respect the integrity and protect the welfare of the people and groups with whom they work. When conflicts of interest arise between clients and psychologists' employing institutions, psychologists clarify the nature and direction of their loyalties and responsibilities and keep all parties informed of their commitments. Psychologists fully inform consumers as to the purpose and nature of an evaluative, treatment, educational, or training procedure, and they freely acknowledge that clients, students, or participants in research have freedom of choice with regard to participation.

a. Psychologists are continually cognizant of their own needs and of their potentially influential position vis-à-vis persons such as clients, students, and subordinates. They avoid exploiting the trust and dependency of such persons. Psychologists make every effort to avoid dual relationships that could impair their professional judgment or increase the risk of exploitation. Examples of such dual relationships include, but are not limited to, research with and treatment of employees, students, supervisees, close friends, or relatives. Sexual intimacies with clients are unethical.

b. When a psychologist agrees to provide services to a client at the request of a third party, the psychologist assumes the responsibility of clarifying the nature of the relationships to all parties concerned.

c. Where the demands of an organization require psychologists to violate these Ethical Principles, psychologists clarify the nature of the conflict between the demands and these principles. They inform all parties of psychologists' ethical responsibilities and take appropriate action.

d. Psychologists make advance financial arrangements that safeguard the best interests of and are clearly understood by their clients. They neither give nor receive any remuneration for referring clients for professional services. They contribute a portion of their services to work for which they receive little or no financial return.

e. Psychologists terminate a clinical or consulting relationship when it is reasonably clear that the consumer is not benefiting from it. They offer to help the consumer locate alternative sources of assistance.

Principle 7

PROFESSIONAL RELATIONSHIPS

Psychologists act with due regard for the needs, special competencies, and obligations of their colleagues in psychology and other professions. They respect the prerogatives and obligations of the institutions or organizations with which these other colleagues are associated.

a. Psychologists understand the areas of competence of related professions. They make full use of all the professional, technical, and administrative resources that serve the best interests of consumers. The absence of formal relationships with other professional workers does not relieve psychologists of the responsibility of securing for their clients the best possible professional service, nor does it relieve them of the obligation to exercise foresight, diligence, and tact in obtaining the complementary or alternative assistance needed by clients.

b. Psychologists know and take into account the traditions and practices of other professional groups with whom they work and cooperate fully with such groups. If a person is receiving similar services from another professional, psychologists do not offer their own services directly to such a person. If a psychologist is contacted by a person who is already receiving similar services from another professional, the psychologist carefully considers that professional relationship and proceeds with caution and sensitivity to the therapeutic issues as well as the client's welfare. The psychologist discusses these issues with the client so as to minimize the risk of confusion and conflict.

c. Psychologists who employ or supervise other professionals or professionals in training accept the obligation to facilitate the further professional development of these individuals. They provide appropriate working conditions, timely evaluations, constructive consultation, and experience opportunities.

d. Psychologists do not exploit their professional relationships with clients, supervisees, students, employees, or research participants sexually or otherwise. Psychologists do not condone or engage in sexual harassment. Sexual harassment is defined as deliberate or repeated comments, gestures, or physical contacts of a sexual nature that are unwanted by the recipient.

e. In conducting research in institutions or organizations, psychologists secure appropriate authorization to conduct such research. They are aware of their obligations to future research workers and ensure that host institutions receive adequate information about the research and proper acknowledgement of their contributions.

f. Publication credit is assigned to those who have contributed to a publication in proportion to their professional contributions. Major contributions of a professional character made by several persons to a common project are recognized by joint authorship, with the individual who made the principal contribution listed first. Minor contributions of a professional character and extensive clerical or similar nonprofessional assistance may be acknowledged in footnotes or in an introductory statement. Acknowledgment through specific citations is made for unpublished as well as published material that has directly influenced the research or writing. Psychologists who compile and edit material of others for publication publish the material in the name of the originating group, if appropriate, with their own name appearing as chairperson or editor. All contributors are to be acknowledged and named.

g. When psychologists know of an ethical violation by another psychologist, and it seems appropriate, they informally attempt to resolve the issue by bringing the behavior to the attention of the psychologist. If the misconduct is of a minor nature and/or appears to be due to lack of sensitivity, knowledge, or experience, such an informal solution is usually appropriate. Such informal corrective efforts are made with sensitivity to any rights to confidentiality involved. If the violation does not seem amenable to an informal solution, or is of a more serious nature, psychologists bring it to the attention of the appropriate local, state, and/or national committee on professional ethics and conduct.

Principle 8

ASSESSMENT TECHNIQUES

In the development, publication, and utilization of psychological assessment techniques, psychologists make every effort to promote the welfare and best interests of the client. They guard against the misuse of assessment results. They respect the client's right to know the results, the interpretations made, and the bases for their conclusions and recommendations. Psychologists make every effort to maintain the security of tests and other assessment techniques within limits of legal mandates. They strive to ensure the appropriate use of assessment techniques by others.

a. In using assessment techniques, psychologists respect the right of clients to have full explanations of the nature and purpose of the techniques in language the clients can understand, unless an explicit exception to this right has been agreed upon in advance. When the explanations are to be provided by others, psychologists establish procedures for ensuring the adequacy of these explanations.

b. Psychologists responsible for the development and standardization of psychological tests and other assessment techniques utilize established scientific procedures and observe the relevant APA standards.

c. In reporting assessment results, psychologists indicate any reservations that exist regarding validity or reliability because of the circumstances of the assessment or the inappropriateness of the norms for the person tested. Psychologists strive to ensure that the results of assessments and their interpretations are not misused by others.

d. Psychologists recognize that assessment results may become obsolete. They make every effort to avoid and prevent the misuse of obsolete measures.

e. Psychologists offering scoring and interpretation services are able to produce appropriate evidence for the validity of the programs and procedures used in arriving at interpretations. The public offering of an automated interpretation service is considered a professional-to-professional consultation. Psychologists make every effort to avoid misuse of assessment reports.

f. Psychologists do not encourage or promote the use of psychological assessment techniques by inappropriately trained or otherwise unqualified persons through teaching, sponsorship, or supervision.

Principle 9

RESEARCH WITH HUMAN PARTICIPANTS

The decision to undertake research rests upon a considered judgment by the individual psychologist about how best to contribute to psychological science and human welfare. Having made the decision to conduct research, the psychologist considers alternative directions in which research energies and resources might be invested. On the basis of this consideration, the psychologist carries out the investigation with respect and concern for the dignity and welfare of the people who participate and with cognizance of federal and state regulations and professional standards governing the conduct of research with human participants.

a. In planning a study, the investigator has the responsibility to make a careful evaluation of its ethical acceptability. To the extent that the weighing of scientific and human values suggests a compromise of any principle, the investigator incurs a correspondingly serious obligation to seek ethical advice and to observe stringent safeguards to protect the rights of human participants.

b. Considering whether a participant in a planned study will be a "subject at risk" or a "subject at minimal risk," according to recognized standards, is of primary ethical concern to the investigator.

c. The investigator always retains the responsibility for ensuring ethical practice in research. The investigator is also responsible for the ethical treatment of research participants by collaborators, assistants, students, and employees, all of whom, however, incur similar obligations.

d. Except in minimal-risk research, the investigator establishes a clear and fair agreement with research participants, prior to their participation, that clarifies the obligations and responsibilities of each. The investigator has the obligation to honor all promises and commitments included in that agreement. The investigator informs the participants of all aspects of the research that might reasonably be expected to influence willingness to participate and explains all other aspects of the research about which the participants inquire. Failure to make full disclosure prior to obtaining informed consent requires additional safeguards to protect the welfare and dignity of the research participants. Research with children or with participants who have impairments that would limit understanding and/or communication requires special safeguarding procedures.

e. Methodological requirements of a study may make the use of concealment or deception necessary. Before conducting such a study, the investigator has a special responsibility to (i) determine whether the use of such techniques is justified by the study's prospective scientific, educational, or applied value; (ii) determine whether alternative procedures are available that do not use concealment or deception; and (iii) ensure that the participants are provided with sufficient explanation as soon as possible.

f. The investigator respects the individual's freedom to decline to participate in or to withdraw from the research at any time. The obligation to protect this freedom requires careful thought and consideration when the investigator is in a position of authority or influence over the participant. Such positions of authority include, but are not limited to, situations in which research participation is required as part of employment or in which the participant is a student, client, or employee of the investigator.

g. The investigator protects the participant from physical and mental discomfort, harm, and danger that may arise from research procedures. If risks of such consequences exist, the investigator informs the participant of that fact. Research procedures likely to cause serious or lasting harm to a participant are not used unless the failure to use these procedures might expose the participant to risk of greater harm, or unless the research has great potential benefit and fully informed and voluntary consent is obtained from each participant. The participant should be informed of procedures for contacting the investigator within a reasonable time period following participation should stress, potential harm, or related questions or concerns arise.

h. After the data are collected, the investigator provides the participant with information about the nature of the study and attempts to remove any misconceptions that may have arisen. Where scientific or humane values justify delaying or withholding this information, the investigator incurs a special responsibility to monitor the research and to ensure that there are no damaging consequences for the participant.

i. Where research procedures result in undesirable consequences for the individual participant, the investigator has the responsibility to detect and remove or correct these consequences, including long-term effects.

j. Information obtained about a research participant during the course of an investigation is confidential unless otherwise agreed upon in advance. When the possibility exists that others may obtain access to such information, this possibility, together with the plans for protecting confidentiality, is explained to the participant as part of the procedure for obtaining informed consent.

Principle 10

CARE AND USE OF ANIMALS

An investigator of animal behavior strives to advance understanding of basic behavioral principles and/or to contribute to the improvement of human health and welfare. In seeking these ends, the investigator ensures the welfare of animals and treats them humanely. Laws and regulations notwithstanding, an animal's immediate protection depends upon the scientist's own conscience.

a. The acquisition, care, use, and disposal of all animals are in compliance with current federal, state or provincial, and local laws and regulations.

b. A psychologist trained in research methods and experienced in the care of laboratory animals closely supervises all procedures involving animals and is responsible for ensuring appropriate consideration of their comfort, health, and humane treatment.

c. Psychologists ensure that all individuals using animals under their supervision have received explicit instruction in experimental methods and in the care, maintenance, and handling of the species being used. Responsibilities and activities of individuals participating in a research project are consistent with their respective competencies.

d. Psychologists make every effort to minimize discomfort, illness, and pain of animals. A procedure subjecting animals to pain, stress, or privation is used only when an alternative procedure is unavailable and the goal is justified by its prospective scientific, educational, or applied value. Surgical procedures are performed under appropriate anesthesia; techniques to avoid infection and minimize pain are followed during and after surgery.

e. When it is appropriate that the animal's life be terminated, it is done rapidly and painlessly.

Appendix B

COMMITTTEE ON SCIENTIFIC AND PROFESSIONAL ETHICS AND CONDUCT: RULES AND PROCEDURES*

TABLE OF CONTENTS

---

*Reprinted by permission of the American Psychological Association.

RULES AND PROCEDURES*

1. Responsibility and Objectives of the Committee

 1.1 *Bylaws*
  1.11 Formulate principles of ethics for adoption by the Association;
  1.12 Receive and investigate complaints of unethical conduct of Fellows, Members, and Associates (hereinafter *Members*);

---

*The Committee on Scientific and Professional Ethics and Conduct adopted in February, 1981 Rules and Procedures to replace its earlier set (which were published in the *American Psychologist*, 1974, pp 703-710). These Rules and Procedures are in major part those adopted by the Committee in February, 1981 with necessary changes made subsequently to reflect changes in the Association Bylaws.

1.13 Resolve complaints of unethical conduct or recommend such other action as is necessary to achieve the objectives of the Association;

1.14 Report on types of complaints investigated with special description of difficult or recalcitrant cases;

1.15 Adopt rules and procedures governing the conduct of CSPEC (hereinafter the *Committee*).

1.2 *Objectives*

The fundamental objectives of the Committee shall be to maintain ethical conduct by psychologists at the highest professional level; to educate psychologists concerning ethical principles; to protect those members of the public with whom psychologists have a professional or scientific relationship; and to aid the Association in achieving its objectives as reflected in its Bylaws.

1.3 *Protection of Public*

While the Committee shall endeavor to take actions toward members found to be in violation of the Association's *Ethical Principles* that are educative and constructive rather than punitive in character, the Committee's primary concern will be to protect the public against harmful conduct by psychologists.

2. General Operating Rules and Nature of Authority

2.1 *Enabling Rules*

2.11 *APA Documents.* The Committee shall base its activities on the Bylaws of the Association,[1] on the *Ethical Principles of Psychologists*, as adopted and amended by the APA Council of Representatives, and on these Rules and Procedures.

2.12 *Rules and Procedures.* The Committee may adopt rules and procedures[2] governing the conduct of all matters within its jurisdiction, and may amend such rules from time to time upon two-thirds vote of Committee members, provided that no amendment shall adversely affect the rights of a member of the Association whose conduct is being investigated or against whom formal charges have been filed at the time of amendment.

2.13 *Power to Investigate.* The Committee has the power to investigate allegations of unethical scientific and professional conduct which may be harmful to the public or to colleagues, or which is otherwise contrary to or destructive of the objectives of the Association.

2.14 *Choice of Procedure.* The Committee shall be the sole judge of whether a matter can be disposed of within the Committee under Section 8.2, whether formal charges shall be brought under Section 8.4, or whether the evidence warrants referral to the Board of Directors under Section 5.

---

[1] Article II, Session 18 and Article X, Section 5 pertain to the Committee specifically.

[2] Rules of Council 60-1 and 60-2 pertain to the Committee specifically.

2.2 *Jurisdiction Over Individuals*

    2.21   *Recommend on Membership.* The Committee has the power to investigate and adjudicate complaints concerning the scientific and professional ethics and conduct of all members of the Association and may make a decision as to whether an individual shall become a member or be readmitted to membership.

    2.22   *Time Limits for Complaints.* The Committee may consider complaints brought by members of the Association against other members only if the complaint was filed within one year from the time the alleged unethical conduct either occurred or was discovered. The time is extended to five years when the complaint is brought by a nonmember of the Association. Any complaint not received within these time limits shall not be considered and the parties involved so notified. This rule may be excepted by a majority vote of the Committee when acceptable cause for extension of time is presented by the complainant.

    2.23   *Additional Evidence.* If additional evidence of unethical conduct is presented after a matter has been closed, the case may be reopened and acted upon under regular procedures.

    2.24   *Time Limits Involving Other Tribunals.* When acting in response to: (a) conviction of a felony; (b) finding of malpractice by a duly authorized tribunal; (c) expulsion or suspension from a state association[3] for unethical conduct; or (d) revocation of licensure/certification by a state board of examiners,[4] the time limit for bringing complaints shall not begin until such actions have come to the attention, or reasonably should have come to the attention, of the Committee.

    2.25   *Litigation.* Civil or criminal litigation pending against members shall be no bar to the consideration of complaints by the Committee. It shall be within the sole discretion of the Committee whether to proceed during the course of litigation or to wait until its completion.

    2.26   *Nonmembers.* Although the Committee has no jurisdiction over nonmembers of the Association, it may cooperate with any agency having jurisdiction by furnishing factual information and consultation.

2.3 *Available Disciplinary Actions*

    2.31   *Expulsion.* Upon recommendation by the Committee, a formal charge, as defined in Section 8.4, may be brought against a member and after the procedures delineated in Section 8 have been satisfied, upon final action by the Board of Directors under Section 9, the member may be expelled or receive some lesser sanction.

---

[3] For purposes of these Rules and Procedures, a state association shall include territorial, local, or county psychological associations; and, in cases of Canadian members of the Association, provincial psychological associations.

[4] For purposes of these Rules and Procedures, a state board of examiners shall include a state board of education in those cases where the pertinent certification is secured from that entity or in states with no licensing authority, a nonstatutory board established for certification.

2.32   *Permit Resignation.* Upon recommendation by the Committee and upon final action by the Board of Directors under procedures delineated in Section 8.3, the member may be permitted to resign under conditions stipulated by the Board of Directors.

2.33   *Committee Action.* Where the Committee chooses to attempt to resolve matters within itself, the Committee may place the member on probation, reprimand or censure the member; it may also request that the member cease the challenged conduct, accept supervision, or seek rehabilitative or educational training or psychotherapy.

2.34   *Delay Resignation on Complaint.* At whatever point the member complained of (hereinafter *complainee*) is notified by the Association that a person has submitted a complaint (hereinafter *complainant*) against him/her, the Committee shall inform the Board of Directors so that the Board may delay action on a tendered resignation while the Committee considers the matter.

2.35   *Delay Resignation During State Proceedings.* When the Committee is informed of disciplinary proceedings against a member by a state association or examining board, it may inform the Board of Directors of such proceedings so that the Board may delay action on a tendered resignation while the Committee considers instituting an action against the member.

2.36   *Void Membership.* The Committee may recommend to the Board of Directors that it void the election to membership in the Association of any person who obtained membership on the basis of false or fraudulent information.

2.37   *Deny Readmission.* The Committee may recommend that the Board of Directors deny readmission of a former member whose membership was terminated under the provisions of Article II, Section 18 of the Bylaws.

2.4   *Meetings and Officers*

2.41   *Frequency and Quorum.* The Committee shall meet at reasonable intervals as needed. A quorum at such meetings shall consist of the majority of the elected members of the Committee.

2.42   *Selection of Officers.* The Chair and Vice Chair shall be elected annually at a duly constituted meeting. The Executive Officer shall designate a staff member to serve as Administrative Officer for Ethics.

2.43   *Vice Chair.* The Vice Chair shall have the authority to perform all the duties of the Chair when the latter is unavailable or unable to perform them.

2.44   *Majority Rule.* All decisions of the Committee, with the exception of changes to the Committee's Rules and Procedures, and notification of other tribunals to protect the public in serious cases, shall be by majority vote of those members present.

2.45   *Secret or Recorded Ballot.* Any Committee Member may call for either a secret or for a recorded ballot. Such a ballot shall be taken if any member so requests.

2.46   *Confidential Session.* Attendance at the Ethics Committee's deliberation of cases is restricted to elected members of the Committee, the Administrative Officer for Ethics and the Ethics Committee support staff except in unusual circumstances when the Committee, by vote, requests the presence of other persons. This does not preclude routine attendance by the Board of Directors' liaison or APA's legal counsel.

2.5 *Confidentiality*

2.51   *Disclosure of Information.* All information concerning complaints against members shall be confidential except that the Committee may disclose such information when compelled by a validly issued subpoena or when otherwise required by law. Additionally, in serious cases which have resulted in a member's probation, suspension or stipulated resignation, the Committee may communicate these actions to:

   a. members,
   b. committees and divisions of the Association,
   c. affiliated state and regional associations,
   d. American Board of Professional Psychology (ABPP) and state licensing/certification boards,
   e. legal counsel of the Association,
   f. staff of the Association's Central Office designated by the Executive Officer to assist the Committee with its work,
   g. American Association of State Psychology Boards (AASPB),
   h. Council for National Register of Health Service Providers in Psychology (CNRHSPP),

   and other individuals or organizations as the committee shall deem necessary to maintain the highest level of ethical behavior by members or to protect the public.

   In addition, the Committee may disclose to any of the above organizations or individuals that an individual is under ethical investigation in cases deemed to be serious threats to the public welfare (as determined by a 2/3 vote of the Committee at a regularly scheduled meeting) and only when to do so before final adjudication appears necessary to protect the public.

2.52   *Notification of Final Action by Committee.* The Committee shall also inform the complainant and the complainee of its action and the rationale for the action when the matter is disposed of within the Committee, including the Principle(s) violated, should there be a violation, and the rationale for its actions. Such parties as have been informed of the complaint shall receive notification of the final disposition of the case. When the Committee deems it necessary for the protection of the Association or the public, or when it deems it necessary to maintain the standards of the membership of the Association, notification of disposition within the Committee may be made to one or more of those bodies enumerated in Section 2.51 above, even though they were not involved in or informed of the prior proceedings.

2.53 *Notification of Closing the Case.* If the Committee votes to close a case, the Administrative Officer shall so inform the complainant; the member in question; and such members, committees, and divisions of the Association; affiliated state and regional associations; ABPP; AASPB; CNRHSPP; and/or state/local licensing and certification boards as may have been involved or may have been informed of the charge.

2.54 *Communication for Investigation.* Nothing in this Section shall be construed to prevent the Committee from communicating with the complainant, witnesses, potential members of factfinding committees, or other sources of information necessary to enable the Committee to carry out its investigative function.

2.6 *Records*

2.61 *Confidential Permanent Files.* Permanent files of the Committee shall be confidential, within the limitations of Section 2.5, and shall be maintained in the Central Office of the Association. They shall be available only to those specifically authorized by the Committee and by the Executive Officer of the Association.

2.62 *Files for Expulsion, Resignation, and Stipulated Resignation.* Files concerning members who have been expelled or permitted to resign shall be maintained indefinitely. For those members who have been readmitted under a stipulated resignation under Section 8.3, records containing personally identifiable information shall be maintained for five (5) years after readmission.

2.63 *Files for Non-Violations.* Except for cases closed for insufficient evidence under Section 8.1, personally identifiable information concerning complainees who have been found not to have violated the *Ethical Principles* of the Association shall be destroyed one (1) year after the Committee has closed the case.

2.64 *Files for Insufficient Information.* In cases where the Committee has closed a case due to evidence insufficient to sustain a complaint of an ethical violation under Section 6.32, records containing personally identifiable information shall be maintained for five (5) years after the Committee has closed the case.

2.65 *Files of Lesser Sanctions.* In cases where the Committee has found an ethical violation but where the sanction is less than expulsion, records containing personally identifiable information shall be maintained for five (5) years after the Committee has closed the case.

2.66 *Files After Death.* All records containing personally identifiable information shall be destroyed one (1) year after the Association is notified of the death of the member.

2.67 *Records for Educative Purposes.* Nothing in this section shall preclude the Committee from maintaining records in a form which prevents identification of the complainee so that it may be used for archival, educative, or other legitimate purposes.

2.7 *Correspondence*

    2.71   *Use of Correspondence.* The Committee shall conduct as much of its business as practical through correspondence. Normally, such correspondence shall be referred to the Administrative Officer for Ethics. Copies of all correspondence concerning complaints of alleged unethical conduct shall be sent to the Chair or the designated case monitor.

    2.72   *Certified Mail.* For purposes of notice, correspondence with the complainee shall be certified-return receipt mail to his/her last known address.

    2.73   *Liaison with Other Ethics Committees.* The Committee shall establish and maintain liaison with the ethics committees of APA divisions and affiliated state and regional associations to enforce effectively the objectives of the Committee.

3. Membership Procedures

The Committee shall review applications for membership upon referral by the Membership Committee or others where there are questions of unethical conduct or false or fraudulent information. Upon such review, the Committee may recommend to the Board of Directors that membership be denied or voided.

4. Membership Procedures – Former Members

    4.1 *Application for Readmission*
    The Administrative Officer for Ethics shall automatically receive from the Membership Committee all applications for readmission by persons who have been (1) expelled or dropped from membership; (2) permitted to resign; and (3) permitted to resign under conditions stipulated by the Committee, agreed to by the member, and accepted by the Board of Directors.

    4.2 *Elapsed Time for Review*
    Applications for readmission by members who have been expelled or dropped from membership shall be considered by the Committee only after five (5) years have elapsed from the date of that action. Applications for readmission by members who have been permitted to resign shall be considered only after three (3) years have elapsed from the date of resignation.

    4.3 *Procedures*
    The Administrative Officer for Ethics shall transmit to the Committee a summary of the application for readmission, including complete copies of the statements submitted by sponsors and the record of the previous case

against the former member. The Committee shall take one of the following actions:

4.31   *Readmit.* Recommend to the Membership Committee that the former member be readmitted;

4.32   *Deny.* Recommend to the Membership Committee that readmission be denied; or

4.33   *Investigate.* Investigate further and, if desired by the Committee, hold a conference; then the Committee shall recommend to the Membership Committee one of the following:

4.331   *Readmit.* The former member be readmitted;

4.332   *Defer.* Application for readmission be deferred for a stated period of time;

4.333   *Deny.* Readmission be denied.

5. Procedures with Members Convicted of or Charged with Felonies or Disciplined in Other Authorized Tribunals

5.1   *Review Record and Suspend*
Where the Committee finds that a member has been convicted of a felony and such member has no further right of appeal, the Committee shall review the record leading to conviction and may thereafter suspend membership without further proceedings.

5.2   *Jurisdiction*
Where the Committee finds that a member has been charged with a felony, such charge shall neither require nor preclude action by the Committee. Delay shall not constitute waiver of jurisdiction.

5.3   *Expelled, Suspended or Delicensed by State*
Where the Committee finds that a member has been expelled or suspended for unethical conduct from an affiliated state or regional associaton, or has had a license or certificate revoked on ethical grounds by a state board of examiners, the Committee shall review the record leading to these sanctions and may suspend membership in the Association without further proceedings.

5.4   *Member Response*
Suspension under 5.1 or 5.3 shall be taken by the Committee only where it appears necessary for the protection of the public. Upon suspension, the member shall be afforded the opportunity, in writing, or, at the Committee's discretion, through personal appearance, to show good cause why he/she should not be expelled from the Association.

5.5   *Recommendation to Board of Directors*
After a member's response, or the expiration of sixty (60) days without response, the Committee shall recommend to the Board of Directors whether he/she shall be expelled from the Association. The Board of Directors may, after a review of the entire record, expel the member or administer a lesser sanction.

5.6 *Decision Not to Recommend Expulsion*
In those cases where the Committee votes not to expel, it has the option to follow its usual procedures for adjudication within the Committee.

6. Procedures with Members: Initial Considerations

6.1 *Time Requirements*
The Committee and complainee shall use their best efforts to adhere strictly to the time requirements specified in Sections 6 through 10. However, failure to do so will not prohibit final adjudication unless the Committee or the complainee can show that such failure was willful and unfairly prejudicial.

6.2 *Complaint*

6.21 *Documents.* Complaints may be submitted by both members and nonmembers of the Association. Upon receipt of a complaint, complainants shall receive a copy of the Association's *Ethical Principles,* the Ethics Complaint Check List and these Rules and Procedures.

6.22 *Previous Remedy.* The complainant shall be asked to inform the Committee of previous steps, if any, that have been taken to remedy the situation.

6.23 *Sua Sponte.* The Committee may proceed on its own initiative when a member appears to have violated the *Ethical Principles* or has engaged in conduct which adversely affects the public or the Association. Materials in the public domain may also lead to sua sponte complaints.

6.24 *Anonymous Complaints.* The Committee shall not act upon the basis of anonymous complaints.

6.25 *Time Limits.* Complaints must be brought within the time limits specified in Section 2.22.

6.26 *Complaints About Nonmembers.* If the complaint does not involve a member, the Administrative Officer shall inform the complainant and may refer the complainant to another agency or association with proper jurisdiction.

6.27 *Counter-Complaints.* The Committee will not accept formal ethical complaints from a complainee member against a complainant member during the course of an investigation of the initial complaint by the Committee. Rather, the Committee shall indicate that all sides of the matter leading to the complaint will be studied and that counter-charges will be considered only after the initial complaint is finally settled.

6.28 *Capricious Complaints.* As a protection for the complainee, members should note that the Committee has the right to bring charges itself if the initial complaint is judged by the Committee to be capricious, or intended to harm the complainee rather than to protect the public.

6.3 *Evaluation of Complaint*

6.31 *Evaluation by Chair and Administrative Officer.* Both the Committee Chair and Administrative Officer shall review each completed complaint. If either determines that the alleged behavior may violate ethical principles, they will take action as outlined in 6.34 below. If both determine that they have insufficient evidence to make such a determination, they will take action as outlined in 6.35 below. If both determine that there is no cause for action, they will take action as outlined in 6.32 below. In addition, they may take the supplemental or alternative action as outlined in 6.35 below.

6.32 *No Cause for Action by Committee.* If the Administrative Officer and Chair determine the conduct alleged, if proven, would not constitute a violation of the Association's *Ethical Principles*, the Administrative Officer shall so inform the complainant but he/she may be allowed to renew the complaint if additional information is provided. If no new information is provided within sixty (60) days from receipt of the request, the matter shall be closed.

6.33 *Insufficient Information*

6.331 *Request Further Information.* If the Administrative Officer and Chair determine there is insufficient information to make a fair determination of whether the alleged conduct would be cause for action by the Committee, the Administrative Officer may request further information from the complainant or others. If the request is made to the complainant, he/she shall be given thirty (30) days from receipt of the request to respond.

6.332 *Committee Decision.* Upon receipt of a response, if the Administrative Officer and Chair are still unable to determine whether there may be cause for action by the Committee, the members of the Committee shall receive all written material on the matter and decide whether to dismiss the complaint or accept it.

6.333 *Close.* If no response is received after thirty (30) days from receipt of the request, the matter shall be closed unless the complainant shows good cause for delay.

6.334 *Multiple Complaints.* When a complaint involves a member against whom a case was previously closed for insufficient information and a complaint is filed by another complainant alleging similar conduct, conduct alleged in the previous complaint(s) may be considered in determining whether to accept the complaint. However, prior complaints may not be used as evidence against the member unless offered in the manner provided for other evidence in Section 8.

6.34 *Probable Cause for Action by Committee*

6.341 *Decision by Administrative Officer or Chair.* If either the Administrative Officer or the Chair decides that there is sufficient information initially, or after additional information has been provided, to indicate the alleged conduct may violate ethical principles, the Administrative Officer shall notify the complainant and request written permission to identify him/her to the complainee.

6.342 *Time for Complainant Response.* The Complainant shall have thirty (30) days to respond to the request and shall be informed that failure to grant permission may preclude further action.

6.343 *Failure to Respond.* If no response is received within thirty (30) days of receipt of the request or permission to inform the complainee is denied, the Committee shall decide whether to proceed on its own initiative, without permission, or close the matter.

6.344 *Waiver of Confidentiality by Client.* The Administrative Officer may request a waiver of any duty of confidentiality in regard to matters that are relevant to the case where the complainant is a client or former client of the complainee.

6.35 *Supplementary or Alternative Action by Committee*

6.351 *Referral to Other Entities.* The Administrative Officer and Chair may recommend that the complainant refer the complaint to a relevant state psychological association, state board of examiners, appropriate regulatory agency or any subsidiary body of the Association, or they may do so on their own initiative. Such referral does not constitute a waiver of jurisdiction over the complaint provided that the Committee opens the case within twenty-four (24) months from the date of referral.

6.352 *Retaining Jurisdiction.* The Committee shall retain jurisdiction until twenty-four (24) months have passed if the entities in 6.351 to which the case was referred have failed to adjudicate the complaint.

6.353 *Right to Adjudicate.* Adjudication by another body does not preclude the Committee from considering the complaint independently.

7. Procedures with Members: Accepted Complaints and Initial Action

7.1 *Communication with Complainee*

7.11 *Notification to Complainee.* If the Administrative Officer and the Chair agree that there is a possible violation of the Association's *Ethical Principles*, the Administrative Officer shall so inform the complainee in writing.

7.12 *Contents of Letter.*

7.121 *Complaint and Principles.* A precise description of the nature of the complaint including the specific section(s) of the *Ethical Principles* which the complainee is alleged to have violated;

7.122 *Request for Reply.* A request for a reply within thirty (30) days of receipt, containing information concerning facts surrounding the complaint as detailed in 7.13 below;

7.123 *Documents.* A copy of the *Ethical Principles* of the Association, and the Committee's Rules and Procedures;

7.124 *Complainant's Name.* The name of the complainant, unless the Committee has for good cause decided to withhold the name, or information that the Committee has proceeded on its own initiative;

7.125 *Future Record.* A statement that information submitted by the complainee shall become part of the record in the case which could be used if further proceedings ensue.

7.13 *Response from Complainee*

7.131 *In Writing.* Information relevant to the complaint shall be provided by the member personally and in writing.

7.132 *Clarification by the Committee on Client Responsibility.* If the complainee believes there is a conflict between his/her responsibility to clients and the Administrative Officer's request for information, the complainee may seek advice from the Committee to resolve the conflict.

7.133 *Respond Personally and Promptly.* The complainee is required to respond, in writing, personally and within specified time limits although he/she is free to consult legal counsel at any time.

7.134 *Lack of Cooperation.* Failure or unwarranted delay in responding or lack of cooperation in the investigation shall not prevent continuation of any proceedings and itself constitutes a violation of the *Ethical Principles.*

7.2 *Information from Other Sources*
The Administrative Officer, Chair, or the Committee may request additional information from persons or witnesses involved, from APA members, from boards, committees and divisions of the Association, from ethics committees of affiliated state and regional associations, from state licensing/certification boards or from ABPP.

7.3 *Action on the Response*

7.31 *Close by Chair and Administrative Officer.* Within thirty (30) days of receipt of a written response from the complainee, the Administrative Officer and Chair may determine that the complaint has no basis in fact, is insignificant, or is likely to be corrected, and may close the matter without further action. The Chair may delegate his/her determination on a case to the designated case monitor.

7.32 *Inform All Involved.* If the matter is closed pursuant to Section 7.31, the Administrative Officer shall inform the complainant, the complainee and all other persons or groups that may have been involved or provided information concerning the complaint.

7.33 *Not Closed.* If the matter is not closed by the Administrative Officer and the Chair (or the Chair's designate), the Committee shall determine whether to:

    7.331 *Close the Case;*

    7.332 *Further Investigate* the complaint by means authorized by the Committee;

    7.333 *Request the Complainee to Appear* before the Committee;

    7.334 *Pursue Dispositions* within the Committee such as are available and appropriate under Section 8.2;

    7.335 *Permit* the member to *Resign under Stipulated Conditions* pursuant to Section 8.3;

    7.336 *Bring Formal Charges* against the complainee with the President of the Association and the Board of Directors pursuant to Section 8.4.

7.34 *Source of Information.* In making these determinations, the Committee shall receive all available information from the Administrative Officer.

8. Procedures with Members: Dispositions of Complaints

8.1 *Closed Case*

After referral by the Administrative Officer and Chair, the Committee may elect to close the case. If the matter is closed, the Administrative Officer shall inform the complainant, the complainee and all other persons or groups that may have been involved or may have provided information concerning the complaint.

8.2 *Disposition Within Committee*

    8.21 *Disposition Within the Committee.* The Committee may decide that the nature of the complainee's conduct is such that it will be resolved most appropriately within the Committee and without formal charges.

    8.22 *Methods Determined by Committee.* If the Committee decides to dispose of the case within the Committee, it may adopt any one or more of the following methods or take any other action it deems necessary:

        8.221 *Cease and Desist.* Require the complainee to cease and desist the challenged conduct;

        8.222 *Reprimand or Censure.* Reprimand or censure the complainee;

        8.223 *Supervision.* Require that the complainee accept supervision;

        8.224 *Rehabilitation, Education or Psychotherapy.* Require that the complainee seek rehabilitation or educational training or psychotherapy;

8.225 *Probation.* Place the complainee on probation;[5]

8.226 *Refer.* Refer the matter to a relevant state or regional psychological association and/or state board of examiners.

8.23 *Time to Accept.* The complainee shall have thirty (30) days after notification to respond, in writing, to the Committee's determination.

8.24 *Notification of Complainant of Informal Determination.* If, within thirty (30) days of receipt, the complainee accepts the Committee's determination, the Administrative Officer shall notify the complainant that the matter has been resolved through a disposition within the Committee stating the set of conditions (if any) specified by the Committee and including the Principle(s) violated and the rationale for its actions.

8.25 *Appeal of a Reprimand or Censure.* If a complainee rejects the Committee's reprimand or censure and furnishes the Committee within thirty (30) days of receipt of that reprimand or censure a written rationale for that non-acceptance, copies of the case file and the rationale for non-acceptance shall be furnished within thirty (30) days of receipt to three (3) members of the Standing Hearing Panel (see 8.48 below) who, within thirty (30) days of receipt, shall independently determine whether:

8.251 There is substance enough to the non-acceptance to reconsider the complaint,

8.252 There is substance enough to the non-acceptance to continue to investigate or,

8.253 There is not sufficient substance to the non-acceptance to withdraw the reprimand or censure.

Should at least two members of this review panel determine that the substance of the non-acceptance is not substantial enough to withdraw the reprimand or censure, the Ethics Committee will be so notified and the case will be closed with that reprimand or censure as the final adjudication.

Should at least two members of this review panel recommend that the reprimand or censure be withdrawn or that the investigation of the case be resumed, this recommendation will be returned to the Committee with the rationale therefor. The Committee shall consider such a recommendation and vote whether to sustain the reprimand or censure, to mandate an appearance before the Committee, to mandate an appearance before a fact-finding committee or to take any other action the Committee deems necessary.

---

[5]Probation is defined as the relationship which the Committee has with a complainee when the Comittee undertakes actively and systematically to monitor, for a specific length of time, the degree to which the complainee complies with the Committee's requirements (8.221, 8.223 and 8.224) above.

8.3 *Stipulated Resignation*

    8.31   *Serious Cases.* When the Committee finds that the complainee has committed a serious violation of the *Ethical Principles*, in lieu of a formal charge, the Committee may recommend to the Board of Directors that the complainee be permitted to resign and reapply for membership in the Association under stipulated conditions.

    8.32   *Complainee Accepts Stipulated Resignation.* In such cases, the complainee shall be notified, in writing, of the Committee's determination and that he/she may accept the Committee's determination within thirty (30) days of receipt. Should the complainee accept the determination, the case continues to be open until the completion of the stipulated time period and the successful discharge of the stipulated behaviors, at which time the complainee may reapply for membership and the new application materials and the case file shall be reviewed for readmission by the Committee.

    8.33   *Complainee Does Not Accept Stipulated Resignation* A complainee who does not accept the stipulated resignation may request a Board of Directors' Hearing Panel under the provisions of Section 8.4.

8.4 *Formal Charges*

    8.41   *Definition.* A formal charge is a statement submitted by the Committee to the Board of Directors after the Committee has concluded that it has probable cause to believe that the complainee has violated one or more of the *Ethical Principles* of the Association.

    8.42   *Choice of Formal Action.* The Committee may elect to take formal action and present it to the complainee and to the President of the Association when one of the following occurs:

        8.421   *Complainee Rejects Stipulated Resignation.* When the complainee rejects the determination that the complainee resign under stipulated conditions pursuant to Section 8.3;

        8.422   *Direct Formal Action.* As an action after consideration of all materials gathered under Section 7.

    8.43   *Complainant Notified.* When the Committee elects to present a formal charge to the President of the Association, the Committee shall so inform the complainant.

    8.44   *Contents of Charge.* The formal charge to the complainee shall contain the following:

        8.441   *Description and Ethical Principles.* A description of the nature of the complaint, the conduct in question and citation to the specific section(s) of the *Ethical Principles* which the complainee is alleged to have violated;

        8.442   *Sanction Recommended.* The disciplinary sanction the Committee recommends;

        8.443   *Documents.* A copy of the *Ethical Principles* of the Association and the Committee's Rules and Procedures.

8.45 *Complainee Requests Hearing.* Within thirty (30) days after the complainee receives a copy of the formal charges against him/her, he/she shall have the right to request in writing a hearing.

8.46 *No Hearing Requested or No Response.* If the complainee does not request a hearing or does not respond within thirty (30) days, the right to a hearing shall be considered waived. The Committee then shall consider all available evidence and make final determination based on the preponderance of relevant evidence at its disposal. The matter shall then be referred to the Board of Directors with the Committee's determination for disciplinary sanction. The Committee's determination shall then be treated as that of the Hearing Committee.

8.47 *Hearing Committee.* If the complainee requests a hearing within thirty (30) days, the complainee shall select, within ten (10) days, a Hearing Committee of three (3) members from the Association's Standing Hearing Panel pursuant to the following subsection.

8.48 *Standing Hearing Panel.* The Standing Hearing Panel shall consist of no less than twelve (12) persons, each serving a term of three (3) years, of whom at least two shall be consumers of psychological services and the remainder members of the Association against whom there are no pending complaints of violations of the Association's *Ethical Principles.* The Panel shall be appointed by the President of the Association in consultation with the Administrative Officer for Ethics and shall not include any present members of the Committee. The complainee, in selecting the Hearing Committee, may choose not to have any public member but, in any event, must choose at least two members of the Association.

8.49 *President Appoints.* If the complainee does not make a selection, the President shall choose the members of the Hearing Committee and their names shall be made known to the complainee.

8.410 *Acceptance of Committee.* Appearance by the complainee before the Hearing Committee without objection to its membership shall constitute acceptance of its composition.

8.5 *Procedures for Adjudicating Formal Charges*

8.51 *Chair of Hearing Committee.* The hearing shall be presided over by the Chair of the Hearing Committee, selected by the President of the Association, who shall be responsible for assuring proper observance of these Rules and Procedures.

8.52 *Date of Hearing.* The President of the Association shall set a date for the hearing within 180 days from the time of the complainee's request for a hearing.

8.53 *Confidentiality.* The Hearing Committee shall not discuss the case with anyone other than at the formal hearing.

8.54 *Legal Counsel of the Association.* The Hearing Committee may use the Association's legal counsel to advice it on matters of procedure and admission of evidence. However, should the Ethics Committee choose to use the Association's counsel to present its case, the Hearing Committee may obtain the services of an independent legal counsel to advise it on procedural and evidentiary matters.

8.55 *Documents and Witnesses.* At least thirty (30) days prior to the hearing, the complainee and the Hearing Committee shall be provided with copies of all documents and names of witnesses to be offered by the Committee.

8.56 *Rights and Responsibilities of Complainee.* The complainee shall have the right to have counsel at his/her own expense, to present witnesses and documents and to cross-examine witnesses offered by the Committee. The complainee must provide the Committee and the Hearing Committee with all documents and the names of witnesses to be offered at least fifteen (15) days prior to the hearing.

8.57 *Adjournment and Rebuttal by Committee.* The hearing may be adjourned for a reasonable time after which the Committee may introduce rebuttal evidence as necessary.

8.58 *Burden of Proof.* The Committee shall bear the burden to prove the charges by a preponderance of the evidence.

8.59 *Rules of Evidence.* Formal rules of evidence shall not apply. All evidence that is relevant and reliable, as determined by counsel for the Hearing Committee, shall be admissible.

8.510 *Hearing Committee Decision.* At the conclusion of the hearing, the Hearing Committee shall have thirty (30) days to recommend whether the complainee shall be cleared of the charges, disciplined, allowed to resign or be dropped from membership. The decision shall be by simple majority and shall be submitted in writing to the Committee and the Board of Directors.

9. Final Action by the Board of Directors

9.1 *Receipt of the Written Decision*

9.11 *Time.* Should there be a formal hearing, the Hearing Committee shall submit copies of its decision within thirty (30) days to the Committee, the complainee and the Board of Directors.

9.12 *Complainee Response.* The complainee shall have fifteen (15) days from the time the statement is received to file a written response.

9.13 *Committee Response.* The Committee shall have (15) days from the time the written statement is received to file a written response.

9.2 *Final Decision*

9.21 *Board of Directors Action.* Within sixty (60) days, after considering the record, the determination of the Hearing Committee, the recommendation of the Committee if no hearing were held, and any statements that may be filed, the Board of Directors shall adopt the recommendation of the Hearing Committee, or of the Committee if no hearing were held, unless it determines that there has been:

9.211   *Incorrect Application.* The *Ethical Principles* of the Association were incorrectly applied;

9.212   *Erroneous Findings of Fact.* The findings of fact of the Hearing Committee were clearly erroneous;

9.213   *Procedural Errors.* The procedures used by the Hearing Committee or by the Committee were in serious and substantial violation of the Bylaws of the Association and the Committee's Rules and Procedures;

9.214   *Disproportionate Sanctions.* The disciplinary sanctions recommended by the Hearing Committee were grossly disproportional in light of the violation.

9.22   *Rehearing.* If the Board of Directors determines that 9.211, 9.212, 9.213, or 9.214 above occurred, it shall order a rehearing before a new Hearing Committee.

9.3   *Reporting the Final Outcome*

9.31   *To Complainant and Complainee.* The Board of Directors shall inform the complainant and the complainee of its final action including the Principles violated, should there be any, and the rationale for the Association's actions.

9.32   *To Membership.* The Board shall report annually and in confidence to the membership the names of members who have been expelled (see Section 5) or dropped from membership (see Section 8.4) and the ethical principles involved.

9.33   *To Other Entities.* The Board of Directors shall notify affiliated state and regional associations, the American Board of Professional Psychology (ABPP), state and local licensing/certification boards, the American Association of State Psychology Boards (AASPB), and Council for the National Register of Health Service Providers in Psychology (CNRHSPP) or other appropriate parties of its final action subsequent to adjudication of a formal charge when the Board deems it necessary for the protection of the public or to maintain the standards of the Association.

Appendix C

BYLAWS OF THE AMERICAN PSYCHOLOGICAL ASSOCIATION*

Article II, section 18
Article X, section 5

ARTICLE II, SECTION 18

18. A Fellow, Member, Associate or Affiliate may be dropped from membership or otherwise disciplined for conduct which violates the Ethical Principles of the Association, which tends to injure the Association or to affect adversely its reputation, or which is contrary to or destructive of its objects. Allegations of such conduct shall be submitted to the Committee on Scientific and Professional Ethics and Conduct (hereinafter "Ethics Committee").

ARTICLE X, SECTION 5

5. The Committee on Scientific and Professional Ethics and Conduct shall consist of not less than six Members of the Association, elected from different geographical areas, for terms of not less than three years. Members of the Committee on Scientific and Professional Ethics and Conduct shall be selected to represent the range of interest characteristic of psychology in all its aspects. It shall be the duty of this committee to receive and investigate complaints of unethical conduct of Fellows, Members, Associates and Affiliates; to endeavor to settle cases privately; to report on types of cases investigated with specific description of difficult or recalcitrant cases; to recommend action on ethical cases investigated; and to formulate rules or principles of ethics for adoption by the Association.

---

*Reprinted by permission of the American Psychological Association.

Index